SOCIAL SECOND EDITION
RESEARCH

AN INTRODUCTION

MATTHEW DAVID AND CAROLE D. SUTTON

SAGE

Los Angeles | London | New Delhi
Singapore | Washington DC

LEARNING
RESOURCES
CENTRE

This edition 2011
First published 2004

SAGE Publications Ltd
1 Oliver's Yard
55 City Road
London EC1Y 1SP

SAGE Publications Inc.
2455 Teller Road
Thousand Oaks, California 91320

SAGE Publications India Pvt Ltd
B 1/I 1 Mohan Cooperative Industrial Area
Mathura Road
New Delhi 110 044

SAGE Publications Asia-Pacific Pte Ltd
33 Pekin Street #02-01
Far East Square
Singapore 048763

British Library Cataloguing in Publication data

A catalogue record for this book is available from the
British Library

ISBN 978-1-84787-012-4
ISBN 978-1-84787-013-1 (pbk)

Library of Congress Control Number: 2009938436

Typeset by C&M Digitals (P) Ltd, Chennai, India
Printed and bound in Great Britain by TJ International Ltd, Padstow, Cornwall

SOCIAL RESEARCH

CONTENTS

INTRODUCTION AND STRUCTURE OF THE BOOK

This book builds upon the success of the earlier *Social Research: The Basics*. The aim of the book is to provide the reader with a practical, balanced and comprehensive introduction to social research. The foundation of the book is that social research techniques are frequently used to underpin the activities of diverse groups, from public sector university researchers and researchers working in local government, through to charitable and commercial agencies. Consequently the intended audience for the book consists of two main groups. We also recognize that it is likely to provide a valuable resource to a diverse range of people outside these two main groups.

The first group are undergraduate students from social science disciplines that include sociology, criminal justice and social policy, who undertake research methods training as part of their studies. The book will also be useful to undergraduate and postgraduate students from these and other more diverse disciplines, for example, education, social work and health, who undertake an independent study research project. The book is designed to be used as part of existing research methods training courses and also to support independent research.

The second group that this book is designed to support are those individuals who work outside higher education, most likely in the public sector, who find themselves having to undertake a piece of research or who are involved in the process of commissioning outside consultants to undertake the research. Here the book provides detail on the different research approaches and methods. The inclusion of a glossary also provides a valuable resource for those assessing tender submissions.

The book can be used in a number of different ways. Indeed as you become more familiar with the social research terminology and jargon, and build your knowledge and experience of conducting research, it is likely that you will switch between them. This book can be used as a core textbook, supporting independent study or a taught programme; alternatively it can also be used as a reference guide or handbook.

The content of the book gives equal weighting to qualitative and quantitative approaches. The book provides a solid foundation of knowledge and a framework for conducting a small-scale research project, for example, an undergraduate dissertation. It is designed for readers with little or no prior knowledge or experience of research, with the aim to provide a foundation sufficient to design, conduct and analyse research. The book provides a level of understanding and practical know-how that will allow you to comprehend more advanced specialist texts, and we have provided suggested readings where appropriate.

Structure of the book

The book is divided into four parts reflecting the different epistemological foundations and processes of social research. Within each part are a number of different chapters. Each of these chapters includes examples with hints and tips to help guide the reader. This book is supported by a website that contains many of the resources mentioned in the book.

In Part I the focus is on getting started with social research. This part is centred on developing a research question from first principles. There are four chapters. Chapter 1 focuses on getting started in research and the development of research questions. Chapter 2 examines the importance of undertaking research that follows ethical principles. It distinguishes key ethical standpoints, drawing practical conclusions on conducting research. Issues of consent, confidentiality and anonymity are discussed, as are how to be ethical at each stage of the research process. Issues of ethics related to qualitative and quantitative approaches to understanding the social world are also discussed. Chapter 3 provides guidance on how to frame and develop your research by undertaking a review of existing literature. The chapter discusses how to structure and conduct a literature search, and how to reference sources correctly. Chapter 4 introduces qualitative and quantitative approaches to research. It focuses on the multidimensional distinctions made between quantitative and qualitative methodology, research design, methods and analysis, and how they emerged from different ontological stances.

Part II focuses on different data collection strategies commonly used by social researchers. The coverage of this part includes both qualitative and quantitative approaches. Chapters 5–11 concentrate on qualitative strategies, and Chapters 12–16 on quantitative strategies. Chapter 17 considers methodological innovation in research with specific reference to the emergence of mixed methods research and internet-based or e-research.

Chapter 5 examines qualitative research and the different approaches of induction, deduction and grounded theory. It looks at sampling in primary research and the availability of existing secondary data sources. Issues of being ethical in qualitative research are also discussed. Chapter 6 looks at interview-based data collection methods. The chapter considers the advantages and disadvantages and the value and limitations of the interview. It details how to design interview questions and interview schedules and considers the challenges of recording data collected. Chapter 7 examines focus group data collection methods, looking at issues relating to group membership, the characteristics of the group members, group size and composition, and practical considerations. The strengths and limitations of focus groups are considered. Chapter 8 defines the historic origins of ethnography and the key stages in conducting ethnographic research. The range of data collection methods that can be employed within the broader ethnographic methodology are discussed. Chapter 9 looks at case study research. The chapter starts by considering the nature of case study research and how a case is identified for research in different fields. The chapter looks at the diversity of purpose of case-based methods and how to define, select and approach cases. Chapter 10 examines how a wide range of textual data can be collected for research purposes. It looks at the different sorts of text used and the ethical debates that accompany their inclusion in research. The advantages and limitations of textual data are also debated. Chapter 11 explores the origins and principles of a grounded theoretical approach to social research, providing a comprehensive overview of key grounded theory terms and the diversity of approaches. Chapter 12 looks at quantitative approaches to social research, distinguishing between experimental and non-experimental designs and the different types of designs used by quantitative social researchers. Chapter 13 outlines the key stages in the hypothetico-deductive process. The chapter focuses on the identification of hypotheses and concepts and the process of operationalization. Within this, different data types are discussed. Chapter 14 looks at the different strategies researchers use to identify research participants. The main probability and non-probability sampling techniques are discussed, together with considerations for sample size. Chapter 15 provides guidance on developing survey questions and examples of different types of questions as well as suggestions for accessing key databases of survey questions. Chapter 16 looks at the practical issues relating to collecting and coding survey data. It takes the reader through the stages in data collection and preparing data for data entry. The chapter provides a practical example of a survey and survey code book. Chapter 17 is the last chapter in Part II and focuses on innovations in methodological approaches to research. The chapter looks at the emergence of mixed methods research and the increasing use of internet or online research techniques.

Part III of the book focuses on different qualitative and quantitative data analysis techniques. Chapter 18 is the first of five chapters that introduce different techniques for analysing qualitative data. This first chapter provides general guidance on how to approach analysing qualitative data. Chapter 19 focuses on the emergence of coding techniques in qualitative analysis. It specifies the range of coding methods available to the researcher and identifies the inductive and deductive features of qualitative coding with reference to content analysis. The chapter moves from simple coding through to more sophisticated methods. Chapter 20 examines a range of non-content analytic forms of qualitative data analysis and conducting forms of semiotic, deconstructive, narrative and conversation analysis.

Chapter 21 provides a comprehensive introduction to using NVivo 8 to manage qualitative data analysis. This includes the importing of data, coding of data and management of NVivo nodes, and undertaking searches. Chapter 22 looks at the emergence of visual analysis in research. It distinguishes between a visual experience and visual analysis, identifies the main areas of attention in visual analysis and considers different methods of visual analysis.

Chapter 23 is the first of five chapters focusing on quantitative data analysis. The five chapters all make reference to IBM SPSS Statistics 19. Chapter 23 covers issues relating to data entry, data file structures, minimizing data entry errors and creating a data file in IBM SPSS Statistics 19. Chapter 24 is the first data analysis chapter and concentrates on the foundations of analysis by examining different analysis techniques for survey data. Chapter 25 concentrates on exploring data to answer research questions using data analysis techniques to explore relationships and differences. The focus is primarily on descriptive techniques to explore between two variables, and the chapter outlines elaboration approaches. Chapter 26 looks at the application of inferential statistical analysis techniques to social data to test hypotheses. This chapter covers commonly used statistical tests and introduces the reader to modelling techniques using simple linear regression. Chapter 27 contains a number of commonly used quantitative data management techniques. This is a rather technical chapter and can be used as a reference guide by the reader when encountering a need to recode data, compute new variables, create multiple response sets and weight datasets.

The final part of the book concentrates on the presentation of research to different audiences in both text and verbal format. Chapter 28 looks at how to present qualitative and quantitative data findings..

Companion website

The new edition of this book is accompanied by a companion website. www. sagepub.com/david. The website contains PowerPoint slides and links to useful websites, as well as additional material.

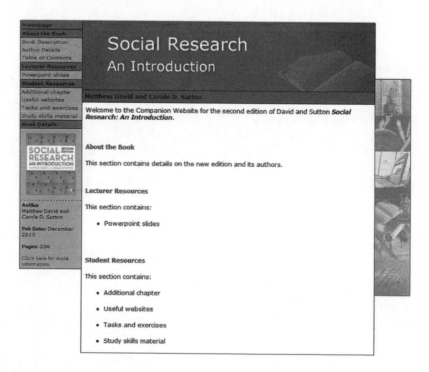

In memory of Christopher David 1938–2010

ACKNOWLEDGEMENTS

We would like to thank friends, family and colleagues for their support. In particular, thanks are extended to Sarah Louisa Pythain-Adams, Lyn Bryant, Loretta Cook, Danny Daniels, Susie Loates, Moira Maconachie, Pete Millward, Chris Rojek and Malcolm Williams for their continued support and encouragement. Many thanks to the Sage editorial staff, in particular Ian Antcliff, Patrick Brindle and Katie Metzler, and to the anonymous reviewers for their constructive comments and suggestions. Particular thanks also go to Jodie Allen, Sue Child, Gesa Kather, Michaela Pyšňáková and Mike Sheaff for their examples. Screenshots from QSR NVivo are reproduced with permission by QSR International Pty Ltd. Screenshots and output from IBM SPSS Statistics 19 are reproduced with permission of SPSS Inc.

GUIDED TOUR

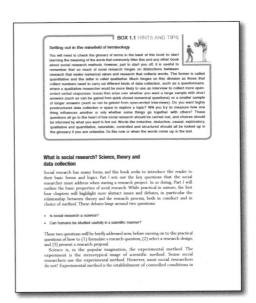

Chapter Aims provide you with the key learning objectives and issues to be addressed in each chapter.

Hints and Tips boxes provide you with practical tips on a range of topics related to carrying out your own research based on the authors' years of experience.

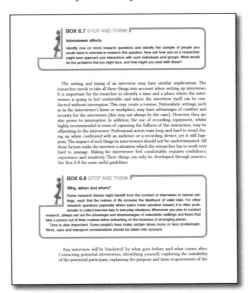

Research Focus boxes provide summaries of examples of real-life research, including both key classic studies and recent research projects.

Stop and Think boxes ask you to stop and reflect on questions raised in the text or more widely on issues which affect your research.

confrontation with difference to reflect upon the weakness of their existing ways of thinking to capture the experience of others. Reflexive field note writing is part of that process. Reflecting on one's experience is one way of telling when it is time to leave the field. Other factors (time, access and finance) also play a part.

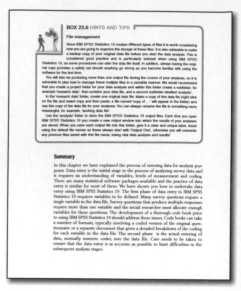
Getting out

A more deductive research strategy will set out in advance the data required to address the question being asked (or the theory being tested). More inductive forms of research cannot specify in advance what and how much data will be sufficient to complete the research. How, then, should the ethnographer decide when to leave the field? One key factor is time. Research funds and access permission have their limits. These constraints may set external limits. Internal criteria can also be developed. As with other forms of inductive research, data collection may be said to be sufficient once a level of saturation has been reached. Saturation refers to the situation the research reaches when new data only act to confirm what the researcher already predicted would be the case based upon their prior research. Once the theories that have developed through the course of data collection and reflection become powerful predictors of future data, there is little reason to carry on collecting data. As has already been noted in the context of focus groups (section 'Conduct and management' in Chapter 7), what would be sufficient

---

Consider This boxes provide you with further examples from research that pose challenging questions for you to consider.

Summary

In this chapter we have explained the process of entering data for analysis purposes. Data entry is the initial stage in the process of analysing survey data and it requires an understanding of variables, levels of measurement and coding. There are many statistical software packages available and the practice of data entry is similar for most of them. We have shown you how to undertake data entry using IBM SPSS Statistics 19. The first phase of data entry in IBM SPSS Statistics 19 requires variables to be defined. Many survey questions require a single variable in the data file. Survey questions that produce multiple responses require more than one variable and the social researcher must allocate enough variables for these questions. The development of a thorough code book prior to using IBM SPSS Statistics 19 should address these issues. Code books can take a number of formats, typically involving a coded version of the original questionnaire or a separate document that gives a detailed breakdown of the coding for each variable in the data file. The second phase is the actual entering of data, normally numeric codes, into the data file. Care needs to be taken to ensure that the data entry is as accurate as possible to limit difficulties in the subsequent analysis stages.

Summaries at the end of each chapter review key concepts and issues covered to consolidate your learning.

Summary

Whilst discourse analysts are critical of the content analytic reduction of qualitative data to tables and charts via coding, discourse analysts often use coding techniques to contextualize the more detailed analysis they seek to carry out on either single texts or small subsamples of material. Discourse analysis can be pursued in a number of different ways, each with a distinct focus of attention. Semiotic analysis focuses on the construction of associations and differences within signs. The analysis of 'mythic' signs seeks to identify the way in which particular texts (words and/or images) carry deeper connotations than are manifestly denoted within surface content. Deconstruction focuses attention on the multiple meanings at work within seemingly coherent and singular textual productions (words or longer segments). Rather than looking for the deeper meaning, deconstruction seeks to show the absence of a deeper meaning below a surface level filled with multiple, often contradictory, meanings. Narrative analysis aims to identify the devices by which a text constructs time, genre, sequence, cause and effect, content and context. If we take someone's life story literally (as a true picture), we might overlook the literary devices at work within their storytelling.

Conversation analysis has its own rules for the presentation and analysis of naturally occurring talk. Most importantly, what is sought is an account of the machinery at work within the talk that relies neither on assumptions about the context beyond the talk nor on the assumed motivations of the talkers. Conversation analysis seeks to analyse the talk itself.

Questions

1 What is a 'myth' in semiotic analysis?
2 What aspects of language are of principal interest in deconstruction or narrative analysis, and how are these analysed?
3 To what extent can such divergent approaches as semiotics, conversation analysis, narrative analysis and deconstruction be used together, or with forms of content analysis?

Further reading

Barthes, Roland (1967) *Elements of Semiology*. London: Cape.

Elliott, Jane (2005) *Using Narrative in Social Research: Qualitative and Quantitative Approaches*. London: Sage.

Kohler Riessman, Catherine (1993) *Narrative Analysis*. London: Sage.

Wodek, Ruth (2007) 'Critical discourse analysis', in Clive Seale, Giampietro Gobo, Jaber Gubrium and David Silverman (eds), *Qualitative Research Practice*. London: Sage. pp. 185–201.

Questions related to the content of each chapter appear at the end to test that you've understood what you've read and to encourage you to reflect.
Further Reading suggestions lead you to resources where you can find additional information.

GLOSSARY

ABSTRACTS AND INDEXES. Abstracts are summaries that sum up the content of a journal article (or other text). Abstracts used to be collected into large bound volumes that could be searched for using parallel volumes of indexes (alphabetical lists by author, title and subject matter). Now, much of this searching can be done on electronic abstracting and indexing services.

ACTION RESEARCH. Research designed not simply to know the world, but to enable change. Action research is more than just policy-driven research; it seeks to implement policy through the research itself. See also *evaluation research*, *participant action research*.

ACTORS. While an actor is said to engage in action, machines, plants, objects and so on only display behaviour (the position of animals is controversial in this spectrum). Action requires a consciousness capable of reflecting upon a course of action. While behaviour can be studied simply in terms of causal mechanisms, understanding action requires a knowledge of what the actor intended to achieve by their action, even if this is not the whole story. The capacity for self-reflection is seen by some as grounds for saying an actor is 'morally' responsible for their actions in the way that, for example, a thunderbolt is not responsible for its behaviour. This view is premised upon the belief that if an action was 'chosen', in the course of 'reflection', the actor could have chosen not to take that course of action. In other words, some believe that actors are at least in part able to determine (cause) their own actions and therefore should be held accountable for those actions. Others prefer to use the term 'subject' to refer to the human individual (consciousness as well as physical being) so as to avoid this attribution of something close to 'free will'. The term 'actor' is closely associated with the term 'agency', which again is often used to attribute self-determination to human beings, rather than seeing them as outcomes of the social arrangements they are a part of. Once again, critics highlight the fact that such a term assumes some kind of freedom of the will, something that cannot be proven, and is almost impossible to conceptualize, except in the base sense of feeling the urge to blame and punish (itself a form of social causation that justifies itself in the language of responsible actors).

ADJACENCY PAIRS. Conversation analytic term referring to forms of talk where the first speaker's talk elicits a predictable response. The expectation built into such

---

The **Glossary** at the end of the book provides a quick reference source for concise definitions of key terms used throughout the text.

PART ONE
STARTING YOUR RESEARCH

ONE

GETTING STARTED: THEORY, RESEARCH QUESTION AND RESEARCH DESIGN

Chapter Contents

By the end of this chapter you will be able to:

- **Understand key elements in formulating a research question.**
- **Distinguish between deductive and inductive research designs, and be able to address the questions that social researchers need to ask when choosing which approach to adopt.**
- **Distinguish primary and secondary data, and be able to critically evaluate their relative advantages and disadvantages.**
- **Identify logical fallacies that recur in research and in everyday life, and which distort understanding.**
- **Comprehend the basic elements of sampling.**
- **Understand key elements of data validity.**

Getting into the water

This chapter, along with Chapters 2, 3 and 4, sets out issues that all social researchers need to think about, decide upon and carry out in order to begin an empirical research project. In some respects this is like getting into the water when going swimming. There is an advantage to just jumping in: the best way to learn is to have a go. But just jumping in without having learnt some basic things might lead to drowning, so here we offer some basic guidelines on what to do. These chapters are about 'getting into the water' safely and with confidence. Doing social research requires that you do a large number of things, seemingly at the same time. This, at first, seems confusing. Those who have been doing research for a while tend to take it for granted, and so they are not always aware of every aspect of what they are doing when they do it. This can confuse the beginner even more. Getting into the loop is about picking up the taken-for-granted routines of the more experienced researcher, and practising them. Once you are familiar with the steps, processes and short-cuts you will no doubt develop your own style, your own routines and your own agenda. The way things are set out here is to help you get started. You will always have to bear them in mind, but after a while you may do things in your own way. This chapter will start with a discussion of how you can generate a research question. It will then discuss how to begin converting this research question into a research design, which involves decisions about testing or exploring; using primary or secondary data; causal or descriptive approaches; interviews, surveys, archival data or observations; issues of validity, reliability and generalization; and evaluation, participatory or action designs. It will finally address the question of writing a research proposal that will allow you to actually do your research. Box 1.1 outlines a few key distinctions that you will need to familiarize yourself with before you read the rest of this book.

BOX 1.1 HINTS AND TIPS

Setting out in the minefield of terminology

You will need to check the glossary of terms in the back of this book to start learning the meaning of the words that commonly litter this and any other book about social research methods. However, just to start you off, it is useful to remember that so much of social research hinges on distinctions between research that seeks numerical values and research that collects words. The former is called quantitative and the latter is called qualitative. Much hinges on this division as those that collect numbers need to carry out different kinds of data collection, such as a questionnaire, where a qualitative researcher would be more likely to use an interview to collect more open-ended verbal responses. Issues then arise over whether you want a large sample with short answers (such as can be gained from quick closed numerical questions) or a smaller sample of longer answers (such as can be gained from open-ended interviews). Do you want highly prestructured data collection or space to explore a topic? Will you try to measure how one thing influences another or only whether some things go together with others? These questions all go to the heart of how social research should be carried out, and choices should be informed by what you want to find out. Words like inductive, deductive, causal, exploratory, qualitative and quantitative, naturalistic, controlled and structured should all be looked up in the glossary if you are unfamiliar. Do this now or when the words come up in the text.

What is social research? Science, theory and data collection

Social research has many forms, and this book seeks to introduce the reader to their basic forms and logics. Part I sets out the key questions that the social researcher must address when starting a research project. In so doing, Part I will outline the basic properties of social research. While practical in nature, the first four chapters will highlight more abstract issues and debates, in particular the relationship between theory and the research process, both in conduct and in choice of method. These debates hinge around two questions:

- Is social research a science?
- Can humans be studied usefully in a scientific manner?

These two questions will be briefly addressed now, before moving on to the practical questions of how to (1) formulate a research question; (2) select a research design; and (3) present a research proposal.

Science is, in the popular imagination, the experimental method. The experiment is the stereotypical image of scientific method. Some social researchers use the experimental method. However, most social researchers do not! Experimental method is the establishment of controlled conditions in which the effect of variables on other variables can be measured. Regulation of inputs allows accurate estimation of causes in the variation of outputs. Experimental method requires an initial prediction about how variation of inputs will affect outputs such that this prediction can then be tested. This prediction is a provisional theory (or thesis). This is called a hypothesis. A variable is anything whose amount can vary, and which is defined in such a way that its variation can be measured (and in an experiment also controlled in this variation). A number of variables may be specified. In the classic experiment (Box 1.2) all identifiable variables are held constant (controlled conditions), bar two variables. These are the independent and dependent variables set out in the prediction/hypothesis. The hypothesis predicts that variation in the independent variable causes variation in the dependent variable. With all other things held constant, the experiment is designed to allow this hypothesis to be tested. The hypothesis is drawn from prior examination of research on the subject. As such the experiment is theory driven (in other words, the data collection is designed to fulfil a need for the information required to answer a theoretical question). This approach to the relationship between theory and research is called deduction. Hence the experimental method is called hypothetico-deductive.

BOX 1.2 CONSIDER THIS

A classic experimental design

It is commonly suggested that students underperform in assessments due to lack of sleep before exams. They stay up all night revising. It would be possible to select a group of students with otherwise similar characteristics (age, gender and previous exam performance, for example). These students could all be given the same amount of preparation in the week before an exam. Then, on the night before the exam, all the students would be kept together in a controlled hall of residence. The group could be divided into subgroups. One group would be required to go to bed 10 hours before the exam, the next 9 hours, the next 8 hours etc., with the time not spent sleeping being given over to exam revision. Who would do best? Those who had 10 hours sleep and did no additional revision, those who had 8 hours sleep and 2 hours revision, those who had no sleep and 10 hours revision? Or would the best performance come from somewhere in between?

It is important to note that much research in the physical sciences is not strictly speaking experimental. Much of geology, astronomy and biology deploy methods of data collection beyond the laboratory. Geological and evolutionary time, galaxies and ecosystems cannot be replicated in controlled conditions. This is also the case for many aspects of social life (Box 1.3). Science cannot be defined exclusively in terms of the classical experiment.

However, despite not always using the experimental method, much of the remaining physical science research does deploy another form of hypothetico-deductive research (that is, research where a prediction is tested through the variation of observed conditions). This may be through comparison over time or between locations. If different levels of a particular variable exist in different locations or at different times, it may be possible to measure the levels of other variables in those times and places to see if patterns (or correlations) exist. Whilst an element of control is lost, it may still be possible to show that variations in one factor go along with variation in other factors (even if what is causing what is harder to pin down). A hypothesis can be stated. The researcher can then go looking for the conditions necessary to test that hypothesis. Data can be collected and results analysed which will then support or challenge the hypothesis. This is still therefore hypothetico-deductive research.

A far greater amount of social research adopts this approach. Proponents of this type of social research tend to see themselves as scientists. However, some forms of social research are not hypothetico-deductive and pursue an exploration-based approach. Sometimes this is to identify what is going on when existing knowledge is insufficient to generate hypotheses. There are plenty of such examples in the physical sciences. Sometimes, this exploratory approach is adopted as a rejection of the hypothetico-deductive method, its predictive process and causal assumptions. This raises the question of whether scientific methods are appropriate to study humans, or whether humans possess qualitatively different characteristics to physical objects (most particularly consciousness and choice) that invalidate predictive forms of research and the predictive model of explanation which hypothetico-deductive research is based upon. These issues will be discussed later (see section 'Testing or exploring?' later in this chapter, and see Chapter 4). These are questions that will recur throughout the research process, but which cannot be resolved at this stage.

Identifying a research question

While a hypothesis is a proposition to be tested, rather than a question to be answered, hypotheses are designed to focus attention within broader research areas or questions. While some research questions are very specific and others far looser in definition, the process of identifying a research question is always an essential first step in any project.

Social problems, political issues, personal motives?

A researcher may enter the process of identifying the research question at a number of different stages. Ironically, the student conducting a research project for their studies and the well-established research professor may have more in common here with each other than either may have with the majority of researchers in the middle. The privilege of starting from first principles, rather than being brought in at the middle or towards the end of the research problem identification process, is most often denied to those neither well established nor researching for study.

Identification of the research question may have many levels, only some of which will be within the researcher's power to alter, at least in the first instance. Issues may become 'ripe' for research in the minds of those able to fund such activities for a number of reasons. Bodies engaged in education, health care, law and order, social work, economics, urban planning, commercial and governmental administration and so on will, for various reasons, come to the view that research may help them address or more clearly identify problems. Research may be funded by charities on issues of concern to them so that findings stimulate awareness and debate about those issues. These bodies will form an opinion about what needs to be researched and such motivations play a crucial role in the identification of research questions.

However, even while such factors play a crucial role in directing research, the question of how such research is to be carried out requires the researcher to develop the identification process from an idea to a practical activity. It is here that the researcher's own interpretations of the 'problem', and the best way to research it, come into play. When the researcher can claim a degree of expertise both in the subject to be studied and in the methods by which such a subject can best be studied, they are in a position to introduce their own definitions of themes and interpretations of 'problems'. To this extent the more developed researcher may become proactive in regard to seeking funding from potentially interested parties for projects the researcher is personally motivated by. In this way the researcher may move 'upstream' in the question identification process. When a researcher's own previous research comes to define how potential research funding bodies perceive an issue, they may consider themselves to have become the source of the stream itself. Most researchers are not in such a fortunate situation, but, as Tim May (1997: 27) points out, the relationship between theories of what problems exist and methods applied to investigate their existence is always a two-way street, even if the density of traffic in each direction varies.

Whether the researcher is contracted to research a particular topic, doing a project within or on behalf of an organization, bidding for funding from a public or private agency, or conducting research as a training exercise within an educational context, the first step in identifying the research question in a practical fashion is to find out what has gone before (see Chapter 3 on Literature Searching and Reviewing. Those interested in the intricacies of gaining funding, and in the politics of such processes, will find many useful discussions (for example, Hammersley, 1995; 2000). Here we will move on to the issue of generating a research question. We will then look at the two types of research question: hypothesis testing and exploratory investigation.

Sources of a research question

Sociologists often refer to the title of C. Wright Mills's (1959) book *The Sociological Imagination* as though this referred to some particular source of creativity that being a sociologist somehow confers upon them. For Mills such an imagination was the combination of two things. First, it was necessary always to ask how what appeared to be personal problems might be better understood as social issues. Second, there arose the application of the researcher's craft required to investigate such suggestions. Mills was famous for collecting newspaper cuttings every day from which he sought to identify contradictions in everyday representations of social life – contradictions that might best be overcome through social research.

The media then may generate issues that can be turned into research questions, but personal experience may do too. Prior research, theory and literature around a topic may generate a question in themselves or in the clash with media representations or personal experience. Newly available access to sources of data (whether these be secondary sources, archives, groups or locations) may make certain questions that were previously hard to answer newly attractive. Just as access opens up questions, so the generation of research questions is bounded by the limits of what data can feasibly be collected. Legal decisions and new policy initiatives may also throw up new questions. In a similar vein, policy and law makers may want research into areas they define as social problems, or to evaluate the consequences and/or effectiveness of their proposals and/or actions. The advent of relatively portable audio and then video recording devices have historically changed the character of research practice, and even opened up new research questions based on new data collection possibilities. The development of personal computing and the internet represents another such transformation in data collection, but also reflects a significant potential change in the character of social reality, not just its 'researchability'. Social change of course represents another key generator of research questions, as do comparisons between different locations.

As such, whilst the origin of a research question may be from many sources and the combination of many different elements, constraints of feasibility and relevance also shape the question formation process. Feasibility refers to access, ethics, time and other resources that the research has to take into consideration. Relevance refers to a combination of factors too. Is the research significant, either in policy terms or in understanding important social issues? Does the research question have any relevance to existing research and literature in the field? Will the question maintain the researcher's own interest? Policy or social relevance, theoretical precedence and personal passion about a topic are essential to getting research off the ground and sustaining it, even while all these elements generate scope for bias that needs to be reflected upon in the process of research design, data collection and analysis.

Talking to people is another key source for generating a research question. This may be informal discussion with colleagues, tutors, family or friends; you may want to organize a discussion group, a focus group or a Delphi group (a focus group of experts in a chosen field); or you may want to set up a discussion board online. Academics and other professional groups routinely attend conferences, often more for the informal 'chatting' opportunities these events provide than for the formal papers they could just as well read at home. Robson (2002: 49, 57) makes the useful suggestions to start where you are but to trawl cognate fields to see if other people do things differently. You might be a geographer, but perhaps the psychologists have something you had not already thought of.

What makes a good research question?

Nicola Green (2008: 47–9) suggests the key to a good research question is that it is 'researchable', and proposes six elements. A good research question will be: (1) interesting; (2) relevant; (3) feasible; (4) ethical; (5) concise; and (6) answerable. Interest to the researcher sustains research practice through the hard times, while relevance to the wider society or to the academic and/or policy community is necessary to maintain funding and esteem. Feasibility in terms of time, topic, place, costs, skills, access and information is crucial. Maintaining ethical standards regarding topic, access, and respect for participants in the collection, analysis and use of data, and in relation to the researcher's own wellbeing, is also essential if research is to be successful. Research must be concise, that is well articulated, conceptually clear, theoretically framed, and able to translate abstract ideas into empirically measurable categories about which data can be collected. Finally, a good research question should be posed in such a way that it would be possible to know what it would take to answer it. Green (2008) notes the importance of mapping the interrogatives – the who, what, when, where, how and why questions. The first four of these are descriptive, the fifth maps process, whilst the sixth refers to causation. As will be seen below, refining the research question allows the researcher to identify whether they are primarily concerned with description, process or causation.

The good research question is always a balancing act. You need to be relevant to what has gone before, but at the same time show that the research you want to carry out will add something new. You need to be concise and yet you do not want to be so pre-emptive as to close down the very originality that new empirical data collection might bring. There is a temptation to be conservative (with a small c) in wanting to ensure that the research is doable, but at the same time there is a temptation to be radical (with a small r) in wanting to do what has never been done before. It is easier to describe, but perhaps more interesting to explain why something is the case. As such, the glory of novelty and the shame/difficulty of biting off more than you can chew should inform your decision as to how you develop your research question.

In reverse fashion it should be pointed out that some things make for a bad research question, and these boil down largely to 'letting the tail wag the dog'. It is not enough simply to do a particular research project because you can. If you formulate your research question simply because you have a particular access, or because you are particularly good or experienced with a certain data collection and/or analysis technique, then the research is likely to be limited and unoriginal. Despite earlier suggestions that research should be doable, it is not enough to just do what is easiest to do. 'Doable' is a necessary condition, but it is not a sufficient condition, and it should be a criterion for evaluating a research question, not the principle on which a question is initially selected. Questions of principle, concerning relevance to social problems, policy and academic development, come first. Practical questions of feasibility (time, money, access, skills) should come second, but are still important.

The value of a good research question

For the same reason that a good research question maps the interrogatives (the what, when, where, who, how and why questions), the value of so doing lies in defining whether your research will explore, describe, explain or even challenge the object of its attention. Exploration seeks to find out what is going on in a situation in the absence of any prior account. Exploration involves description, but exploration involves not even knowing in advance the full range of what it is you will seek to describe. Description seeks to capture the what, where, when and who of a situation, often in the absence of any prior or sufficient explanation of what is going on. Explanation requires a descriptive mapping of the situation, but involves the addition of seeking to explain relations between the phenomena being described, in particular the possibility that certain features of a situation cause others. Critical researchers may go one step further in seeking to suggest that research can identify the causes of problems and encourage improvements. The value of a good research question in the first place lies in helping clarify what your research is seeking to achieve.

The establishment of a research question will act as something of an anchor during the course of subsequent stages in the research process. Your research question will guide the search for prior literature (see Chapter 3) and inform the way you filter and review such work found. The research question, perhaps reframed in the light of your literature review, will then determine the research design you select, which itself determines your data collection, analysis and interpretation. Each step along the way will involve reflection, and may involve modifications, but a well-formulated research question should guide you from beginning to end. It is too easy to be moved off along various tangents. Difficulties in data collection may lead to certain data being easier to collect or certain groups easier to collect from. Without a robust research question to guide the research process it is easy to be swayed by such conveniences and complications. Your research question should act as a guiding star, something to navigate by. In this regard it is not something that should change at every twist and turn.

Refining your research question: from research question to research design

Keith Punch (2005: 33) usefully distinguishes between areas, topics and questions. A research area is very broad (such as 'class', 'work' or 'family'). A research topic will be narrower (such as 'social mobility within a class structure', 'the relationship between skill and reward at work', or 'divorce'). Research questions operate at an even more specific level. What is it about mobility, skill or divorce that you want to find out about? Punch observes that a general research question may define the key relationships and issues you want to investigate, whilst specific research questions and actual data collection questions involve a further level of focus and detail. This is the transition from research questions to research designs.

Nicola Green (2008: 50–9) suggests a four-step movement from general interest to something narrow enough to have moved from a research question to being the basis for a research design. Whilst step one involves going as wide as possible in terms of sources of ideas and discussions/brainstorming to develop these, step two involves narrowing the list, noting recurrent themes and less common ones, themes that seem to go together and those that seem at odds, core elements and less significant ones, clusters and nested themes that can be merged together, those that are answerable and those that are too abstract or ephemeral. The third step involves drawing out the character of the question you want to ask (descriptive or causal etc.) and, from this, addressing the question of what information (data) would be needed to answer such a question. Step four, a review, involves asking whether the revised research question meets the six criteria for a good research question set out earlier. If so, the research question should naturally flow into providing the basis for a research design, a practical strategy for collecting data.

Turning a research question into a research design is sometimes referred to as 'operationalization'. Sometimes this term is used to refer more narrowly to the process of taking theoretically informed concepts and turning them into empirically recordable objects. The concept of class for example is elusive, and to measure its relationship to health for example would require that each individual be assigned a 'class' value based on a robust scale that could be clearly measured by collecting particular pieces of information. Operationalization in its narrow sense refers to the move from ideas into the realm of empirical measurement. In deductive forms of quantitative research a variable such as class would require definition in advance to allowed individual cases to be measured along a scale of values within the variable. Essentially, in such research concepts have to be translated into variables that are both internally homogeneous and externally discrete. Internal content should be sufficiently 'the same', and 'the same' things should not be able to fit into two values of a variable. How and where the boundaries are to be drawn is therefore fundamental. If you can specify these in advance of collecting any data, you can reasonably conduct a quantitative and deductive research design. If the content of meaningful categories and the boundaries between them cannot be clearly and confidently asserted in advance it is better to adopt a more inductive and qualitative exploration of the research question, whether in the form of a pilot exercise in advance of a more deductive project, or as a stand-alone piece of qualitative research. Qualitative forms of inductive research seek to operationalize concepts only in the process of data collection. It is in the act of exploring that provisional categories are fleshed out into substantive classifications of the field. These forms of operationalization will be discussed in greater detail in Part II.

Testing or exploring?

Researching the existing literature (see Chapter 3) will give you some sense of what has been said before, what the key findings and key disputes are, and perhaps will have left you with a sense of what is missing or still needs further investigation or clarification. Similarly, whether the original motivation for your research was personal, moral, political or intellectual fascination, or the interest of the organization funding the research, this will have given some focus and direction to the research, even if only to establish some of the initial keywords used in your literature search. So, your research will have some degree of focus already, but the degree and nature of that focus must now be clarified further.

At this stage you will need to ask yourself the following questions:

- Do I have a hunch (in other words a hypothesis) about what is going on here?

- Does that hunch/hypothesis suggest to me what the key causes and effects are?

You do not need to be sure. If you knew for sure that increasing amounts of X led to increasing amounts of Y, it would not be necessary to research it. The purpose of at least one type of research (hypothetico-deductive research) is to test hunches. Whether the hunches are supported in the final research or not, we have a result. Research that is based upon the idea of testing hunches is to be distinguished from research where we are setting out only to explore what is present in a particular situation.

Testing a hunch requires that we can state it in such a way that it can be compared with reality. This formulation of the hunch is then a prediction. This is not the same as a question. A question is open ended, while a prediction states an expected outcome. What is open ended, in the case of a prediction, is whether this expected outcome conforms with the actual outcome. Will the prediction be correct? A hunch is a theory that has not yet been supported with evidence. In research terms this is called a hypothesis. What distinguishes a hypothesis from other kinds of ideas is that a hypothesis is designed to be tested, and so must state clearly the elements involved (measurable categories of actions, objects or actors) and the nature of the relationship between them that is being predicted (cause, mediation or correlation). These practical matters will be dealt with in greater detail in Chapter 4. Here it is only necessary to be aware of the distinction between testing and exploring, and the logic behind choosing either one or a combination of the two. So what is exploratory research and why choose not to test a hypothesis?

On completing a review of the literature you may feel that there is a reasonable case for suggesting that X has a relationship with Y, and even that the relationship is a causal one. This may not have been actively tested in the previous research you looked at, or such testing may have been long ago or in a different location, thereby warranting your wish to carry out such tests. Alternatively, you may feel that the literature does not leave you with a hypothesis that can be tested, only a series of open questions about what is going on. If this is the case, it is not going to be possible to draw up a testable hypothesis. You have no tentative predictions, only questions. In this instance you will want to adopt an exploratory approach. Without a prediction to test, the design of exploratory research will be more open ended. Because of this, exploratory research tends to collect more qualitative (interpretive) data, though this is not always true. Testing a hypothesis is more often associated with the use of quantitative (numerical) methods. Chapter 4 examines the qualitative/quantitative distinction in more depth.

The key to hypothesis testing is the belief that the existing literature is a reasonable source of predictions. Exploratory research designs tend to occur when predictions cannot be gleaned from the literature. However, some argue that it is not just a question of 'if and when' the literature cannot generate reasonable predictions, but a question of principle, and that theory should not determine the structure of research in such a rigid way as is required for hypothesis testing. Such researchers argue that theory should be built up from exploration of reality, not used to predict it in advance. This is an inductive (as opposed to a deductive) approach to theory building and research. Here it is enough to say that all good research combines elements of prediction and exploration even without using the terminology. In using a literature review, all researchers to some degree are guided in their work by predictions of what is useful to research, where and how to look and what to look out for. Even the most 'inductive' researcher cannot avoid this. Yet at the same time the use of some form of exploratory research is standard practice in even the most rigid hypothesis testing research. The pilot study, where researchers seek to explore the extent to which those they seek to research support the hypotheses, may take many forms. Some are more open than others, but all are forms of preliminary exploration (see Chapter 4). For now, suffice to say, while differences are great, they are not always as great as might first appear. So then the question for the researcher is: should I generate a hypothesis or adopt a more exploratory approach? In part this will depend on what you have found in your review of the literature, but it will also depend on your stance concerning the nature of human action – causation or choice (see sections 'Causes, meanings and probabilities?' later in this chapter; and 'The deeper divide' in Chapter 4).

Primary and secondary sources

The process of social research outlined in this text focuses predominantly on the designing, processing and analysing of data collected by the researcher, known as primary research. Depending on the area of research and the research question, it may be appropriate to consider using and searching for existing data. These data can then be examined and analysed, a technique called secondary analysis.

It is worth taking a few lines to discuss what exactly is defined by secondary data analysis. Compared to primary research, much less has been written on secondary analysis. Hakim provides the traditional definition of secondary analysis as 'any further analysis of an existing data set which presents interpretations, conclusions or knowledge additional to, or different from, those presented in the first report on the inquiry as a whole and its main results' (1982: 1). Dale et al. (1988) suggest that secondary analysis is a broader term that simply entails data being analysed by someone else other than the original researcher. The most famous piece of secondary data analysis in the history of sociology is Emile Durkheim's (1952) use of suicide statistics from various regions of Germany and France in the mid nineteenth century to highlight that patterns were consistent over time, but varied across location, such that certain social facts clearly increased or decreased the incidence of self-inflicted death. In the UK, secondary analysis emerged during the 1960s and 1970s as a product of the large surveys undertaken by government departments and agencies. These developments were paralleled in other industrial societies across the world. Surveys such as the General Household Survey, Family Expenditure Survey, British Crime Survey and British Social Attitudes Survey and the 10-yearly Census were conducted by government to inform economic and social policy. The UK government did, of course, collect data on the population before this date. The first Census was in 1801. Since the 1960s, the number of surveys and the coverage of the surveys have broadened considerably and the availability of data for secondary analysis has been improved through the development of websites detailing the original survey and data, for example, the Economic and Social Research Council (ESRC) Data Archive at Essex University (www. data-archive.ac.uk).

The decision to undertake a primary or secondary research design should be determined by the theoretical and conceptual nature of the research question. Beyond this, secondary analysis can often be restricted by the availability and quality of existing data. Given the historical nature of secondary analysis, with its roots in government surveys, the majority of data available are quantitative, numerical data, derived from questionnaire and structured interview-based surveys. Ongoing initiatives are being undertaken to redress the balance through funding for a qualitative data archive (www.qualidata.ac.uk) which aims to collect interview transcripts, diaries, participant observation notes and so on.

Causes, meanings and probabilities? Logic, relationships and people

A naïve or simple conception of causation suggests that when X is said to cause Y, what is meant is that X makes Y happen. This implies a mechanism at work, and this idea of mechanisms is not accepted by many in the social sciences who suggest human action is either too complex or too qualitatively distinct from physical events which seem more easily reducible to mechanistic accounts. Are these objections legitimate? Statements like 'X causes Y' seem to suggest either that every instance of Y is the result of a prior instance of X, or that every instance of X will result in the production of an instance of Y. The first is a logical fallacy. The second is false on the grounds that no singular action is ever 'sufficient' to explain an outcome. First, it is logically incorrect to say that because X causes Y, all Ys must result from Xs. Exams cause stress, but not all stress is caused by exams! Second, in conditions of complexity (reality) it is incorrect to assume that because X causes Y, all instances of Xs will lead to Ys. Exams cause stress, but not all exams are experienced as stressful because intervening factors can influence the outcome in some cases.

As mentioned above, the first example is an instance of a logical fallacy: the fallacy of 'reversal'. Just because something may cause another thing to happen does not mean it is the only possible cause. Other logical fallacies are those of 'composition' (that is, if one woman can become prime minister then all women can, or if one person is bad then all in that group must be bad), and 'association' (that is, if storks nest before babies arrive, storks must cause babies to arrive). Logical errors of this sort characterize much of everyday consciousness and political rhetoric as well. Social researchers are not immune, so care must be taken to avoid such logical pitfalls when posing a hypothesis or deciding whether to pursue a causal hypothesis. For further discussion of logical fallacies, see Sayer (1992).

The second example (where a causal agent does not lead to the same effect every time) is a manifestation of complexity, and raises the issue of necessary and sufficient conditions of causation. Sometimes when a light switch is flicked the light comes on. Sometimes it does not. It is not enough to say that flicking the switch causes the light to come on, although it is a part of the causal process at work. There are other links in the chain, and if any of these are out of place the sequence is not completed and the effect does not happen. Necessary conditions are those that are required for an event to occur, but no single one of them is sufficient on its own. As such, causation in conditions of complexity never operates by means of single links where X will always cause Y. The weather is a complex set of interacting systems and subsystems. Because of the extent of its complexity it is not possible to predict with absolute certainty what certain conditions will lead to. Causation is too complex to map outcomes with absolute certainty. Within such complex systems prediction is not always possible, even where a fairly clear idea of the causal factors and mechanisms has been developed. Open systems defy absolute prediction, but this is not because they are beyond causation.

Tendencies are one way of describing the existence of forms of causal association that are never absolute because of the complex interaction of many necessary conditions. There is a tendency for class background to affect educational performance, but this is never absolute, as there are many factors in an individual's life that may alter their chances, even if these factors are largely stacked in favour of those from more affluent backgrounds. Intervening factors are often called mediations. Tendencies can be expressed in the form of probabilities rather than in terms of absolute causation. Modern statistical techniques were largely developed to aid researchers in the human sciences deal with the fact that complexity never allows for singular causal agents to have 100 per cent outcomes.

So far, then, the objection to simplistic (X makes Y happen) causal explanations of human action can be accepted on the grounds that reference to mechanisms may imply too simplistic a set of causal processes than are in fact at work. However, if we avoid logical fallacies of causation and recognize complexity, while limiting the scope of prediction and prohibiting the use of simple monocausal models, these objections are defused. Are there other grounds for resisting causal explanations in social research?

One suggestion is that human action is intentional, and that intentions are future oriented. Can a future state that motivates a present action be called a cause? As causes must come before effects, the future cannot cause the present, and so, it is argued, intentional action is best not understood in causal terms. This is a logical error, as it is not the future that causes an intentional action, but the intention itself, which can be firmly located prior to the intentional act. Another suggestion is that causes refer to external forces acting upon an object. Human actions emerge from the workings of inner states. It is suggested that it is meaningless to suggest that something caused itself. Could this argument be applied to a video-recorder? Having a complex inner mechanism, a video-recorder acts upon itself. Causal mechanisms operate inside the box. A third suggestion is that beliefs and meanings are linguistic entities rather than physical ones. Whilst language may have rules, structures and even devices and mechanisms, these are not the same as physical rules and mechanisms. As such, using the term 'causation' to describe the influence of an idea or the strength of a belief may be misleading. Certainly, using the kinds of mechanism appropriate to physics to explain language would be unduly reductionistic. Many biologists would say the mechanisms in physics are not sufficient to explain biological phenomena. It may be that language is simply another level of causation that has its own set of mechanisms. Perhaps it is fundamentally distinct. It is not really important to decide here whether language, human consciousness and intentionality really transcend causal logic and explanation. Language and conscious intentionality can be seen either as mediations in the causal process or as something distinct from causal mechanics. Either way, language and conscious intentionality play a part in the outcome of social affairs, even if the extent to which this is the case is open for dispute. Whether you reject causation as key to understanding social life or accept it, there will always be a role for asking people what they think is going on, even while it may well be the case that other important processes operate 'behind their backs' as it were. A false belief as much as a true belief, and a caused belief (if such a 'thing' exists) as much as a freely chosen belief (if such a 'thing' exists), have implications for the behaviour of the believer and their social world.

Data: asking, looking, reading and recording

What are data? While there is a great deal going on beyond that which researchers record, what goes on 'out there' is not data. Data are not what is out there to collect. Data are what is actually recorded by the researcher. As such, data are not naturally occurring 'stuff'; they are in a very important respect what researchers manufacture in their work as researchers. Why make this distinction? Well, fundamentally it is to remind you that what the researcher records is not reality itself but a 'reflection' of that reality, shaped by the tools they use to generate and record it. This is important to remember. It is nice to imagine that the camera or the human eye gives a 'picture' of the world that never lies. This is not true. The camera must be pointed in one direction rather than another. The human eye (and the sensory system of which it is a part) is selective. How the researcher chooses to direct and select will shape the data they collect. How they choose to record what they collect will involve classification, and this classification also shapes the data that are collected. How they choose to sample will affect what it is they collect. How they choose to frame their questions or structure their observations will influence the form and content of their data. In this respect, data are a product of research and not something that researchers simply collect. Data are the output of research, not the input. Research is in many respects therefore a kind of manufacture, and requires all kinds of tools and apparatus. This may also be called a form of technology. These tools may be physical objects (such as cameras, tape-recorders and computers, or in the case of the physical sciences, microscopes and spectrometers). Tools refer also to forms of structured interactions, such as the interview or the observation. The survey questionnaire and the experiment are tools that fuse both physical and social elements (a carefully structured text on paper or a controlled laboratory). All of these tools (or technologies) act to stimulate and filter events and actions so as to generate materials that can then be recorded as data. Even the most naturalistic forms of research (such as an ethnographic field trip where the researcher lives with a community to observe their everyday lives) involve complex designs and tools (choices over where to visit, how to live, how to ask questions and how to record findings). There is no such thing as the totally unstructured interview or observation, even if some forms of research adopt far less pre-emptive structuring than others.

As will be discussed in the following chapters, all forms of social research involve a lot of planning. All data collection requires the development of tools and technologies of both a physical and a social kind. While social research can be divided in terms of the type of data collected and the degree and form of structure imposed in the collection and recording of those data, all data are manufactured. The types of data are observational based, question asking, and the collection of 'textual' materials (these materials may be diaries, letters, photographs or receipts and so on). The degree of structure refers to the deductive and the inductive forms. This allows the generation of six ideal-typical forms of primary data collection (research designs):

1 deductive observation: such as the experiment

2 inductive observation: such as the ethnographic study

3 deductive questioning: such as the survey questionnaire

4 inductive questioning: such as the in-depth interview

5 deductive textual study: such as quantitative newspaper content analysis

6 inductive textual study: such as qualitative content analysis or discourse analysis.

Research projects may adopt a combination of methods to achieve specific ends. This is often called triangulation. Observation records what people are doing at the point of observation. Interviews and questionnaires record what people say or write at the point of response. These two things are different. Your choice of method needs to reflect whether you are more interested in action or talk, or your best judgement as to what method will best give insight into an issue. It should always be borne in mind that what people do and what they say they do are not always the same thing. Similarly, what people say and do and what people say and do when they are being observed are not always the same things.

What, and how much, is good enough? Validity, reliability and generalizability

Spending a large amount of time observing or interviewing a small number of people offers greater opportunity to know them better. Spending less time with each person or group, and so allowing the research to involve a larger number of people, offers greater opportunity to claim that what one finds is not idiosyncratic. This tension cannot be washed away with a single formula. What is to be done? The tension is often described as one between validity and generalizability (or between internal and external validity).

Validity refers to the closeness of fit between data and reality. Are your data really showing what is 'out there'? Validity can be divided into two parts. The first part refers to the fit with those you actually studied. Do your data actually express the reality of their lives and beliefs? This is what is called internal validity. The second part refers to the fit with the wider world. Do your data really show the reality of the wider population from which your sample was selected? This is external validity (sometimes called generalizability). Population does not refer to everybody. Population refers to everybody in the group you claim to be researching. If you claim to be studying the French, then your population is everyone who is French. We do not need to worry too much about this here, but defining such a group, or any group, is not a straightforward exercise. If you claim to be researching the homeless in Plymouth, your population is every homeless person in Plymouth. What counts as homeless and Plymouth requires interpretations that can be practically measured and defended as accurate. This is not always easy, especially when the group researched is not readily identified. Criminals and racists are not always forthcoming to be recorded, so these populations are largely hidden. (See section 'Reliability and validity' in Chapter 15 for more detail about types of validity.)

In-depth interviewing and long-term observation allow for greater internal validity (though they do not ensure it). Inductive approaches may also allow greater depth of understanding as the researcher is freer to allow the researched to dictate the direction of the research. However, the downside to this is that time spent focused on a small group limits scope for a greater number to be included. This may lead to a loss of external validity. In addition, inductive forms of research that do not impose a strict order on interviews and observations generate problems of reliability. If each interview is different, each interviewee may have greater scope to develop their own interpretation of reality, but it becomes harder to compare one interview with the next. A structured observation or interview/ questionnaire allows clearer comparison. Deductive researchers tend to emphasize the value of reliability (or uniformity) in generating comparable results. They also place greater emphasis on the need to gain a sufficient number of respondents to allow reasonable claims about the whole population concerned. Both these concerns hinge around an emphasis on external validity. Inductive forms of research tend to emphasize internal validity. In so far as inductive research is less concerned with testing a hypothesis than it is with exploring a field, it is less concerned with making generalizable claims.

Gaining external validity is not just about getting as large a number of respondents as possible. A well-chosen but relatively small sample is far more useful than a larger but badly chosen group of respondents. A census, where every member of a population is researched, may sound ideal, but it is rare to have the opportunity, and as rare to have the time to analyse all the data that would be generated. So what counts as a well-chosen sample? A well-chosen sample seeks to mirror the population the researcher is interested in. The first question here is whether it is possible to say who the members of a population are. It is far easier to say who the prison population is than it is to say who the criminal population is. Even if we could define what a criminal is (do you count all those who have ever broken a law?), they are not a group who openly advertise their identity. The most valid sampling method is called the random sample. This requires that the whole population have an equal chance of being chosen, and this requires that we can identify them all. A sampling frame is a list (or even a hat) containing the names of the whole population from which a sample can then be drawn in such a fashion that all have an equal chance of being chosen. This is the meaning of 'random' in a random sample. Random in this context does not mean stopping the first person you meet on the street. A school register is an ideal sampling frame if your population is all the children at that school. Other such lists exist for other populations. But many populations do not have such records, or where they do exist you may not always be allowed access, and in such cases random sampling (strictly speaking) is not possible. Researchers have devised numerous approximations of the random sample to deal with different situations, and these will be discussed in more detail as the book develops (see Chapter 14 for a full account of sampling methods). Here it is only necessary to mention the extreme opposite of the random sample. This is the snowball sample. Where a population is hidden and not much is known about who is and who is not a member, it may be suggested that exploratory/inductive methods be best used. The snowball sample is highly inductive. Where no sampling frame exists and so where a more prestructured selection of sample members cannot be achieved, the researcher may use their first respondent's personal networks as a means of gaining access to other members of the population. This raises many serious questions about external validity, but in an exploratory research project it may be the only way to generate a sample.

Finally, how big does a sample need to be in order to be a good sample? As was said above, size is less significant than good selection methods, but having enough respondents to fulfil the purposes you require is still essential. This will be discussed in more detail in Chapters 5 and 14.

Evaluation, participation and action research

Evaluation research seeks to measure performance. In social research this will usually involve the evaluation of an organizational strategy or the delivery of a service. Performance may be measured in terms of objective indicators (increased sales, declining absenteeism or the reduction of crime in an area) or in terms of more subjective perceptions (customer satisfaction, employee contentment or perceptions of safety). Evaluation research is more interested in practical objectives than in purely theoretical motives, but of course it is the researcher's job to design the best method, and this will involve consideration of past research and theory in the area being researched. As such, evaluation research follows the same processes as other forms of research. In so far as evaluation research tends to start with a clear sense of what is of interest, it will tend to be more deductive in nature. However, especially with regard to the more subjective indicators of performance (which may be less easy to establish in advance), more inductive and exploratory forms of research may be adopted to investigate perceptions and experiences. For more detailed discussions of evaluation-based research, see Rossi et al. (1999), Pawson and Tilley (1997) and/or Clarke and Dawson (1999).

Participatory research takes two basic forms, though a combination of these two creates a third. In the first, the researcher seeks to participate in the everyday practices of those researched in order to gain a better understanding of their life and experience. Such observation by participation is generally led by the routines and practices of those researched. It therefore tends to be inductive, but more deductive forms of participant observation can be used. Participant observation is an extension of the classic ethnographic method of non-participant observation. However, a researcher may take up the role of participant observer with a pre-structured set of questions they want answered, but which they feel can best be investigated by means of observation in natural settings rather than via question-naires or surveys. Participant observation may be overt, covert or partially covert. It can be claimed (on 'consequentialist' ethical grounds: see section 'Sensitivity in the conduct of research' in Chapter 2) that not telling those being observed that their fellow participant is a researcher may be justified. This may, in certain situations, be true. However, as a first-time researcher it is not advisable to choose a topic (such as researching the cultural practices of international gunrunners) where revealing your identity as a social researcher may undermine the validity of the research (and the viability of your health).

The second form of participatory research involves the recruitment of those researched in the conduct and even the construction and evaluation of the research. Involving participants in this way may allow insights not available at the outset, and is a logical extension of inductive principles. Nevertheless, just as inductive methods can sometimes be used at the start of a research project to get a sense of the field prior to the development of a more deductive design, so the initial involvement of participants in developing the research agenda can give way to more deductive forms of participatory research. Such research is almost always overt.

A combination of these two strategies may be adopted. Here the researcher participates in the routines of the researched, and the researched participate in the routines of the researcher.

Action research is an extension of evaluation research. Action research is designed to facilitate the development of the goals of an organization rather than simply to measure the level of success in achieving such goals. Such a form of research presumes both that the goals of the organization are clear and that they are goals the researcher feels are appropriate for them to become involved in pro-moting. Where funding is involved this may lead to pressure on researchers to accept goals as defined by those in the organization in a position to offer the funds. It should be remembered that organizations are not homogeneous and those at the bottom may not see things in quite the same way as those at the top (David, 2002).

One particular brand of research is participant action research. This is the com-bination of action research with a form of participation (Whyte, 1991a; 1991b). The researcher seeks to facilitate the goals of those they are researching. This is the meaning of the term 'action research'. The researcher also seeks to participate with those being researched and to recruit the researched into the process of research design and conduct. This is the meaning of participatory research. Participant action research is a form of advocacy research and assumes the legitimacy of the standpoint of those being researched. If the researcher aims to facilitate the goals of those researched, there must be a presumption that these goals are legitimate. This fusion of research and advocacy parallels many debates within feminist research over the most appropriate research methods to take forward feminist intellectual and political goals.

Writing a research proposal

For various reasons students, professionals of various kinds, academics and others will find themselves wanting or needing to apply for either permission or resources or both for the conduct of a research project of their own. This is the business of writing and submitting a research proposal. Approval may be needed to access certain groups and locations, or to work with various organizations. Whether you are working for an organization or seeking to work within an organization, or aiming to gain funding or other support and approval from particular organizations (such as government departments, businesses, universities, hospitals, schools and charities), these organizations will have particular rules and procedures that you will need to work within. Your research proposal will often involve an up-front demonstration of your awareness of such rules and of your willingness to work within them.

Your research proposal is the way to convince others of the validity and value of your suggested project, but it is also an important means of bringing together these two elements in your own mind. The question of validity relates to the 'truth' content of what you seek to undertake. Does the research question translate into a design that will provide the data capable of answering it? The value question relates to the usefulness of such research, whether in advancing pure knowledge or in developing some kind of policy/practical problem solving application, or both. The questions of 'What?' (what to study), 'How?' (how it will be studied), and 'Why?' (for what purpose it will be studied) come together in the research proposal, just as they do in the movement from a research question to a research design, only with one additional feature. This time you have to convince someone else. As such, you have to make the proposal both clear and impressive.

To write a research proposal involves outlining elements of theoretical and empirical background, design, data collection, ethics and analysis that are yet to be discussed here, and which make up the rest of this book – so don't jump straight in. One thing that a research proposal needs to demonstrate is the prospective researcher's grasp of the field. As such, you will want to have worked your way through this book, at least to a degree, before actually attempting to submit your own proposal.

Whether you are an undergraduate student undertaking a small piece of research within a single course or module, or preparing for a final-year dissertation project; whether you are a professional conducting research within your own organization;

whether you are in the process of applying for funding to conduct a graduate-level research degree (such as an MPhil or a PhD); or whether you are an academic seeking funds or authority to empirically investigate theories in your field; the first administrative hoop will be getting approval for your research proposal. However, you should think of the exercise as your way of proving to yourself that your project is worthwhile, and in the process of getting approval you are likely to increase the actual validity and value of the project. There is no better way to get something clear in your own mind than to have gone through the process of explaining it to someone else. If you can convince someone else that the exercise is worthwhile, you can be very confident that it is. Unless you really are your own harshest critic (and few people are) then the approval of others, particularly those with some qualification to pass judgement, is better than just convincing yourself.

What do they want?

The first thing to think about when constructing a research proposal is the framework and regulations of the organization and system you are submitting the application to. There are seven elements to think about:

1 *Format.* Is there a set application form or guidance on formatting your application? Are you given guidance/instructions regarding how to write and the length required (minimum and often more importantly maximum word lengths)? Are you required to break the proposal down into specified sections with a specified sequence? Where applications are competing for acceptance/funding, the best way to have your application rejected at the first hurdle is not to conform to the guidance/instructions.

2 *Deadlines.* Is there a cutoff point after which applications are no longer accepted for consideration? Again, if there is stiff competition for acceptance/funding you are as well to put your application directly into the recycling bin if you can't get it in on time. Where the penalty for late submission is a deduction of marks or a delay in getting under way, it is only you who loses out. It is sensible to keep an eye on the clock.

3 *Entry criteria.* Does the organization to which you are applying have entry criteria for approval/funding? Do you have to have certain prior qualifications/experience? Some funding bodies and organizations are only accessible to certain nationalities, age groups etc. Check the entry criteria before applying.

4 *Focus.* Does the organization specify the parameters of the work it approves, the topics it is interested in funding or approving, the methods it accepts as valid or useful? There is no point applying to do a sociology dissertation in the physics department. They won't like it.

5 *Resources.* How much time and/or money is available? You have to take resources very much into consideration when constructing your research proposal. You will be turned down if your project cannot be achieved in the time frame being applied for (such as for an undergraduate dissertation or a doctoral degree), irrespective of whether it has other merits. One person funded for three years is not able to do what

three people might in the same time. You need to cut your clothing according to the cloth on offer. If you don't you may end up with embarrassing holes, or no clothes at all.

6 *Coverage.* What's covered? Does the funder or approver provide or pay for equipment, people, space and other resources for travel and related fieldwork expenses? Will you get the time off to do the work required in the project you'd like to do? Will your university fund that overseas trip your undergraduate dissertation really needs? If not, it is unlikely the project is going to be approved, unless you want to pay for it yourself.

7 *Ethical/political orientation.* What are the ethical and social/political principles held by the organization you are applying to? There is no point asking for approval for work that is at odds with these principles, as the answer will be no. You may then wish to consider which other organizations might say yes, but if you are already embedded in a particular company, department or university, you may find yourself having to play by their rules. Knowing what the rules are gives you greater scope to work the rules to your advantage. Rules are open to interpretation, so you may be able to make your case if you give sufficient attention to how to square your plans with your organization's rules.

Presenting yourself

The art of presenting a research proposal is to be clear and authoritative. Show that you know what you are talking about, but avoid jargon and verbiage. Be brief. There is usually a word limit, so practise the art of precision persuasion. People are grateful if you pay them the courtesy of not wasting their time. Don't treat the reader as a fool either. They hold the strings and, even if they don't know as much as you do about your specialist subject, if you can't explain that topic and its importance to them then you have failed, not them. Say what you intend to research, how and why, before you explain the background literature. Put yourself first, but link your ideas to those of others. Be ambitious but don't be unrealistic. Connect with the here and now, but avoid becoming a hostage to fortune (yesterday's headlines are today's waste paper).

Be:

- brief but not sketchy
- authoritative but not condescending
- original but not unrelated to what has gone before
- up to date but not just a flash in the pan
- realistic but not conservative.

How long have you got?

You need to impress upon the person you wish to approve your project that you know what you want to do, how this can be done and why it should. Central to the 'How?' question is whether you have a realistic estimation of the time it will take to get the job done. If you appear unrealistic in your estimation of time management, the person granting approval may get cold feet. Derek Swetnam (2004: 21–2) gives an outline of the timeline for a 10 month undergraduate final-year dissertation. I have translated this into percentages of your total research time.

- reading, planning and setting up   30%
- searching and reviewing the literature   20%
- refining methodology and method/design   10%
- data collection   10%
- data analysis   10%
- preparing conclusions and recommendations   10%
- proofreading, corrections and binding   10%

Note the length of time taken before data collection begins. Don't imagine you will be jumping straight off at the deep end. Give yourself time. If you consider that only 10 per cent of your time will be spent in data collection, scale up the overall time it will take to carry out the project you have in mind. How many interviews a week? It soon adds up, and that time is only a small fraction of the overall time you will need. Don't be naïve. Take time seriously. Whilst there are significant differences between qualitative and quantitative research in terms of the distribution of time, the same general principle applies. Where fieldwork may require longer in the field and less time to calibrate in advance, the overall key is never to underestimate the time it takes to do research. The mark of an experienced researcher is that they appear confident enough to ask for more time to collect fewer data. The novice will often try to do too much too quickly and fail to deliver as a result.

Sequence

The first rule is to follow the guidance on formatting given to you by the organization you are applying to. If there is no specific guidance, Table 1.1 offers a standard default sequence.

Note that the length allowed determines the length of the sections, but whereas the title, the abstract and the aims and objectives tend to remain relatively similar in length irrespective of the overall length of the proposal, the research design and the background will be the sections to take up the additional length if extra words are available. Scale up your sections according to how much space you have to play with. A typical undergraduate final-year dissertation may only ask for a one- or two-page research proposal, whilst an application for a PhD place/funding will usually require (allow) three times this length. Research proposals within non-educational contexts

TABLE 1.1 Sequence of a research proposal

Sequence	Length	Content
Title	Usually about a sentence in length	The what question in a nutshell
Abstract	Usually about a paragraph in length	The what, the how and the why questions in essence
Aims and objectives	Usually a couple of paragraphs	The how and the why questions in a little more detail
Research design	Usually the largest part, as much as you have space to say	Detail the collection, analysis and ethical dimensions (and timeline)
Background	Around half the design section	Practical experience and where the research sits in relation to past and up-to-date developments in the field

may vary somewhere in between. An academic applying to research councils for grants may have to fill in dozens of pages.

All of the above may seem rather daunting and offputting. Nevertheless, it should be seen as an opportunity to clarify your own ideas rather than as an exercise in jumping through other people's hoops.

Summary

Social research takes many forms. The classical experimental method is rare in social research, but in other respects much social research adopts a scientific approach. Deductive research seeks to test a proposition, while more inductive research seeks to explore a research question or field. Hypotheses and research questions emerge from social and political issues and from the researcher's own personal and theoretical motivations. However, research needs to demonstrate that its findings are the result of rigorous methods and not simply the motives of the researcher or those funding them. Are human beings 'free' agents, or 'social' beings? Answers to such speculation shape the kinds of question we might want to ask and the hypotheses we might formulate, as well as the level of prediction/ explanation we might expect our accounts of society to give us. Social life is never fully predictable. 'Data' are what the researcher collects – by asking questions, observing situations or reading human records. Validity, reliability and generalizability are all criteria by which the 'truth' of research can be judged. The quality of the selected sample in relation to the population in question, as well as the quality of the data collection instruments, will determine the depth and scope of the findings. Some research seeks not only to know the world, but also to help change it. This approach raises certain ethical and validity questions. Such approaches offer their own solutions as well as limitations. The development from research question to research design and their combination within a successful research proposal should form a logical progression, even as each step along the way will lead to reflections and adjustments of the steps that have gone before.

 ## ■ Questions

1 How far can social research motives be separated from research methods?
2 What is the relationship between empirical research design and forming a research question?
3 Should social researchers emulate the natural sciences?

■ ■ Further reading ■

Becker, Howard (1967) 'Whose side are we on?', *Social Problems*, 14: 239–47.

David, Matthew (2002) 'Problems of participation: the limits of action research', *International Journal of Social Research Methodology: Theory and Practice*, 5 (1): 11–17.

Hammersley, Martyn (1995) *The Politics of Social Research*. London: Sage.

Whyte, William Foote (ed.) (1991a) *Participatory Action Research*. London: Sage.

TWO

BEING ETHICAL

Aims

By the end of this chapter you will be able to:

- **Distinguish key ethical standpoints and draw practical conclusions about how to, and how not to, conduct research in an ethical way.**
- **Distinguish forms of consent, anonymity and confidentiality.**
- **Outline and comprehend the ethical issues confronting the social researcher at each stage of the research process.**
- **Relate ethical positions to more theoretical stances in the social sciences, and to the division between qualitative and quantitative approaches to studying the social world.**

Sensitivity: being ethical at every stage – before, during and after

The term 'ethics' refers to the systematic study of or formalization of rules concerning the separation of good conduct from bad. Ethics is distinguished typically from morals, which are the principles and practices people actually display. Morals and morality can be seen to have historical and cultural variability, and so are linked to norms and values, though norms and values refer to all the particular tastes, preferences and practices of different groups, whilst morals would only be those that are specifically what one culture or society considers to be good as distinct from evil. Flared trousers might be in this year. This is an issue of norms and values, given that they were not in last year, or elsewhere. They are not moral or ethical issues. That morals vary across time and place has led to discussion over whether ethical systems can ever attain the character of universal prescriptions that might be legitimately imposed either across a whole community or from one community to another. Democracy, human rights, women's rights, universal education, freedom of expression are all contested universals. Ethicists debate whether it is right to claim such principles are universal when some people and societies do not appear to respect them (yet?). Ethicists debate whether morals are just another set of norms and values that vary and which cannot be judged better or worse. Relativists claim that moral systems cannot be judged better or worse, only different. Others defend the idea that judgements as to what is appropriate can be generalized, even in the face of opposition from those who would do otherwise.

One group that has often 'done otherwise' are social researchers, who have applied all manner of justifications for the conduct of research that others have condemned as immoral. Is it ever ethically justifiable to pry into other people's lives, perhaps even deceiving them, causing them inconvenience and perhaps even suffering in the name of science? This chapter seeks to address the areas where social science must consider the ethical character of its practice, and to highlight the highly problematic character of social science in relation to ethics.

During the process of designing and implementing your piece of research, you need to consider the ethical implications of undertaking the research. 'Ethics is the science of morality: those who engage in it determine values for the regulation of human behaviour' (Homan, 1991: 1). Collecting information about people raises ethical issues in the focus of attention chosen, in the methods adopted and in the form and use of the findings. These three areas of concern are examined below. A number of controversial cases of social science are described in Boxes 2.1–2.4. Ask yourself whether you agree that such research should have been allowed. In particular cases you may agree, and in others you may not. On what basis should we make the decision, and who should decide?

BOX 2.1 RESEARCH FOCUS

Studies in obedience to authority: using deception

Perhaps the most controversial study in the social sciences is Stanley Milgram's 1961 experiments into obedience to authority (Milgram, 1974). Milgram asked a sample of people whether they would be prepared to administer electric shocks to another person as part of an experiment, even up to 450 volts (which most people are aware is likely to kill). The vast majority of respondents said they would refuse. This was in the United States only a relatively short time after the Second World War. Milgram wondered whether Americans were somehow different from the Germans, who had been more willing to comply with and participate in genocide during the war, or whether it was simply that people say they wouldn't do such things but would in the 'right' circumstances. Milgram advertised for participants for an experiment in learning, and paid nine dollars to each person who took part. The experiment was a fake. The participant was asked to administer at first mild electric shocks to another alleged participant who was in fact an actor. The actor was asked questions by the director of the experiment and when they got answers wrong the participant was to administer a shock, supposedly to motivate their learning. The shocks were increased each time a mistake was make, up to a maximum of 450 volts. Participants showed visible signs of distress as they were asked to administer ever greater shocks, but when the experimenter told them that he was responsible, that the experiments were important, that the participant had taken the money, and/ or that the other alleged participant had also been paid, the vast majority of participants carried on up to the full (and if real, fatal) 450 volt shocks. This was even after the actor (who in the initial design was in the next room) started screaming and protesting that they had a heart condition and a family. Even whilst complaining, asking that someone check on the recipient of the shocks and questioning the value of the research, the participants continued to comply under the 'authority' of the experimenter. Milgram's research suggested that most Americans would have made compliant participants in genocide if only they were told to do so by someone in authority. As Milgram's earlier questionnaire had demonstrated, people would not believe in or admit to such things if asked, but such data were useless as a predictor of what they would actually do. When Milgram carried out versions of his experiment where two experimenters argued over whether or not the participant should continue administering the shocks, the participants typically sided with the resister and ceased administering the (fake) shocks. Milgram concluded that his research was valuable as it showed that it was not something pathologically unique in German people, but rather the character of totalitarian authority structures that engendered such unethical actions. Milgram believed his findings, which could not have been obtained if he had been honest at the start with his participants, were ethically important, and that such findings justified the deception and the suffering he inflicted on his participants. If we are to stop genocide in the future then we need to know that people can be manipulated in particular conditions. If we do not learn the lessons of human weakness in research, perhaps we will continue to suffer the consequences of such weaknesses in real life. Critics of Milgram can point to some of his participants who claimed later that they knew all along that the electric shocks were not real. Were Milgram's participants pretending to him, just as he was pretending to them? One problem with deception in research is that it may weaken the validity of the data. However, it may be that the participants were in fact lying about knowing the shocks were not real. Perhaps they just wanted to make themselves feel better after what they had done.

BOX 2.2 RESEARCH FOCUS

The Lucifer effect? The right to withdraw and protection from harm

Philip Zimbardo (2008), an old school friend of Stanley Milgram, conducted perhaps the second most notorious social science experiment in 1971 at Stanford University in California. He selected a group of 24 students and divided them into prisoners and guards. The two groups were then placed into a controlled space in which they were to enact their roles. Those playing guards soon began displaying sadistic attitudes and behaviour towards those playing prisoners, and those in prisoner roles began to show signs of depression and fatalism. Zimbardo took the role of prison superintendent and became involved in attempts to break the will of the prisoners by various means. Various violations of the prisoners' expressed will were undertaken in the name of prison discipline. It was only with the intervention of an outsider that the whole dynamic of the 'experiment' was called into question and the 'prison' was closed after only six days of what was supposed to be its two-week duration. Zimbardo was keen to show how 'role' rather than some inner personality or identity could lead to cruelty and inhumanity, and, like Milgram, he believed that in order to achieve this it was necessary to create in an artificial context what might lead to such behaviours in real life. The prisoners were at least under the impression that they could not leave, even if they wanted to, and many were damaged by the research. Not only were those playing the 'prisoner' roles hurt by their treatment, but the behaviour of the 'guards' led to later feelings of shame and anxiety. It is interesting to note that the experiment was repeated by the BBC in 2001–2, and was also terminated early on ethical grounds. Most university ethics committees would have refused to allow such work, though 'The Experiment' did manage to secure ethical approval from one university. Zimbardo himself was called as a witness in 2004 at the trial of a US Army prison guard at the Abu Ghraib prison in Iraq after repeated torture and humiliation of prisoners had been filmed and photographed and shown around the world. Zimbardo's research was cited as evidence that a person in such a role may not be fully responsible for their own actions, and that the conditions they were placed in had the potential to turn anyone into a torturer. Staff Sergeant Ivan 'Chip' Frederick was however convicted and sentenced to eight years in prison.

BOX 2.3 RESEARCH FOCUS

Being sane in insane places: the researcher's protection from harm

David Rosenhan (1973) recruited eight individuals with no history of mental illness to report to their doctors hearing voices. All eight were admitted to psychiatric institutions. All eight then proceeded to behave 'normally', and were instructed to wait until they were discharged. Whilst around a third of the other patients recognized the pseudo patients as imposters, none of the psychiatric staff did. The pseudo patients were retained in their respective hospitals for between one and seven weeks with an average of just under three weeks. All were discharged with a diagnosis of schizophrenia in remission, itself a technically incorrect medical term even if the individuals were schizophrenics, which none were. Rosenhan used notes kept by pseudo patients to map the process of labelling by which perfectly normal behaviours were interpreted as signs of what the staff in the mental hospitals were trained to look out for. As such he claimed the pseudo patients were being labelled as mentally ill because that is what psychiatrists expect. Psychiatry then is said to be only a pseudo science, no more a science than were the pseudo patients 'mad'. The very act of taking notes whilst in a psychiatric hospital became evidence of obsessive compulsive behaviour, and was incorporated into the diagnosis which appeared already to exist and simply required fleshing out with evidence. Rosenhan goes on in his account to document the powerlessness and depersonalization of patients in psychiatric institutions. It is on the basis of his eight sane researchers' experiences of such distressing feelings and conditions that Rosenhan sought to bring to the world's attention the suffering of those whose plight might wrongly be put down to their illness. Is it ethical to inflict suffering on one's researchers in the hope that such suffering might then be relieved for others?

BOX 2.4 RESEARCH FOCUS

Project Camelot: social science as social engineering

In 1965, the United States Congress ordered the closure of a research programme involving sociologists and anthropologists that had been funded by various defence and intelligence agencies through US universities. It focused upon the causes of revolutionary action in developing societies and the scope both to develop counter-insurgence strategies and to build pro-American development in such countries. The name of the project was taken from the Arthurian legend of Camelot and its round table (Horowitz, 1967). The government officials and presumably the researchers recruited believed that the promotion of American values of tolerance, reason and justice would be best served by a programme of research designed to identify threats to such values and the causes of such threats. The claim has been routinely made that anthropologists have been used as spies in foreign countries, and that spies have claimed to be anthropologists (Boaz, 1919, cited in Bulmer, 2008: 147). In the years after 2001, the US 'War on Terror' has seen calls for more 'intelligence' about cultures and communities that might wish harm to the United States and its interests. This has seen a large swelling of government intelligence agencies. There has been a recognition of the limits of technical intelligence (collecting information via various forms of technical surveillance) as such information still requires interpretation. Interpretation has been seen as the work of anthropologists, and they are best placed to go to the places where electronic eavesdropping is just not enough. Does such 'research' breach ethical principles, or does it become ethically imperative as an alternative to other sources of intelligence gathering? If social science should have an impact, make a difference, can it therefore be justified to use social science as intelligence gathering? If Rosenhan, Zimbardo and Milgram could claim they were serving the greater good in using deception and allowing their subjects to suffer, can social scientists then reject the calls from their own governments to use their skills to serve the 'greater good'? One of us, in our first ever class as a seminar leader, asked our students what they wanted to do with their sociology degree. Only one student knew for sure: she wanted to work for British intelligence. The student pointed out that MI5 (the domestic branch of British military intelligence) studies society, and as such a sociology degree was the best qualification for that line of work. Is it possible to question the logic of her argument?

Ethical issues in the decision to research

What should deserve our attention? Can the values that direct our attention towards some questions and away from others be warranted on objective grounds, or do they inevitably stem from particular biases and perspectives? Can values be based upon facts? Can good research help us decide what our values ought to be, or are facts and values fundamentally distinct?

It is generally believed that the success of the physical sciences lies in the separation of facts (positive propositions) and values (normative propositions) and the prohibition on the use of values in the evaluation of 'truth'. This separation of facts and values is said to enable objective research that is free of values (value freedom). It presumes that the physical world is devoid of ethical content, and that the introduction of values constitutes an inappropriate projection of human sentiment. This position has been criticized, but that is not our business here. In the realm of social research, such an assumption that what we wish to study is devoid of ethical content is untenable. Researchers and the researched alike hold, attribute and claim ethical status. Ethical beliefs both motivate research and are one of the things researchers investigate.

Social researchers who seek to emulate the success of the physical sciences claim at least the possibility that social science can generate 'positive' ('non-normative') knowledge about the social world. Positivists tend to also propose 'naturalism', which in this context refers to the assertion that human actions and physical events are both subject to causal mechanisms, even if the particular mechanisms at work are different. If human actions are best understood in terms of causal processes that lead to such actions, then these processes can be studied in a value-neutral way, just as one might study the causes of volcanoes without any value judgements concerning the negative consequences of such eruptions. Naturalism seeks to remove moral judgement from accounts of human action. From such a perspective, human beings cannot be understood to have been the cause of their actions; rather, they are caused. Society may use 'punishment' to cause people to avoid certain actions in the future. All societies engage in such attributions of responsibility (Barnes, 2000) but, for a naturalistic positivist, such attributions and punishments/rewards are simply mechanisms serving to cause desirable outcomes instituted by society. If such a positivist were to 'help' society to learn what best causes certain behaviours this might be to cross the line between science and engineering, but positivists believe they are able to simply explain social causes. Just as in physical sciences, positivists in social science have often referred to 'the doctrine of neutrality' (David, 2005a), asserting that they just find the truth, and it is for society to decide what to do with such knowledge. Critics of positivism suggest that as humans are not simply the product of external mechanisms, the choice to focus on elements that may foster control over people is an ethically laden choice, one that binds positivists to the engineering model of science that has been dominant in Western societies in the modern era (Adorno and Horkheimer, 1979). Nevertheless, the strength of evidence that shows the susceptibility of people to external causation (as was demonstrated in the above cases) is taken by positivistic researchers to justify research that applies the very ethically questionable practices that critics see as unjustifiable reductions of human beings to machines.

Social researchers who reject the causal model of naturalism and positivism assert that human action is the result of meaningful interpretation rather than causal mechanisms, and that such processes do leave the human subject responsible for their own actions. As such, understanding why someone acted as they did does not explain such action away. Just as such a view elevates human agents in ethical capacity, so it tends to raise their position as recipients of ethical consideration. Rather than seeing the individual as victim of external causes that they are often ignorant of, and which can therefore only be studied by methods that replicate such ignorance, interpretive researchers tend to the view that it is only through the research participants' understanding that we can understand their actions. As such, research using deception would be less useful, and so unjustifiable. Rosenhan's (1973) research (Box 2.3) is interesting here. Rosenhan relied on the active knowledge of the real nature of the research by the pseudo patients. Unlike Milgram, Rosenhan's participants were not deceived. Rather the deception was practised upon the medical staff, whose positivistic models of illness Rosenhan sought to expose as pseudo scientific labelling. Ironically, Rosenhan's interpretive approach used non-deception of one group to help study by deception the practices of those who would themselves routinely justify deception in the name of positive science.

What can be seen in the last example is that those less prone to believing that deception is necessary tend to emphasize its invalidity as a method. Those who believe in external hidden causes tend to believe in the value of research that replicates them. Where an interpretivist researcher did believe in the value of deception, despite deception being more ethically problematic for someone holding this view of human beings, they decided to allow their epistemology (theory of how to get to the truth) to override their ethical position. Researchers often construct ethics to fit their desired research, and when such research requires a bending of their ethical principles, the temptation is to claim the common good as a defence. Social researchers are not naturally any more ethical than anyone else, and the pursuit of truth is a powerful motivator to bend the rules. As this chapter will suggest, it is precisely for this reason that social researchers need ethics committees to regulate their conduct, just as they need peer review processes to regulate the claims they make regarding the validity of their research.

So there is a tension here. Will values inevitably undermine factual research, or should our choice of research reflect our moral concerns? What is the relationship between facts and values? Functionalists, Marxists and feminists hold the view that values can be derived from the facts of human nature and social life. To correctly understand what it means to be a society or an individual human allows us to judge whether particular conditions or practices are right or wrong. However, these theorists disagree over what the correct interpretation of social reality and human nature is. Those who adopt a more interpretivist/constructivist view of social order and human nature tend to suggest that humans are relatively plastic. There is, for interpretivists/constructivists, no fixed human nature and so no best social order in which they could all live. The ethical conclusion to draw here might be that one cannot come to a single set of ethical conclusions about what is right and wrong from the facts of social life. Ironically, this is the same conclusion that is drawn by those social researchers keen to preserve the legacy of the physical sciences by suggesting that social research should avoid values and only deal with positive facts. The irony lies in the fact that such positivists (those that believe in the neutrality of science) and constructivists are otherwise diametrically opposed to each other in all other respects. So there is certainly no simple solution.

Objectivity in the positivist tradition and subjectivity in the interpretivist tradition appear to mirror each other in the view that the researcher should not and cannot make ethical judgements about the social world they study; yet as has been seen, both traditions appear to draw ethical conclusions regarding the justification for researching people in one way rather than another. Beneath claims to positivistic objectivity and the doctrine of neutrality often lies a kind of social epidemiological ethic of 'cure' that merges science with a medical model of 'care', whereby the medic is charged with the duty to make people better. Critics of this approach to social science (Bauman, 1991) suggest that such an approach often becomes a form of social engineering that, in claiming simply to make people better, is in fact engaged in attempts to make better people. The history of medicine is haunted by such attempts to 'cure' the group by culling the deviant individual. Such 'eugenic' programmes of social medicine were taken to their most extreme form in the Nazi holocaust, where medical science was deeply implicated in the drive to purify and cure (Jacobsen, 2000). Beneath interpretivist claims to *verstehen*, the orientation to understanding without judgement of the 'lifeworld' of meaning that different cultures and communities live by, is a deeper conception of what it means to be human, as meaning makers. From this perspective it is the ability to make meaning, and hence to create different values and beliefs about what is important, that makes humans special, and which it is the ethical duty of the social researcher to defend against reductionism to external causal accounts (whether these be from biologists, economists or positivistic sociologists). As was noted in the previous paragraph, this is often qualified in interpretivist accounts by the suggestion that whilst reductionism is wrong (epistemologically and ethically), there is no universal good society, just a diversity of possible ways of life. Critics of this tradition (Habermas, 1987) reject the assumption that cultures can only be understood in terms of their own internal system of values and beliefs, such that one cannot criticize one culture's values by reference to those of another culture or from any universalistic ethical stance. To say so implies that the meaningful experience of one lifeworld cannot be translated into the language of another lifeworld. To say this invalidates the very social science model that interpretivists seek to undertake. Whilst something may still get lost in translation, to suggest that cultures cannot communicate is a gross exaggeration; and to go further, in suggesting that it is never possible to critically evaluate a culture except from within its own value system, is in fact a contradictory suggestion for an interpretive researcher to make. Given the interpretivist's critique of positivistic social science and their defence of human meaning making, surely such meaning making – the orientation towards understanding rather than the attempt to reduce people to causal processes and the mechanisms by which they can be manipulated – would form the basis for an ethical orientation to different forms of social life in which such manipulation is applied.

The tradition of critical theory (found in the work of Adorno, Marcuse and Habermas amongst others) arose from the attempt to move beyond both positivism and interpretivism. Critical theory develops elements of Marxism, though it tends to reject the rather positivistic elements of Marx's account of economic forces determining historical development. Critical theory took on board elements of interpretivism's critique of positivism, but at the same time sought to resist its subjectivism. Critical theory rejects the separation of facts and values. From within this tradition, values can be deduced from the substantial reality of being human, and of being human in conditions of inequality and domination that undermine the capacity of human beings to realize their humanity. As has been pointed out, positivists, interpretivists and critical theorists draw their ethics from their understanding of the facts of what it means to be human. It is just that they differ in their understanding of what these facts are. In part the differences over what the facts of being human are lies in prioritizing certain characteristics over others, and this is a question of values. Positivists emphasize the extent to which human beings are the product of external causes. Interpretivists emphasize the capacity of humans to create meaning and to live by meaningful systems of belief. Critical theorists emphasize the tension between human creativity in both material work and cultural meaning and the constraints placed on such creativity by social processes that they do not control. Each tradition highlights the extent to which the facts claimed by other traditions are themselves influenced by the values they bring to their research, in their choice of topic, methods of data collection and interpretation of results. As such, again, facts and values cannot be readily separated.

Nevertheless, however the researcher believes that facts secure their values, it is still the case that they must seek to conduct research in such a way that it will not be rejected by others as *simply* the projection of the researcher's prior beliefs. This is especially true when funding comes from bodies with values and interests in the field. If the values of funders directly influence results, then the purpose of doing social research is lost. Max Weber (1949) distinguished *value freedom* and *value neutrality*. He suggested that while all social research is motivated by values (and so can never be value free) the researcher is obliged to conduct their research in such a way as to ensure that such values do not dictate the outcome. In other words, the methods chosen must be *value neutral*. If values drive the choice of topic, the job of the social scientist is to be neutral in its conduct. This is an ideal, at least for many, but can never be fully attained. It remains a benchmark around which researchers can reflect and debate the merits of particular research projects. Does value neutrality prohibit the researcher from taking sides? No. However, it forces the researcher to defend their methods and reflect hard upon them. Honesty and reflection on these issues are the best policy as there is no magic formula.

Howard Becker (1967) argued that social researchers should seek to understand the outlook of those whose voices are under-represented. 'Underdogs' and 'outsiders' are more prone to being misunderstood. Becker suggested that presenting a view of the world from the point of view of society's 'underdogs' will always draw the criticism, from those in authority, that the researcher has become biased, an advocate of those they seek to present. Whilst Becker advocated methods that 'got close' to the lives of those being researched, he rejected the claim that presenting an outsider view was the same as advocating it. Many took Becker to be suggesting that because the accusation of bias was inevitable, so bias itself was inescapable. Marxists and feminist researchers, alongside many who work with those they consider to be disadvantaged, exploited and/or oppressed, have advocated a standpoint approach to research. Standpoint approaches suggest there can be no neutral way to conduct research, and no neutral choice as to what to study or how to study it. Ethical decisions about what to study merge with political choices over how to study. In this view research is always a form of advocacy. Social research is seen as a political weapon to empower the 'underdog', not as a neutral science seeking to objectively 'map' them. This was not Becker's view, but the question remains as to whether and how the researcher can avoid taking sides. *Participatory action research* is one extension of the logic of advocacy (see section 'Evaluation, participation and action research' in Chapter1). Boxes 2.5 and 2.6 also flag up issues to do with taking sides and trying to be useful.

BOX 2.5 CONSIDER THIS

The politics of social research

David (2005b) highlights the problem of 'impact'. The British government in the early 2000s promised to listen to social researchers when they, the government, were designing policy. This was referred to as 'evidence-based policy'. In exchange the then home secretary, in a speech to the UK's largest funder of social science research, the Economic and Social Research Council, demanded that social researchers should engage in policy-based evidence collection. Rather than conducting research into theoretical, abstract, impractical or radical questions, researchers should conduct research that would answer the questions that the government felt needed to be answered. In order to be listened to, social researchers had to say what the government wanted to hear, or at the very least avoid questions the government was not interested in knowing about. In this framework social science would very much become a form of social engineering, directed towards solving problems as defined by the powerful. Michel Foucault (2001) argued that each social science was a form of engineering. Each discipline acted to regulate a field of human deviation from what the dominant regime defined as appropriate and each field constructed a space in which disciplines could practise their regulation. Prisons, schools, hospitals and psychiatric institutions, barracks and other regimes of knowledge/power became the sites in which disciplined bodies were made fit to serve society. For Foucault social sciences are tools of power, not forms of enlightened knowledge acting to liberate people from ignorance. Many social scientists reject Foucault's bleak account of their professional snooping, but if they do not reject the position of social engineer, can they really avoid the charge?

BOX 2.6 CONSIDER THIS

The problems of participation: local environmental movements

David (2002) highlights one problem with participation-based social research. In researching local environmental movements in East Kent as a PhD student, Matt joined in with a range of groups signed up to the local environmental network. The purpose of the research was to see how the concepts of environment, locality and movement were articulated. Who would align with whom? And in alignments, how were issues defined such that different groups could see themselves as joined or in opposition? One organization sought to promote eco-tourism by developing a holiday centre within ancient woodland. The organization claimed their project was environmentally friendly as it would reduce foreign travel and promote a variety of conservation projects within the forest and nearby. Opponents claimed the project would demolish a part of the ancient forest to build the centre and would cause increased pollution and congestion on local roads. The developers claimed to be part of the environmental movement, and had the support of some groups within the network in which Matt was a participant observer, but were opposed by others in the network. Having gone to a local meeting and signed an attendance sheet, Matt had his name (somehow) passed on to the developers, who then wrote to the A level college where Matt was then working part-time to ask them whether they (the college) really thought it right to be employing someone who was actively campaigning to undermine the local economy. In gaining the trust of the local environmental network Matt had been able to access a range of people and events he would otherwise not have been able to interview and/or observe. However, when Matt wrote to the company proposing the development plan to ask for an interview, this was turned down. Participatory research has the danger of opening some doors, only to encourage others to close their doors to you.

In essence, the choice to conduct social research at all, and the choice of adopting a particular 'epistemological' (theory of knowledge) stance (positivistic, critical theoretical or interpretivist), will be grounded in assumptions about the basic character of being human. 'Ontology' (the theory of being or what reality fundamentally is) in the social sciences is deeply laden with ethical implications. If you believe in naturalistic causation, meaningfully directed action or the tension between meaning and constraint as the basic underlying reality of social life, you will hold different values in terms of how best to study society, and over what is ethically acceptable and unacceptable in social life and in social research. Considerations of what is ethical and unethical in society will have a strong impact on the questions that get researched. Considerations of how best to study humans and considerations of which methods are ethical will determine how such questions are subsequently researched. As we have seen, social scientists often confuse the last two elements, and have to be reminded that just because a technique is the best one for answering the question they really want to answer, this does not make such a technique ethically acceptable; and just because a technique might be ethically problematic, this does not make its results necessarily false. Because social scientists' ethics are tied up with their epistemological outlook such that values are never fully detached from facts in social science, it is easy to forget that the best way to collect data is not always the most ethical and that the best way to be ethical may not always be the best way to get to the truth. It needs to be recalled that sometimes the truth is less important than being ethical and that social scientists have no automatic right to manipulate others in the name of science or any other 'higher' value. As different traditions define truth differently, and ethics too, it cannot be assumed that one single truth or one single ethical framework could ever determine an absolute answer to how to balance competing claims. As in Milgram's experiments, when there was more than one experimenter overseeing the participant who was being asked to administer electric shocks, and when the two experimenters argued over what was right and true, it was then that the participant seemed best able to resist the tendency towards obedience and do the right thing. Perhaps in the social sciences it is the existence of dispute over absolute principles of both knowledge and ethics that prevents abuses in the name of one extreme principle or another. This is not relativism as such, rather simply the institutional absence of absolutism.

Sensitivity in the conduct of research

The development of ethical oversight

Mark Israel and Iain Hay (2006) chart the history of ethical oversight in the conduct of research involving human participants. They note that whilst various moves had been afoot prior to the Second World War, the most significant developments happened in the light of the Nuremberg trials of doctors and scientists in Nazi Germany who had conducted experiments using concentration camp prisoners. Such medical, psychological and biological experiments shocked the world, and shamed the medical and scientific community. Israel and Hay point out that experiments with convicts and those held in psychiatric institutions were not restricted to Nazi Germany, and many doctors and scientists in other countries, including the United States, France and Sweden as well as the UK, had undertaken experimental research on human subjects without their expressed consent. They document an array of such 'abuses'. However, or perhaps because of such complicity in abuse, it was convenient to present Nazi Germany as the 'other' and for all countries to agree in future to reject such practices that the Nazis took to extreme levels. The Nuremberg trials led to the Nuremberg Code in 1946. The code contained 10 principles, the most significant of which was the principle of *informed consent*, the doctrine that research involving human subjects must be based on the full, free and knowing understanding and consent of those taking part in the research. This principle was set against the doctrine defended by those on trial at Nuremberg who had claimed that their work as scientists and medical researchers was to uphold and develop the species, even if that meant the sacrifice of the individual. Experimentation on human individuals against their will went hand in hand with the eugenic policy of the Nazis, which was to selectively promote the reproduction of some people whilst actively preventing the reproduction of others (whether through sterilization or killing). The belief that the greater good was being served and that this justified the 'lesser evil' of violating individuals was condemned in the Nuremberg Code. Researchers are required to treat their participants with respect, the first principle of which is that they have the right to decide whether or not they wish to participate, and to make that decision in the full knowledge of the research methods and goals in advance. Subsequent ethical codes, such as the Helsinki Declaration of the World Medical Association (Israel and Hay, 2006), develop the principles of autonomy and respect for the rights of the research participant. The increased emphasis upon working within an ethical framework, and on developing such frameworks at institutional, disciplinary, national and international levels, has drawn attention to two related dimensions of ethical conduct: the philosophical principles upon which ethical systems should be based; and the practical dimensions of such ethical responsibility.

Basic ethical positions

Malcolm Williams and Tim May (1996) as well as Mark Israel and Iain Hay (2006) distinguish two fundamental philosophical positions that have tended to define disputes over what is and is not ethically acceptable in social research. Drawing from the utilitarian tradition in philosophy, itself strongly associated with positivism and with attempts to quantify human values, practices and outcomes such that they can be weighed against each other, the *consequentialist* tradition in ethics argues that actions should be judged relative to the overall outcome. If the benefits of an action outweigh the harm, and assuming no alternative was available which would have realized a similar or greater benefit with less harm, such an action can be said to be ethically justified. In essence the consequentialist position regards ethical judgement as requiring an acceptance of the tradeoff between benefits and harms. The notion of trading benefits against harms assumes that units of good and bad can be measured such that so much of one can be offset against so much of the other. Utilitarian philosophy is premised upon the view that the good is that which brings about the maximum happiness for the maximum number of people (or animals). Jeremy Bentham (1879), a founder of the utilitarian tradition, argued that if ethical action was oriented to maximum happiness and minimum suffering, and as animals could feel pleasure and pain, so the principles of utilitarian ethics should be extended to include at least the more sentient animals. Peter Singer's (1990) founding text for the contemporary animal rights movement rekindled Bentham's eighteenth-century extension of ethics to animals. Within utilitarian consequentialist ethics, debates exist over the measurement of relative suffering and benefit as well as over trading relations such that one group's suffering might 'buy' another group's benefit. Does the greater good of the greater number justify harm to the smaller number? Under the doctrines established in Nuremberg and Helsinki, it might be assumed that the answer must be no, but in fact the principle of informed consent does allow a person to volunteer to take risks if they are given a clear outline of what these might be. When might this be justified? Consequentialism tends to be the ethic of choice for more positivistic and quantitative researchers, but some ethnographers argue that covert research is legitimate if the benefits gained by exploring a group outweigh the morally problematic act of deceiving them. More validity may have the effect of being more ethically problematic (see Box 2.7).

BOX 2.7 CONSIDER THIS

The crash-test dummies: when validity and ethics collide

If you want to carry out potentially damaging research on a group because they are representative of a wider population for whom you wish to reduce the future incidence of similar damage, it must be concluded that precisely because this sample is like the general population, the validity of researching them also underpins the claim that it would be unethical to do so. In medical research, the very reason that testing a drug on group *X* might tell you whether it is safe for the general population must be premised upon group *X* being sufficiently similar to the general population as to allow findings from group *X* to be used to predict what the drug would do to everyone else. If we test animals, it must be assumed that these animals are sufficiently similar to humans for the research to be of value in measuring human safety. To conclude that such a similarity does exist challenges the claim that such research should be conducted on animals as to do so is not unethical. To say animal testing is ethical, where it would be unethical to test humans with experimental drugs, is to assume that animals are fundamentally different from humans. If that were true, why then is it useful to test animals, as the results from such animal studies could not be generalized to humans? Car safety is often tested using crash-test dummies – manikins that resemble humans to some degree at least. It would be unethical to put real people in such crash tests, so the dummies appear to be the nearest ethical alternative. The claim that various aspects of animals (such as particular organs and body parts) are similar to their human equivalents is often used to suggest that animals are similar in utility even whilst they remain different ethically. This rather convenient argument does not really stand up to scrutiny, as the possibility of testing specific body parts and tissues could be carried out *in vitro*, and would not require that procedures be carried out on whole, living and sentient animals. If it is suggested that the whole, living and conscious animal is required to make the test valid, the claim that it is only certain particular mechanisms and elements that need to be similar is undone.

In contrast to consequentialist ethics, deontological ethical frameworks start from the premise that what is ethical cannot be traded for other benefits. As such, if something is wrong it cannot be made right when set against the benefits that might arise from such wrongdoing. The deontological view is that ethics are to be deduced not from expedient reality but rather from principles, whose very nature stands above vulgar interests. The classic statement of this view is from Immanuel Kant's *Critique of Practical Reason* (1997). Kant asserts that ethics must be deduced from what he calls the categorical imperative. For an act to be ethical it must be such that its conduct could be generalized into a universal rule. For Kant this boils down to the principle that ethical action is action that treats others as ends in themselves and not as means to an end. In relation to human beings, whose consciousness and reason make them capable of a form of autonomy that is not possible for 'mere objects', we are ethically bound to respect their self-aware and self-directed nature. To violate a human being's capacity to self-directed will, to reduce them to the status of an object, a thing whose purpose is to serve our ends rather than their own, is for Kant ethically unacceptable. It should be noted that Kant's construction of what it means to be human is fundamentally different from the utilitarian and positivist construction. For Kant, human beings are worthy of ethical treatment because they have the autonomous reason to think and to choose. For utilitarians and positivists, human beings are like other animals. They can feel pain and are the products of causal mechanisms like everything else.

The anatomy of ethical conduct in social scientific research

Controlled conditions, detachment and manipulation are the hallmarks of physical science, but may have negative connotations when applied to humans. Respect for those you research can be diminished in the act of treating them as research material. The development of ethical codes of conduct for research involving humans developed most significantly after the Second World War, and was centred around the principle of informed consent, but other principles allied to this have also been developed. This section is divided into three parts: informed consent; privacy, confidentiality and anonymity; and protection from harm. The section concludes with a note on ethics committees.

Informed consent

The principle of informed consent is generally agreed to be the ideal mode of operation when enlisting others in a researcher's designs.

> Informed consent means the knowing consent of individuals to participate as an exercise of their choice, free from any element of fraud, deceit, duress, or similar unfair inducement or manipulation. (Berg, 1998: 47)

While there are occasions when researchers feel it is justified to deceive those they are researching, either with outright lies, or in not informing them that they are being researched, or in not informing them fully of the purpose of the research, these circumstances are fraught with ethical difficulties and require substantial justification and scrutiny. The question of whether it is ever justified to proceed without the informed consent of those researched hinges around the question of whether the ends ever justify the means. Those who adopt a consequentialist ethical position suggest that if the greater good can be best served by research that is not explicit about its intentions or even its very existence, then the ethical violation of those deceived is outweighed by the good that might flow from the research findings. This is the justification usually given for the double-blind trials of new medical drugs where half the test subjects are given the drug while the other half are given a placebo. The parallel here with social research lies in the possibility that knowing one is being researched, or knowing the objectives of the research, might lead those researched to act differently. As such, covert observation, or not giving a full account of one's motives, may allow the researcher to get a more accurate impression of real life. Those that adopt a deontological ethical position suggest that the benefit of the many does not justify the violation of the few. Such arguments have been used to successfully challenge the ethics of double-blind medical trials in both the US and parts of Europe (see Collins and Pinch, 1998: Chapter 7). It is suggested that once it is accepted that the benefit of the majority justifies the abuse of the few, there is no ethical boundary stopping those in authority doing whatever they like in the name of 'the majority'. The deontological ethical stance defends the ideal that human rights are universal, absolute and cannot be traded.

Laud Humphreys's (1970) study of male homosexuals using public toilets to meet for sex was conducted without informing those observed that they were being researched. Humphreys claimed that his research served to prove that those engaged in 'the tearoom trade' were not perverts or child molesters, as was typically assumed in the media at that time. Covert research allowed Humphreys to claim that his research avoided the possibility that those researched were hiding their true behaviour whilst being watched. As such, he claimed that deception served the greater good in the long run. Nigel Fielding's (1981) research into the racist National Front political party in the UK was partially covert in that Fielding sought to give the impression of sympathy for the organization upon entry and then did not fully disclose his researcher role to most of those he encountered during his fieldwork. Exposing the racism within that organization could be said to justify such a limited openness. However, would we support such methods if the organization being researched, and which might lose a significant amount of credibility as a result, was one we had more sympathy with? For a more developed account of consequentialist and deontological views, see Malcolm Williams and Tim May (1996).

While this dispute over the basic principles of social research ethics is of great importance, it should not worry you unnecessarily at this stage. If you are just starting out, and especially if you are doing a research project as part of a training or educational programme, you should stick rigorously to the principle of informed consent. As was pointed out in the discussion of Milgram's experiments, the research participants may have caught on to their being deceived and may have just been playing along with the experimenter. A problem with deception, especially when the research is covert, is that there is little scope for the researcher to check the validity of their results. The claim that deception can increase validity (as Humphreys suggested) can be offset by the claim that deception reduces validity. However, it is not possible to discount deception on grounds that all such research is invalid. This would make life a lot simpler as ethics and epistemology would become one. What was ethically good would be epistemologically good and researchers would not suffer the temptation of trading a bit of one for a bit of the other. Such a simple life does not exist. Validity may be increased by honesty. It may not. Researchers have to weigh up the claims and counter-claims, and if they feel deception would increase the validity of their data collection they still have to decide, or approach an ethics committee to decide, whether such a gain should be made at the expense of fully informed consent. If you are just starting out it is unlikely that you will be given approval to deceive, so it is best to think how your research can be achieved without deception.

It might be asked how informed a person needs to be to give genuine informed consent. Is the person who agrees to be part of a drugs trial, and who has been told that they will receive either the experimental drug or the placebo, fully informed or only really partially informed? In ethnographic research the researcher may not fully know in advance what they will find, so how possible is it to gain consent that is fully informed if the researcher cannot say in advance exactly what they will focus on? In such research the researcher may not know who they will encounter, and in observational research in natural settings (everyday places) the researcher may not be able to predict in advance who they will encounter. How then can they gain consent? Some research investigates topics that many people will not fully grasp even if they were explained at length. The questions of how much information is required to enable being informed, and how much understanding and time are required to allow someone to be said to have truly consented, are open to much debate. Given such complexities, one solution is to provide a written consent form which outlines the nature of the research and informs the research participant of their rights and the researcher's responsibilities (see later). One option is to ask participants to sign such forms if they are prepared to be researched, and for these forms to be countersigned and dated by the researcher. This is one way to ensure a significant level of informed consent. Time should be given for the participant to be able to digest what they are being asked to participate in. This level of consent may not be necessary where the participant's involvement is relatively limited, and where they are not asked to record their names and other identifying information. Where a researcher collects information in a clipboard opportunity sample (such as in the street) the researcher may give the potential participant an information sheet and they may talk through the nature of the research, but as personal identity is not to be recorded, it is not necessary to gain signed consent (which would defeat the purpose of not recording names: see the next section on privacy etc.).

This non-necessity for written and signed consent may be extended in ethnographic research to those whom the researcher does not identify and whom they do not directly engage with, at least if this inadvertent inclusion takes place in a public space. Where a researcher is observing in a public space, such that they do not need permission to be where they are, and where those present could not reasonably say they were expecting 'privacy', it might be legitimate to record behaviour as long as this was not recorded in such a fashion as could identify those individuals. If an ethnographer wanted to interview people, they would have to abide by the principles of informing discussed above. If they wanted to conduct observations in private spaces, then they would need to gain consent from those being observed, as these people could reasonably expect privacy in a private space, which the researcher would be infringing. The question of what constitutes a private space is an interesting one. Do internet discussion boards constitute private spaces? What about shops, cafés and public houses? You do not need permission to enter such places, but they are still private in some senses of the term. In such situations where a location is ambiguous as to its public/private location, it is common practice for the researcher to gain strong (i.e. written and signed) consent from the chatroom moderator, shopkeeper or café/bar licence holder. As long as this is granted, the researcher would be able to observe interactions in that semi-public space without having to announce themselves to every person they observe. If however they wish to engage directly with someone, they should seek more explicit consent. Some ethnographers have been criticized for assuming that certain geographic locations which are formally public spaces are not also the territory of certain communities. Should they seek permission from informal community leaders who claim that territory as their own? In such situations, it is often the case that there are competing claims to the right to offer access. Who should be given the status of gatekeeper?

The question of gatekeepers becomes most significant in relation to informed consent in the context of those groups and individuals who are not deemed able to make a fully informed decision for themselves. Such individuals are said to be incapable of giving consent either if they are not able to understand the implications of what they are consenting to, or if they are not in a position to choose freely, for example in institutions such as prisons, schools or hospitals where refusal to participate may lead to subsequent disadvantage, or at least the perception that this might be the case. Some groups, such as those under a certain age (the actual age varies from country to country), are deemed legally incapable of giving consent on issues of sexual behaviour, voting or entering into military combat duties. In these matters such groups are prohibited from undertaking what they are said not to be capable of fully comprehending. In other areas, such as participation in research, the question of how consent might be managed involves identification of those who have the right to decide on the person's behalf, such as parents, school teachers or other care providers. If your research requires that you collect data from such groups, it is important that you negotiate such consent issues carefully and in line with the rules and ethical procedures of the institutions you are dealing with. There is no blanket formula for getting this right.

Another extension of the principle of informed consent arises from the level of involvement the researched have in the direction of the research. Researchers who adopt a principled stance on the use of inductive methods of exploratory research argue that hypothetico-deductive research adopts a position of superiority over those being researched, in so far as it fails to involve the researched in defining the issues as they experience them. To research people in the way you would research things may be considered in itself unethical. Researchers from a more deductive tradition (one more at home with the claim that human actions can best be explained in terms of causes and effects, even to the extent that those affected are not always aware of the causes of their behaviour and/or circumstances) would respond by suggesting that it is not that they do not respect human beings, only that they understand human beings differently. They might even suggest that if people are sometimes victims or products of forces they are not fully aware of, it would be unethical to address only those things that those people were aware of, as if the hidden forces did not exist. As you may well have gathered, those using deductive forms of research (grounded in a causal approach to social life) are more likely to adopt a consequentialist approach to research ethics. Inductivists (who are more likely to account for events in terms of intentional actions and beliefs) are more likely to adopt a deontological approach. The former will accuse the latter of a superficiality that fails to get to grips with the unseen influences which shape the lives of individuals, and of being ethically complicit with the continuation of those hidden forces. The latter will accuse the former of using claims of unseen social forces to justify an image of ordinary people as hapless dupes incapable of making up their own minds. There is no simple solution to this dispute, so the best advice is to be aware of it and to reflect upon the role you think you are performing when you conduct social research yourself. Such reflection is best achieved through discussion with tutors, colleagues and ethics committees, even where the latter are often seen as intimidating, bureaucratic and alien impositions.

Privacy, confidentiality and anonymity

It is important to recognize and respect the privacy of those you are researching. In so far as you are following the principle of informed consent, you will need to gain the permission of those researched for you to 'invade' their privacy. In addition it is essential that you protect that privacy in the storage and use of any data collected. This can be by means of either anonymity or confidentiality. Anonymity refers to the situation where you do not know or do not record the personal details (that is, name, address and so on) of those researched. Confidentiality refers to the situation where that information is known and recorded by the researcher, but is not disclosed in the reporting of the research. In line with data protection protocols and laws, it is essential that if any personal details that could identify an individual are to be stored by the researcher (electronically or on paper), this information is kept separately from other data collected. This is best achieved by assigning research participants an identifying code. This code is used in the filing of data, while a separate list is kept linking real names with their assigned code reference. In this way the likelihood of those researched being personally identified is kept to a minimum. It is often essential that those researched are assured that their confidentiality will be maintained, and it is your responsibility as a researcher to do your utmost to ensure that this is so.

It is important to think through what is meant by confidentiality, and to inform research participants what you mean by the term, as the expression means different things in different contexts. Do you promise not to disclose personal identifiers to anyone at all, or are you only promising not to reveal such information to people outside the data collection process? If you have conducted focus groups or public observations, it may be hard to ensure that other people present will be unable to identify people in the research. You cannot protect the confidentiality of a focus group participant at least from the other people in the group. You can ask other persons present to respect the confidentiality of the discussion, but you cannot promise on behalf of other people. You need to make this clear. Are you going to keep the research data confidential from everyone outside the research collection context, or are you going to discuss data with supervisors and co-researchers? Again you need to explain to participants what boundaries of confidentiality you are going to uphold.

Just because you have gained consent to carry out your research, you do not have *carte blanche* to expose the private lives of people, or to collect information that is highly sensitive private information if it is beyond the scope of what your research is about. It is also the case that even where a participant has given the researcher consent to collect certain information it is still the researcher's duty to protect the participant from harm. If a research participant discloses highly intimate details about themselves, and they have not requested full confidentiality, it should still be expected that the researcher does not reveal such information, or allow them to be identified. There is a tension between informed consent and protection from harm. Even with consent it would still be wrong to expose a person to harm. Whether or not you believe that a person should be allowed to harm themselves (binge drink, smoke, eat junk food to excess or even attempt suicide), even if such practices are totally legal, it would still be unethical to ask people to engage in them for the purpose of research. Whether it is legitimate to recruit people who are already doing these things rather muddies the water, but the main point here is that protection from harm applies even where someone consents to being acted upon.

Protection from harm

It is essential to be aware of the sensitivity of many topics researchers are keen to investigate. Research may become damaging to the research participant's sense of self if sensitive topics are pushed without consideration. If sensitive topics are to be addressed (and it is important to remember that what is sensitive may be understood differently by the research participants than it is by the researcher), the research subject's right to withdraw must be respected. This needs to be explained in advance as part of the process of gaining informed consent. It is best practice to introduce the themes of the research prior to its conduct to forewarn the research subject and so to allow the choice to withdraw. In the conduct of more open-ended observation or interviewing, these issues become more complex. Further guidance can be found in a number of useful books (for example Lee, 1993; Renzetti and Lee, 1993). At the end of an interview, experiment, questionnaire or observation it is important also to 'debrief' participants, to explain issues that were raised, and to ask if there are questions the participant wants to ask you about the motives, content or intended outcomes of the work they have contributed to.

Protection from harm has a number of dimensions. First, there is protection from physical harm. This is more commonly a problem in medical and biological research, but may be significant in some forms of social and psychological research. One line of argument suggests that research participants must not be exposed to any physical harm, whilst another line of argument suggests that a participant should not be left any worse off as a result of participation than if they had not participated. The second line of argumentation is used to justify the harm that might be said to occur if a person was assigned the placebo in a drug trial, when they might have had the chance of improvement using the experimental drug. If of course there are problems with the experimental drug, the participant might end up worse off than if they had had nothing at all. Such research typically relies on the principle of informed consent to say the participant had been made aware of the risks. Social researchers rarely take this view, and tend to the opposite, such that research would not be undertaken if there is a significant chance that participants would be left worse off than when they started. A stronger ethical stance is taken by those who claim that it is not enough to leave some people no better off at the end of a research project where some, including the researchers, have benefited. If you were researching an educational strategy and you compared a new strategy with an existing one and the new strategy was very successful, those on the new scheme have benefited and the researchers have benefited. Might the researchers owe a moral obligation to give the group who had been denied the improvement the chance to benefit from it? Where time might have passed, and where such time would have most likely led to improvement (development of various kinds), to leave someone where they were before might in fact be to have hampered their growth.

Beyond physical harm, there are also possibilities of emotional and legal harm. Research conduct may damage a person's self-esteem if problematic issues are raised, and if criminal actions are revealed the researcher may find themselves in possession of data that could also be seen as 'evidence'. For a beginner it is best to avoid topics that are likely to unearth such things, but in time you may wish to research such sensitive issues. If so, you will have to weigh up what you might consider appropriate. If you have promised confidentiality, should you then give a caveat to this by saying in advance that you do not wish participants to explicitly implicate themselves in any criminal actions, and/or that you promise not to record such details?

Ethics committees

It is important to be aware of the ethical codes of practice that have been established by various professional bodies involved in social research, as well as institutions such as universities and schools. If your research takes you beyond the bounds of these codes of practice you could easily get yourself into trouble with those you are researching, those that are supervising your research, the professional bodies themselves, the law, or any combination of these. As a beginner, it is easy to make mistakes, so it is all the more important that you are aware of the boundaries of good practice and stick well within them. Before undertaking a piece of research it is strongly advisable to consult the professional organization most closely associated with your topic area. Most organizations have a website where their ethical statements can be accessed, for example: British Sociological Association (www.brit-soc.org.uk); American Sociological Association (www.asanet.org); Market Research Society (www.market-research.org.uk); British Psychological Society (www.bps.org.uk).

In addition, conducting research in large organizations will often require the researcher to submit the project proposal to an ethical approval committee and may involve the completion of specific forms. For example, health-related research undertaken in the UK National Health Service requires the completion and submission of ethical clearance forms for the appropriate primary health care trust. The process can be time consuming, especially as the ethical approval committees may meet at certain fixed times in the year, and this needs to be accounted for when planning the project.

If you are conducting a piece of research as part of an educational course you may also be required to complete an internal ethical clearance procedure in addition to any external organization's requirements. You should seek advice from your project supervisor as to the exact process at your institution. For a more in-depth discussion of the ethical and legal issues in social research, see Dawn Burton (2000: Part II).

Sensitivity over the use of social research findings

Deductive researchers are more prone to believe that the purpose of research is to identify causes not always visible to those they are researching. One consequence of such research findings might be the call for interventions that seek to address these unseen causes. These calls may come from the researchers themselves, from those who funded the research, or from other interested parties. More inductive researchers tend to the view that their research serves more of a translator's function, seeking to understand those who are different from 'us', rather than seeking to explain their actions in terms of causes underlying their own intentions. Nevertheless, publication of such research may be used to argue for interventions and policy changes, again not always from the researchers themselves. Once research is published it may be taken up and used for a variety of purposes. The researcher must be aware of the potential for their work to be used in ways that are not their own. It is therefore essential that the researcher writes up their work in such a way that:

- Those researched are protected from personal identification.
- The researcher is responsible about the claims they make.

Whilst it is not possible to fully control the way a published work will be used or interpreted, the social researcher must reflect on how their work might be used and guard against abuses. In the decision whether to take on certain forms of research, or to take funding from certain agencies, these questions must be asked. Whilst certain topics may be interesting for a researcher to investigate, sometimes it is better not to research or publish at all rather than risk abuse. Sometimes a researcher must resist the temptation to publish interesting materials they have worked hard to collect and analyse if there is a significant risk of harm. For example, research into work may show that workers who feel themselves to be underpaid or overworked or both may sometimes take extra breaks, slow down the pace of work deliberately, or even steal from their employer. The researcher may desire to show that such actions are a legitimate response to bad conditions, but this may result in those conditions becoming worse for those workers, and may even result in them losing their jobs. For a more in-depth account of this danger, and for a useful set of examples, see Roger Homan (1991: 140–59).

Nevertheless, whilst it is not appropriate to reveal personal details about a research participant that would identify that person, and would embarrass them, it may be the case overall that information about groups of people should be revealed, even if it is damaging to them. If research showed that middle-class parents were successfully able to gain better access to state-funded educational resources, should this not be revealed? Is this not why research of this kind is carried out in the first place? If the research found that middle-class parents did not gain such additional resources for their children, but that these children still outperformed children of working-class parents, would these parents not want the results too? If the former case was found, would not working-class parents want the truth to be revealed? Deciding who has the right not to be criticized is as political as the question of who should be researched and what should be looked into about them. If a research question was such that its answer was so problematic as to make it better not to be asked, it is likely to be a question posed in a problematic fashion. Focusing attention on a particular group and investigating their potentially problematic behaviour would require justification relative to other groups. Why ask the questions: 'Does group X engage in crime?'; 'Does group Y support violent political protest?'; 'Does group Z claim social security benefits they are not entitled to?' Such questions might be problematic. Surely the question of who commits crime, supports violent political protest, or claims benefits they are not entitled to would better be researched in a non-directed fashion. Research that asks appropriate questions is less likely to produce prejudicial data. However, what counts as appropriate will be politically contested. Nevertheless, how such research is presented and how findings are interpreted and selected for publicity are important issues of integrity for the researcher. It is easy to grab headlines with exaggerated claims that distort research findings. This may have a short-term benefit for the researcher, but is likely to damage their credibility and their ability to do future research, so it is not a sensible thing to do. Even if it could be used to gain publicity and future funding, exaggerated and distorted representation of findings is still unethical and should not be done.

Integrity, plagiarism, fabrication and falsification

As has been pointed out above, researchers have an obligation to those that they research, but they also have an obligation to society to reveal social processes at work. As such, there may be a tension between revealing the truth and protecting the reputation of the social groups being studied. It would be unethical to *falsify* results, but it is also important not to reveal specific details about individuals in the research. Disguising identities in the reporting of research is not generally considered *falsification*. To censor comments in an interview so as to disguise identities and locations is one thing. It is quite another to censor relevant information and thereby create a false impression. Discretion may involve being less than fulsome with the truth. This is generally distinguished from lying and making up things that did not happen or hiding things that did happen. The creation of results that did not exist at all is *fabrication*. Increasing the numbers of people in a survey by either filling in extra questionnaires or entering the same data more than once is very tempting, but highly damaging to the reputation of anyone who is caught doing so. In addition to *falsification* and *fabrication* there is *plagiarism*. If the first two involve deception at the level of manipulation of data, plagiarism involves deception over the origin of work done. Taking credit for other people's work is a form of intellectual theft, and undermines the foundations of academic life, where researchers make their work available to others for free circulation and criticism. Academics are rarely paid for publishing in academic journals and do so in the hope that their names will be noticed and cited by others. This process of citation increases the reputation of the author and advances their position in their respective fields. This kind of gift economy encourages people to make great efforts in the hope that their names will be noticed and their reputations built. Plagiarism undermines this system of reward and so undermines the whole academic system. *Don't do it!* Plagiarism has two main forms, voluntary and involuntary. When names are added to academic papers of people who made no significant contribution to the work, this is voluntary plagiarism, at least to the extent that the person who did the work 'agrees' to the action. It may be that they are not in a strong position to refuse, such as where a supervisor insists that their name gets added, or where a team develops a culture of mutual adding of each other's names to papers. This practice is widespread, even whilst it is equally widely condemned. Involuntary plagiarism is where someone takes someone else's work and claims it as their own without the consent of the person who did the original work.

To conclude, it is essential to bear in mind that ethical considerations influence all aspects of the research process and that there are no magic formulas. In so far as social research is a part of the same social world it seeks to research, and this social world is deeply divided both materially and ethically, social research becomes political. Yet the systematic attempt to clarify and reflect upon its methods and its motives may give social researchers some additional capacity to understand the world, to do so in an ethically informed way, and to aid in the making of ethically sensitive and socially responsible decisions.

Summary

Research involving human subjects needs to be ethical in its selection (design), in its conduct and in the use/distribution of its findings. Ethical approaches to research connect with fundamental understandings of what makes society and individuals what they are. As such, ethics is linked to epistemology and politics. The attempt to separate these elements may be justified to offset the impact of bias on the conduct of research, and to ensure that research practicalities do not come to justify dubious ethical practices, but the three cannot be fully disentangled. As such, what some consider to be ethical, others will criticize. Whilst this is not an ideal state of affairs, the tensions between positivists, interpretivists and critical theorists over the connections between and separations of ethics, epistemology and politics create a space in which researchers are forced to justify what they do. To the extent that they feel the need to justify their actions, this is a good thing. The existence of ethics committees formalizes the sense that you are not just answerable to yourself. Being forced to be reflexive is a valuable thing in itself.

 ■ **Questions**

1 Is it ever appropriate to mislead people in the conduct of social research?
2 What distinguishes anonymity from confidentiality?
3 How does the adoption of a consequentialist or a deontological ethical stance alter what the researcher considers to be acceptable methods of researching humans?

■ ■ **Further reading** ■

Homan, Roger (1991) *The Ethics of Social Research*. Harlow: Longman.

Israel, Mark and Hay, Iain (2006) *Research Ethics for Social Scientists: Between Ethical Conduct and Regulatory Compliance*. London: Sage.

Lee, Raymond (1993) *Doing Research on Sensitive Topics*. London: Sage.

Renzetti, Claire M. and Lee, Raymond M. (1993) *Researching Sensitive Topics*. London: Sage.

Williams, Malcolm and May, Tim (1996) *Introduction to the Philosophy of Social Research*. London: UCL.

THREE

LITERATURE SEARCHING AND REVIEWING

Chapter Contents

Aims

By the end of this chapter you will be able to:

- **Locate and identify sources of literature useful in framing and developing your research.**
- **Structure and conduct a literature search.**
- **Carry out a literature review.**
- **Reference sources correctly.**

Researching the literature

One definition of a literature review is as follows:

> The selection of all available documents (both published and unpublished) on the topic, which contain information, ideas, data and evidence written from a particular

standpoint to fulfil certain aims or express certain views on the nature of the topic and how it is to be investigated, and the effective evaluation of these documents in relation to the research being proposed. (Hart, 1998: 13)

This is all very well in theory, but it sounds a tall order. Researching the literature comes in two parts, although these parts feed into each other:

- *Searching for literature.* A literature search seeks to find materials related to a topic.
- *Analysis of its content.* A literature review seeks to analyse the content of that material in more depth.

Of course, what counts as part of the literature of interest depends upon its content, and knowing its content depends upon finding it first. The two parts feed into each other. A chicken and egg scenario! So where to begin? As with starting a job, moving to a new town or learning any new skill, we are confronted with the novelty of what those more established there take for granted. The established researcher in a field knows who the key players are, what they have written, the journals to keep an eye on, as well as the conferences and presentations to attend. They are in the loop. Their social networks in the field are a crucial asset in keeping their fingers on the pulse. In one of the authors' own research for the British Library into literature searching (David and Zeitlyn, 1996; Zeitlyn et al., 1999), it was found that more established researchers were quite unlikely to use the technical literature searching services available to them, while younger researchers did (Box 3.1). Just as an established resident is unlikely to use a map of their town, so the more established researchers draw upon experience and personal networks to find their way around. So how to get into the loop? This is where more technical searching services come in, but such searching services are only as good as the questions asked of them. Computers might be the answer, but what is the question? How do we identify the crucial themes, concepts and theories?

BOX 3.1 RESEARCH FOCUS

The hungry rats syndrome

Jane Keefer (1993) compares the behaviour of students looking for things to read in the maze of shelves within a library and the behaviour of rats in laboratory mazes looking for food. She notes research that showed that when rats are hungry they search more rapidly than when they have only recently eaten. As the rats become increasingly hungry the speed of their darting around the maze increases, but after a

(Continued)

(Continued)

certain point their hunger begins to interfere with their recall and the rats' search patterns become increasingly random. Keefer notes that students who are looking for books in the library display similar patterns. When their essay is not due in for a long time, students are rather leisurely in their searching behaviour, but as deadlines approach their desperation increases, as does the speed with which they race around looking for the materials they need. Past a certain threshold the urgency of the need starts to impair students' abilities to locate materials and they find it increasingly difficult to find the right shelves and once there to see the item on the shelf. Keefer concludes that increased motivation can be offset by the stress of leaving things to the last minute. Combine this with the fact that if you do leave things to the last minute there is an increased likelihood that the material will not be available, it is never too early to start searching for literature.

Searching the archives

Bouma and Atkinson counsel that: 'A good librarian is the finest resource available to anyone undertaking social science research' (1995: 35). And Keefer states: 'The basic "information problem" revolves around the fact that the inquirer knows enough to know that he or she needs information, but doesn't know enough to ask the "good" questions that would produce the needed information' (1993: 336).

Before searching the archives, it is essential to discuss your topic with peers, tutors and librarians. This is the best way to identify the keywords that are going to assist you in wading through the near infinite mass of literature that exists (Box 3.2).

BOX 3.2 HINTS AND TIPS

How to ask a question when you don't already know the answer

It is often assumed that a rhetorical question is not really a question at all. When you ask a question because you already know the answer, and are only asking in order to elicit the response you wanted to hear, you are only using the question form to get someone else to make a statement that you were keen to have said, but wanted the other person to be the one to say it. As such, it might be assumed that if rhetorical questions are only that – rhetorical devices – then real questions are always those where you don't know the answer in advance. This might be true, but some questions are so open ended that the person asking not only does not know the answer in advance, but is not really sure how to pose the question in the first place.

In social research the formation of a research question (as discussed in Chapter 1) may leave you with a very clear idea of what you need to find out or it may leave you with a very wide-ranging set of ambiguities. Typically, a deductive research project will formulate a research question with very strict limits and a clear sense of the concepts and evidence needed to generate an answer. More inductive research will tend to the opposite extreme.

When you are setting out to research the literature, just as when you are setting out to design your data collection strategy, the issue of how tightly defined your question is in advance is very significant. In the physical sciences, researchers are required to specify their research questions in terms of very strictly defined sets of keywords which have narrowly defined meanings. Each discipline and subfield has its own set of such keywords, and often the journals in that field will require authors to identify very clearly which keywords their work should be catalogued under. This rigour does not exist in the social sciences. To simply wish that such rigour did exist ignores the fact that there is much less agreement in the social sciences as to what the core concepts and keywords should be, or what such terms mean. Because of the diversity of theoretical and methodological traditions, simply to agree the keywords would create a superficial consensus underneath which authors would continue to mean different things by the same words. When setting out to undertake a literature search and review, it is important to recall that words mean different things to different people. What might appear to be a systematic search (reading all the articles and books where one or two or more keywords appear) may be rendered unsystematic if you have not managed to find all the research where alternative terms have been used to refer to your key themes, and where you have not managed to discount all the research where the same terms are used to refer to things you are not interested in.

The social scientist cannot rely on mechanical forms of rigour. Whilst many very helpful search tools have become available in recent years that help the social researcher trawl through the mass of research literature out there in the archives, it is still essential that the social scientist learns the skill of asking questions that take account of the fact that they can never be sure in advance what the answers might be.

This is one reason why it is always useful to talk to supervisors, colleagues, librarians and others when seeking to formulate the questions you want to ask, and the search strategies and keywords you are going to use.

Once you begin to accumulate texts from within a field, new keywords may begin to stand out, initial ones may drop out, and others may take on additional significance. Keeping records of what you have read, and of the central arguments and keywords used within these texts, is therefore an essential task. Traditionally researchers would keep a card index of all texts read (usually ordered alphabetically by author, but sometimes ordered by other criteria). Nowadays, such indexes can be stored electronically, either in straightforward word-processing files or in more specific indexing software. Either way, it is essential to establish your own indexing system (Box 3.3). This enables the streamlining of content and the storage of essential information, and allows for comparison. Another key consideration when developing an indexing system is how you are going to organize the content of each text's respective card or file (see section 'Reviewing content' later in this chapter).

BOX 3.3 HINTS AND TIPS

Taking notes and storing them

The art of taking notes is to reduce the content whilst retaining the important details. The key details within any text are discussed in the 'Reviewing content' section below. In relation to the conduct of literature searching, it is important to create a storage structure in advance, so that basic details can be recorded to be fleshed out in the transition from search to review. When you identify a text (whether it be a book or a journal article or whatever) you should record the bibliographic details in a filing system. Bibliographic information is the information by which texts are located:

- authors' names
- date of publication
- title of publication
- editor's name and title of book if edited collection
- book publisher's location and address or journal title
- volume and issue numbers and page references if relevant
- location where the text was found and can be accessed for future reference
- other information (such as web address).

Beyond bibliographic details, you will also want to record a basic synopsis of the work:

- topic
- questions asked
- methods used
- data collected/used/sampled
- location
- date
- analysis undertaken
- conclusions drawn.

In addition to this, you should add your own critical evaluation of the research:

- What are the strengths?
- What are the weaknesses?
- What are the omissions?
- What are the similarities and differences from other research?

The critical evaluation should be built upon the elements of the synopsis in conjunction with your accounts of other materials. This will require coming back to such notes and adding to them once you have looked at other works. This is the transition from literature searching to literature reviewing. Keep your notes in electronic files, and make backup copies of these.

Once you have identified your provisional keywords, established how you are going to store the reference details of the texts you uncover, and prepared some means of ordering and storing the actual materials you uncover (shelves, filing cabinets and piles on the floor are popular), you are ready to begin formal searching.

Searching for books, articles, theses, web materials, newspapers and other sources

Most of us, when we think about literature, think first of books. However, in conducting an efficient literature search, it is often more productive to begin with journal articles, theses and reports from bodies concerned with the subject we are interested in. This is for a number of simple reasons. Articles, theses and reports are usually shorter than books, are more tightly focused, and so are more rapidly published and read. The latest journal articles, theses and reports will be more up to date and their bibliographies are likely to be the best source of references for older research, and particularly the older research that has become core reading in the field in question. Reading the latest articles, theses and reports is therefore the fastest and most effective method of getting to grips with a field.

Almost all libraries now have online public access catalogues (OPACs) that enable the researcher to identify the volumes shelved in the library. Academic and research libraries often have these OPACs networked, allowing the researcher to search catalogues of libraries around the world via a networked computer. However, some OPACs only catalogue volumes and not their contents. Such OPACs are not the best vehicle for identifying journal articles. In such circumstances it will be necessary to use alternative databases. However, many academic libraries now integrate their shelving catalogues with full-text journal services, such that you can not only identify journal articles electronically, but also read them electronically in a full-text format. The advent of full-text journal services has made the use of journal articles more attractive than was the case in the past.

Abstracts and indexes for articles, theses and reports

Abstracts and indexing services enable the researcher to search the content of articles, theses and reports (usually not books). This requires that the researcher identify keywords by which to search. The wrong keywords may lead you in the wrong direction. Keywords that are too general will generate references to too many texts, and the researcher will get swamped. Too specific keywords may not generate enough references. Keywords may be the names of authors, places, dates, names of journals, academic fields and disciplines or concepts (such as gender or crime). Discussion with peers, tutors and librarians is the key to getting past this problem of which keywords to start with. Once you get going, additional (and sometimes better) keywords will present themselves. When publishing an article, authors are asked by journal editors to select the keywords that best reflect their piece (see Figure 3.1). In addition to keywords, the bibliographic details (date of publication, author name(s), title and journal title and so on) are stored as keywords in the abstracts and indexing system. Your job is to second-guess these. The physical sciences have a more systematic process of allocating keywords than is found in the social sciences, so second-guessing in the social science abstracts and indexes is harder.

Traditionally indexes were large bound volumes organized alphabetically by author, title and keywords from the text. Each index would cover a specified academic

David, Matthew (2002) 'Problems of participation: the limits of action research', *International Journal of Social Research Methodology*, 5(1): 11–17.

Abstract

Alvin Gouldner (1979) suggests knowledge is both culture and capital. Knowledge enables meaningful action. Capital is culture privatized. Culture is capital generalized. This raises the question of ownership in social research. Detachment in social research is praised as a virtue but also viewed as a source of difficulties, epistemologically and ethically. Participatory action research offers a critique of detachment and advocates its opposite, 'commitment'. This may not necessarily involve 'political' advocacy. However, commitment to involve participants, and to further their goals through the conduct of research, does become a form of 'advocacy'. This paper draws on problematic experiences as a 'participatory action researcher' in social movement and evaluation research. Drawing on the recent work of Steve Fuller (2000), I will suggest, rather bluntly, that when asked 'whose side are we on', academics might be more bold and suggest we are on our own side.

Keywords: PAR, participatory action research, advocacy, detachment, instrumentalism, social movements, evaluation research, telematics, social exclusion, politics

FIGURE 3.1 A typical social science journal abstract

field for a specified period. Specific indexes were devoted to academic journal articles, academic theses or commissioned reports. A researcher seeking to find materials would search the relevant indexes for references to texts that might be of interest to them. Each entry in the index would then reference the location of an abstract of that article, thesis or report. An abstract is a short summary of the text, as shown in Figure 3.1.

By reading the abstract, the researcher gains a better idea of whether the text might be worth finding and reading in full. Bound volumes of abstracts relating to the bound volumes of indexes would usually be kept in the same section of the library, and in some cases the abstracts and indexes would be within a single bound volume. This was a laborious process and was seen as one of the 'rites of passage' in 'becoming a researcher'. One of the most tedious aspects was cross-referencing between keywords. For example, if you were interested in the use of 'illegal drugs' by 'women', you would want to identify all articles that refer to both. This would mean listing not only all the articles that had keywords related to 'women', but also all the articles that contained keywords related to 'illegal drugs'. Each keyword link had a code linking it to an article. Once you had written down all the codes for one keyword you would then have to go through all the codes for the other keywords. Where two keywords had the same code, that was an article that referred to both keywords.

There may be thousands of articles with each keyword, and so too many to read. You may want only those articles that contained both. This is an AND type search. Sometimes you will want a NOT search, where you might request, for example, all articles about drugs NOT those relating to medication. Such AND, NOT, OR and other types of search are called Boolean searches, and form one strand of qualitative data analysis (see Chapters 18–21). See Box 3.4 for how such an AND link differs from other types of search.

BOX 3.4 HINTS AND TIPS

Boolean searching

When you were at school, it is likely you were at some point required to draw Venn diagrams. Venn diagrams display the principles of set theory, which underlies Boolean searching.

If a box is meant to represent all the people in the class, and a circle represents all the pupils with blue eyes, another circle can represent all the students with brown eyes. These two circles will not overlap, as membership of one circle precludes membership of the other (unless you have one of each perhaps). Assuming these two circles are discrete, we can still imagine another circle representing all those pupils who belong to the swimming club. If this group includes pupils with blue eyes and pupils with brown eyes, then the swimming club circle will overlap both the other two circles. The area where the swimming club circle overlaps the blue eye circle represents pupils who belong to both sets.

The logic of Venn diagrams allows a visual representation of sets of members of different sets, and of how much crossover there is between sets. We can see in Figure 3.2 that members of the dive club are all members of the swim club, but most members of the swim club are not members of the dive club. Where one circle sits within another, this represents a subset. Where two circles overlap, this represents cases which belong to more than one set. Where multiple circles overlap, we have cases of multiple membership. There are some pupils who swim, dive, have brown eyes and are in the nature club. But there are not many. If you asked who is in the brown eye circle AND the nature club circle AND the swim club circle AND the dive club circle, that would be a very small group. AND searches are exclusionary as they require only cases where individuals belong to one set and another (etc.). AND might seem to be inclusive, but in Boolean searching AND will get you only those where all the keywords (or sets) apply. If you wanted all those in a club, you would use an OR type search (swim club OR nature club OR dive club). This would give you an 'inclusive' search. NOT would allow you to, for example, select those who were in the swim club but NOT the dive club.

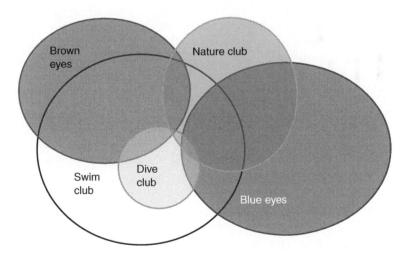

FIGURE 3.2 Venn diagram

(Continued)

(Continued)

If you were searching for all the articles on violence, but were interested only in those linked to drug crime, you could use an AND type search. If you were interested in articles on violence and domestic abuse (which is a term that may be used to refer to a certain form of violence), you could use an OR type search. If you were interested in violence but not that involved with military conflict, you could use a NOT search.

It is essential to identify alternative keywords when searching for a particular theme. For example, if you were interested in poverty, many articles may be of use to you that do not have the term 'poverty' as a keyword. These articles may have terms like 'social exclusion', 'inequality' or 'deprivation' as keywords. While these words do not have identical meanings, their meanings overlap. In any keyword search it is important to think of as many such overlapping terms as possible in order to be comprehensive. These terms can be generated by the researcher in advance, in collaboration with colleagues and others, or new keywords can be generated as the researcher goes along (looking at the other keywords in the abstracts of articles found along the way). Once keyword searches point to potentially useful abstracts, these abstracts can be read and a decision made as to whether it would be useful to find and read the full articles.

This narrowing down used to require seemingly endless trawling backwards and forwards, between pages within the abstracts and then between the indexes and the abstracts they referred to. Things have changed radically in recent years. Though some paper abstract and indexing services still exist, and may be useful, electronic services have now largely taken the place of paper. Electronic services allow searches that once would have taken days to be carried out in minutes. Of course, being easier does not ensure that searches done electronically are better.

Electronic abstracts and indexing services have evolved rapidly. The earliest electronic systems emerged in the physical sciences (for example, Chemical Abstracts Service), medicine (MEDLINE) and law (Lexus). They involved centrally stored databases that could be accessed online. These services charged for time online and were complex and expensive. Researchers would usually get a specialist (librarian or other) to do searches quickly on their behalf. The advent of the CD-ROM enabled the data to be held locally at a fixed price. This meant that researchers could do their own searches without per-minute costs. CD-ROMs are still a popular medium for abstracts and indexing services, but updating requires replacement each time. The next stage in the development of electronic abstracts and indexing was the rise of consortia which brought together numerous databases within a single search format, and then charged institutions (usually academic and research-based libraries) fixed rates (usually per year) to access their service. This meant a high initial fee, but no per-minute charges. This enabled these institutions to give open access to these services to all their members (or end-users) without fear of excessive costs. In this way the 'liberated end-user' has access to the most up-to-date version of the database without their institution having to continually buy new CD-ROMs. The next development was the availability of many of these services through the World Wide Web, thus easing access and improving interface quality (Box 3.5).

BOX 3.5 HINTS AND TIPS

Social science databases for literature searching

http://www.scopus.com/home.url. Scopus claims on this website to be the 'largest abstract and citation database of research literature and quality web sources'. It contains materials on around 15,000 journals dating back to 1996, with almost 3000 of these being social science journals. Scopus is based in the USA.

http://www.lse.ac.uk/collections/IBSS/about/about_IBSS.htm. The International Bibliography of the Social Sciences has approximately the same number of social science journals as Scopus, but has only these; its catalogue goes back to 1989, so it has a little more history than Scopus. IBSS is based at the London School of Economics and is funded by the UK Economic and Social Research Council.

http://wok.mimas.ac.uk. Based at Manchester University and funded by the UK's Joint Information Services Committee, Web of Knowledge provides access to the International Science Index service, which includes the Science, Social Science and Arts and Humanities Citations Indexes along with a range of other services. Citation indexes map who is referencing whom. This is often taken as a proxy indicator of a researcher's importance. Citation indexes have become very important in all domains of research as the sheer volume of research means that nobody can hope to keep up with the actual content of everyone else's work. The attempt to map citations to see whose work is the most influential has proved controversial, as it is not always clear that the person who is cited the most is the most original person, or simply the person either whom everyone disagrees with or who was the first to make the original work of someone else comprehensible to a large number of other people. Being truly original might be one way to ensure that you are not cited very often. If you stick with the mainstream, and cite all your colleagues in a little 'cluster', perhaps they will all cite your work as well. You will feel very important, but are you? If citation indexing were to be seen as the scientific equivalent of democracy it would be an electoral system where everyone gets to vote as many times as they want to. Increasingly governments want to measure research impact, and they want to use citation indexes as a fast and efficient way of doing so. Many researchers think this is a foolish thing to do, but as a way of searching for interesting things to read, we may as well piggyback on all the money that was spent in developing the systems.

It is worthwhile learning how to use these services as they give you a gateway to huge amounts of material that you would neither know about nor be able to select between without the use of their Boolean search capabilities. You will use the techniques discussed in Box 3.4, but you will have to also learn a few particularities in each such service. One common feature of such literature searching databases is the abbreviation function. If you want to find all the articles on tourism, tourists and touristic, then you are often able to simply search for 'Touris*'; the * function limits the search to all items with a keyword starting with those six letters, irrespective of what comes later. Your library will have lots of information about the services available to you within your institution and they will be able to give you specific instructions on how to access and use them from your location.

Pay-per-minute services, CD-ROMs and fixed-fee-based systems all exist, but, as a beginner, you are likely only to use the latter two. These systems are all fundamentally similar to the traditional paper services. You have to identify the keywords you want the system to search for, and then cross-reference, but electronic services offer increased scope, speed and range of peripheral services. Abstracts found electronically can be saved to word-processing files. Journals store their articles in electronic format. Some journals allow these to be made available via the electronic search services, so in addition to an abstract you may be able to get the full text. If your university or college has a good library it will most likely have entered into a licensing agreement with publishers. This means that for a flat fee (often very high) all staff and students can access electronic versions of the publishers' materials (journals and many books). If you want to access such materials from outside the university or college you may either be blocked or asked to pay a per-item fee. As such, it is worth finding out what your institution has to offer. Not everything is available online, and some items identified electronically may be in a paper copy in your library. If not you may find that your library is prepared to order copies of articles, books and other published materials for you via interlibrary loan. You will need to see what your library can offer. Sometimes you will have to pay a small fee, but this varies from library to library and sometimes it will vary depending on whether you are a first-year undergraduate, a final-year undergraduate doing a dissertation, a research student or a member of staff.

Similar services exist for newspapers and magazines. Your library will be able to show you how their particular deals with media sources work, but there are a number of useful databases for newspapers from particular countries and from around the world. Most newspapers also have web pages of their own and these contain their own archives, which you might want to use instead. Some such services require a subscription or for you to register. Each such system will have its own quirks, and not all will be available to you through your home computer or via the institutions you either work or study in. Once again your librarian is your best friend in this regard and it is they (not us) who can best advise you on what is available to you, and how best to access and use it. Technical networks do not replace social networks when it comes to doing social research, and especially when it comes to knowing how to ask a relevant question. Other kinds of news media, such as television and radio, also have websites and archives of content, and these are often free to access.

Once you have found material and stored it you will want to move on to the detailed and critical analysis of its content.

Reviewing content

Reviewing the content of literature gathered is a form of research in itself. It is a form of secondary data analysis, and as the content we are dealing with here is textual, this form of secondary data analysis is a form of qualitative data analysis. All these themes are discussed in greater detail in Chapters 18 to 21. At this stage it is useful to suggest five possible sets of questions that can be addressed to the content of specific pieces of literature (Box 3.6). These five approaches feed into each other and are drawn from the work of Hart (1998). As one becomes more confident as a researcher, these practices may become habits that take on a less formal quality. The more seasoned researcher may trust their 'instincts' and adopt a more holistic approach to reviewing texts. Whether this is healthy or just laziness is a matter for speculation, but the seasoned researcher can get away with it more easily, while the beginner cannot. As such it is best to start with some degree of formal ordering. When you are a famous social researcher you can do your own thing.

BOX 3.6 HINTS AND TIPS

How to read a book, chapter or article

Confronted with a large amount of literature, you may be wondering how it would be possible to read it all. Reading a novel or short story for pleasure is a very different kind of reading from what you want to do when looking to extract the content from research literature. There are a number of useful techniques to help this extraction process. When you pick up a book, read the title, the subtitle and the back cover. The contents page will tell you what each chapter is about. This will give you an instant impression of the structure and content of the book. Then read the opening page or two, which should give you some idea of the argument that the book will make and the evidence being used to make it. Then, look at the index to identify the keywords that have been indexed. This should give you an idea of which terms have been deemed most central to the book and which have been used the most. The index will give page references for each time a term or author is cited. Just looking to see which terms and authors have the longest list of page references will tell you a lot about the book's content. The bibliography will also tell you a lot about who the author is drawing upon, which traditions and approaches they have been influenced by, and whose work they appear not to have used (relative to what you find in other people's bibliographies).

Use these skimming techniques to help inform yourself of whether a book is useful or not, and make a few notes in your filing system (see Box 3.3).

This combination of techniques should tell you whether a book is going to be useful, and which parts are going to be the most valuable. You may want to work through the book from beginning to end or focus on just the chapters and sections that appear most relevant. This may depend on your time constraints, the amount of material you have to get through, and whether or not you are interested in the fine details or the general findings. It is alright to be selective, but just be aware of the danger of skimming. You save time, and have more chance to cover a greater range of material, but you will lose some of the depth and detail. Be careful.

Whether you are reading a chapter or a journal article, the opening abstract or introduction and the conclusions will give you the most concentrated information, and unlike a good novel it is not cheating to read the end before you've read the middle. Its alright to spoil the surprise, and as you will no doubt know from films, TV dramas, plays and novels, it is often the case that things make more sense once you look back from the end. If you struggle with someone's argument, look at their introduction and conclusion and then try to make sense of how they got from one to the other. Another tip is to map out the subheadings and major segments of the chapter/article. If you know the major points along the route, it is easier to avoid getting lost in the mass of details.

1 Defining parameters: how does the particular text define the field of study? What are the key elements included, what are the boundaries drawn around the topic, and what are the elements explicitly excluded?

2 How are the findings of the work classified? What framework of categories is being used to define the objects identified in the research? What distinctions and variables are being used? What methods are being used?

3 Argumentation analysis: logic and argument. What is the argument being developed in the work? How is evidence used to build towards a conclusion? What are the conclusions drawn?

4 Organization and expression of ideas. What theoretical models are being used?

5 How best can the text's content be represented? Here the researcher may wish to use mental maps, flow diagrams and compressed summaries of the piece.

Once specific texts have been treated in this way it is possible to move on to the more synthetic task of evaluating the relationship between them. A firm grasp of the elements will enable you to ask the questions:

• What do some or all of these texts have in common?

• What do some or all of these texts contain that distinguishes them from each other?

These questions will return you to the five question areas above. How is the definition of the field established and/or disputed? What are the key categories and variables being deployed, and how far is their use agreed and/or disputed? How is evidence used to establish or dispute findings? What are the theoretical lines of dispute and agreement that operate within the field? How best can such disputes and/or consensus be represented? (Timelines and mental maps are particularly useful in representing how disputes and/or agreements develop historically, within and between different theoretical traditions and in different locations – localities, states and larger geographical areas.

In asking and seeking to answer these types of question, you begin to move away from cataloguing towards critical evaluation. In time and with regard to different fields of study you will come to develop your own interrogation strategies. The job of a literature review is to focus, find, catalogue and evaluate. Each step may turn up issues that require going back a step to widen, narrow or shift the direction of the review, but the aim is that of evaluation. It is only at this stage that the researcher can claim to have a grasp of their chosen (and to a degree self-generated) field. It is only at this stage that the researcher can claim to occupy a vantage point from which to identify the gaps and crucial lines of conflict which require further investigation. Even where research is contracted and comes with a high degree of prespecification about its aims, the translation of these aims into practical research objectives requires the researcher to know what has gone before – partly to avoid reinventing the wheel, but also to enable the research meaningfully to contribute something new to the field.

Systematic review, meta-analysis and narrative review

Mary Ebeling and Julie Gibbs (2008: 67) distinguish three main types of literature review. A systematic review seeks to define the parameters of searching, selection and analysis in a fully explicit and deductive fashion. Where very clearly defined keywords characterize a field (such as in chemistry or physics), and where terms are used in a highly routine fashion, it is possible to carry out such a deductive search, and to select literature purely on the basis of such shared keywords. Where methods are clearly specified and carried out either in laboratory conditions or in a style approximating such repeatability (in principle), the movement from research question to method to analysis and conclusions in each study can be compared and contrasted with a degree of methodical repetition that allows the literature review to resemble a questionnaire survey in which each case is asked the same questions and where responses are compared against a common benchmark. Where this approach is taken to its full extent, and where data collected from a range of similar studies can be compared, systematic review becomes meta-analysis, a form of qualitative secondary data analysis. Where the literature is so detailed as to include its data, and where such data are comparable with data from similar research, the boundary between literature and data breaks down. This is rarely achieved except in very quantitative research fields, and most often in the physical sciences. Whilst the term 'meta-ethnography' is used to refer to literature reviews where the reviewer seeks to give an overview of a range of qualitative studies, such qualitative data rarely get presented in the literature in such a form that a reviewer could analyse them in the way a meta-analysis involving numerical data might. Most social science literature reviews are what Ebeling and Gibbs (2008) call narrative reviews, where a range of previous research is compared and contrasted, but where it is not possible to be either as systematic in selection or as integrated in analysis as are required in systematic review or meta-analysis. The diversity of means by which keywords are selected in the social sciences, and the divergence of methods and theories in this domain of research, mean that narrative reviews are as much engaged in noting the differences in conceptual and methodological construction as they are in comparing outcomes from similar studies across time and space. It is one thing to aspire to the apparent rigour of systematic review or of meta-analysis. It is another to place naïve faith in such methodical approaches. Their rigour can easily become problematic when the literature being reviewed is not sufficiently well structured to warrant it.

BOX 3.7

SYSTEMATIC REVIEW

A systematic review or systematic research synthesis is a review of the literature that uses a systematic approach to identify and synthesize the research evidence. In a normal literature review the views of the author are taken as an accurate reflection of the research. In a systematic review

(Continued)

the actual methodology, methods and research findings are included in the review. Systematic reviews have emerged from clinical medicine and the development of evidence based practice or evidence informed approaches. The use of systematic reviews has been adapted by the social sciences (see Victor, 2008) to meet the needs of the discipline particularly in the areas of applied research and practice. The purpose of a systematic review is to provide a rigorous evidence base that can be disseminated, often to policy makers, public organizations and the general public.

Victor (2008:1) summarizes a systematic review as one that '... should be comprehensive in its coverage of the literature; pay careful attention to the quality of included evidence; take a clear, systematic approach to the synthesis of the data; and generally follow transparent and rigorous processes. These features are designed to allow greater validity and reliability to be attributed to the synthesised findings.'

Systematic reviews can be considered as small pieces of research of their own, with an agreed approach and methodology. Clear inclusion and exclusion criteria for the consideration of different evidence are stated with clear stages of development. In its simplest form the review will start with some broad criteria from which potential articles are identified and from which subsequent criteria (for example: keywords; dates; type and size of study; geographical location) are applied. Further criteria can assess the quality and clarity of individual research findings; evidence that does not meet these strict criteria is again excluded from the review.

A record of all included and excluded sources is kept. The methodology for the review is provided in order that the results can be accountable, replicable and updateable (EPPI, 2009).

Example of a systematic review

Oliver, S., Kavanagh, J., Caird, J., Lorenc, T., Oliver, K., Harden, A., Thomas, J., Greaves, A. and Oakley, A. (2008) *Health Promotion, Inequalities and Young People's Health: A Systematic Review of Research*. London: EPPI-Centre, Social Science Research Unit, Institute of Education, University of London.

In this study Oliver et. al. (2008) describe how much health promotion and public health intervention research has focused on inequalities in young people's health, and what methods have been used to define and measure inequalities. They undertook a review of the existing evidence of health promotion and public health research in areas that young people experience health inequalities, for example, mental health; physical health; teenage pregnancy; healthy eating.

For further details see http://eppi.ioe.ac.uk/cms/Default.aspx?tabid=2410

Further Reading

Victor, Liz (2008) 'Systematic reviewing', *Social Research Update*, 54, Summer. http://sru.soc.surrey.ac.uk/SRU54.pdf

Evidence for Policy and Practice Information and Co-ordinating Centre (EPPI-Centre), Social Science Research Unit, Institute of Education, University of London, http://eppi.ioe.ac.uk/

Referencing your sources

As you collect materials and as you take notes on what you have collected, you should ensure that you are recording the bibliographic details along with your notes on the content and your critical and comparative observations. This is for your convenience when you come to write up your research, and for your protection in the event of your using other people's work as though it were your own and thereby being guilty of plagiarism (see Chapter 2). The rules on plagiarism are not always the same and have changed over time, and vary from institution to institution. It was once common for the act of plagiarism to require evidence of intention to deceive, the deliberate attempt to pass off other people's work as your own. This is not so common now. Today, in many universities, it is enough to have used significant amounts of someone's work without referencing it correctly to be found guilty of plagiarism. Ignorance is not a defence in most institutions. The question of what counts as 'use' varies, as many institutions rely upon the identification of identical passages of text, whilst others use software that can detect high levels of similarity (such that just changing a few words here and there is not enough to avoid being caught). Even in the absence of direct verbatim quotation, copying the structure of an argument when this represents the whole structure of your essay can draw the accusation of plagiarism in some institutions. How much of a piece of work is copied also influences the decision as to whether an essay or other assessment is deemed to have been plagiarized, or is 'just' poor scholarship with a minor slip. How many identical words in a string are sufficient to make it plagiarism also varies from institution to institution. For all these reasons you have to learn what the rules are where you are, and follow these. You need to understand the rules as best you can, as to be caught out for simply not having understood can still lead to significant punishment and stigma.

How then should you reference correctly? The basic premise is that you must ensure that the person reading your work does not gain the impression that you are the originator of expressions and ideas that are not yours, and that all the work you have drawn upon in the construction of your work is clearly identified both in the text and in some form of collection (as footnotes, endnotes, a bibliography, a reading list or a set of references). Here we start by outlining the linkage between references in the body of your text and a bibliography, reading list or reference section.

Referencing in the text allows you to flag up sources at the point at which they have been used in your work. There are three levels of such referencing in the text:

1 If you make a statement of your own, but it has been influenced by other work or is based upon the evidence you found in a particular source, that other author's family name and the date of the work's publication need to be placed in brackets at the end of the sentence e.g. '(David and Sutton, 2011)'.

2 If you are referring directly to an author in the text, then you place the date of the publication being referred to in brackets immediately after the author's name. For example, 'David and Sutton (2011) suggest this is a good idea.'

3 If you are using a direct quotation from a text you need to add the page reference within the brackets and after the date. For example, 'How then should you reference correctly? (David and Sutton, 2011: 69).'

There are some minor variations in different institutions and in some publications, so find out what you are expected to do. Whether the full stop at the end of the sentence goes before or after the brackets when the bracketed information is at the end of the sentence is one such case. However, the general point is to ensure that wherever your work has been based on someone else's work, whether or not it is a direct quotation or whether you have mentioned them by name, you have to make a reference. Students often ask whether this means that they have to repeatedly reference the same source over and over at the end of every sentence if they have based a large part of an essay on one author. The answer to this question is that the student should not rely so fully on one source.

The above style of referencing in the text applies to all sources – books, articles, chapters, websites, encyclopaedias, reports etc. – where there is a bibliography, reference section or reading list at the end of your work. Where there is no identified author, such as for some newspaper articles, you cite the name of the newspaper along with the date (and page numbers if citing a quotation). This system is efficient and clear as it requires a minimum of repetition. The author's name and date allows the reader to note that a reference has been made. These names and dates must then correspond to their compilation at the end of the work.

A bibliography may include works not directly cited in the text, where a reading list or reference section only contains material that is contained in the text itself. Whilst a seasoned author may wish to add material to their bibliography which does not appear in the text, this is not really a good idea for a beginner. If your work has been influenced by certain pieces of work, you should be very careful to say so in the text itself via citing the author and date where the connection exists. You gain marks for doing so, and might lose marks for not doing so if it is felt you are not being fully clear about your sources in the text. The term 'bibliography' to this extent should be seen as pretty much synonymous with 'references'.

As your text has made citations based on author names and dates, the bibliography, references or reading list at the end of your text should be organized sequentially by these criteria. You could then have everything organized by date, starting with all the references from the earliest year going up to the present. This is unusual. More common is to order references alphabetically by author name. If there are multiple 'Sutton' entries then these should be organized by date. If there are two different people called 'David', then their initial should be used to put one ahead of the other. If there are many items by the same author, then use date order to sequence them. If there are more than two authors it is common to simply give the first author's family name in the text followed by the expression 'et al.' (which indicates 'and others'), but you will have to give all the names in the bibliography/reference section.

Here are some examples:

David, Matthew (2005) *Science in Society*. London: Palgrave.

David, Matthew (2008) 'You think Bart Simpson is real: I know he's only an actor!', *Current Sociology*, 56 (4): 517–33.

David, Matthew (2010) *Peer to Peer and the Music Industry: The Criminalization of Sharing*. London: Sage.

David, Matthew and Kirkhope, Jamieson (2006) 'The impossibility of technical security: intellectual property and the paradox of informational capitalism', in Mark Lacy and Peter Witkin (eds), *Global Politics in an Information Age*. Manchester: Manchester University Press. pp. 88–95.

In these you can see that the full first name has been given. This may not always be required and sometimes only initials are required. Also note that where there is a co-author, the material is cited after all the single-authored items by the first author, whether or not this is the correct date sequence. Recall that if you are ordering alphabetically by author name then the second author will make the alphabetical listing come after, in the same way that 'hat' comes before 'hatch' in the dictionary.

The four items cited above show a particular set of conventions regarding format that are not universal. Note that the titles of books and journals are in italics, whilst articles within journals and chapters within books are in single inverted commas. This is a particular convention, and different institutions and publications have variations on this. The punctuation between the title, location and publisher, for volume and issue numbers for journal articles, and for page numbers of chapters and articles, are again open to some variation. Even the sequence is not always the same. Some formats require the location of a publisher to be placed ahead of the name of the publishing company, whilst other formats reverse this. You need to be aware of the quirks, and the regularities.

If you are citing a web page, or an online publication, you need to add the URL as well as the date at which you accessed the site. This is in addition to the date at which the material was first uploaded. Much confusion lies around the expression 'Harvard referencing system'. In essence this refers to having a set of references at the back of the text organized by author name and date, with links by these identifiers to the main body of the text. There are no universal rules for the Harvard system apart from this basic principle. It is said that the Harvard system is the most popular system worldwide, but given the diversity within the so-called system, and given that the system did not start at Harvard and simply catch on elsewhere, it is not quite clear whether this is a fair description. Rather as with the origins of football or the River Thames, there are many tributaries, so to claim absolute origin is a little mythic.

Alternative referencing systems exist. The Chicago referencing system is commonly associated with the use of footnotes at the bottom of pages where citations have been made. The footnote contains the bibliographic information for the material being referred to in the text and is linked to the text by means of superscript numbers, as at the end of this sentence.[1] The Chicago system also has a bibliographic version almost identical to the Harvard system, only typically with the date at the end rather than just after the author's name. The Oxford referencing system requires that the writer use both footnotes (which may use 'ibid.' and 'op.cit.')[2] and a bibliography at the same time.[2] The advantage of this is that the reader can check references as they go along without having to jump back and forth between text and bibliography, but also has a collected set of references at the end to refer to.

The two footnotes identified by the superscripts numbers in this paragraph might appear at the foot of the page as follows:

1 David, Matthew and Sutton, Carole (2011) *Social Research: An Introduction*. London: Sage.

2 'Ibid.' refers to the same text as in the previous footnote, though if it was a quote the quotation might carry a different page reference. Where you want to refer to an item previously footnoted but which was not the last one cited, use the expression 'op. cit.', as for example in 'David and Sutton, op. cit.' (please imagine that this was not the previous footnote – it's just that there are only two).

All sorts of conventions apply to the use of footnotes and these can be extended to endnotes, which compile references at the end in order of their appearance in the text, rather than by alphabetical and date order. Footnotes and endnotes can combine bibliographic and additional notes that the author wishes to add to their main text. It is not recommended that you use such additional text options. If you have a word length for an assignment, and you use footnotes to cut down on your word count, these words will also be discounted from your assessment and so will not count for anything. You need to decide what is relevant and what is not.

At the end of the day, if you are working within institutional constraints, you must pay attention to what the institution requires. Some universities require that you follow a particular system and even a particular style within that system. You need to pay attention, learn that particular set of conventions and work with it.

Summary

Depending on whether your research question gives you a highly structured, deductive theory testing hypothesis or a very open-ended inductive and exploratory research question, your approach to the literature will be very different, somewhere on the spectrum between a very organized and preplanned systematic review and a more emergent narrative review. The relationship between your research question, the search for literature and the review of its content will also vary, but these three elements are always bound together. The conduct of a literature search and the review of content are usually, for social scientists, something of a chicken and egg game, and the review may even lead to the reformulation of your research question (see Chapter 1), even whilst the act of getting started on a literature search requires that you have some idea of what you want to be looking for. The way to find material to read requires that you learn how to use a range of search systems, from paper abstracts and indexes to the latest databases and search engines. Reading the bibliographies at the back of books and articles is also a very good way to identify the keywords that are going to help you use more sophisticated search strategies. The principles of Boolean searching, set theory and Venn diagrams will help you to think through how you might want to select, include and exclude from your searching. Reading texts and taking effective notes require a degree of organization in reading, storing and comparing. The act of critical review requires you to draw out the essential features of work and use them to identify what has been done, and how and what needs to be done in the future. In writing up your review you must be able to document the materials you have used through the use of referencing in the text and typically also at the end of the text.

In everything that you do it is essential to refer to the rules and guidance in operation where you are located. There is a great variety of different systems and you need to learn the ropes as they are applied where you are.

 ■ **Questions**

1   What is the relationship between empirical research, literature searching and literature reviewing?
2   What is the difference between a bibliography, a reading list, footnotes and endnotes?
3   Try to specify the Boolean AND, OR and other search operators for a particular topic.

■ ■ **Further reading** ■

Ebeling, Mary and Gibbs, Julie (2008) 'Searching and reviewing literature', in Nigel Gilbert (ed.), *Researching Social Life*. London: Sage. pp. 63–79.

Hart, Chris (1998) *Doing a Literature Review*. London: Sage.

Hart, Chris (2001) *Doing a Literature Search*. London: Sage.

FOUR

THEORY AND RESEARCH: QUALITY AND QUANTITY

Chapter Contents

By the end of this chapter you will be able to:

- Comprehend the multidimensional distinctions made between qualitative and quantitative research designs, data and analysis.
- Distinguish different and fundamental ontologies and outline the methodological and epistemological consequences that flow from such positions.
- Identify common features that unite quality and quantity in all social research.
- Outline the strengths and limitations of mixed methods research.

Introduction

The second part of this chapter focuses on the distinction between qualitative and quantitative social research methodologies, but this distinction between methodologies needs to be located in the wider framework of sociological theory. The first part of the chapter therefore sets out the range of approaches and dimensions of such theory. The narrow conception of 'theory' refers to the overall accounts of the social world held by different sociological traditions. This narrow sense of the word 'theory' equates with what is called 'ontology': the theory of fundamental reality. The term 'theory' in the broader sense refers to the linkage between general ontologies and related theories of knowledge, data and data collection that exist within each theoretical tradition. This wider framework of different traditions and dimensions within each is set out in Table 4.1.

Ontology, epistemology, methodology and method

The four traditions outlined below – scientific naturalism, Marxism, constructionism and constructivism – have many subdivisions. Social scientific naturalism emulates the materialism of the physical sciences. Marxism is materialist, but emphasizes the human capacity to reflect and resist control. Within Marxism, critical realists place their attention on the material constraints operating in society. Critical theorists place their attention on the forms of meaning and belief systems operating in society which act as ideologies masking reality and keeping people in their place. Constructionists focus on how people create meaningful social reality for themselves through their interactions and thereby create a sense of order through shared beliefs rather than from real external 'structures'. Constructivists focus upon the structural characteristics of language, which they see as having a determining effect on the ordering of social life and human subjects.

Naturalism

This approach is also called 'scientism', applying the principles of natural science to society. The fundamental ontology of naturalism is 'objectivism', the belief that

TABLE 4.1   Theoretical traditions and their dimensions

| Traditions | Scientific naturalism | Marxism | | Constructionism | Constructivism |
		Critical realism	Critical theory		
Ontology	Objectivism	Historical materialism	Dialectical materialism	Hermeneutics, phenomenology	Discursive anti-humanism
Focus	Structural associations	Mechanisms	Ideologies	Meaning and interaction	Linguistic structures
Epistemology	Positivism (empiricism)	Intervention to expose mechanisms	Identification of contradictions in reality	Interpretivism (*verstehen* – understanding)	Linguistic self-referentiality
Methodology	Quantitative	Primarily quantitative	Philosophical analysis	Qualitative	Qualitative
Method	Surveys and experiments	Surveys and experiments	Critique	Interviews and unstructured (naturalistic) observation	Textual analysis
Purpose	Prediction and control	Explanation	Emancipation	Understanding	Relativism
Variations	Structural functionalism	Variations across the biological and social sciences	Adorno, Marcuse, Habermas	Symbolic interactionism, phenomenology, ethnomethodology	Structuralism, poststructuralism

everything is the result of prior causes. Such an 'objectivist' ontology is linked to a 'positivist' epistemology, a theory of knowledge that asserts the possibility of generating objective knowledge through the value-free collection of empirical data. Such a 'positive' knowledge requires the non-normative, non-judgemental detachment of the researcher in relation to what they are studying, and the commitment to 'evidence' and the rejection of all speculation and conjecture that cannot be grounded and/or tested with reference to evidence. Positivism is associated today with deductive research, the testing of theories, formulated into hypotheses. Early positivism in nineteenth-century Britain and France used more inductive data collection and subsequent theorizing. Positivist epistemology holds that data are neutral, and can be used to objectively judge competing theories true or false. Positivist epistemology is 'empiricist', rejecting the claim that all evidence is theory laden. Critics of positivism challenge this epistemological premise. The methodological consequence of naturalism, objectivism and positivism/empiricism is the need for data that can measure relationships between possible causes and effects. Methodology refers to the sort of data required to follow up on one's epistemological approach. Naturalism requires quantitative data as these allow for measurement and statistical analysis. The methods best suited to generating such data are questionnaires (in surveys) and experiments. Through ontological objectivism, epistemological positivism/empiricism, methodological quantification and the methods of surveys and experiments, the naturalistic researcher seeks to explain social relationships. This allows for practical policy interventions, just as the physical sciences enable technology. Critics suggest 'objectivism' objectifies humans for the purpose of social engineering/control.

Marxism

The essential ontology of Marxism is materialism, a form of naturalism, exploring causal processes at work in society. Marx was rejecting 'idealist' (anti-naturalist) accounts of history. Marx drew upon the positivistic traditions in British economics and French social and political theory, but retained an element from German anti-positivism, seeing history as the product of social conditions and the actions of people in such conditions. For Marx the material is dialectical, driven by contradictions within society.

Critical realists focus upon historical development and the mechanisms at work beneath the everyday appearance of social and economic relationships. Critical realists share with naturalism and positivism an emphasis upon causal structures, but reject empiricism. For critical realists, explanation lies beneath appearance and empirical phenomena are only surface reflections of deeper mechanisms. Critical realist epistemology asserts the need to apply rationalist thought to map potential mechanisms to be explored or tested for by empirical means. It is not enough to simply measure surface events. Critical realists use quantitative methodologies to measure surface expressions of what they believe to be deeper forces at work (Bhaskar, 1979; Pawson and Tilley, 1997; Robson, 2002).

Critical theory emerged in Germany after the First World War, and was influenced by (1) the failure of historical processes to deliver social progress; (2) rejection of the Soviet Russian version of Marxism and socialism; (3) the apparent power of ideologies in blinding people to their own material interests; and (4) German anti-naturalistic social theories, such as would develop into today's 'constructionism'. Critical theory focuses on the ideologies that sustain domination. As such the ontology of critical theory is that of dialectical materialism, combining attention to material conditions with a focus on the ideological beliefs that allow such conditions to continue. Critical theory tends to use a philosophical methodology to engage in the identification of contradictions within both reality and representations of reality, and the method of dialectical critique to highlight those contradictions. It rejects naturalism, objectification and positivism. Throughout, the ontology, epistemology, methodology and method of critical theory seek to disrupt common sense and so foster emancipation (Adorno and Horkheimer, 1979; Marcuse, 1991; Habermas, 1992; 1984; 1989; Lowith, 1993). Critical theory influences social research less in its data collection techniques and more in the questions it asks.

Constructionism

The term 'constructionism' was popularized in the United States with adaptations of German phenomenological ideas, but also covers symbolic interactionism, which also rejected quantitative approaches. Both traditions drew upon the work of Max Weber. The ontology of constructionism is that the social world is built on the shared meanings and coordinated actions of rational actors, not by external structures, causes and hidden mechanisms. The epistemological foundation for the researcher is their ability to share and understand meaning as a social actor. *Verstehen* is the ability to reconstruct the meaning that social life has for those engaged in it though the researcher's own ability to comprehend meaning and belief. This epistemology is fundamentally distinct from positivist or realist approaches, and would be taken to its most pure form by Alfred Schutz (see section 'Phenomenological ontology' later in this chapter). Where Schutz rejected structural accounts entirely, Weber's earlier formulation of interpretivist epistemology sought to combine its insights with more structural ones. Methodologically constructionism adopts qualitative approaches focused on recording meaning; and at the level of method, interviews and unstructured observation are preferred. In addition to Weberian interpretivism, phenomenology (Schutz, 1967) and symbolic interactionism (Blumer, 1956), this tradition also produced the radical version of phenomenology called ethnomethodology (Garfinkel, 1984; and see companion website for more detail).

Constructivism

This tradition sits between constructionism and naturalism rather as Marxism does, only taking the reverse aspects from each neighbour. Constructivism rejects naturalistic explanation in favour of discursive (cultural) determinism of social life, thereby also rejecting human agency in favour of linguistic determination of human meaning, belief and behaviour. Constructivism adopts a 'theoretically anti-humanist' ontology in direct opposition to phenomenology. Constructivism's focus is on meaningful systems, linguistic structures and discursive regimes. Typically, this focus is upon 'serious text', the constructions of social reality generated by dominant groups, such as experts like doctors or authorities like teachers, the police, lawyers and the prison system, government officials, the mass media etc. Constructivism's epistemology is fused with its ontology, as it uses language to study language. Radical versions of constructivism assert that there is nothing outside language (David, 2005a). A less radical version of constructivism suggests that our knowledge of the non-human world is always shaped within language (Delanty, 2002). All constructivists believe that the social world is build upon linguistic structures. Constructivists adopt qualitative methodologies, and the primary method is textual analysis. The primary purpose of constructivism is to generate reflexivity, the awareness that what we think is objective, concrete and universal is not so. Structuralist versions of constructionism emphasize the coherent character of linguistic systems. The anthropology of Lévi-Strauss (2001), the psychoanalysis of Lacan (2001) and the early semiotics of Barthes (2000) sought to show how meaning exists within the system, rather than within the heads of the individuals who express it. Later poststructuralist versions of constructivism highlight the power of language even where such systems are fractured and multiple and

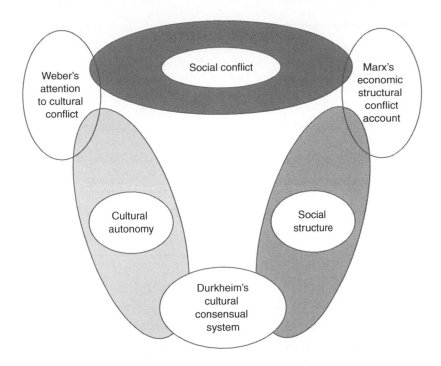

FIGURE 4.1 The fabrication of the 'founding fathers' as a symmetrical provocation to ask questions (after Giddens, 1971)

lead to the generation of conflict and contradiction. Michel Foucault (1977; 2001) highlighted how expertise on sex, health, mental illness and criminality fabricates the very 'subjects' it claims to know. Jacques Derrida's (1972) deconstructive approach focuses upon the double meanings embedded within language which ensure that meaning always evades reduction to any reality external to it.

How theory 'sensitizes' empirical social research

Anthony Giddens (1971) combined Marx, Weber and Durkheim to create a synthetic framework for asking sociological questions (see Figure 4.1). Marx and Durkheim emphasized social structure, whereas Weber emphasized methodological individualism. Marx and Weber emphasized social conflict, whilst Durkheim emphasized consensus. Durkheim and Weber argued culture was not reducible to economic forces, whilst Marx believed in the primacy of economic forces. The symmetry of this triptych requires that each author is reduced to a rather crude approximation of their complex thoughts. The triptych sets up polar potentialities that provoke the social scientist to ask: what is actually the case? In setting Marx, Weber and Durkheim up as the 'founding fathers' of sociology, Giddens framed the discipline in such a way that its founding claims were disputes, not conclusions.

The tension between these three retrospectively appointed founders generates a permanent set of questions to be applied to every topic and event that any sociologist might seek to research. Where Parsons (1951) had sought to solve the 'problem of order', to explain society in theory prior to doing any empirical research, Giddens's reformulation leaves things open to be investigated.

Giddens (1986) presents another kind of three-way invitation to sociological theory, or thinking sociologically. Here he proposes three ways to place any particular aspect of social life into question, upsetting the taken-for-granted character of everyday life and our way of living:

- *Thinking historically* is to compare life today with the past. Fertility rates, mortality rates, educational levels, employment relationships, leisure activities and just about everything else have changed. In seeing this it is hard to imagine any social relationship is natural or can be taken for granted any more.

- *Thinking comparatively* is the art of comparing what goes on in one location with the way life is lived in other locations, whether this be comparison between nation-states, regions or whole continents. Again, what might seem natural and necessary here may seem bizarre and even perverse/criminal in other places.

- *Thinking philosophically/critically* involves comparing the social world with the ideals that society claims to live by. If we claim to be a democracy, what does this term mean, and how does our society size up when set against the principles it claims to uphold? What about equality, justice, freedom, opportunity? Terms like risk, success, class, intelligence and virtue are constantly used, but need to be questioned.

C. Wright Mills (1959) proposed a 'sociological imagination' in seeking to see personal problems as social issues. Unemployment, poverty, illness, depression and divorce are experienced by individuals, but the resources that allow some people to cope better and to avoid negative outcomes are socially distributed. One only has to look at the impact of 'natural disasters' such as hurricanes and earthquakes in poor regions compared to wealthy ones to see that whilst natural events can be disastrous, the harm done is best explained in terms of social failures. Part of the sociological imagination is to ask the question: who had the power and is therefore to blame? Those with the most power have the greater responsibility. This inversion of the common-sense tendency to blame the victim is a significant factor in the importance of social theory. If unemployment, poverty and inequality are problems, perhaps we need to focus upon employers, the wealthy and dominant groups first.

Stanley Cohen (1985) started his career as a social worker, likening this to standing by a river looking for those in trouble. He fished them out, dried them off and sent them back upstream. But the same people kept drowning, so he decided to go upstream to find out who was throwing them in. The shift from managing problems to identifying their cause is a shift from a therapeutic approach to a theoretical one. A therapist tries to make people fit back into society, but the theoretical focus might be to ask why society does not work for so many of the people in it.

Double meanings

Words can be used to mean more than one thing, so try to avoid confusion. Two examples are given here. However, beware: in social research there is no consensus on the basic fabric of social life (ontology), or on how best to study society (epistemology, methodology and method). Social researchers cannot even agree on the words they use.

- *Naturalism.* Naturalism holds to the view that everything that exists is governed by fundamentally similar causal relations. From within such a perspective, the notion of free will, the idea of an uncaused and autonomous human agency, appears as 'scientifically' alien as the idea of divine intervention as an explanation for earthquakes might appear to seismologists. This is to say not that culture is to be explained in terms of atomic or molecular structures etc., but rather that such phenomena require explanations in terms of social and cultural structures. Naturalism is popular with those adopting a positivist or realistic approach, and tends to be associated with quantitative methodology. The term 'naturalism' has a very different meaning for those with a more phenomenological ontology, interpretivist epistemology and qualitative methodology, and in particular for those that use ethnographic and participant observation forms of data collection methods. Naturalism in this context refers to the collection of data in naturalistic settings, such that the data are said to reflect the natural conditions of life for those being studied and not the controlled conditions and/or structured questions that are required in quantitative experimentation and survey designs.

- *Constructionism, constructivism.* These two words are not identical, but are close enough to cause confusion and are often used interchangeably. Constructionism refers to the maintenance of social life, and at least the impression of order by means of nothing other than the interactions and interpretations made by human actors. In its strongest phenomenological and ethnomethodological forms, constructionism rejects the concept of social structure entirely; whilst less radical forms of interpretivist and interactionist constructionism place emphasis upon the significance of action in the maintenance of institutions and organizations. Constructivism refers to the view that social order is constructed within the linguistic structures of discourse and that these structures shape individual actions. Constructionists say 'actors' whilst constructivists say 'subjects'. Constructionism sees people as the producers of social life. Constructivism sees people as the product of discourse.

Quality and quantity: beyond the wars of religion?

The terms 'quality' and 'quantity' in social research have come to mark a distinction. This distinction has led to passionate arguments over the nature of social research and social life itself. The force of this divide has led some to suggest that it represents a fundamental ideological split within social research, one that cannot be resolved by facts and arguments, as each side is not prepared to accept that the other side's 'facts' and 'arguments' stand up. At one level this distinction is relatively easy to identify. At another level meaning becomes elusive.

- *Qualitative research* usually emphasizes words rather than quantification in the collection and analysis of data. As a research strategy it is inductivist, constructivist and interpretivist, but qualitative researchers do not always subscribe to all three of these features (Bryman, 2008: 697).

- *Qualitative methods*: methods of social research that employ no quantitative standards and techniques; based on theoretical and methodological principles of symbolic interactionism, hermeneutics and ethnomethodology (Sarantakos, 1998: 467).

- *Qualitative observations*: scientific observations that are not recorded in any standardized coding format (Ellis, 1994: 377).

- *Qualitative data*: data which express, usually in words, information about feelings, values and attitudes (Lawson and Garrod, 1994: 218).

- *Quantitative research* usually emphasizes quantification in the collection and analysis of data. As a research strategy it is deductivist and objectivist and incorporates a natural science model of the research process (in particular, one influenced by positivism), but quantitative researchers do not always subscribe to all three of these features (Bryman, 2008: 697).

- *Quantitative methods*: methods employing quantitative theoretical and methodological principles and techniques and statistics (Sarantakos, 1998: 467).

- *Quantitative observations*: scientific observations that are recorded in a numeric or some other standardized coding format (Ellis, 1994: 377).

- *Quantitative data*: data which can be expressed in numerical form, for example, numbers, percentages, tables (Lawson and Garrod, 1994: 218).

Four distinctions are at work here, between numbers and meanings, deduction and induction, objectivism and subjectivity, and between generalizability and depth validity.

Numbers and meanings

Quantitative data refer to things that have been or which can be counted and put on a numerical scale of some kind. This requires that these things can be specified in such a way that they can be counted and scaled. Reality has to be viewed in such a way that elements within that overall reality can be specified as individual units, whether this means people, plates or television sets. The number of such units present can then be recorded (for example, centimetres in a person's height or portions of fruit in a person's daily diet). Qualitative data refer to the collection of materials in a linguistic form, a form that has not been translated into a location on a numerical scale. Numbers require that the world can be broken down into units. Attention to meaning raises the question of whether beliefs can similarly be broken down into units. It is perfectly possible to ask people about beliefs in a fashion that can be measured in units. *Do you believe in organized religion? Yes or No.* That is quite easy. The qualitative researcher is more interested in the fact that meanings come in packages, wholes, ways of life, belief systems and so on. Attention to 'meanings' in this sense is a reference to the 'holistic' fabric of interconnected meanings that form a way of life and which cannot remain meaningful if they are extracted and broken down into separate units outside their meaningful context. What organized religion means may be very different from one culture to the next, or even in the opinion of different individuals. This question can also be approached in very different ways (see Box 4.1).

BOX 4.1 RESEARCH FOCUS

Approaching the same issue using different methodologies

In 2005 the journal *Sociology* published a series of articles on religion in the United Kingdom. Of particular interest here were one article by David Voas and Alasdair Crockett and another by Paul Chambers and Andrew Thompson. Voas and Crockett used quantitative data from the British Household Panel Study (BHPS) to test the proposition that whilst religion might be in decline at the level of attendance and formal belonging, religion might still be said to be 'strong' at the level of belief. Grace Davie's work is cited in this regard. Where it had been common to assume that the decline in attendance and formal belonging was indicative of secularization, Davie suggested that this assumption was flawed and that perhaps what was in fact happening was a shift from public to private belief. If religious belief in modern society is associated with what a person believes and not their public displays of such belief, then to measure such public display might be to take a measure of one thing as an indicator of something else entirely. However, using the BHPS, a longitudinal panel study collecting information from the same households year after year, Voas and Crockett found that variables designed to measure religious belief showed a decline that was in line with the decline in measures of both attendance and formal affiliation. There is a 50 per cent decline in both from each generation to the next. Using qualitative interviews, Chambers and Thompson examined the public engagement of religious organizations and found that members of religious organizations were more likely to engage in public and political processes than were non-members. Whilst public religious life might be in decline, other forms of public engagement are declining even faster. As such, if there is a general decline in public engagement then, despite their decline, religious organizations become more important in public life. If religious belief and attendance declined by 50 per cent in a generation, but political parties saw their faithful drop by three-quarters, this would in fact mean that religious organizations would have grown in significance despite having shrunk in actual size. Whilst Voas and Crockett use numbers to demonstrate trends over time, interview data highlighted new relationships that had not been conceived prior to such data being collected.

Deduction and induction

As was discussed in Chapter 1, deductive research sets out to 'test' a hypothesis, while inductive research sets out to explore a field. As such, deductive research requires a greater degree of pre-emptive structure in the data collection process. If you are seeking to test a hypothesis you will want to measure the relationship between variables. Does the increase in variable *X* go hand in hand with the increase in variable *Y*? A variable, as you will recall from Chapter 1, is any class of event or thing (height, shoe size, likelihood of voting) that can be different (across time, between places, or in different people). Variables require some method of measuring variation and that requires counting and numbers. Inductive methods are exploratory, seeking to build accounts of what is going on from the data collected. This does not require the establishment of preset measures and methods of counting. In fact, it is often the case that the researcher chooses exploration over hypothesis testing precisely because they do not know what the 'right' measures might be. Quantitative research is associated with the deductive approach, while qualitative research is associated with the inductive approach. However, some exploratory research is quantitative (identifying and developing units and measures as one goes along, rather than in advance), while some qualitative research starts from the formulation of a hypothesis. In some respects this blurring is always the case. Things are never cut and dried. As will be suggested below, this last fact raises some serious questions about what is really at stake in the distinction between quality and quantity.

Falsification and/or theory-laden (paradigm-dependent) seeing

A significant criticism of induction is that building a theory from a set of examples can never fully confirm the theory. It was Karl Popper's (1935) great contribution to the philosophy of science and social science to observe that while a disproving example will falsify a theory, no amount of confirming instances will ever fully verify it. Popper drew from this the conclusion that science should always seek to test theories against evidence rather than build them up from evidence. Popper's deductive approach was to start with a theory and seek to identify what it was that would falsify it. The theory (or hypothesis – the name for a theory that is to be tested) should assert a claim which the researcher should then seek to knock down. If the testing cannot discount the theory, then it can be retained. Otherwise it can be said to have been falsified. Popper suggested that this hypothetico-deductive method should be applied in both the physical and the social sciences. Any claim that could not identify the conditions by which it could be falsified could not be considered a candidate for scientific scrutiny, and any theory that had not survived such an attempt to be falsified could, likewise, not be called scientific. Many social researchers who use quantitative methods have sought to follow Popper's approach.

Social researchers with more qualitative dispositions tend to reject Popper's strong claim that there is a fundamental asymmetry between the inability to verify and the decisive character of falsification. What Popper requires to make this distinction is that there is an absolute difference between verification and falsification. No amount of confirmation can absolutely guarantee the universal nature of a claim; but does a singular falsification offer such an absolute guarantee that the theory is totally wrong? Popper's famous example is the claim that all swans are white. Any number of confirming instances do not guarantee that the next swan will not be black, but one black swan would appear to discount the theory. Is this asymmetry really so black and white? Well, to assume that it is requires that the empirical observation by which the theory is being tested is valid, and that such observations are not in any way influenced and/or biased by the theory being held by the researcher. Qualitative researchers have drawn heavily on the work of Thomas Kuhn (1962) in questioning this fundamental assumption of Popper's and therefore of more deductive forms of research. Kuhn's research into the development of knowledge in physics pointed out the high levels of socialization which trainee physicists have to undertake in order to qualify. They learn to see the world in a particular way, and to ask certain kinds of questions. These ways of seeing and these questions form what Kuhn calls a 'paradigm' – a frame of reference and a puzzle within which to operate. Kuhn asserts that evidence cannot be disentangled entirely from the way questions are posed and the way researchers have been socialized to interpret their results. This theory dependency, such that evidence cannot independently confirm or falsify a theory if the theory is so deeply embedded in the way evidence is interpreted, casts doubt on Popper's absolute asymmetry between the possibility of empirical falsifications and the impossibility of inductively logical universal confirmations. If we see a large black bird that resembles a swan, who is to say that it is a swan?

Qualitative researchers tend to see human cultures as meaningful constructions in which each element is dependent for its meaning upon the other elements within the cultural system. As such, it is not possible to tease out singular elements as isolated facts to be tested against other facts. Thus qualitative researchers see something akin to Kuhn's interdependency theory of knowledge in society itself as well as in the way such a society can and should be researched. Popper's strong claim that facts can and should be tested with independent evidence stands in contrast to Kuhn's paradigm dependency theory. Both authors recognized that it would be a mistake to exaggerate their positions. Popper recognized that a perfect falsification was only ever an ideal, and that all real-world research is less certain. Kuhn also came to regret the way his paradigm dependency theory was taken up by those who sought to claim that all knowledge was relative and that truth was a social construction.

Objectivism and constructionism/phenomenology

Quantitative research is associated with a belief in the objectivity of the social world, and the idea of causation in social processes. This is linked to the belief that social research can draw on the methods of the physical sciences, in particular the use of numbers to measure the relationship between 'things'. The notion of the objectivity of the social world is associated with this view that the social world is populated with 'facts', 'things' and 'objects'. While these are different from those that exist in a physical sense, objectivists and realists argue that social structures and social mechanisms constrain and enable those who live within them. Qualitative research tends to be associated with the idea that social life is the product of social interaction and the beliefs of actors, that the social world is populated not by things but by relationships and actions. The focus on meaning reflects this emphasis on the subjective and the constructed nature of events. Objectivism is associated with the notion of social structure as the key cause of social reality and the key site for understanding, while subjectivism or constructionism places a greater emphasis on micro-interactions as the source from which to gain information about the creation of social life. Measuring the relationships between large things or large numbers of things requires the use of numbers. Attention to the relationships between individuals may not. The distinction between a macro and a micro focus is often associated with that between quantity and quality. The question of whether society is made up of objects or actions begs the question of whether we should describe social phenomena as nouns or verbs (see Elias, 1978).

Generalizability and depth

As the earlier quotes suggested, quantitative research is associated with the use of standardized methods of data collection and data analysis, while qualitative research is associated with less structured formatting. As was pointed out in Chapter 3, quantitative researchers tend to emphasize the need for research to be reliable and generalizable. Given their tendency to believe in macro-patterns and social causation, quantitative researchers will tend to be more interested in establishing generalizations than are qualitative researchers. As such, quantitative researchers are keener to be able to claim that results from their limited sampling can apply to the population from which the sample was drawn. The use of standardized questions that can be answered in a numerical fashion, as well as the use of random samples, allows statistical methods to be used. These enable the researcher to evaluate the likelihood that their results came about by chance. When the relationship between the variables is strong enough, it is possible to claim that the likelihood of a result being by chance alone (such as throwing 100 consecutive heads with a coin) is remote enough to be discounted. To conduct research in such a fashion requires a great deal of ordering. Questions must be structured and repeated without deviation. Laboratory conditions must be superficially contrived to achieve control over all possible deviations. Such conditions are highly artificial. Qualitative research is often associated with the critique of such conditions. Will such conditions not distort responses? Can such standardized questions get at the particularity of individual experiences? Does fitting people's lives into the researcher's pigeonholes give any real understanding? Qualitative research is associated with the prioritization of depth validity over generalizability. This can be linked to the discussion of deduction versus induction, and is also associated with debates over the macro and the micro. If you believe that people are the product of social conditions, you will need a macro focus and therefore you will need a generalizing approach, which will more often than not need to be deductive in nature. If you believe that people are the producers of social conditions, you will need a micro focus and may be less interested in generalization.

Problems and complexities

As we have seen above, the distinction between qualitative and quantitative research is not simply between meaning and numbers as such. Simple meanings, such as yes and no answers, can be quantified. What qualitative research is interested in is meaning as something holistic from which elements cannot merely be broken off and measured out of context. This is said to set qualitative data apart from things that can be broken down into discrete units of measurement. Yet, as we have seen, quantitative research is associated with objectivism, the belief that social structures have a causal influence on individuals, while qualitative research is associated with a more subjectivist (or micro) approach that looks at the actions of individuals and small groups as key sites of social construction. This seems curiously at odds at first glance. Qualitative research seems interested at one level in micro-interactions and personal meanings, while at another level it seems interested in what cannot be broken down and detached from context. Quantitative research on the other hand seems interested in breaking things down in order to get at the big picture.

The question of induction and deduction maps onto these apparent tensions. While induction allows the researcher to explore the wider context from the actor's point of view, does the qualitative focus upon the holistic nature of meaning, and the presumption that the actor's own beliefs represent the best route to understanding social life, constitute a hypothesis in itself? Conversely, to what extent can the deductive researcher escape from the fact that they, as researcher, and those they research are engaged in a constant negotiation of meaning between themselves, interpreting questions, observations and responses in the micro context of the questionnaire, experiment or interview situation?

The deeper divide: it's not just about how to research people, it's about contrasting beliefs over what makes people what they are!

As can be seen above, there are a number of themes around which the distinction between qualitative and quantitative research hinges. These themes are a mix of methodological questions about how best to find out about people, and ontological questions about what it is we are looking at in the first place (what does it mean to be human?). As has been pointed out above, there are compromises in every choice that has to be made when conducting research. A larger sample may increase generalizability. However, increasing the number sampled decreases the amount of time that can be spent with each person or group. Structured questions or observations that are repeatable and which generate answers that are quantifiable make it easier to conduct comparison and generalization. However, the rigidity of the questions may act to distort the recording of individual lives and experiences that are not best categorized within the prescribed pigeonholes of the researcher. On the other hand, more open-ended questioning or observing, in a more inductive style, gives the advantage of openness to the specifics of individual lives and their general context, but such a method is hard to generalize from, with the results from each interview or observation hard to compare with the next. Large-scale research that seeks to identify macro patterns in society might be helpful in showing the existence of correlations (things that seem to go together), but their meaning is hard to pin down when data are only recorded in numerical form. For example, to say that X per cent of the population has experienced stress over the last 12 months, or that this figure is up or down relative to previous years, tells us little about what stress actually feels like or whether that experience is the same for any two people.

At one level it would seem rather obvious that the solution is to conduct research of both a qualitative and a quantitative kind, either as separate projects or as an integrated whole. While this seems to be very good a common sense, it is not always what happens. Why is this? Well, it is because a great many social researchers are committed to a particular kind of research approach (either qualitative or quantitative) for more than just methodological reasons. The choice of seemingly 'pure' qualitative or quantitative research (though appearances are deceptive, as will be shown later) often reflects the researcher's fundamental beliefs about the nature of human beings. Beliefs about how best to know people will depend on what it is you think they really are. The most basic opposition in the social sciences is between a numerical ontology and a phenomenological ontology.

Numerical ontology

For Pythagoras the universe was made of numbers. Beneath surface appearances, reality seemed to follow a series of patterns which could only be represented in numbers. Earth, wind, fire, water and spirit were seen to be merely the three-dimensional manifestations of numerical patterns (pure forms). Modern science comes close to the view that the universe is made of numbers and patterns. Whether in the work of Newton, Galileo, Einstein or Hawking, there is a sense that numbers speak the language of the universe because the universe is somehow fundamentally numerical. The world is a matrix of numerical relationships that create patterns. The development of science in this sense is the development of a method for mapping numerical patterns beneath the qualities of surface appearance. Just as the universe is a code waiting to be cracked, so the social world is a code. Beneath the surface of words and actions there are patterns that are not always apparent. Only through mapping those patterns will the truth be revealed, a truth that can only be told in numbers. People are not always aware of the influences upon them, or even of the patterns their own actions are a part of. To the extent to which people are the product of patterns and routines they do not control, and of which they are not always aware, the role of the social researcher is to go beneath everyday understanding, language and action, to identify the big picture. For this approach science is the search for patterns beneath appearances, and these patterns are revealed through numerical relationships. For those in the social sciences who adopt this approach, social research can and should adopt methods that are similar to those in the physical sciences, even if these similarities are never absolute.

Emile Durkheim's (1952) classic sociological study of suicide is based upon a presentation of numerical differences between countries, regions and social groups. While it may appear obvious that people commit suicide because of their personal sadness, loss or failure, Durkheim sought to show that this is not true, and that social forces operate above the level of individual experience to generate patterns of behaviour in social groups. The fact that women are more regularly diagnosed with depression, but are many times less likely to commit suicide than men, suggests that there is something at work beneath the level of personal experience. Erik Olin Wright (1997) draws together research from across the world to suggest that social inequality displays systematic patterns – patterns that are not fundamentally altered by the attitudes and beliefs held in different societies about whether or not inequality is high/low or good/bad in that country. The Black Report (see Whitehead et al., 1992) shows that poor people die younger than the more affluent, and that this is not the result of the choice to live an 'unhealthy lifestyle'. Cigarettes kill and so do poverty and discrimination, whether you are aware of it or not, or so the parallel runs.

Phenomenological ontology

The basic premise of phenomenology (Schutz, 1972) is that for humans at least reality is not something separate from its appearance. The way that humans think about themselves is fundamental to what they are. Humans are conscious beings and their consciousness shapes their reality. While a stone is what it is and has no conception of itself, a human being is shaped by his or her conception of themselves. Phenomena, the appearance of things, and nomena, things as they really are, might be separate in the physical realm (a stone is a stone regardless of whether it is perceived), but in the realm of humans phenomena and nomena are intimately linked together. Self-perception, an awareness of one's self, is not a perception of something separate; it is the fusion of appearance and actuality. A human who is not aware of her or his own existence would not be human in the full sense of the term. In the realm of human life, beliefs are not abstractions from the real; they are part of the reality of being human itself. This leads to the suggestion that to understand humans it is best to discover what they think and how they behave, rather than to dig deeper for some hidden truth that lies beneath action and awareness.

Max Weber's (1905) study of Protestantism's 'elective affinity' with the early capitalism of Western Europe makes the case that beliefs played a crucial part in driving people towards radical social change, just as beliefs play a key role in the maintenance of social roles, institutions and relationships. Weber's (1949) methodological writings defend a *verstehen* approach, which means the attempt to see the world from the point of view of the person or group being studied, as their outlook is an essential element in understanding why they do the things they do, even while Weber retained the need to study social 'structures' in a more objectivist fashion to complement the *verstehen* approach. Schutz's phenomenology sought to extend the *verstehen* approach, using Husserl's (1962) phenomenological philosophy, to the point where institutions were understood as a set of relationships held together by actions and beliefs held in common and taken for granted by groups and individuals.

So, at one level we might suggest that different methods for conducting social research are just different ways of getting to the reality of human life, but at another level there is a dispute over the very nature of social life. This is what has given the debate over qualitative and quantitative research methods their passion. This debate has become polarized between philosophical extremes. Below it will be suggested that this polarization ignores a fundamental fact: all social research relies upon qualitative and quantitative aspects. All social research requires some form of classification. All social research requires some form of measurement to identify the existence and prevalence of those things that have been classified. Classifications register the existence of distinctions. These distinctions can be called qualities. Some qualities of an orange, for example, would be that it is round and that it is orange. Measurements register the existence of quantities. But quantities have to be quantities of something, and these somethings are qualities. At one level this may simply be to note the existence of a quality (one rather than none). It may, however, register the degree of its existence (large or small, high or low and so on). It may register this existence in a more exact numerical form (in 25 per cent of cases, half the time, 25 individual cases, 1 metre 60 centimetres and so on). The dispute between quality and quantity in social research obscures the fact that there is always a degree of quantification in any form of qualitative research and that there must always be a qualitative dimension in any attempt at quantitative research. All research is qualitative and quantitative.

The qualitative inside all research: classification

To ask a research question or to make a set of observations requires the capacity to make and record distinctions. The simplest distinctions are binary in nature: yes or no, present or not present, black or white, X or not X. More complex distinctions may have many more gradations, classes or types. However complex a set of distinctions might be, they all require one basic capacity: that is, the capacity to identify the boundaries between the gradations, classes or types. Classification requires the capacity to identify the qualities that make a particular response; action or object go into one classification rather than another. The capacity to make such qualitative distinctions is the basis upon which any subsequent quantification can take place. It is impossible to measure the amount of something if you cannot specify how to identify the presence of that something, in other words to distinguish it from other things. Two important factors enable the identification of qualities. One is internal homogeneity and the other is external discretion (Blumer, 1956). Internal homogeneity is the requirement that all members of a particular category share something. In some sense (if not in every sense) they are the same; they have a common quality. External discretion is the requirement that if a certain quality is what makes those with that quality into a meaningful category, this quality must be theirs alone. For example all human males have warm blood. This is a quality they all share. In this sense all human males are the same. This is internal homogeneity. However, having warm blood is not sufficient to distinguish human males from human females, who also have warm blood. Warm blood is not sufficient on its own to make the category of human males externally discrete. While having warm blood would be a sufficient quality to distinguish humans from reptiles, other qualities would be needed to distinguish meaningful classifications within the human species (see Box 4.2).

BOX 4.2 CONSIDER THIS

Reality or just how it appears?

Class, race, ethnicity, sex, gender and sexuality are all highly contested systems of classification. Marx argued that class relationships exist objectively. If a person thinks they are middle class because they have a mortgage on their house, yet they are employed and earn their living from their labour and not from managing others, selling goods they own or charging rent on assets and/or professional qualifications, for Marx they would be working class. Measuring class would be an objective exercise based on relatively quantifiable indicators (see Wright, 1997). From a Weberian perspective, class is a combination of the work a person does and their ability to organize themselves into a group to fight for greater rewards for such work. From this perspective it would be essential to ask people to describe their self-belief. The equal opportunity forms people are often asked to fill in when applying for jobs contain a variety of classifications for race/ethnicity from which a person is asked to pick a classification they feel applies to them. The lumping together of racial classifications (themselves simply a superficial classification of people by skin colour and other skin-deep markers of identity) and ethnicity (usually a loose collection of religious, national, linguistic and other cultural clusters) in such schemes is no way of defining a person's identity, except to the extent that these might be the identifiers by which a person might be discriminated against, which is of course what equal opportunities monitoring forms are designed to monitor. W.I. Thomas famously suggested: 'If men define situations as real, they are real in their consequences' (1928). Yet, does that mean that ethnicity is only in the eye of the person viewing another person? The extent to which groups are shaped internally and externally is again hotly contested and has profound implications for how such groups and group identities should be researched. Regarding sex, sexuality and gender, the question of identities, their substantial content and the boundaries between them is hotly contested, and differences over ontology (such as debates over the existence of a 'gay gene') lead to significant differences in epistemology and methodology.

The formulation of such classifications of qualities has led to great controversy within the human sciences. To pursue deductive forms of research, where one is seeking to test a hypothesis, requires that classification occur prior to the collection of data. This allows the data to be collected in such a way that they can be used to test the relationships the researcher believes are important. More inductive forms of research seek to allow classifications to emerge through the course of the data collection process. There are advantages and disadvantages here. Those who seek to classify their qualities prior to data collection can be accused of imposing their own priorities, while those who seek to allow classifications to emerge during the research process are thereby unable to use the data collection period to test their subsequent theories. They too can then be accused of imposing their own priorities because it is hard to confirm or disprove their interpretations as no 'testing' has been done.

As will be pointed out in the discussions of quantitative and qualitative research, it is always essential that any classification scheme that is developed is evaluated prior to its application. This may mean the conduct of a set of pilot surveys in a more quantitative research format, or in the conduct of open-ended cumulative interviews/observations in qualitative research. In either case the purpose is to evaluate the validity of the qualities one has identified as the key indicators of difference.

A second aspect in the controversy over classification in the human sciences concerns the objectivity/subjectivity of human qualities. In what sense are the qualities of interest to social researchers real objects? To what extent are any of the classifications of interest to social researchers externally discrete and internally homogeneous? Attempts to classify humans into economic classes, races, nationalities and ethnic groups have all run into very significant difficulties. While it is accepted that the objects in the physical world are relatively stable (this may be less so than is often presumed), those in the social world are prone to modification and dispute, not least by those classified. When does a person without a home of their own become 'homeless'? When does a person without official and/or paid employment become 'unemployed'? When does an impairment become a 'disability', and when does that 'disability' make the person with it 'disabled'? When does a person become an 'adult'? When does 'love' become 'abuse'? These are not just questions for researchers. These are the kinds of questions that are asked and fought over in everyday life.

Those who adopt the position of phenomenological ontology (discussed above) argue that we cannot assume that such things as class, race, unemployment and abuse 'exist' outside our beliefs about them, and that these beliefs are generated and sustained though the interactions between people. As long as we take these things for granted we can go on believing that the relationships our actions sustain are in fact objective realities. For social research to look for the true classifications by which human actions can be mapped and predicted would only be to repeat the everyday misconception: that is, the search for explanations for our actions outside those actions. For those who start from phenomenological ontology (we are what we think we are), the task is to study how people come to construct the routines, practices and meanings of their lives through action and interaction with others. *Researchers seek to map the maps used by actors.*

For those who adopt something closer to the numerical or realist ontology (which suggests the existence of either patterns or mechanisms beneath the level of consciousness that are the frameworks which individuals and groups are required to act within), social reality does contain limits that can best be understood as objective constraints. These limits affect the life chances of individuals differently depending upon their 'race', 'ethnicity', 'class' and/or 'gender'. While social realists might generally dispute the existence of objective 'races', many would point out that 'institutional racism' operates against those not classified as 'white'. By 'institutional' it is suggested that discrimination operates in many countries through institutional structures and rules that are not necessarily reducible to the conscious actions of individuals (see Box 4.3).

BOX 4.3 RESEARCH FOCUS

Educational research: structures and interactions

A long-standing debate within the sociology of education is over the relative significance of the school experience in a child's future success in life relative to the background from which they come. Samuel Bowles and Herbert Gintis (1976) concluded, based on survey data, that educational outcomes are of little significance as children from middle-class families get middle-class jobs irrespective of their educational performance. Whilst middle-class children tended to get better grades and better jobs, even those who got poor grades still ended up in better-paid jobs than the small number of children from poorer homes that did do well at school. Mike Savage and Muriel Egerton (1997) carried out secondary analysis of data from the UK National Child Development Study to examine the relative significance of cultural and more direct economic resources in the success or failure of working- and middle-class boys and girls. Interestingly, they found that whilst middle-class children were much more likely to get good educational qualifications and better-paid jobs than working-class children, middle-class boys typically gained better-paid jobs than working-class boys even if they performed badly at school. Middle-class boys appear to benefit from family success without having to translate such advantage into educational success first. Middle-class girls, however, were even more likely to outperform working-class girls at school and in employment. However, middle-class girls who did badly at school were less likely to get a well-paid job than were the minority of working-class girls that did better than average for their sex. In other words, the translation of family capital into future employment success has to be mediated through educational success for girls in a way that is not true for boys. As such, it might be concluded that school plays no significant part in boys' future success. This view has been criticized by qualitative researchers who suggest that the internal experience of school life plays a very significant part in socializing children into the future positions society wishes them to occupy. Labelling theory suggests that personal interaction enforces social identities and reinforces structural inequalities (Matsueda, 2007).

Likewise the operation of markets, bureaucracies, states, the law and other institutions (such as the family or the school) form frameworks that are not controlled by individuals, that establish routines to which the individual must adapt, and so act as external constraints upon their lives. Rosemary Crompton's (in Crompton et al., 1996) work with large datasets from more than one country is designed to identify patterns of employment and non-paid domestic work that may inform the choices of individual women. While many women make personal choices to have children, and pursue less ambitious careers to fit around this, these choices are made within conditions where alternatives (such as good quality and affordable childcare, or a culture where men take an equal responsibility for raising children) are limited. For the realist (such as Crompton) it is essential that the researcher develop classifications that capture the underlying reality. They seek to identify the manifest qualities (the surface appearances) by which such hidden realities can best be identified. *Researchers seek to map the realities that shape actors.* As can be seen here, the dispute between quality and quantity is not between those who focus on qualities and those who do not. All research focuses upon the qualities by which the world can be classified, even if there are significant differences in how such qualities are sought and understood.

The quantitative inside all research: measurement

The fact that all forms of social research use forms of quantification, in other words measurement, is unavoidable. As will be discussed in Chapter 13, there are various levels of measurement, these being nominal, ordinal, interval and ratio levels. Elements of all these levels of measurement are deployed in both qualitative and quantitative research, though 'qualitative' research more typically deploys the former two types, while the latter are most often the preserve of 'quantitative' research. Nominal data refer to things that have no necessary numerical order, for example, hair colour, style of clothing, country of birth. Ordinal data can be put in order, but not on a more sophisticated numerical scale, which allows the size of the differences between levels to be registered. An example of this might be a scale between very happy and very unhappy. While happy might be less happy than very happy, it is not possible to say by how much. If one song is at number 8 in the music charts and another is at number 12, we can see which has sold more, but such ordinal data do not tell us by how much. Interval data are ordered, and are on a scale whereby one can say 'how much' the difference is between points. An example of this might be shoe sizes or temperature. Ratio data are ordered and have numerical intervals, but here the scale must pass through a zero that registers complete absence of the thing being measured (even if no actual zero results are recorded). Height is a good example. Nobody is zero centimetres tall, but because height can be measured on a scale on which zero equals no height, it is possible for different heights to be measured in a ratio form (that is, 2 metres to 1 metre is a ratio of 2:1). As has been pointed out already, quantitative data allow for the use of statistical methods of calculating the probability that observed results could have come about by chance, and the strength of the relationships between variables. Statistical analysis can be conducted on data at any of the four levels of measure. The more mathematical the level of measure (the lowest being nominal and the highest being ratio level), the greater the scope for statistical analysis; yet data collected at any level of measure is open to mathematical manipulation. Of course, the units of analysis (areas of residence, levels of belief, temperature or wealth) all require qualitative definition before the incidence of that particular quality can be measured.

It is often suggested that qualitative research is not open to statistical analysis. This is not true. What is true is that qualitative data are not usually collected with the primary purpose of applying statistical techniques. However, qualitative research collects data that are usually nominal or ordinal in nature, and this requires some mode of measurement. In the case of nominal data, it may simply be a matter of registering the existence or non-existence of a particular variable. Noting whether the person interviewed or observed is male or female is to record a nominal piece of data. Identifying the characteristics of a group or setting in the conduct of ethnographic research involves noting what is present and perhaps what is absent. This is often a form of nominal data collection. This may become ordinal or even interval data collection if the researcher identifies or records the existence of levels of belief, or loose accounts of differences in the incidence of certain actions, attitudes or rewards. In recording the talk and interactions of others, the researcher will be collecting many instances of the research subjects' own classification systems, evidenced either in words or in action, which will most often be of nominal or ordinal level. The ways in which a racist divides up the world, or how a sexist male classifies women, or how a middle-class teacher classifies working-class students, are fundamental to the organization of their own lives and may have profound effects upon those so classified. The qualitative researcher may wish to explore (inductively) the meanings at work in the classifications being used in everyday life, rather than impose a classification scheme of their own in order to (deductively) test it (as is said to characterize more quantitative approaches). However, the qualitative researcher must still engage in measurement at either the nominal or the ordinal level just to be able to record whether particular qualities are present (nominal) or are greater or lesser in their presence, intensity, longevity and so on (ordinal). If the qualitative researcher notes that household X spent twice as much on electricity as household Y, they are engaging in ratio data collection. This is a less significant part of the routines of qualitative research, but the use of measurement at the nominal and ordinal levels is inescapable.

Quality and quantity: distinctions and parallels

Once again it is necessary to point out that the boundary between qualitative and quantitative research is not simply between the use of numbers and the use of meanings, or between the use of measures and the use of qualities. The divergence between qualitative and quantitative research methods involves a number of blurred distinctions, none of which are absolute. All forms of research involve the construction and recording of qualities and quantities. The distinction is best defined in terms of a tension that is both practical and philosophical. Those who adopt the more numerical approaches tend to give greater practical emphasis to reliability and generalizability. This tends to flow from the philosophical belief that fundamental characteristics of human life lie in the influence of often hidden macro 'structures' or 'processes' upon individuals and groups. Those who adopt the more phenomenological approach tend to give more practical emphasis to issues of depth validity. This tends to flow from the philosophical belief that the social world is not external to the actions and beliefs of actors, and that it is the product of human interaction. When it comes to the generation of classifications (qualities) and measurements (quantities), there is a tendency for the former to adopt a more inductive approach, while the latter tend towards a more deductive approach. This maps onto the distinction between exploring and testing, and that between an anti-causal understanding of human actions and the recognition of causation in the social world.

It remains the case that within the social sciences disputes rage over the broad philosophical question of 'causation' versus 'freedom' in human action. Human beings display behaviour that is at one level predictable (to some degree). This level is that of overall averages. The children of the more affluent gain, on average, higher educational qualifications. Women in Europe are, on average, less likely to commit suicide than men. Divorce rates in some countries are systematically higher than divorce rates in other countries. These 'facts' suggest that there are 'macro' processes at work that influence the choices and actions of individuals. Some might choose to use the term 'causal influence'. However, while averages show the existence of patterns, individual behaviour displays a level of complexity that makes prediction hard. Individuals in seemingly similar situations react differently.

Mixed methods, pluralism and triangulation

The above discussion has already made clear that there can be no absolute separation between the qualitative and the quantitative in social research and that the boundary between qualitative and quantitative research is not fixed by any single or agreed set of principles. Yet, as has also been pointed out, the prioritizing of depth validity or generalizability, and the philosophical principles that stand behind such prioritizing, lead those who tend towards the former priority to a more inductive, more naturalistic and less mathematical approach to research design and data collection, while the latter tend to more deductive, structured and mathematical approaches.

Nevertheless, all research is both qualitative and quantitative. There are advantages to be had in both the inductive and the deductive approaches. Induction allows for exploration and a greater insight into the lives of those studied, while deduction, due to a tighter focus, allows for greater reliability and generalizability. To combine the benefits of both emphases is, of course, therefore attractive. Malcolm Williams (2002) suggests that all research must claim some degree of depth validity and generalizability if it is to be called research rather than art. As such the inevitability and the necessity of combining qualitative and quantitative research leave room only to ask how such a combination is best effected in particular circumstances and in reference to particular questions. Williams concludes:

Indeed Weber (1975) speaks of nomothetic and ideographic approaches, not as scientific versus nonscientific modes of inquiry, but both as forms of scientific inquiry. The nomothetic Weber equates with the abstract generalizable law like statements, whereas the ideographic he regards as the science of *concrete* reality, of specific instances. Moreover, he expressed the view that with the exception of pure mechanics and certain forms of historical inquiry all 'science' requires each mode of inquiry ... The view that sociology (or any other social science) can be only ideographic would therefore be antipathetic to Weber (and of course the opposite would be true). While Weber did not go on to recommend methodological pluralism, this seems to be an inevitable conclusion if we can accept that sociology has a nomothetic and an ideographic dimension. (2002: 139)

When (quantitative) survey researchers conduct a pilot survey with follow-up interviews, they are attempting to get a better sense of how their prospective respondents think and live. The researcher here is trying to gauge what their questions might mean to those they hope will answer them. There is no point asking people questions they will not understand. Even if respondents think they understand a question, if the understanding is not that which the researcher intended then the answers may be misunderstood in return. The quantitative researcher may wish to carry out a deductive hypothesis testing exercise, but would be wise to do some inductive exploration first. Piloting one's questionnaire is an essential first step. Alternatively, the survey researcher may wish to conduct a short spell of ethnographic fieldwork, living with those they seek to survey, in order to improve the kinds of questions they will ask. Of course, the survey researchers may not wish to carry out such work themselves. Different researchers with different skills may be employed to carry out different aspects of a research project; or, the researcher may consult secondary sources (using the existing literature). Similarly, the researcher may begin with the collection of statistical data concerning the field they wish to research. The data once collected may give rise to questions that the researcher feels can best be explored using a less mathematical form of data collection.

In reverse fashion, a researcher who has conducted in-depth interviews may find that certain patterns exist in their data and set out to clarify their findings with a more numerical questionnaire. Alternatively, at the end of a survey the findings might be made available to some of the researcher's sample and a focus group discussion might be held. This would allow for some in-depth feedback that might help the research team clarify their findings or iron out any misinterpretations (or at least highlight any differences in interpretation that might otherwise not have been noted).

Such approaches can be called mixed methods, pluralism or triangulation. While all research is both qualitative and quantitative in nature, specific methods exist along the spectra of induction/deduction, linguistic/numerical, depth/generalizability, naturalism/control and so on. The use of mixed methods is the explicit attempt to gain some benefit from different methods from across the different spectra. It is an attempt to get the best of all the available options. The use of mixed methods is not just about the balance of quality and quantity. An experiment may be combined with a survey to gain two different takes on a theme. Both 'takes' in this case sit on the quantitative end of the spectrum. Ethnography may be combined with in-depth interviews to give a triangulation of qualitative methods. While the use of mixed methods is often cited as a means of getting the best of both worlds (quality and quantity), it is not always used for that purpose and is not a guarantee of success. How the results of mixed methods can be compared or rendered compatible is often profoundly challenging and may be no less problematic, or rewarding, than trying to cull the existing literature for suitable concepts and usable measures.

Summary

The distinction between qualitative and quantitative approaches to social research has many meanings and many dimensions. The distinction has become a central point of contention within the social research community. While much energy has been expended defining the value of one approach over the other, as much energy has been expended seeking to overcome the divide. The dispute hides the fact that all research has a qualitative dimension, that of identifying conceptual categories that are meaningful units, and a quantitative dimension, that of measuring the scale or incidence of such units (even if only to register presence or absence in some cases). The deeper divide lies between those who hold to an objectivist view of the social world, one which sees social institutions and 'structures' as 'fact' like constraints shaping the lives of human beings, and those who hold a more social constructivist or phenomenological view, in which it is social actors who create the patterns of social life through their beliefs and actions. The selection of research methods often reflects these deep-seated ontological beliefs.

 ■ Questions

1 What is the range of meanings given to the distinction between qualitative and quantitative methodology in social research?
2 What are the fundamentals of objectivist and constructivist/phenomenological ontologies?

■ ■ Further reading ■

Bauman, Zygmunt and May, Tim (2001) *Thinking Sociologically*. Oxford: Blackwell.

Bryman, Alan (1988) *Quantity and Quality in Social Research*. London: Routledge.

Savage, Mike and Egerton, Muriel (1997) 'Social mobility, individual ability and the inheritance of class inequality', *Sociology*, 31(4): 645–72.

Williams, Malcolm and May, Tim (1996) *Introduction to the Philosophy of Social Research*. London: UCL.

PART TWO
DATA COLLECTION STRATEGIES

FIVE

INTRODUCTION TO THE PROCESS OF QUALITATIVE RESEARCH

Aims

By the end of this chapter you will be able to:

- Distinguish a number of different forms of qualitative data collection methods.
- Identify issues specific to qualitative research when selecting a sample.
- Outline the range of different approaches to research design emerging from choices over induction, deduction and grounded theory.
- Specify crucial ethical issues that must be addressed by the qualitative researcher.

Induction and exploration

As has been suggested already, the distinction between qualitative and quantitative research at best is hard to define, and at worst can be positively misleading. It is wise to use the distinction with caution. In what follows the research methods described will be those which give emphasis to the collection of primarily non-numerical data, that is, thick descriptions of events, in-depth interviewing and the use of written or recorded evidence and artefacts. What has come to be understood as qualitative research involves more than simply the lack of emphasis on quantification. Qualitative research is also strongly associated with induction and exploration in research, rather than with the more deductive testing of preconceived theories. Induction and exploration imply that the researcher sets out with a more tentative idea of what is important. The researcher attempts to be more sensitive to the priorities held by those whom they will interview or observe, or whose texts and artefacts they will attempt to 'read'. As such, the process of research design involves the deliberate attempt to leave a certain degree of openness in the structuring of the research questions, in the formulation of the research sample, and in the design of interview questions, observational schedules and so on. In the section 'From literature review to a research question' later in this chapter, this openness is examined in the movement from literature review to research question and then on towards research design, conduct and analysis. This movement is, crucially, not a one-way street. The relationship between literature, question formation, data collection and theory building in qualitative research often involves ongoing modification, with data collection leading to emergent theories which themselves redirect the data collection process. It is important to examine the relationship between induction and prior literature. While induction and exploration are key elements within the qualitative tradition, this tradition is itself carried forward within the background literature each researcher carries with them as they enter the field. To what extent can the qualitative researcher suspend such theoretical baggage, and to what extent should they do so? This fluid relationship between theory and data collection is examined in the section 'Degrees of grounded theory and sampling in qualitative research' with reference to the notion of grounded theory. Grounded theory offers a particular approach to theory building in the conduct of qualitative research. While formal processes of qualitative data analysis will be examined in Chapters 18 to 22, this chapter outlines how ongoing data analysis during the conduct of data collection has become a near standard practice within much qualitative research (see Box 5.1). The section 'Ethics of qualitative research' addresses the specific ethical issues raised by qualitative research.

BOX 5.1 STOP AND THINK

Do you know what it is you really want to know?

It might seem an odd question to ask at this stage, but when you are about to choose the methods of your data collection, you will need to ask yourself again whether you know what it is you really want to know. Surely you should have sorted this out at an earlier stage. Shouldn't your review of the literature and your identification of a research question have already settled this for you? Well, yes and no. If your research question was very precise in terms of the data that would be required to answer it then you are in a position to design relatively specific data collection instruments (such as very narrowly prescribed questions in a questionnaire, or very particular measurements taken from observations in controlled conditions or in other contexts). If, however, your review of the literature and the formation of your research question leave you feeling that the kind of information you need to answer your question is still rather vague, and that the very parameters of the question are still so broad as to require further exploration even in the data collection process itself, you need to choose data and data collection tools that will enable this. The relatively open-ended research question will most likely require more qualitative forms of data collection, and this will be explored in the next few chapters. Asking relatively open-ended questions is one way of being qualitative. Changing the order of your questions, or even changing the kinds of questions you ask as you go along, is another form of being qualitative. Not asking questions, but rather watching people in their everyday lives so as to identify what is significant to them without presuming in advance to know (as would be required if you were to have formulated questions in advance), is another way of being qualitative. Finally, selecting a sample of one case to study in depth rather than selecting a sample that it is hoped will represent the general population, or selecting your sample as you go along rather than in advance, is another way of being qualitative. As you will have noted from Part I, qualitative research is associated with a focus on meaning over numbers, but is also associated with induction over deduction, the micro over the macro, and description over explanation. Robson (2002) suggests it might be better to use the word 'flexible' to describe this cluster of research strategies, rather than 'qualitative'. As such, ask: does answering your research question require that you be flexible, or is it better to adopt a more structured approach?

Primary data collection or secondary sources?

In the past, and still today, critics of qualitative research have argued that one of the major limitations of such methods is the difficulty other researchers have in getting hold of the original 'data' of qualitative researchers. The relatively open methodology characteristic of qualitative research leaves little in the way of a transparent trail and so is harder to replicate. To a degree this is changing with the advent of large-capacity computer archives; however, it is in the nature of qualitative research that it will rarely generate the kind of uniformity and transparency characteristic (or at least idealized) in quantitative forms of data collection. Having said this, it should be pointed out that in so far as qualitative research is about the collection of primarily non-numerical data for the purpose of linguistic analysis (the search for interpretive patterns rather than statistical patterns), evaluation of previous qualitative analysis and the data presented in such work constitutes a form of secondary qualitative analysis.

Many of the techniques of qualitative data analysis parallel those of literature reviewing (discussed in 'Reviewing content' in Chapter 3). Likewise, in archival forms of qualitative data collection the methods deployed are very similar to those employed in the conduct of a literature search ('Searching the archives' in Chapter 3; see also Box 5.2). Whether it be ethnographic monographs, media discourse analyses, the writing up of interview-based research or any other form of qualitative research, attempting to locate and decode the qualitative research findings of others constitutes a form of qualitative research in itself. Of course, one may wish to go deeper and seek access to the researchers' original field notes, interview transcripts and other texts and artefacts. While rare in the past, this is becoming increasingly possible (see Box 5.3).

BOX 5.2 CONSIDER THIS

Are they data or is it literature?

The analysis of language, the attempt to make sense of meaningful signs and symbols organized into systems, applies to reading text, whether that text be an interview transcript or a researcher's interpretation of all the transcripts they collected.

There are many useful ways to extract meaning from text, and these can be applied whether the text concerned is data or literature. Neither is the difference between data and literature that between numbers and language. If I asked 100 people for their height, the 100 heights would be data, but I might provide an average in my written discussion of the research. This average would be part of the literature. However, if I collected the averages from a number of such studies I could convert these averages into data of my own. Do averages vary from place to place or across time? Data might consist of 100 statements in response to the question: 'How do you feel about your height?' This would be qualitative data. My interpretation of these responses, if I wrote up this research, would become part of the literature. Newspapers may conduct surveys, or they may report the results of research carried out by other people. If a social scientist is interested in the surveys themselves, then referring to the newspapers that discussed them might be part of a review of the literature. This assumes that the newspapers were giving a reliable account. This is problematic. It is more likely that the researcher would be wanting to look at newspaper reporting to see how they construct events including their reporting of research. As such, these newspaper articles would become data, something to be studied, rather than a reliable source of information about something else to be studied.

BOX 5.3 HINTS AND TIPS

The archiving of qualitative data

http://www.esds.ac.uk/qualidata/about/introduction.asp

This web link takes you to the home of the Qualidata Archive. This archive is run by the Economic and Social Data Services team at the University of Essex. ESDS was set up to house the huge and growing array of large quantitative datasets that are produced each year by government-funded researchers in the UK. In addition, the UK government and the research funding councils who allocate money for research projects felt that the same kinds of secondary research that are enabled by the making available of datasets online could also be undertaken for qualitative research. In the past, and still, it is a common criticism of qualitative research that the data on which researchers conduct their analysis are rarely open to critical re-evaluation by other researchers. Qualidata is a service designed to enable such secondary analysis of qualitative data. This service is relatively easy to access if you are based in a UK educational institution. The service allows you to explore the research designs and the data collected. It is very well worth exploring, not least as it would enable you to find out if the question you want to research has already been investigated. If so, you may want either to carry out secondary research or try to adapt your own work in the light of what has been previously identified.

Interviews, observations, archives

Interviews, observations and archives are types of data collection, each of which takes many forms; this diversity will be described in further detail as this chapter develops. Chapters 6 and 7 will deal with the two fundamental forms of the qualitative interview, first the more traditional one-to-one interview and then the focus group or group interview. Each approach has its advantages and disadvantages. You will need to evaluate these in relation to the research you wish to carry out and the resources and experience you have at your disposal. Chapter 8 examines the ethnographic method: here the researcher spends time with a group of people, observing a way of life. Ethnography will usually also involve interviewing, and often the collection of artefacts for analysis. Given the attention to interviewing in Chapters 6 and 7, it is the observational element of ethnography that will receive most attention in Chapter 8. Sociologists often prefer to use the term 'participant observation' to describe what anthropologists have traditionally called ethnography. The distinction is porous, but examining it will allow some important themes to emerge (such as between participation and 'passive' observation, and between covert and overt observation). The term 'case study' can apply to any research that is not comparative in nature, that is, where there is only one case. This case may be an individual, an organization or an entire community or culture. Interviews, observations and the collection of texts and artefacts may be used. Chapter 9, on case studies, addresses how such techniques are used in the particulars of biographical, life history, organizational and community studies, sometimes ethnographically. Case studies may form the basis of a research design, or may be one part of a wider design. Also, whilst the primary rationale for case study research is to give emphasis to the internal character of the case, this does not mean that comparison cannot be undertaken between cases. Chapter 10 examines the collection of textual data. The term 'text' has come to mean any artefact that contains or has been given meaning by a culture. From the collection of straightforward printed texts (such as newspapers, government reports, diaries and letters), textual data have come to include television programmes, photographs, art works and so on. As will be seen in Chapter 18 concerning qualitative data analysis, discourse analysis and 'semiotics' have opened the field of textual interpretation and hermeneutics (the study of meaning) to all things human. In recent years, the development of still and video cameras both as a means of primary data collection and as a source of archival data (other people's images, whether these be private individuals or media companies) has led to a rising interest in visual methods. As such visual data are analysed as text, their collection will be addressed in Chapter 10, alongside other forms of textual data collection. Conversation analysis (CA) (see Chapter 20) can be seen as a fusion of innovative observation and textual analysis techniques, being the unobtrusive recording of naturally occurring talk for purposes similar to those of ethnomethodology. Both ethnomethodology and CA challenge mainstream social research to work in radically different ways and to different ends.

From literature review to a research question: degrees of closure

As has been pointed out already, qualitative research tends towards a more inductive and exploratory form. This need not be the case. Research that is designed to collect non-numerical forms of data, whether by means of interview or observation or by the collection of archival materials or artefacts, may be deductive. It is perfectly possible for a researcher to formulate a research question that takes the form of a hypothesis (a prediction that can be tested) and to then seek to test that hypothesis by collecting qualitative data. For example, a researcher might, on the basis of a review of existing literature, hypothesize that male and female students attach different meanings to their education. By interviewing male and female students the researcher may seek to test that hypothesis. The researcher may choose in-depth (that is, qualitative) interviews if they feel that this may offer the best means of identifying the 'meanings' held by students. Other forms of qualitative research methods may be similarly employed to investigate a hypothesis if they are deemed most useful (see Box 5.4).

BOX 5.4 CONSIDER THIS

Qualitative hypothesis testing

Hypothesis testing is commonly associated with quantitative forms of data collection. Quantitative research is more likely to be deductive, where the research is designed to test a theory, and numerical data are more easily analysed for patterns of association, strength and significance (see Part III). Nevertheless, qualitative data can be used to test hypotheses, as well as being useful in the prior exploration of a topic that might itself help in the formation of hypotheses for subsequent investigation. The two qualitative dimensions of hypothesis testing are most clearly visible in 'grounded theory' and in 'focus group' research, but the principles can be extended to any kind of qualitative research. In grounded theory, the first round of exploration in the field is followed by a period of reflection where the researcher seeks to theorize the field, to generate an account or explanation of events. This forms a provisional hypothesis, to be taken into the next round of data collection. Does the provisional hypothesis 'fit' the new encounters and interactions? If not, then the researcher needs to reformulate their hypothesis for the third round. Grounded theory involves a constant movement back and forth between exploration and hypothesis testing. Such a movement is common in ethnography, and in the more open-ended forms of interviewing where the researcher may shift the focus of subsequent interviews on the basis of what prior interviews have led them to believe is significant. In such situations, the hunches that emerge in the field act as hypotheses to be tested in each new encounter. This is a form of deductive research, as each new encounter has a purpose, directed by the researcher's belief about the field. A purely inductive research process would allow each encounter to shape the data collection process, and is relatively rare. As such, most qualitative research involves an element of grounded (sometimes called emergent) hypothesis testing. The second dimension of hypothesis testing is made most explicit in focus groups, which are rather like qualitative experiments. Here the focus group acts almost like a laboratory for the researcher to pose certain questions and to bring certain people together (the composition of the group will of course impact on the dynamics of the discussion). Both the choice of question and the composition of the group will be based on the researcher's prior 'hunches' about what is and is not important to explore. These hunches may be relatively modest hypotheses, but they might also be quite bold presumptions about what is going to be significant in determining what people say and how the group conversation will unfold. One-to-one interviews will also carry a degree of preconception about what is being examined and which relationships are to be interlinked. For focus groups or one-to-one interviews to avoid any form of hypothesis testing, they would have to give free rein to naturally occurring discussion. To do so would mean that what was produced was not really an interview at all. All interviews are conversations with a purpose, and this purpose will always contain a hypothesis, however tentative. Whilst qualitative researchers can work with very tentative hypotheses, and quantitative researchers will require more structured and narrow ones, it should not be assumed that the latter use hypotheses and the former never do. It is worthwhile locating your research agenda on a spectrum, and your data collection also.

See Grim et al. (2006) for a more detailed exploration of qualitative hypothesis testing.

The reason qualitative research tends to be associated with more inductive and exploratory (that is, non-hypothesis-driven) research projects is because the kinds of depth which qualitative methods are said to enable allow the researcher to explore issues by following the priorities and actions of those they are researching. Conversely, quantitative research methods require the researcher to have a well-defined focus so as to enable them to identify exactly what it is they need to measure. Such a focus can relatively easily be framed in the form of a hypothesis. Quantification does make testing simpler, as what counts as a positive or negative result is more easily identified in numbers. However, simplicity is not always best. On the basis of a review of existing literature the researcher may be left with a very strong sense of what needs to be measured, a weak sense of the general area that needs to be investigated, or something in between. All empirical research requires the researcher to identify the basic issues and locations they need to investigate. In the loose sense of the term, all researchers start with a 'hunch' of some kind, even if many of these 'hunches' would not be sufficiently precise to be called 'hypotheses'. Where a hunch is not precise enough to be 'tested' (and the researcher may deliberately choose to avoid such precision in order to remain open to new 'leads'), the researcher should adopt a more inductive approach.

Inductive research seeks to build theory on the basis of empirical research (see section 'Deduction and induction' in Chapter 4). This means that the relationship between literature review and data collection will be less prescriptive. There is a greater degree of openness. This, however, does not mean that such forms of qualitative research fail to build upon rigorous foundations within the existing literature. It may well be the case that it is precisely the findings of past research in the particular field in question that suggest to the researcher the need to adopt a more open and exploratory approach. This may be through particular findings or the lack of them. The choice of a more open research design may also flow from existing literature at a higher level of abstraction. The researcher's choice may stem from general theoretical commitments (recall 'The deeper divide' in Chapter 4) developed through that person's career as a social scientist and itself grounded in their past reading, rather than simply their evaluation of research related to a particular topic. In this regard research is never fully inductive, just as it can never be fully open. As was suggested above, openness and closure are the opposite ends of a spectrum. All research sits somewhere between these extremes (see Box 5.5).

BOX 5.5 RESEARCH FOCUS

What leads a qualitative researcher to study what they do, and how?

Elizabeth Aries and Maynard Seider (2005) explored the experience of university students from relatively low-income families in the United States. They adopted a qualitative approach in order to explore how these students described their educational and personal development. The motivations for the research combine academic with policy-based literature. The issue of low entry from poorer families into elite universities and colleges is cited in the authors' literature review as an issue for academic researchers and administrators, as well as for politicians. Aries and Seider's paper cites a wealth of prior literature both to locate the problem and also to warrant their approach to exploring their sample group's experience. The choice of only white students from lower-income backgrounds is justified in terms of prior literature which suggested the educational experience of non-white students from poorer backgrounds is very different from that of white students from similar income backgrounds. As the sample was relatively small (15 students from each of two colleges), something that was driven by the in-depth data collection methods used, it was necessary to purposely sample students who (the researchers claim) could be meaningfully contrasted with each other. Just as the research was driven by prior theoretical assumptions, so too was the sampling technique. Most qualitative research is driven by such prior theoretical and methodological motivations and choices – choices that structure the research. Whilst the choices that structure quantitative data collection are often more explicit and more rigid, it should not be assumed that there is a choice between prestructuring and 'open-ended' research. Again, there is a spectrum upon which research can be located. There is very little that sits on the extremes. Most research is somewhere in the middle.

Cassandra Phoenix and Andrew Sparkes (2009) carried out a series of interviews with a 70-year-old man called Fred. From these interviews the authors draw out examples of narrative storytelling which allow them to engage with currently popular theories of narrative and similarly contemporary approaches to researching and collecting data about such storytelling. There is no policy agenda here, despite the significance of ageing as a policy concern in developed societies. Rather, Fred is an opportunity for the researchers to explore the field of prior theories and popular methodologies in qualitative research. The data collection is textual and relatively open ended, but the researchers' motives remain very much driven by prior theoretical and methodological concerns. It is not entirely clear whether the authors subscribe to the 'life is what you make it' narrative structure that Fred routinely deploys, but they are certainly sceptical of any attempt to map ageing as a real process that acts as an objective constraint on individuals.

Returning to the example of male and female students and the meaning they attach to their education, the suggestion that males and females may differ in this regard constitutes a very weak hypothesis in itself. If this proposition were bolstered by more precise predictions (such as predictions about the nature of those differences, their manifestations in expressed attitudes, beliefs and behaviours, and their strength), this prediction would begin to take on the characteristics of a fully formed and so testable hypothesis. If not, then the weak prediction is best not called a hypothesis at all, and may be better called a research question. The former is more open to numerical data collection. The latter is best suited to a more qualitative approach.

It should, however, be recalled (see Chapter 4) at this point that even the most precise hypothesis cannot be translated into a testing instrument without being piloted. Piloting in deductive research (testing the test) will often involve a degree of reformulation. This is usually at the level of the questions to be asked or the observational measures to be taken, rather than of the hypothesis to be tested. However, piloting may throw up new insights that force the researcher to reconsider their hypothesis. As such, this represents an inductive moment (the generation of theory on the basis of empirical observation) even within the most rigorous forms of deductive research (the use of empirical research to test a prespecified but as yet tentative theory). In qualitative research the tendency is to extend this moment by means of more fully inductive data collection techniques. These techniques are what will be explored in this chapter.

Degrees of grounded theory and sampling in qualitative research

The term 'grounded theory' has taken on an almost mythic status in qualitative research. Barney Glaser and Anselm Strauss's *The Discovery of Grounded Theory* (1967) sought to demonstrate how theory could be built through the conduct of qualitative research. By theory, Glaser and Strauss mean concept formation. While the conduct of deductive and quantitative research requires that the researcher operationalize their concepts (identifying how abstract concepts can be turned into measurable categories or variables) prior to then 'going out' and measuring the incidence and/or levels of them, grounded theory offers a methodology for allowing concepts to be generated in the course of empirical research. Emergence refers to the way in which the researcher seeks to formulate and clarify a picture of the world they are studying by identifying categories that capture what is going on. Through various forms of qualitative data collection (and even the collection of numerical data), the researcher seeks to identify patterns. They then seek to formulate concepts that capture such patterns, in other words which best describe what is going on in the data. 'Best' is not a static term. On reflection, after initial investigations the researcher formulates what they think are strong descriptive tools – concepts that seem to capture the situation. The researcher then needs to further investigate the power of such descriptions through further research. This will often require that initial concepts be reformulated or even abandoned. New or refashioned concepts may then emerge to face a new round of examination. Grounded theory thereby seeks to build a picture of events that best fits that situation.

Grounded theory is an explicit reaction to the kinds of deductive research that seek to apply 'grand theory' empirically by means of hypothesis testing. It should be noted, however, that grounded theory is not simply a form of inductive theory building. A straightforwardly inductive form of theory building would conduct data collection and then seek to build theories afterwards. Grounded theory seeks to fold induction into deduction, back and forth, collecting data, formulating tentative theories and then seeking to test these theories with new data collection and analysis, which itself may lead to more than just testing (as it may lead to the generation of new concepts). This cycle of data collection, theory building, testing and reformulation carries on (ideally) until saturation. Saturation refers to the point at which the currently held set of concepts seems reasonably able to describe and even predict the situation they seek to theorize. Of course, no theory can fully predict every aspect of a situation or field, and likewise, no research project can go on forever. As such the researcher must make a judgement about the validity of their theory relative to the resources they have available to continue their research.

Whilst grounded theory is not the only approach to qualitative research, it does highlight a more general characteristic of qualitative research, which is the fluid relationship between data collection and data analysis. Whilst piloting in quantitative research often involves the reformulation of how research questions are to be posed empirically, it is less common that the research question, and the basic concepts and categories being used, are reformulated. This is precisely what grounded theory seeks to facilitate. In grounded theory, data collected at each stage require analysis prior to moving on to the next round of data collection. Whilst forms of qualitative data analysis are to be discussed in more detail in Chapters 18 to 22, it is important at this stage to point out that data analysis is an essential stage in the development of more grounded forms of data collection. Where data are not collected in a fully structured way, the researcher is required to think at each moment about what are useful data, and what lines of enquiry to continue or to move on from. Each of these decisions involves a form of micro data analysis.

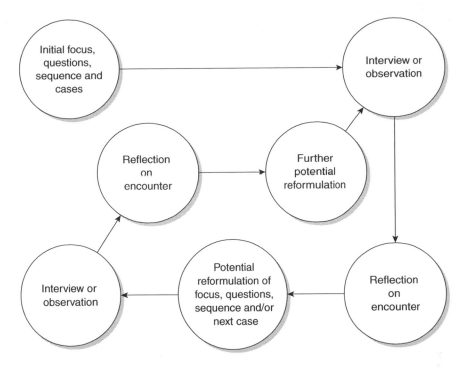

FIGURE 5.1 Flexible designs: shifting the focus, questions, sequence and cases

Flexibility in data collection is represented in Figure 5.1. Flexibility may be in terms of the focus of research, the questions to be asked or which direct the researcher's attention, the sequence and/or priority of such questions, and the sample to be studied. Flexibility may be in one or more or all of these areas. This includes the initial formulation of the research question, the way these questions are to be answered (whether by asking or by looking, the degree of structure to be imposed on such asking/looking, the sequence of what gets attended to or asked first, second etc.), whether or not the sequence of asking/attending will stay the same from one encounter to the next, and whether the sample will be selected before data collection begins or whether new members of the sample are to be added on the basis of details gained from data collection itself.

Sampling

The conduct of quantitative data collection requires a clear and pre-emptive specification of the key concepts and their translation into measurable categories and variables. Qualitative research more often seeks to retain a degree of openness such that data collection enables the formulation of such concepts rather than their testing. As such the process of sampling in qualitative research design tends to differ in its aims and its method from sampling in quantitative research. Qualitative research tends to be exploratory. One aspect of this may be to explore the identity of those you are seeking to research. It is often not possible to specify in advance exactly who you are interested in. Research into issues such as homelessness, racism and alcoholism does not present the researcher with target groups whose members are 'registered' or even easily identifiable. Part of the exploratory process may be to find these people. It is not possible in such cases to draw a random sample, as there is no sampling frame (a list of all members) from which to randomly select (see Chapter 14 for a discussion of formal sampling methods). Of course, a non-random sample group can be researched using a quantitative questionnaire, just as a statistically random sample group can be researched using qualitative interviews. How one generates a sample does not dictate the subsequent research instruments used. However, the use of qualitative data collection methods may be useful in the generation of subsequent members of a snowball sample. In-depth interviewing or participant observation and so on may enable the researcher to identify where to look next or who to talk to next. In the same way that responses to open-ended questions may generate theoretical insights, so they may offer new leads in the identification of research subjects. As such, qualitative research is often associated with exploratory, or snowball, sampling. In such situations, where a sample is built up through information provided in the last stage of data collection, the same principles of validity and saturation (discussed earlier in this section) apply as they did in the case of concept formation and theory building. A sample would be sufficient when the current round of theory building provides sufficient insight such that subsequent sample members' identities and responses or behaviours are predictable. Even in the conduct of a case study, where one organization or group is chosen – and so, in terms of statistical sampling theory, the results cannot be readily generalized from – it is still possible to sample respondents within that group or organization in a formally random fashion if a sampling frame can be devised or found. It is essential that the social researcher choosing qualitative methods understands quantitative techniques, and vice versa. This is true not only when using mixed methods, but even when one approach is selected. A choice based on understanding is far better than doing only one because you don't understand the other. Regarding sampling, it is therefore essential to read Chapter 14. See also Box 5.6.

BOX 5.6 RESEARCH FOCUS

Examples of qualitative sampling

Aries and Seider (2005), discussed in Box 5.5, selected two groups of 15 students, one group from an 'elite' private university college and one group from a less exclusive state university college. The composition of each group was specified in advance in strict terms. For a student to be included their parents' income had to be below a specified level, and all those interviewed were white, to avoid the complicating factors of income and ethnicity. The two groups were balanced equally by gender.

Pete Millward (2006) sought to examine the language used in football supporters' online discussion boards (e-zines) to describe local, national and European identification. Becoming a member of the e-zine 'threads' of conversation would automatically be sent to the researcher, in very large volumes. In total over 1200 such threads developed over the 14 month period in which data were collected. The first wave of sampling was then the selection of teams and their e-zines. The next stage was in selecting the time period. As each thread amounted to a conversation of hundreds or sometimes thousands of words, it was necessary to sample further within this dataset of 1200+ threads. It was decided to draw a quarter sample of days (107 in total), and so a random number generator was used to select 107 days from the total number of 426 days (14 months).

Michael Heaney and Fabio Rojas (2006) used ethnographic methods to explore the framing of anti-war protest and pro-war counter-protest. They selected a single site, the Airborne and Special Operations Museum outside Fayetteville, North Carolina, outside of which a series of anti-war protests was held in 2005–6. Having attended a number of anti-war protests in various US states, the researchers selected the Fayetteville site for more prolonged attention as the largest US anti-war coalition had itself decided to give particular attention to that location in mounting protest events. The researchers thus selected a single case as it was seen to be central to the anti-war coalition's approach to campaigning. The researchers made four visits of three days each time between March 2005 and March 2006. They networked at events and thereby identified and interviewed 15 leaders. Shorter interviews were carried out where opportunities arose, with 52 protest participants. A brief survey was distributed at events and 253 responses were collected. The researchers also used independent media video footage and media coverage of the events as data.

Cassandra Phoenix and Andrew Sparkes (2009) – see Box 5.5 – sampled Fred.

Ethics of qualitative research

As has been discussed in Chapter 2, social research requires ethical consideration at all stages: in the decision to research one topic over another, in choosing one method over another, in the conduct of data collection and analysis, and in the dissemination of findings (as well as in limiting the dissemination of such identifiers as might damage research participants). Qualitative research offers advantages but also presents difficulties at each of these stages in the research process.

The traditions of qualitative research arose largely as a reaction to the positivism of quantitative social research and its attempts to replicate the methods of the 'natural' sciences. Many qualitative researchers see their methods as an active attempt to avoid the reduction of their participants to the status of objects. The more inductive approach favoured in much qualitative research is said to give more of a voice to those being researched, allowing them a greater power to direct the flow of the research. The use of more open-ended forms of data collection enables the words of the researched to come through, rather than for their beliefs, values and behaviours to be tightly filtered and boxed through the deductive researcher's prescriptive categories and scales.

Perhaps the most famous (if very often misunderstood) article published on the subject of the ethics of qualitative research is Howard Becker's 'Whose side are we on?' (1967). As noted in 'Ethical issues in the decision to research' in Chapter 2, Becker suggested that by researching society's 'underdogs', and in unearthing their way of looking at the world by means of in-depth interviewing, participant observation and so on, the researcher will inevitably be accused by those in authority of being biased in favour of the researched (the accusation of 'going native'). Presenting 'their story' from 'their point of view' will often be taken to be advocating rather than simply representing. However, many subsequent researchers have taken Becker to be suggesting that the researcher cannot be neutral and so must choose to use their research to support either authority or the underdogs. Qualitative research is seen as ideally suited to the task of demonstrating the validity of ways of life and beliefs that might otherwise be misunderstood. Forms of participant observation allow the researcher to combine research with involvement within an organization or a movement they feel is worthy of their support. Participatory action research (PAR) involves the researcher conducting research in order to actively forward the goals of an organization (Whyte, 1991a; 1991b; see also section 'Evaluation, participation and action research' in Chapter 1). As such the researcher is involved with the goals of the organization and the members of the organization are actively involved in shaping the direction of the research. Many qualitative researchers investigating new social movements (such as feminism, ecology and so on) have argued that the role of advocate is not at odds with the role of social researcher (Harries-Jones, 1991). They suggest that the idea of value freedom is a myth and that the detachment of the researcher from the researched simply allows the researcher to become a social engineer, researching in order to better manage society's troublesome misfits and outcasts. However, not all feminist writers accept that only qualitative forms of research can fully grasp the truth about women's lives in a manner that does not distort or even oppress (Maynard, 1998; Oakley, 2000). Similarly, not all qualitative researchers are comfortable with the idea that social research needs to abandon any commitment to standards of objectivity and neutrality in the conduct of research. Becker himself was keen to assert that while qualitative research was always likely to be accused of bias in favour of those being researched, it was still the job of the researcher to present that way of seeing and way of life in as truthful a fashion as possible (Hammersley, 2000; David, 2002).

This raises the ethical question of 'truth'. While the qualitative researcher may wish to claim greater depth validity, more quantitative researchers often claim that their ability to deliver greater reliability and generalizability offers 'more' truth. This is a thorny dispute that cannot be resolved here (Box 5.7). It is only possible to note the importance of truth as an ethical criterion in social research. It is questionable as to whether social research would be worthwhile if truth were not a goal, even if one that could never be fully achieved (Hammersley, 2000; David, 2002).

BOX 5.7 CONSIDER THIS

Ethics committees and qualitative research

Mark Israel and Iain Hay (2006) point to the problematic relationship that tends to arise between research ethics committees and qualitative research (see Chapter 2). In recent years the conduct of research in universities, hospitals, government departments and other settings has become increasingly regulated by research ethics committees. Institutions are motivated by a combination of reduction of harm caused by the conduct of research, and avoidance of liability for the consequences of a researcher's abuse of their position. For these two reasons institutions increasingly require researchers to specify in advance exactly what they are going to do, what they want to find, why and who they will research and how. Not only are such outlines required to be submitted, but research will not be permitted until the institution's appointed committee gives its approval. This may be withheld if research is said to be ethically problematic, or if it is not clear exactly what is being proposed. Many qualitative research-ers have felt this to be a major problem for their approach. Inductive research, which may shift its attention, may not define fully its data collection methods in advance and may adopt rather open-ended data collection techniques, which make it hard to specify in advance (or sometimes at all) who it is that is going to be researched, does not conform easily to the demand to define everything clearly in advance. The very essence of a flexible research design makes it hard to apply the param-eters of ethical approval, which are based on the assumption that the researcher will not deviate from what they set out to do at the start. Ongoing processes of negotiation between institutional committees that are often based on medical and bioscientific approaches to deductive research and more inductive researchers in the social sciences are taking place in universities and other settings across the world. Some institutions have developed more flexible procedures. In other institutions it is necessary for qualitative researchers to structure their research within parameters that define the what, the who and the how in general terms (particularly in terms of themes, meth-ods and sample participants that will be excluded), so as to 'fit' into dominant models of approval. It is essential to know how things work where you are planning to do your research.

While advocates of qualitative research have tended to advance the virtues of depth as a means both of gathering data and of retaining an ethical relationship with those who are being researched, it is important to note that there are ethical difficulties with such an approach to data collection. The conduct of in-depth inter-views, ethnographic observation and so on gives a greater opportunity for those researched to expose themselves to harm by revealing damaging or threatening facts and opinions. This may, in the first instance, be to the researcher. However, the smaller sample size characteristic of qualitative research makes it harder to hide the identity of respondents in subsequent dissemination of research findings. Where the respondents to a written questionnaire may be able to avoid personal disclosure, the face-to-face interview offers less protection. The researcher in such situations must be all the more conscious of the dangers involved in researching sensitive topics (Lee, 1993). Likewise, the qualitative researcher must be doubly conscious of the need to protect the confidentiality of those they research, both from the wider audience and from other participants in the research. This latter task is particularly problematic as it is in the nature of qualitative research to offer depth, whilst at the same time the researcher needs to prevent such depth insight rebounding negatively upon those researched. It is not possible in the context of a focus group interview to avoid disclosure to other participants what is disclosed to the interviewer. It is therefore not advisable to deal with highly sensitive subjects using focus groups.

Finally, there is the issue of consent, which raises some particular problems for certain forms of qualitative research. The qualitative interview (whether one-to-one or in a focus group format) offers the researcher plenty of opportunity to clarify issues with the interviewees. However, forms of archival research and observational research are more problematic. The classical experimental form of observation has been criticized as often the research subject is not told the purpose of the research until debriefing, giving them no opportunity to withdraw. Forms of overt participant observation, where the researcher is open about their role as researcher, allow a greater dialogue. However, even the most overt participant observer may find it hard to inform everyone they meet in the course of their research about their researcher role. As such, not everyone is able to give informed consent. This is, of course, all the more true in covert forms of participant observation where the researcher does not disclose their researcher identity. Quantitative archival data will tend to be in a format that does not identify individual respondents. However, qualitative archival materials, whether these are primary sources such as diaries and letters, or secondary sources such as field notes and interview transcripts, may contain more explicit personal identifiers. Often the advantage of archival materials is that the authors are not otherwise accessible (the older the archives, the more likely this is to be the case). Whilst this makes the archive a useful source, there is still the question of whether it is right to unearth personal details about people who have not consented to this taking place (see Box 5.8).

BOX 5.8 STOP AND THINK

The ethics of the unexpected

If one of the rationales for qualitative research is that it allows the researcher to explore a topic rather than to pursue a predefined agenda, this may be seen to have ethical merit. If you are following the priorities of those you are researching, following the themes and connections, as well as perhaps sampling people who your research participants put you in touch with (snowballing), then this may be seen as giving a greater ethical weight to the values and beliefs of those you research. The researcher can be said to be respecting not only the people they research, but the complexity of their world. However, the very respect for such complexity means that the researcher cannot predict in advance what they are going to ask, when, how or to whom, and the possibility exists that they will unexpectedly stumble upon issues and events that are highly sensitive, secret or intrusive. There are a number of cases where ethnographic research has stumbled across criminal activity when this was not intended. What then does a researcher do? How should a researcher deal with the disclosure or discovery of information of this kind? In the conduct of flexible research the researcher may encounter people who do not know the researcher's research identity and as such are unable to give informed consent, or who may be children or people with other issues that limit their capacity to give consent. If the researcher did not sample in a structured fashion at the start, they cannot predict who they will meet. Whilst inductive forms of qualitative research are often harder to regulate in ethics committees, this is often for reasons that mean they are all the more in need of ethical oversight. It is very important to keep such dangers in mind.

Summary

Qualitative research design is commonly associated with more exploratory and descriptive forms of research design, though this need not be the case. Forms of grounded theory, where inductive exploration precedes more deductive forms of testing theories emerging from earlier exploration, are also common, and some forms of qualitative research test hypotheses and/or seek to identify causal relationships. Qualitative forms of research have been advocated on the grounds that the more open-ended forms of data collection are ethically (as well as empirically) advantageous, giving those researched a stronger voice and say in the direction of the research. However, qualitative data collection techniques and the data themselves also generate greater scope for intrusion upon privacy, non-informed consent and exposure to harm through the revelation of potentially damaging personal information either at the point of data collection or in subsequent publication/presentation.

 **■ Questions**

1 Why is qualitative data collection most often associated with exploratory and descriptive research questions?
2 In what ways are the practical advantages of qualitative research also the sources of significant ethical dangers?
3 What is grounded theory?

▓ ▓ Further reading ▓

Aries, Elizabeth and Seider, Maynard (2005) 'The interactive relationship between class identity and the college experience: the case of lower income identity', *Qualitative Sociology*, 28 (4): 419–33.

Becker, Howard (1967) 'Whose side are we on?', *Social Problems*, 14: 239–47.

Glaser, Barney and Strauss, Anselm (1967) *The Discovery of Grounded Theory: Strategies for Qualitative Research*. Chicago: Aldine.

Hammersley, Martyn (2000) *Taking Sides in Social Research: Essays on Partisanship and Bias*. London: Routledge.

SIX

QUALITATIVE INTERVIEWING

Chapter Contents

Aims

By the end of this chapter you will be able to:

- **Identify the advantages and disadvantages of interview-based data collection methods.**
- **Distinguish the value and limitations of interviews in relation to particular research questions.**
- **Outline key elements within the design of interview questions and interview schedules.**
- **Specify the range of choices that exist, and the reasons for choosing between them, when sampling for qualitative interviews.**
- **Understand the difficulties involved in recording and transcribing interview materials and the steps required in order to limit those difficulties.**

Qualitative interviewing

Interviewing involves asking people questions, but it is equally about listening carefully to the answers given. Not all questions are best answered by means of an interview. In some cases, observations or records may be better. The qualitative (or in-depth) interview takes many forms. Such interviews may be one-off and one-to-one. Alternatively, interviews can be cumulative (returning to the same person a number of times) or group based. They may be a combination of the above. Qualitative interviewing may be combined with observational and archival research. Ethnography and case study research often involve qualitative interviewing. Qualitative interviews are most often face-to-face, but may be carried out over the telephone or by computer. The thing that makes an interview qualitative lies in the formatting of the questions and the scope made available for the interviewee to answer.

We can distinguish structured and unstructured interviews, as well as standardized and unstandardized interviews (see Figure 6.1 and Box 6.1). Structure refers to the

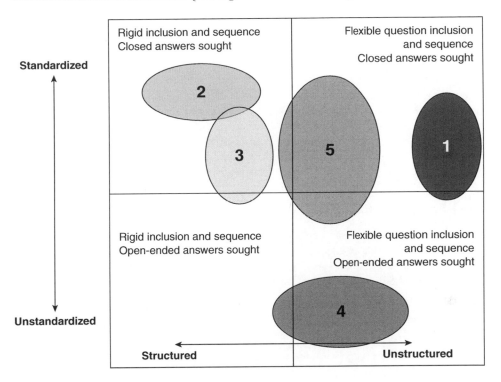

1 Sequence, wording and inclusion are all flexible, whilst questions are designed to elicit a mix of open and closed responses.

2 Wording and sequence always kept to, and questions seek closed and fixed responses.

3 Wording and sequence always kept to, but mix of questions seeking open and closed responses.

4 All questions designed to gain open-ended responses, but there is a mix of core structured questions and some that are flexible in relation to inclusion and/or sequence.

5 A mix of open standardized and unstandardized questions and a semi-structured mix of fixed and flexible question formation, sequence and inclusion.

FIGURE 6.1   Degrees of closure in questions and answers

degree to which the form and order of questions asked are kept identical from interview to interview. The structured interview seeks to maintain high levels of reliability and repeatability. The more unstructured interview seeks to emphasize the depth validity of each individual interview – the attempt to let the interviewee tell their story and so determine to a greater extent the flow of the dialogue. Standardization refers to the level of closure placed around the answers interviewees can give. Closed answers allow greater scope for quantification. Open answers allow for greater depth and personal detail, but are harder to compare numerically. The qualitative interview is that which tends towards the unstructured and the unstandardized, though the spectrum from semi-structured to unstructured and from semi-standardized to unstandardized is a broad one. Some interviews are formally arranged and timetabled as interviews. Other kinds of interviewing may be less formal and almost spontaneous (for instance, an unscheduled exchange that occurs between a participant observer and an informant). The more informal, unstructured and unstandardized an interview is, the more the interviewer needs to work during the conduct of the interview. Berg (1998: Chapter 4) refers to the drama of the interview. The interviewer is performer, audience and choreographer. When the script is flexible, the qualitative interviewer must be all the more prepared for the role they are to perform.

BOX 6.1

LEVELS OF STANDARDIZATION

Standardization requires that the researcher frames a question in such a way that all possible or permissible answers can be defined in advance. Semi-standardized questions are those where the scope to answer is fairly limited, but the researcher does not fully close down the possibility of alternatives. Unstandardized questions seek to elicit answers that are open ended and which cannot be simply placed in a prescribed box.

Standardized questions

1 Please state your age in years: ......
2 Have you visited the United Kingdom in the last three years? Yes/No
3 How afraid are you of being robbed?

   (a) Not at all
   (b) A little afraid
   (c) Afraid
   (d) Very afraid

Semi-standardized questions

1 What type of accommodation do you live in?
   (for example a house, flat, hotel, caravan etc.)
2 What is your favourite sport?
3 What university clubs and societies do you belong to?

Designing open-ended questions and semi-structured interview schedules

So what is it that you want to know? Whilst a qualitative interview is unlikely to start from the desire to test a specific hypothesis, it is still necessary to start with an outline of what you are seeking to investigate. This reflection allows the researcher to draw up a list of key themes around which interviews can be built with varying degrees of structure and standardization. These reflections will be, in part, on the background literature you have identified and your own interpretations of this material. Reflections may also be on previous data collection, whether in the form of interviews, observations or archival materials. It should be remembered that grounded theorists recommend that the qualitative researcher should shift the emphasis of their questioning as they go along, based on their previous rounds of data collection. Once a set of key themes has been identified, the researcher will then want to take each key theme one at a time and identify specific questions that may allow them to probe that theme in more detail. In the course of an interview the researcher may choose to follow the set of themes and subquestions in a relatively structured fashion. However, they may prefer to keep the set of themes and subquestions as an *aide-mémoire* to which they can return during the course of the interview but which does not dictate the order (Box 6.2). In highly unstructured interviewing (such as where a participant observer engages in spontaneous conversations with informants) the value of the setting out of key themes and subquestions in advance lies in giving the researcher a sense of order from which to draw questions from unplanned encounters. Even when no written record of such questions is to hand, the process of reflection in advance aids the researcher's sense of clarity. In this sense even the most seemingly unstructured interview involves a degree of structure. This element of structure is what distinguishes an interview from a casual conversation. An interview is a conversation with a purpose (Burgess, 1984). The purpose is clarified in the act of setting out themes and subquestions, even if these do not become a formal interview schedule (or a questionnaire). The questions set out in Box 6.2 could be asked one after the other in exactly the form written, or the questions could be used as prompts to be ticked off in any order in which they may best be fitted into a less structured discussion.

SEMI-STRUCTURED INTERVIEW *AIDE-MÉMOIRE*

Training, strategy, information and local knowledge: a study of small and medium sized enterprises in Cornwall, Devon and Somerset
Dr Matthew David, Senior Lecturer in Sociology, University of Plymouth

1   Brief introduction to you and the business.
2   Issues of size, number of employees, types of employee (age, qualifications, geographical recruitment and so on).
3   How do you identify the skills that people need to work here?
4   How do you expect/encourage those who work here to gain the skills required?
5   How do you find out about training provision, if at all?
6   How do you gauge the success of your 'on-the-job' training?
7   For 'off-the-job' training, what are the issues that you have come up against when trying to set training needs against other needs?
8   What support have you been able to get in promoting staff development?
9   Does your company have a formal training strategy? If so, how is this strategy identified and put into effect?
10 Does your company have a training manager? If so, how does their job fit within the overall management of the enterprise?
11 Does your company have a training budget? If so, how is this calculated and allocated?
12 Do you or your company have 'networked' computing facilities (most particularly the ability to access the World Wide Web on your computer/computers)? If so, who uses them, how did they get trained, do others working here learn from them, and what is it that these machines are used for?
13 If you were able to ask for tailor-made training, what is it that you would ask for, and how would you like it to be delivered?
14 When you need to know something about training, who are the people you talk to (for example, friends, people you work with, local agencies, government bodies, local and national associations)?

Question types

Questions may be of a number of different types (see Box 6.3). Warm-up questions seek to establish trust and rapport with the respondent. Demographic questions elicit factual data about the respondent (age, sex, occupation and so on). Core questions address key themes of the research. Prompts and probes seek to elicit additional information about a core question (for example, 'Can you say a little more about that?'). Clarifying questions seek to check the meaning of a response (for example, 'What do you mean by that?'). Clarifying questions may ask a different question that approaches the same theme from another angle. Practising the generation of core, clarifying and probing questions and so on increases the ability of the researcher to react creatively to the answers they are given. Just as in music, practising the elements better enables the performer to play 'spontaneously' and in tune with those around them.

QUESTION ORIENTATION

1 Warm-up questions to establish rapport.
2 Demographic questions.
3 Core questions covering all key themes within the research question.
4 Prompts and probes to elicit more detail and depth than are initially forthcoming.
5 Clarifying questions to check interviewee's understandings of what they have been asked.

Piloting

Once the researcher has generated a set of questions relating to each of the key themes, it is necessary to pilot these questions (see Boxes 6.4, 6.5). These questions are the basis for the researcher's interaction with their interviewees. Questions are a bridge between the two sides. Faults in the questions may lead to faulty information passing between the two sides. The first step in the piloting process will involve showing your provisional themes and questions to colleagues and experts in the field for their critical review. Second, it is important to interview a small number of people from your target population. Language is the key to the interview. It is the medium through which qualitative interview data are generated and collected. It is essential that questions be asked in a language that the interviewee can make sense of, and which is understood in the sense that the interviewer intends. An essential part of the piloting process is to conduct the interview and then talk over with the interviewee what (if anything) they understood by each question. If you are interested in what people believe, rather than their behaviour, it is important that this be clearly communicated. If you are interested in what people do rather than what they say, you have another serious issue. This concerns motivation. What motivates an interviewee to answer questions? How can the interviewer put their respondents at their ease, win their trust and gain their interest and enthusiasm? Piloting may highlight hidden resentments and

Operationalizing research questions

However much you think that you have been successful in translating the themes that make up your research question into a language that will be readily understood by the people you want to interview, it is very likely that some of the terminology you use will be unclear to those who have not read the literature you have, or who have not studied research methods as you have. As such, the process of turning your research question into a set of actual questions to ask people requires some interaction with the kinds of people you want to make up your sample.

resistances. Questions may give rise to offence. Asking people about social status, money, sexuality, religious beliefs, the success (or failure) of their children at school and so on all require the greatest tact and sensitivity.

BOX 6.5 STOP AND THINK

Gauging your target population

It is a popular claim in the mass media that nobody ever went bankrupt underestimating the intelligence of their audience. The general suggestion here is that the most successful media products (films, television programmes, newspapers, books etc.), in commercial terms at least, tend to orient towards the 'lowest common denominator'. Successful soap operas never develop plot lines that could not be understood by a typical 11-year-old. The higher the pitch, the more potential audience share you will lose. If you want to sample from across the social spectrum, in terms of age, education and other factors, you need to avoid anything that will exclude sections of that target population. Even if you are seeking to research sophisticated questions that involve complex relationships between obscure concepts, it will be the mark of your talent as a social researcher that you can translate these complexities into questions that can be readily understood. Good luck.

Understanding the question and wanting to answer are not the only potential weak points in an interview. It is possible that questions may address things that the interviewee is unable to answer. A respondent may not have access to certain kinds of information, even about themselves. Interviewing people about their own lives is not always able to generate all the detail you might wish for. People's lives are not entirely transparent even to themselves.

Finally, it is essential to ask pilot respondents whether they felt the interview was leading or biased in any way (see Box 6.7). Of course, the purpose of the interview directs it to some extent, but it is important to ask the pilot interviewees how they experienced the interview. Did they feel they were able to express their point of view effectively? Did they feel the questions asked addressed the core features of the area as they see it? There is a great danger that questions contain built-in bias. Feedback from experts, peers and pilot interviewees should be directed to this issue. Also, the tendency to introduce bias in prompts and probes is something which, at least in part, is the result of inexperience. In everyday conversation we seek to support or disagree with the person we are talking to. Whether it is in body language or in words we often encourage or discourage lines of discussion without really knowing we are doing it. It may be necessary to learn to avoid saying 'Yes' or 'No' or 'That's right!' when an interviewee comes to the end of an answer. It may be necessary to learn to say more neutral things such as 'That's interesting' or 'Can you tell me more about that?' Piloting may be an opportunity to learn about yourself in relation to the topic at hand and the people you will be interviewing, and to confront your own biases and preconceptions. Piloting also allows the researcher to gain a reasonable idea of how long interviews are likely to take. This is important when arranging interviews as locations, interviewees and interviewer need to be coordinated and informed (and in some cases booked).

The conduct of qualitative interviewing

As has been already mentioned, the interview situation is itself a social interaction. Both parties in an interview are playing roles in a situation loaded with many potential meanings (Box 6.6). The notion of interviewer bias does not simply refer to the way in which questions might be asked and how answers are responded to. Interviewer bias refers to the whole character of the interviewer and the impact this may have on the responses of the interviewee. The sex/gender, class/status, ethnicity and appearance/behaviour of the interviewer may impact on the interviewee's sense of the interview situation. This in turn may impact on their 'talk', or lack of it. The sense of social difference or distance may create tension and defensiveness. Depending upon the nature of the questions to be asked it may be more or less possible (for example) for women to interview men, middle-class interviewers to interview working-class respondents, or white researchers to interview black interviewees successfully (Box 6.7). Such interactions may generate talk that is as much the product of the dynamics of the interview situation as it is a reflection of the interviewees' everyday lives. Postmodern social theorists have suggested that all data are only ever the product of such dynamics. Others seek to identify methods of reducing such bias. One such method might be to use more than one interviewer (male and female for example). This would enable comparison of results to identify interviewer effects. Having more than one interviewer raises serious issues about interviewer training, but these are not directly relevant to this text. As beginners, you are unlikely to be asked or able to recruit your own team of interviewers.

BOX 6.6 HINTS AND TIPS

Ten commandments of interviewing

On the basis of extensive practice as a qualitative interviewer, Berg (1998: 87–8) suggests Ten Commandments of interviewing:

1. Never begin cold: always warm up with light, chatty conversation.
2. Remember your purpose.
3. Present a natural front.
4. Demonstrate aware hearing: be attentive and be seen to be so.
5. Think about appearance.
6. Interview in a comfortable place.
7. Don't be satisfied with monosyllabic answers: use probes and prompts.
8. Be respectful.
9. Practise.
10. Be cordial and appropriate.

The setting and timing of an interview may have similar implications. The researcher needs to take all these things into account when setting up interviews. It is important for the researcher to identify a time and a place where the interviewee is going to feel comfortable and where the interview itself can be conducted without interruption. This may create a tension. Naturalistic settings, such as in the interviewee's home or workplace, may have advantages of comfort and security for the interviewee (this may not always be the case). However, they are also prone to interruption. In addition, the use of recording equipment, whilst highly recommended in terms of capturing the fullness of the interaction, may be offputting to the interviewee. Professional actors train long and hard to avoid drying up when confronted with an audience or a recording device, yet it still happens. The impact of such things on interviewees should not be underestimated. All these factors make the interview a situation which the researcher has to work very hard to manage. Making the interviewee feel comfortable requires confidence, experience and sensitivity. These things can only be developed through practice. See Box 6.8 for some useful guidelines.

Any interview will be 'bracketed' by what goes before and what comes after. Contacting potential interviewees, identifying yourself, exploring the suitability of the potential participant, explaining the purpose and time requirements of the research, asking for participation, arranging time and location and so on, are all performances designed to win trust, display integrity and establish rapport. It is as well to set out an *aide-mémoire* for the recruitment process, as this interaction is very similar in nature to the interviewing it pre-empts, and is prone to many of the same pitfalls. It is essential that the right to withdraw from research, the right to informed consent and the right to confidentiality and anonymity are explained to potential interviewees in advance (see section 'Sensitivity in the conduct of research' in Chapter 2). When recruiting an interview sample from a sampling frame it is often the case that contact is made by letter (paper or electronic) when requesting participation. This letter should outline the above information clearly (for a further discussion of the construction of covering letters, see Chapter 16). You also need to arrange a place to carry out the interview (see Box 6.8).

In this sense, warming up starts long before the microphone is switched on. Creating the interview situation may involve booking rooms, arranging soft drinks and snacks (preferably non-crunchy ones, which challenge even the best tape-recorders), getting to locations in good time, having functioning recording equipment (check and check again), having all the necessary paperwork to hand (prompts, interview schedule or *aide-mémoire*, identification documents and/or any explanatory materials you may need to clarify issues with the interviewee). Maintaining all this while appearing unflustered is something that requires plenty of practice and a good bag.

In the case of informal interviews, such as conversations that crop up in the course of participant observation, all the above preparation cannot be set in motion in advance of the encounter. Nevertheless, establishing a strong sense of what you are interested in and of how to ask questions in a manner meaningful to the other person and which are not biased allow even the most spontaneous encounter to generate fruitful data. In such situations one may ask if it is possible to record the interaction (either on audiotape or on paper). However, when this is not possible it may be necessary to write extensive notes on the encounter immediately after it occurs. A good bag is essential in which to keep tape-recorder and/or paper and pen.

Once an interview gets under way, the interview schedule or set of prompts or *aide-mémoire* should allow you to set the course of the conversation without forcing the pace or direction of the talk unduly. As a beginner, you may feel more comfortable with fully scripted questions, but with practice you will gain more confidence. Confidence is most fully expressed in the ability to keep silent, or to gently encourage the respondent to carry on with what they are talking about. Being attentive to both the interviewee's talk and your own themes requires a level of skill that comes only with practice. Having a go and making mistakes is part and parcel of becoming a researcher. Don't expect to get it right first time. Your first few interviews will teach you more about yourself than about the person you are talking to. Luckily, piloting offers some scope to practise before formal data collection. And it will give the interviewee the chance to reflect, speak and ponder their answers (see Box 6.9).

BOX 6.9 HINTS AND TIPS

Let people speak, even if it takes a while to come out!

This title says really all that needs to be said, so do your best to stick to it. You may have carried out a large number of interviews and feel you know the topic, but you have to do all you can to give the interviewee the time to form and express their opinions. You are not trying to show what you know, and you must never treat an interview as an opportunity to show that you know more or better than the person you are interviewing. This might seem obvious, but it is very easy to get carried away with your own importance. Always remember that the interviewees' answers are what you are interviewing for, so this is always your absolute priority.

The length of qualitative interviews (even with the same set of questions) may vary considerably. Take spare tapes and batteries. Check your tape-recorder as a way of helping the interviewee feel comfortable (see Box 6.10). Try to book a time and a space that will allow for a degree of spillover. Nevertheless, it is respectful to avoid pushing the respondent to go beyond a loosely agreed time limit. It is useful to give an estimated time limit when arranging an interview, but suggest the need to be flexible in advance. It may be the case that you will want to speak to the same respondent again after an initial interview. This may be part of a design for cumulative interviewing, or it may be something that turns out that way. Be flexible, grateful and polite. If you find a particular respondent fascinating, tell them so at the end. If you found them deadly boring, it is better not to tell them.

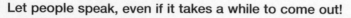

BOX 6.10 HINTS AND TIPS

Have a warm-up with the equipment

If anyone has ever come up to you at a birthday party or at a wedding and pushed a video camera in your face and asked you to say a few words or to act naturally, you will know that this will typically leave you tongue-tied and unable to remain casual and yourself. The same is often true when a researcher starts to record an interviewee. One way to overcome this anxiety is to have a quick test of the equipment, where you turn on the recorder and ask a few very simple questions ('Where were you born?', 'Can you please state your name and date of birth?' etc.). Then stop the recorder and play back the sound. This will usually elicit a nervous laugh as most people are not used to hearing the sound of their own voice, but it does have the effect of breaking the ice.

Once an interview is over and the tape-recorder is switched off, ask the interviewee what they felt about the interview. This may elicit very valuable material, both about the subject being researched and about the handling of the interview itself. Both types of information may be more freely given once the tape-recorder is turned off, and you may want to ask if you can take a few notes. If this request is made in terms of how useful the interviewee's comments would be to the research, and to the researcher, it is usually not a problem, but this is not always true and consent should never be taken for granted. After thanking the interviewee, and separating, it is essential that you write down your own experiences of the interview. This gives you the chance to reflect upon the strengths and weaknesses of your own practice, and allows you to identify things that might be improved upon, as well as emerging themes to build into future data collection. It is also insurance against a faulty tape-recorder.

The recording, transcribing and storage of qualitative interviews

All forms of data collection are prone to complications. One of the key features of qualitative interviewing is that the direction and duration of the interview are relatively open. As such the interviewer needs to be prepared for an interview that may go on for longer than initially expected. Always take additional tapes if you are going to record an interview. Also, as has been mentioned, check your recording equipment (see Box 6.11).

BOX 6.11 HINTS AND TIPS

Always check your recording equipment!

As a researcher, one of the authors was once asked to carry out a set of interviews. The project director was confident that his tape-recorder was very sturdy and reliable. It had been up mountains, into swamps and through forests and thickets. In the event the first interview, when played back, sounded as though it had been conducted in a combination of all the above locations. A new tape-recorder was immediately acquired.

The same person conducted a focus group interview. It took some time to arrange. Sadly, it was forgotten that the microphone had a separate on/off switch in addition to the record button on the tape-recorder itself. Apart from handwritten notes of the event, the discussion was lost. It is always a good idea to take some written notes during an interview and to write up your experiences as soon as the interview is over. It is an even better idea to turn your microphone on. Best of all, do both!

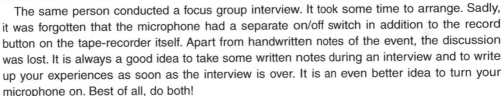

Transcription of interview data is time consuming and often highly taxing. Even with a good transcribing machine it is still likely to take between three and six times as long to transcribe an interview as it took to record. If there is a lot of background noise or if the voices are not clear on the tape, you can add extra time. It is possible to get transcription done for you by a professional typist, but this is expensive and takes you one step away from your own data. The hours of listening required to transcribe a tape are often the best way of gaining a fine-grained knowledge of your own data. While software can now assist you in qualitative data analysis it cannot bypass the need to have a feel for the talk, which only time can provide.

Always keep in mind that in-depth interview data are rich in the personal details of those from whom they are collected. As such there are ethical implications to be considered when storing them in a form that others may be able to access. It is worth recalling that it is best practice to ensure that personal identifiers are separated from other data and stored in a separate format (see Chapter 2).

Summary

Interview techniques (whether one-to-one or group based) seek to draw inferences about social life from talk generated in research-driven encounters. Qualitative interviewing requires the researcher to pay great attention to the nature of the questions they ask and the place and time in which they set their interactions. This attention is to ensure a balance between the researcher's focus of attention and the priorities and interpretations of those being interviewed. The ability to ask open questions and to create an open environment in which respondents feel comfortable to answer comprises a difficult and complex set of achievements. A balance between the researcher's prior agenda and the interviewee's own interpretation of the topic has to be struck. How far the researcher's initial sequence of questions remains in that order, the extent to which these questions are all included, and whether the questions are always posed in exactly the same way, will depend upon how much the researcher wants to retain their initial conception of 'the topic' and how far they wish to be led into an exploration of the alternative constructions held by interviewees. The same issue will determine how standardized the questions asked ought to be. Always remember that an interview is a human relationship and not a one-way street.

 **Questions**

1 What issues need to be addressed when designing interview questions and interview schedules?
2 What are the main types of question to be found in an interview schedule or *aide-mémoire*?
3 The interviewer's presence causes more harm than good. Discuss.

Further reading

Collins, P. (1998) 'Negotiating selves: reflections on "unstructured" interviewing', *Sociological Research Online*, 3 (3). www.socresonline.org.uk/3/3/2.html.

Harding, J. (2006) 'Questioning the subject in biographical interviewing', *Sociological Research Online*, 11 (3). www.socresonline.org.uk/11/3/harding.html.

Kvale, S. (2009) *Interviews: An Introduction to Qualitative Research Interviewing*, 2nd edn. London: Sage.

Silverman, D. (2006) *Interpreting Qualitative Data*, 3rd edn. London: Sage. Chapter 4.

SEVEN

FOCUS GROUPS

Chapter Contents

Aims

By the end of this chapter you will be able to:

- **Identify the origins and diversity of focus group research.**
- **Weight the ethical and practical pros and cons of this method.**
- **Balance the relative merits of naturalistic and researcher composed groups.**
- **Distinguish group designs for opinion and group dynamic research.**
- **Evaluate the pros and cons of homogeneous and heterogeneous groups.**
- **Engage with the pragmatics of organization, moderation and recording.**

Focus group interviewing

Some research questions can best be addressed by actually asking people questions directly (in interviews or questionnaires). Other topics may be better suited to more unobtrusive or observation-based methods. When asking questions directly, it may not always be best to ask these questions in a one-to-one interview format. Sometimes asking a group of people to discuss a question, or a set of questions, may generate more useful and interesting data. An example of a focus group interview prompt sheet is given in Box 7.1.

BOX 7.1

FOCUS GROUP INTERVIEW PROMPT SHEET

Dr Mike Sheaff, School of Sociology, Politics and Law, University of Plymouth, UK

Interview schedule

Italicized headings and questions in bold indicate the main themes and focus for the discussion at each stage. Subsequent questions in parentheses are illustrative follow-up questions.

Introduction

Focus of project on inter-professional relationships within multi-disciplinary team working in the field of learning disability – discussions being conducted in three locations. Interest in work relationships and systems – not interpersonal relationships. Project organized through the University of Plymouth on behalf of the South West Association of Learning Disability. Confidentiality and right to withdraw. Informal, semi-structured, discussion.

Experiences

What difference has the co-location of teams meant for your own work?
(Do you think client experiences have changed?)
(What have been the positive and negative aspects of the change?)
(Have there been differences within the team – for example, between different professional or administrative groups?)

Relationships

What impact has the changed system had on work relationships within the team?
(Are professional boundaries and roles less clearly defined?)
(What changes have occurred in communication and understanding within the team?)
(What have been the benefits and difficulties in having a single manager across disciplines?)

Change process

What involvement did you have in the process of change?
(Was any involvement as an individual or as a team?)
(Were there any particular problems or issues that arose?)

General

How would you assess the changed working arrangements overall?

Form and function

The focus group is a group interview rather than the more stereotypical one-to-one interview. Formally developed in the social sciences in the 1940s, the focus group method of data collection was taken up mainly in market research in the decades that followed. The focus group has become more popular again in the social sciences only since the 1980s. The focus group takes a number of forms. While this diversity has led some to argue over what should and should not be counted as a focus group, David L. Morgan (1997) argues that such debate is not helpful and it is most useful to reflect on what form best suits the research you want to carry out. Focus groups may be relatively highly structured to generate data that can easily be compared with those from other focus group interviews (with different types of interviewees). This enables strong comparison between the groups selected to participate. Focus groups may be relatively unstructured to enable exploration rather than strict comparability. Those selected to participate in the interview may be experts in their field. Such interviews are designed to elicit debate at the cutting edge of that particular field, and these focus groups are called Delphi groups. Other groups consist of non-experts. Such groups may be made up of individuals with certain common characteristics (age, gender, ethnicity or class, for example). This enables the researcher to compare the characteristics of these groups with reference to the issues being discussed by comparing the discussions in different groups. Alternatively, the groups may be made up of individuals with a diverse array of characteristics. This may enable the study of how such differences play off against each other in the individual group interviews. Groups may vary in size. Groups may be made up of strangers or of people who already know each other. Groups may be assembled by the researcher, or the researcher may 'take advantage' of naturally occurring group interactions, which they may either intervene in or observe more passively. Of course, presence in a group may have an effect; therefore no observation is totally passive.

The purpose of focus groups is to use the interaction between a group of interviewees to generate discussion about a topic. This discussion, it is hoped, will be more detailed and wide ranging than would result from a one-to-one interview. Focus group interviews also hold out the possibility of giving the interviewees greater control of the talk as they bounce off each other, rather than simply with the interviewer. The focus group then works by means of creating a group dynamic. This dynamic (people feeding off each other) may be a means to an end, a way of generating more data on the topic being discussed. Alternatively, the group interview may seek to study group dynamics as a social phenomenon in itself. How do individuals react to others? How might consensus or conflict emerge in a group? What is the role of leaders in group opinion formation? These are fascinating questions. However, group dynamics in focus groups tends to be the means to other ends (getting data about topic X), rather than being the subject of study in itself. This is unfortunate, as much of the debate over the value of focus group methods hinges on whether group dynamics generates depth or bias.

The focus group is used in a number of ways. It may be used as a piloting device to explore a topic area or to investigate the validity of a survey that is being prepared.

It may be used as a post-primary research tool, to clarify results generated by other means. Alternatively, the focus group may be used as a part of a multi-method approach. Also there is the use of the focus group to study group dynamics (as mentioned above). Finally, focus groups can be used as a means of consciousness raising; here research is designed not simply to increase the researcher's knowledge of the group being studied, but to increase the group's understanding of themselves (see Chapter 2). It can be argued that the focus group is democratic and participatory, giving more power to the interviewees. The ethics of focus groups are discussed in the next section along with the advantages and disadvantages in general.

The advantages and disadvantages of focus groups: ethical and practical

The long-standing and extensive use of focus groups in market research, and their more recent adoption by political parties looking to tailor their language and policies to 'key' voter groups (those most likely to switch their votes), have led many to suspect focus groups of being a cheap and superficial device, open to abuse in:

- selecting participants
- directing discussion
- interpreting responses in a biased fashion.

All three abuses exist, and it is not in the power of textbook authors to change the motives and manipulations of those who would abuse research for economic or political advantage. That similar abuses can be effected in the design of public opinion and marketing questionnaires (through the use of leading questions, unrepresentative samples and selective interpretation of results) does suggest that the problem is with the user, not with the method used.

While focus groups offer the ethical advantage of giving the participants greater control over the direction of the discussion, the ethical downside is that given the group nature of the talk, the researcher is unable to offer the degree of confidentiality available in a one-to-one interview format. This may have more than just ethical implications, as members of the group may not give full accounts of sensitive issues in such a setting, thus weakening the depth validity of any data collected.

As mentioned above, the group interview offers the advantage of allowing the talk of members of the group to stimulate other members of the group. However, there is the danger that dominant individuals within a group may control the discussion, either in terms of setting the tone or in terms of the amount of time they spend talking. This may lead to a discussion in which less dominant individuals either don't say very much or tend to go along with the views of more vocal participants. This possibility requires that the focus group leader (often referred to as the facilitator or moderator) works hard to counter the dominance of particular individuals in the group (Box 7.2). It may be the case that the facilitator can use the strong opinions of one participant to draw out alternative views from others. This requires that the facilitator be prepared to intervene. Just as in the one-to-one interview where the use of prompts and probes can be used to keep a fairly open-ended dialogue within the broad boundaries of the researcher's remit, so even a fairly unstructured focus group may require a strong degree of management. This involves setting ground rules before the discussion gets under way so that the group can, in part, manage itself. Degrees of self-management or facilitator intervention vary. The need for ground rules does not (see Box 7.4 for a basic set of such rules). The focus group is not an open forum.

BOX 7.2 STOP AND THINK

What do you want to get out of your focus group data?

It is essential to ask yourself what you want from a focus group. To allow dominant voices to direct the discussion may be highly problematic if what you really want is to know what each person came to the group thinking, but if you are interested in group dynamics, then allowing dominance to emerge is not a problem. If you want to see how prior beliefs change in group discussion then you would need an initial period where the moderator controlled the discussion to ensure that everyone expressed their view. This would be followed by a period where the group was given a freer rein to develop as it will. At the end it might be necessary for the moderator to close down the discussion and encourage each individual to speak so as to gauge how individual expressions might have changed.

Another related issue is the way different groups may generate different responses. If the group know each other this may have effects on what they say or don't say. There is evidence that men say different things about women if there are women in the group, and vice versa (Wight, 1994, cited in Morgan, 1997: 12). People brought together as members of a particular group are more likely to conform to stereotypical characteristics that are associated with that group (Morley, 1980). The tension between a group dynamic that encourages group identification and one that encourages differentiation cannot easily be resolved. The next section on group composition and size will seek to address the issue in more detail.

Once the focus group facilitator recognizes the need to 'manage' the group dialogue, they must confront the danger of the group tending towards pleasing the facilitator in their discussion. While the facilitator may wish to avoid letting dominant individuals in the group enforce a pre-emptive consensus, they must also avoid the tendency of imposing their own 'correct' responses, even as they still seek to set the broad framework for discussion. This requires a high degree of preparation in setting out prompts and probes that are stimulating but which do not direct the group to one opinion or another. Just as with any research instrument, designing good questions is as important as getting them answered.

Focus groups are not a cheap and quick data collection method. They require a great deal of preparation and organization. Data are also hard to record, transcribe and analyse. However, such groups do offer a way of talking to a number of people at the same time, and getting them to interact may stimulate insights. One hour spent with eight people (group size will be discussed shortly) may generate more data than one hour spent with one person. However, one hour spent with eight people in a focus group does not generate as much detail as eight one-hour interviews with eight individuals. Fern (1982) found that a focus group generated only about 70 per cent of the 'original ideas' that were generated by a set of one-to-one interviews with the same number of individuals. Of course, this still means that one focus group interview generates more ideas than a single one-to-one interview, but a focus group with eight participants is not equivalent to eight separate interviews.

Composition and size

The central questions around focus group composition are:

- Strangers or existing groups?
- Homogeneity or heterogeneity?
- Naturalistic or researcher constructed?
- Group size?

Strangers or existing groups?

If a focus group is made up of people who know each other already, there is the possibility that existing knowledge of each other will enable members of the group to feel comfortable with the group environment and so feel at ease when talking. This may make the discussion easier. However, there is always the danger that such a group will take each other for granted. In one sense this is an advantage, as members will not have to take time to 'settle in' to the discussion. The danger is that members will be 'too settled'. This may lead to a conversation where too much is taken for granted and so not expressed. While being confronted with strangers may at first be a challenge to individual members, it is this very challenge that encourages exploration of assumptions and beliefs. Such a challenging environment requires careful management by the facilitator, but is generally regarded as a more productive environment for data collection (Box 7.3). The facilitator must encourage participants to feel comfortable, but not so comfortable that they feel they have nothing to add. Another factor that might inhibit open discussion is the desire not to disclose sensitive information to people you know, and who may pass such revelations on to others in the participants' social networks. As already mentioned, this is an ethical as well as a data collection issue. Once again it is generally agreed that 'stranger' groups offer less fear of embarrassment and so are a richer and more ethical means of data collection. This is not to say that groups who know each other cannot be useful, especially in the context of case study research and ethnography, where the focus of the research is a particular group and where focus groups might be adopted as a means of supplementing other methods. In expert focus groups (Delphi groups) it is harder to bring people together who are not in some way already known to each other (as being an expert in a field usually entails an awareness of other experts). In such situations it is essential that the researcher reflects on the dangers and difficulties outlined above in order to minimize both the ethical and the methodological weaknesses. Again, this will often involve setting ground rules and creating a non-confrontational environment. One such ground rule would be for participants to sign up to an agreement to respect the confidentiality of other participants (see section 'Structure, organization and location' later in this chapter).

BOX 7.3 STOP AND THINK

Question the easy option

It is far easier for a researcher to work with existing groups, especially where such groups regularly meet to discuss things. In these cases, the researcher already has most of their preparation work done for them. All they need to do is gain consent to attend the group and to put some questions to them. If a researcher wishes to carry out totally naturalistic focus groups, they would attend meetings where particular topics are to be discussed and they would not even have to intervene. However, the downside of existing groups is that the researcher has less control over the group and the direction of the questions. The way members of the group respond will rely on prior knowledge of each other, and the researcher will not know what this prior knowledge is. As such, whilst it is easier to get started, such a strategy will produce data that are harder to analyse. Unless you are particularly keen to generate data about a particular group of people, the extra effort of creating your own groups will most often be worth it. That is, of course, if you have the time and other resources to do so.

Homogeneity or heterogeneity?

The dynamics of a group will be affected by the degree to which participants are selected as representatives of a particular category of people. However, these effects are not fully predictable. Set in a group of women, a single male may adopt a less masculine tone than might be the case if he was in an all-male group. However, the reverse may be true, as being the only male may encourage him to take a more 'masculine' tone. Morgan (1997: 12) cites Wight's findings that young males expressed more 'macho' attitudes towards women in all-male groups than was found in mixed groups. Is it the case that one of these results is true, while the other is false? Does one of the group compositions get to the real, while the other encourages the men to disguise their true feelings? Perhaps these young men have mixed feelings! Perhaps such beliefs are context specific and not fixed outside social interaction. David Morley's

(1980) study of audience interpretation of the UK news and current affairs programme 'Nationwide' used relatively homogeneous focus groups to represent different social groups (for example, separate groups for trade unionists, managers and Afro-Caribbeans). While the groups appeared to interpret the same programmes in very different ways, were these expressions as much the product of the group identity given to them in the interview situation as the product of their 'true' beliefs? Does such a group environment realistically capture the everyday dynamics of opinion formation? Are people's everyday lives and communities so homogeneous? If young males spend most of their time interacting with other young males, a focus group of young males may best capture the everyday social dynamics of opinion formation. If young males spend most of their time in mixed groups, then a mixed group may be more appropriate. In this regard the question of homogeneity or heterogeneity in focus group composition is one of naturalism: does the group come close to the everyday dynamics of interaction or is it artificial? If you feel the issue at hand is one that is likely to be highly open to peer pressure, you may prefer one-to-one interviews, or you may use focus groups to study consensus formation and pressure to conform. In this latter situation, the data you would be interested in are not the attitudes expressed, but the processes of interaction that led them to be said. The question of naturalism takes us on to the use and usefulness of self-generated groups.

Naturalistic or researcher constructed?

If it is advantageous for a focus group's composition, at least in part, to reflect the composition of everyday interaction, it might seem obvious that naturalistic focus groups (where the researcher arranges to conduct their focus group interviews with pre-existing groups) would be the ideal focus group form. Naturalistic focus groups do not require the researcher to create the group, and members will usually be easier to bring together than would a group of strangers. Members are familiar and so will find it easier to talk to each other. The researcher is not imposing an identity on the group. The group has already identified itself. The boundary between naturalistic focus groups and ethnographic observation is highly porous. Attending group meetings (whether these be, for example, in the study of social movements, patient self-help groups or sports supporters), and addressing questions to those groups rather than to individuals, comes close to naturalistic focus group interviewing. However, as has been noted, there are ethical and validity difficulties in interviewing groups who already know each other. These difficulties need to be weighed against the potential bias that may be introduced by the artificial construction of a group. Such a balancing of ethical, practical and methodological issues is inevitable. There is no one blueprint to fit all situations.

Group size?

David Morgan (1997: 34) suggests that, in the conduct of social research, groups of between 6 and 10 people work best. Market researchers have tended to use larger groups (8–12). It is generally suggested that the more group members know about or are motivated by the topic at hand, the smaller the group needs to be. Expert focus groups (Delphi groups) may have only four participants, but are likely to have a lot to say and are likely to be able to feed off the comments of others more readily. Groups of consumers discussing their experience of a new product may have less to say, so a larger group, if well managed, may be better. Smaller groups are more challenging to participants as there is greater pressure to contribute, while larger groups offer greater opportunity to sit back and not say much. The latter case requires that the moderator acts to involve all participants and to avoid individuals coming to dominate the discussion (unless the research is more concerned with group dynamics and leadership in opinion formation than with individual opinions).

Structure, organization and location

The conduct of effective focus group research requires well-organized sampling, a well-prepared interview guide or *aide-mémoire*, clear instructions for the participants, and an environment (both physical and social) that will enable dialogue and recording. Sampling methods will depend upon the nature of the subject groups you wish to recruit. If a random sample can be drawn, this has many advantages (see Chapter 14). However, this is not always possible and the whole range of alternative sampling methods, used in social research generally, is equally applicable in the context of focus group research. If you wish to recruit a group with a particular range of characteristics, you will need to use a stratified sampling method (whether random or not). The choice will depend upon the goals of the research, the nature of the groups sought, and the practicalities of the particular situation. Wilkinson (1998) suggests the precautionary principle of over-recruitment, due to the added complexity in group interviewing of getting all members of the group to arrive at the same location at the same time. If you are hoping to conduct a group interview of seven people, it is best to recruit eight or even nine to be safe.

Again as in other forms of interview-based research, the production of an interview schedule/guide or *aide-mémoire* is essential, and again, as in qualitative interviewing more generally, the extent to which this is structured or relatively unstructured will depend on the interest of the researcher. The extent to which the moderator wishes to structure the flow of talk will determine the nature of the schedule/guide. The situation where the researcher sits in on naturalistic group discussions and hardly intervenes at all represents an extreme. However, this may not be considered a focus group at all by many. It may better be described as straightforward ethnography. The inexperienced focus group moderator will tend to require a tighter hold on events, as they have developed fewer of the subtle interview management skills that come with practice. As such, the inexperienced focus group moderator is best advised to have a relatively well-structured interview schedule, even if they should be careful not to use such a security blanket too dogmatically. Experience enables flexibility.

In addition to a well-thought-out interview guide, it is often useful to prepare 'stimulus materials'. These may include video materials, paper-based materials, objects, photographs or even spoken presentations. Where participants cannot be expected to be highly informed and/or highly motivated about the topic of interest to the researcher, it is often useful to provide some introductory background to the issue to generate interest and reflection. Of course, this requires attention to the danger of bias in the material presented. Often it is advisable to present material explicitly as a range of perspectives, rather than to give the impression that these are 'the facts'.

Clear instructions to participants are essential. This has been mentioned already with reference to the ethics of confidentiality, but it is essential that the participants be given certain ground rules that will enable the discussion to run smoothly, and to allow recording (see Box 7.4). These instructions need to be clearly outlined in advance. This will aid greatly in encouraging the group to regulate itself. This leaves the moderator with less need to intervene, except in introducing the research themes.

BOX 7.4 HINTS AND TIPS

Basic ground rules for focus group participants

(adapted from Berg, 1998: 115)

1   Only one person should speak at a time.
2   No subgroup discussions.
3   Allow others to speak.
4   Respect the right of others to express views that are not your own.
5   Speak clearly.
6   Respect the confidentiality of other members of the group.

Setting ground rules is essential in the creation of a positive environment in which participants feel comfortable in expressing their views. Also essential in the creation of a positive environment is the choice of interview location (and timing). Not only is it essential to secure a location that is quiet, it is also important to identify a time and a place that are convenient to those whom you wish to participate. This requires some level of background research into the routines and commitments of those you seek to recruit, or of those you have provisionally recruited. Morgan (1997: 55) offers the useful reminder that a table, which everyone can sit around, is an essential aspect in the choice of location. Finally, it is often useful to lay on soft drinks and snacks. If you are conducting organizational research and wish to interview a group of people from a particular organization, it may be useful to use lunch breaks as a time when groups can get together. In such situations you may want to provide a light lunch to compensate. It is best here not to lay on crunchy food as this may interfere with recording.

Conduct and management

How long should a focus group meeting be? Focus groups vary in duration from around 45 minutes to 90 minutes, though the more open-ended discussions may last for up to two hours. The greater the number of themes and the more open ended the form of discussion, the longer the focus group will tend to be. When recruiting participants and securing the location, it is important to have a clear idea of how much time will be needed. Preparation, outlining the ground rules and dealing with any issues that might need to be dealt with at the end of the session all add to the required time. When conducting focus groups for the first time it is usual to opt for shorter sessions. For a 45-minute discussion it is realistic to inform participants that they will need to 'give' you around 90 minutes of their time. It is advisable to book your location for a longer period again.

Once a group has been constructed and brought together, the tape-recorder has been set up, turned on and checked, and the purpose and ground rules of the discussion have been outlined, the moderator has to manage the event itself. It is useful to have a second researcher who takes charge of recording and takes a second set of notes on the proceedings, as this frees the moderator to engage fully with the group. However, this is not always possible.

Moderator involvement with the group takes a number of forms and serves a number of purposes. The first question is the level moderator involvement. If the research is primarily interested in the dynamics of group interaction and influence, it is likely that moderator involvement will be kept to a minimum. If the primary aim is to elicit the opinions and experiences of the individual participants, it is likely that the moderator will take a more active role in encouraging all to speak and in curbing the more dominant participants. The researcher needs to ask themselves where on the spectrum between individual expression and group process their interest lies (Figure 7.1).

The moderator needs to listen carefully in order to identify where the discussion is going, in order both to take notes on what is being said and to direct the flow if necessary. Careful listening will often allow the moderator to direct the flow of talk along the broad lines they are interested in by picking up on comments and feeding these back to the group. This avoids the need for blunt redirections. Of course, the flow of talk will not always present the moderator with such opportunities, but the more attentive the listening, and the better the note-taking, the greater the likelihood that such opportunities will not be lost. The degree to which such opportunities are taken advantage of will, of course, depend on the degree to which the researcher seeks to follow a relatively narrow focus (with the need to keep things on track) or wishes to keep things open. This will depend on the research question being asked and the way it has been formulated.

How are questions to be asked? The best advice is to ask about experiences and opinions rather than about facts. Questions should encourage reflection and exploration. This may best be elicited by asking about the context in which certain experiences occurred and where certain opinions developed. The moderator may

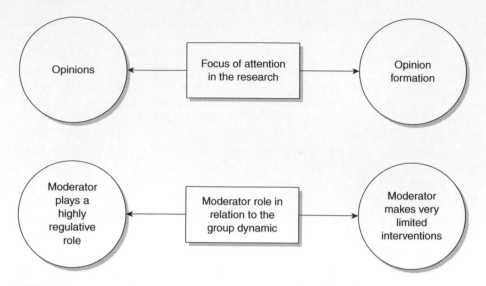

FIGURE 7.1 How tight a rein should you keep on the group?

highlight contrasts in the accounts given and ask the group to reflect upon these. The moderator needs to be careful here not to give priority or support to one opinion or experience over another. It is important in this context for the moderator to avoid playing the part of an interviewer. This means avoiding one-to-one discussions between the moderator and individual participants (though single questions can be directed towards specific individuals).

The flow of the discussion can best be set in motion with icebreakers and warm-up questions. These need to be easy and everyone needs to be brought into the process of 'getting to know each other'. From such easy questions it is then possible to move towards general themes. From these, it is hoped that leads may emerge that the moderator is then able to reintroduce to the group at a later point. The movement from general themes to particular issues is important, as the reverse may close off debate or direct it too readily in one direction rather than another.

Drawing a focus group to a close is best facilitated with a round-up, where each person is asked to contribute their experience of the session and the things they feel have emerged. This is a useful data collection device: it brings the event to a close and it allows the participants a sense of closure. It is also an opportunity for the moderator to identify any last points that may need elaboration before things are wound up.

How many focus groups are needed? Morgan (1997: 43) cites the arguments of Zeller (1993) for social science research and Calder (1977) in marketing. Both claim that more than five focus groups with similar members rarely generate more significantly new data than can be generated by three to five groups. The variation between three and five will depend upon the composition of the group and the level of structure. The more diverse the group composition and the more open ended the structure, the greater the number of groups required. The 'three to five' rule of thumb applies to research into one segment of the population. Of course, many research projects will seek to compare the beliefs and experiences of different segments of the population (such as between older and younger people or between men and women). In such instances it would be ideal to carry out three to five focus groups with each segment. Some research would seek to use mixed groups rather than homogeneous groups. In the case of researching the attitudes of males and females, one could opt for either five mixed groups or six single-sex groups (three male, three female). Perhaps in this case it would be best to conduct three male, three female and two mixed, if resources allowed. If one was interested in age and gender, one would need more groups still as the number of segments starts to multiply once you introduce more variables. Just dividing 'age' crudely into 'young' and 'old', and crossing this with male and female, would generate four segments (young male, young female, old male and old female), and this would require at least 12 focus groups if Morgan's formula were applied dogmatically. However, for practical reasons, this multiplication is rarely fully adhered to. Morgan (1997) cites Calder's (1977) suggestion that the number of focus groups actually carried out should not be determined strictly by a formula. Rather, the researcher should apply the grounded theory method of gauging *saturation* as they move from one focus group to the next (see section 'Degrees of grounded theory and sampling in qualitative research' in Chapter 5). Saturation is the realization that after so long the researcher begins to be able to predict what will come out in the next group. Once the researcher comes to hear nothing significantly new from one session to the next, the purpose of continuation starts to diminish.

Recording and transcription

Good quality tape-recording is essential, but it is also important to write notes during the conduct of the sessions, both for the management of the discussion and to enable immediate reflections after the group has ended. Good notes and a written summary of the researcher's experiences and reflections immediately after the session enable the researcher to transcribe more easily (especially where parts of the dialogue are unclear on the recording). When the moderator is not the person transcribing, such notes and comments can be equally useful. Transcription is a very time-consuming process. A professional transcriber may require at least three times the duration of the session to transcribe its recording, and a non-professional may take twice as long again. As is the case with one-to-one interview recording, the temptation to get a professional to do the transcription (to save time) should be tempered by the fact that time spent transcribing is a very useful way for a researcher to 'get close' to the data (Box 7.5). Knowing every word of the conversation is a great advantage when it comes to qualitative data analysis.

BOX 7.5 HINTS AND TIPS

Getting a feel for the data

Transcribing a focus group is very hard work. Unlike in a one-to-one interview where the microphone can be located in the optimal position to pick up on the interviewee's voice, in a focus group there will be many voices, all coming from slightly different places. This is another reason why the person transcribing the interview is often best being the person who carried out the focus group, as they will have the best chance of decoding any obscure expressions. This is another reason why it is useful for the moderator or their assistant to take notes. If some part of the discussion is hard to make out on the recording (you can be sure that someone's chair will squeak just at the point where something valuable is being said) then those notes, and the experience of the event that such notes will reinforce, will be extremely valuable. In addition, transcribing the recording of a focus group is one of the best ways to get really close to the discussion and to pick up on the subtle developments and processes at work in the discussion. The time taken to transcribe words and sentences is like watching something in slow motion.

Summary

Focus groups should not be seen as cheap and quick ways of conducting 8 to 12 interviews when you don't have enough time to carry out the same number of one-to-one interviews. Rather, focus groups have a particular value in researching the views of individuals in context, or the dynamics of opinion formation in groups. The time it takes to organize a focus group should be taken into account, as coordinating a group of people to be in the same place at the same time is often harder (and takes longer) than it would take to see each of those individuals on their own. Focus groups can be likened to qualitative experiments, where the researcher sets out a range of controlled conditions (the content of the group, the questions to be asked and the way they manage the interaction). Such control is at odds with some commonly assumed features of qualitative research, and as such highlights the multiple and ambiguous meanings of the term. More naturalistic forms of focus group come closer to all the common features of qualitative research, but not all social researchers would consider the recording of a naturally occurring group discussion as a focus group at all. The thing to remember about focus groups is that they serve a number of useful purposes, but cannot be used for everything. You have to be aware of the potentials and the limits when choosing whether to adopt such an approach and whether to adopt a relatively regulated or unregulated approach to group dynamics.

Questions

1 What are the relative merits and limitations of one-to-one interviews and focus group methods of data collection?

2 What are the ethical grounds on which a researcher might choose between one-to-one and focus group interviews, and how do such grounds relate to the questions they are seeking to research?

3 What issues need to be considered when deciding how to sample and structure the participants within focus groups, and how do these factors affect the researcher's choices for focus group composition?

▉ ▉ Further reading ▉

Fern, Edward F. (1982) 'The use of focus groups for idea generation: the effects of group size, acquaintanceship, and moderator on response quantity and quality', *Journal of Marketing Research*, 19: 1–13.

Morgan, David, L. (1997) *Focus Groups as Qualitative Research*. London: Sage.

Morgan, David L. (1998) *The Focus Group Guidebook*. London: Sage.

Wilkinson, Sue (1998) 'Focus groups in feminist research: power, interaction and the co-production of meaning', *Women's Studies International Forum*, 21 (1): 111–25.

EIGHT

ETHNOGRAPHY

Aims

By the end of this chapter you will be able to:

- **Define ethnography and identify its historical roots.**
- **Identify the key stages in the conduct of ethnographic research.**
- **Specify the strengths and limitations of ethnographic research.**
- **Understand the relationship between ethnography and related research designs.**
- **Understand the relationship between the range of different data collection methods that can be deployed within the broader ethnographic methodology.**

What is ethnography?

Berg (1998: 120) cites a range of definitions of ethnography: 'unfettered or naturalistic enquiry' (Lofland, 1996: 30); 'cultural description' (Wolcott, 1973); 'thick description' (Geertz, 1973); and 'subjective soaking' (Ellen, 1984). Hammersley (1998: 2) suggests five central aspects of ethnography:

- the study of people's behaviour in everyday contexts
- largely based upon informal observation and conversation
- being relatively unstructured
- using a small number of cases
- offering more description than causation.

John Brewer writes:

> Ethnography is the study of people in naturally occurring settings or 'fields' by methods of data collection which capture their social meanings and ordinary activities, involving the researcher participating directly in the setting if not also in the activities, in order to collect data in a systematic manner but without meaning being imposed. (2000: 6)

Ethnography is based upon a belief in the value of naturalistic methods of data collection in natural settings. Ethnography involves time spent 'within' a culture or group. This location 'within' leads to it often being referred to as field research. Ethnography often involves living with those the researcher is studying, and this living may involve the researcher living as a participant within that field. As such, some ethnography is called participant observation. Not all field research or ethnography involves the researcher in taking a role as participant, though the line between participation and non-participation is often, perhaps always, blurred. Not all ethnographic data collection is based upon observation (as participant or not). Ethnographic data collection may involve interviews and the use of documentary sources. As such the term 'ethnography' covers a wider range than the term 'participant observation', which may be one aspect of an ethnographic project.

Ethnography can be deductive (designed to test a specific hypothesis), but tends to be inductive (theory building in the course of data collection or after). Being in the field offers great scope to explore a culture or group 'way of life'. This focus on a 'way of life' means that ethnography tends to be 'holistic' rather than 'mechanistic'. This combination of exploration and holistic interest means that the ethnographer tends towards description over causal theories as the aim of their research (Box 8.1). The word 'ethnography' is used to describe both a form of data collection (that is, field research) and a form of written account (the monograph or account of fieldwork and analysis).

BOX 8.1 CONSIDER THIS

Discovery, appreciation, immersion

Various reasons are given for the use of ethnography. These reasons circulate around three interconnected elements: discovery, appreciation and immersion. Discovery relates to the sense that ethnography exposes the researcher to the possibility of being confronted by things and ideas that they had not thought would be important at the outset. As such, discovery is linked to the idea of inductive research. Appreciation refers to the ability to understand the particular features of the lives of those you meet during ethnographic fieldwork because you are able to understand their lives in general and from the point of view of the person living that life. To this extent ethnography can be seen as an ideal method for interpretive research. If the word *verstehen* (understanding) has often been associated with the ability to stand in the other person's shoes, what better way to do that than to live as close to that other person's life as it is possible for a researcher to do? Finally, the idea of immersion relates to the sense that the researcher should seek to experience the world they are researching in a way that takes them beyond the actions of a detached researcher. Rather as when someone throws themselves into the swimming pool 'at the deep end', so the notion of immersion suggests that it is only when your feet do not touch the bottom that you can really be said to be 'in the water'. The interrelated concepts of discovery, appreciation and immersion act as regulative ideals in ethnography. Whilst it is rare for the researcher to ever fully lose touch with prior research questions, their own prior beliefs and values and their sense of being an outsider, taking on the ethnographic role places all this prior knowledge under some degree of suspicion. Having said that, the researcher who fully abandons their prior intentions and beliefs will be said to have 'gone native', and whilst this might have some advantages, it is also considered a significant problem (see Box 8.9).

Origins of ethnography

The term 'ethnography' originated in anthropology and referred to the conduct of 'fieldwork' within 'cultures' other than the anthropologist's own. This tended to mean research by white Europeans within the European colonies in Asia, Africa, Australia and New Zealand, the Pacific and the Americas. In the late nineteenth and early twentieth centuries, such research was largely carried out by colonial administrators and geographers, and focused upon what were seen to be small-scale and geographically specific 'cultures'. Such research rarely involved living as a part of that 'culture'. Bronislaw Malinowski (see Kuper, 1973: Chapter 1) established the modern ethnographic tradition in the early years of the twentieth century with his suggestion (though not always in his practice) that to live with and within a culture was the only way to really understand it.

Within sociology a similar strand of research method developed in the 1920s. The Chicago School of sociology popularized methods of researching urban life by means of time spent with people, learning about their lives, routines and experiences. This type of research paralleled early studies of urban life (for example, Henry Mayhew's studies of the life of London's poor in the late nineteenth century, reprinted 1961) but built upon them. Such research did not involve living in a faraway 'field', but did emphasize and develop field-based empirical data collection methods (Bulmer, 1984). This research tradition was often called 'participant observation' rather than 'ethnography', which was a term used mainly in anthropology. In recent decades the distinction between participant observation in the researcher's own 'society' and ethnography in the 'culture' of 'others' has broken down, even whilst the two terms are not fully synonymous. Where Malinowski proclaimed the virtues of living within the community under study, the scope to live as a member of such a culture was less than it was for a Chicago sociologist to take part in the routines of life within other parts of their own city, even if significant barriers of gender, class and ethnicity limited full participation still.

Finally, the tradition of community studies fed into the development of 'field research'. The community studies tradition sought to research specific towns, cities or regions as organic entities. Research involved time spent in the specific location, building a picture of life in that place by means of interviews, observation work and the collection of documentary sources (Bell and Newby, 1971) (Box 8.2).

BOX 8.2 RESEARCH FOCUS

The changing face of ethnography

Ethnography as a method was pioneered by Franz Boaz and Bronisław Malinowski amongst others. Boaz was a German, then American, researcher who moved from the physical sciences through geography to the study of human cultures in context. Finding himself isolated in the polar darkness of an arctic winter appears to have been a decisive moment in Boaz's development of respect for cultures deemed not to be modern. Bronisław Malinowski was a Polish-born researcher who eventually settled in London. Malinowski's trip to the Trobriand Islands (near Papua New Guinea) coincided with the outbreak of the First World War. His Polish citizenship led the Australian authorities to 'exile' him on the islands for the duration of the conflict, thus encouraging his development of the 'in-depth' approach to living amidst the group studied. Whether it was survival in harsh climes or the sophistication of supposedly 'primitive' cultures in navigating vast oceans, Boaz and Malinowski came to believe it was necessary to overcome the perception that cultures deeply different from those of academic Western researchers were simply pathological, inferior and backward. They argued the best way to achieve this was to get to know such ways of life from the inside. The 'classic' ethnographic method moved away from theorizing the reports of explorers and colonial agents to that of 'living amongst' those that were being studied. Within the sociological tradition of participant observation, William Foote Whyte's study of an Italian American 'slum' neighbourhood in Boston in the 1930s pioneered techniques similar to those developed in anthropology by Boaz and Malinowski. Whyte spend almost four years 'in the field'. The publication in 1943 of his book *Street Corner Society* documented this time, Whyte's experience and the findings that emerged out of this experience. Ethnography underwent an upsurge in British sociology in the 1970s, as part of the reaction against 'positivistic' and quantitative traditions that had dominated until that time. A classic British urban ethnography of that period was Paul Willis's study of how working-class kids get working-class jobs. Willis's monograph *Learning to Labour* (1977) documents the use of ethnographic fieldwork in a particular school over

(Continued)

(Continued)

a number of years. Willis got to know a particular group of working-class 'lads'. He sought to understand the world in which they lived and in particular how rebellion against school values of academic achievement and the celebration of its opposite, manual labour, acted to feed those working-class lads into low-paid and insecure employment. Willis brought a critical dimension to ethnography, not simply giving a voice to the underdog (such as in earlier versions of qualitative interpretive sociology). For Willis, ethnography offered a way of placing such voices in the context of the worlds out of which they emerged. Critical ethnography sought to question the power relations in operation within everyday interactions. Nigel Fielding's (1981) ethnographic study of the racist National Front party in Britain in the late 1970s was another example of critical ethnography. Fielding's research was covert, and most of the party members he interacted with had no idea that they were being studied. Unlike Boaz and Malinowski, or even Whyte or Willis, who would not have been mistaken for Italian migrants or school children, Fielding was able to blend into the research environment, and this raises serious ethical questions. In more recent years the question of 'lurking' – conducting research in public spaces where those observed are not aware of the researcher's presence or at least their researcher role – has been heightened with the large-scale development of online ethnography. The existence of discussion boards, chatrooms, web forums and social networks has created a vast array of virtual spaces in which the researcher can immerse themselves, rather (it is suggested at least) as do field researchers in alternative cultures. Christine Hine (2000), as well as Don Slater and Daniel Miller (2000), provided early examples of this new form of 'ethnography'.

The pros and cons of ethnographic methods: ethical and practical

The same ethical issues (both advantages and disadvantages) which were raised in Chapters 6 and 7 apply to ethnographic methods.

Not all 'fields' are open to the ethnographer. Some are only accessible if the researcher enters covertly (pretending to occupy a non-research role), and this presents problems. Not all aspects of life are open to routine observation (the bedroom and the past being two examples). Nevertheless, ethnography offers a powerful means of data collection and theory building. 'Being there', on location, on the inside, offers a range of opportunities which are not available to those using other methodologies such as the interview or the experiment. Field research offers the chance to see what people 'really do', not just what they say they do, or what they do in artificial situations. Of course, this assumes that people will behave naturally in their everyday circumstances, even when in the presence of a researcher. It is dangerous to overly romanticize ethnography as being a royal road to 'how things really are': the possibility of the researcher having an effect on the data they collect is common to all research strategies. Martyn Hammersley (1998) offers a useful summary of the pros and cons of ethnography. He suggests there have been three defences of the ethnographic method against those who argue that field research lacks the control, reliability and transparency of experimental forms of observation. First, naturalistic methods can be said to be more valid than methods dependent upon artificial situations when researching humans. Second, field research offers a greater scope for exploration. Finally, ethnography is useful for describing specific cases in detail and should not be criticized for not generating comparisons and generalizations if that is not its aim. Hammersley argues that the sacrifice of generalizability for depth is a legitimate tradeoff as long as the loss involved is not ignored. The inability to prove causation in the complexity of field situations may be regarded as an unacceptable limitation only if one sees experimental physics as the only model for good science (though proving causation even in laboratory physics is highly problematic) (see Box 8.3).

BOX 8.3 CONSIDER THIS

There's more to life than physics and stamp collecting

Lord Ernest Rutherford (founder of nuclear physics) famously asserted that: 'All science is either physics or stamp collecting.' This rather dismissive remark suggested that unless a science sought to reduce explanation to the lowest level possible it was merely engaged in surface descriptions of different patterns. This distinction between causal explanation at the most elementary physical level, and mere superficial description, has been largely rejected by most scientists, who accept that the organization of simpler building blocks into more complex structures both allows these structures to influence the elements from which they are composed, and creates a non-reducibility to such elements. It is unhelpful to become heavily entangled with debates over causal explanation versus ethnographic description. The complexity that can be experienced by ethnographic observation is different from the control that can be exercised within laboratory conditions over a relatively narrow set of elements. The complexity of the former makes the things observed less predictable, but this is not the same as saying that there is less 'causation'. An awareness of the reality of complexity in what makes society what it is, is not to reject causal processes as such, only to recognize the insufficiency of causal explanations that seek to boil complexity down to what can be fitted into controlled conditions. For some ethnographers, the non-reducibility of complexity is taken to mean the suspension of simple forms of causation. Human cultures are said not to be explicable in terms of any lower or prior biological or physical necessities. This is to say not that humans don't need to eat or sleep, but rather that such needs do not determine how the variety of human cultures develop, as human variety manifestly demonstrates. For some, recognition of complexity is best dealt with by accepting Rutherford's insult and inverting it, celebrating the refusal to reduce the world to physics and instead embracing description and interpretation. Other ethnographers seek to develop explanations at levels, such as language and social structure, that are still causal but which are simply not reducible to atoms.

Description may be a legitimate goal as long as description is not then falsely passed off as explanation. If one wants to investigate the possibility of a specific causal relationship, there are other methods, though ethnography may still have a part to play even in them. Interestingly, as Hammersley suggests, there are critiques of ethnography that suggest it is too scientific. The idea of naturalism as a means of getting to the truth of what is really going on can be criticized. The idea that the ethnographer can see the truth and then report it may be too simplistic. Paul Atkinson (1992) has pointed out how much ethnography relies on a naïve belief that things can be seen as they really are if you just spend enough time looking. He also points out the genre styles that characterize ethnographic writing, and which are used to convince the ethnographic monograph's reader of the researcher's account. The ethnographer is forced to use storytelling (narrative) devices and metaphorical (redescription) devices both to construct their own 'experience' and to convey that 'experience' to the reader (Box 8.4).

BOX 8.4 RESEARCH FOCUS

Being there

Sarah Delamont (2007: 205) begins her discussion of ethnography and participant observation with a quote from James Lee Burke: 'Down the canyon, smoke from meat fires drifted through the cedars and mesquite trees, and if I squinted my eyes in the sun's setting, I could almost pretend that Spanish soldiers in silver chest armor and bladed helmets or a long dead race of hunters were encamped on those hillsides. Or maybe even old compatriots in butternut brown wending their way in and out of history – gallant, Arthurian, their canister-ripped colors unfurled in the roiling smoke, the fatal light in their faces a reminder that the contest is never quite over, the field never quite ours.' Ethnography draws heavily on the ability of the ethnographer to found their claim to have experienced the situation, to have really been there. Yet, such evocative expressions of experience highlight the deep vein of interpretation such experiences carry. The combination of sensations, selections and interpretations in Burke's words might persuade us that the author has the authority of experience, but they are clearly bringing a great deal of historical and academic baggage into their viewing. The romantic linkage of past peoples including the former waves of butternut-clad ethnographers should also draw our attention to the way the ethnographer is keen to write themselves into the account. Whilst ethnography may allow the researcher to experience what it is like to be a part of another culture, it is also true that ethnography allows the researcher's experiences to become the focus of attention, even at the expense of the 'reality' they enter into. Ethnography's claim to be a form of naturalistic observation should be set against the observation that any form of writing about 'nature' will itself be 'unnaturally' composed.

Description always involves selection and interpretation. The truth of a culture, group or way of life cannot simply be passed directly into another culture's (the ethnographer's own) words, and there are almost always competing claims as to what is important, and how things are to be understood even within the group being researched. Even identifying the boundaries of 'the group' or 'culture' to be studied requires selection (Box 8.5). To talk of cultures or groups as objects with discrete boundaries is to copy the language of physics, and this is highly misleading. Ethnography, while a powerful social research approach, should not be assumed to be unproblematic. We should not be naïve about naturalism! Porter's (2002) discussion of critical realist ethnography outlines one, perhaps two, attempts to balance extremes, but such views are by no means universally accepted.

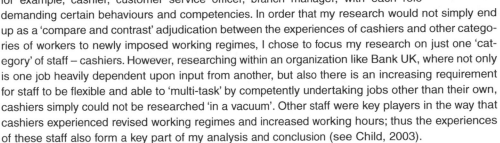

BOX 8.5 RESEARCH FOCUS

A rationale for ethnography

Dr Sue Child, School of Sociology, Politics and Law, University of Plymouth, UK

Within the archetypal domestic banking branch, staff engage in a multiplicity of jobs: for example, cashier, customer service officer, branch manager, with each role demanding certain behaviours and competencies. In order that my research would not simply end up as a 'compare and contrast' adjudication between the experiences of cashiers and other categories of workers to newly imposed working regimes, I chose to focus my research on just one 'category' of staff – cashiers. However, researching within an organization like Bank UK, where not only is one job heavily dependent upon input from another, but also there is an increasing requirement for staff to be flexible and able to 'multi-task' by competently undertaking jobs other than their own, cashiers simply could not be researched 'in a vacuum'. Other staff were key players in the way that cashiers experienced revised working regimes and increased working hours; thus the experiences of these staff also form a key part of my analysis and conclusion (see Child, 2003).

To answer questions of this nature, I used a variety of classic ethnographic data gathering techniques, for example, participant observation, interviewing, oral life histories and focus groups. Ethnography is not a particular method of data collection but 'a certain style of research distinguished by its objectives to understand the social meanings and activities of people in a given field or setting' (Brewer, 2000: 11), traditionally encompassing 'some amount of genuinely social interaction in the field with the subjects of the study, some direct observation of relevant events, some formal and a great deal of informal interviewing, some systematic counting, some collection of documents and artefacts; and open-endedness in the direction the study takes' (Fielding, 1995: 157).

'The value of adopting an ethnographic approach to workplace relations is that it can illustrate and begin to explain the complexity of social change to a degree which other research techniques cannot' (Scott, 1994: 29). Thus: 'This choice of research method may be seen as my response to the self-interrogative: "If I want to understand what it is like working under JIT [just-in-time management] and TQM [total quality management], shall I sit in my office and mail out questionnaires or shall I go and observe it, experience it, and ask people about it first hand?"' (Delbridge, 1998: 15).

Over a 16-month period from May 2000 to August 2001, I endeavoured to record every aspect of a cashier's working life, both business and social, through the adoption of a variety of ethnographic research methods: completion of field diaries, participant observation, oral life histories, increasingly focused individual and group interviews, and participation in 'out-of-work' social activities. In order to be in a position to explain events within the context in which they occurred, I chose to 'go native'. In quintessential 'Chicago School-esque' ethnographic style, I went out and 'got the seat of my pants dirty in real research' (Park, cited in Bulmer, 1984: 97). By wearing the uniform and working alongside other cashiers, enduring continuous, unwarranted public rudeness and frequent, unpleasant male sexual advances in response to the 'flirtatious' expectations of selling – all simply part of 'just doing business' for Bank UK – I strove to integrate myself as a 'useful part' of the social fabric of all my research sites. I ensured that I adopted and continuously used the dual languages of both 'bank-lingo' and the strong local colloquial language of the area, both of which served to demarcate not only those 'inside' and 'outside' the organizational culture, but also those considered 'inside' and 'outside' local social culture. In classic ethnographic style, I needed to cement relationships with people in whose natural environment I was researching, and I needed to show trust by using their language, speaking as they speak and doing as they do (Brewer, 2000: 85).

(Continued)

In order to capture 'hidden' data not apparent from the mere physical side of working, I 'bitched' and 'gossiped' in 'the ladies' – going 'backstage' with members of the team, where audiences could not see us, often ridiculing the audience in a way that was inconsistent with the face-to-face treatment normally reserved for them (Goffman, 1959: 169). I sat in various staff rooms, joining others in the escapism of lunchtime 'soaps' and dissemination of holiday brochures. Alongside fellow workers, I endured relentless sales and service directives from head office, and subjected myself to individual performance-related assessment through participation in a variety of sales-related activities, appearing to require a combination of both selling and flirting skills.

Preliminary rounds of semi-structured interviews enabled the testing of early data analysis, and as the ethnographic study developed and findings were progressively analysed, increasingly structured questions tested emergent hypotheses.

Stages in the ethnographic method

John Brewer (2000: 58) suggests a checklist for enabling open and reflexive fieldwork research:

1 Outline aims and objectives.

2 Justify choice of site and cases.

3 Identify resources and needs (time, money and so on).

4 Identify sampling scope (time, people and places).

5 Identify gatekeepers, contacts and access issues.

6 Negotiate role.

7 Identify analysis methods.

8 Exiting strategies.

These elements may shift during the course of field research, but it is useful to monitor all these elements to map change in the research strategy over time. These issues are addressed below, though not in the sequence outlined by Brewer.

Choosing a topic

In so far as ethnography tends towards inductivism, holism and naturalism, the nature of the research topic could be the exploration of the particular group, 'culture', community, organization and so on without too much further focus being set in advance. Nevertheless, ethnography, like any other form of social research, draws upon past work in the formulation of the 'who' and the 'how' as well as the 'why' questions about a research project. Choosing to engage in a 'pure' form of exploration by means of ethnographic fieldwork is slightly misleading. To choose such an approach is, in some ways, to follow in the footsteps of an established tradition and body of work, itself contained within a wealth of existing ethnographic monographs (books that detail particular fieldwork projects). The written ethnographies of earlier researchers are often what the new ethnographic researcher starts from when developing a research topic. These texts will contain details about duration of fieldwork, accessing issues, role issues as well as discussions of findings, theories that emerged and conclusions about the group studied and similarities/differences with the findings of other researchers.

Ethnographers do not always choose strictly inductive and exploratory approaches in which the topic of the research is to explore the life of one group or case without further specification or focus. A researcher may choose to study a group for specific reasons. They may be funded to research particular issues within a particular organization. This may be a form of action research, where the researcher interacts and assists the organization in addressing an issue it sees as problematic. The researcher may be keen to research a particular group because they wish to test a theory or compare particular characteristics with those found in another group, or by means of a different research method. These approaches are more deductive and specific. Ethnography is not always inductive and holistic.

Selecting cases

The selection of cases for research is intimately bound up with the nature of the topic the researcher wants to research. It is also bound up with the question of access. To a degree the selection of cases depends upon their suitability for researching the researcher's chosen topic, but the reverse is also sometimes true, that is, that the topic may be changed to fit the characteristics of the case or cases the researcher actually managed to gain access to. Brewer (2000: 76) refers to Stake's (1998: 88–9) suggestion that there are three types of case selection:

- *Intrinsic case*s are selected and studied for their own sake, without the intention to generalize from the results.

- *Instrumental cases* are selected to represent a set of similar settings. It is believed that it is possible to generalize from the findings of such cases.

- *Collective cases* are selections from different settings designed to allow comparison.

Of course, it is not just a question of choosing whom you would like to study and then going and studying them. The issue of access is highly problematic. Ernest Gellner (1992) went so far as to suggest that the debate within anthropology over whether ethnography was worthwhile, given the difficulties of translating the reality of one culture in such a way that it would be genuinely understood by another culture, has its origins in the increasing difficulty anthropologists found in getting visas to visit other societies once those societies were no longer colonies. Being unable to gain access to other cultures, many anthropologists seemed to decide that it was not really useful going there anyway. Ethnographers have found it very hard accessing elite groups in their own society, while those lower down the social scale have often been easier to gain access to. This may be said to have biased the nature of ethnographic research. Ethnography has also tended to focus upon small-scale 'places' rather than larger regions, countries and even continents. This is because it is possible to access a small location, while it is hard to observe a large space. This may lead the ethnographer to give more emphasis to micro-interactions rather than to interactions that occur over long distances. Once again, access may bias the orientation of the ethnographer. It is important to balance the advantages of ethnographic method with an awareness of its limitations.

The term 'case' within ethnography tends to be used to refer to the setting or location of the research. Cases might be a school, a village, an organization or a region. Such units would be the large-scale units of the research, the case being the space where the researcher researches, as well as being a place, the boundaries of which are set and maintained by the actions of those being researched. Such units are never fully bounded, separated social worlds unconnected and not overlapping with other places, groups and cultures. Whilst early anthropological ethnographers tended to focus on small-scale societies in relative isolation from other cultures, this was often exaggerated, and cannot possibly be conceived in contemporary sociological contexts.

Even the most bounded unit of research cannot be researched exhaustively, as the researcher has to sleep and they cannot spend every minute of every waking hour with every person and in every possible location within their field of study. As such, the researcher has to select cases within their wider case. Within the wider case the selection of more particular cases will involve some elements of sampling. An ethnographer might deploy a random sample if they can draw up a sampling frame of all those within their wider case. This is rarely what happens, and the ethnographer will tend to rely upon a combination of purposive, theoretical, convenience and snowball sampling (see Chapter 14) (Box 8.6).

BOX 8.6 RESEARCH FOCUS

The most famous snowball sample in the sociological 'canon'

More will be said about gatekeepers later on, but here it is simply worth noting that the most famous example of a snowball sample was William Foote Whyte's introduction to innumerable interviewees via his primary gatekeeper 'Doc'. Doc has become a legendary figure in the history of participant observation and within sociology more generally. Finding someone who is able to introduce you to all the right people, get you access to people who would otherwise refuse to talk, and generally smooth the path generating a sample is something akin to being given the keys to the city. Nevertheless, reliance upon a single key informant in the construction of a snowball sample is a dangerous thing. Reliance upon a single gatekeeper may have a serious distorting impact upon the data collected.

Getting in

The nature of the field determines the nature of the researcher's entry problems. Going to live in a village in the Amazon rainforest will present a different set of entry problems than becoming a participant observer in a car factory, or spending time with a street gang. Is the place you wish to enter a public space or a private space? Do you need formal permission to be there? Formal permissions must be sought from authorities of various kinds and this requires a degree of tact and negotiation. Organizational leaders may want to recruit you to do research for them. You need to retain a degree of independence, though you may agree to show them your finished research findings. If you do, it is essential that the confidentiality of other contacts is upheld, and that you make it clear at the start that you are not prepared to breach that confidentiality. If you are suspected of being a management spy, your data collection will be much diminished, as people will not be so willing to talk to you.

In such instances, the first-time researcher should ask the advice of someone more experienced either with research or with the particular organization whose 'private' space you want to enter. The latter group are called gatekeepers. These may be people in the organization or location whose help and consent will enable your research to develop. They may be people from outside the group you are interested in, but who have connections within. Some gatekeepers are official gatekeepers, such as ethics committees and public relations managers. Others are semi-official or unofficial, e.g. community, organizational or gang leaders.

Many public spaces are effectively privatized through the practices of groups and cultures. While you may not need permission to go to a particular village, hang out on particular street corners, or attend a particular religious building, your uninvited presence may not grant you much access to the lives of others present. A stranger may be shunned or ignored. Suspicion may lead people to act differently in the presence of a stranger. Real life may be conducted in the private spaces hidden within the public realm, while the stranger is treated to a front. Access to a culture is more than just spending time in a place. Contacts are important. Gatekeepers might be met in the course of conducting prior or preliminary fieldwork in public settings or they might be cultivated in advance.

Beyond the gatekeepers are the guides and informants whose advice will enable the researcher to get a deeper kind of access, often by means of snowball sampling. At this stage it is only important to recall that the point at which you start will affect where you end up. Consent at one level of an organization or from one set of people within a community may make contact at other levels or with other groups harder (David, 2002). Cultivating relationships is always a balancing act, and this balancing act begins with the cultivation of your first contacts and gatekeepers.

Roles

One way to short-circuit a number of access and gatekeeper problems is to assume the role of a member of the group you are interested in and conceal your researcher role. This is more realistic in some situations than in others, and raises a range of ethical and methodological questions. Covert research involves deception. Can this be justified, ever or in particular cases (see Chapter 2)? Covert research cannot

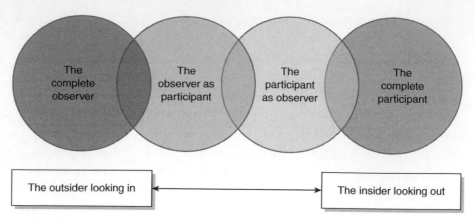

FIGURE 8.1 The ethnographer's role

employ overt research techniques such as formal interviewing or even certain kinds of observation without arousing suspicion. Field notes, the record of the researcher's observations and conversations, cannot be written up in public. These limitations may weaken the research. Alternatively, the covert researcher may gain access to locations unavailable to an overt researcher. Those being researched may react more 'normally' in the presence of a covert researcher, thinking the researcher is 'one of them'. As such there is always a tradeoff. Nevertheless, as a first-time researcher it is highly advisable not to be covert. Being honest and avoiding situations that require deception makes life a lot easier and potentially a lot safer.

Martyn Hammersley and Paul Atkinson (1995: 104) refer to Junker's (1960) elaboration on Gold's (1958) fieldwork role spectrum. Four points on a spectrum are set out (Figure 8.1):

1 *The complete participant.* Here the researcher researches from the position of a full participant – for example, a teacher conducting ethnographic research on school life or a police officer on police work.

2 *The participant as observer.* Here the researcher assumes the role of a member of the group they are interested in and lives as a member for the duration of their research. An example would be of a researcher becoming a research assistant in a chemical laboratory to study the construction of scientific knowledge.

3 *The observer as participant.* Here the researcher spends time and may even live with a group, but is never really a full-time participant, though they may get involved in certain rituals and events. An example of this would be the anthropologist who goes to live in a village in Papua New Guinea for two years and is invited to participate in a variety of customs and everyday activities.

4 *The complete observer.* Here the researcher is not a participant. Of course, just being around may have an effect and so all researchers participate in the situation they are present within, but in this case the researcher does not formally take up a role within

the group other than that of being a researcher. An example of this might be from more traditional forms of ethnography where the anthropologist observed from the sidelines and did not seek to take part in the 'native' way of life.

The complete participant and the participant as observer roles offer scope for being covert, though the roles do not require a covert approach in most cases. Moving along the spectrum towards the complete observer increases the necessity for an overt researcher status. In any research project it is likely that the researcher will move back and forth across the spectrum at different times unless, of course, they are completely covert and so must stick to their participant role. The researcher's role as insider/outsider requires the constant management of marginality (Hammersley and Atkinson, 1995: 109).

It is important to remember that any researcher role involves some degree of performance or even theatricality. This is all the more manifest in the case of ethnography. It is important for the researcher to fit in even if they are not trying to pretend to be someone they are not, or not to be someone they are. Choice of clothes and appearance (suit or jeans, high heels or trainers, long hair or short, make-up and so on) may all play a part in establishing whether you fit in. Trying too hard (trying to be too fashionable, or trying to give the impression of being too interested, knowledgeable or impressed) may be as bad as not making an effort at all. The researcher is there to learn, not to judge. It is not necessary to compete with members of the group to see who has the most local knowledge or street credibility.

Data collection

Watching, doing, listening, reading, asking, thinking. The ethnographic researcher may build towards an understanding of the social situation they are in through participation. They may observe passively. They may ask questions. These questions might be in the form of informal conversation or more formal interviews (usually fairly unstructured, but not always). Interviews may even take the form of focus groups. The ethnographer may use written sources (diaries, letters, local newspapers, organizational communications and so on). The ethnographer can draw upon a range of methods for collecting data. Ethnography is a broad umbrella, referring to the presence of the researcher for an extended period within, for example, a community or an organization. What the researcher does when in the location varies depending upon what works and what is possible. We have discussed interviews at length in Chapter 6. The use of existing written materials will be the topic of Chapter 10. Here, therefore, the focus will be upon observation in fieldwork research.

Field-based (or naturalistic) observation

The experiment is observation in highly controlled conditions. Naturalistic or field-based observation sacrifices control for the hope of greater internal validity (the belief that behaviour observed in natural settings is less likely to be changed by the research process). However, it is important to appreciate that field observation is not totally unstructured. The selection of fields for the conduct of research already involves choices about sampling. Once in the field the observer needs to organize the when, where, who and how of observation. They also have to devise a method of identifying what they are looking at (classification) and what they are looking for (focus). Also they must identify methods of recording their observations. One cannot observe everything that is going on, even at one moment in a relatively small space. One cannot record in full even the things that one is able to observe. Perception involves selection. Becoming reflexive about selection is important. Once in the field, and even beforehand when negotiating access, it is important to reflect upon the range of times and locations that exist within a field. Schools are different places at different times of the day and night. What goes on at the front desk of a police station is not the same as what goes on behind locked doors. Fieldwork observation requires access to the range of whens and wheres. Time and place need careful consideration. This is a form of sampling that may be organized before and/or during the field research period. Likewise, the researcher may want to observe (or interview and so on) a range of different people. Initial gatekeepers and contacts are not necessarily typical and may give a one-sided impression of the scene. Others may present themselves, or need to be sought out.

Recording observations involves the use of classification. This may be in the generation of lists or in the writing of detailed descriptions. Classification is the process of distinguishing things and defining what makes some things go together and what separates some things from others. Classification may draw from prior reading of the literature, or from established classifications (such as male/female). Alternatively, a more inductive form of classification can emerge from time spent in the field. Starting out without clear classificatory schemes, the researcher may come to see patterns after a while spent in the field. These they then explore, sometimes elaborating, sometimes rejecting, as they steer through the field according to what emerges as they go along. This issue of steering, the choice of where to go, what to look for/at, who to talk to and what about, is the question of focus. Once again this will in part derive from the researcher's survey of existing literature (the desire to study gender relations in the police force may motivate the researcher to conduct an ethnography inside and around a police station), yet the focus will develop during the course of the fieldwork.

Finally, there is the question of recording field observations. Field notes are a written record of the ethnographer's observations, as well as of their other data collection methods. The traditional advice to the anthropologist, that they should keep their hard-bound notebooks inside biscuit tins to protect their writings from insects and moisture, may not always apply, but the writing and preservation of field notes still present many problems. The covert participant observer cannot take notes easily in view of others. This may lead to a great many visits to the toilet to scribble down notes, or to a loss of valuable data as things get forgotten between events and the next convenient writing-up time. It is advisable to write up events as soon after they happen as possible, and always on the same day.

Building time into your fieldwork schedule to take notes is essential, even if this is hard. The more inductive approach makes planning hard as the researcher may find themselves following unexpected routes at any moment, but making time to write up field notes is essential. Box 8.7 provides a useful checklist.

BOX 8.7 HINTS AND TIPS

A checklist for taking field notes

Berg (1998: 147–8) suggests a five-point checklist for field notes:

1 Record people's keywords and key phrases in the field.
2 Make notes about the sequence of events as soon as possible.
3 Limit time spent in the field, as the ratio of field time to writing up may be 1:4.
4 Write up 'full' notes immediately after exiting the field. Exiting means at the end of each day or session and at the end of each period of fieldwork. Fullness means an account of events and people and the relationships between them.
5 Get notes written up before showing them to others.

The regular writing up of field notes offers the researcher the opportunity to reflect upon what they have found. This reflection encourages elementary theorizing, thinking about the connections and the interesting new issues that have arisen. From such reflection the researcher may derive new ideas about what is important in their research, and about the location they are researching. They may begin to think they can see what is really going on. This is where data collection links into inductive forms of theory building.

Building theory

As will be discussed in greater detail in Chapters 18 to 22, and as has been mentioned in Chapters 4 and 5, the processes of data collection and data analysis are not separate in many forms of qualitative research. The inductive approach to theory building, where theory develops out of the conduct of empirical research rather than being developed in advance for the purpose of 'testing' by means of empirical research, may leave theorizing till after the data collection has been done. However, given that inductive approaches do not specify so rigidly in advance what their focus is going to be, the selection of topics and the sampling of events, people, places and times develop as the research moves along. As such, choices as to what is important and what is not are made during the course of the research. Such choices express emerging theories – theories that flow from the research and begin to move it in particular directions. This is what grounded theorists call theoretical induction. Ethnography tends towards the use of such an approach to theory building. Ethnography is best suited to such an approach, as being in the field provides the greatest number of opportunities to be struck by the unexpected, those things that may or may not lead you in directions not previously thought of. The theory building process of theoretical induction requires that the researcher can be highly reflexive. Well-written and full field notes are an essential foundation for this. Howard Becker (1986: ix; in Brewer, 2000: 133) suggests that 'writing is thinking'. As can be seen from Berg's set of reminders for writing field notes (Box 8.7), the process of building from initial descriptions of events, times and places, to a more developed description of the processes involved, parallels the development of theoretical induction (see Box 8.8). All of these methods of data analysis will be discussed in greater detail in Chapters 18 to 22.

BOX 8.8 HINTS AND TIPS

Building theory from field notes

David Fetterman (1998: Chapter 5) identifies a range of strategies for building theory out of field notes:

1 Content analysis (what categories are contained in the data). The distinction between quantitative and qualitative forms of content analysis will be discussed in Chapters 18 and 19.
2 Noting patterns (what keeps happening in different places and or times?).
3 Common use of language (note similarities and differences in use and context).
4 Interpreting key events in terms of the routine and the extraordinary in that field.
5 Maps (plot the space between people and events that create a sense of 'place').
6 Flow charts (plot the time lines and gaps between events in the field).
7 Organizational charts (plot the lines and relationships that bind people together).
8 Matrices (draw up cross-tabulations between types of people and/or events and other types of people and/or events: see Chapter 19).
9 Statistical analysis of the instance of key variables (the move beyond matrix diagrams towards more sophisticated mathematical examination of the data).

An important point to note is that theoretical induction can never be pure induction. This is intimately bound up with the nature of perception, language and writing. To take field notes presupposes we have a language that can describe the things we see. This language will reflect our established ways of seeing. We bring existing systems of classification to novel situations. Are such ways of dividing and labelling appropriate to describe cultures and settings different from our own? Ethnographers struggle with the question of how to write about other cultures. Can we see the world as others do? How would we know if we were doing so? The grounded theorists argue that through saturation in the life of others we can begin to build a picture of the world that maps the 'native' experience (Box 8.9). However, the researcher can never be totally grounded; they can never start at some base level of raw experience without theoretical expectations. There will always be theories the researcher brings to the field. The best that can be expected is that the researcher uses their confrontation with difference to reflect upon the weakness of their existing ways of thinking to capture the experience of others. Reflexive field note writing is part of that process. Reflecting on one's experience is one way of telling when it is time to leave the field. Other factors (time, access and finance) also play a part.

BOX 8.9 CONSIDER THIS

'Going native' and 'whose side are we on?'

The expression 'going native' originates amongst colonial traders and administrators, fearful that time spent in the colonies would corrupt the mental and moral superiority of the 'civilized' incomers with the seductions of 'savage' conditions and customs.

In relation to the works of early ethnographers, the suggestion of 'going native' implied a researcher who had given up their detachment and reflexivity in favour of full immersion in the world of those they studied. Where early ethnographers sought to classify the societies they studied, into either evolutionary schemes or functional systems (such as around kinship and exchange), it was feared that over-immersion into the 'native' worldview would prevent the researcher understanding the underlying history or structure of the people they studied, as it was generally assumed that the people under investigation were themselves unable to understand themselves. The twentieth century saw long-running disputes in anthropology and sociology over the 'rationality' of human actions. Ethnography today takes a far more measured attitude to the view that those being studied are prey to social processes beyond their comprehension. As such, the accusation of 'going native' today lacks much of the negative force it once possessed. Still, as Becker (1967) points out, when the researcher seeks to show the world as it is seen from the point of view of outsider groups, they will more than likely be accused of losing their detachment and of 'going native'. From a strong interpretivist perspective, this might not be considered a bad thing. Interestingly, critical ethnographers retain the sense that the world as it appears to the actor in everyday life may remain deeply distorted and in need of analytical detachment before it can be fully made sense of.

Getting out

A more deductive research strategy will set out in advance the data required to address the question being asked (or the theory being tested). More inductive forms of research cannot specify in advance what and how much data will be sufficient to complete the research. How, then, should the ethnographer decide when to leave the field? One key factor is time. Research funds and access permission have their limits. These constraints may set external limits. Internal criteria can also be developed. As with other forms of inductive research, data collection may be said to be sufficient once a level of saturation has been reached. Saturation refers to the situation the research reaches when new data only act to confirm what the researcher already predicted would be the case based upon their prior research. Once the theories that have developed through the course of data collection and reflection become powerful predictors of future data, there is little reason to carry on collecting data. As has already been noted in the context of focus groups (section 'Conduct and management' in Chapter 7), what would be sufficient predictive power for one researcher might not be sufficient for the next. There are no agreed procedures for evaluating how predictive is predictive enough. This creates scope for variation. At the end of the day it is likely that in most cases the external constraints of money and time will apply sooner than the internal constraints of indisputable theoretical saturation.

Leaving the field requires careful management of relationships established during the course of the research. Trust relations that have been set up need to be respected and participants in the research need to be reassured that they will not be abused, misrepresented or exposed to potential harm by the researcher's use of the data. Contacts are often retained for the purposes of subsequent clarification or in the event of subsequent research. Sometimes relationships are maintained because time together has developed into friendship.

Summary

Ethnography seeks to identify holistic patterns of belief and action within the 'culture' of small-scale communities, groups or organizations. It is important to recall that field research (ethnography) may draw upon the techniques of interviewing and textual or non-intrusive data collection in addition to forms of naturalistic observation and participation. The same is true of community and organizational case study research. What makes ethnography or case study research distinct is the primary focus upon one site, rather than the primary concern with comparison. The intimacy of fieldwork relationships can be the greatest advantage of ethnography, but it is also the source of its greatest ethical difficulties. Insight may also represent invasion of privacy.

 ■ **Questions** ▬▬▬▬▬▬▬▬▬

1 **Can covert forms of fieldwork ever be justified ethically or practically?**
2 **What are the advantages and disadvantages of ethnographic focus upon single groups, rather than upon comparisons between groups?**
3 **In what different ways is the relationship between data collection and theory building managed within ethnographic research?**

▬▬▬ ■ ■ **Further reading** ■▬▬▬▬▬▬▬▬▬▬▬▬▬▬

Atkinson, Paul (1992) *Understanding Ethnographic Texts*. London: Sage.

Brewer, John (2000) *Ethnography*. Buckingham: Open University Press.

Hammersley, Martyn and Atkinson, Paul (1995) *Ethnography: Principles in Practice*, 2nd edn. London: Routledge.

Whyte, William Foote (1943) *Street Corner Society: The Social Structures of an Italian Slum*. Chicago: University of Chicago Press.

NINE

CASE STUDY RESEARCH

Aims

By the end of this chapter you will be able to:

- **Identify the range of fields in which case study research has been applied.**
- **Distinguish a range of different forms of case-based data collection.**
- **Understand the diversity of purposes and uses that case-based methods are designed to serve.**
- **Make choices as to how best to define, select and approach 'cases'.**

Case studies

Case studies are in-depth studies of specific 'units'. Units may be individuals, organizations, events, programmes or communities. Case studies are distinguished from experiments in that they are not conducted in controlled conditions and are not specifically designed for comparison. Case studies are distinguished from surveys in that they are primarily designed to investigate specific cases in depth. Case studies may draw upon a range of methods, such as interviews and questionnaires, focus groups, observation (participant and non-participant), document and artefact collection and analysis. In this regard case studies share many characteristics in common with ethnography in particular. With regard to the study of organizations and communities, case study and ethnography often mean the same thing. Case studies, however, are not the same as ethnography in all cases. In-depth analysis of particular events, organizations, individuals and communities may be carried out in ways other than ethnographic field research. We have already discussed focus groups, interviews and ethnographic methods of data collection, and documentary sources will be discussed in Chapter 10. Here, the focus will be on the purpose and value of case-based data collection.

Case studies may involve a range of methods, a range of purposes and a range of sampling techniques. Robert K. Yin (2009: 2) suggests that case study research can seek to explain an individual, outcome, event or community situation; it may seek to explore, or it may seek to describe. Explanatory case studies tend to be more quantitative and deductive. Exploratory and descriptive case studies tend to be more inductive and qualitative. Methods of design, data collection and sampling will be chosen accordingly. Case studies in the physical sciences and in medicine tend to be explanatory, as they are in economics and psychology. In sociology there is greater variety.

What is a 'case'?

Problems immediately present themselves when defining a 'case' once it is noted that there are no absolutely isolated units of social life. Anthropologists gave themselves the naïve luxury once of imagining that the groups they studied existed in pristine isolation, were previously uncontacted by other people, and could be studied as singular and bounded units. The simplicity of such a view stood in contrast to the often complex relationships such 'tribes' actually had with wider cultures and communities, as well as with the Europeans who imagined they had 'discovered' them. Within case study research, the question of what makes up a case is a complex one. Robert Stake (1995: 2) suggests that a 'case' must represent a 'bounded system', a unit of social life that can be studied as a coherent entity, in its own terms. In other words, the 'case' must have its own internal regulative structure that can be studied. As such, human individuals, families, events, organizations, locations and durations (eras) can be studied as 'cases'. Yet, any such case is never fully 'bounded'. As Bill Graham (2000: 1) suggests, a case 'can only be studied or understood in context'. Whilst for Stake the case is the context, for Graham the context is the setting in which cases operate. This does seem rather confusing, but the tension can be resolved if we consider that cases are units of analysis (individuals, groups, places, organizations) that have some degree of self-regulation, but which also require reference to wider realms of social interaction and organization to be understood. The notion of a case then assumes that cases have a degree of internal coherence, but at the same time are not totally bounded. Boxes 9.1 and 9.2 illustrate these tensions.

BOX 9.1 CONSIDER THIS

The Polish Peasant: Cases within a case

Arguably the first major study within the Chicago School of urban sociology was William Thomas and Florian Znaniecki's (1919) work, *The Polish Peasant in Europe and America*. This study was an examination of migration experiences and the relationship between those who had migrated to the United States and those they left behind back home. The research involved the collection of hundreds of letters sent across the Atlantic (one way and the other), a number of diaries kept by migrants documenting their experiences, and one long and detailed autobiography. The question then arises as to what constituted the 'case' under examination in this study. Was it the community of Polish migrants who had moved to the United States in the early years of the twentieth century? Was it the individual migrant whose autobiographical account formed a core part of the research? Were the dyadic letter writers individual cases, rather than each individual? As many letters were written to and by groups of people, or on behalf of others, the boundaries of the individual should not be assumed to represent the boundaries of a case. 'The Polish peasant' (singular) and 'The Polish peasant' (collective) intermingle in *The Polish Peasant* (monograph) as well as 'the Polish peasant' (research project).

BOX 9.2 CONSIDER THIS

The Jack Roller: Two ideas of a case

In Jennifer Platt's (1992) history of case study research, she notes a curious double meaning in the term 'case' as used in Clifford Shaw's famous case study *The Jack Roller* (1930). Shaw picked one case from a caseload of 200 juvenile offenders who were being dealt with by the social work department where the research was being carried out. The individual that formed the focus of Shaw's study, 'Stanley', was initially defined as a 'case' for treatment, and only became a 'case' for research later. Shaw selected this one individual, as he felt that Stanley's story was capable of 'empathetic generalization'. Stanley's story was one that Shaw believed would allow others to understand the conditions that produced juvenile crime, even whilst at the same time not shying away from the violence, selfishness and criminality that characterized the life of this particular 'case'. Platt suggests the contrast between a treatment case and a research case, as well as between the case as unique individual and the case as basis for providing greater understanding of a wider condition, are well illustrated in *The Jack Roller*.

Recognition that cases always contain a degree of bounded self-regulation, but are never completely autonomous, leads to an important observation. Cases can be selected at smaller or larger levels of scale and size. On the dimension of scale a case might be a human individual, a family (for which individuals would be members), a group (made up of individuals), an organization (made up of individuals and groups) or a locality (in which there are numerous individuals, groups, organizations and families). On the dimension of size a case may cover only a short period, a narrow space, a small number of individuals or groups and so on. It may extend further in all these dimensions. Charles Ragin (1992: 3–9) notes that this scope for the bounds of a case to vary in both scale and size leads to two significant tensions. The first is between a notion of the case as a naturally occurring unit of analysis and the sense in which the researcher is always forced to make choices as to the level of organization they choose to study (individuals, groups, families, organizations, time frames and locations). The second tension is between the generic and the specific. When a case is chosen, is it chosen because it represents a unique social situation to be studied in its own terms and for its own sake, or because it represents a wider range of similar cases, of which we can learn from the study of the particular?

What constitutes a 'case study'?

Robert Stake (1995: xi) writes: 'A case study is expected to catch the complexity of a single case.' The emphasis then is upon the internal validity of such an account. In this sense the case study can be contrasted with what has been called 'variable analysis' (Elliott, 2005). Variable analysis is the kind of research where data are collected in the form of values for numerous question variables. In variable focused research, cases are the units (most often individuals) to whom this multi-tude of questions is posed. Variable analysis takes place when the responses to particular variables are compared to the responses given to other particular varia-bles. For example, in a survey of 10,000 university students it might be found that the answer to the gender question (male or female) correlates with the answer to the question on subject studied. In this kind of variable analysis thousands of cases are investigated, but the analysis focuses upon the variables and their relationship, not upon the particular characteristics of each of the many thousands of cases. Case study research gives emphasis to the internal character of the individual case, rather than breaking cases down into a set of variables which allows for the vari-able analysis typically found in surveys. As such, for Stake (1995: xv), the value of case study research lies in exploring cases in a qualitative 'naturalistic, holistic, ethnographic, phenomenological and biographic' fashion, rather than breaking cases down into quantifiable variables. Robert Yin (2009), however, points out that with a case study it may be useful to carry out forms of quantitative data collection and analysis. This may allow for internal analysis of what is going on within a par-ticular case, or it may be used for comparing the situation in one case with that of another case. Whilst case study research gives emphasis to the internal validity of its investigations of particular cases, this has not meant that case study researchers have not undertaken comparative studies involving more than one case. It is how-ever true that a comparative case study method would select only a very small number of cases relative to the number of cases that are typically selected to participate in a survey.

> [C]ase studies investigate real-life events in their natural settings. The goal is to practise sound research while capturing both a phenomenon (the real life event) and

its context (the natural setting). One strength of the case study method is its usefulness when phenomenon and context are not readily separable ... Another strength is that the method enables you, as a social scientist, to address how and why questions about the real-life events, using a broad variety of empirical tools. (Yin, 2004: xii)

For Yin then case study research balances the accounting of complexity and the attempt to identify causes, and he concludes (2009: 1) that differences of emphasis exist not only across different fields within the social sciences, but also from case study to case study, depending upon the researcher's intentions and research questions. Economists and psychologists tend to set aside elements of complexity in order to identify causes and so tend towards greater use of quantitative analysis within their case studies. Sociologists and anthropologists tend to emphasize holistic complexity and so focus more upon qualitative description. Other social sciences are more mixed.

A range of fields of focus

The range of fields in which case study research is undertaken is broad, and the range of different forms such research takes is therefore also very wide (see David, 2007 for a detailed introduction to this field of study and for an extensive collection of the most significant examples of such research). The history of medicine, psychiatry and psychology was largely built upon case-based research methods. These methods are still significant, even with the greater part played today by experimental methods. In these fields, 'case study' methods refer to clinical-treatment-based encounters rather than purely research-based interactions, and where the 'cases' are patients/clients. In legal studies the use of case study methods refers to the exploration of particular legal cases when seeking to examine how the law is being interpreted and developed. In countries such as the United States, the UK and many Commonwealth countries, which have legal systems where law is made through case precedent set by trial verdicts rather than only through statutes passed by government, the study of case law is particularly important. The study of such cases requires the ability to interpret the way that a trial has come to a conclusion and to interpret the verdict and the statement of the judge when summing up the case. As these verdicts and summaries become the basis for future legal arguments, such interpretations are of academic interest and also form the basis for subsequent legal defence and prosecution cases. Where medical case studies may draw upon a mix of qualitative and quantitative data collection and analysis, legal case study research is almost exclusively a form of qualitative analysis of legal arguments. Legal case study methods are focused on explaining not the causes of decisions, but rather their meaning and the arguments used to construct such meaning. The Harvard Business School developed a case-study-based form of teaching and research when examining success and failure within companies. This case-based approach to examining business at the level of the company involves the collection of qualitative and quantitative data. Researchers in social policy, planning and administration, civic design, social work, sociology and public administration have also adopted the case study research method for examining the process of policy making and implementation. Such policy-oriented case study research adopts an evaluation-based approach rather than a purely intellectual interest, but as the focus is on whether a particular organization or policy succeeds or fails, the detailed attention to one organization over the time taken to set a policy in place makes the case study method ideal. The use of case study methods has been most heavily adopted in educational research, in part because of the apparently relentless desire of policy makers to change educational systems of provision and the equally relentless inability of those involved in such actions to agree on what works and what doesn't. Studies within classic anthropology and participant observer or community sociology tend to adopt a less instrumental approach to selecting their location. As their focus tends to be communities rather than organizations and they are less often focused on answering particular policy questions, they tend to be far more holistic and qualitative than the kind of case study methods adopted in medicine, business and public policy research. In political research the case study method has come to occupy a position somewhere between the statistical research of 'political scientists' and the theoretical models created by 'political philosophy'. In political research the case study method has been adopted for two main types of research: first, the unique and unrepeatable event; and second, the in-depth analysis of what might otherwise appear to be the mundane routines of political life that operate below the level of statistical analysis of election results or general theories of political action, authority and legitimacy (see Box 9.3).

BOX 9.3 RESEARCH FOCUS

Is grounded research tautological?

Robert Dahl's (1961) case study of the democratic process in the Connecticut city of New Haven (home of Yale University) sought to identify what democratic politics actually meant, rather than viewing it on the basis of election statistics or via the abstraction of political philosophical principles. What Dahl sought to do was examine the nuts and bolts of local organization, campaigning and decision making. He was interested to use the case study method to identify how issues arose, and how a plurality of issues and activists shape and are shaped by the political process and the political institutions of American life. Dahl was concerned to challenge the view, propounded by C. Wright Mills (1956) and others, that the United States was governed by a military-industrial elite, whose control of the economic, cultural, political and military institutions created a system of control over the general population. Dahl's study of New Haven convinced him that American political life was far more pluralistic than elite theory tended to suggest it was. For Dahl it was the diversity of different voices that meant America could still claim to be a democratic society. Dahl's use of case study research to get to the empirical roots of what a term like 'democracy' really means was heavily criticized by Herbert Marcuse (1964). Marcuse argued that it was tautological to draw up an account of what democracy is by studying a particular case, and then to claim that what goes in that case is democratic because it accords with your definition of democracy. Dahl felt that New Haven had a diversity of voices and issues within its political process; but without contrasting those voices and issues with all the other voices and issues that were not heard, it is not really possible to say whether New Haven was more open than it was closed. Only by comparison to other places, and in contrast with theoretical accounts of what democracy ought to mean, can it be said whether New Haven is democratic or not. Dahl's critics suggested that he had heard many voices, but did not really appreciate that they were all speaking with a similar accent.

A brief history of case study research

Whilst case-based research had been going on in medicine, law and psychology for much longer, and whilst ethnographic methods were developing at the start of the twentieth century, sociological 'case study' research began and was named as such only in the 1920s. The name was coined within the Chicago School of urban sociology, and was as much influenced by biological 'ethological' studies of animals in their natural habitat as it was by other social sciences. Just as ethology examined the natural environment, so social research would study the urban environment and the impacts this would have on the people who lived in such habitats. It was Robert E. Park, founding figure in the Chicago School, who introduced the concept of ecology into sociology, and the notion of urban ecology led to attention being paid to the ecological space in which people lived, rather than to particular characteristics (such as race, class, religion and nationality) being studied in isolation. Within the Chicago School, case study research included the study of autobiographical writings and letters of migrants, the autobiographical study of life as a vagrant, in-depth studies of individual criminals, in-depth accounts of time spent in marginalized communities, and studies based upon time spent living amongst those that were being studied. One of the most famous Chicago School influenced studies was that of Muncie, Indiana (see Box 9.4).

BOX 9.4 RESEARCH FOCUS

Is Middletown a representative town?

The medium-sized but rapidly growing Midwestern town of Muncie, Indiana, was the focus of Robert and Helen Lynd's iconic (1929) case study research project *Middletown: A Study in Modern American Culture*. Muncie had been selected because it had experienced the kinds of rapid migration and urbanization that were seen to have caused so much dislocation across other North American cities in the early twentieth century. However, what the Lynds did when they selected Muncie was to choose a place that had experienced these two phenomena, but which had not experienced the kind of ethnic diversification

(Continued)

that was typical of other bigger places. As such, they sought to study the impact of growth as a separate variable from that of ethnic diversification. Were the social tensions caused by rapid urbanization alone, or was it only the mix of growth and diversity that led to conflict? Middletown had witnessed growth from other parts of the northern United States, rather than people from Eastern and Southern Europe or Black Americans from the rural deep south. This attempt to separate out key variables stands rather in contrast to the Lynds' own suggestion that the case-based method was best suited to overcoming fragmented approaches to social problems: 'The stubborn resistance that "social problems" offer may be related in part to the common habit of piecemeal attacks upon them. Students of human behaviour are recognizing increasingly however that the different aspects of civilization interlock and intertwine, presenting, in a word, a continuum' (Lynd and Lynd, in Yin, 2004: 27). If the value of the case method is that it attends to the complexity of the unique situation, it would be problematic to assume that the findings from such a case could be used to explain other situations, whose additional complexities were deliberately deselected when choosing the case actually studied.

Whilst notable case studies were carried out in the period after the Second World War, such as Robert Dahl's (1961) study of democracy in New Haven, and Seymour Martin Lipset et al.'s (1956) study of union organization amongst US typographical workers, the case study method of social research in sociology witnessed a decline for a number of decades as social and political sciences came to be dominated by quantitative methods and general theories. The declining confidence in grand statistical and/or theoretical models in the period from the end of the 1960s saw a revival in the fortunes of qualitative research in general and of case study research in particular.

Case study methods: strengths and weaknesses

The strength of the case study method lies in the time and attention given over to the processes and interactions operating within the case. This attention to the complexity of the particular case does limit the scope for identifying singular causal processes within the complexity of naturally occurring events. It may be suggested that this is a strength, to the extent that the kinds of variables that might be said to 'cause' particular 'effects' when manipulated under controlled conditions do not operate in such a simple fashion in real-world situations. However, the benefit of escaping such simplicity must be paid for by not being able to identify robust patterns (correlations) that might exist across a large number of cases but which might have been identified in a survey (Box 9.5). Herein lies a curious paradox. Within social science, and outside laboratory conditions, it is not the case that quantitative methods can identify causes; rather they can only demonstrate the existence of correlations between variables. Whilst the case study research method does not have the generalizability of a survey, its attention to the particular situation does allow for a deeper attention to how events came to turn out as they did. Whilst many case study researchers adopt an interpretive approach to description rather than causal explanation, realists argue that attention to the particular processes by which events unfold is as important to causal explanation as statistical correlations.

BOX 9.5 CONSIDER THIS

Are children the same all over the world?

Jean Piaget developed his model of child educational and development stages through the detailed study of a very small number of case studies. These children were all Swiss and all grew up in roughly the same place and the same time (see Scholz and Tietje, 2002: 19). It is very easy to suggest that any findings drawn from such a limited sample might be unrepresentative, and that it would have been better to seek more robust sampling techniques and testable, perhaps quantitative methods of measuring ability and development. It is therefore interesting to note that Piaget's models have stood up to considerable scrutiny whilst more statistical and large-scale studies of human intelligence have been no less prone to criticism. The kinds of questions and tests used to produce numerical measures of a supposed general intelligence (or IQ) have proved no less controversial and no less prone to the accusation of eurocentrism.

One of the founders of case-based research in sociology, Florian Znaniecki (1934), argued that case-based research methods are ideally suited to what he called 'analytic induction': the process of building causal theory from the continued reformulation of the researcher's account of events based on ongoing engagement with the case under investigation. Znaniecki suggested that this is far more typical of what goes on in the physical sciences than statistical theory testing. Of course, such an inductive approach to theory building, as opposed to theory testing, falls prey to Karl Popper's (1935) assertion that no amount of inductive verification will ever prove a theory 'true'. This has led some to suggest that case-based research, and analytic inductive methods of theory building from individual cases, can only ever be used to develop theories that would then need to be tested by more quantitative survey or experimental methods. Others reject Popper's critique and point out that science (physical and social) does not fit his account, whilst others still point out that it is perfectly possible to conduct forms of statistical testing within a case study, or to carry out statistical tests to measure similarities and differences even between a small number of cases.

What Znaniecki was suggesting was that the case study researcher should explore the case to identify what they consider to be significant events with particular outcomes (Box 9.6). It would then be necessary to identify the variation in such outcomes and to search within the case for possible candidate theories to explain why such variations in outcome might have come about. These explanations can then be evaluated relative to the evidence gathered from the case study. This data collection may be before or after the formulation of the theories. Where data collection is undertaken after initial theories have been developed, the method Znaniecki is suggesting is rather close to that put forward in grounded theory (see Chapter 11). Grounded theory, whilst often deeply misunderstood, does suggest a method that moves beyond either inductive theory building or deductive theory testing.

BOX 9.6 CONSIDER THIS

What can we 'learn' from unique events?

It is commonly suggested that if we do not learn the lessons of history, we will be more likely to repeat history. The paradoxical consequence of such a suggestion is that by learning from history we reduce the likelihood that history will contain valuable lessons for us to learn. This can be seen in the curious case of political science using case study methods to research revolutionary events and in so doing seeking to understand the general character of such events. Theda Skocpol's (1979) book *States and Social Revolutions* carried out in-depth analysis of three revolutionary cases, those of France in 1789, Russia in 1917 and China in the period up until 1948. These events were of course specific historical events and as such could not be studied either in any kind of laboratory conditions, or through any research method other than historical documentary case study research. Skocpol's fundamental conclusion from her case studies was that in each case it was not the internal conditions of society or the political organization of the revolutionaries that was sufficient to explain events. Only when the state in that society had been fundamentally undermined by external events, in particular defeat in war, was it possible for internal conditions and conscious revolutionary activity to combine in successful social revolution. Skocpol's book was published in 1979, just as the revolution in Iran overthrew a Western-backed dictator and established a new Islamic republic. Faced with no external threat, and at a time when oil price rises had flooded the old regime with wealth, the Iranian revolution appeared to be a new case that undermined the lessons of previous cases even before the ink had dried on their most in-depth analysis. Skocpol (1982) was quick to reconsider the situation and to point out that she had not claimed that the lessons of France, Russia and China were set in stone. She was forced to radically redefine her theory. She was able to show that, in fact, there were significant similarities between Iran's regime and earlier doomed regimes in its detachment from the rest of Iranian society. Nevertheless, we should always remember that one of the things that make case study research useful is that significant cases will very likely confound previous predictions. Case study research may show common features, but where it really comes into its own is in highlighting the unique and confounding elements.

Life histories and auto/biographical approaches

Individual life histories use a biographical approach to understanding particular individuals and the times they lived in. Life histories offer insights that may be either theoretical or therapeutic. Freud's psychoanalysis is often referred to as 'the talking cure', a reference to the suggestion that talking about one's life, in particular early traumatic events, offers the chance to bring to consciousness hidden anxieties and conflicts whose unconscious existence causes psychological illness. Once brought to the surface, such issues can be addressed and overcome. This is a therapeutic form of case study research.

Robert Atkinson (1998: 4) refers to Eric Erikson's studies of the lives of Gandhi and Luther. These texts sought to explore both the individual and their social context through the study of their lives. Ethnographers often rely upon key informants in their fieldwork and it is often the case that extended interviews with these key informants about their lives enable the researcher better to understand the field in which that person lives as well as the relationship their key informant has with that situation. The Chicago School of urban research pioneered the use of life histories as ways of exploring social life (Bulmer, 1984).

Yin (2009) suggests that the case study method is best applied to the study of contemporary events by methods that are naturalistic in form (that is, which gather data in natural settings or via relatively open-ended interview and observation techniques). While this might be true, the use of documents and life histories allows the case study researcher to explore past events through the study of key events and key individuals or through the recollection of ordinary lives.

While the life history/biographical interview shares many characteristics in common with other interview forms, Robert Atkinson (1998: Chapter 3) offers a number of useful suggestions as to the topics that may shape the course of a life history interview. These include birth and family origins, cultural settings, upbringing and traditions, family, friends, siblings, schooling, media experiences, hobbies and interests, love and work, relation to and recollection of historical events, retirement, inner life and spirituality, major life themes (gifts, decisions, learning, mistakes, difficulties, disappointments, relationships, influences, achievements and fears) and visions of the future. To this might be added political beliefs, actions and affiliations. These themes need to be narrowed or broadened to take in the person being interviewed. As such they are only suggestions and not instructions. Catherine Kohler Riessman (1993) suggests that what distinguishes the narrative focus of life history research as a method is a research design that gives the respondent as much time as they need to tell their story. This requires open-ended questions and a degree of flexibility in the questioning (see section 'Designing open-ended questions and semi-structured interview schedules' in Chapter 6). Life history as a form of case study research may draw also upon the use of textual data sources such as diaries, biographies and letters. As John Scott (1990) suggests in relation to textual sources such as diaries, letters and other personal archives (see Chapter 10), the stories being told occupy an ambiguous position in relation to the lives of those who compose and store them. It cannot be assumed that such records are simply statements of fact. Nor can it be assumed that such texts are simply fabrications. The researcher needs to think carefully about using such records as resources that allow access to a reality beneath such accounts, or as social constructions. Quite how self-representations relate to the lived experience of the person constructing such accounts is again an open question (Box 9.7).

Whether such texts can be studied independently of the lives of their authors, or whether there must be at least some kind of triangulation with their 'real' lives, is an interesting debate between those who see auto/biographical and life history research as part of a wider case-based method (that might include wider historical or ethnographic contextualization) and those who research the textual account as the case.

BOX 9.7 CONSIDER THIS

The use of autobiographical sources

Jodie Allen, University of Cambridge

Recovery from an eating disorder is a complex and personal process, and unfortunately one that remains poorly understood. Research in this area is dominated by outcome studies which rely on the perspective of the researcher who uses the individual's response to confirm or deny an already predefined notion of 'recovery'. As Garrett (1997: 64) underscores, 'potentially complex answers are simplified to fit categories chosen by the researchers; a relatively small group of fairly like-minded people'. However, any useful definition of recovery should incorporate the individual's subjective account of their experience (Redenbach and Lawler, 2003). Studies that have explored the subjective accounts of those with eating disorders draw our attention to a number of factors that individuals perceive as integral to recovery, such as willpower (Hsu et al., 1992), developing relationships (Matoff and Matoff, 2001) and feeling understood (Hsu et al., 1992). While there is no doubt of the importance of such findings, these 'isolated elements' leave us with 'no clear understanding of the *process*' (Weaver et al., 2005: 1890).

In my research on recovery, I use eating disorder memoirs to explore individuals' subjective accounts of recovery from an eating disorder. Using this form of 'autobiography' to research people's experiences of recovery from mental illness offers a number of advantages. Most importantly, due to the temporal requirements of the writing process, these isolated elements are rendered meaningful by the author who situates them within a series of moments that together form a story from illness to recovery. In contrast to personal narratives gathered through interviewing, these first-person accounts of illness come with a unique layer of self-reflection afforded by the writing process. This reflexivity is often explicitly apparent when an author switches from first to third person, for example, by including a raw diary entry written in the midst of illness alongside their reflection on it at the time of writing. Thus, the researcher is privy to the individual's *own* extensive interpretation of their experience which she can use when making her analysis. This is of particular importance in a context where the voices of those who suffer from mental illness have been somewhat absent (Foster, 2007), and where their knowledge is often subjugated by hegemonic medical and psychological discourses. By considering these stories as vital to expanding our knowledge of recovery, we reinforce the notion of the sufferer as expert – as someone who has an equal but unique contribution to offer alongside professional expertise. This approach is in line with the 'person-centred focus of recovery models' (Ralph et al., 2002, as cited in Roberts and Wolfson, 2004). In addition, on a practical level, researching recovery through illness memoirs allows us to learn from those individuals who may have not entered the medical system because they are unable to access treatment, or have a subclinical form of disordered eating, or have chosen not to seek 'professional' help. These voices are often left unheard by studies that recruit solely from clinical service-user populations.

Alongside these advantages, it is also important to consider some of the issues that may be raised by using this kind of method. The researcher is unable to ask questions or clarify assumptions – something

---

that is made possible by the interview process and can lead to richer data. There can also be a concern as to the 'truthfulness' of these accounts if we consider that writing is always done with a particular audience in mind, and that editorial input can sometimes impact on the degree to which the book reflects the story as told by the author. This issue is deemed mute by the proliferation of self-publishing and print-on-demand (POD) publishers in which editorial input is nil. However, with third-party publishers these issues still need to be considered by the researcher of autobiography. Arthur Frank (1995: 22), author of the seminal text *The Wounded Storyteller,* reminds us that the 'stories we tell about our lives are not necessarily as they were lived, but these stories become our experience of those lives'. Furthermore, the 'social scientific notion of reliability' is not valid here because 'stories are true to the flux of experience and the story affects the direction of that flux'. Thus, stories can be seen as constitutive of experience as much as a reflection of it. Frank (1995: 22) explains how it is possible to view stories that 'evade' certain issues, events, or ways of telling as 'false', but really that 'evasion' *is* 'their truth'. In other words, we can learn as much from what is *not* told as we can from what is. Moreover, we are reminded that these texts are simultaneously 'cultural documents' and personal stories (Sayre, 1994: 13), and the *way* in which a story is told (mode) can tell us as much as the story itself (content).

Summary

Case study research operates in a diversity of ways: (1) in defining a case as or in relation to a context; (2) in choosing a naturally occurring or a researcher-defined unit; (3) in considering the relationship between internal exploration or explanation; (4) in focusing exclusively on internal dynamics or in comparison; (5) in viewing the case as unique or as a means for developing more general propositions; (6) in analysis for internally instrumental 'action research' purposes or for purely academic interest; and (7) in using a primarily qualitative or a form of mixed methods research. As cases may be individuals or whole societies, the case-based method can be the most micro-sociological form of research or one of the most macro-structural approaches. This diversity might suggest the very coherence of the term 'case study research' should be brought into question. However, the emphasis on the internal dynamics of each case rather than on the correlation of variables across large numbers of cases, alongside the orientation towards naturally occurring events relative to controlled conditions, does provide a significant degree of continuity. Moreover, diversity within case study approaches forces the researcher to be reflexive about the methods they choose rather than being able to fall back on a prescribed set of tools and techniques.

 ■ **Questions**

1 Is biography a useful resource for or topic of social research? What does this distinction mean?
2 When does the advantage of focus on the unique case outweigh the limits of generalization?

3   Do the differences in form outweigh the similarities in case study research across the social sciences, or does such diversity simply add to the value of such a family of techniques?

4   What are the issues and questions a researcher should ask when seeking to define a 'case', and in particular their case?

■ ■ Further reading ■

Atkinson, Robert (1998) *The Life Story Interview*. London: Sage.

Kohler Riessman, Catherine (1993) *Narrative Analysis*. London: Sage.

Roberts, B. (2002) *Biographical Research*. Buckingham: Open University Press.

Yin, Robert K. (2009) *Case Study Research: Design and Methods,* 4th edn. London: Sage.

TEN

COLLECTING TEXTUAL AND VISUAL DATA: PUBLIC AND PRIVATE

Aims

By the end of this chapter you will be able to:

- **Define the meaning of the term 'text' as it is used in social research.**
- **Identify a range of types and sources of 'textual' data.**
- **Evaluate the strengths and limitations of 'textual' data.**
- **Engage with ethical debates concerning the use of 'textual' data.**

Textual data

The great value of textual data lies in their abundance. Written materials, and materials that can be 'read' as a text, are all around us. Some of these materials are already well archived and available for researchers even after their authors are long dead, or otherwise unavailable. However, not all archived materials are readily accessible or well ordered. In addition, whether in archives or not, available textual material may be either unrepresentative or invalid or both.

Purpose and varieties of textual data

'Textual data' refers to any form of meaning-laden objects that the researcher can collect for the purposes of analysis. There are a range of sources and forms. The term 'text' is used to refer to anything that can be 'read'. This has allowed images (paintings, photographs, postcards and so on) and other traces of meaningful human activity (such as buildings, clothing and furniture) to be used as 'textual' data (Box 10.1).

BOX 10.1 STOP AND THINK

See the illustrative case by Alison Anderson in the accompanying website for this book for a discussion of the relationship between the number of times a word or theme is mentioned and the way such language is given meaning within the wider context of the overall text in which it is embedded.

Here discussion is restricted to words and images. For a more wide-ranging discussion of 'unobtrusive methods' (that is, reading artefacts rather than directly researching people), see Lee (2000). For a detailed introduction to visual data in the social sciences, see Emmison and Smith (2000), Banks (2001) or Pink (2001).

Why collect textual data? Textual data provide what John Scott (1990: 3) calls 'mediated access' to the lives of those who produced the texts. Why would we wish to use mediated access as opposed to directly accessing people by means of interviews, observations or other methods? Scott suggests two reasons. First, textual data often outlive their producers. Historians have long relied on textual records of the lives of people no longer available for interview. Second, textual data are 'non-reactive'. Whereas humans react to the fact of being researched, texts offer less reaction. Such documents may open a window to parts of life that the researcher would otherwise not have access to. The minutes of corporate board meetings, the discussions of government officials, or the diary of a drug addict may offer insights otherwise unavailable (Box 10.2).

BOX 10.2 CONSIDER THIS

Online textual data

The viral character of communication online can be captured in part at least in a way that would have been harder to trace in relation to other forms of communication. An interesting example of this is the proliferation of parody materials circulating online. One of the authors (David, 2010) is interested in file-sharing and the attempts to criminalize sharing in an information age. Corporate lobbies have produced an array of campaign materials designed to persuade people that file-sharing is wrong, illegal, dangerous and liable to cause problems to society, the individual or the future of music. One particular example of this was a campaign which sought to draw an analogy between downloading music from the internet, stealing a car and stealing a handbag. A short promotional film uses a repeating motif with a recurrent musical soundtrack to attempt a reinforcing of this suggestion, starting with the statement, 'You wouldn't steal a car!' followed by the statement 'You wouldn't steal a handbag!', and goes on to suggest that by association you should not file-share. This 'campaign' was widely circulated, but its impact is harder to pin down. The internet is full of examples of people who have made parody films using the same repetition motif and music, but with comic or subversive effect. An examination of such parody websites demonstrates a deep understanding and familiarity with the material and with the structure of its composition, but to the extent that this knowledge is used to invert the intended meaning, the sites provide a useful data source for an examination of the relationship between content and discourse. It is one thing to be imitated, but it is quite another to assume that being constantly referred to is evidence of the persuasive power of what is being referred to.

There are many types of textual data. Scott (1990: 14) offers a system of classification based upon authorship and access. Scott first identifies modes of authorship:

- personal
- private (for example, business, media, charities and so on)
- state.

He then outlines four levels of access:

- closed
- restricted
- open (archival)
- open (published).

A diary may be written for a closed readership of one, or for a restricted readership (as are personal letters). However, a diary may be written with an eye to being made more widely available later (via an archive or by publication). Diary and autobiography merge at this point (Box 10.3). A letter to a newspaper is intended to be more openly accessed than a letter to a best friend. An official letter to or from a bank or government department will be recorded institutionally. Postcards and birthday cards are sometimes kept and sometimes thrown away or lost. Private and state bodies keep records of routines and of special events. These are sometimes made available (via archives or publication) but are sometimes closed, restricted, lost or even destroyed. Written documents are not the only forms of material that people and institutions keep. Individuals keep photographs and films (cine, video and so on). Institutions also may keep photographic or film archives (surveillance video footage, for example). The media (television, radio, print and new media) generate huge quantities of textual (word and image) data, which are often easy to access, record and thereby analyse.

BOX 10.3 HINTS AND TIPS

Vocabularies of motive

It is worth remembering that the way people present information about themselves says as much about how they wish to present themselves as it does about who they really are and/or what they really think (and maybe more). The only thing you can be sure of is that such textual representations have involved a degree of self-reflection in their composition. Writing something down will have involved the writer thinking and changing their words as they go along. This is also true in speech, but in writing the opportunity to check oneself and to modify what finally gets written is greater. This is all the more true in an age of computers, though text messages and e-mails are said to contain a greater degree of unchecked 'honesty'. Whilst textual data have the advantage that they are generally generated prior to the research encounter, and so do not suffer from interviewer effects (the interviewee giving answers in part shaped by the impression they want to give the interviewer), it should not be forgotten that textual material generated for non-research purposes, and which can then be collected by a researcher after its creation, was still written for a purpose. C. Wright Mills (1940) addresses the extent to which motivation can be shaped by the language through which we articulate our actions, not only to others but also to ourselves. The things that are acceptable to use as 'excuses' change over time, and are different for people of different ages, for men and women and in relation to all sorts of other social positions. As such, reading autobiographies, letters, application forms, sick notes and court transcripts can tell us a great deal about what society considers legitimate motivations and explanations. Explaining that your essay is late because your goldfish died is (apparently) today considered a legitimate 'excuse' in many British universities. In the past, and elsewhere, such goldfish-related bereavement may have been treated with less sympathy, and as such few applications were received in which this circumstance was cited.

Raymond Lee (2000: 66–81) offers an array of interesting examples of how textual data can offer insights into social life. The choice of children's names over the years is recorded in registers of births and religious initiation. Personal advertisements may tell us a lot about the way we live (Box 10.4). How obituaries are written in different times and places may offer comparative and longitudinal insights. Radio and television schedules may offer insights into changing lifestyles and attitudes. Job descriptions, advertisements and representations of work in the media all contribute to an understanding of social life. Lee cites fascinating research that draws upon school yearbook entries, personal curricula vitae, published autobiographies and suicide notes. Many will be familiar with 'reading' other people's holiday postcards and photographs for 'clues' of things we might feel it would be rude to ask bluntly about. Lee (2000) devotes particular attention to the internet as a new source of unobtrusive data. Whether it be e-mail, chatrooms or the World Wide Web, internet activity leaves a textual trail that the researcher can follow and record (Box 10.2). It should be remembered that such activity is not evenly spread throughout the population and this raises the question of sampling and selection. Surveillance of the internet is currently an ethical hot topic. However, the ethical issues related to using the internet to collect textual data (often from people who are not aware that they are being researched) are in many respects the same as those raised by social research more generally. The ethics of documentary research will be touched upon later in this chapter.

BOX 10.4

TEXTUAL REPRESENTATIONS OF SELF

'WELL TO DO GENTLEMAN in early forties wishes to correspond with southern lady of refinement. Object matrimony. Box …' (Vedder, 1951: 219)

'Attractive M, muscular, high flier, 6', gym, music, art, seeks slim open-minded fun female for adventures.' (Jagger, 2001)

These two examples of men advertising in lonely hearts columns tell us a great deal about the social context in which they were placed, or at least the wide range of such texts does so. These individual cases are indicative of such texts in general, but it is only through their systematic collection that such patterns can be identified. Lonely hearts columns do not tell us what people are really like. We do not know the material circumstances of either of the two persons above. Rather, what we can know from the collection of such textual data is something of the 'acceptable' rules of representation and of what appears best to say about yourself in different eras and countries. Vedder notes that the first advertisement received 13,000 replies! One imagines that a call for an open-minded female for adventures would have been less successful in 1950s America than in modern Britain, though there is no record of how many responses the second ad received. The way that men represent themselves, as above, is distinct from the way women do, and again this can be a useful way to investigate gender stereotypes. That a person seeking a relationship would seek to present themselves one way or another is a very good way of measuring the social pressures and norms by which individuals imagine they are being measured by others, and to which they therefore feel required to conform, at least in how they describe themselves. That people pay money to put this information into the public domain is of great benefit to social researchers, as such data are readily available and relatively ethically safe. In particular, the personal details of the senders are already concealed despite the public nature of the advertisements; this means the researcher is not impinging on privacy even though the topic being researched is of a highly personal nature.

Sampling

Sampling tends to refer to the selection of materials such that the selected group is 'representative' of the population the researcher is interested in. John Scott (1990) identifies four criteria for selecting and evaluating the usefulness of textual materials:

- authenticity

- credibility

- representativeness

- meaning.

Authenticity relates to

- whether the 'text' is what it claims to be (that is, that it is not a forgery)

- whether the author of the text is whom we think it is.

Credibility refers to the level of trust we can place in the contents of the 'text'. Is it trustworthy? Is the source reliable? Was the author sincere and/or accurate? The question of representativeness refers to how typical the text is, and how typical the author is. Not all texts survive and not all that do are made available. As such, those texts that the researcher gains access to may be highly unrepresentative. At the same time, certain texts are more likely to be produced about or produced by certain types of people. Diaries in seventeenth-century England were mainly written by the middle and upper classes. Police surveillance today is more heavily concentrated on the less powerful. 'Meaning' refers to what the text actually says. Scott (1990: 36) points out that the meaning of a text can be used as either a resource or a topic. The contents of a diary may be an accurate portrayal of the life and world of the writer. If so, the diary is a resource, a window to the life it was a part of. Alternatively, reading Victorian cookbooks may tell us little about the real diet of people in the nineteenth century, but it might tell us a lot more about the attitudes and beliefs of their middle-class authors. Here the text is a topic in itself. Much analysis of mass media content focuses on what the texts (words and images) are seeking to convince us of. It is rarely assumed that such coverage is itself 'credible' as a resource. All textual material is generated within the author's framework of 'moral accounting', whether this be a diary, a letter, or a government's record of births and deaths. Texts will always reflect the context of their production. Whether they accurately represent the world they seek to record is a more complex question. For a wide-ranging and insightful discussion of the value of auto/biographical work as a research resource and as a topic in the social sciences, it is worth reviewing the collection of articles contained in volume 27, number 1 of the journal *Sociology* (1993), edited by Liz Stanley and David Morgan. The use of biography, autobiography and clinical case notes as textual data link textual analysis with case study methods, discussed in Chapter 9.

The actual selection and collection of textual materials vary according to text type and research context. Materials may be accessed directly from those being researched or from archives (Box 10.5). Personal texts (such as diaries, letters and photographs) may be sought directly from those being researched or from archives. The books, magazines, newspapers, music recordings and video cassettes which an individual accumulates constitute a personal archive that may speak volumes about them. The letters, birthday cards and bills they choose to keep may also constitute a revealing personal archive. Museums and libraries often contain specialist collections of personal documents. Formal texts from private or public institutions will more usually have to be accessed from archives, though the type of archive might vary. Some institutions keep archives of their own textual production, which the researcher may seek permission to access. Other materials (such as mass media production) may be archived by other institutions, such as libraries or research institutes. Accessing archive materials may constitute the first stage of a research project, as a parallel to a literature review. It may constitute the main substance of a research project. Alternatively, in more ethnographic research the researcher may accumulate textual material in a more grounded fashion from those they observe, participate with and interview. Asking for personal materials (diaries, letters, photographs and so on) may be built into an interview schedule or questionnaire. Research projects relating to education, health or the law may wish to draw upon institutional records of individuals or groups. These materials can then be compared to the experiences and personal archives of students, patients and those enmeshed within the legal process (such as lawyers, police officers, criminals, those accused, witnesses, jurors and those convicted). Media researchers may wish to compare media output with the experiences of audiences, or the practices of those involved in the process of media production (journalists, actors, producers and editors, owners and shareholders, as well as pressure groups and institutional actors who seek to influence media content). Historical records in all these areas can be used to compare the past with the present.

BOX 10.5 CONSIDER THIS

The availability of textual data

It is now abundantly easy to collect archival textual materials, such as newspaper articles, by going to the websites of the newspapers you are interested in, or using a collating service, of which there are many. This makes it very easy to engage in a range of research projects. Here are three examples of research projects created for undergraduate sociology research methods classes.

First, the search terms 'student' and 'university' were put into the archive search engines for a range of UK daily newspapers with a time range from a year ago to the present. This generated a large number of newspaper articles. After these were screened for erroneous articles in which one or both terms appeared but only tangentially, a sample was selected at random. This provided the basis for a study of the representation of students. For more liberal newspapers, students were hard working and poor; for more conservative newspapers, students were lazy and either drunken or open to various forms of antisocial radicalism (religious or political).

Second, the making available online of an archive of *The Times* newspaper made it possible to carry out a longitudinal study of representations of similar events at different times. Late in 2006 a series of prostitutes were murdered in Suffolk. Collecting newspaper articles from the period immediately after the murders, and a set of articles from the same newspaper from the late 1970s which concerned the murder of students and prostitutes by the so-called 'Yorkshire Ripper', allowed a comparative study of how such crimes are reported.

(Continued)

Third, in 2008 Liverpool was European Capital of Culture. How would this impact upon the representation of the city? Collecting articles from four leading national newspapers via their respective web archives allowed comparison to be carried out.

It should be noted that some of the detail contained in paper newspapers is lost in their online electronic archive form. It was once the case that pictures, graphs and tables were usually lost, but increasingly these materials remain. However, page referencing is very often lost, and the position on the page is also lost. In newspapers it is commonly seen as a significant thing whether or not an article is above or below the fold. Being in the top half of the page marks something as being important, so its position is worth knowing, and may remain unknown if an article is simply recovered from a web page. Similarly, if an article is relegated to the middle pages it is less likely to be read. Where back pages are reserved for sports news, and when some people go straight to that section, being on the back may increase the likelihood of being read. Where a newspaper has sections, knowing which section an article is contained within is important context in which the text might be better understood. These things, if lost in an electronic article, may limit the full understanding of the text's meaning.

Collecting visual 'texts'

Just as cheap, and relatively mobile, recording devices revolutionized the conduct and collection of interview materials, so the proliferation of cameras has generated increased interest in the value of visual images in the research process. It is increasingly possible to take and record images, both still and moving, without significant preparation. Where once a posed photograph was something that took a great deal of time to prepare and could only be undertaken in very limited and controlled conditions, and by expert photographers and film makers, now the researcher can 'point and click' with an array of devices. As such material is now often digitally recorded, it is also available for immediate analysis and for very simple storage and replication for subsequent dissemination and analysis.

Not only are cameras now available for researchers to record everyday life in ever increasing detail, so too are such devices available and actively deployed in the routine recording of life by those whose lives are being recorded. With cameras now built into mobile telephones, and with the popularity of social networking sites, millions of people routinely add images of themselves to the internet every day. In addition to this most people collect archives of images of themselves, the people in their lives, the places they have been and the things they have done or bought or made. As such, visual images become an essential part of how many people communicate and represent themselves to others, and how they construct and record their own personal accounts and memories of life.

In addition to such personal archives, the social world is also awash with organizational images and recording. Whether this be visual media such as film and television, or other media such as commercial billboards, glossy image-centred magazines, and the photographic and visual content in newspapers, manufactured and often readily collectable visual data surround us.

Organizations and individuals give considerable attention to self-representation, whether this is when a company engages in the construction of a brand image and identity, or when an individual seeks to construct their image through cosmetics, exercise or clothing. Whether a researcher goes out and photographs objects, logos and individuals, or collects existing images of such things, attention to what people do when they engage with other people though appearance is growing.

As can be seen above, the collection of 'visual text' – images that are collected for the meaning they hold for those who construct and circulate them – can be by means of (1) primary data collection, i.e. going out and recording images; (2) primary archival data collection, i.e. drawing upon existing stores of such images collected by people for non-research purposes (whether these be private and personal collections or organizational ones); or (3) secondary archival collection, where images are those that have already been generated and stored for earlier research purposes.

The ethics of documentary research

The use of textual materials raises some serious ethical issues (as briefly mentioned earlier). To begin with, there is the problem of consent. Gaining consent from an archive to research the materials held there is one thing. It is another to claim that such an institutional consent represents the consent of those whose materials are contained within that archive. Materials written by or written about the dead raise the ethical problem of whose consent should be sought. Does death annul all ethical obligations? Were the documents meant for circulation beyond a limited circle? How were the documents acquired by the archive, and with what provisos concerning their use? The researcher is obliged to address these questions. If authors or people mentioned by an author are still alive, should the researcher seek to gain their consent to use the material? Health, education, employment, tax and legal data are protected by law. Is it enough to retain confidentiality, or should formal and informed consent be sought? For legal as well as moral and methodological reasons, researchers should seek guidance about the specifics of any proposed use of archival materials. Academic and professional associations in different countries offer guidance tailored to specific contexts. These should be investigated (see Chapter 2). Regarding personal materials gained by researchers directly from those they research, it is easier to ask for informed consent; this should be done, once again, in accordance with the ethical guidelines of the relevant professional and/or academic association.

In relation to visual material it is particularly important to note that, rather as with ethnography, one of the advantages of such material also presents a serious ethical danger. Visual images of people are much more likely to reveal identities than are responses on a questionnaire. Just as time in the field allows the researcher the opportunity to really get to know those they are researching, and so potentially to infringe their privacy, so the nature of ethnographic fieldwork makes it harder to maintain confidentiality. Similarly, a photograph can provide depth and detail about a person, event or place that might be as ethically problematic as it is epistemologically valuable. It is important therefore to gain consent from those whose images are being used, so that these images can be displayed to the readership of the research; or, if such consent is not granted, care should be taken to protect the identities of those pictured.

Recording and storage

Notes taken from, or transcripts of, written materials can be recorded and stored in the same way as one would take notes from any other source in a literature search. Some archival materials may be available electronically and may be recorded and stored as such. Other archival materials may be available on loan or have to be noted from within the archive itself, as is the case with much library reference material. Such material may or may not be reproduced (via scanning or photocopy). Personal documents and images may be viewed, borrowed and even reproduced with consent. In a field context, storage of artefacts is problematic, and recording (in text or via photography, scanning, video or photocopy) raises all the problems encountered in the earlier discussion of taking field notes (see section 'Data collection' in Chapter 8). In an archival context, storage issues are those discussed in respect of doing a literature review (Chapter 3). In each case, the purpose of recording and storage is to allow subsequent analysis. As qualitative analysis is based upon the analysis of meaning, the recording and storage need to facilitate subsequent access to meaning. This requires the recording of the text and its 'context' (that is, source, time, place, author and other information that will locate the text in the social conditions of its production and retention in either a personal or a formal archive). Just as it is essential to record the demographic details of people interviewed (age, sex, social position and so on), it is similarly important to record the corresponding characteristics of texts. When storing visual material, the need to record context is an interesting question. As the 'visual text' is not 'text' in the actual written sense of the word, context may have to include a good deal of information that might in one sense be said to be within the image, but in another sense can only really be attributed to it or said about it.

Summary

Primary text-based data collection generates data by non-intrusive data collection methods that do not primarily involve direct interaction with the producers of the texts collected (though accessing such materials may involve such interaction). While avoiding many of the practical and ethical difficulties involved in interviewing and field research, textual data collection presents the reverse difficulties of distance and detachment. The questions of source reliability, validity and representativeness are the same as for all research methods, but lack of access to the producers of texts may limit the researcher's ability to provide answers. This is balanced against the greater scope to cross-reference different texts and to be able to access sources where their producers may be either dead or otherwise unavailable. Whether textual materials offer a window on reality, or only into the minds of their producers, is another question that must be addressed by the researcher.

 ## ■ Questions ■

1 When might primary textual data collection be used either instead of or in addition to other forms of qualitative data collection?
2 On what ground should a reflexive researcher question the validity of any textual data they collect?
3 What different sorts and sources of textual data exist?
4 With regard to issues of sampling, what are the advantages and disadvantages of textual data?

■ ■ Further reading ■

Banks, Marcus (2001) *Visual Methods in Social Research*. London: Sage.

Emmison, Michael and Smith, Philip (2000) *Researching the Visual: Images, Objects, Contexts and Interactions in Social and Cultural Inquiry*. London: Sage.

Lee, Raymond (2000) *Unobtrusive Methods in Social Research*. Buckingham: Open University Press.

Scott, John (1990) *A Matter of Record: Documentary Sources in Social Research*. Cambridge: Polity.

ELEVEN

GROUNDED THEORY AS AN ABDUCTIVE APPROACH TO DATA COLLECTION

Aims

By the end of this chapter you will be able to:

- Identify the origins and principles that underpin the grounded theoretical approach to social research and its critique of alternative approaches.
- Understand what grounded theorists mean by theory and how such conceptualization emerges from data.
- Comprehend the meaning of key grounded theory terms such as emergence, constant comparison, abduction, theoretical sampling and saturation.
- Recognize the diversity of grounded theory approaches in terms of their relationship to empirical discovery, theoretical pragmatism and social constructivism.
- Work with an awareness of the strengths and limitations of the grounded theoretical approach.

Origins

The term 'grounded theory' is used widely in social research. In its more general usage, the term 'grounded' may simply imply that an idea is located in context, or has emerged from active engagement with the 'real' world of empirical enquiry. We often refer to something or someone as being 'grounded' to imply that they have their feet on the ground and are not too arrogant or detached from real life. I recently walked past a Gothic cathedral and noticed its tower had a large wire coming down the side. This 100 metre tower had been 'earthed' to ensure that if it was struck by lightning, the energy would be passed into the ground safely. When we talk about grounding in social research we typically imply the former meaning rather than the latter. Grounding is designed to allow reality to filter up, but at the same time being grounded ensures that research is not just the projection of a lightning bolt from the blue (imposing our ideas on reality).

The term 'grounded theory' in the more restricted sense refers to the now 40-year-old tradition initiated by Barney Glaser and Anselm Strauss with their 'classic' text *The Discovery of Grounded Theory* (1967). Kathy Charmaz (2006) suggests that Glaser and Strauss's 'grounded theory', which developed from the two researchers' collaborative investigations into palliative care services (nurses and their relationship to death and the dying), combined Glaser's Columbia University sociology's emphasis on empirical positivism with Strauss's Chicago School of sociology and its combination of pragmatism and symbolic interactionism. Corbin and Strauss (2008: 1–5) outline the basic premise of pragmatism as an approach to understanding the world as being real and yet only ever knowable through our particular and practical engagements with it. Symbolic interactionism extended the pragmatism of Dewey and James (which saw social life as both real and the result of practical activity). Glaser and Strauss (1967: 10) rejected the idea that social research should be an attempt to 'master great-man theories and [to test] them in small ways' – the idea that sociological theory could set a correct, single and true framework in which questions could be formulated and then tested empirically by means of social research. For Glaser and Strauss, theories were only ever partial, practical and temporary accounts. What they sought to do in their book *The Discovery of Grounded Theory* was to reset the relationship between theory and empirical enquiry, such that theory emerged from data rather than drove the collection of data into answering predefined research questions (Box 11.1). Grounded theory is not quite a purified empiricism. Neither is it a pure form of induction. Rather, it is an attempt to rebalance social research in the direction of empirical induction. However, as Paul Hodkinson (2008: 81) suggests, grounded theory is never followed 'to the letter'. As a pragmatic approach to social research, this is only appropriate. However, those who write about grounded theory often do so with such devotion that it does sound more dogmatic than its practice ever allows it to be.

BOX 11.1

MOTHERING ON CRACK COCAINE: A GROUNDED THEORY ANALYSIS

Margaret H. Kearney, Sheigla Murphy and Marsha Rosenbaum

Abstract

Mothers who use crack cocaine are commonly believed to be selfish, uncaring, and neglectful of their children. For this paper, the grounded theory method was used to analyze 68 semi-structured depth interviews with cocaine-using mothers. These women's views of motherhood, the strategies they used to manage mothering on cocaine, and the contextual influences on mothering outcomes were explored. Contrary to popular assumptions, the women highly valued motherhood and held firm standards for childrearing. Mothers were concerned about the possible risks to their children and used a process of defensive compensation to protect both their children and their maternal identities from the negative influences of crack cocaine.

Social Science & Medicine, 1994, 38 (2): 351–61

If the value of grounded theory lies in the possibility of counter-intuitive conceptualization, then the above article certainly can claim to be achieving this possibility.

Meaning and principles: discovery, grounded and theory

By 'discovery', Glaser and Strauss seek to distinguish their approach from approaches that seek to bring theory to the empirical data collection process. Deductive models or research develop their theoretical model from previous literature and then seek to design research in order to test the theory. Glaser and Strauss seek rather to allow theory to emerge from data, through a series of manoeuvres that will be detailed in the next few sections. The principle of discovery however is not only set against the idea of theory testing. It is also set against what Glaser and Strauss see as descriptive sociology, which does not seek to discover theory at all, but rather strives to provide detailed descriptions of the social world. Glaser and Strauss are more ambitious that this, even whilst they reject the pre-emptive ambitions of purely deductive researchers. It should be noted that the process of discovery is not simply one of passive encountering. As will be seen below, the grounded theorist seeks to build theory and to test tentative theories as they develop. Discovery is an active process that shapes the direction of the data collection process even if it does not determine fully how that process gets started or which theoretical leads will set the ball rolling.

The term 'grounded', as has been pointed out in the previous section, relates to the way grounded theory seeks to resist pre-emptive shaping of research and theory development. Grounded theory starts with data, and moves towards theory. Grounded theory starts with its feet on the ground, even if it seeks to build higher-level and more general accounts of social life. Grounded theory is also grounded in the sense that theory building and data collection remain interlinked from the very earliest entry into the field to the final point of departure (which is said to be enabled at the point of saturation: see below).

The term 'theory' in grounded theory is not quite theory in the sense other social scientists use the term. Glaser and Strauss seek to avoid grand total theories of the social world. For them, theory should be a more modest but still significant account of the world. For them, data allow for the emergence or discovery of patterns that can be coded for in the data collected. These codes can be studied and their links explored. Such links between codes or categories of action and expression (for grounded theory, actions in particular) should direct the researcher to explore in more detail and in diverse settings and combinations such codes or categories. In so doing the researcher can build from codes or categories to more abstract concepts and conceptual models that best account for what is going on in the data. Such models represent 'grounded theory' rather than an abstract theory with universal ambitions. For Glaser and Strauss, theory should be pragmatic – both useful and specific. It is more than just a description of a singular set of observations; however, it should never claim to be all there is to say about the social world.

Key concepts: constant comparison, theoretical sampling and saturation

As has already been mentioned in the previous section, 'discovery', 'grounded' and 'theory' carry particular meaning in relation to grounded theory. In addition to this, three key concepts emerge that further specify the conduct of grounded theory as distinct from other forms of social enquiry.

The idea of *constant comparison* refers to the key difference between grounded theory and either deductive research or purely inductive research designs. Constant comparison refers to the requirement of the grounded theorist to start their data analysis from the very first moment they collect data. Constant comparison refers to the comparison between units of data collection, i.e. cases, whether this means observation periods, persons, events or locations, and between the codes that the researcher develops in order to provisionally account for such cases or units of data collection. Constant comparison involves asking what makes one case or unit different from the next; or asking why the coding that emerged from one case or unit is different from that which the researcher felt best explained another. Constant comparison is between units of data, and between data and provisional explanations. Each round of data collection should be reflected upon, and such reflections should force the researcher to clarify their tentative theories in relation to previous data and the theories (coding, into categories, into concepts) that emerged from them. Constant comparison is the ongoing and continuous act of provocation, by which each new empirical case challenges the completeness of what until then appeared to be a workable explanation (theory) of what was going on. Glaser and Strauss (1967: 107, cited in Hodkinson, 2008: 88) write: 'The constant comparison of incidents very soon starts to generate theoretical properties of the category. The analyst starts thinking of the full range of types of continua of the category, its dimensions, the conditions under which it is pronounced or minimized, its major consequences, its relationship with other categories, and its other properties.'

Theoretical sampling takes forward the logic of constant comparison. It is not simply a question of lining up a set of cases. If you were interested in student experience in twenty-first-century higher education you might start with some provisional interviews with students, and from these you might feel a pattern begin to emerge in what you are being told. Grounded theory does not simply suggest the researcher keep interviewing more and more students until they are certain they have honed their theory to perfection. Rather, as a pattern within the coding starts to suggest a conceptual model to the researcher, the researcher should ask themselves what such a model (theory) predicts. At this point, grounded theory begins to engage in a form of qualitative hypothesis testing. In asking what the as yet tentative theory would predict, so it is possible to select further cases (to observe or to interview) that might challenge the validity of such a theory. The researcher should deliberately choose new cases for empirical examination which would stretch the boundaries and limits of their provisional prediction. New rounds of data collection will allow new instances of constant comparison and thereby of discovery (often called emergence). By means of the combination of constant comparison and theoretical sampling, the grounded theorist seeks to build, test, challenge and reformulate their account through numerous iterations (Box 11.2). The intention of course is to arrive at a point where the theory that has been discovered can be stabilized (though grounded theorists tend to avoid a sense of total closure).

BOX 11.2 RESEARCH FOCUS

The discovery of the 'mainstream': the value of using grounded method in contemporary research of 'post-revolutionary' consumer generation in the Czech Republic

Michaela Pyšňáková, Masaryk University

Since the collapse of communism in the former Czechoslovakia in 1989, there has been an increasing recognition that the experience of the post-revolutionary young generation in the Czech Republic offers a useful indicator of changing social, cultural and political trends. When I started my research on youth consumption, the issue had not been given sufficient attention and tended to be restricted to the domains of media representation and marketing. In order to contribute to a debate on the 'post-revolutionary' generation drawing upon theories of risk and individualization, I focused my research on young people's experience of consumption as a response to social change. The grounded theory method provided a set of useful research strategies for analysing young people's experience of consumption. Particularly, the emergence of the concept of 'mainstream' presented a challenge to the predominant conception of young consumers, which tended to dismiss them as a materialistic, hedonistic and egocentric generation.

The key feature of grounded theory is that it provides a framework for generating conceptual theory from data in a process of continuous exploration for discovery (Glaser and Strauss, 1967). The methodological stance is based on the method of *constant comparison* and the use of *theoretical sampling*. Building grounded theory is an iterative process of data collection, coding, analysis, theoretical saturation and theoretical sensitivity in planning what to study next. This means that the researcher is led in 'all directions which seem relevant and work' (Glaser, 1978: 46) and must be flexible enough to allow for modifying the study design to accommodate issues that emerge as the study progresses.

For example, in the initial stage of my project I conducted exploratory research among students of Masaryk University from different faculties and departments, aged between 20 and 24 years. This step provided a significant insight into young people's experience of consumption. Respondents were asked to write an essay entitled: 'What does it mean "cool"?' I identified several potential relevant concepts and labelled them with codes such as 'sheeple' (people who behave like sheep or herd-like behaviour), 'mainstream' (always the others, or the antithesis of individuality), 'poseur' (stylization, lack of authenticity) and 'brand devotee' (mostly teenagers, whose self-identity was constituted through the brand). To understand what the students meant by 'sheeple', 'mainstream', 'poseur' or 'brand devotee', it was necessary to carry out further theoretical sampling. This involved a series of focus groups and two small-group semi-structured interviews.

The selection of the focus group participants was based on young people's attitudes towards consumption, especially brands. All discussions drew on previous concepts, but at the same time a new cluster of categories connected closely to the meaning of mainstream emerged, such as 'individualism', 'non-conformity', 'choice', 'freedom' and 'brand-reflexive individual'. Semi-structured interviews provided a deeper insight into the question of what role consumption plays in the conflicting nature of young people's individual choices.

In order to identify and visualize crucial concepts, the categories emerging from gradually collected data and the relationships between them, I used ATLAS.ti, a software program designed to facilitate the organization, work and analysis of qualitative data and to support researchers interested in grounded theorizing. The semantic network in Figure 11.1 captures emerging relationships between mainstream and individualism.

The common thread running through the data was a systematic demarcation of young people against the mainstream, which was described as the opposition to one's individuality. The strategies of grounded theory yielded a new perspective on the relationship between individualism and the mainstream. Formulation of emerging concepts and capturing relationships between them, in other words questioning 'what was going on in the data' (Morse and Richards, 2002: 113), led to a discovery of the mainstream which reflects individualism as a norm, rather than opposing it. Within the debate on the 'post-revolutionary generation' in the Czech Republic, the grounded theory method 'discovered' mainstream as a useful concept for understanding young people's relationship with social change. Within a broader context of sociology of youth, the 'discovery of the mainstream' challenges established assumptions underpinning the sociology of youth's conception of consumption.

(Continued)

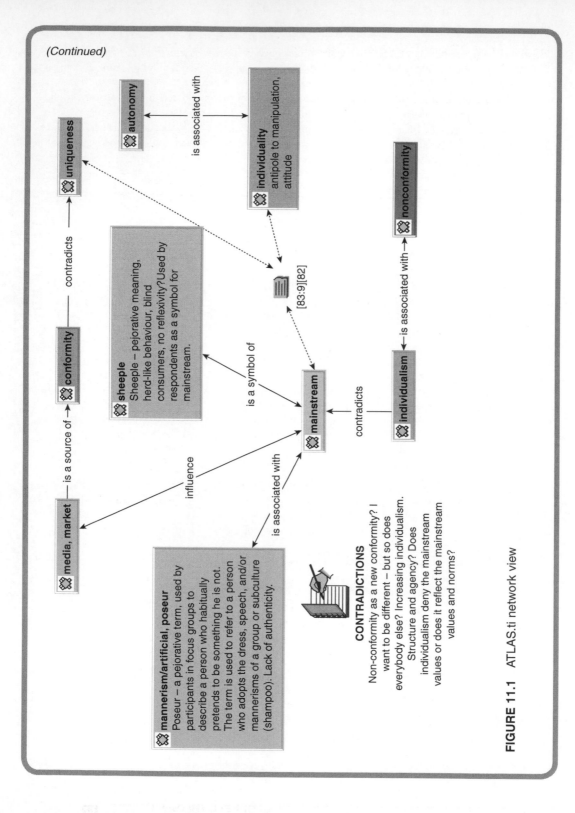

FIGURE 11.1 ATLAS.ti network view

The question of when grounded theory comes to an end is more ambiguous than would be the case for purely deductive or inductive approaches. In a deductive research project the initial research hypothesis and design determine the data to be collected and, once this volume of data has been collected, analysis begins. In more inductive research, data collection occurs largely prior to data analysis and theory development. In the case of grounded theory, data collection and data analysis mix together and each provokes the next round of the other, rather than each occurring in its own discrete and separate time frame. When can such a process be legitimately drawn to a close? Glaser and Strauss put forward the notion of *saturation*, the point at which data collection no longer generates new and significant challenges to the explanatory capacity of the emergent theory. Saturation is not the same as 'nothing new happening' (Charmaz, 2006: 113). Barney Glaser suggests: 'Saturation is not seeing the same pattern over and over again. It is the conceptualization of comparisons of these incidents which yield different properties of the pattern, until no new properties of the pattern emerge. This yields the conceptual density that when integrated into hypotheses makes up the body of the generated grounded theory with theoretical completeness' (1992: 191).

The folding in of data collection and analysis: not pure induction!

As has been highlighted repeatedly above, grounded theory is not a pure form of induction. It tends to start from a relatively inductive position, allowing initial rounds of data collection to be relatively unstructured and aiming at the emergence of themes from the data, rather than for data collection to be structured by an initial research agenda. However, through the process of constant comparison and theoretical sampling, grounded theory moves on from initial induction to a far more deductive process of selecting and testing. Variation exists within grounded theory practice as to how far the stick should be bent towards the more inductive allowance for emergence or the more deductive processes of selection and focus. This tension hinges around the very meaning of the term 'discovery'. Whilst the term implies a relatively passive process by which theory is revealed to the researcher without their prior conceptualization of it, the term also implies the explorer's endeavours to cut a path through the near infinite density of the 'unknown'. As will be seen later in the discussion of diversity within grounded theory, tension exists over how much the explorer can bring with them to their explorations from the start. This is a tension that led Glaser and Strauss to part company over the very meaning of grounded theory. Here, it should be pointed out that even assuming the researcher entered the field in a total state of innocence, they would soon find themselves having to choose between remaining open ended in their data collection and choosing to follow certain leads rather than others. Kathy Charmaz (2006) suggests that one grounded theorist's legitimate selection is another's 'forcing of the data'. She writes: 'A potential problem with ethnographic studies is seeing data everywhere and nowhere, gathering everything and nothing' (2006: 23). Constant comparison and theoretical sampling are said to aid in overcoming this superficiality and lack of focus. However, Charmaz goes on to suggest: 'Some researchers who use grounded theory methods discover a few interesting findings early on in their data collection and then truncate their research. Their work lacks the "intimate familiarity" with the setting or experience that Lofland and Lofland (1995) avow meets the standards for good qualitative research' (2006: 84). Finding a balance between inductive openness and deductive focus is problematic as there is no 'correct' point on the spectrum, and there are competing grounds for bending the stick one way or the other. Charmaz writes: 'The particular form of reasoning invoked in grounded theory makes it an abductive method, because grounded theory includes reasoning about experience for making theoretical conjectures and then checking them through further experience … In brief, abductive inference entails considering all possible theoretical explanations for the data, forming hypotheses for each possible explanation, checking them empirically by examining data, and pursuing the most plausible explanations' (2006: 103). By abductive reason is meant making educated guesses as to what a number of events have in common, or what explains particular differences. These guesses or hunches are then used to encourage further explorations and new directions (Box 11.3).

BOX 11.3 RESEARCH FOCUS

Discovering chronic illness

Kathy Charmaz's (1990) use of grounded theory in research into chronic illness experience and adaptation has sought to challenge the dominant biomedical model of the patient as a passive recipient of biological processes beyond their control. The value of grounded theory lies in allowing the research to focus on how patients engage with their condition and how they seek to overcome the obstacles such conditions generate. Charmaz's work highlights the impact of chronic illness on patients, and in particular on how such conditions damage not just the physical body but also the person's sense of self-identity and control in relation to themselves and their wider social position. However, a grounded approach also allowed for themes of adaptation and adjustment to emerge, accounts of restoration as well as simply damage to self-identity. In adopting a grounded approach Charmaz allows the chronically ill to have a voice for their suffering but also to be seen as active respondents in their relationship with their conditions.

Process of data collection and theory building: coding and memos

Key to the process of grounded theory, and its cycles of data collection and theory building, is the process of coding and building up from simple coding to more elaborate forms of theoretical coding. Coding will receive much greater attention in Part III of this book, in particular in Chapter 19 on qualitative content analysis. However, as grounded theory integrates data collection and analysis, it is necessary to mention coding here, in the particular fashion in which it is undertaken within this approach. Initially, coding is the attempt to draw out the particulars from within each empirical case or instance of data collection (text, interview or observation). This represents a relatively low-level translation of events into units of meaning, and this is designed to allow the researcher to reflect on what is going on in that event, unit or case. It also enables the process of constant comparison as codes (units of meaning assigned to data) can be compared and contrasted in the attempt to identify emergent patterns. These patterns can be used to suggest initial hypotheses, which in grounded theory allow for the selection (by theoretical sampling) of subsequent cases by which these tentative theories can be explored and tested further.

Paul Hodkinson (2008: 90–1) suggests three levels of coding in grounded theoretical data collection and theory building. The first level of coding is 'open coding', which seeks to flag up everything that is in the data. This is sometimes called systematic coding (see Chapter 19), and may involve coding word by word, line by line, incident by incident etc. to truly capture the depth, detail and diversity of the data. Remember that in grounded theory, the initial data collection that will undergo such coding will be relatively small in size. It may consist only of the very early encounters, and as such can be analysed with a very considerable level of detail. Giving particular attention to the actual words spoken by participants is referred to as *in vivo* coding (see Chapter 19). Hodkinson's second level of coding is 'axial coding', where the researcher seeks to identify patterns across the data, and to pay particular attention to those themes that appear to be significant and therefore deserve closer attention. Glaser (1978) uses the term 'focused coding' to refer to the more selective form of coding that emerges after the initial phase of open coding. Corbin and Strauss use the term 'axial coding' to mean roughly the same things, though the two terms reflect differences between Glaser, who tends to keep closer to open coding for longer, and Strauss and Corbin, who are willing to move faster towards the adoption of more selective forms of coding (which reflects the general difference between Glaser's empiricism and Strauss's pragmatism). Somewhat similar to the more deductive end of what Corbin and Strauss call axial coding is what Glaser calls theoretical coding, which seeks to identity overarching patterns within the data. Glaser remains more suspicious of how far such theorization should go, and his conception of theory is more limited than most sociologists would consider. He is interested in identifying not grand theories but only adequate and useful explanations. Hodkinson's third level of coding is what he calls 'selective coding', the identification of key examples and illustrations of the patterns that have emerged in the earlier stages of coding.

The act of writing memos, and attaching these both to chunks of data and to emerging codes, acts as a form of proto-coding, a way of logging emerging ideas and connections before they reach the point where the researcher feels they are secure enough to be used (as codes) to structure the organization and explanation of the data. Memos will be given much greater consideration in the discussion of qualitative data analysis in Part III. Grounded theorists integrate such memo taking into the process of coding and therefore of constant comparison and theoretical sampling; and as such, unlike other forms of research, memos (like coding) become a part of the data collection process.

Diversity

Whilst grounded theory emerged as a reaction to quantitative and deductive forms of research, and defined itself also in opposition to what it saw as descriptive forms of purely inductive qualitative research, the unity of the approach soon collapsed. The primary division arose between Glaser's desire to cleave more to the empiricist critique of theoretically driven forms of deductive research, and Strauss's interest in the pragmatic utility of grounded theory in addressing research themes not discovered as such in the data, but which informed the researcher's approach to what and how they researched. This conflict can be seen to hinge around a narrow and a broad conception of what is meant by the term 'sensitizing concepts'. This term comes from Herbert Blumer's (1956) version of symbolic interactionism and refers to the kinds of framing device that a researcher might use to engage with and select data without being too pre-emptive. The most basic sensitizing concepts would be those of what, how, where, when and why. These concepts form a basic palette of conceptual probes that act to interrogate data beyond the level of simple description. Beyond such very rudimentary sensitizing concepts, debate continues as to what kinds of framing devices or concepts can legitimately be introduced to direct research in grounded theory, in directing constant comparison and therefore theoretical sampling. Whilst Barney Glaser held to a more limited conception of what was legitimate in not 'forcing the data' and as such held to a notion that grounded theory should remain concerned with theories that emerge only from the data, and not which organize and direct data collection in advance, Anselm Strauss (with Juliet Corbin) took a more pragmatic line. For them the purpose of grounded theory could not be to seek pure truth. Rather it allowed the exploration of issues that were of concern to the researcher, even if once so directed the researcher was keen to allow for as much discovery as was possible within the confines of the selected 'topic'. Whilst claiming to agree with Glaser, Kathy Charmaz (2006: 48) seems to cleave closer to Strauss in supporting Ian Dey (1999: 251) when he writes: 'There is a difference between an open mind and an empty head.' Whilst Glaser can be presented as a naïve empiricist, who believes in the possibility of entering the field like a 'blank slate', this is unfair. Nevertheless, the value of grounded theory does rather rely upon the claim that such an approach can render the researcher more open to emergence and to discovery than if they were to adopt a pre-emptive hypothesis testing approach.

A second divergence can be seen in Kathy Charmaz's (2006) constructivist version of grounded theory. This in turn challenges the empiricism and pragmatism of Glaser and Strauss. 'Glaser and Strauss talk about discovering theory as emerging from data separate from the scientific observer. Unlike their position, I assume that neither data nor theories are discovered … We construct' (2006: 10). Many qualitative researchers, in their opposition to natural scientific models applied to social research, may feel comfortable with this constructivist suggestion that data and theory are constructed and not discovered externally from the researcher. The sense that data and theory are invented rather than constructed is in fact not entirely dissimilar from what either Glaser or Strauss would accept. However,

Glaser would suggest that it is the purpose of the grounded theory methodology to help ensure that the real empirical world beyond the researcher's mind and actions plays as great a part as is possible in the construction process, even if of course the researcher is active in drawing together and interpreting their data, codes and memos. Strauss's pragmatist leanings would also suggest that whilst all knowledge is active and shaped by practical goals and choices, this does not leave such constructions as solely the creations of the researcher's preconceptions. However, the stronger versions of constructivism, such as Charmaz appears at times to advocate, would make it hard to see the value of grounded theory, if even such a grounded methodology could not break out of the researcher's preconceptions.

Strengths and limitations

The professed benefits of grounded theory lie in the claim that such an approach avoids 'forcing the data' and reduces the disparity between overarching theory and a diminished research process, where data are simply packaged to test predefined theoretical models. Attendance to what happens in your data, and the attempt to build theoretical models from the ground up as it were, are said to challenge and surpass existing forms of deductive research in both validity and utility, as such theories that emerge from the data are driven by the priorities that exist for those being researched, rather than those of the researcher and their abstracted agenda.

Paul Hodkinson (2008: 91–5) suggests three main weaknesses in the grounded theoretical approach. First, he suggests that grounded theory is too prescriptive. The process of developing theory through constant comparison and theoretical sampling, whilst being better focused than purely inductive forms of ethnography, and less deductively structured than a purely prestructured questionnaire or experiment, requires a very high level of structure and selection once the initial period of open data collecting and open coding has evolved into more selective and testing mode. As such, whilst not gaining the scale that would be possible in a large-scale survey, grounded theory approaches tend to lose the openness characteristic of more open-ended forms of qualitative and inductive research. This may be seen as a balance between two problematic extremes or the failure to escape from the limitations of both. The second weakness Hodkinson suggests is the limited explanatory force of grounded theory accounts. Whilst claiming to be moving beyond simple description, the formulation of theory in grounded theory is really only ever the best account of the relatively small dataset being researched. Whilst grounded theory claims that the researcher should continue to research until they reach saturation, it is unlikely that any small-scale researcher could ever exhaust all the possible explanations and alternative combinations of circumstances possible, unless of course they limit the scope of their claims to a very tiny number of people and situations. In either case the researcher's claims can only ever be very modest unless the research was very extensive and intensive (which is often not possible within the research budgets and timetables afforded to researchers who do not offer funders a clearly defined research question in advance). Finally,

Hodkinson questions what he calls the 'God Trick', by which he means the appearance of something from nothing. Can the researcher really generate theory from data alone, rather than through the prism of prior theory? Even ardent grounded theorists like Charmaz suggest this is naïve, and even one of the founders of the perspective moved a long way from the strong initial stating of this position.

Despite these criticisms, which might all be seen as statements of limitation rather than as fundamental criticisms, the approach set out by Glaser and Strauss in 1967 still offers an attractive way to engage in qualitative research by steering a path between extremes, those of pure deduction and pure induction.

Summary

Grounded theory is neither coherent, nor capable of addressing what many social scientists believe in advance to be the key research questions that require attention. It is rarely ever possible to start from a blank slate, when researchers and sponsors want answers to questions that have been posed in advance. It is rarely possible to engage in open-ended enquiry. Nevertheless, grounded theory offers a rationale and a method for engaging in research from the ground up, and even when few have the freedom to engage in a purified form of grounded research (if such a pure form could ever be defined), the suggestion that new insights (or theories) can emerge from data offers a useful corrective to established intellectual and policy-oriented agendas.

 ■ **Questions**

1 How does grounded theory 'fold' data collection and data analysis into each other?
2 How is grounded theory divided on the relationship between discovery and theory?
3 Some people see grounded theory as flexible, whilst others see it as highly rigid. How can the same approach generate such divergent perspectives?

■ ■ **Further reading** ■

Charmaz, Kathy (2006) *Constructing Grounded Theory: A Practical Guide through Qualitative Analysis*. London: Sage.

Corbin, Juliet and Strauss, Anselm (2008) *Basics of Qualitative Research*, 3rd edn. London: Sage.

Dey, Ian (1999) *Grounding Grounded Theory*. San Diego: Academic.

Glaser, Barney and Strauss, Anselm (1999 [1967]) *The Discovery of Grounded Theory*. Chicago: Aldine Transaction.

TWELVE

INTRODUCTION TO QUANTITATIVE RESEARCH DESIGN

Aims

By the end of this chapter you will be able to:

- Understand what is meant by the term 'research design'.
- Distinguish between experimental and non-experimental designs.
- Outline the different types of quantitative research design available to the social researcher.

- **Understand the difference between primary data collection and the use of secondary data.**
- **Consider ethical issues associated with research including confidentiality, anonymity and informed consent.**

Research design

Quantitative research design is based within the positivist traditions of the natural sciences. The purpose of a research design is to provide a framework for the collection and analysis of data. In the natural sciences research is often performed using experiments that are designed to control for all known factors that could influence the data collection. These experimental designs are concerned with controlling and manipulating a specific characteristic, called a variable, and measuring any changes that occur as a result of an external stimulus being applied. An example is applying heat to a container of ice and measuring the change in the state of the water from solid ice to liquid water.

In social research the quantitative research design ideally should stay within the traditions of positivism and naturalism. However this is problematic, as it would be almost impossible to manipulate characteristics in a social setting. For example, in a study that wished to investigate changing political opinions at different ages, the researcher could record an individual's political opinion but would be unable to change their age to then record any change in that political opinion. The natural passage of time would have to elapse before recording political opinion at an older age.

In some instances it may be possible to adopt the techniques of the natural sciences, but to do so would raise serious ethical issues. An example is randomly placing children into two separate groups and allocating them into different educational settings where one group is more disadvantaged than the second group.

In response to the difficulties of the experimental design, social research has developed alternative non-experimental approaches that focus on collecting data from already occurring groups in social settings. Statistical analysis techniques are used to compare the data from these different groups. The best known of these non-experimental designs is the cross-sectional design. The logic of the experiment with its focus on analysing the relationships between characteristics is maintained. In the experimental design the change in one variable as a result of the application of a stimulus is measured, whereas in the non-experimental design, data on a number of different characteristics or variables are collected and analysed to explore the possible relationships and associations between those variables. The main method of collecting these data is the self-completion survey or structured interview.

There are a number of experimental and non-experimental designs available. This chapter will detail the main experimental and non-experimental designs. Chapter 13 will discuss variables and the testing of relationships between variables, the key stages in the research process, and the development of a research question, hypotheses and operationalization. Chapter 14 discusses various sampling techniques for selecting participants in a study. Chapter 15 concentrates on the two main research methods in quantitative research, the self-completion survey and the structured interview; key issues in question development, format and sequencing, piloting, data collection and preparing question responses for analysis by a computer are discussed.

Primary data collection or secondary sources?

The main emphasis in this chapter is on the collection of primary data. This is research where the researcher undertakes all the stages in the research process, from research question to final data analysis. In many cases this is the most appropriate method for the topic under investigation. There may be some topic areas that can be researched and explored further using existing data that have been collected, coded and entered into data files. The use of such sources is called secondary data analysis. The decision whether to undertake primary research or to use secondary data sources will ultimately be determined by their availability and appropriateness for the research area.

Research design: experimental and non-experimental

Research design provides the logical framework upon which the research project is conducted and enables the researcher to gather evidence that will allow the research question to be addressed.

The function of a research design is to ensure that the evidence obtained enables us to answer the initial question as unambiguously as possible. Obtaining relevant evidence entails specifying the type of evidence needed to answer the research question, to test a theory, to evaluate a programme or to accurately describe the phenomenon (de Vaus, 2001: 9).

Research design is often confused with research method. The two are intrinsically linked but are distinct from each other. 'Research method' refers to the actual techniques of data collection, for example, self-completion surveys, interviews, focus groups and participant observation. Experimental research designs are based upon the natural sciences. Non-experimental research designs have been developed to take account of research undertaken in social settings. Frequently used non-experimental designs include the case study design, the cross-sectional design, the longitudinal design and the comparative design.

The classic experimental design

The classic experimental design involves randomly allocating subjects into two groups, the experimental group and the control group. Observations of the characteristic to be measured, known as a dependent variable, in both groups are undertaken at the start of the research, often referred to as the pre-test. The experimental group is then subjected to the manipulation or stimulus, known as the independent

Groups	Observation 1	Experiment stage	Observation 2
Experimental group	Pre-test	Experiment performed	Post-test
Control group	Pre-test	No experiment	Post-test

←——— Compare and analyse ———→

FIGURE 12.1 The classic experimental design

variable, while the control group is not subjected to the stimulus. A second set of observations of the measured characteristic is then taken from both groups, often referred to as the post-test (see Figure 12.1). Pre-test and post-test observations of both groups can then be compared and analysed.

There are variations on this experimental format: see Black (1999) for a detailed discussion. There are a number of issues to be considered in relation to the experimental design. The first is the application of such a design in the social world. It is often not possible to be able to allocate subjects randomly into two groups, and even where it is possible, there is an issue of other external factors influencing the measured observations. The second issue is that introducing a manipulation or stimulus can be very difficult.

Quasi-experimental design

In situations where a classic experimental design cannot be achieved, the researcher may decide to use a quasi-experimental design. While not adhering to all of the characteristics of an experimental design, it endeavours to meet certain characteristics of the approach and is often applied in situations where subjects cannot be allocated to an experimental or a control group. There are many variations on the quasi-experimental design. The main feature of a quasi-experimental design is that the subjects are allocated to groups according to already occurring features and are not randomly allocated by the researcher. The two main types of quasi-experimental design are non-equivalent control group designs and before-and-after designs (Schutt, 2001: 185). Non-equivalent control group designs have experimental and control groups that the subjects naturally belong to. The same process of pre-test and post-test is undertaken and the experimental group is subjected to the manipulation of the independent variable. Before-and-after designs differ in that there is no control group. Subjects are measured pre-test, subjected to the manipulation of the independent variable, and measured again post-test.

Experimental and quasi-experimental designs have been used by policy makers and government departments to assess the impact of a policy or programme initiative. Examples of such initiatives are an assisted return to work programme to help support the long-term unemployed back into the workplace; and an awareness raising programme aimed to reduce the level of young people who engage in criminal activity and decrease their risk of entering the youth justice system. For the former, in a quasi-experimental design, workless individuals who have been in receipt of state benefit support for 12 months could be randomly selected for inclusion in the research. Half of the participants could be allocated to the programme intervention, known as the experimental group, while the other half continue with the normal services offered, forming the control group. Here, the control group is sometimes referred to as the counter-factual. The term 'counter-factual' refers to what would have been likely to happen to the group of individuals who were not exposed to the intervention or policy initiative. The outcome of the control group is used as an estimate of the counter-factual. For the second example, a quasi-experimental design could be used to assess the outcomes of two groups of young people: an experimental group who have been convicted of a crime and had direct experience of the youth justice system, and a control group who have no first-hand experience of the youth justice system. Here data can be collected over time, perhaps using existing databases of information collected on young people and compared over time.

Case study design

A case study design is concerned with the detailed examination of a single case. It is commonly associated with qualitative research techniques (see Chapter 5), though it can be used in quantitative approaches. The case study can seek to explore a topic where there has been little prior knowledge or understanding. It can also involve following one case over a period of time, for example, researching an individual's life history. The key element here is the definition of the term 'case'. A case could be an individual, an organization, an institution, an event or a geographical area.

One of the difficulties of case study design in quantitative research is defining the case. There are occasions when a research project may be described as employing a case study design, yet the defining characteristics of the case are not the key objects under study. For example, the case study may be identified as a work organization, though the focus of the research is the individual employee. Yin (2009) provides a full discussion of undertaken case study research, including the design, case selection, data collection and analysis of results.

Cross-sectional design

A cross-sectional design is the most recognizable research design in social research. It is concerned with collecting data on more than one case at a single point in time and is often referred to as the 'social survey design'. Take care not to confuse this term with the term 'social survey' that is used to refer to the self-completion survey, which is a method of data collection. While a cross-sectional design is typically associated with a social survey, this is not the only data collection method that can be used. A cross-sectional design can be used in qualitative research, for example, when undertaking structured observations and content analysis.

In a cross-sectional design the researcher is concerned with selecting many cases on the basis of variation in identified characteristics, known as variables. An example is selecting individuals or households by geographical area. Data recording different characteristics are collected from each case and used to describe and explore relationships through the detecting of associations between the characteristics. For example, a questionnaire survey records a respondent's age and income. The association between age and income can then be described and analysed using a variety of statistical techniques. For this reason, adopting a cross-sectional design needs consideration of who and how many are included in the research (see Chapter 14 on sampling). Research on small numbers of cases is unlikely to yield sufficient data for patterns and associations to be detected. See Box 12.1 for examples of cross-sectional design research.

BOX 12.1 RESEARCH FOCUS

Cross-sectional design research

British Social Attitudes survey (www.britsocat.com)

The British Social Attitudes (BSA) survey began in 1983 and has been run annually with the exception of 1988 and 1992. The BSA is conducted by the National Centre for Social Research. The purpose of the survey is to collect attitudinal data on social, political, economic and moral issues. The annual nature of the survey means that patterns of attitudinal change, continuity of attitudes and attitudinal movements over time can be monitored. The BSA contributes to the International Social Survey Programme (see section 'Comparative design' later in this chapter), allowing for some of the questionnaire data to be used for cross-national comparisons.

The survey questions are in two parts. One part is a self-completion questionnaire and the second part is administered by a researcher as a face-to-face structured interview. There are core topics that are covered each time, and other topics are raised on a less regular basis. The core questions include defence, the economy, labour market participation and the welfare state. A wide range of questions is also asked to gather background information on the individuals.

The fieldwork is conducted between June and November each year. A stratified random sampling technique is used to identify households from the Postcode Address File (PAF).

British Crime Survey

The British Crime Survey (BCS) started in 1982 and since 2001 has been run as an annual survey. The latest BCS is conducted by the British Market Research Bureau. The purpose of the survey is primarily to collect data on victimization and involves asking respondents about their experiences of property and personal crime in the previous 12 months. This includes crimes that may have not been reported to the police and so provides an evidence base for unreported crimes that are not detected by other systems. Data on attitudes to crime, fear of crime and avoidance of crime are also collected. Since the survey findings report on actual experiences of crime they provide a consistent measure that is not affected by non-reporting or changes in police measurements of crime. Detailed information on each crime incident is recorded. The survey is also used to identify particular groups of individuals who may have a higher likelihood of being a victim of crime, allowing authorities to target crime reduction intervention measures accordingly. As with other repeated surveys, the questions are constant to enable comparisons between years and to identify trends.

The survey questions are in two parts. One part is a self-completion questionnaire and the second part is administered by a researcher as a face-to-face interview. The self completion survey in 2007–8 examined topics on drug use, drinking behaviour, stolen goods and interpersonal violence.

The fieldwork is conducted across 12 months from April to March. A stratified random sampling technique is used to identify private households across England and Wales.

In cross-sectional design the exploration of relationships and associations between variables needs to be carefully thought through. In experimental design the independent variable is that attribute which is being manipulated to measure variability in the dependent variable. In contrast, with cross-sectional design there is no pre-test/post-test measure to compare, as the data are collected at one point in time. Instead the researcher has to use the knowledge gained, through an extensive literature review and prior experience, to determine the independent and dependent variable(s). In many instances the independent variable will be a characteristic of the case, for example where an individual sex, marital status and age. Changes in the dependent variable, for example income, can be explored by examining the differences between men and women, or plotting the variation in income by age. Variables and the testing of relationships are discussed in more detail in the section 'Variables and levels of measurement' in Chapter 13. Within cross-sectional designs the actual collecting of data can take place as a one-off research project, for example a survey of university students where a sample of students receive a questionnaire at the same time. Alternatively, the data collection can take place across a wider period of time. These are used in large surveys, typically those conducted by government departments and where the survey is repeated at regular intervals. Data can be collected either continuously throughout the year or at set points in the year. These approaches are particularly useful where there are likely to be variations in the topic being researched. For example, students' fear of crime around a university campus may vary according to the time of year, with shorter periods of daylight and dark evenings increasing fear compared to the longer daylight hours of the summer term.

Longitudinal design

Longitudinal design involves collecting data over time and is particularly useful when studying social change. The design will involve data collection from the same sample at two or more points in time. The data from each collection period can be compared to assess social change. Longitudinal studies are financially more expensive and time consuming, and consequently are not frequently undertaken by individual researchers. They tend to be conducted by government-based organizations and use self-completion surveys or structured interviews as the method of data collection.

The design of the longitudinal study tends to be a cross-sectional design. The Longitudinal Study, established in 1973, was designed to collect information on a randomly selected sample of half a million individuals in England and Wales. This was about 1 per cent of the entire population. Information is collected on these individuals from a variety of official sources. The National Health Service Central Register (NHSCR) is used to identify and track individuals. Data from the vital statistics indexes (births, marriages, deaths) and census data are linked using the NHSCR register (Marsh, 1988). Studies that involve surveying representative samples at two or more points in time are known as panel studies. A high level of consistency across the questions and the representative samples will allow the researcher to analyse the data for changes over time or time trends (Ruspini, 2000). Studies that involve returning to the sample participants are known as cohort studies. For a fuller discussion of the issues relating to longitudinal design, see Hakim (2000), de Vaus (2001), Marsh (1988) or Menard (1991). In the UK a new longitudinal study has been commissioned and started in January 2009: see Box 12.2 for more details.

BOX 12.2

UNDERSTANDING SOCIETY LONGITUDINAL STUDY

Starting in 2009, the Understanding Society project uses a longitudinal research design. The following is an extract from the Understanding Society website (http://www.understandingsociety.org.uk/).

The Economic and Social Research Council (ESRC) has commissioned a definitive study of how British households respond to regional, national and international change. The study will equip decision makers with a deeper understanding of society as they assess the impact of the recession and look ahead to longer term challenges like climate change and our ageing society.

ESRC's Understanding Society study is tracking 100,000 people from 40,000 households over time seeing how their economic and personal situations change year after year. It is capturing the key data telling us *Who the people participating in the survey are?* – whether they are young, old, working class, have a disability or are from an ethnic minority.

The study is sweeping across a wide spectrum of questions that extract information to tell us *about people's circumstances* – like our state of health; have we just lost our job, have we been a victim of crime; are we in debt, are we involved in our local community?

Understanding Society will tell us *how we are living our lives*. We will look at people's ambitions for their children, their trust in government, their use of social media to communicate with friends, do we take drugs and are children staying out without their parents' knowledge.

What researchers can then do is stand back and make links between these quite distinct pieces of information and *draw out key patterns to inform policymakers*, so we get a much fuller profile about:

- Does a whole section of the community experience deteriorating health if they are out of work for months and months?
- Does relationship breakup now have an even bigger financial impact on women than it has in the past?
- Are some children more influenced by their friends at school than their parents, whether it be about drugs or career ambitions?
- How far are people changing their environmental behaviour as we face the onset of climate change?
- Are black teenagers in London more likely to feel education can give them a better life than Pakistani counterparts in the North West and why?

As we track people over the years we will build up an understanding of their past that will enable us to see how different routes took them to different situations, whether it be to family breakup, poverty in old age, setting up a business or dropping out of university.

Comparative design

Comparative research design has been developing and growing in recent years. The focus of comparative research is to identify differences and similarities between different groups, for example, nation-states. A research project could examine the similarities and differences in deprivation experienced by rural populations in different countries in the European Union. The growth in comparative research has taken place at a time of increasing globalization and the development of mass communication systems. Information and data on a variety of aspects, particularly nation-states, are more widely available through the development of government sponsored surveys and censuses. Other organizations that also collect data are corporate businesses and non-government organizations. Comparative research encounters a number of research issues relating to the design, fieldwork and analysis which may not be consistent across different countries. This is a particular issue to consider in relation to cultural differences and language/translation. The International Social Survey Programme (ISSP) is an annual programme of cross-national collaboration on social surveys covering topics of importance to social science researchers. The programme enables national projects, for example the British Social Attitudes survey (see Box 12.1), to include an international cross-cultural comparison dimension to the research. Research topics are agreed cross-nationally and the topics, known as modules, vary year by year: some modules are repeated at intervals of three to four years; others are new and may be one-off. As part of this process there is a methodological research team that focuses on cross-cultural methods to ensure equivalence in survey questions across nations. More information on the ISSP can be found at www.issp.org.

The ethics of quantitative research

A general discussion of ethical issues in social research can be found in Chapter 2. The following highlights the central ethical issues when undertaking quantitative research.

Confidentiality and anonymity

Confidentiality refers to the researcher ensuring that no one outside the research team will be able to identify the participants in the study and that responses of individuals are not directly repeated to others. Anonymity refers to the practice of ensuring that no one will be able to identify the participants in the study. Anonymity is the more challenging ethical issue to address. The process of confidentiality begins with the contacting of the sample, which should be undertaken by the research team, although administratively this is not always possible. Care needs to be taken during the data collection process to record sensitive data, such as names and addresses, separately from the question responses. The normal practice for confidentiality is to allocate each participant a unique identifying code.

The researcher does need to be aware that even these procedures do not always ensure anonymity, as an individual with specific knowledge of the sampling frame may be able to identify individuals through careful scrutiny of the final research report. In an organization it may be possible to identify individuals through other characteristics, for example, position in the company, sex and length of service. In these cases the researcher needs to give careful consideration to how the research findings are reported.

Informed consent

It is the duty of the researcher to provide the potential participant with information on the nature and purpose of the research to be undertaken. In obtaining informed consent the participant should be given enough time to consider their participation in the research. Ideally details should be given before the completion of the data collection. In the case of a mail survey, this can take the form of a covering letter. For research involving face-to-face interviews, participants should be sent a covering letter prior to the interview and the interviewer should check that the respondent has received this and understood the research before starting the interview. In the case of interviews, it is also important that documentary evidence is collected to confirm that informed consent has been obtained, and this can take the form of signing an agreement. This is increasingly important to avoid any future litigation issues. For surveys, completion and return of the questionnaire can be taken as evidence of consent.

There is an issue of how much detail to pass on to the respondent. This is difficult to stipulate, as it will vary according to the nature of the project. It may also be necessary to obtain informed consent from 'key others' who may act as gatekeepers to access. For example, a study involving school children completing a questionnaire survey may require the informed consent of the headteacher, the classroom teacher, the parents/guardians and the school children themselves.

Conduct of the researcher

The researcher should at all stages in the research process conduct themselves in a professional manner.

The researcher should accurately record the data and process the data accordingly. The fabrication or falsification of data is a serious misconduct offence. In order for the researcher to ensure confidentiality and anonymity, the privacy of the data collected needs to be protected. The data should be recorded anonymously. If data are recorded with respondents' personal information, they should conform to the Data Protection Act legislated in the relevant country. Details of the United

Kingdom Data Protection Act (1998) can be found at the Information Commissioner website (http://www.dataprotection.gov.uk/). Details on privacy legislation in the US can be found at the Federal Trade Commission (www.ftc.gov).

Ethics and internet-based research

In addition to the ethical issues that have been discussed so far, using the internet for research raises some specific that need to be considered. The first is that of anonymity. Respondents who e-mail completed surveys back to the researcher can be identified by the reply e-mail address. Surveys based on websites can record the internet protocol (IP) address of the computer that is accessing the web page. It is technically possible for this address to be located. Websites can also set cookies – requests for information – which can gather additional details about the user's computer. Respondents who use computers in public access areas, internet cafés or libraries reduce the technical possibility of being traced. An additional concern to the researcher is the issue of ensuring confidentiality through not disclosing data collected to any third parties. This is subject to the security software system installed on the web server. Security could be breached by hackers who can access and corrupt data files. (Also see Ethics and E-Research in Chapter 17.)

Summary

Quantitative research design provides the framework for the social researcher to undertake a research project based on the positivist traditions of the natural sciences. This chapter has detailed both experimental and non-experimental designs that are available for the collection of primary data. The adoption of an experimental design would follow most closely those adopted in the natural sciences. However, the social researcher needs to consider both practical and ethical issues as to the feasibility, or indeed the desirability, of adopting such a design. The majority of quantitative researchers maintain their theoretical position within positivism and naturalism by adopting non-experimental research designs. The most commonly used design is that of the cross-sectional or social survey design. Cross-sectional designs and longitudinal designs are adopted in the large government-based surveys that researchers use to undertake secondary data analysis.

 ■ **Questions**

1 What is the difference between primary data and secondary data?
2 What are the main features of an experimental design?
3 Describe the different types of experimental and non-experimental quantitative research designs.
4 What are the ethical issues associated with quantitative research?

Aldridge, Alan and Levine, Ken (2001) *Surveying the Social World: Principles and Practice in Survey Research*. Buckingham: Open University Press.

Black, Thomas (1999) *Doing Quantitative Research in the Social Sciences: An Integrated Approach to Research Design, Measurement and Statistics*. London: Sage.

May, Tim (2001) *Social Research: Issues, Methods and Process*, 3rd edn. Buckingham: Open University Press.

Robson, Colin (2002) *Real World Research: A Resource for Social Scientists and Practitioner-Researchers*, 2nd edn. Oxford: Blackwell.

Sarantakos, Sotirios (1998) *Social Research*, 2nd edn. Basingstoke: Macmillan.

THIRTEEN

HYPOTHESES, OPERATIONALIZATION AND VARIABLES

Aims

By the end of this chapter you will be able to:

- **Understand the key stages in the hypothetico-deductive process.**
- **Describe what is meant by the terms 'hypothesis' and 'concept'.**
- **Understand the process of operationalization.**
- **Distinguish between independent, dependent and control variables.**
- **Describe the four different levels of measurement.**

Formation of the research question: theory, hypotheses and operationalization

Formulating a research question involves stating clearly what the researcher wants to find out. The research question will be a product of theories drawn from the literature review, discussions with professionals or experts in the area of study, and the 'hunches' or theories of the researcher. A full discussion of this process can be found in Part I. The key factor in formulating the research question is that it must clearly state what exactly is to be researched. It is often the hardest aspect for the new researcher to grasp, as it requires a level of focus that is not initially easy to find. The development of a research question is the first stage in the research process.

The hypothetico-deductive research process is summarized by a number of stages (see Figure 13.1). At the first stage the literature review and knowledge gathered from other sources allow for a theory to be developed, and from the theory a hypothesis may be constructed which can, in turn, be tested. A hypothesis states the expected causal relationships between concepts. A concept is a unit that allows a researcher to organize an idea or observation, for example, the concept of the family or a healthy lifestyle. Before the hypothesis can be tested the concepts need to be operationalized, requiring the development of an operational definition and measurable indicators. Without an operational definition of the concept it would not be possible to collect data to accept or reject the relationship stated in the hypothesis. For example, if a project were examining family structures, how would the concept of family be defined? If a project were going to explore variations in healthy lifestyle amongst different social classes, the concepts of both healthy lifestyle and social class would need to be defined.

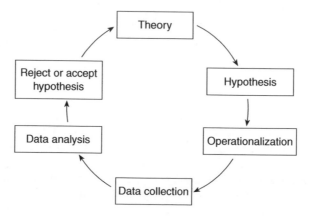

FIGURE 13.1   The research process in a hypothetico-deductive research model

The next phase in the hypothetico-deductive model is the collection of data. After data collection, the data can be analysed to explore the relationships stated in the hypothesis. From the analysis the initial hypothesis can then be accepted or refuted, and subsequent alterations to the initial theory made.

The research process as shown in Figure 13.1 is an idealized model. The reality for the social researcher is that the research process is frustrated by the complexities of the social world. As Bryman states:

> Quantitative research is invariably much more messy. It tends to involve false trails, blind alleys, serendipity and hunches to a much greater degree than the idealization implies. Nor does the idealized model take sufficient account of the importance of resource constraints on decisions about how the research should be carried out. (1988: 21)

However, the idealized model of the research process does provide valuable structure and rigour for the researcher. The importance of addressing the issues at each stage in the research process should not be underestimated.

Operationalization: measuring concepts and developing indicators

Concepts need to be operationalized through the development of an operational definition and measurement tools. Operationalization is the process of turning abstract theoretical concepts into observable and measurable entities. Some concepts are easier to provide an operational definition for than others that are more abstract and difficult to 'pin down'. The key issue for the researcher is that there is often no consensus on the definition of concepts and the measurement tools or indicators developed for them. The literature review should provide the researcher with information on how previous research conducted in a particular subject area defined and operationalized the concepts used. This can be used as a foundation for the development of the measurements in your own research.

De Vaus (2001) provides a framework for developing the measurements called the 'ladder of abstraction'. The first step is to define the concept; one or more definitions may already exist and the researcher will need to decide which one to use or to develop their own definition. In either instance, a clear rationale for the decision needs to be stated. The next stage is to decide on the different dimensions through which the concept can be measured. Within each dimension, subsequent subdimensions may exist. The next stage is then to devise an operational or working definition of the dimension that can be observed and measured. Through the operational definition of the dimension, the development of appropriate indicators can be achieved.

Where a concept has more than one dimension, multiple indicators can be developed. The issue for the researcher is then what indicators to use and how many of the indicators to include in the data collection and analysis stages. Many indicators already exist and have been developed amongst academic and professional researchers over many years. It makes sense at both the practical and the methodological levels for the first-time or student researcher, with limited experience, to make use of existing indicators. Use of these indicators, where appropriate, will also allow the researcher to make comparisons between their own research findings and those of others. Where new indicators are developed, with slightly different definitions, comparisons become problematic. Indicators exist in a wide range of fields and particularly in relation to areas that are strategic to government policy decisions. These indicators are likely to have been developed from their application in government sponsored surveys, such as the General Household Survey and the Family Expenditure Survey. Further details on the Office for National Statistics programme to harmonize the data collection of standard concepts across UK government departments can be found at the 'Harmonisation' website at http://www.ons.gov.uk/about-statistics/harmonisation/index.html.

Example of a process of operationalization: students, grades and paid work

Some people suggest that students undertaking paid work during their studies gain valuable experience that enhances both their future employability and their academic performance. Others argue that paid work interferes with study and leads to reduced academic performance and hence has a detrimental effect on future employment prospects. In order to investigate this issue it is essential to operationalize the concepts of 'student', 'paid work', 'academic performance' and 'employability'.

By 'student' we would need to clarify whether we were referring only to undergraduate degree students or whether we also wished to include other groups, such as pre-higher-education students, those on other kinds of higher educational studies, and/or postgraduate-level students. In addition, we would need to clarify whether we wished only to focus upon full-time students, or whether we would also want to include those who study part-time. What would count as full-time and part-time then becomes a key issue. It may be important to consider whether different institutions of learning adopt different definitions of full-time and part-time study, which might affect the comparability of the data.

By 'paid work' we would need to decide whether we were only interested in work carried out during academic term time or semester time, or whether work during holidays and vacations would also be taken into account. The time of day at which work takes place may alter the effect it might have on studies, so this may be a factor. Should work carried out at weekends be recorded, or are we only interested in work that took place during the week, when students might otherwise be attending to their studies? The type of work carried out may also be significant: the question of how to classify different kinds of work would require serious attention. The number of hours spent at work may be more difficult to record than might be imagined, and the rate of pay should also be recorded as poor pay may influence quality of life and hence performance.

By 'academic performance' do we only mean formal grades, or are there other elements to be taken account of? How might these be measured? Frequency of attendance, contribution to tutorials and seminars, involvement in student-centred self-support groups, and fulfilling deadlines and performance targets may all be affected by time spent in paid work. Should we measure these, or simply measure final grade outcomes? Should we record students' self-perception regarding grades and other indicators, or seek institutionally held secondary data?

Post-study employability is, of course, something that happens some time after a student's study time. How long should one wait to test the relationship between study, grades, paid work and future employment? Would it be better to measure current students and wait till they graduate, or might it be best to approach those already in employment and trace back their educational performance and employment record while they were students. And, what criteria should be applied to 'measuring' employment success? Is it enough simply to measure income, or are other factors significant? What might these be and how might they be measured?

Before any quantitative data can be collected, the issues raised around the above four concepts need to be resolved. Each concept needs to be operationalized into a measurable data collection tool (Box 13.1).

BOX 13.1 STOP AND THINK

Pro-environmental behaviour

Pro-environmental behaviours are a particular interest for the UK government Department for Environment, Food and Rural Affairs (DEFRA). The department supports policy developments in the areas of a healthy natural environment, a sustainable and low-carbon economy, a thriving farming sector and a sustainable, healthy and secure food supply (www.defra.gov.uk). DEFRA has undertaken research across all of these areas. One particular focus has been on identifying the evidence base of consumer behaviour in the UK population. In 2007 the Survey of Public Attitudes and Behaviours toward the Environment was undertaken. The concept of pro-environmental behaviour covers a wide range of issues and topics. The survey's aim was to capture data on people's thoughts about and behaviours towards a range of issues relating to the environment, including transport and recycling.

The survey operationalized pro-environmental behaviour to focus on the following areas:

- attitudes and knowledge in relation to the environment
- transport
- energy and water efficiency
- recycling
- eco-friendly purchasing.

In each area questions were asked that captured data on attitudes, behaviour and barriers.

Select one of the five areas listed above. Consider how you would operationalize the concepts in the area. Once you have completed this, visit the DEFRA website for more information on the survey. Further information can also be found at the Office for National Statistics (www. statistics.gov.uk).

Variables and testing relationships

A hypothesis is a statement that expresses the proposed relationship between two variables, an independent variable and a dependent variable. There are three different types of variable in the describing and testing of relationships set out in the hypothesis. A variable is defined as a characteristic, an attribute or a single unit of information collected on a case. A case is the individual respondent, for example, a person, a business or an educational institution. If the case were an individual, some of the variables would contain data that describe their attributes, for example, age, sex or marital status. Alternatively, if the case were a business some variables would contain characteristics that would describe the company, for example, the business sector, the number of employees and the annual financial turnover. Additional variables would also contain data that related to the topic area to be studied.

To establish a relationship between two variables, as stated in a hypothesis, requires the use of statistical techniques to establish if there is an association between the two variables. By association we mean here whether a change in the observed value of one variable corresponds to a change in the observed value of another variable. Variables can be assigned three different roles depending on the complexity of the hypothesis or model of the relationship: independent variable, dependent variable or control variable. The hypothesis represents what the researcher proposes as the relationship between the variables. Variables can take on one or more of these roles according to the relationship that is being described and tested.

The independent variable, also referred to as the cause, is assumed to be the variable that is influencing a second, dependent variable. The independent variable is presented as the X variable in mathematical notation. The dependent variable, also referred to as the effect variable, is the variable that is being influenced by the independent variable. The dependent variable is presented as the Y variable in mathematical notation. In many instances there is a time order associated with the independent variable and dependent variable relationship. The relationship between the independent and dependent variables is shown in Figure 13.2.

The control variable is a variable that the researcher 'suspects' may have an influence on the relationship between the independent and dependent variables. The exact nature of the influence may not be understood. It is often presented as the Z variable in mathematical notation. Figure 13.3 shows the possible influences that the control variable can have on the relationship between the independent and dependent variables. The control variable can have a direct influence on the independent variable X. Alternatively, the control variable may intervene or mediate in the relationship between the independent X and dependent Y. These are shown in Figure 13.3 as a and b respectively.

Figure 13.2 Independent and dependent variables

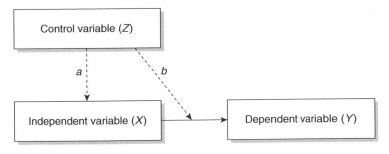

Figure 13.3 Control variables

The process of analysing the relationship between an independent and a dependent variable while controlling for the effects of a third, control variable is referred to as 'elaboration'. When the relationship between the independent and dependent variables disappears as the result of the introduction of a control variable, the original causal association between variable X and variable Y is said to be spurious.

While it is possible for the researcher to undertake analysis of all possible relationships between all variables in their dataset, it is not a recommended or efficient practice. Attempting to embark on such a task will result in too great a volume of results that are unmanageable and ultimately meaningless. Instead the strategy should be to collect data relevant to the original model of the relationships and to map out the relevant relationships between variables.

In mapping out relationships between variables, care must be taken to assess the time order of the variables. You need to avoid exploring relationships between two variables where the independent variable naturally occurs in time after the dependent variable. For example, an analysis of a relationship between income and sex has a time order of sex occurring before income. The individual is born with a specific sex, the independent variable; income, the dependent variable, can only occur once the individual is a working adult. Likewise, in the relationship between number of years of formal education and income, the time order is formal education years, the independent variable, and then income, the dependent variable. Chronologically the individual should complete some schooling before entering the labour market. Assessing the time order is a useful technique at the data analysis stage.

Of course, when the researcher reaches the data analysis stage, the idea of setting out a formalized relationship between two variables may seem abstract to the real social world where many factors or variables will influence particular outcomes. For example, one only needs to think of the wealth of literature and research that has been undertaken on widening access and participation in higher education. The focus of much of this research has been on the choices that potential students make and how these choices are 'infused with class and ethnic meanings' and different individuals' biographies and 'opportunity structures' (Ball et al., 2002: 51). Reducing the analysis to a simplistic cause-and-effect relationship between two variables would hardly seem sufficient. The data analysis would need to reflect the range of factors identified from the literature review. The use of a cause-and-effect relationship model, though, does provide a useful structure at the data analysis stage.

Variables and levels of measurement

Variables can be defined into four different data types, known also as levels of measurement, according to the particular features of the data. The four data types are nominal, ordinal, interval and ratio. It is important that the researcher is able to distinguish between them as the data type or level of measurement will influence the type of statistical analysis techniques available at the data analysis stage.

Scale or interval/ratio

Scale or interval and ratio variables contain data that are measured on a continuous scale. They are also referred to as quantitative variables, since the data can be subjected to mathematical operations. Both interval and ratio variables can be placed in rank order of importance and the distance between observations is known and can be calculated. Interval variables have no true zero point; they include measures such as time and temperature. Ratio variables have a true zero point; examples include measures of length, height, weight, age and number of persons in household. For convenience, interval and ratio variables are often referred to as simply interval or scale variables. It is important to note the difference between interval and ratio levels of measurement at the analysis stage, particularly if the researcher decides to manipulate the original data.

Ordinal

For ordinal data, response categories can be placed in a rank order. No calculation can be made as to the distance between the different categories, though it is possible to judge one category to have a higher order than a second category. A common example of ordinal data is a scale measuring attitudes: for example, a five-point scale of strongly agree, agree, neutral, disagree, strongly disagree.

Nominal

Nominal or categorical variables result from questions that ask a respondent to select a response category from a list of named items. For example, a question asks the respondent to select the newspaper that they read on a daily basis from a list of 10 different newspapers. The response categories cannot be placed in any order and no judgement can be made about the relative size or distance of one category to another. Consequently, no mathematical operations – addition, subtraction, multiplication or division – can be performed on these variables. In the literature nominal variables are sometimes referred to as qualitative variables because they have no mathematical properties. Variables that have only two responses, for example 'Yes' or 'No', are known as dichotomies.

Hierarchical order with levels of measurement

Nominal, ordinal and interval/ratio variables can be placed into a hierarchical order. Nominal variables are the lowest, ordinal variables are in the middle, and interval/ratio variables are the highest. This is an important hierarchy to remember, as it is possible to recode, or adjust, the data. Interval/ratio variables can be recoded into ordinal variables or nominal variables. Similarly, ordinal variables can be recoded into nominal variables. However, a lower-order variable cannot be recoded to a higher-order variable. Ordinal variables cannot become interval/ratio variables and, likewise, nominal variables cannot become ordinal or interval/ratio variables.

When developing survey questions it is important that the researcher considers the data type of the question response and the likely analysis to be undertaken (Box 13.2). For example, a question that asks for last week's salary to be recorded to the nearest whole pound, euro or dollar can be analysed using an array of techniques appropriate for interval/ratio data. It can also be manipulated into an ordinal or a nominal variable at a later stage if required. A salary question that has response categories of salary ranges and therefore generates ordinal data can be analysed using ordinal techniques and can be manipulated into wider salary range categories or into nominal data. The researcher needs to balance the analysis techniques available for different levels of measurement against the appropriateness of questions and responses. In the earlier example of salary, would asking someone to specify his or her salary for last week be more likely to result in a refusal to answer than being asked to tick an appropriate salary range?

BOX 13.2 STOP AND THINK

Below are examples of survey questions and the response categories.

1 Are you:

(a) Male

(b) Female?

Level of measurement: nominal. There are two response categories. There is no rank order to the categories, they are just different. This is also an example of a dichotomy, where there are only two categories to select from.

2 What is your personal current yearly salary, before taxation?

(a) Less than £10,000

(b) £10,000–£14,999

(c) £15,000–£19,999

(d) £20,000–£24,999

(e) £25,000–£29,999

(Continued)

(Continued)

    (f) £30,000–£34,999
    (g) £35,000–£39,999
    (h) £40,000 or more

Level of measurement: ordinal. Here there are eight response categories. These eight categories are placed in an ascending order from lowest to highest salary. Therefore the categories can be placed in a rank order.

3 How many months have you been working for your current employer?

    _____ months

Level of measure: scale (interval/ratio). Here the response given is a numeric value recording the actual total number of months. The unit of month is known. The responses can be placed in a rank order, from lowest to highest number of months working for the employer, and the distance between each month is known and equal. So, for example, we know that an individual who has worked for their employer for six months has an employment service record that is twice that for a second individual who has worked three months.

Summary

In the hypothetico-deductive research process, the research moves through a number of defined stages from knowledge gathering, development of a theory, and construction of a hypothesis to the operationalization of concepts, data collection and analysis. The operationalization process turns concepts into observable and measurable entities that are then stored as variables for the purposes of analysis. The subsequent analysis undertaken involves exploring relationships between different variables, and requires independent variables, dependent variables and control variables to be identified.

 ■ **Questions**

1   **What are the key stages in the process of operationalization?**
2   **Give three examples of variables that a researcher may construct to record information about an individual person.**

■ ■ **Further reading** ■

Bryman, Alan (1988) *Quantity and Quality in Social Research*. London: Routledge.

Balnaves, Mark and Caputi, Peter (2001) *Introduction to Quantitative Research Methods: An Investigative Approach*. London: Sage.

Fielding, Jane and Gilbert, Nigel (2006) *Understanding Social Statistics*, 2nd edn. London: Sage.

Office for National Statistics (2009) Harmonisation Programme website. http://www.ons.gov.uk/about-statistics/harmonisation/index.html.

FOURTEEN

SAMPLING

Chapter Contents

Aims

By the end of this chapter you will be able to:

- **Describe the terms 'population', 'sampling frames', 'sampling technique' and 'sample size'.**
- **Understand the difference between probability and non-probability samples.**
- **Outline the different sampling techniques available.**
- **Understand the factors that will influence sample size selection.**

This chapter discusses the decisions about who will participate in the research project. It will cover the issues of population, sampling frames, a variety of sampling techniques and sample size.

If the group to be studied is small, it may be possible to survey the entire group; otherwise a selection of the group will be surveyed which must be representative of the entire group. The first stage in this process is to define the population that is to be surveyed; depending on its size the researcher will then take a sample – a selected number of cases from the population to survey. Consideration of how the cases are selected and the appropriate number of cases to select needs to be addressed.

Population and sampling frames

A population is simply every possible case that could be included in your study. It will be defined by the nature of your enquiry. For example, in a study of first-year student debt the population would all be first-year students. If the research question were further refined to focus on two degree programmes, BSc Geography and BSc Sociology, the population would then be defined as first-year students on BSc Geography and BSc Sociology. In this example the population refers to individuals, though this is not necessarily always the case. The individual units within a population will be defined by the research question and could be companies or households; where quantitative content analysis is being undertaken, the units might be policy documents, media news coverage or minutes of meetings.

When the population is too large to undertake a census, that is, to survey every individual case, then a representative group, called a sample, needs to be selected. As long as the sample is representative of the population, surveying only a fraction of the entire population can still yield results that would, on the whole, be found if the entire population was surveyed. In order to select a sample, a sampling frame needs to be drawn up.

A sampling frame contains every unit in the population and the subsequent sample is drawn from it. The units that are selected are known as sampling units. The main issue facing social researchers is whether they are able to define and locate the population. In the above example, the educational institution should have a definitive list of students enrolled at stage one on either the Sociology or the Geography programmes.

There is a practical distinction that can be made between a population and a sampling frame. While the population is every individual case, the sampling frame is inevitably defined by specific criteria and has the possibility of being out of date (Black, 1999: 119). For example, the list of enrolled students is established at the beginning of the academic year. Students who leave their course of study prematurely may not be accurately recorded and removed from the list.

Defining the population for research purposes in some areas may not be so apparent. For example, a research project wishes to compare the leisure activities of the over-75s that live in rural and city locations. The population would be defined as the over-75s that live in city and rural locations. The first stage would be to define 'city' and 'rural' and from this locate all over-75s within each. This sounds straightforward; however, in reality it is extremely unlikely that a definitive list of all over-75s in rural and city locations exists. The researcher will have to access other sources to build a list, perhaps gaining access to local doctors' lists or finding support organizations that have contact with over-75s. While these may allow a list of individuals who are over 75 years of age to be established, it will be a list of over-75s who *also* have contact with these organizations, and *not* all over-75s.

Types of sampling

One of the key requirements of sampling is that the selected sample is not biased by either over- or under-representing different sections of the population. Consideration of the different characteristics within the population needs to be included in this process. In the earlier example of research into first-year student debt, the researcher may want to ensure that they have a sample that represents the different social backgrounds of first-year students. For example, there may be students who attend university straight from school or college, older students returning to study after a period away from education, students who have parental responsibilities or students who have to travel significant distances to attend lectures on campus.

The different sampling techniques available can be divided into two classifications. Probability samples are based on each case in the population having an equal chance of being selected. Non-probability samples are used when it is difficult to identify all potential cases in the population. There are a number of sampling techniques available within probability and non-probability techniques, each of which will be examined in the subsequent sections.

Probability sampling

There are four main types of probability sample:

- simple random sampling
- systematic sampling
- stratified sampling
- cluster and multi-cluster sampling.

The decision as to which technique to use will depend on 'the nature of the research problem, the availability of good sampling frames, money, the desired level of accuracy in the sample and the method by which the data are to be collected' (de Vaus, 1996: 61).

Simple random sampling

Simple random sampling involves randomly selecting individual units from a sampling frame. The term 'random' refers to a selection based on a mathematical formula that will consistently give all units an equal chance of being selected; it is not just a matter of a researcher randomly selecting units from a list! The mathematical techniques are also employed at the analysis stage and form the basis of inferential statistics and parametric tests (see Chapter 26).

There are a number of defined stages in undertaking a simple random sample (Black, 1999; Fink, 1995b). The first stage is to obtain a complete sampling frame: for example, a list of all first-year degree students. The second stage is to assign each unit, in this instance a student, with a unique number. The third stage is to randomly select the appropriate amount of random numbers. There are several ways of achieving this. One can make use of random numbers generated through a computer or use random number tables. Random number tables contain rows and columns of random numbers. An extract from a random number table is shown in Table 14.1.

TABLE 14.1 Extract from a random number table

29	32	95	99	57	98	08	36	97	08
12	11	80	16	17	01	03	97	59	73
87	58	22	25	55	35	72	79	28	15
02	92	42	87	57	53	53	34	55	75
69	28	63	73	98	45	61	10	43	20

Source: Kmietowicz and Yannoulis, 1988

A systematic selection of random numbers across the table should be made until enough random numbers have been selected for the total sample size required. Deciding on the required sample size is discussed in the section 'Sample size' later in this chapter. The final stage is to match the random numbers with the number of each unit in the sampling frame. The units that match the selected random numbers are included in the final sample.

Simple random sampling works well as a sampling technique when there is a large population with a quality sampling frame. There are some practical considerations when deciding whether to employ this technique. The most obvious and practical issue is linked to the method employed. If the population is large and spread over a large geographical distance, how feasible is it to conduct face-to-face interviews? A mail survey may be more practical in these circumstances, although this then brings in the other issues specific to this method (Box 14.1).

BOX 14.1 STOP AND THINK

Scenario: postal survey of local club runners

You have been asked to conduct a survey of runners who belong to three local running clubs. Fortunately the membership secretary in each club records each member's name, date of birth, sex and home address on the club database. Since your research has obtained the appropriate ethical clearance, the membership secretary is happy for you to have access to the database to draw your sample.

The total membership across the three clubs is 1200. You have sufficient resources to conduct a survey of 300 runners. The table shows the profile of the three clubs.

	Club 1	Club 2	Club 3
Men	400	200	0
Women	200	100	300
Men <35 years old	200	75	0
Men 35+ years old	200	125	0
Women <35 years old	50	40	100
Women 35+years old	150	60	200
Total membership	600	300	300

Selecting a sample of 300 club runners using a simple random sampling technique

A simple random sampling technique would require that a lottery method was used. The researcher would construct a sampling frame of the 1200 club runners. Each sampling unit would be assigned a number and a lottery or random number method to select the sample of 300.

Selecting a sample of 300 club runners using a stratified sampling technique

The research team want to ensure that there is adequate representation of runners from each of the three clubs and from the men and women within each club. A stratified sampling technique is adopted. The sampling frame would be organized by running club, and then within each club further divided into men and women respectively. As with simple random sampling, each sampling unit would be assigned a number with a lottery or random number method used to select the sample. The sample would be selected by using a random technique within each of the stratified variables (club and gender) and with sample size for each as follows:

- Sampling for Club 1: a total of 150 runners will be selected of which 100 will be male and 50 female.
- Sampling for Club 2: a total of 75 runners will be selected of which 50 will be male and 25 female.
- Sampling for Club 3: a total of 75 female runners will be selected. This is a women-only running club.

Systematic sampling

Systematic sampling is an easier technique for sample selecting than simple random sampling. Again the first step is to define the sampling frame. The next stage is to decide upon the sample size and to work out what fraction of the total sampling frame this represents. For example, if there were 1000 first-year students and the sample size was to be 100, then this represents 10 per cent of the population. The first unit would normally be selected by random numbers and every subsequent tenth unit would then be selected.

Systematic sampling is a quicker technique than simple random sampling; however, there is one inherent weakness. It can be easy to inadvertently select units with 'like' characteristics: for example, in a sampling frame of first-year students the student records may have been arranged into a male then female order. If the sample size required you to select every fourth unit and if the randomly selected unit were male, all subsequent case selections would also be male (see Figure 14.1). This can be overcome by careful checking of the characteristics of the sampling frame prior to sample selection.

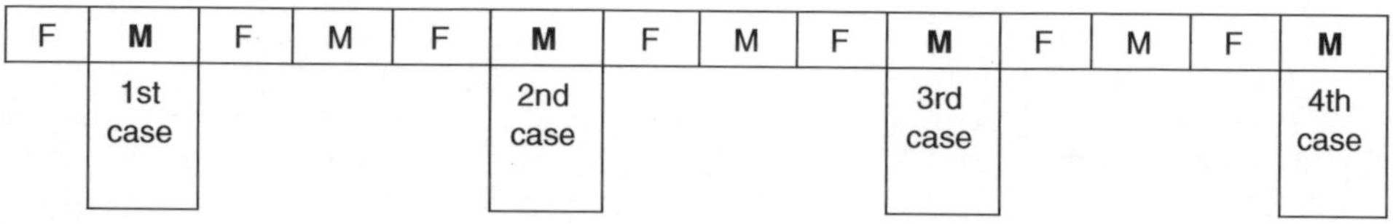

F	**M**	F	M	F	**M**	F	M	F	**M**	F	M	F	**M**
	1st case				2nd case				3rd case				4th case

FIGURE 14.1   Systematic sampling

Stratified sampling

Stratified sampling is designed to produce more representative samples. The sampling frame is constructed according to a characterizing variable. This variable is also referred to as the 'stratified variable', for example, sex or social class, age group or ethnicity. The selection of the variables will be determined by the characteristics required for survey. The sampling frame is then organized according to these variables. For example, in the survey of first-year students we want to select a representative sample based on sex. The first-year students would be organized into two groups, male and female. The next stage is to determine the proportion of male and female students to select. In the population of 1000 students the percentage of men is 60 per cent, the percentage of women is 40 per cent and the sample size is to be 100. Sixty per cent of the sample size should be male and 40 per cent female; thus we need to select 60 male students and 40 female students. A systematic sampling technique can be used to select the male and female students. More complex stratified sampling techniques can be adopted to sample across more than one stratified variable; for a more detailed explanation, see Moser and Kalton (1971).

Cluster and multi-stage sampling

A clustered sampling technique involves selecting a sample based on specific, naturally occurring groups within a population: for example, randomly selecting

20 universities from a list of all universities in England, Wales and Scotland. Cluster sampling is a convenient sampling technique often used when the geographical spread of the population is large and where time and cost issues are of importance. Multi-stage sampling refers to a technique where cluster sampling is repeated at a number of different levels, from general to more specific groups. For example, rather than sample all first-year university students in England, Wales and Scotland, the sampling procedure would be staged. The first stage would involve randomly sampling universities according to different regions in England, Wales and Scotland. The second stage would then be to randomly sample students from each selected university.

Non-probability sampling

Non-probability sampling can be used when no convenient sampling frames of the population are available, or when time or cost restrictions make the surveying of a widely dispersed population impractical.

Convenience, availability or opportunity sampling

Convenience, availability or opportunity sampling is simply a sample that is selected for ease of access. Examples are conducting a survey involving stopping pedestrians in a city centre; stopping students as they walk around a university campus; or magazine or newspaper surveys that ask their readers to complete and return a survey. They are useful when the population is unknown or when a researcher is exploring a new research setting (Schutt, 2001: 130). The disadvantage is that they are not generalizable to the population, making problematic any analysis beyond simply describing the sample.

Quota sampling

The quota sampling technique involves selecting cases, by opportunity-based selection methods, according to some predefined characteristics of the population. These predefined categories are referred to as quotas. The quotas can be selected in order to reflect the population's profile. In the earlier example of a survey of first-year students, if the researcher was unable to obtain a student list from the university they could ascertain from university central reports the proportions of the current new student intake that are male and female. If the proportions were 60 per cent male and 40 per cent female and the sample size was to be 100, then the researcher would need to select 60 male and 40 female first-year students.

The sample selection could be defined further with the introduction of a second quota, for example age. If the university profile of the student population age indicates that two-thirds are 21 years or under and one-third over the age of 21, the selection of male and female students could reflect this. In the sample of 60 men,

40 men should be 21 years or under and 20 men over 21 years. In the sample of 40 women, 27 women should be 21 years or under and 13 women over 21 years.

The difficulty with a quota sampling technique is that the sample is selected according to specified characteristics used in the quotas and excludes other population characteristics, for example, ethnicity and social class. This can be further complicated by not knowing the full population characteristics. Unlike availability sampling, quota samples do at least allow the researcher to establish characteristics that provide for a sample that will allow for comparisons between different groups within the population to be made, for example, comparing men to women.

Purposive or theoretical sampling

In purposive or theoretical sampling, the units are selected according to the researcher's own knowledge and opinion about which ones they think will be appropriate to the topic area. For example, in a study on rural poverty the researcher decides to sample key individuals within local communities, such as local councillors and voluntary group leaders. These individuals are judged by the researcher to hold specific knowledge on this issue. The sample selection is based entirely on their opinion of who are the most appropriate respondents to select.

Snowball sampling

Snowball sampling is a particularly useful technique when a population is hidden and thus difficult to identify. It involves the researcher making contact with one appropriate case from the population who, in turn, is able to put the researcher in contact with other 'like' cases. Snowball sampling is based on social networking and provides an informal method of accessing the required population (Atkinson and Flint, 2001).

The difficulty with snowball sampling is that the technique will inevitably result in a biased sample. The researcher is reliant on others to make appropriate contacts. The sample is self-selecting and will reflect the social networks of those that choose to participate (Griffiths et al., 1993). Since the population is hidden, its characteristics are likely to be unknown and it will be virtually impossible for the researcher to make a judgement as to its representativeness. The sample characteristics will reflect only those that agree to participate and will fail to reflect those cases who refused or were not approached to contribute to the study. Lee (1993) provides a detailed discussion on the different strategies for sampling rare or deviant populations. There is considerable innovation in techniques to access hard to reach populations. These include time–space sampling, time location sampling, respondent driven sampling and capture–recapture techniques (see Marpsat and Razafindratsima, 2010, for a fuller discussion of these techniques).

Sampling and the internet

Sampling in internet-based surveys brings its own set of issues. As with many other areas in the social sciences, there is a problem in being able to define the population and consequently the sampling frame. Adopting a sampling technique is immensely problematic, as there is no definitive list of e-mail addresses. Even if such a list existed, there is scope for sampling bias towards those who have regular access to and usage of the internet. In recent years internet usage has risen dramatically. In the UK 18.3 million households in 2009 had access to the internet, representing 70 per cent of households, with 63 per cent of all households having broadband connection. There are regional differences, with 80 per cent of households in London having access compared to 62 per cent in Scotland (UK National Statistics Omnibus Survey, 2009).

Online research companies offer services in relation to the development of online surveys and fieldwork services. These can include access to established panels of respondents that they manage and select to the requirements of your research. Panels of respondents are basically a database list of participants who are normally paid a small fee for participating in an online survey. The internet company will hold demographic information on the panel members. This information is then used to select the sample for the research. This will typically involve using a probability sampling approach to ensure that the final sample is representative of the target population. This process may also involve setting quotas (sometime referred to as hard quotas) to ensure that sufficient numbers of participants from specific categories or groups are included in the final sample. Commissioning online research companies is useful when the research is of broad interest to the general population and is particularly useful if the research needs to take into account regional variations. An example is the gathering of information on research into organic food purchases or attitudes to local policing strategies. However, the composition of the panel may not always meet the needs of the research and there is an obvious financial cost associated with using these services. Where no convenient sampling frame or database of online respondents exists, the researcher will need to adopt different strategies that are appropriate to the topic. For example, a snowball sampling technique can be an effective strategy to build a sample. The researcher can e-mail topic-appropriate newsgroups and bulletin boards, inviting interested parties to access a web address that contains the self-completion survey. Coomber (1997) provides a solid discussion of some of the issues relating to internet research and sampling.

Sample size

Sample size is an issue that often provides the most concern to first-time researchers. The question often is, 'How large should my sample be in order for it to be representative?' Unfortunately there is no simple answer, as 'the larger the better' does not apply. There are many different elements that contribute to the size of the sample. Some considerations are statistical while others are more practical in nature, with time and cost constraints playing a major role.

The quality of the final sample will depend on the following:

- a well-defined research problem

- a clearly defined and identifiable population to be researched

- the availability of a suitable sampling frame that holds an accurate list of the sampling units in the population

- the use of a probability sampling technique

- identifying a sample size large enough to gather enough evidence on the target group and any subgroups of interest

- identifiable bias in the response and non-response of the sampling units

- other as yet 'unidentified' forms of bias in the research process.

A smaller sample size, with careful attention to the accuracy of the sampling frame and sampling technique, may be more representative than a larger sample selected without consideration of the sampling frame and sampling technique. The exact size of your sample will depend on the research you are undertaking. For quantitative research approaches a probability-based sample with an accurate sample size calculated to enable more complex comparative analyses, that involve estimating population characteristics, will require a detailed calculation to maximize representativeness. Quantitative or qualitative studies that focus on an exploratory analysis of the research topic may not require such a high degree of accuracy and a smaller sample size can be considered. Determining the adequate sample size is therefore dependent on a number of factors: the purpose of the research, the availability and accuracy of the sampling frame, the level of analysis required by the research, and how much error you are prepared to accept in your sample (Box 14.2).

BOX 14.2 RESEARCH FOCUS

The Northern Ireland Life and Times Survey (NILT) 2006

The 2006 NILT survey was designed to gather data from a representative sample of men and women aged 18 years and over in Northern Ireland. The Postcode Address File (PAF), a database of all known households, was used as the sampling frame. The Northern Ireland addresses were stratified into three geographical regions, Belfast, East of the Bann and West of the Bann, which is a standard approach used in Northern Ireland social surveys. A simple random sampling technique was used to identify households. An advance warning letter was sent to the households to inform them that they were invited to participate and that a researcher would be contacting them. When the researcher called, the adult whose birthday was next in the household was selected as the interviewee. Regarding non-responses, researchers were instructed to try five times to make contact before a refusal could be recorded. Where refusals were encountered the researchers were then provided with an alternative addresses. The NILT team obtained a total of 2162 addresses; 175 were found to be derelict/vacant or commercial properties, as the PAF is unable to provide household information to this level, leaving a total of 1987 households approached. The breakdown of response is shown in the table, together with the calculated percentage for each category.

	N	%
Achieved	1230	62
Refused	479	24
Non-contact	227	11
Other	49	2
Total	1987	

Source: Northern Ireland Life and Times, 2006, technical notes, www.ark.ac.uk/nilt

There is a statistical approach that allows you to calculate an adequate sample size. It is based upon assumptions of the normal distribution curve, the amount of variation in the characteristic being measured in the population, confidence intervals and significance. Two terms often used to describe variation in a population are heterogeneity and homogeneity. Heterogeneity refers to there being a large amount of variation in a population. Homogeneity refers to there being little variation in the population. The amount of variation will depend on what is being measured and also the coverage of the population. For example, a project that looks at women's career aspirations across a wide range of occupations will have a high degree of heterogeneity. On the other hand, research that looks at women's career aspirations in one specific occupation will be more homogeneous.

The basic notion is to select a sample size that will allow you to state, with a certain level of confidence, that the sample findings would also be found in the population. The sample size required minimizes the difference between the true population value, called a parameter, and the sample value. This difference is known as the sampling error. While in general a larger and well-selected sample will have a smaller sampling error, beyond a certain point a large increase in the sample size does not translate into a large gain in the reduction of the sampling error. Different formulas are used depending on the type of probability sample. In general a sample size that approaches around 1000 cases produces results with an acceptable sampling error of approximately ± 3 per cent. This is why political pollsters use samples of around 1000. The general formula used for calculating sample size is based on the central limit theorem and confidence intervals and the sampling technique to be used. See Moser and Kalton (1971: 146), Fink (1995b) or Mazzocchi (2008) for a more detailed explanation. Probability sampling is based on the properties of the normal distribution curve (see Chapter 26 for more information).

Some statistical tests require a minimum number of expected cases. Expected cases are calculated from the observed cases. The researcher therefore needs to ensure that the sample of observed cases is sufficient to meet this requirement. The chi-square test, a frequently undertaken hypothesis test, requires a minimum expected observation of five in each cell of a table (see section 'The chi-square test for categorical data' in Chapter 26).

From the discussion of these main issues in relation to sample size, the question still remains: 'How big should my sample be?' If you do not know the variation in a population characteristic, then the mathematical calculation of a sample size is problematic. An alternative is to use some of the rough rules of thumb or to take guidance from other more experienced researchers. Certainly for student research projects guidance should be sought from your tutor, who will have a more in-depth knowledge of your research topic and will be better placed to offer advice. Consideration of the type of analysis to be undertaken will be a factor in this decision. In reality other non-statistical factors will be important considerations, especially resources in terms of financial costs and time.

Beyond basic description it would be difficult for the researcher to undertake more complex statistical analysis, as most of these analyses require a minimum sample of 30. Ideally the sample size should be greater than 30, otherwise the observations when exploring relationships between two variables will be small. One suggestion is to look at the variables derived from the survey questions and at the relationships you wish to explore. Since many of the variables are likely to be nominal or ordinal, the sample size could be based on the minimum expected observations of five required for the chi-square test (an appropriate test for two categorical variables: see Chapter 26). A two-by-two (2 x 2) relationship of sex by work full-time or work part-time would require a minimum sample of 20, though 30 should ideally be the minimum. A minimum sample of 20 would comprise five expected observations for each relationship: male and working full-time; male and working part-time; female and working full-time; female and working part-time. Examination of the number of categories in other categorical variables will allow you to extend this principle. For example, examining the relationship between age, grouped into six age categories, and a variable recording the daily newspaper read, containing nine different newspapers, would produce a 6 x 9 table requiring a sample size of 270 units (54 cells in the table times the minimum value of 5). If this relationship were going to be explored further, by controlling for sex, then the sample required would ideally be 540. Others have suggested alternative minimum observations for each category in an independent variable. Sapsford (1999) suggests 20 and Aldridge and Levine (2001) suggest 50.

One further consideration in establishing the size of your sample is that of non-response. When one is undertaking research, approaching research participants is likely to result in some declining to take part. The difficulty with non-response is that the level of non-response likely to be encountered is simply an unknown quantity. Increasing the original sample size to take account of anticipated sample non-response is usual; however you will still need to consider that non-response will impact on your results even if you meet your target sample size (see Box 14.4).

BOX 14.4 CONSIDER THIS

Response rates and non-response

Response rates refer to the proportion of cases who participate in a research project compared to those who were invited and refused. This sounds quite straightforward until you consider that a refusal can take a number of different forms. A straightforward refusal would be where a respondent declines to participate from the outset. This could be measured as a 'no thank you' in a structured interview or the non-return of a postal questionnaire. Here non-response could be measured as the total number of returned questionnaires or the total number of individuals who participated in a structured interview divided by the total number of surveys mailed out or the total number of individuals asked to participate in the interview.

There are other forms of refusal to be considered though. A participant could initially agree to participate, for example in an interview, and then after a few questions will ask for the interview to stop. An alternative form of refusal is where the interview takes place but the respondent refuses to answer some questions, or where the self-completion survey respondent skips some questions. Managing response and refusal requires careful consideration at the data entry and analysis phase. In general where respondents have refused from the outset to participate, they are not recorded as missing cases in the data file. Where there has been a refusal to answer some question, and thereby a partially completed dataset is gathered, the data responses are entered and the type of missing data is accurately recorded (see Chapter 16).

Non-response can become problematic when particular groups and/or subgroups within your research are either over- or under-represented in the final dataset. The technique of weighting data can be used to adjust the data responses accordingly (see section 'Weighting' in Chapter 27 for more information).

Summary

Sampling refers to the process of deciding who will participate in the research project. When the population is known and is small enough, it may be possible to survey the entire group. However, for the majority of research the population either is too large or is unknown at the outset of the research. In these instances a small group or sample will be selected for the research study. Where the population can be identified and a sampling frame drawn up, it is possible to select individual sampling units using a probability sampling technique that will seek to represent the population. In instances where the population is hidden or difficult to locate or access, non-probability sampling techniques are employed. Probability sampling techniques aim to reduce the sampling error, this being the difference between the true population data findings and the sample data findings. Determining sample size is a complex issue that is determined by a number of factors including the level of acceptable sampling error, the size of population, the variability in the characteristic to be measured, and time and cost considerations.

 **Questions**

1 Why is it important for the social researcher to consider the most appropriate sampling technique for a particular research project?
2 Describe the difference between probability and non-probability sampling.
3 Define these terms: population, sampling frame, sampling unit.

Further reading

Fink, Arlene (2002) *The Survey Kit: How to Sample in Surveys*, 2nd edn. Thousand Oaks, CA: Sage.

Lee, Raymond (1993) *Doing Research on Sensitive Topics*. London: Sage.

Marpsat, M. and Razafindratsima (2010) 'Survey methods for hard-to-reach populations: introduction to the special issue' *Methodological Innovations Online*, 5(2) 3–16. http://www.pbs. plym.ac.uk/mi/pdf/05-08-10/2.%20Marpsat%20and%20Razafindratsima%20English2%20 (formatted).pdf Accessed 24/10/2010

Moser, Claus A. and Kalton, Graham (1971) *Survey Methods in Social Investigation*, 2nd edn. London: Heinemann.

Mazzocchi, Mario (2008) *Statistics for Marketing and Consumer Research*. London: Sage.

Sapsford, Roger (1999) *Survey Research*. London: Sage.

FIFTEEN

SURVEY DESIGN

Chapter Contents

| **Aims** |

By the end of this chapter you will be able to:

- Understand the advantages and disadvantages of conducting research using a self-completion survey or a structured interview.
- Distinguish between different types of survey questions.
- Identify existing sources of survey questions.
- Identify the key issues relating to the structure and organization of survey questions.
- Understand issues of reliability and validity in relation to the development of survey questions and indicators.

The survey: the self-completion survey and the structured interview

The two traditional methods of data collection used in quantitative research are the questionnaire survey and the structured interview. Both approaches require the respondent to complete a series of questions that have been designed by the researcher.

The delivery and return of the self-completion survey can be undertaken using a number of different methods. The traditional and most widely used approach is to send the self-completion survey through the postal service, when it is known as the mail survey or postal survey. Increasingly self-completion surveys are included within a wider data collection process, where the researcher is present, involving a combination of a self-completion survey and face-to-face interview: see Boxes 15.1 and 15.2 for an example of how this method has been used. The self-completion element may be paper based or could involve computer assisted self-interviewing (CASI) where the respondent is asked to complete questions on a laptop that the researcher has brought with them to the interview. The advantage of this over a paper-based method is that entered responses are automatically coded into a data file, and a CASI approach allows for more complex routing to enable questions to be better tailored to the respondent. Although in this approach the researcher is present, there will be little or no dialogue between the two parties beyond explaining the process for completing the CASI survey.

BOX 15.1 RESEARCH FOCUS

The Northern Ireland Life and Times Survey (NILT) 2007 (www.ark. ac.uk/nilt/)

Background

Launched in 1998, the Northern Ireland Life and Times Survey is an annual survey that monitors the attitudes and behaviour of the people of Northern Ireland. It provides a time series dataset on public attitudes towards a wide range of social policy issues relevant to Northern Ireland. The questions are divided into a series of modules. Every year the same three modules concerning political attitudes, community relations and background information on respondents are run, and the remaining modules vary annually. The aim is for all of the modules to be repeated over a longer period.

In 2007 the question modules were:

- background information on the respondents
- community relations
- attitudes to minority ethnic people and migrant workers
- identity
- political attitudes
- public services
- role of government.

Data collection method

Face-to-face interviews in the respondents' homes were conducted from October 2007 to January 2008. The main interview was conducted by the researcher using the Blaise computer assisted personal interviewing (CAPI) package installed on a laptop.

There was a separate self-completion module which contained more potentially sensitive questions on role of government; community relations; public services; and attitudes to minority ethnic people. This was competed in one of three ways:

- Computer Assisted Self Interviewing (CASI) method: the respondent completed the self-completion on the computer.
- Computer Assisted Personal Interviewing (CAPI) method: the interviewer completed the self-completion on the computer.
- Traditional pen and paper method: the respondent completed the self-completion in a paper booklet. Where a pen and paper method was used, the data were subsequently entered into the CASI database using Blaise.

BOX 15.2 HINTS AND TIPS

Finding out more about NILT and accessing the NILT data files

The NILT survey is used in the data analysis Chapters 23–27. We suggest that you go to the NILT website (www.ark.ac.uk/nilt/) to find out more about the survey before you proceed to those chapters.

Survey data files containing anonymized responses by year are available on the NILT website. These can be downloaded, following the web links and instructions on the NILT

(Continued)

The structured interview involves an interviewer asking questions and recording the interviewee's responses. Where the interview is conducted in person with both the interviewer and the interviewee present, it is called a face-to-face interview. An alternative method is to conduct the interview by telephone, known as telephone interviewing. As with the self-completion survey, the structured interview as a method of data collection has seen developments in survey computer software. Computer assisted telephone interviewing (CATI) involves the interviewer reading instructions and survey questions from a computer screen and recording the interviewee's responses directly onto the survey form on the screen. There data are then automatically coded and stored into a data file for subsequent analysis.

In more recent years the internet has become one of the main forms of communication, and in part as a response to this it is increasingly being used as the vehicle to conduct survey-based research, particularly by market researchers. As with all research, the different methods throw up different methodological, practical and ethical issues.

The general advantages and disadvantages of using self-completion surveys and structured interviews for data collection are detailed in the following sections. (As with all research, the different methods throw up different methodological, practical and ethics issues, see Chapter 17.)

Self-completion survey: advantages and disadvantages

Postal or mail survey

A postal or mail questionnaire involves distributing the questionnaire by post with a covering letter and normally a pre-addressed postage-paid envelope for the respondent to return the questionnaire. A follow-up letter to boost response rates may be required; sometimes the questionnaire may include incentives to return the questionnaire, such as entry to a prize draw.

The first advantage of the postal or mail survey is that the relative costs associated with its completion have traditionally been lower than with other methods.

The main costs are the reproduction of the questionnaire, envelopes, postage costs and data entry costs. Time and resources committed to data entry can be reduced by the use of closed-ended questions that can be pre-coded, allowing for easier data input. Specialist software applications are also available to automate all or part of the questionnaire design and help facilitate the data entry phase. The second advantage is that data from a large sample, possibly distributed over a wide geographical area, can be surveyed within a limited timespan. It would be difficult to gather data from such a sample using a face-to-face interview method unless the research team consisted of a large number of interviewers with a sufficient timescale. In this situation the issues of interviewer effect and bias would require specific focus to ensure consistency between interviewers. The third advantage is that there are no interviewer effects. The responses given by the interviewee can be affected by the presence of the interviewer, who influences the replies made by their wording of the questions, their tone of voice, their mannerisms or their general characteristics (age, gender, ethnicity). The fourth advantage is that a self-completion survey may be a particularly useful tool when collecting data on sensitive topics that the respondent may otherwise be too embarrassed or reluctant to respond to. Other advantages often mentioned include that the respondents can complete the questionnaire at a time convenient to themselves, and that questionnaires can be completed and returned anonymously by the respondent.

The main disadvantage of a mail survey is the often low response rate obtained. A response rate of 50 per cent or less can be the norm. Reasons for this low response rate are varied and can include factors such as 'the subject matter of the survey, the target population under study, the recipients' perception of its value, and the ease of completion of the questionnaire' (Simmons, 2001: 87). However, good question development and layout, together with clear instructions on the nature of the study and why it is important to complete and return the questionnaire, can dramatically improve response rates.

Response rates are also difficult to assess as they are related to the sampling technique used and knowledge about the target population. 'Response rates will be underestimated if questionnaires have been sent to people who are not part of the target population or who have moved address' (Aldridge and Levine, 2001: 52). The issue for the researcher is that it is not possible to distinguish between non-response due to a refusal and non-response due to an inappropriate sampling unit, such as the wrong individual being selected. (See section 'Non-response' in Chapter 16 for further discussion of factors that affect non-response.)

There is also an implicit assumption with self-completion surveys that the targeted respondents' literacy level is sufficient to provide written responses. The advice to restrict the structure of individual questions (that is, simple, not cumbersome, short; not too many open-ended questions; careful use of contingency questions to direct respondents to specific questions according to set criteria) can restrict the data that are collected and, depending on the nature of the research, a questionnaire may simply not yield the information required for the research.

Other disadvantages often cited include the inability to control the context within which the questions are completed; respondents may jump between questions and not complete in the intended order. The researcher is also unable to determine if the targeted sampling unit, for example a named individual, was actually the person who completed and returned the questionnaire.

Internet-based survey

Developments in computing technology and software have enabled surveys to be distributed by electronic mail (e-mail) and on the World Wide Web. The advantage to web-based questionnaires or online surveys is that the data can automatically be placed in a data file that in turn can be imported into a suitable analysis package. The data collection period can be quite short, allowing for a quick turnaround. The online survey can be written in such a way that the accidental selection of an inappropriate number of categories or failure to respond can be avoided: for example, when a question states to tick one response only, this can be ensured; or failure to complete all the questions in the survey can be brought to the attention of the respondent by displaying an alert message directing them to the incomplete questions.

Questionnaires can also be distributed via e-mail, or respondents can be e-mailed and invited to complete a survey at a website. It is also possible to use a pre-questionnaire to screen out respondents who fall outside the target sample characteristics required. This can be particularly useful if that level of information about the sample is not available. For example, you may have a database of all users of a local swimming pool, but the focus of your survey may be on those aged between 30 and 50 years living in the city boundaries. A pre-questionnaire asking for the respondent's age and home postcode could be used to screen out those that do not meet the focus of the study. Online surveys are also useful if the sample base has a wide geographical coverage, particularly if it includes respondents that are based outside the country where the researcher resides. There are specialist market research companies that recruit individuals to panels or groups of individuals. The database of these individuals is then monitored and refreshed to ensure that the panel is representative for the needs of their client: for example, the panel may have the characteristics of the population of England and Wales. As with paper-based questionnaire surveys, inducements to complete the questionnaire can be offered, such as entry into a prize draw.

There are difficulties with online surveys, particularly related to sampling and technical support. While the researcher can aim to achieve a representative sample based on identified characteristics, the sample will only ever be based on internet users who are also willing to take part in online surveys. The researcher needs to consider the level of technical expertise and support required for internet or web-based surveys. Either this will require them to gain the necessary technical expertise in the area of web survey construction, accessing a sampling frame of e-mail addresses, and managing the survey databases together with the respective hardware and software; or they will need to access appropriate technical support. Such support may be available in-house within a university department or specialist research support unit; where there are no in-house support facilities it is possible to access support services via the web as either a free-to-use service or a professional fee-paying service (for an example see www.surveymonkey.com). When using external services, careful consideration needs to be given to the type of services offered to ensure that they meet the requirements of the research project (see Box 15.3 for details of two online services). As with telephone interviews, there is also the issue of excluding certain social groups from the sample if they do not have access to the relevant hardware/software or user skills for the World Wide Web. For a fuller discussion of the issues associated with using internet-based surveys, and the wider use of E-research, see Chapter 17.

BOX 15.3 HINTS AND TIPS

Online surveys

If you are not fortunate enough to have easy access to online survey software, one possibility is to search the web for no-cost services. These are often services that allow a very limited range of usage for free; they then charge users if they require a more comprehensive service.

Check out the following survey websites:

> www.surveymonkey.com
> http://freeonlinesurveys.com/

Structured interviews: advantages and disadvantages

Face-to-face interviews

Face-to-face interviews offer a number of advantages over a postal survey. The first is that, depending on the research topic, a greater response rate can be achieved. The direct personal contact between the researcher and the potential interviewee to arrange a convenient interview time can, as long as it is conducted in a professional manner, result in the building of both rapport and respondent commitment to the research study. The personal contact is often combined with other forms of communication, including introductory letters, information leaflets, postcards on research updates and thank-you notes. Together with the optional use of incentives, this can all help to boost the response rate for the study. The researcher needs to balance striving to achieve a good response rate against being too pushy in getting reluctant interviewees to participate, and will need to use their experience and common sense to achieve this in a professional and ethical manner (see Box 15.4).

BOX 15.4 STOP AND THINK

Keen to participate?

As part of a study examining gender difference in students' sports participation, you identify the chairperson of a number of different university sporting clubs to interview. To date you have interviewed 10 out of the potential 30 chairs. The chair of the men's rugby club has expressed that he is very keen to participate as he is especially interested

(Continued)

(Continued)

in the research topic. However, he cancelled the first interview at short notice because of a last-minute change to the rugby club training session; the second interview was similarly cancelled. Despite two follow-up telephone calls and three e-mails you have not been able to get in touch with this person. You have since found out that the rugby team is now into the final of a local cup competition and is training hard in preparation for the big match. The final is only one week before the hand-in date for your research report. What do you do? What impact will your decision have on your research?

One of the biggest advantages of face-to-face structured interviews is that there can be a greater use of open questions, where the respondent's own words are recorded, and the interviewer can provide additional explanation, if required, to aid the respondent's understanding of the question. Prompting can be included with the questions and, if a question is inappropriate, data on why no response was made can be recorded. This enables the question sequencing to be more complex if required, and greater use can be made of routing or funnelling questions for specific targeting of different groups of respondents. To aid the navigation by the interviewer, precise instructions for the interviewer to aid completion will be included. Here the responsibility for navigating the appropriate questions for the respondent to answer is with the interviewer, and this places less of a burden on the respondent. The respondent will not be aware that the schedule contains a vast number of questions as they will only complete those of direct relevance to them. This type of sequencing can most easily be seen by looking at existing interview schedules from large surveys, often government sponsored, such as the UK's General Household Survey, the British Social Attitudes survey, or the USA's General Social Survey. See Box 15.5 on how to access an archive of online resources in the United Kingdom. These studies often use a combination of face-to-face interviews and self-completion questions (see Box 15.1). Instructions for prompting by the interviewer are included in the questionnaire schedule. Additionally, the use of show cards containing the response categories for closed-ended questions or other visual aids can provide accurate and swift completion of the questions. The non-verbal cues of human interaction can also be recorded, such as facial expressions.

BOX 15.5 RESEARCH FOCUS

The Survey Resources Network (http://surveynet.ac.uk)

This is a web-based resource service, launched in April 2009, whose aim is to coordinate a wide range of activities related to survey research methods. One aspect of this resource is to develop further the existing Survey Question Bank (SQB) database of questionnaires used in a wide variety of surveys. SQB can easily be accessed via the SRN website.

SQB provides a range of online resources related to quantitative social research methods and can be used to assist in the design of new survey questionnaires.

The online resources can be searched for potential questions using two approaches. The first is to access actual past questionnaires directly. These questionnaires are stored and downloadable as pdf files. The second is to search by thematic topics (for example, health) that are then linked to appropriate surveys and questionnaires.

There also exists a bibliographic resource which discusses a variety of issues relating to data collection using a survey method.

Example of using Survey Question Bank (SQB)

A student wants to undertake a survey to examine university students' fear of crime in and around the main teaching campus.

SQB holds questionnaires from the British Crime Survey (BCS) and also has a topic section on crime and victimization. From either of these links information on the BCS for previous years and the types of question asked can be accessed. The questionnaires are available as pdf files which are bookmarked to allow easy navigation of the respective sections of the questionnaire. In the main questionnaire there are sections on 'feeling safe' and 'worries about crime'. Both of these questions ask respondents to assess their feelings and worries on respective attitudinal scales.

Potentially relevant questions for the student crime survey are listed below. The BCS questions need to be understood within the overall research design and sampling. An important aspect to understanding these questions is that respondents were interviewed, face-to-face, in their own homes, and the questions below relate to their area of residence.

For 'Feeling safe'

How safe do you feel walking alone in this area after dark?
How safe do you feel walking alone in this area during the day?
How safe do you feel when you are alone in your own home at night?

These questions use a 4-point attitudinal scale:

1 Very safe
2 Fairly safe
3 A bit unsafe
4 Or very unsafe?

For 'Worries about crime'

How worried are you about … having your home broken into and something stolen?
(How worried are you about) … being mugged and robbed?
(How worried are you about) … having your car stolen?
(How worried are you about) … having things stolen from your car?
(How worried are you about) … being raped?
(How worried are you about) … being physically attacked by strangers?
(How worried are you about) … being insulted or pestered by anybody, while in the street or any other public place?
(How worried are you about) … being subject to a physical attack because of your skin colour, ethnic origin or religion?
And now thinking about all types of crime in general, how worried are you about being a victim of crime?

(Continued)

These questions use a 4-point attitudinal scale:

1 Very worried
2 Fairly worried
3 Not very worried
4 Not at all worried.

Source: http://surveynet.ac.uk/sqb/qb/surveys/bcs/06mainqbcs.pdf, accessed 31 March 2009

The advantages of face-to-face interviews have to be balanced against the disadvantages. Obviously in a face-to-face interview the issue of anonymity no longer applies, though the interviewer can make assurances of confidentiality. There is also the potential for both interviewer effect and interviewer bias. The age, social background and sex of the interviewer are all interviewer effects that could influence the responses given by the interviewee. The general awareness, prior experience and communication skills of the interviewer – directed towards making the interviewee feel comfortable, willing to participate and talk honestly – will be key factors in limiting the potential interviewer effect. Interviewer bias can occur through both the verbal comments and the non-verbal cues of the interviewer. In order to minimize interviewer effect the researcher should draw up precise details on how the interview should be conducted. Earlier we mentioned that the interview schedule should include clear instructions to the interviewer for completion. If the research is being carried out by more than one researcher then there needs to be a 'team' briefing event where issues of consistency can be discussed. In a professional research setting this would involve the lead researcher briefing the interviewers and going through a practice interview. If it is a group of students completing a group research project then this would be the entire group meeting, going through the interview schedule to ensure a consistent approach is taken.

Compared to a postal or telephone interview survey, the costs of a face-to-face method can be much more. A considerable amount of researcher time is involved in arranging the interview, and sometimes having to rearrange the interview to accommodate the interviewee's daily schedule. Contacting interviewees is initially often by letter or, where appropriate, by e-mail. This will then be followed up with phone calls to arrange a suitable day and time for a researcher to visit a convenient place for the interviewee, often their own home or other private setting.

One also needs to consider issues relating to the potential risk to the researcher. This is in terms not only of physical personal safety but also of potentially psychological and traumatic situations. A discussion of issues relating to the potential for increased risk associated with going into the field should take place with senior staff or, for students, with the relevant academic staff member. Risks should be anticipated and assessed accordingly. Once in the field the researcher themselves must exercise due care and diligence at all times. For these reasons where face-to-face interviews involve visiting the home addresses or other private settings of the participants, the researchers will ideally work in pairs and always leave a record of where they are going with someone else. Further details on awareness of personal safety can be found at The Suzy Lamplugh Trust website http://www.suzylamplugh.org/, and the Social Research Association also has a code of practice for the safety of social researchers which can be found on their website at http://www.the-sra.org/.

Telephone interview survey

The telephone interview survey can be a favoured method when funding is sufficient to cover telephone costs. As with the mail survey, it is also possible to obtain a large sample over a wide geographical area. Some of the issues of interviewer effect are removed, as there is no visual contact, although the tone and pitch of the interviewer's voice may introduce some interviewer bias. Depending on the research topic and potential participants, cold calling participants can lead to a straight refusal to participate, especially if the recipient has already had personal experience of telephone canvassing for marketing purposes. To minimize this occurrence the researcher should think carefully about the opening words used, and also be prepared for an immediate refusal before the purpose of the project is properly explained. Maintaining a friendly and engaging tone on the telephone may help win over an initial hostility.

The disadvantages of the telephone interview are that the guidelines for self-completion questions must still be adhered to. Questions should be short and simple and the number of response categories specified must not be too great, as the interviewee will be unable to remember all the list items from which to choose. Open questions can be included, though not too many, to enable the respondent to express their responses in their own spoken language and terminology.

Undertaking telephone interviews also introduces an element of bias in the sampling as it will automatically exclude those without a telephone and, if using publicly available directories, those that are ex-directory. Furthermore, people are often unwilling to participate in cold-call telephone interviewing, raising questions about the quality of data collected (Thomas and Purdon, 1994). This can be overcome by approaching respondents initially to participate in the research and to arrange a suitable time for the telephone interview to be conducted. It is also very important that you maintain accurate records of who you have called, and the date and time, and make relevant notes; see Chapter 16 for a practical checklist for conducting telephone interviews.

Developing survey questions

The development of questions is a time-consuming process that requires sufficient allocation of time and effort. At first the development of questions for a questionnaire or interview schedule will seem relatively unproblematic; however, a researcher who thinks like this seriously underestimates the complexity of the process. The questions must be carefully thought through in a systematic manner, piloted, then reviewed and edited before the full survey commences. A rushed, ill-thought-through set of questions will inevitably fail to collect the data required. This will result in the researcher being unable to explore relationships or test the hypotheses from the original research question. Once the survey is conducted there is no possibility of revising badly worded questions, or questions that fail to collect data relevant to the research question.

The following section provides an overview of the process of developing questions and the main issues to consider.

Getting started on question development

The purpose of developing questions is to enable the researcher to collect data in order to investigate the research question through the exploration of hypotheses. The data collection process requires the development of survey questions and measurements. Some of the questions will be open ended, enabling the respondent to provide their own written or spoken responses, while other questions will be in a closed-ended format with specific responses, also known as categories, to select from. The development of these categories will be undertaken in conjunction with topic-specific knowledge of appropriate responses and also different measurements. One would also need to develop questions that are appropriate to the target population that you are surveying and the characteristics of the individual units in your sampling frame.

Knowledge about the topic can be collated from a variety of sources. The most obvious source is the review of the literature (see Chapter 3). When there is less background literature available, or where a particular local context needs to be carefully considered, it may be appropriate to conduct some limited fieldwork by interviewing key individuals in the area to be studied, or to invite suitable individuals together for a focus group discussion to discuss the key issues. The context-rich data from both interviews and focus groups can help fill in any gaps in knowledge and understanding that you have from the literature review. The adoption of a qualitative phase before the main survey can allow the researcher to formulate their research ideas in more detail and to arrive at a better position to be able to formulate hypotheses.

An additional source of useful information is to access existing archives that contain details of previous studies. These studies are generally from large government studies whose surveys have been subjected to robust and rigorous testing, and which for repeated surveys are subject to the retesting of survey questions and response categories over time. They represent a very useful resource to replicate questions for use in your own research project or as a starting point to develop new questions (see Box 15.6).

BOX 15.6 STOP AND THINK

1 How could you develop the questions in Box 15.5 for the student survey?
2 How would you adapt the question wording to make it relevant to the university campus and the student population?
3 Could you keep the same response categories?
4 What other questions would you need to ask in order to identify how different groups of students fear and worry about crime on their campus?

From the literature review a range of concepts and indicators for measuring these concepts will have been developed in relation to the research question. Together with past research studies and/or your own hunches you may have developed one or more hypotheses about how the indicators may vary between different groups and are influenced by other factors. For example, a student's fear of crime when on a university campus may differ depending on whether the student is in halls of residence on the main campus or in private accommodation off campus; and, on whether they are a frequent user of university facilities at different times of the day.

An alternative example is a study that is exploring poverty and deprivation in rural and urban areas. The characteristics of the concepts of 'rural' and 'urban', and how they relate to a measurable entity, need careful consideration. In the 2001 UK Census, 'urban' was defined as a settlement of population of 10,000 or more (Office for National Statistics, 2004). A variety of indicators for measuring deprivation may cover household income, number of waged earners and income from state benefits, and not just such economic factors but also those relating to access to services, location of post offices, location of food supermarkets, distance to bus stops, frequency of bus routes, location of banking services and so on. See Box 15.7 for details on indices of deprivation used by local governments in England.

BOX 15.7 CONSIDER THIS

Indices of deprivation

Within England the indices of deprivation have been calculated to provide a single measure for deprivation that is used by local governments to plan services and interventions appropriate for the neighbourhoods in their areas. The measure is available to a small geographical area, known as a lower super output area (LSOA), which contains between 1000 and 3000 individuals. The 2007 indices of deprivation combine 37 different indicators across the following areas:

- income
- employment

(Continued)

(Continued)

- health and disability
- education, skills and training
- barriers to housing and services
- living environment
- crime.

Source: Using the English Indices of Deprivation 2007 Guidance, http://www.communities.gov.uk/documents/communities/doc/615986.doc

Access the 'Using the English Indices of Deprivation 2007 Guidance' to find out more about how the indices of deprivation were constructed.

Types of questions

There are a number of different types of questions and question formats. A combination of these is likely to be used in a survey. The questions can be classified into three broad groups. Questions can be factual, concentrating on a behaviour or knowledge. Questions can focus on gathering attributes about the respondent: for example, an individual's age or marital status. These questions are primarily concerned with collecting background information on the respondent for the purposes of classification and comparison at the data analysis stage. Since the collecting of background or demographic data is a routine aspect of survey design, it is worth considering accessing existing surveys for ideas on how to construct suitable questions. Again, resources like Survey Resources Network (http://surveynet.ac.uk) are useful. Questions can also be concerned with gathering data on opinions, beliefs and attitudes; for example, in a survey of knowledge about and use of local bus services there could be a series of questions gathering both factual data on usage and attitudes and opinions relating to the service provided (see Figure 15.1).

The development of survey questions needs to be understood within the framework that the potential participant will respond in. Background information on the topic area needs to be thoroughly researched in order to develop questions

---

Factual – behaviour: 'In the last week, have you used local bus services?'

Factual – knowledge: 'How frequent is the bus service to your nearest town?'

Opinion: 'Do you think that bus services should be operating in this area?'

Attitude: 'How would you rate local bus services?'

Personal attribute: 'Are you male or female?'

FIGURE 15.1   Example of different types of questions

that are appropriate and clearly worded with a logical layout in order for the participant to interpret them and respond accordingly.

Closed-ended or open-ended questions?

The format of a question can be open ended or closed ended. Open-ended questions, also known as unstandardized questions, enable the respondent to enter a response in their own words. Closed-ended questions, also known as standardized questions, require the respondent to select from a range of stated answers. The advantages of closed-ended questions are that with a clearly stated question they enable the respondent to provide a quick response. Respondents are generally more willing to complete a series of questions if the response time is minimal and requires less effort in completion, though the issue of false data being collated can then become a concern. Another useful aspect is that closed-ended questions are simpler for the researcher to deal with when it comes to the data entry and analysis stages. Fixed answers are easier to code, and pre-coding the answers can save time once the completed survey is returned for data entry and analysis.

A number of disadvantages must be considered when developing closed-ended questions. The main issue relates to the fact that they can force the respondent to select one of the responses when, in fact, they would not have spontaneously offered either any response or that particular response. For example, an individual might respond to an attitudinal question by expressing an opinion that they do not necessarily hold.

Concerns about potential false responses with closed-ended questions may influence the decision to make use of open-ended questions. Open-ended questions enable the respondent to express their response in their own words and allow for the possibility of issues arising that the researcher had not previously considered. There is the issue with open-ended questions that they are reliant on the respondent being sufficiently interested in or knowledgeable of the question to provide an answer and being able to express their response in a written format. Open answers are also more time consuming for the researcher to code and analyse as they require post-coding (see section 'Coding for open-ended questions' in Chapter 16).

Ultimately, the choice between closed-ended and open-ended questions is dependent on the area being researched, the type of question, background considerations on the motivation of respondents and how and where the survey is administered. A self-completion survey will be completed in a different environment to a structured interview.

Format of closed-ended questions

When developing closed-ended questions you will need to decide upon the format of the response categories. The development of these needs to be considered

Version 1

How old are you? Please tick one response only:

Under 21   ☐

21 or over   ☐

Version 2

How old are you? Please tick one response only:

Under 21   ☐

21–30   ☐

31–40   ☐

41–50   ☐

51–60   ☐

61–70   ☐

71 plus   ☐

Version 3

Please enter your current age, in years:

———————— years old.

FIGURE 15.2 Three questions that would record a respondent's age

in relation to the data type or level of measurement of the data to be collected. There are four types: nominal, ordinal, interval and ratio (as outlined in the section 'Variables and levels of measurement' in Chapter 13). At the analysis stage the data type determines the statistical techniques available. How a question is worded will determine the response given and so in turn the level of measurement of the data. It is worth spending a few minutes to consider this point with an example.

In Figure 15.2, the researcher wishes to ask a question about an individual's age. Three different ways are displayed in which the question could be asked, together with the respective responses. The format of the responses will impact on the statistical analysis available.

In version 1 the age question requires the respondent to select one of two categories: under 21, or 21 or over. Beyond this the question response will not allow the analysis to distinguish between respondents of different ages within each of those categories. Consequently, if in the subsequent analysis the researcher wanted to focus on responses made by those aged 71 or over, this would not be possible as they did not collect the age data in a format that allowed them to identify this subset of the sample. The level of measurement is nominal and, since there are only two categories, it is referred to as a dichotomy. In version 2 there are seven age categories available. The categories can be placed in rank order of ascending age and the data type is ordinal. Each category must be mutually exclusive, also known as externally discrete, which means that the age ranges do not overlap. This version of the age question would allow the researcher to distinguish at the data analysis stage between a respondent who was 71 or over and one who was aged 31–40 years. However, within each category the researcher would be unable to determine the actual age of the respondent.

In version 3 the question is open ended with the respondent being asked to enter their actual age in years. Here the data are interval/ratio. With interval/ratio data a greater range of statistical analysis techniques is available. The hierarchical order of the levels of measurement means that an interval variable, for example age in years, can be recoded or collapsed into an ordinal variable, for example categories of age ranges, or into a nominal variable, two age categories (a dichotomy). While collecting the respondent's actual age in years can offer the greatest flexibility at the data analysis stage, it must be balanced against the difficulty that this can be a sensitive issue which may result in a large number of non-responses. A tradeoff between issues of sensitivity and the restrictions on the range of analysis techniques available needs to be considered by the researcher. The majority of questions asked by researchers when investigating the social world have response categories that are of a nominal or an ordinal level.

Developing closed-ended question responses

The development of question responses should consider the guiding principles of exhaustiveness, exclusiveness and balancing categories (de Vaus, 2001: 100–1).

Exhaustiveness refers to the need to ensure that an appropriate range of responses is made available. The question would fail if relevant responses were omitted, resulting in the respondents not responding to the question. While every effort should be made to ensure that the list of responses is exhaustive, it is common practice for questions that list a number of responses to include a final category that allows the respondent to indicate that none of the listed categories were appropriate. A final response of 'other' with a qualifying 'please state' can be used. Sometimes it may be more appropriate to include a response stating 'none of the above'. For attitudinal responses, a category of no opinion or neutral should be included.

Exclusiveness means that response categories are exclusive in the sense that respondents can select only one of the categories. In the earlier example of the respondent being asked to select the age category, there are no overlaps in the age categories. For example, if a researcher had wrongly set the first two age categories as '21 and under' and '21–30', a 21-year-old respondent would fall into both categories. In this example the issue of exclusiveness is easy to deal with; however, questions that have a list of responses from which to choose, and the respondent can select more than one, need to be given more consideration and thought.

In the following example there is a question about mode of transport used to get to work:

How did you travel to work this morning?

Car ☐
Bus ☐
Coach ☐
Taxi ☐
Train ☐
Other ☐

There is the possibility that a respondent may use more than one mode of transport: for example, train and bus. There are a number of ways in which you can deal with this. The first would be to create mutually exclusive category combinations, for example, car only, bus only, coach only, taxi only, train only, car and bus, train and bus, and so on. Where there is a long list of categories and potential combinations this can be inappropriate. When there are only two categories, the inclusion of a third category 'Both' would suffice. The second, if appropriate to the research, is to reframe the question to focus on the main mode of transport used, for example, 'What was the main mode of transport that you used to get to work this morning?' However, in this example you are requiring the respondent to define the term 'main mode'. The third option is to alter the format of the question to allow for multiple responses, where the respondent ticks all categories that are applicable. The fourth option is to split the original question into a number of separate questions with responses of 'Yes' and 'No'. For example, 'Did you use the bus to travel to work today?', 'Did you use the train to travel to work today?'

Balancing categories refers to simply ensuring that when using a series of categories that can be placed in a rank order, for example, attitudinal scales, the categories are balanced with equal numbers of positive, or high, and negative, or low, categories. More categories at one end of the scale could distort the responses given. The scale is normally balanced by including a neutral category in the middle position. For example, on a scale of importance the categories might be very important, important, neutral, unimportant and very unimportant.

Different formats of closed-ended question responses

In this section some of the common formats used for closed-ended question responses are outlined.

Questions with only two responses

One question format has only two response categories, known as dichotomies. Such questions can be useful when gaining basic factual information or to provide structure to a questionnaire by directing respondents to complete certain sections of a questionnaire (see section 'Routing questions and funnelling respondents' later in this chapter). Beyond this their use should be carefully considered, especially in relation to questions asking about a respondent's opinion, as the nature of the dichotomies may force the respondent to express a view that is greater or less extreme than their true view. For example:

Do you think that degree students should pay tuition fees?

Yes ☐
No ☐

How would a respondent answer this question if they felt that the payment of tuition fees should be subject to parental income? The respondent may also not have considered this issue before and have no immediate opinion. Consideration of the inclusion of a 'Do not know' category should be made.

Questions with a list of responses

These questions list a number of responses, or categories, from which a respondent can select. Clear instructions need to be included with the question as to whether one or more of the responses can be selected.

Figure 15.3 contains two examples of the format of questions that have a list of responses. Both questions ask the respondent to state the daily newspaper that they read. In example 1 there is a specific instruction that states 'Tick *one* only' to indicate that only one of the listed categories should be selected. In example 2 the instructions accompanying the question state 'Tick all applicable' to indicate that the researcher is allowing for respondents who read more than one newspaper a day. When more than one response can be selected the questions are multiple response, requiring special attention at the coding and data entry phases.

Additional categories have also been included at the end of the list. The inclusion of an 'Other' category allows the respondent to enter a newspaper that is not included on the selective list provided by the researcher. In addition, the final category of 'Do not read a daily newspaper' has been included. This category could have been omitted by the introduction of a preceding routing question that asked if the respondent read a daily newspaper, which would have filtered out those that did not; only those that replied 'Yes' would then complete the full newspaper question. More details can be found in 'Routing questions and funnelling respondents' later in this chapter.

When listing the categories it is important that the researcher spends time considering what the relevant categories are. For questions on individual attributes, consider spending some time looking at existing survey examples such as those undertaken by the large government surveys. Such surveys focus on data collection for mainly social policy decisions and thus contain many questions relating to various aspects of the individual, for example, income, health, education and employment.

Piloting of the survey questions may reveal additional categories not considered by the researcher and which can be included in the final survey. In order to fulfil the requirement of exhaustiveness it is wise to include a final all-encompassing 'Other' category followed by an open response of 'Please state'.

Example 1: Selecting only one response

Which of the following daily newspapers do you normally read?

Tick *one* only:

Financial Times	☐
New York Times	☐
Washington Post	☐
Melbourne Age	☐
Times of India	☐
South China Morning Post	☐
Le Monde	☐
Other	☐ (Please state) _____
Do not read a daily newspaper	☐

Example 2: Selecting one or more responses (multi response)

Which of the following daily newspapers have you read in the last week?

Tick all applicable:

Financial Times	☐
New York Times	☐
Washington Post	☐
Melbourne Age	☐
Times of India	☐
South China Morning Post	☐
Le Monde	☐
Other	☐ (Please state) _____
Do not read a daily newspaper	☐

FIGURE 15.3   Questions with a list of response categories

Attitudinal or opinion question responses

Questions that seek to gather data on a respondent's opinion will make use of a rating scale. A number of different rating scales have been developed and can be used to create formal scales to measure concepts by combining responses from a multitude of statements. This section will first examine some of the frequently used rating categories and then describe the application of Likert scales.

Rating question responses   Rating question responses are simply response categories that are presented in a rank order between two extreme positions, normally positive and negative. The number of categories in the scales can vary, with three and five categories the most common. Rating questions with three categories could be less, same or more. Rating questions with five categories are shown in Figure 15.4.

Very important	Strongly agree
Important	Agree
Neutral	Undecided
Unimportant	Disagree
Very unimportant	Strongly disagree

FIGURE 15.4 Examples of five-point scales

The 10-point and 100-point numerical scales These scales involve presenting a numerical scale with extreme positions at both ends. The respondent then circles the number that most closely represents their position on the continuum. They are similar to the five-point scale except that labels are not applied to each of the numerical points on the scale, leaving individual respondents to decide where their position is on the scale.

A frequently used scale is the 10-point scale, which will run from 1 to 10, or from 0 to 9 (Figure 15.5). An extension of this scale is to increase the range of points on the scale. Occasionally questionnaires may ask individuals to position their response on a 100-point scale, which may be represented as a thermometer with a scale from 0 °C to 100 °C

Bad	0	1	2	3	4	5	6	7	8	9	Good
Dull	0	1	2	3	4	5	6	7	8	9	Fun
Low	0	1	2	3	4	5	6	7	8	9	High

FIGURE 15.5 Examples of 10-point scales

Semantic differential scales Semantic differential scales are used to assess individuals' responses to particular statements that have been developed to measure one or more concepts. Responses would be made by circling the numerical position on the scale that most represents the respondent's feelings, attitude or belief in respect of a particular item under study (see Figure 15.5). Each end of the scale represents an extreme position: bad to good, dull to fun, low to high. Its application is particularly useful in research that involves comparing the attitudes of one group of individuals to another: for example, employees' rating of line management or supervisory staff.

Likert scales These are a convenient method of collecting data on a concept from a number of different approaches (Oppenheim, 1992). They also allow the researcher to obtain more information about a respondent's opinion or feelings on a particular topic that is beyond simply obtaining a disagree/agree or yes/no response.

		Strongly agree	Agree	Neutral	Disagree	Strongly disagree
(1)	I have enjoyed studying this module.	5	4	3	2	1
(2)	The aims and objectives of the module were clear to me.	5	4	3	2	1
(3)	It was difficult to access the student portal for course related materials.	1	2	3	4	5
(4)	Access to university computers outside of workshops was difficult.	1	2	3	4	5

FIGURE 15.6   Example of a Likert scale

The structure of the Likert scale is to write a number of statements, known as scale items, each with the same standard set of responses. The scale items will consist of a mix of positive and negative statements. The responses would be on a rating scale with two extreme positions, positive and negative, at either end of the scale. A Likert scale consists of five points: strongly agree, agree, undecided, disagree, strongly disagree (see Figure 15.4). Each of the response categories is given a score from 1 to 5. Scale items (statements) that are positive require response categories that are scored 5 for strongly agree to 1 for strongly disagree. Scale items (statements) that are negative require response categories that are scored 1 for strongly agree to 5 for strongly disagree. An example of four scale items and the scores assigned to each of the respective response categories is shown in Figure 15.6. Scale items 1 and 2 are positive statements. Scale items 3 and 4 are negative statements.

Once the respondents have completed the scale items, the next stage would be to enter the individual scores into a data analysis package (see Chapter 23). The final stage is to calculate a final score by the addition of all of the scale items. Taking the example in Figure 15.6, a respondent who has answered for statement 1, agree, scored a 4; statement 2, agree, scored a 4; statement 3, disagree, scored a 4; and statement 4, agree, scored a 2. The total score for this respondent would be 4 + 4 + 4 + 2 = 14. The computation of the total score is easy to complete in the data analysis package IBM SPSS Statistics 19, using the 'compute new variable' commands (see Chapter 27).

One of the difficulties with the computation of a total score is that the process of aggregation makes it difficult for the researcher to interpret scores that are in the middle range. Are they slightly disagreeing or slightly agreeing? A further difficulty is that the total score can be reached by a wide range of differing responses. Look again at Figure 15.6 and consider how many different combinations of responses could be used to obtain a total score of 14. In addition to computing a total score, the analysis of responses to each of the individual statements can reveal further information to the researcher.

Specialist texts are available on design scales for specific purposes. For example, a number of complex scales have been developed in relation to measuring health and quality of life. These include the Short-Form 36 General Health Survey Questionnaire, SF-36 (Ware and Sherbourne, 1992), Sickness Impact Profile, SIP (Bergner et al., 1981) and Quality of Life Index, QL-Index (Spitzer et al., 1981). For a general text on measuring health and medical outcomes see Jenkinson (1994) and McDowell and Newell (1996).

Ranking question responses Ranking question responses are used when the researcher wishes to collect data on how respondents rank a list of items in relation to each other. This could involve ranking the importance of access to public services or a range of environmental issues. Ranking questions can be structured in two different ways. The first is to list a series of items and ask the respondent to rank all of them in order of importance from 1 to the maximum number of items listed. The item of most importance should have a 1 entered next to it, the item of second importance would have a 2 entered next to it, and so on until all items have been ranked.

The second is to list a series of items and ask the respondent to rank only the top three items of importance from 1 to 3. Items not deemed of sufficient importance do not have a numerical rank entry entered for them. Figure 15.7 has an example of both approaches. Each of the questions contain detailed instructions for their completion.

Multiple response questions Multiple response questions are simply any question that requires the respondent to indicate more than one response or answer. These would include questions that require all relevant categories to be selected from a list and also the ranking questions mentioned in the previous section. It is important that the researcher recognizes when they are asking a multiple response question as it will impact on how the data will be coded and analysed. The key to multiple response questions is that enough variables have to be created in the dataset to accommodate the maximum number of question responses made by an individual case. In the second example of a ranking question, Figure 15.7, the respondent was required to rank their top three items in order of preference and hence would require three variables in the data file. More information on coding multiple response questions can be found in the section 'Coding for multiple response questions' in Chapter 16.

Matrix question structure Where there are a large number of rating questions it can be appropriate to organize them into a matrix question structure. It is advisable to organize the rating questions into specific related areas and make

Example 1

Below is a list of local facilities that could be improved. Enter a number, from 1 to 9, in the box next to each of the facilites listed to rate the importance of improving each of the facilities. The most important facility to be improved should be given a value of 1, the second most important a value of 2, repeat this until you get to the value 9 for the least important facility for improvement.

Indoor sports facilities	5
Outdoor sports facilities	3
Children's play centre	4
Swimming pools	1
Libraries	7
Local parks and green spaces	2
Cinemas	8
Theatres	9
Local Community Centres or Halls	6

Example 2

Below is a list of local facilities that could be improved. Select the three most important facilities that in your opinion should be improved upon. Place these three into order of importance, 1 for most important, 2 for second important and 3 for third important.

Indoor sports facilities	
Outdoor sports facilities	3
Children's play centres	
Swimming pools	1
Libraries	
Local parks and green spaces	2
Cinemas	
Theatres	
Local Community Centres or Halls	

FIGURE 15.7 Example of two ranking questions

use of more than one matrix question if there are a large number of rating questions on a variety of different topics. Separate matrix questions should be used if the rating scale is different for some questions. The advantage of matrix questions is that they allow for a large number of questions or statements to

	Strongly agree	Agree	Neutral	Disagree	Strongly disagree
The module aims were clearly stated.	☐	☐	☐	☐	☐
The course materials accompanying this module were clear and easy to follow.	☐	☐	☐	☐	☐
It was easy to gain access to university computers outside of formal sessions.	☐	☐	☐	☐	☐
I have enjoyed studying this module.	☐	☐	☐	☐	☐

FIGURE 15.8 Example of a matrix question structure

be condensed into a smaller area in the questionnaire. An example of a matrix question is shown in Figure 15.8.

Developing the wording of questions

The development of the question needs to be carefully assessed and scrutinized before conducting the main survey. The formulation of the questions will often precede the decision as to whether questions are open ended or closed ended.

The first steps in survey question construction would be to identify the key areas for data collection. These areas will be identified from the process of operationalization. The literature review may have revealed some questions used in previous studies that you could include, with or without modification, in your questionnaire.

General guidance on question construction concentrates on the following areas:

- *Clear question wording.* The wording of questions needs to be clear, direct and simple. There should be no ambiguity.

- *Question length.* Questions that are too long are likely to put off the respondent. Questions can also be too short and fail to provide adequate guidance and information on the data required from the respondent.

- *Terminology.* Avoid terms where there is not one universal definition or a term that not all respondents may be familiar with. Equally one needs to ensure that the question itself cannot be interpreted in more than one way. For example, 'Do you have a car?' Does this mean, do you have your own car? Do you have access to a car? Do you have a company car? Is the issue one of car ownership or usage of a car?

- *Double questions.* When first constructing questions it is very easy to word a question that is in fact asking two questions. For example, 'How would you rate the frequency *and* cleanliness of local bus services?' It is important to avoid such occurrences.

- *Leading questions.* Question wording needs to avoid bias and leading the respondent to give a particular response. The wording of the question may hint at the 'correct' or 'desired' response.

- *Questions that require a very specific memory recall.* Respondents may not always be able to remember exact events, particularly frequency of events, over a specified timescale. For example, asking the question 'How many times have you used the local bus services in the last year?' is unlikely to result in an accurate response. In these instances the time period can be shortened, for example, 'How many times in the last week have you used the local bus services?' However, there is then the issue of defining 'last week': does this mean the previous seven days or the previous working week? An alternative method of dealing with these types of question is to replace the open response of actual frequency with a series of closed responses. For example: every day, 4–6 times a week, 2–3 times a week, once a week, never.

Collecting demographic information

Earlier in this chapter we mentioned the need to collected background data on the respondents or participants in your research study. Background information will include asking demographic questions, for example, age, gender and educational qualifications. The exact demographic data to be collected will depend on the research topic. For example, in a study of university students, collecting data on the student's year of study and the mode of study may be of relevance. Where existing research has been undertaken it may be useful for comparative purposes to take into account the classifications used in the previous research. For example, if your research needed to collect data on educational qualifications then using one of the standardized questions from a large survey such as the Census would enable a comparison of your sample characteristics with the Census data returns (see Box 15.8). The advantage of using an existing question format is that questions from repeated surveys are often subject to rigorous test and retest methods to ensure the validity of the question (see section 'Reliability and validity' later in this chapter). In structured interviews a show card can be used for potentially sensitive questions, for example on income. The respondent is given the card and asked to state the number next to the relevant category. The interviewer records the category on the questionnaire form. In a structured interview an alternative strategy is to combine the structured interview schedule with a short questionnaire that contains questions specific to gathering demographic information. The respondent is asked to complete a short questionnaire containing these questions at the end of the interview.

Examples of existing demographic questions commonly used

From the UK Census 2001

Which of the following qualifications do you have?

☐ 1+ O Levels/CSE/GCSE (any grade)
☐ 5+ O Levels, 5+ CSEs (grade 1), 5+ GCSEs (grades A–C), School Certificate
☐ 1+ A levels/AS levels
☐ 2+ A Levels, 4+ AS levels, Higher School Certificate
☐ First Degree (e.g. BA, BSc)
☐ Higher Degree (e.g. MA, PhD, PGCE, Postgraduate certificate/diploma)
☐ NVQ Level 1, Foundation GNVQ
☐ NVQ Level 2, Intermediate GNVQ
☐ NVQ Level 3, Advanced GNVQ
☐ NVQ Levels 4–5, HNC, HND
☐ Other qualifications (e.g. City and Guilds, RSA/OCR, BTEC/Edexcel)
☐ No qualifications

From the Northern Ireland Life and Times Survey 2006

What is your *personal* income *before* tax and national insurance contributions?

Include all income from employment and benefits

Under £3,000 per year	(less than £60 per week)	☐
£3,000 – £3,999 per year	(£60 – £80 per week)	☐
£4,000 – £6,999 per year	(£80 – £135 per week)	☐
£7,000 – £9,999 per year	(£135 – £195 per week)	☐
£10,000 – £14,999 per year	(£195 – £290 per week)	☐
£15,000 – £19,999 per year	(£290 – £385 per week)	☐
£20,000 – £25,999 per year	(£385 – £500 per week)	☐
£26,000 – £29,999 per year	(£500 – £580 per week)	☐
£30,000 – £39,999 per year	(£580 – £770 per week)	☐
£40,000 – £49,999 per year	(£770 – £960 per week)	☐
£50,000 + per year	(£960 + per week)	☐
I do not wish to answer this question		☐
Don't know		☐

Further details on the Office for National Statistics programme to harmonize the data collection of standard concepts across UK government departments can be found at the 'Harmonisation' website at http://www.ons.gov.uk/about-statistics/harmonisation/index.html.

Survey layout

The presentation and layout of the self-completion survey and questions need to be considered carefully. Failure to allow time for this in your planning schedule could result in a poor completion rate for a mail survey and confusion for the telephone interviewer or face-to-face interviewer. It is important that the survey is professionally presented to convey a sense of importance to the respondent, who in turn will, hopefully, be more willing to complete and return the document. A survey that fails to convey this is unlikely to receive the response desired.

Organization and order

The organization of the questions needs to be carefully considered. It is important that the questions are organized by similar topic areas. This makes it easier for the researcher to visualize and manage the relationship between the questions and measurement tools used for each question and the original questions and hypothesis. At the development stage it may be useful to sketch out the relationship between these two using a simple organization chart.

Routing questions and funnelling respondents

Routing or funnelling questions are a convenient method of directing or funnelling respondents to particular sections of questions. They are appropriate to use when it is known that some groups of questions will not be applicable to specific respondents. For example, in a survey of healthy lifestyles, a series of questions on participation in sporting activities undertaken would be not applicable to those who do not participate in any sporting activity.

Directing respondents away from completing questions that are not applicable to them will reduce completion fatigue; ticking 'Not applicable or relevant' to a series of questions can become very tedious! The use of routing questions can reduce the time required to complete the overall questionnaire. Routing questions also have the advantage of making the researcher think through carefully why they are asking particular questions and how they relate back to the original research question.

Routing questions typically place the respondent into a particular category. The question will normally consist of a 'Yes/No' or 'Tick all applicable responses' followed by clear instruction to then progress to a particular set of questions. Two examples are given in Figure 15.9.

Reliability

The use of indicators and tests raises issues of reliability and validity.

Reliability is the degree to which the indicator or test is a consistent measure over time, or simply whether the respondent will give the same response at a different

Example 1: yes/no response

In a survey of residents' use of a local sports facility, respondents were asked what facilities they made use of.

Q1. Have you used the facilities at the Forestview Leisure Centre in the last month?

Yes ☐   If Yes go to Q2.
No   ☐   If No go to Q3.

Q2. Which of the following facilities have you used?

Swimming pool   ☐
Multigym   ☐
Activity classes, e.g. aerobics, boxercise, pilates   ☐
Crèche   ☐
Five-a-side football pitches   ☐
Badminton courts   ☐
Tennis courts   ☐

Q3. Have you used any other leisure centres in the last month?

Yes ☐   If Yes go to Q4.
No   ☐   If No, go to Q5.

Q4. Please name the other leisure centre(s) that you have used: ☐

Q5. Can you please tell me if you are

Male   ☐
Female   ☐

Example 2: tick all applicable, followed by directions to different sections of the survey

Do you participate in any of the following sporting activities, either competitively or for leisure? (Please tick all applicable)

Swimming   ☐   Please complete section 2
Tennis   ☐   Please complete section 3
Badminton   ☐   Please complete section 4
Running/jogging   ☐   Please complete section 5
Cycling   ☐   Please complete section 6
Football   ☐   Please complete section 7
Rugby   ☐   Please complete section 8

FIGURE 15.9 Examples of routing questions

time. The importance of accurately measuring an indicator is that it will allow for the detection of differences, or variance, between different groups of cases. It is inevitable that the data collected in a measurement tool or indicator will consist of the true measure plus an error measure. The reliability of a measure is judged by consistency in response and the limitation of the error measure. It is not possible to totally eliminate error. Even when one is taking measurements in the natural sciences, errors will occur. For example, measuring a length of string will always be an estimate according to the skill of the scientist, the accuracy of the rule and the number of decimal places used in the length unit. Reliability is an important issue as a large error or unreliability will impact on the analysis of relationships between the variables. 'When a measure has low reliability, some of the differences in scores between people which it produces are spurious differences, not real differences' (Punch, 1998: 100).

The only way of assessing the reliability of the measurement tool or question is the test–retest method where the respondent is asked the same question at different intervals. Correlation techniques can then be used to assess the consistency in the answers given. A correlation coefficient of 0.8 or higher is taken as an indication that the question is reliable (de Vaus, 1996: 55). The difficulties with the test–retest method are that it is often not practical to ask the questions to the same sample on two or more occasions, and that respondents may remember their previous response. The test–retest can then become a measure of respondents' memory and not the reliability of the measurement tool. Reliability can be improved by the careful construction and piloting of the questions, making use of existing questions from reputable surveys. For structured interviews the skill of the interviewer is important, particularly where two or more interviewers are used. The use of multiple indicators can also improve reliability.

Validity

Validity refers to the degree to which a measuring instrument actually measures and describes the concept it was designed to. Validity is a more complex issue to understand as it is separated into a number of sub-divisions.

Criterion validity involves the researcher undertaking some initial analysis of the measure to check that it performs in the way that it would be expected to. For example, a tool has been devised to measure an attitudinal difference between men and women. The measure fails to show any difference in attitudes between the two groups. This suggests that either the measure is not performing as expected, or there is no measurable difference between men and women. If existing surveys suggest that those differences between the attitudes of men and women do exist, then perhaps the measurement tool is not measuring the variation. However, this is based on the existing measurement being accepted.

Predictive validity involves a time lag between the research itself and its prediction for future findings. If the predicted findings are measured at a later date, then the measure has predictive validity.

Face validity refers to the assessment of whether the measure is a suitable measure of the concept. This assessment should be undertaken by the researcher in a critical self-evaluation and by referring the measure to identified experts in the area.

Content validity is concerned with assessing how well the measurement claims to measure all of the different dimensions of the concept. For example, in the measure of religiosity, a measurement tool that only collected data on ceremonial attendance would have poor content validity as it would not take into account the other dimensions of religious belief.

Construct validity involves assessing how well the measurement conforms to the theoretical model. The assessment of construct validity is dependent upon the strength of the original theory.

Two other more general validity terms are internal validity and external validity. Internal validity focuses on establishing that there is no evidence that other factors, on which data may or may not have been collected, are responsible for the variation in the dependent variable. The sampling technique and the measurement tools used for data collection can compromise internal validity. Establishing internal validity is a difficult processes and is linked to the processes of elaboration and spuriousness (see Chapter 25). External validity is the extent to which the research findings can be generalized to larger populations and applied to different settings. It is determined by the representativeness and size of the sample from which the findings are derived.

Summary

The questions the piece of research attempts to answer and the geographic location of those to be surveyed will be major factors in the decision to conduct a self-completion survey or structured interview. There are advantages and disadvantages to both methods that the social researcher will need to consider. Both methods require the development of survey questions. The literature review will identify appropriate concepts and indicators from which survey questions can be developed. The survey questions are the data collection tool that will enable the researcher to investigate the initial research question and hypothesis. Depending on the nature of the study, it may be appropriate to use existing survey questions from established large-scale repeated studies. Survey questions seek to obtain factual information, personal knowledge, attributes, beliefs and opinions. The format of the survey question can be open ended or closed ended, depending on the type of data to be gathered. Attention needs to be given to the structure, wording and format of the questionnaire survey and the structured interview schedule.

 ■ **Questions**

1 Under what circumstances would a self-completion survey be preferable to a structured interview?
2 How can the categories selected for closed-ended questions restrict the subsequent data analysis?
3 What do you understand by the terms 'reliability' and 'validity' and how do they relate to question construction?

Aldridge, Alan and Levine, Ken (2001) *Surveying the Social World: Principles and Practice in Survey Research*. Buckingham: Open University Press.

Belson, William A. (1981) *The Design and Understanding of Survey Questions*. London: Gower.

Cicourel, Aaron (1968) *Method and Measurement in Sociology*. New York: Free.

Fink, Arlene (2003) *The Survey Kit: How to Ask Survey Questions*, 2nd edn. Thousand Oaks, CA: Sage.

Fowler, Floyd (1995) *Improving Survey Questions: Design and Evaluation*. London: Sage.

Jenkinson, Crispin (ed.) (1994) *Measuring Health and Medical Outcomes*. London: UCL.

McDowell, Ian and Newell, Claire (1996) *Measuring Health: A Guide to Rating Scales and Questionnaires*. New York: Oxford University Press.

Oppenheim, A (2000) *Questionnaire Design: Interviewing and Attitude Measurement*. London: Continuum.

SIXTEEN

COLLECTING AND CODING QUANTITATIVE DATA

Chapter Contents

By the end of this chapter you will be able to:

- **Understand the importance of piloting a survey.**
- **Understand the administrative aspects of conducting a survey.**
- **Identify issues associated with non-response.**
- **Construct a code book appropriate for different variables and types of question.**
- **Identify potential sources of secondary data.**

Piloting

The piloting stage of the survey questions allows the researcher to assess the main elements of the data collection process. Basically it is concerned with making sure that the survey questions are understood by respondents and return meaningful and usable data that will enable you to answer your research question. A common mistake made by the student researcher is to focus solely on ensuring that the question wording and structure are understood by the respondent and forgetting to check that the data collected are actually useful in addressing the research question. The survey questions should be piloted on a test group of cases from the target population. It is important that this test group reflects the characteristics of the actual sample cases. For example, a survey that is intended for distribution to final-year undergraduates should be piloted on a small group of students from their final year.

The piloting of a self-completion survey will allow the researcher to gather information on the appropriateness of the questions, the predefined response categories for each question, and how the overall survey format and structure actually function. Aldridge and Levine (2001: 91) suggest that the following 'warning signs' are an indication of problems with surveys that will need to be addressed:

- multiple answers to questions where only one was required

- only one response given to a multiple response question

- ranking question inadequately completed

- uniformity of answers, i.e. the same answers from all respondents

- no answers given to a question

- completion time lengthy.

The incorrect completion of questions suggests that any instructions for completing the questionnaire are inadequate. This can be particularly challenging if the survey has routing and funnelling questions included within it. Failure to answer suggests that either the question is inappropriate or the question needs rewording. Sometimes respondents will write comments over survey questions to indicate the difficulties they experience in completing the question, and these prove a valuable resource in determining how to reword the question or in deciding to remove the question entirely.

In structured interviews, similar issues as for self-completion surveys may occur. The skill of the interviewer will play an important role in teasing out difficulties and problems. Where questions are inappropriately answered, the interviewer can make specific follow-up questions to ascertain the reasons why. This is of particular value where questions are unanswered. Unlike in a self-completion survey, in a structured interview the interviewer is in a position to assess the wording of questions and appropriateness of predefined categories and where appropriate probe the respondent for other more appropriate categories.

Administering the survey

Administering a survey is an important stage in the research process, requiring the researcher to ensure that a number of related matters are addressed. Once the survey questions have been developed, arrangements need to be made for their reproduction. For mail surveys, envelopes need to be purchased, together with postage stamps or franking. The mail survey will need to include an introductory letter explaining the nature and purpose of the study. Consider including a pre-paid return envelope to maximize the potential response. Another consideration is the use of a follow-up or reminder letter to be sent a few weeks after the initial survey to remind those sampled of the importance of returning the survey. For surveys involving telephone interviews, the sending out of a letter to explain the purpose of the survey and likely contact timings should be considered. This would avoid the 'cold-call' approach and hopefully boost response rates by minimizing an instant refusal.

Covering letters and statements

A covering letter is a short piece of explanatory text that introduces the nature and purpose of the study. The exact content of the covering letter will be determined by the nature of the study and contact method being used. As a minimum the letter should address the following points:

- identify who is undertaking the research
- explain the aim of the study
- convey the importance of the completion and the valuable contribution the respondent is making to the study
- stress the importance that as many people as possible should participate in the study
- give assurances of confidentiality and anonymity in the reporting of the research

- confirm that the study has been approved by an ethical clearance protocol
- provide contact details should additional information be required
- include completion and return details (self-completion survey only)
- include details of the interview date/time and location (structured interview only)
- include the dates that telephone interviewing will be undertaken (telephone interview only).

Figure 16.1 contains an example of a covering letter that would be sent out with a self-completion survey. Figure 16.2 contains an example of a covering letter that would be sent out to interviewees.

Date: <date>

Dear <name>,

We are part of the Sociology and Social Policy Research Unit at the University of Smithstown. We are currently undertaking a study of the participation of the local population in a range of social and sports-based physical activities. The research has been commissioned by the Local Strategic Partnership to help them plan local service provision that meets the needs of the local area.

You have been randomly selected for inclusion in this study. The enclosed questionnaire seeks to gather information on your own participation and those that live in your household with you.

The research has been approved by the university's Ethics Committee. All information gathered from the survey will be recorded in accordance with the research ethics policy. All survey responses will be treated confidentially and individual responses are anonymized to ensure that no one is identifiable. The data will not be passed on to any third parties.

In order to gather information from across the population it is important that we receive as many responses as possible. We would appreciate if you could complete and return the questionnaire in the pre-paid reply envelope as soon as possible. As a token of our appreciation, all questionnaires returned by 31 August 2011 are eligible to be entered into a prize draw to win £100 of gift vouchers. In order to be entered into the prize draw, please make sure that you complete the personal details postcard attached to the back of the questionnaire. This card will be entered into the draw.

If you would like further information on the research or have any concerns you would like to discuss, please contact the Active Participation Research hotline on 01234 567890.

We thank you for your participation in this survey and look forward to receiving your completed questionnaire.

Yours sincerely

Carole David

Research Officer

FIGURE 16.1 A covering letter for a self-completion survey

We are part of the Sociology and Social Policy Research Unit at the University of Smithstown. We are currently undertaking a study of the participation of the local population in a range of social and sports-based physical activities. The research has been commissioned by the Local Strategic Partnership to help them plan local service provision that meets the needs of the local area.

Thank you for agreeing to participate in this study. Your interview will take place at your home on Friday 31 August 2011 at 10 a.m. The interview will last for approximately one hour and will consist of the interviewer asking you a series of questions. There will also be a short questionnaire for you to complete. The researcher will be carrying a university identification card and a copy of this letter.

Your participation in the research remains voluntary throughout. You can stop the interview at any time. You should not feel under any pressure to participate in the study, and you are able to withdraw from the study at any point.

The research has been approved by the university's Ethics Committee. All information gathered from the survey will be recorded in accordance with the research ethics policy. All information collected will be treated confidentially and individual responses are anonymized to ensure that no one is identifiable. The data will not be passed on to any third parties.

As a thank you for participating in the study, we will enter your details into a free prize draw to win £100 of gift vouchers.

If you would like further information on the research or have any concerns you would like to discuss please contact the Active Participation Research hotline on 01234 567890. If the above interview day and time are not convenient, please call that number.

We thank you for your participation in this survey and look forward to meeting you.

Yours sincerely

Carole David
Research Officer

FIGURE 16.2 A covering letter for a structured interview taking place in the participant's home

Incentives

You will notice that in Figures 16.1 and 16.2 the statement includes an incentive to participate in the study. This can be quite a contentious issue in academic social research circles. In market research the practice of incentives is quite wide. The rationale is that you are compensating someone for their time in completing the study – as well as, hopefully, increasing your response rate. Careful consideration needs to be given to whether the offering of an incentive is appropriate and how best it can be achieved. The availability of sufficient research funds is also, of course, an issue.

In the following sections a number of specific issues relating to the management of different types of surveys are considered (see also Box 16.1).

BOX 16.1 HINTS AND TIPS

Researchers' contact details

Including contact details for the participant to get in contact with the research team is a normal feature of maintaining a good relationship with research participants. If you are conducting a student research project, particularly if it is part of a taught course and if you are working as part of a team, then you will need to consider what type of contact is appropriate. For example, you could substitute a telephone number with an e-mail address. The use of your personal home or mobile telephone number requires careful consideration. It is important that your own privacy is balanced against the requirements to complete the research. For example, for a survey of school pupils, including your personal mobile number would be ill-advised. If you were conducted depth structured interviews with school teachers, including your mobile number might be less of a risk. Here it is advisable to talk to your academic tutor for their views and the research guidance of your institution.

Internet-based surveys

Administrating a survey that is based on the internet involves a number of different stages. Where the survey is to be distributed via electronic mail, the questions need to be placed into a suitable file that is attached to the message or included within the main body of the e-mail message. The e-mail message should also contain the same information as in the covering letter for a mail survey, plus technical details on how to complete and return the completed survey questions. The e-mail is then sent to the addresses in the sample or, where a snowball sampling technique is adopted, to bulletin boards or newsgroups inviting people to participate in the survey.

Where the survey questions are going to be placed on the World Wide Web, the first stage is to transfer the questions and response categories in a suitable file format, for example HTML (hypertext markup language), onto a web server. This is likely to involve the support of local technical staff who will need to ensure not only that the survey can be viewed on the web, but also that responses made are collected into a suitable data file. Any technical difficulties need to be addressed during the pilot phase. An e-mail can then be sent to the addresses of those in the sample and should contain the same information as for a mail survey covering letter. Where a snowball sampling technique is adopted, an e-mail can be sent to newsgroups and bulletin boards inviting participation in the survey.

Structured interviews

In structured interviews the interviewer is available to answer any concerns about participation directly. However, if possible a written introductory statement should be sent to the participant prior to the interview to allow the respondent time to decide on participation and consider any arising matters. Figure 16.2 contains

Instruction to the interviewer: to be read to the interviewee at the start of the interview.

Thank you for agreeing to participate in this study. My name is <name> and I am part of the research team at the University of Smithstown. We are currently undertaking a study of the participation of the local population in a range of social and sports-based physical activities. The research has been commissioned by the Local Strategic Partnership to help them plan local service provision that meets the needs of the local area.

Thank you for agreeing to participate in this study. Your interview will take place at your home on Friday 31 August 2011 at 10:00 a.m. The interview will last for approximately one hour and will consist of the interviewer asking you a series of questions. There will also be a short questionnaire for you to complete. The researcher will be carrying a university identification card and a copy of this letter.

Your participation in the research remains voluntary throughout. You can stop the interview at any time. You should not feel under any pressure to participate in the study, and you are able to withdraw from the study at any point. If you are unhappy, you can request that the data are not included in the study. The research has been approved by the university's Ethics Committee. All information gathered from the survey will be recorded in accordance with the research ethics policy.

All information collected will be treated confidentially and individual responses are anonymized to ensure that no one is identifiable. The data will not be passed on to any third parties.

Do you have any questions? Are you happy to participate in the study and start the interview?

Thank you. Could you please sign the following consent form.

Consent Form

I have received details of the study and have had the study explained to me. I understand that all the information gathered will be held in the strictest confidence. I am aware that I may withdraw from the study at any stage.

Signed (participant):

As the researcher I confirm that I have explained the purpose of the research study to the participant above.

Signed (researcher):

Date:

FIGURE 16.3 An introductory statement read at the beginning of the interview

a copy of a covering letter sent to interviewees before the interview, as we have seen. It is the same research project as used in the covering letter for the self-completion survey (Figure 16.1). You can see the slight difference in wording since the researcher will be meeting the participant.

Figure 16.3 contains an example of the introductory statement read by the interviewer at the beginning of the interview, and a consent form. With a questionnaire, the actual completion of the survey questions is often used as a form of consent. This is the equivalent of the consent that you give when you go to the dentist: opening your mouth is taken as implicit consent without you actually signing any document. However, for some studies, particularly of a sensitive nature or when dealing with vulnerable groups, a more formalized consent form is used, and may be a requirement of the local ethics committee. As a minimum the consent form would consist of a checklist of statements confirming that the interviewee understands the points made in the covering letter. The consent form would be signed by both the participant and the researcher before the interview starts, to confirm that the study has been explained to the participant and has been understood. In order to adhere to anonymity the consent form is held separately from the research data. With regard to research involving children, consent may need to be obtained by parents or by those acting *in loco parentis*, such as school teachers. Again, this will depend on the exact nature of the research project.

A practical checklist for interviews is given in Box 16.2. In addition, ensure that the interviewer has enough survey forms if conducting more than one interview on a given day, together with spare pens and pencils.

BOX 16.2

PRACTICAL CHECKLIST FOR CONDUCTING FACE-TO-FACE STRUCTURED INTERVIEWS

Managing the arrangements for the interview

- Record the interviewee's contact details.
- Where contact is made and a date arranged, record the details.
- Send a confirmation letter: see Figure 16.2.
- Check the travel arrangements for the interviewer to the venue.

Day of the interview

- Take contact details for the interviewee.
- Check that copies of the interview schedule or questionnaire are packed.
- Take enough pens and pencils.
- Make sure that the interviewer carries an identification card.
- Arrive promptly.

Safety of the interviewer

- Ensure that someone else knows when and where you are conducting your interview.
- Depending on the nature of the topic and where the interview is taking place, you may need to take someone with you.
- You will need to take advice from your academic tutor and follow any local protocols.

Telephone interviews

There are some practical issues in managing a telephone survey. These relate to ensuring that the process is accurately recorded, and that appropriate systems are in place to clearly identify a successful call; the need for a follow-up call, for example where it is necessary to call back at a more convenient time; and finally, a straight refusal. A checklist of these and other aspects can be found in Box 16.3.

BOX 16.3

PRACTICAL CHECKLIST FOR CONDUCTING TELEPHONE INTERVIEWS

Managing the telephone call

- List the contact details, name, telephone number, identification number.
- Log first attempt to call, when, date, time.
- If contact made:

  o Refusal, absolutely no further contact. Record this clearly to ensure no embarrassing follow-up call.

  o Refusal but willing to be interviewed at later date/time. Record a convenient time to call back and check that you should call back on the number you have on your database.

  o Contact is made but the relevant individual is not available. If you were phoning to ask to speak to a person in a role (for example, head of finance), try to find out the name of the person and their direct telephone number. If a named individual, record date/time of call. Ask the person who answers the phone if they know a better time to call back (reassure that you are not a marketing person). Log these details.

- No answer. Log call attempt details and call back later. Vary the time of day of the call-back. Decided how many call attempts you will make before abandoning. Two? Three? Four?

Working as a group

If you are undertaking research as part of a group, you will need to work out a system for how you are going to manage the calls and call-backs, particularly if another member of the research team will be calling back to a named individual. You will need to decide who is responsible for managing this process.

Other useful details worth recording

As you go through the interview schedule with each respondent, record any other information that may be useful to you when you come to the data analysis phase. This information should be recorded next to the respondent ID in order that you can link to the data file at a later stage. An example is where the response categories did not 'fit' a respondent's circumstances.

Should you track participation?

The issues of confidentiality and anonymity have been raised in Chapter 2. During the administration and access of the sample you need to consider if you are going to track those that have responded to a request to complete a self-completion survey or structured interview. Keeping track of those that have responded allows the researcher to monitor response rates and to target those who have not responded with a follow-up letter reminding them to return the survey form or respond to a request to participate in an interview. For postal or mail surveys, questionnaires can be numbered before distribution and a note kept of the corresponding name of the recipient. The difficulty with this is that it enables the researcher then to link the returned questionnaires to respondents, thereby breaking anonymity. For purposes of both anonymity and conforming to data protection, care must be taken to ensure that the two sets of information (contact details and returned survey forms) are kept separate. An alternative strategy is simply to send a follow-up letter to all respondents in the sample, even though this does incur additional financial expense.

Non-response

Non-response is defined as the failure to collect data from a sampling unit. The response rate is calculated as the ratio of the actual sample size obtained to the total sample size selected. For example, if 75 individuals are surveyed from a total sample size of 100, the response rate is 0.75 or 75 per cent. Alternatively, this could be specified as a non-response rate of 0.25 or 25 per cent. Non-response is important as it affects the representativeness of the research results and introduces an error or bias into the findings (Fink, 1995b).

Decisions as to how to proceed with the issue of non-response will be constrained by the timescale of the research project. It is difficult to estimate the level of non-response that you may get; even government-based surveys with a large resource base experience non-response. The non-response rate for the General Household Survey (2000–1) was 33 per cent and for the Family Expenditure Survey (1999–2000) it was 37 per cent (National Statistics Office).

Arber (2001) identifies two main sources of non-response: refusals and non-contacts. Refusals are from respondents who simply do not wish to participate in the study. They may consider the study to be uninteresting, or may not perceive the study as important or as having legitimacy. In the case of interviews, non-response can be influenced by the skills of the interviewer, and in mail surveys by the quality of the questionnaire design and the explanation in the covering letter. Non-contacts occur when the respondent is not at home when the interviewer calls; or the respondent cannot be interviewed due to illness or communication issues; or, in the case of a named respondent, they have moved home. Non-contact rates can be improved by the interviewer 'calling back' or by the researcher providing follow-up letters encouraging completion and return of the questionnaire. Depending on the study the offering of an incentive, for example, entry to a prize draw, may improve rates. Where the respondent is non-interviewable it may be appropriate to arrange an advocate or a proxy to help complete the survey or interview.

Arranging for proxy interview is particularly important in surveys of very old people, because the needs of the most frail would otherwise be under-represented. It may also be important to employ interviewers who speak appropriate languages or interpreters, otherwise the sample would be biased against those with least fluency in speaking English (Arber, 2001: 75).

Once measures have been put in place to limit the rate of non-response, there is little that the researcher can further do to enhance data collection. The next step is to assess the impact that non-response has on the overall representativeness of the sample. Take the key characteristics of the sample, for example, age, sex and occupation, and compare the proportions of each with the population characteristics. The population characteristics can be found from Census data or other large, often government-based, surveys. In the UK, with the exception of the 10-yearly Census, government surveys do not survey the entire population. For example, the General Household Survey 2000–1 surveyed 19,266 individuals in 8221 households (UK Data Archive, 2002). Sophisticated sampling techniques are employed in these surveys to represent the population. Where differences in proportions are found, for example where a particular group is underestimated in a sample survey, weighting techniques can be used to multiply by an appropriate ratio (see section 'Using IBM SPSS Statistics 19 to compute a new variable' in Chapter 27). The assumption of employing this technique, however, is that there is uniformity between those cases that responded from the group and those that did not.

Developing a code book

You have already been introduced to the concept of levels of measurement in Chapter 13. There are four levels of measurement: nominal, ordinal, interval and ratio. Interval and ratio are often combined together and referred to as just interval in the literature, as they have similar properties. A code book, also called a coding frame, provides the framework of how the responses given to survey questions are prepared for analysis in a computer package. A code book needs to be developed for all methods of quantitative data collection. For closed-ended questions it is possible to include the codes next to the response categories on the actual survey itself. This will help by increasing the likely speed of data entry and decreasing the likelihood of a data entry error. In addition, the coding of closed-ended questions before the survey is administered allows the researcher to check that the level of measurement of the data will be appropriate for the envisaged analysis.

Coding for nominal variables

Nominal variables are coded numerically. The starting code is normally 1. The categories can be coded in the order that they are listed in the questionnaire. Codes for subsequent categories are simply incremented by 1 on the previous category. Since there is no order to the categories, one could code in any order; however, the norm is to code in order of appearance. This makes intuitive sense and is likely to reduce the potential for coding errors at the data entry stage. Dichotomies are sometimes coded as 0 and 1. The following shows three examples of coding for nominal variables:

Variable: Sex
Coding: 1 = male; 2 = female

Variable: Have you read a newspaper today?
0 = no; 1 = yes

Variable: Which newspaper did you read?
Coding: 1 = *Financial Times*; 2 = *New York Times*; 3 = *Washington Post*; 4 = *Melbourne Age*; 5 = *Times of India*; 6 = *South China Morning News*; 7 = *Le Monde*; 8 = other

Coding for ordinal variables

Coding ordinal variables is similar to that for nominal variables. Coding will normally start at 1 and increase by a count of 1 for each category. The categories should be coded in rank order to maintain the hierarchical order. The coding can run in either direction. In the first example below, the code for very important is 5 to reflect that it is more important than 1, very unimportant. However, remember that it is not possible to make a statement that very important is five times the size of very unimportant. In the second example, the coding is in reverse order where 1 is the highest educational qualification and 6 the lowest educational qualification.

Variable: Importance scale
5 = very important
4 = important
3 = neutral
2 = unimportant
1 = very unimportant

Variable: Highest educational qualification
1 = degree or higher
2 = diploma in HE
3 = certificate in HE
4 = A levels
5 = AS levels
6 = GCSE

In the coding of attitudinal questions, the coding can be reversed where question statements run in opposite directions. For example, in a list of statements there may be a combination of negative and positive statements. For the positive statements it would be appropriate for the strongly agree to be given a higher value of 5, whereas in the negative statements it would be appropriate for the strongly disagree to be given a higher value of 5. Assigning values in the appropriate direction is a particular issue for psychologists who may want to combine the responses to a list of statements into one total, or index, for analysis purposes (see section 'Different formats of closed-ended question responses' in Chapter 15).

Coding for interval/ratio variables

Coding for interval and ratio variables simply requires entry of the data value. For example, if a respondent is 23 years of age, the value of 23 will be entered in the data file. If the number of persons in a household is 3, this value will be entered in the data file.

Coding for multiple response questions

The coding of multiple response questions requires the researcher to identify the maximum number of responses that any one individual could potentially give to the question. Below are the responses to a question asking the respondent to indicate which of the daily newspapers they read. Potentially a respondent could tick all of the responses.

Most questions in a survey require only one response to be given. Where one response is made, only one variable is needed to contain the data in the data file. Multiple response questions produce many responses and therefore require more than one variable in the data file. The easiest method of coding multiple response questions is to treat each category in the list as if it were a single variable. Responses for each variable, in this example each newspaper, are then coded as a dichotomy of 1 = yes and 2 = no. The response 1 (yes) states that they have ticked that newspaper and 2 (no) states that the newspaper has not been ticked.

Financial Times	☐
New York Times	☐
Washington Post	☐
Melbourne Age	☐
Times of India	☐
South China Morning Post	☐
Le Monde	☐
Other	☐ (please state) _____

Coding for ranking questions

Ranking questions require the respondent to place two or more categories into a rank order (see Figure 15.7 for an example). These questions are also multiple response questions and require additional variables. Two or more variables, according to the number of categories to be ranked, need to be allowed for and the code for each variable would be the entered rank value.

Coding for open-ended questions

The coding of open-ended questions, also known as post-coding, is determined by the nature of the question and the variation and depth of the responses given. Where responses are short with some uniformity, within a given range, it can be possible to place the responses into 'like' categories and for these categories to be coded in turn. The level of measurement and coding would be nominal. However, the difficulties with coding open response questions are that the responses may not be appropriate for categorization and that the in-depth self-expression contained within the respondent's answer is removed by this process, thus removing the very rationale for including such a question in the survey. An alternative strategy for dealing with the responses from open-ended questions is to record in the data file a variable that indicates that a response was made and to record the actual response within a separate word-processed document. Included with the actual response should be the unique identifying number for that case, as this would allow for the response to be matched to the other data for that case at the analysis stage. The layout of such a document can follow the format for transcribing interviews, and the subsequent analysis of the open response could employ techniques used within qualitative analysis (see Chapters 18 to 20).

Coding for non-response or missing values

During the construction of a code book, consideration needs to be given to how you will deal with non-response, as it constitutes missing data. Respondents may not provide responses to all of the questions because they either choose not to respond or do not have to respond because the question is not applicable to them. In most data analysis packages it is possible to simply leave a blank entry for all data that are missing. The problem with doing this is that it will not allow for the researcher to distinguish between the two types of missing data at the analysis stage. This could be important if question responses have a large proportion of non-responses. Failure to answer the question could signify problems with the question. A common coding strategy for non-response is to divide the different types of non-response into discrete categories and assign a code that is remote from the positive response codes. Some researchers prefer to code using a negative number: for example, –9 = did not respond, –8 = not applicable. These codes can be set at the data entry stage to be excluded from the results (see section 'Defining a new variable' in Chapter 23).

What should a code book look like?

In this section we offer some suggestions on how you can organize and record your code book. Code books can take a number of different formats.

One approach is to use a copy of the questionnaire as the code book and type in the coding, the missing values and the data type against each question. This can be an effective and time-efficient approach where the survey structure is not too complex. Embedding the codes onto distributed questionnaires can also help to minimize errors at the data entry phase, as researchers responsible for input of survey responses into a data file see the correct code next to the selected answer. However, it is not always appropriate to include the codes. It will depend on the complexity of the survey, the format and the question structure.

Figure 16.4 shows an extract from a survey on students' experiences and concerns relating to crime and personal safety around a university campus. The

We are conducting a survey to explore university students' experiences and concerns relating to crime and personal safety in and around the university campus. We are interested in finding out the views of as many students as possible and would be grateful if you could complete the following survey questions. The questions should take no more than 5 minutes to complete.

Q1.   During term time how many days a week, on average, do you visit the university campus?

Please tick one box only

[DAYS]

1.   1 day   ☐
2.   2–3 days   ☐
3.   4–5 days   ☐
4.   6–7 days   ☐

[−9= Did not respond]

Q2.   Have you visited the campus during daylight hours? Please tick one box only

[CAMPUSDAY]

1.   Yes   ☐   If YES please now answer Q3.
2.   No   ☐   If NO please now answer Q4.

[−9 = Did not respond]

Q3.   How safe do you feel walking alone around the campus during daylight hours? Please tick one box only

[SAFEDAY]

1.   Very safe   ☐
2.   Fairly safe   ☐
3.   A bit unsafe   ☐
4.   Very unsafe   ☐

[−9 = Did not respond]
[−8 = Not Applicable, skipped]

Q4.   Have you visited the campus after the dark? Please tick one box only

[CAMPUSDARK]

1.   Yes   ☐   If YES please now answer Q5.
2.   No   ☐   If NO please now answer Q7.

Q5.   How safe do you feel walking alone around the campus after dark? Please tick one box only

[SAFEDARK]

1.   Very safe   ☐
2.   Fairly safe   ☐
3.   A bit unsafe   ☐
4.   Very unsafe   ☐

[−9 = Did not respond]

[−8 = Not Applicable, skipped]

(Continued)

Q6. How worried are you about any of the following incidents occurring to you when you are on the university campus after dark? Please select one option for each type of incident.

	(1) Very worried	(2) Fairly worried	(3) Not very worried	(4) Not worried at all
(a) Being mugged or robbed [MUGROB]	☐	☐	☐	☐
(b) Being verbally insulted or pestered [INSULT]	☐	☐	☐	☐
(c) Being physically attacked [ATTACK]	☐	☐	☐	☐
(d) Being sexually assaulted [ASSAULT]	☐	☐	☐	☐

[−9 = Did not respond]

[−8 = Not Applicable, Skipped]

Q7. Are you

Please tick one box only

[GENDER]

☐ 1. Male

☐ 2. Female

[−9 = Did not respond]

Q8. What type of course are you studying

Please tick one box only

[COURSE]

☐ 1. Undergraduate

☐ 2. Postgraduate research

☐ 3. Postgraduate research

☐ 4. Other

[−9 = Did not respond]

FIGURE 16.4 A questionnaire with code book details included

variables and codes for each survey question have been typed in and are printed in bold text.

Using this approach is efficient and can certainly act as a separate reference guide. However, as the researcher you will need to assess if including all code book details is problematic for surveys that are self-completed by participants who will see the coding. For instance, in the questionnaire in Figure 16.4 the variable names have been included in square brackets, e.g. [DAYS]. These could be distracting to the respondent of a self-completion survey, although they would not cause problems if the survey was administered face-to-face by a researcher.

Where coding onto the original questionnaire is considered inappropriate, an alternative is to construct a separate code book in a tabular format. This is particularly useful when you are working in a small team or may have to pass on the resulting survey data file to a third party. Each row in the table records a separate variable. The question number, description of the variable, codes, missing values, and data type can be recorded. Table 16.1 contains an example of a separate code book based on the questionnaire in Figure 16.4.

One of the advantages of compiling a separate code book is that you can record additional information or detail easily without it interfering with the questionnaire format. For example, in Table 16.1 we have included a column to record the data type or level of measurement of the variable. This provides an easy point of reference when analysing the data and checking that you are undertaking the correct statistical analysis for that type of data.

Locating and accessing secondary quantitative data

The analysis of existing, secondary, data can prove a valuable resource for a research project. Depending on the nature of the research, analysis of an existing dataset can provide background information and/or can be the main focus of the project analysis. Consideration of the inclusion of secondary data sources in a research project will be influenced by the theoretical and conceptual nature of the research project. Secondary data are available in a number of different formats. Dale et al. (1988) categorize these into three different groups: aggregated data, sample surveys and cohort studies. These distinctions provide a useful framework for deciding when and how to incorporate secondary data into your research project.

Aggregated data are probably the easiest data to access and incorporate into research. They are data that have already been manipulated and condensed into summary tables. The predefined format allows the researcher to then present the data as tables or charts in a report. Often the aggregated data are derived from one or more sources, and are available on a wide range of topic areas. Examples are economic indicators, births, marriages and deaths, national and regional crime statistics, and environmental issues, to name but a few. Aggregated data from government sponsored surveys, often referred to as official statistics, have increasingly been made more freely available via the internet. In the UK this is via the National Statistics Office website (www.statistics.gov.uk), for the European Union via the Eurostat website (www.eurostat.com), and for the US via the Federal Statistics website (www.fedstats.gov). The level of public access varies at each website, with access to some aggregated datasets requiring registration as a user.

Aggregated data are a resource that should not be undervalued within the research process. The tabular data have a robustness and a reliability that cannot be matched by undertaking a primary piece of research. Even where there may not be a dataset that exactly matches the research requirements, there will often be associated datasets that provide a valuable and comprehensive base against which

TABLE 16.1   Example of a code book or coding frame

Variable	Question number/ description	Codes	Non-response, missing values	Data type
IDCase	Questionnaire number	Enter actual number	–	–
DAYS	Q1. Number of days on campus per week	1 = 1 day 2 = 2–3 days 3 = 4–5 days 4 = 6–7 days	−9 = Did not respond	Ordinal
CAMPUSDAYS	Q2. Visit campus during daylight hours?	1 = Yes 2 = No	−9 = Did not respond	Nominal
SAFEDAY	Q3. How safe do you feel walking alone around the campus during daylight?	1 = Very safe 2 = Fairly safe 3 = A bit unsafe 4 = Very unsafe	−9 = did not respond −8 = Not applicable, skipped	Ordinal
CAMPUSDARK	Q4. Visit campus after dark?	1 = Yes 2 = No	−9 = Did not respond	Nominal
SAFEDARK	Q5. How safe do you feel walking alone around the campus after dark?	1 = Very safe 2 = Fairly safe 3 = A bit unsafe 4 = Very unsafe	−9 = Did not respond −8 = Not applicable, skipped	Ordinal
MUGROB	Q6a. Worried being mugged or robbed	1 = Very worried 2 = Fairly worried 3 = Not very worried 4 = Not worried at all	−9 = Did not respond −8 = Not applicable, skipped	Ordinal
INSULT	Q6b. Worried being verbally insulted or pestered	1 = Very worried 2 = Fairly worried 3 = Not very worried 4 = Not worried at all	−9 = Did not respond −8 = Not applicable, skipped	Ordinal
ATTACK	Q6c. Worried being physically assaulted	1 = Very worried 2 = Fairly worried 3 = Not very worried 4 = Not worried at all	−9 = Did not respond −8 = Not applicable, skipped	Ordinal
ASSAULT	Q6d. Worried being sexually assaulted	1 = Very worried 2 = Fairly worried 3 = Not very worried 4 = Not worried at all	−9 = Did not respond −8 = Not applicable, skipped	Ordinal
GENDER	Q7. Gender of respondent	1 = Male 2 = Female	−9 = Did not respond	Nominal
COURSE	Q8. Course of respondent	1 = Undergraduate 2 = Postgraduate taught 3 = Postgraduate research 4 = Other	−9 = Did not respond	Nominal

to compare primary research results. Of particular value within the UK National Statistics website is a geographical tool that enables the researcher to identify key population characteristics for a particular neighbourhood area (see www. statistics.gov.uk).

Sample survey data refers to the data from specific, often government initiated, surveys. Many of the surveys are undertaken on an annual or biannual basis, though one-off surveys are also included within this group. Examples of UK-based sample surveys include the General Household Survey (GHS), the Family Expenditure Survey (FES) and the Labour Force Survey (LFS). The data collected can be accessed as anonymized individual records, enabling the researcher to manipulate the data in a statistical and data analysis package such as IBM SPSS Statistics 19. The data can be analysed to specific geographical areas (in the UK to ward or postcode area), enabling the data findings to be compared to other statistical sources.

Cohort studies are a very specific type of study in that they are concerned with taking repeated measures from individuals over a longer period and are used within a longitudinal research design. In the UK two well-known cohort studies are the National Child Development Study (NCDS) and the British Household Panel Study (BHPS). The NCDS started in 1958 and took approximately 17,000 individuals from all those born between 3 and 9 March 1958 who lived in Great Britain. There have been five subsequent waves (1965, 1969, 1974, 1981, 1991). The data collected are multi-disciplinary, covering the physical, educational, social and economic development of these individuals. Patterns of change over time can be described, controlling for age and historical events, and detailed analysis of relationships between variables undertaken. Complex data analysis can be undertaken that takes into account the developmental, age and historical events of an individual's life course.

Advantages and disadvantages of secondary data

There are a number of issues to be considered when deciding to use secondary data. The survey data should not be viewed as free-standing, as they are a product of the subject area that the original study focused on. This is of particular concern for one-off surveys that have a specific focus, and less so for government-based surveys that have a wider coverage. When one is considering specific data, the sampling technique, sampling frame, research design and method of data collection should be considered together with the conceptual framework. How were concepts operationalized? What measurement tools were used? How were they defined? How were question responses coded?

The advantage of using secondary data is that their use has been established within the social sciences. Examples include the use of official suicide statistics by Durkheim (1952) and the use of socioeconomic and health data in the Black Report on poverty and inequalities in health (see Whitehead et al., 1992). In the UK, working within a higher-education setting allows the researcher to have privileged access to such data through the UK Data Archive. The search catalogues are easy to use and data access is mostly cost-free. In relation to government sponsored surveys and subsequent datasets, the National Statistics Office has developed a high level of data and statistical expertise, and the data are subjected to test and retest methods for validity. The datasets generally contain a much larger and broader sample than could be realistically obtained by a researcher on their own, particularly if the research forms part of a course of study. In turn, the financial costs associated with the secondary analysis are much lower than for primary data collection, with no data collection, coding or data entry to be undertaken.

The disadvantages of using secondary data are, first, that its use will be dependent upon the availability of accessible datasets in the UK and applicability of existing datasets to the area of your study. While catalogue search engines are easy to use, it may take some time for the exact data file you require to be located; indeed, such a dataset may not exist. The time saved in not undertaking primary data collection will instead be spent on the time-consuming task of downloading the datasets or subsets of data, and familiarization with the data and the coding used. The conceptual frameworks used as the basis for the original data collection may be different to those in your current project. If using more than one secondary data source, there may be differences between the studies that need to be considered. It is important that time is spent examining the original purposes of the study, the questions and the categories coded. Depending on the nature of the data analysis to be undertaken, it may require a higher level of technical, data handling and statistical expertise. This is particularly the case when using cohort studies for longitudinal analysis where issues such as missing cases need to be considered. Additional difficulties with using secondary data sources are well documented within the literature on using official statistics and the different methods of measurement (Atkinson, 1978).

Accessing datasets in the UK

The main route for searching and obtaining data for secondary analysis in the UK is via the Economic and Social Data Service (ESDS) (www.esds.ac.uk) (see Box 16.4). The Office for National Statistics also provides social and economic data (www.ons.gov.uk) that include neighbourhood-level statistics. Many datasets are stored at the UK Data Archive (which can be accessed via www.esds.ac.uk, see Box 16.4) where information on the catalogue and accessing protocols can be found.

> ### BOX 16.4
>
> ## ACCESSING USEFUL INFORMATION ABOUT EXISTING SURVEYS
>
> Information about existing data is available from a variety of websites, many of which cross-link. Collectively the archives store information on the topic, methodology, methods, sampling, survey questionnaires, findings and, depending on the study, the raw data file that is available for secondary analysis to bona fide users.

Summary

Collecting and coding survey data are both key stages in the research process. Piloting a survey enables the social researcher to identify the appropriateness of the survey questions and to make subsequent amendments to these questions as required. Once the main survey is undertaken there is a certain amount of administration which accompanies this process, for example, the production of covering letters and introductory statements. If one is undertaking a structured interview, show cards containing the response categories for closed-ended questions enable the interview to be conducted smoothly and with clarity. A key stage in the research process is the development of a code book that details how the collected data are going to be transferred, mainly in a numerical code format, into a computer for analysis by a statistical package. As has been shown, the level of measurement of the data collected determines the coding of these responses. These data are stored as variables in the final dataset. The number of variables needed varies according to the question structure, with multiple response questions requiring more variables. Development of the code book provides a structured concise framework for the data entry phase of the research process.

 ■ **Questions**

1 What factors can influence non-response, and how can you take steps as a social researcher to minimize non-response?
2 How would you code nominal, ordinal and interval variables and non-response?
3 What factors would you need to consider if undertaking secondary analysis of an existing dataset?

▨ ▨ Further reading ▨

Aldridge, Alan and Levine, Ken (2001) *Surveying the Social World: Principles and Practice in Survey Research.* Buckingham: Open University Press.

Dale, Angela, Arber, Sara and Procter, Michael (1998) *Doing Secondary Analysis.* London: Unwin Hyman.

Fielding, Jane and Gilbert, Nigel (2006) *Understanding Social Statistics*, second edition. London: Sage.

Gilbert, Nigel (ed.) (2001) *Researching Social Life*, 2nd edn. London: Sage.

SEVENTEEN

METHODOLOGICAL INNOVATIONS: MIXING METHODS AND E-RESEARCH

Chapter Contents

By the end of this chapter you will be able to:

- Understand how social research design and methods have been applied innovatively in mixed methods and e-research
- Distinguish between different types of mixed methods research
- Understand the purpose of evaluation research
- Understand how the internet has enabled the development of e-research

Introduction to mixed methods

Mixed methods research is concerned with combining different research methods in order to understand a particular research problem. The term 'mixed methods' could refer to using more than one quantitative method in a quantitative research design, or similarly more than one qualitative method in a qualitative research design. For example, in a quantitative design the method could entail the use of structured interviews, self-completion questionnaires and an online survey. In a qualitative design the method used could include a combination of focus groups, unstructured interviews and observation. However, more frequently the term 'mixed methods' is used in research approaches where a combination of quantitative and qualitative methods is adopted, although this position is by no means universally accepted (Moran-Ellis et al., 2006).

Mixed methods in the social sciences came to prominence in the 1980s as part of a more pragmatic approach to research, linked to the 'real-world' problem-based research particularly found in evaluation research (see section 'What is evaluation research?' later in this chapter) and educational research (Tashakkori and Teddlie, 2008: 9). It is sometimes referred to as the third methodological approach. Since it is relatively new, mixed methods as a research approach is still developing in terms of both methodological debates and practical issues. Mixed methods are not without controversy; these centre on whether it is appropriate for different methods to be combined in research. The debate is one that is essentially epistemological in origin – questioning whether one can ever combine the differing approaches to understanding and making sense of the social world that positivist and constructivist perspectives offer. These differing perspectives have been debated at length in Part I together with the blurred distinctions between data based on numbers and those representing meaning; between deduction and induction; and between depth and generalization. From these preceding chapters you will now be aware that the research problem should guide the methodological approach and methods utilized; and that different research approaches bring with them a variety of research methods, each of which has a variety of strengths and weaknesses. Rather than adopting one approach, either qualitative or quantitative, the researcher can choose the more pragmatic view of methodological pluralism in order to capitalize on the strengths of both. This is not to suggest that a mixed method should always be considered, as it should be the research problem that is central to the decision-making process.

The whole debate around mixed methods can be confusing as the terminology is often used interchangeably (Moran-Ellis et al., 2006): for example, mixed methods, multiple methods, multi-method, and the term 'triangulation' for using more than one method. Textbooks on mixed methods and journal articles (see the suggested reading at the end of this chapter) discuss issues relating to the selection of a mixed method strategy and how that strategy is implemented. If you are considering adopting a mixed methods approach it would be advisable to refer to these texts and journals as this will allow you to engage with the most recent innovative developments in this area.

Why use mixed methods?

Researchers are attracted to using mixed methods as they are seen as a way of finding out more about the subject that they wish to understand. As summarized by Williams (2003: 182), there are essentially three broad approaches to implementing mixed methods: as a sequencing of methods, qualitative–quantitative or quantitative–qualitative; the use of different methods to explore different aspects of the research question; and the use of different methods to corroborate the research findings of each, also referred to as triangulation (see Box 17.2). For example, using depth interviews or focus groups allows the researcher to develop an understanding that is based on the respondents' everyday experiences, meanings and language, from which robust survey questions can be developed. Alternatively the analysis of generalizable data from a quantitative survey identifies emerging themes that can be explored in more depth in interviews. Different methods can be used separately to understand different aspects of the research, for example, a broad survey of many service users and depth interviews with the small number of service providers. A triangulation of methods can be used to provide breadth and depth, for example, through a survey. The results can be used to corroborate evidence from the two methods.

The design of mixed methods research should focus on the methods to be used and time order or sequencing of the methods. Debates on the order and prioritization of methods have been subject to much debate (see Morgan, 1998b; Bryman, 2004; Creswell, 2008). Decisions on research design are linked to all aspects of the research itself, from theory and the existing literature, methodology, data collection and analysis. Researchers can use innovative combination of different methods to find solutions to their research problems. These can include autobiographical writing, documentary evidence, longitudinal and quasi-experimental design and new e-research technologies.

Purposes of mixed method research

One approach to understanding how you can utilize a mixed method approach in your research is to consider how others have used mixed methods to answer specific research questions (Box 17.1).

Thinking of implementing mixed methods in your research?

Mixed methods are relatively new in social research; consequently new areas of methodological and practical research debate are emerging. The *Journal of Mixed Methods Research* would be a good starting point to gain an understanding of the current issues and to locate previous topic-specific research. Also see the suggested further reading at the end of this chapter.

In a review of 57 empirical mixed method evaluation studies, Greene et al. (2008) identified five different purposes for mixed method research. These are summarized in Table 17.1. First, mixed methods are used for triangulation purposes, by which data collected from more than one method can be used to help verify or authenticate research findings (Box 17.2). Data collected using different methods

TABLE 17.1   Purposes of mixed method research

Purpose	Rationale
Triangulation: seeks convergence, corroboration, correspondence of results from different methods	Used to increase the validity of the results by counteracting or maximizing the heterogeneity of irrelevant sources of variance attributable especially to inherent method bias but also to inquirer bias, bias of substantive theory, biases of inquiry context
Complementarity: seeks elaboration, enhancement, illustration, clarification of the results from one method using the results from another method	To increase interpretability, meaningfulness, and validity of constructs and inquiry results by both capitalizing on inherent method strengths and counteracting inherent biases in methods and other sources
Development: seeks to use the results from one method to help develop or inform the other method, where development is broadly constructed to include sampling and implementation, as well as measurement decisions	To increase the validity of constructs and inquiry results by capitalizing on inherent method strengths
Initiation: seeks the discovery of paradox and contradiction, new perspectives on frameworks, the recasting of questions or results from one method with questions or results from another method	To increase the breadth and depth of inquiry results and interpretations by analysing them from the perspectives of different methods and paradigms
Expansion: seeks to extend the breadth and range of inquiry by using different methods for different inquiry components	To increase the scope of the inquiry by selecting the methods most appropriate for multiple inquiry components

Source: adapted from Greene et al., 2008, Table 5.1 'Purposes for mixed-method evaluation designs'

can be used to verify the results, leading to greater accuracy of understanding. Second, mixed methods are used as a way of complementing each other, where data collected are used to gain in more detail a multi-level understanding of the research subject by exploring the different dimensions of knowing about the social phenomenon. The data can be used to elaborate, enhance and add clarification to findings. The use of mixed methods is seen as building strength into the research and balancing out the weaknesses in individual methods. Third, mixed methods are used as part of a development process to enable the researcher to build robust, valid and reliable measurement tools, for example, using an in-depth case study to develop a subsequent questionnaire. Fourth, mixed methods can be used to initiate new research areas or the explore existing research from new perspectives. Finally, a variety of different methods may be adopted to expand upon different aspects of the study. This approach enables researchers to build a broad research project that has multiple aspects, each of which is explored using an appropriate method. For example, in an evaluation of the implementation of a government initiative by a local government body, documentary evidence could be used to assess the implementation of a policy, in-depth interviews with managers to understand how the policy was implemented in the local context, a questionnaire of key stakeholders/users to gather data across a larger representative sample, and follow-up depth interviews of a smaller representative subsample of stakeholders to gather rich data.

BOX 17.2 STOP AND THINK

Triangulation

In social research, triangulation can be understood in terms of inter-method triangulation using two or more different qualitative or quantitative methods, or intra-method triangulation where two or more research method techniques from within either a quantitative or a qualitative approach are used. Triangulation can be used to overcome difficulties with the particular qualitative or quantitative approach, or a difficulty with a particular method within an approach. Triangulation can also be extended to the actual researcher, where more than one researcher working on a project can provide valuable insights at the fieldwork, analysis and reporting stages of the research (Denzin, 1978).

Similarly, Bryman (2006) undertook a content analysis of 232 journal articles that reported findings from mixed methods research. The analysis explored the rationales for combining qualitative and quantitative methods and a coding scheme was developed from which 18 different rationales for the use of mixed methods were identified (see Bryman, 2006; or for a summary, Bryman, 2008: 609). The classifications provide a useful reference point for the different ways in which mixed methods have been used by professional academic researchers. The most common rationale given for using mixed methods was enhancement to augment the research findings through collecting qualitative or quantitative data.

Starting out with mixed methods

So far in this chapter we have discussed different frameworks and strategies for implementing mixed methods. In this section we are going to outline the key stages that you need to consider when designing your own mixed methods research project.

The starting point for any research is to establish the research question, and from this to consider the most appropriate method or methods to adopt.

Key stages in developing a mixed method approach

The key elements for considering the adoption of mixed methods approach are:

1   Appropriateness to the research topic. You can decide this by identifying the research question(s) and considering how different approaches and methods may provide you with different evidence and research data.

2   How may using more than one method offer more insight into the topic?

3   If you are going to use different methods, how are they going to be organized in terms of the sequence of the research process?

4   There are also practical aspects of the research to consider. What resources are available to conduct the research using more than one method? Are there sufficient resources to undertake a mixed methods research project? Resources include both money and time. The latter is a particular consideration when undertaking a time-limited piece of research that forms part of your academic studies. In these circumstances, careful consideration must be given to the viability of undertaking a mixed methods approach, and undertaking multi-methods to a high level of proficiency is required.

5   Do you have the necessary skills set to be proficient in both qualitative and quantitative methods?

6   Sampling. As with any research, decisions need to be made on who you are going to include in your study and how you are going to select them. In mixed methods, decisions need to be made regarding if there are the same or different participants at different stages of the research (see next section).

7   Data analysis and reporting of findings. The nature of the research, together with the decisions made in relation to the implementation and priorities of the research, will be a key factor in how the research data are analysed and reported. You will have a combination of qualitative and quantitative data. The techniques for analysing these data separately can be found in Part III. Data collected from a mixed methods approach will require you to consider how the different data relate to both the research question and the different phases of the research. Consideration will also need to be given to the selection of participants and how this relates to the generalizability of research findings. In a concurrent mixed method approach the quantitative research element may have utilized a probability sampling technique and the qualitative phase a convenience sample,

each drawn from a different population. By contrast a sequential approach, involving first a quantitative method utilizing a probability sampling technique, from which participants were drawn for the follow-up qualitative phase, will have different data reporting considerations.

Sampling in mixed methods

In Chapter 14 the different types of sampling techniques used by researchers were discussed. From this chapter you will be aware that there are two broad approaches to sampling: probability sampling and non-probability sampling techniques. While probability samples are associated with quantitative approaches, the social sciences are often faced with the problem of not having a sampling frame of the target population to select from. Similarly, not all qualitative research uses a non-probability technique.

In mixed methods, 'who' is included in each element of the research design needs careful consideration at the design phase and will be related to the research question, the sequencing and the priority of the methods.

For example, consider a research project exploring public confidence in the local police. The research design involved a concurrent method of a large-scale survey and focus groups. The survey was completed online by a representative sample of 1200 participants across the nine government regions of England. Individuals were drawn from an online survey panel operated by a commercial research agency using a probability sampling technique. The 18 focus groups were run in nine urban locations across the regions. Participants for the focus groups were recruited directly by a research team using a variety of media including local posters, radio broadcasts and dissemination via local community networks. Each focus group contained 10 participants with quotas based on gender and age for each group set by the research team. The quantitative data collected were representative of the population and the analysis included the use of inferential statistics (see Chapter 26). The qualitative depth data collected in the focus groups was analysed using the techniques discussed in Chapters 18 and 19. The findings from each element were carefully considered, with results suggesting commonality or areas of difference assessed in relation to the participants and sampling issues.

Weaknesses of mixed methods

Much of what we have discussed so far in this chapter presents mixed methods in a positive light, allowing the researcher to overcome some of the weaknesses of a single approach, and thus allowing a research question to be explored from a multidimensional perspective. However, mixed methods are not without critics. The controversies regarding the epistemological foundations have been discussed in the introduction, and some of the additional concerns are presented below.

There are issues relating to the validity of combining quantitative and qualitative research findings. The researcher may encounter difficulties in interpreting findings within the context of different methods. Managing conflicting data findings can be confusing, and their occurrence will require the researcher to consider carefully the data collection and measurement tools used in the different phases of the research. For example, quantitative research uses closed-ended questions whereas qualitative research uses open-ended questions, allowing for greater respondent interpretation. Rather than adding additional depth, understanding and validation to research findings, conflicting results can cause confusion, adding a complexity that is difficult to understand and interpret (Creswell, 2008). This can lead to further complications in reporting findings and how they are presented to the intended audience. Rather than a seamless blending of research results, the findings are often presented separately or with emphasis on one methodological approach (Bryman, 2008). At a practical level, mixed methods research can be expensive in terms of researcher time, the number of participants needed, and the time the participant is required to engage with the research (Gray, 2009).

What is evaluation research?

Evaluation research is concerned with assessing the value or effectiveness of a particular programme or intervention on individuals, groups of individuals and/or organizations. It will involve collecting evidence or data that will enable systematic judgements to be made on the programme. Unlike other types of research whose focus may be on uncovering new knowledge about the social world, evaluation research specifically focuses on the assessment of a particular programme or intervention. Evidence from the evaluation can be used to inform the future direction of the programme or other initiatives. The research outcomes from the evaluation will be used to both assess the research and make recommendations for changes to improve future programme developments.

Evaluation research will typically draw upon different subject disciplines and make use of more than one research method. For example, an evaluation of a government intervention programme to reduce alcohol-related criminal activity may draw upon expertise from the fields of psychology, sociology, medicine and economics. A university will evaluate taught undergraduate courses at a number of different levels by asking students to complete a survey, gaining feedback from the student–staff committee, undertaking an internal review of course curriculum and standards, and submitting to a review involving external assessors.

Evaluations can take many different forms and use a variety of different methods within them (Shaw et al., 2006). As evaluation research has developed, the evaluation designs have varied in their methodological stance. Initially evaluations were positivist, seeking quantifiable data conducted by external evaluators; however in recent years, as part of a wider move to action research, evaluation is now more often seen as part of an ongoing organization-based process. The focus is more on 'what is being evaluated, why and for whom' (Gray, 2009: 279). In evaluation research consideration needs to be given to the role of the evaluator. Evaluators can be external and/or internal to the programme or organization.

Some evaluation designs will involve external evaluators working closely with individuals in the organization in order to support them to develop appropriate evaluation systems. Examples of evaluation research can be found on a number of different UK government websites (see Box 17.3).

BOX 17.3 HINTS AND TIPS

Finding out about existing evaluation research

UK government departments routinely commission research to evaluate various government-led policy initiatives. The reports from this research can be found on most government departments websites under 'Research' and/or 'Statistics'.

Particularly useful websites for social researchers are as follows.

Business, employment and work

Department of Work and Pensions, http://www.dwp.gov.uk/
Department for Business, Innovation and Skills, http://www.bis.gov.uk/

Health and care

Department of Health, http://www.dh.gov.uk/
Care Quality Commission, http://www.cqc.org.uk/

Family, children and education

Department for Children, Schools and Families, http://www.dcsf.gov.uk

Environment and food

Department for Environment, Food and Rural Affairs, http://www.defra.gov.uk/
Food Standards Agency, http://www.food.gov.uk/

There are different types of evaluation research (summarized from Gray, 2009: 286–92):

- *Experimental evaluation.* Used to evaluate a programme where the aim is to change the behaviour or outcome. The researcher will seek to use experimental or quasi-experimental research designs to measure before-and-after effects, often with a control and treatment group. Priority tends to be given to quantitative data that will enable the evaluation team to draw statistical conclusions on the before-and-after effects of the intervention. An experimental evaluation design has been used to assess the impact of education and training programmes.

- *Systems evaluation.* The focus of a systems evaluation is on gathering evidence on whether the planned outcomes of a particular intervention have been met. The researcher will identify specific evaluation objectives that map directly to the outcomes of the intervention.

- *Goals-based evaluation.* The purpose of a goals-based evaluation is to identify where there are differences between the planned goals of a programme and the actual goals/outcomes that were achieved. Rather than stating whether the original goals have been achieved, as in a systems evaluation, the goals-based evaluation takes into account what has been achieved.

- *Decision-making evaluation.* The focus of a decision-making evaluation, as the name suggests, is on those who made decisions, for example, policy makers and managers who implement policy. The evaluation will explore the decision-making process of this particular group of individuals.

- *Professional review – validation and accreditation.* Now often a routine part of professional working life, a professional review evaluation involves professions reviewing their processes and programmes against an agreed professional association standard. For example, the Market Research Society qualifications are subjected to the UK's National Qualifications Framework (see 'Qualifications' at the website www.mrs.org.uk). A university offering a BSc Social and Market Research programme can accredit their programme to the MRS validation standards. This process involves the programme team providing the evidence to demonstrate that the programme meets the necessary standards. These can include academic teaching curriculum and standards, administrative processes, student support and mentoring, assessment and feedback.

- *Illuminative evaluation.* This form of evaluation is linked with case study research. The focus of the evaluation is on understanding the views of all stakeholders in the programme. For example, an illuminative evaluation of a children's centre would focus on the researcher evaluating the centre's role from multiple perspectives including the centre manager, parents/carers, children, health visitors, centre workers and social workers.

- *Goal-free evaluation.* Goal-free evaluation is undertaken by the researcher who has no pre-research aims or objectives and has no prior knowledge of the programme to be evaluated. For example, a goal-free evaluation of a children's centre would require the researcher to enter the organization with no prior knowledge of the aims and objectives of the centre. This approach has close synergies with constructivism.

- *Responsive evaluation and action research.* This evaluation involves the researcher working closely with the programme and its key stakeholders to develop an evaluation approach that accurately follows what the programme has actually done. The motivations and decision-making processes are examined as part of the process of understanding how the programme has developed in relation to the requirements of the different users.

Cost–benefit and cost-effectiveness analysis in evaluation research

Some evaluation research, particularly where evaluating large government-funded programme initiatives, requires the researcher to undertake an evaluation of the effectiveness of the programme in terms of the funding allocation received, or how much the programme cost, and the positive outcomes or benefits of that programme. These can be used to assess whether the programme represented 'good value for money'. There are two main terms associated with an economic assessment of effectiveness: cost–benefit analysis and cost-effectiveness analysis (Rossi et al., 2004: 339–41). These are defined as follows:

- *Cost–benefit analysis.* In a cost–benefit analysis the costs of the programme together with the benefits of the programme need to be calculated in a standard monetary unit. Both direct and indirect costs and benefits need to be included. For example, the direct costs of a smoking cessation programme would be the cost of the posters, nicotine replacement drugs, counselling and staff time. The indirect costs could include patient travel costs to local clinics or support groups. The benefits of non-smoking could be calculated to include factors such as reduced doctor appointments over the lifetime of the individual due to better health; reduced life insurance policies for the individual; and better quality of life. Assigning a financial amount to the complexities of everyday living can get very complicated and the application of economics to the understanding can cause moral and ethical debates.

- *Cost-effectiveness analysis.* In a cost-effectiveness analysis the costs of the programme are calculated in a standard monetary unit. However the benefits, or outcomes, of the programme are measured or expressed in outcome units. For example, the introduction of a new drug treatment costing £1000 for the average patient reduced the average amount of time spent by a patient in hospital from 30 days to 20 days. Each drug treatment reduced the average number of patient hospital bed days by 10, and the cost-effectiveness of the drug is expressed in hospital bed days.

Examples of research using a mixed method approach

In this section we present three different examples of mixed methods research. The first example outlines the methods used in a research project undertaken for the Electoral Commission exploring public attitudes to the Scottish Parliament and local elections. It uses a combination of quantitative and qualitative research methods, each designed to gather a broad understanding of the issues from members of the public, and more depth understanding and exploration of issues in the focus groups. The research involved a quantitative survey and a series of focus groups.

The second example reports on research undertaken to explore the occupational culture of drinking habits in the US Navy. The research involved a combination of qualitative and quantitative methods across multiple time periods. The research had a longitudinal design with the fieldwork conducted over a four-year period. The research first used initial pilot face-to-face interviews with key US Navy personnel to develop the research team's understanding of the US Navy and occupational culture issues. From the analysis of data from these interviews various research measurement tools, including survey questions, interview schedules, focus group schedules and observation schedules, were developed that were used for the data collection over the subsequent three-year period.

The third example reports research undertaken to explore rural deprivation in the UK. This was a piece of research commissioned by a local council with two distinct aims: to provide statistical evidence and to provide insights into people's lived experiences of rural life. The reporting of the data findings reflected these specific aims.

Public attitudes towards Scottish government

http://www.electoralcommission.org.uk/__data/assets/electoral_commission_pdf_file/0005/16169/Scot-PollPosition_23369-17390__E__N__S__W__.pdf.

Professor John Curtice and GfK NOP Social Research undertook research to explore public attitudes towards Scottish devolution, the Scottish Parliament, local government and election voting by the Scottish people. The research aims were to inform the Electoral Commission's efforts to:

- raise awareness of the 2007 Scottish elections

- further voter understanding of the voting procedures being used in the elections

- encourage people to register in advance of the elections.

The objectives of the research were to examine:

- public attitudes towards the Scottish Parliament

- public understanding of the role and responsibilities of the Scottish Parliament

- attitudes towards local government in Scotland

- public understanding of the role and responsibilities of local government

- factors that might encourage voting in the Scottish parliamentary elections and local government elections.

The research used a mixed methods approach. The methods used included a scoping study of recent opinion research and primary research that used a survey and focus groups.

The scoping study examined existing survey evidence on public attitudes to the Scottish Parliamentary and local elections. Data on voter turnout in the 1999 and 2003 Scottish parliamentary elections were analysed and compared to the new survey research conducted in the study to assess how turnout might change for the next election.

A total of eight qualitative focus groups were undertaken across Scotland, representing each of the eight Scottish parliamentary regions. The fieldwork took place 3–7 May 2006. A total of 70 participants took part in the focus groups. Quotas were set within each of the eight locations to ensure a mix within each group of those who had not previously voted, those not registered to vote and those who intended to vote in the 2007 elections. Findings from previous research linking likelihood to vote with family voting behaviour, education and a sense of duty to vote were explored in more depth in the focus groups.

The public opinion survey research was conducted by the research agency GfK NOP Social Research. A total of 1034 computer assisted telephone interviews (CATIs) were conducted. Quotas were set by age, working status and gender. The sample was selected using a random sample of Scottish postcode sectors and a random sample of telephone numbers within each sector. The fieldwork took place between 25 May and 7 June 2006. The survey data were weighted to adjust for age, gender, working status, social class and region of the Scottish population. The data from the survey were compared with the data identified in the scoping phase. The survey findings were also used to provide a broad breadth to the qualitative research findings.

Drinking habits in the US Navy

Ames, Genevieve M., Duke, Michael R., Moore, Roland S. and Cunradi, Carol B. (2009) 'The impact of occupational culture on drinking behaviour of young adults in the US Navy', *Journal of Mixed Methods Research*, 3(2): 129–50.

Ames et al. (2009) use a mixed method approach to study how work culture and drinking norms affect heavy drinking patterns of young people during the first three years of US Navy service. The purpose of the research was to describe the impact of work culture and drinking norms on drinking patterns. It also allowed the multi-disciplinary research team to discuss the opportunities and challenges of undertaking a mixed methods approach. The methodological approach drew upon research approaches used in social psychology, public health and anthropology. The fieldwork was conducted over a four-year period using a mix of qualitative and quantitative research methods in a longitudinal study design. The fieldwork is represented diagrammatically in the research paper and is reproduced in Figure 17.1.

At the start of the research (Y1) pilot qualitative interviews were conducted with key participants who had a unique insight into the US Navy around issues of policy, employment and rituals that may influence drinking behaviour. These participants included medical personnel, officers, chiefs and counsellors. The interviews allowed the research team to illuminate 'the dimensions and characteristics of alcohol use in the Navy, to uncover pertinent themes and workplace vocabulary pertaining to Navy life, and to provide data for developing a heuristic model of military work-related alcohol use that would guide the remainder of the study' (2009: 133). Data from these interviews were used to development measurement tools for a survey and interview schedule in years 2 and 3 (Y2–Y3). Data from these initial interviews were also used to develop the overall research model to adapt it to the particular aspects of Navy life. The qualitative and quantitative research elements at Y2–Y3 and then at Y4 were carried out concurrently.

The quantitative survey, administered at Y2–Y3, was completed by 2002 new Navy volunteers. The survey was administered two years later to Navy personnel with 1132 responding. In addition to the initial pilot interview, qualitative data were collected using observation and face-to-face interviews on five military bases

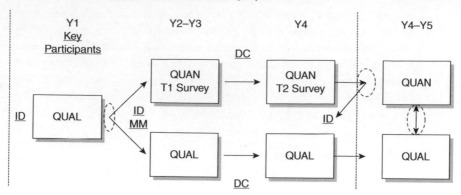

Figure 17.1 Research Implementation Sequence, With Nodes of Qualitative/ Quantitative Integration. Taken from Ames et al. (2009)

Note: Nodes of integration are represented by ovals.
Source: Reproduced from original source. Ames et al. (2009) Figure 1, p. 133.

in the US. These interviews were carried out across the fieldwork period of Y2–Y3 and Y4. The ovals in Figure 17.1 represent how the data collected at each time point were analysed and subsequently integrated into the next phase of the research process. A total of 50 semi-structured interviews were undertaken across five large military bases. Naturalistic observations were also undertaken by the research team.

This project with its longitudinal design collected a substantial amount of quantitative and qualitative data. The quantitative data analysis involved sophisticated analysis across the different time periods to identify predictors of frequent heavy drinking. Qualitative data were thematically analysed with initial themes drawn from the key variables in the survey data. This allowed the research team to better link the quantitative and qualitative results reported. The quantitative data identified risk factors for heavy drinking which were explored in the qualitative data with in-depth descriptions of the cultural and social context.

Rural deprivation in a UK district

Bryant, Lyn, Evans, Julie, Sutton, Carole and Beer, Julian (2002) *The Experience of Rural Deprivation and Exclusion*. Social Research and Regeneration Unit, University of Plymouth.

Bryant et al. (2002) used mixed methods to examine the experience of rural deprivation within the boundaries of a district council in England. The research undertaken contributed to various policy decision-making processes within the district council.

The aims of the research project were twofold. The first was to build a detailed statistical picture within the district council boundaries to describe and analyse the extent and characteristics of rural deprivation. The second, and main, focus of the study was to gain an understanding of individuals' experiences of rural economic deprivation and their access to networks of support. The nature of the two aims generated different research approaches, thus making the use of mixed methods appropriate.

The first aim of building a statistical picture involved the collating and analysis of secondary quantitative data. A comprehensive literature review was undertaken from which appropriate data sources were indentified. Many of these data were already in the public domain and were supplemented by data provided by the council's own information department utilizing geographical information systems (GIS) software at both electoral ward and parish council level. The main measurement tool used to assess the deprivation of different areas in the UK, normally at ward level, is an index of multiple deprivation (IMD). IMD data were used in this study, supplemented with a limited amount of data on household incomes which were anonymously accessed through a local voluntary support group that helps households in financial crisis. Mapping quantitative data to geographical areas is known to mask areas of deprivation and to fail to convey an understanding of the experience of deprivation. These issues were in part addressed through the use of a qualitative approach.

A qualitative methodological approach was also adopted in order to meet the second research aim. This involved the collation of some of the existing qualitative research on rural deprivation, at both national and local level, together with information gathered through interviewing key local people who have expert knowledge of the issues. In addition, primary data were collected through face-to-face interviewing at a household level on the experiences of deprivation and the effects on household members of distance from a variety of services and facilities. The data gathered from the interviewees also included data on all members of the household. The interviews also provided 'rich insights into people's experiences, opinions, attitudes and feelings' (May, 1997). A self-completion postal survey would not have resulted in the same depth of data, or allowed for the interviewer to gain additional knowledge about areas not previously considered of importance by the research team. A semi-structured interview schedule was used with the specification of questions based on the key issues highlighted from the existing literature and research. The topic areas covered were determined by existing literature, previous research, summary data findings from analysis of the quantitative data, and interviews with active members and leaders of the local communities. The main areas covered in the interviews were: employment, including access to work, choice and opportunities; economic support, including access to housing; education and training, access and needs; social life, activities, leisure and recreation; family networks; young people; access to all services and to transport. In addition, the semi-structured interviews allowed issues not covered in these main areas to be discussed with the researcher.

The analysis of the quantitative data was undertaken separately to the qualitative phase. The IMD and other ward-based data were used to rank wards at national and local level. Data at a local level were used to provide a statistical foundation for the council. A more detailed analysis of the data is contained in the full research report.

The qualitative phase of the research had a total of 55 households participate, and a total of 66 individuals from these households took part in the interviews. Over half of the participants were male and almost a third had children under the age of 18 years. Almost half of the participants had lived in the council area all their lives. Owner occupation accounted for almost three-quarters of the sample.

A summary of the results from the interviews has been divided into a number of themes with transport and employment particularly highlighted. The nature of the original research aim meant that the final report analysed the quantitative and qualitative research in distinct sections, with some of the overlaps at a local level, for example, data on employment rates and transport, being used to support the everyday lived experiences of people in rural communities.

E-research: the new technologies

This section explores how the internet can be used for social research purposes. The focus is on using the internet to undertake various forms of primary research. The internet can be used as the focus of the research itself or as a method of communication with research participants.

The internet is a global network of host computers that individuals access via the World Wide Web (WWW). The expansion of the network now means that the internet is routinely accessed by large sections of the global population. Globally there are estimated to be 1.7 billion users. Estimates of internet users as a percentage of population by different regions are USA 74, Australia/Oceania 60, Europe 52, Latin America/Caribbean 31, Middle East 28, Asia 19 and Africa 7 per cent (Internet World Stats, 2009)

The internet hosts information in a variety of different ways. Websites are used by organizations and businesses to promote their activities. There are online databases that include library catalogues, newspaper archives, data archives, government sites and institutional archives. Individual users can access the internet to perform tasks for both professional and private purposes. The development of Web 2.0 digital technologies has seen the emergence of more interactive websites, including social networking sites. For example, Facebook and MySpace are used for social communication by users, and LinkedIn for professional communication and networking opportunities. These sites provide synchronous (real-time), and asynchronous (non-real-time) discussion opportunities. In addition there are subject-specific discussion lists, formally known as listservs, that are used by groups of users with specific subject interests.

Using the internet for primary research

Using the internet for primary research is increasingly being explored across subject disciplines by social researchers. Historically the internet has been used extensively by market researchers particularly to conduct online (e-mail and web-based) surveys of consumers, and their use has become increasingly widespread amongst the academic community.

Web 2.0 digital technologies, which allow for greater interactivity between individual internet users, are being increasing explored and utilized by social researchers to undertake interviews, focus groups, observations and ethnography.

E-mail and web-based social surveys

Surveys distributed via the internet have seen considerable growth in both social and market research. The internet enables researchers to undertake both targeted surveys on specific social groups and larger surveys of groups or multiple groups. Online surveys are cheaper to administer than postal surveys. The data collection and analysis phases of the research can be reduced, enabling shorter periods between the commissioning of research and the reporting of survey findings. The extent of the growth in online surveys is demonstrated by the UK government's use of an online survey for the 2011 UK Census. Households will have a choice of either submitting a paper-based questionnaire or completing the online version. Online surveys do require consideration of how the end-user, or research participant, is supported. Typically online surveys will include an e-mail or telephone support line. For example, the 2011 UK Census will have a telephone support helpline to deal with queries as well as online video and audio support (Office for National Statistics, 2009).

While online surveys are typically seen as cost effective, there is considerable debate on the differences between internet-based surveys and traditional paper postal surveys, particularly in relation to the validity of the survey data collected. Concerns are most often raised about response rates, sample bias and the quality of question completion. Dolnicar et al. (2009) considered the format effects of a tourism survey that was conducted both online and as a paper survey. The analysis of respondents and responses concluded that online respondents had a lower drop-out rate and produced less incomplete data. In terms of sample response, the results did show that there was a significant difference in the survey responses between the two methods of administering the survey. Respondents are quicker to complete an online survey than to complete and mail back a paper postal survey. However, evidence suggests that responses rates for online surveys have been declining in recent years (Sheehan, 2001) with the proportion of non-deliverable e-mails increasing (McDonald and Adam, 2003). Greenlaw and Brown-Welty (2009) compared the relative costs of a paper-based and a web-based annual survey, concluding that while web-based survey costs are on average less, the use of the web needs to be balanced with the appropriateness of the administration process for the particular research topic and the type of likely respondent. A mixed mode approach using both paper and online surveys may yield a higher response rate and allow the researcher to balance maximizing the response rate against survey costs.

The term 'online survey' refers to both e-mail-based and web-based surveys. E-mail-based surveys are questionnaires that are sent as an e-mail to a designated person who then replies with the completed survey. A web-based survey is a questionnaire that is hosted on a website. The respondent is invited to participate in the survey and is directed to the website via a live link.

Constructing a simple text-based e-mail survey requires little technical expertise on behalf of either the researcher or the respondent. The survey can consist of simple text-based questions, with some limited use of graphics. The respondent can click on the <reply> button and respond to each question accordingly. The simplicity of an e-mail survey is also one of its downfalls. The format of the survey questions is limited and respondents are free to respond in a format of their choosing, even with clear instructions. The data contained in the e-mail will need to be manually taken from the body of the message and entered into a data file for analysis. Further complications of e-mail-based surveys are that it can be difficult to track participation; e-mail addresses need to be known (see section 'Sampling and the internet' in Chapter 14); and it is difficult to gauge the type of non-response, for example, due to not reading the e-mail or not wishing to participate (Hewson et al., 2003).

Web-based surveys require more technical expertise and also access to a website to host the actual survey and collect the survey responses. Basic web surveys can be created with some knowledge of HTML (hypertext markup language). There is also survey development software available that allows the researcher with little technical knowledge to build complex surveys, for example, SNAP Surveys or SurveyMonkey. In a web-based survey it is possible to develop question-and-response formats that can be visually more interesting to the respondent (see Figure 17.2 for an example). For example, a closed question can have categories listed with a tick box or radio circle next to each category that the respondent simply clicks, or a list of categories in a dropdown menu from which the researcher selects one. Open questions will have an open text box into which a response can be typed. Questions can be organized into sections and the survey organized into 'page-like' format that the respondent moves through. The software can allow for complex routing of questions where only relevant questions are displayed onscreen for the respondent to complete. This can reduce the respondent burden as they remain unaware of the extent of the survey; and, the inclusion of a progression bar can provide a visual acknowledgement of how much of the survey they have completed. This level of complexity can also enable the questions to drill down to issues that are relevant to specific groups of individuals identified through the response(s) they have given to earlier questions. Additional help and advice/query links can be included to assist in maximizing the response rate.

Quantitative data from the completed surveys are downloaded into a database that can be easily uploaded into software analysis packages such as IBM SPSS Statistics 19, STATA, MS Excel and MS Access. Qualitative data can be downloaded into a text document and analysed using one of the qualitative data analysis packages such as NVivo and ATLAS.ti.

By hosting a survey on a website there may also be the opportunity to monitor the site usage statistics. Usage statistics are routinely collected on websites and can provide a useful insight into how the site has been accessed. Phippen (2007) considers the use of analysis of the log files from websites, known as web analytics, in relation to response rate:

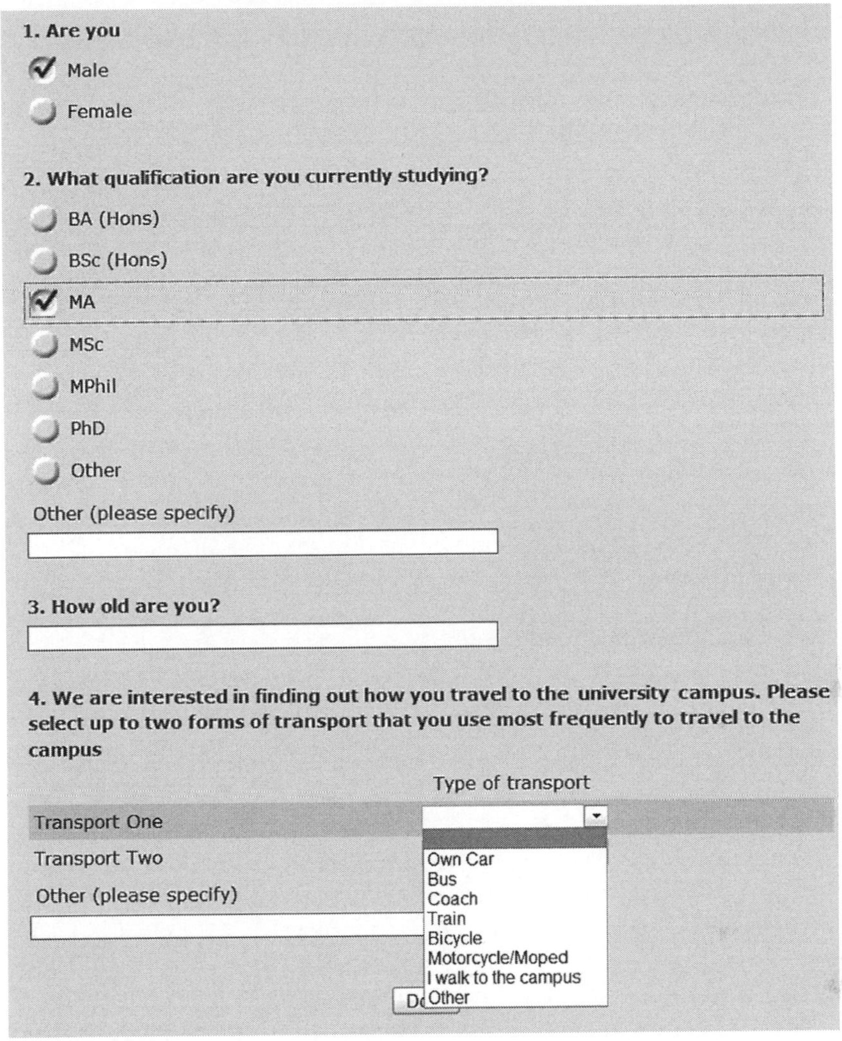
1. Are you

Male

Female

2. What qualification are you currently studying?

BA (Hons)

BSc (Hons)

MA

MSc

MPhil

PhD

Other

Other (please specify)

3. How old are you?

4. We are interested in finding out how you travel to the university campus. Please select up to two forms of transport that you use most frequently to travel to the campus

Type of transport

Transport One

Transport Two

Other (please specify)

Own Car
Bus
Coach
Train
Bicycle
Motorcycle/Moped
I walk to the campus
Other

FIGURE 17.2 Example of web-based questions

A consistent problem with survey based research is response rate – who has received the invitation to participate, who has looked at the survey and decided not to participate, how many people who have seen the survey actually return it? ... the log files can show how many people have read the email. If they click through to the survey from the email, an entry will appear requesting the survey page. By matching IP address from the email being opened to the survey page request, we can show an individual has read the email and gone to the survey page. Finally, the submission of the form will also result in an entry in the log file. Therefore, we now have a record of a respondent reading the invitation, viewing the survey, and submitting it. In instances where a respondent has viewed the survey but not submitted, this too will be reflected in the log file.

Online discussion boards, blogs and social networking sites

Online discussion boards or internet forums are websites that contain discussion software where users can exchange views and ideas either synchronously or asynchronously. Posted messages are normally subject to some form of censorship by a moderator to ensure offensive materials do not remain posted. Blogs are another form of message-based website that are maintained by individuals who can post commentaries, videos or graphics. In more recent years social networking sites such as Facebook and MySpace have provided an easily accessible and digitally more interactive format that can include text, video, graphics and audio. Registered users organize their online lives around a series of friends, other member users, and can build a complex social network that encompasses the multiple facets of people's lives in a global society. Collectively the new internet-based technologies are known as Web 2.0 with the key feature of interactive user involvement. All of these technologies normally require the user to register to use the website features. These emerging digital technologies present new opportunities and challenges and are being used by researchers in a variety of different ways (Murthy, 2008).

Internet interviews and online focus groups

Internet interviews can take place using e-mail, discussion boards, internet forums and chatroom technologies. In addition there is specialist web conferencing software that can be used on dedicated websites. These can incorporate text, audio and video.

One consideration when using these technologies is the visibility, and hence privacy, of e-mail interviews that involve researcher and participant. In a secure conferencing software environment, the exchange of e-mails can take place in private and be sent over a period of time, enabling structured, semi-structured and unstructured question formats. While a similar exchange can take place across discussion boards, one needs to consider that a discussion board will be open to the public or other invited members and may therefore be better suited to online focus groups. Chatroom technology enables the researcher and one or many participant(s) to chat synchronously in real time.

Denscombe (2007) identifies the following benefits and drawbacks of using discussion boards in research:

- Responses are not time dependent. There are reduced costs as the difficulties of geographical distance and time zones are overcome.

- Bulletin boards and discussion groups (and now internet forums) are organized around particular themes, enabling researchers to identify a group of individuals who have a strong interest in the research topic.

- Responses are likely to be considered, thoughtful and reflective, resulting in quality data.

- Many boards archive their posts, enabling this material to be considered in the research.

- There is a reduction of interviewer effect, and the communication becomes more equal.

- They are particularly useful for sensitive or embarrassing topics where the participants could feel uncomfortable or normally unwilling to take part.

However, what are seen as advantages can also be considered as drawbacks. These include:

- The loss of visual clues from a face-to-face interview or focus group. The researcher is unable to see facial or body language clues. Links to age, gender and socioeconomic background are less immediate. Participants can also assume an 'online' role that may be different from their everyday reality.

- Loss of spontaneity in response, which may be a particular problem for online focus groups.

Discussion boards also provide a useful data resource for researchers who want to explore topical issues. Instead of developing specific research tools to collect data, for example, a questionnaire or an interview schedule, the researcher adopts an observation method. This can involve the researcher as a 'lurker', watching, observing and recording activity, or as an active participant where they announce their participation. The 'lurking' role raises similar issues to those of the undisclosed observer in more traditional forms of research. Box 17.4 provides an example of how the content for an online discussion forum was used to explore Islamophobic postings amongst football fans.

BOX 17.4

EXAMPLE OF USING ONLINE DISCUSSION FORUMS

Millward, Peter (2008) 'Rivalries and Cacisms: "Closed" and "open" Islamophobic dispositions amongst football supporters', *Sociological Research Online*, 13(6), http://www.socresonline.org.uk/13/6/5.html.
    From the 1980s onwards fanzine magazines were established in English football as a medium through which football fans could express their voices. From these, e-zine message boards have emerged as an online version. These message boards contain contributions from a wide variety of football club supporters who both attend and do not attend football matches in person. Millward used e-zines to explore fans' discourse after an Islamophobic incident against a professional football player at a league match. Millward accessed data from two e-zines, one for each of the rival football teams' fans, and maintained the anonymity of the 'posters' in the subsequent reporting of findings. Islamophobic postings were often subject to moderation whereby the original postings were removed soon after they had first appeared on the discussion board. The text postings were analysed using Goffman's frame analysis to develop both qualitative and quantitative data. Quantitative data on the framing of postings were extracted and presented with the actual textual data from the postings.

Ethics and e-research

Research involving the internet needs to adhere to the same ethical principles as all social research, and of particular consideration are confidentiality, anonymity and informed consent. The ethical issues in relation to e-research are emerging as Web 2.0 technologies are adopted. As the British Sociological Association guidelines note:

> Ethical standards for internet research are not well developed as yet. Eliciting informed consent, negotiating access agreements, assessing the boundaries between the public and the private, and ensuring the security of data transmissions are all problematic in internet research. Members who carry out research online should ensure that they are familiar with ongoing debates on the ethics of internet research, and might wish to consider erring on the side of caution in making judgements affecting the well-being of online research participants. (2002: 5–6)

The Market Research Society provides guidelines on internet research and offers particular advice for internet research involving children (http://www.mrs.org.uk/standards/internet.htm).

At each stage of the data collection process the researcher needs to consider these issues in specific relation to the internet technology that they are using. Some ethical issues can be part of good administrative procedures while others can be more complex, requiring the balancing of research methods with ethical considerations.

For example, in a web-based survey the researcher may send an e-mail inviting participation to a sample of individual e-mail addresses. In order to ensure anonymity the researcher must make sure that if a standard e-mail (the equivalent of a covering letter) is sent out to multiple addresses, then the individual e-mail addresses are not included in the heading of the e-mail for all participants to view.

At the 'live survey' phase of the research, data from completed web-based surveys may be stored temporarily on a web server, and the researcher needs to ensure the security of these data. The correct encryption software needs to be used and adequate safeguards against hacking should be in place.

The emergence of research involving social networking sites presents new ethical challenges, especially as such sites represent private/public space where issues of privacy require careful consideration (Sveningsson Elm, 2009). While a potential source of secondary data, much of the content on members' pages of social networking sites available in the public domain is personal information. Phippen et al. (2009) undertook an analysis of profile data available in the public domain on three social networking sites and conducted subsequent experiments to see how much personal information could be gathered about users. The aim of the research was to assess information security amongst naïve users. The first experiment involved gathering publicly available information from users' profiles. The second experiment involved the creation of two users who made subsequent contacts or friends on the social networking sites. Data on these contacts were gathered. In order to fulfil the needs of this research, consent was not obtained. As Phippen et al. (2009) noted, this was particularly problematic for the second experiment, and yet to have requested consent and to have informed the subjects of the research aims would have interfered with the everyday use of the sites by those users.

Summary

In this chapter we have explored the emergence of mixed method research and examined some strategies for undertaking a mixed methods design. Mixed methods provide a pragmatic approach to addressing the methodological strengths and weaknesses of quantitative and qualitative approaches. This chapter has highlighted strategies for designing a mixed methods piece of research, and three examples have provided an insight into how mixed methods have been implemented in three very different research projects. We have looked at different types of evaluation research that will typically use mixed methods in the research design; and also considered the emergence of internet-based research that presents new opportunities and challenges for the social researcher.

 ■ **Questions**

1 In mixed methods research, what factors will be considered in relation to sequencing of the research methods used?
2 What are the advantages and limitations of internet-based research?

■ ■ **Further reading** ■

For general mixed methods

Bryman, Alan (2006) 'Integrating quantitative and qualitative research: how is it done?', *Qualitative Research*, 6: 97–113.

Gray, David E. (2009*) Doing Research in the Real World*, 2nd edn. London: Sage.

Rossi, Peter H., Lipsey, Mark W. and Freeman, Howard E. (2004) *Evaluation: A Systematic Approach*, 7th edn. Thousand Oaks, CA: Sage.

For internet-based research

Hewson, Claire, Yule, Peter, Laurent, D. and Vogel, Carol (2003) *Internet Research Methods: A Practical Guide for the Social and Behavioural Sciences*. London: Sage.

Dillman, Don A., Smyth, Jolene D. and Christian, Leah Melani (2008) *Internet, Mail, and Mixed-Mode Surveys: The Tailored Design Method*, 3rd edn. London: Wiley.

PART THREE
DATA ANALYSIS

EIGHTEEN

INTRODUCTION TO QUALITATIVE DATA ANALYSIS

Chapter Contents

Aims

By the end of this chapter you will be able to:

- Identify the variety of qualitative data sources and their relationship to the diverse array of qualitative data analysis techniques.
- Distinguish qualitative content analysis and discourse analysis.
- Specify the significance of direction and purpose in the conduct and organization of qualitative data analysis.
- Outline key steps and guidelines for the conduct of qualitative data analysis.

Doing qualitative data analysis

In this chapter it will be suggested that the two dominant and competing forms of qualitative data analysis – content analysis and discourse analysis – require each other and are combined in one way or another in all forms of qualitative data analysis. Qualitative data analysis (QDA) is often mentioned but rarely specified. Those involved in qualitative research or those pursuing mixed methods are inevitably engaged in some kind of QDA. Those also engaged in forms of quantitative research are conducting forms of QDA in the act of interpreting prior literature, and in identifying the concepts and categories that will structure their quantitative data collection instruments (questionnaires, observation schedules or experimental designs). Any attempt to draw meaning from the world is a form of qualitative data analysis even when it is not formally given that name. Likewise, much of what is carried out in the act of collecting qualitative data is QDA, even if it is not formally classed as such. In this sense, as has already been mentioned on a number of occasions, the distinction between qualitative data collection and QDA is not so clearly defined as is often the case in forms of quantitative research. As such, data collection and data analysis often fold into each other in exploratory forms of qualitative research. This form of folding is most often associated with grounded theory (see Chapter 11; and see section 'Degrees of grounded theory and sampling in qualitative research' in Chapter 5). However, even those who adopt elements of a more deductive (see Chapter 4) or prescriptive data collection process agree that the value of qualitative research lies in the ability to constantly compare one's latest findings with the tentative explanations generated from the previous round of findings. In this process the researcher may change the emphasis of the research and in so doing change the focus of the next round of data collection (Box 18.1).

BOX 18.1 RESEARCH FOCUS

The art of ethnography: how to analyse cultural data

Gesa Kather (PhD), University of Liverpool (2009)

What is so special about ethnographic data analysis?

Ethnographic data are collected through ethnographic research, usually through fieldwork where the main research methods of participant observation and ethnographic interviews are applied. What is very particular for ethnography is the fact that the quality of ethnographic data relies heavily on the kind of access gained to the 'field', i.e. the social groups to be researched. Here, the ethnographer's ability to build trusting relationships with the researched is of vast significance. The analysis of ethnographic data, in turn, is connected to this particularity of the data collection process. Yet, the approach to the sampling and selecting of data is linked not only to the data collection but also to the choice of the research site and question. This results from the fact that the main objective of ethnographic research is, contrary to the approach in the social sciences of explaining a social phenomenon, to explore it in depth. Hence, the final products of ethnographic research are cultural texts – accounts of cultural phenomena that explore the logics of social actions and the meanings attached by social actors. The key elements used in the process of ethnographic data analysis are case construction, triangulation and interpretation. Drawing from examples of my own research, I will show that there is no prescriptive approach or formula to follow; ethnographic data analysis, just like ethnographic research as a whole, is a skilled art.

Ethnographic data on Burnley and Harrogate

For my PhD research I conducted ethnographic field research in two northern English towns, Burnley and Harrogate. The aim of the research was to produce a comparative account of the different political practices of marginal groups in both towns. I collected data differing in nature on youth and migrant groups which I supplemented with data on the political, economic and cultural life of the two towns. The final thesis, titled '"Good"/"bad" citizens on the margins? An ethnographic study of political participation in two northern English towns', is a cultural account of the facets of formal and informal political participation in marginal social spaces in Burnley and Harrogate. It explores the political practices of marginal cultures and their relationships to the practices of the state. The types of data collected during six months of residence in each town included field notes on participant observation and informal conversations, transcribed semi-structured in-depth interviews with 60 research participants, local newspaper articles, and statutory publications and reports. I ended up with hundreds of pages of material that had to be analysed. Now, how did I tackle this? Is there a helpful formula at all?

Unique to the method of data analysis in ethnography is the fact that it is an ongoing process which begins with the early days of the research, the planning, and continues until the achievement of the final product, the ethnographic text. This challenges the research process of social sciences such as sociology, where research design, data collection and data analysis are treated as entirely separate consecutive stages of the research project. Thus, it is commonly prescribed for the production of a PhD thesis in sociology to write the literature review and the methods chapter *before* conducting the data collection. However, this does *not* work for ethnography.

Constructing the case of northern English towns

Due to the particular nature of ethnography, analysis is an ongoing process which does not begin only after data collection but is already under way during data collection and even before, with the sampling of the field and the groups to be researched. It continues with the selection of interview partners and the cultural phenomena to be studied, and finishes with the sampling of the final data that go into the ethnographic account, the final text. Through this continuous process of sampling the ethnographer is actively constructing the case (Ragin, 1994; Ragin and Becker, 1992). This means that the ethnographer has to decide how to study the selected groups and how to place the focus in the research. There can be a whole range of aspects that s/he is interested in, with the central objective being the study of social practices and the attached meanings. As a consequence, the focus is sharpened not through the study of theory but through the collection and study of ethnographic data (Glaser and Strauss, 1967). A key impact on the sampling of the fields and groups is also access. The quality of the data depends on the forms of access the researcher has found. This method of selecting the site for the research (labelled 'random' by the social sciences) continues during the actual fieldwork. Only during the actual fieldwork does the ethnographer find out about the actual local everyday practices that people use; only thus can s/he understand the significance of practices for the researched, how social networks are constructed and how observed social practices (for example events, meetings, street interactions) are meaningful in varying ways.

(Continued)

Let me give you two examples from my research. I noticed that in both towns, Burnley and Harrogate, young people from a working-class background are seen as alienated and disconnected from society, but that at the same time their practices have an impact on society. Because I found access to gaining ethnographic data on them, I decided to construct the case of 'Chav gangs' and their politics of resistance. In Burnley I found that one particular group of young Asian men were visible in the political arena of youth and community policy. Because I gained very good access and rapport with this group, as well as because of the current climate of Islamophobia, I decided to construct the case of the policy of the 'Asian gang'.

Implicitly triangulating 'Chav' and 'Asian gangs'

Now, what is the ethnographer looking for when analysing the data? And how does s/he go about it in the first place? Data analysis – the thinking about what practices mean for individuals – is ongoing and begins during the data collection. And again, ethnography does something very different to most of the other social sciences. It is not interested in verifying theory. The ethnographer does not focus on aspects that confirm theories previously produced by other social scientists. Rather, s/he is interested in dissent (Flick, 1992) – in aspects and practices that diverge from 'the normal'. Only through this will it be possible to develop new theory that relates to the local everyday practices of people. So for my research, I was not interested in finding marginalized groups that participated particularly well or were particularly alienated. I was interested in groups and their practices that seemed to be in some sort of dissent with sociological and political science debates on participation and alienation. I was interested in groups that maybe looked like they were not participating in the legitimate political practices at first glance, but with the intention to show that their practices were still meaningful and that they were likely to participate according to their own cultural rules. Similarly, I was also interested in showing that groups who are seen as participating well can also be of very little political impact when their participation is mainly based on economic participation and silent consent to formal politics.

So what did my actual practice as an ethnographic researcher look like? I lived in Burnley and Harrogate and mixed and participated with different social groups on an everyday basis and used the spaces and resources of the town just like any other resident. And I took as many field notes on my participant observation as possible, found interview partners through my overt participation and through snowballing, and did semi/structured interviews with them that I then transcribed. And after my fieldwork I just read and read through my data and tried to make sense of them. I did a literature review on political participation debates and ethnographic studies of marginal groups and the state. Every time I came across dissent within my data and the theory I paid special attention and tried to work out what was going on. When I found dissent I would try to establish the rule and occurrence of this by triangulating it with other data and theory. This going back and forth between the data and theory at varying times of the research (Glaser and Strauss, 1967) requires a lot of skill and the ability to perceive the wider picture. There is often talk about the danger of ethnographers becoming lost in the data.

Hermeneutics 'on the margins' of northern English towns

The final step in ethnographic data analysis that makes it a unique research method is interpretation. Whereas for the triangulation of data certain kinds of software (NVivo) can be used, the researcher cannot rely on any modern technology for interpreting his/her data but has to use her/his own skills. The experienced researcher will use his/her cultural knowledge and empathy to interpret the studied practices. This will bring out the underlying meaning of people's actions which they are often only implicitly aware of, and this cannot be put into words. The researcher will produce a cultural account of the studied phenomena, a cultural text (Clifford, 1988). The required antecedents for this are empathy, experiences in different cultures and cultural translations, and an understanding of the culture that is being described, i.e. longer field research in this culture. An important notion for the production of cultural text is 'thick description' (Geertz, 1975). This tool helps the ethnographer to produce a comprehensive account of cultural practices by giving a detailed description of the practices and the deep structures of meaning attached. In relation to my own study, I produced an account on the practices of resistance by 'Chav gangs' in northern towns and tried to explain the deeper political meaning of vandalism of public property, for example, and I was able to show that 'Chav gangs' are deeply engaged in the norms and values of society by expressing their dissent. I was able to show how they connect to the formal forms of participation in mainstream society when they use their practices of dissent.

Having pointed out the more fluid and cyclical tendency in qualitative data collection and analysis, we still face the question of what such analysis actually involves. Fluidity has often generated the impression that QDA is a rather *ad hoc* process of cumulative impressions. How the results emerged from the data is often obscure. It is true to say that such vagueness is commonplace, but it is not the task of this volume to explore, critique or explain this. Here it is intended to offer guidelines on good practice, transparency and reflexivity.

In this chapter the diversity of qualitative data will be highlighted, but their common features will also be highlighted. In Chapters 5–12 interviews and observation-based data collection were distinguished from data collection based on collecting existing textual materials. However, because all qualitative data can be and usually is 'transcribed' into a text form, all QDA is a form of textual analysis. In this sense at least, the text of an interview, a research diary and the contents of a series of newspaper articles are the same. While the more experienced researcher may want to explore the subtle differences in more detail, the beginner may rather acquire the general tools that allow basic analysis of all that can be qualified as 'textual' data. Basic characteristics of qualitative analysis and a set of 'rules of thumb' are given to guide the research process. Inductive and deductive approaches and their mixing are then outlined. This raises the issue of whether QDA should best be carried out by means of content analysis or discourse analysis. The distinction between content analysis and discourse analysis will be made.

Types of qualitative data: diversity and unity for purposes of analysis

While there is a diversity of forms of qualitative data, for the purposes of an introduction to data analysis, it is possible to identify a sufficient degree of unity to allow a fairly general outline. What defines qualitative data is the ability to extract meaning from their content, as distinct from (though not exclusively) the extracting of numerical relationships between elements of the data. As such, the process of data analysis is the attempt to identify the presence or absence of meaningful themes, common and/or divergent ideas, beliefs and practices. A number of issues arise at this point concerning the nature of the data to be analysed and the relationship between such data collection and their analysis.

The cyclical process

As has already been pointed out, qualitative data can be gathered in a number of ways. Ethnographic fieldwork will generate a large quantity of field notes, observations and reflections, narratives and descriptions alongside attempts to provide provisional explanations of events to which the researcher has been exposed or of which s/he is a part. Field notes will also contain records of events and accounts of the researcher's own strategies and research plans, which will almost inevitably change over the course of a period in the field. Such notes are themselves a form of qualitative data, and can be analysed as such. However, the data in this case are the most explicit example of the ongoing process of analysis within the data collection process itself and in the resulting data. The researcher's field notes are always selective accounts of events, and selection will depend upon the researcher's choices of where to go, what to observe or participate in and whom to talk to. Such choices will be based upon the interpretations the researcher makes of the situations they have already been party to. Not only are such field notes dependent upon the researcher's ongoing analysis of the situation (just as the survey researcher's questionnaire is the result of prior analysis of existing literature and provisional piloting), but also such notes will, or should, contain explicit analytical accounts and comments. The ethnographer or participant observer should maintain a separate account of such analytical reflections, often in a separate book or computer file. A clear linking by date, location, participants, event and so on should be maintained. This is to enable clearer reflection on the process when later rounds of analysis take place. Depending on the nature of the fieldwork situation, the field researcher needs to take time to maintain a record of this cyclical process of data collection and provisional analysis, and subsequently refocused data collection. This process of keeping memos about ongoing and provisional analysis forms a certain feature of grounded theoretical approaches to qualitative analysis (see Chapter 11), but is useful in all qualitative data analysis.

Due to the nature of fieldwork data collection, where a large part of what are collected as data is the researcher's own notes, the researcher's influence upon such data is more explicit than in other forms of data collection. The fact that such data are more explicitly filtered through the mind of the researcher before being 'recorded' (on paper) is a constant reminder of the 'analytical' input that goes into what is recorded, and how this content then influences what the researcher does next, where they go and who they interact with. This cyclical process is a common feature in most of what counts as qualitative data (Box 18.2).

BOX 18.2 CONSIDER THIS

From memos to analysis in research on training use/non-use

Evaluation research into the takeup and value of training courses for people in rural areas was undertaken by one of the authors (David, 2002; 2003). Funding had enabled the development of a series of training modules by a number of colleges and universities, all of which were located in large towns and cities. These modules were designed to be studied by users in telecentres or telecottages in rural areas. The idea was that the modules would be studied online and without direct teaching contact. Interviews and time spent with developers of such modules, with those running the telecentres and telecottages, and with unemployed and underemployed individuals in rural areas (at whom the modules were supposed to be targeted) allowed comparison to be made between the perceptions of each different group. Memos taken after each interview and observation generated a distinction between a lack of knowledge and a knowledge of lack. Product developers always framed their discussions in terms of the knowledge that was lacking in rural areas, whilst telecentres and local unemployed people tended to frame their accounts of events in terms of their knowledge of what was lacking in material resources and opportunities. Where those writing the modules imagined rural populations would benefit from packages of information, telecentre and telecottage managers felt money would have been better spent on tutors, printers and the other resources necessary to keep each centre open into evenings and weekends. Unemployed people and those in low-skilled and seasonal employment pointed to the lack of employers in rural areas who would value skills and training, especially as the rural and seasonal economy of the region (which had a large tourism sector) tended not to invest in trained staff. The distinction between lack of knowledge and knowledge of lack emerged from reflections on the data as they were collected, and this was made possible by constant use of memos.

Notes and transcriptions

Ethnography usually involves talking to people as well as observing and interacting or participating in other activities. These may be informal conversations or formal interviews. If such talk is not recorded verbatim (for example, on audiotape), the question of what gets 'saved' in the form of written notes again raises the issue of analysis in the act of data collection. Just as interview schedules may be more or less structured, so too is what is to be noted down. In most cases, barring the most informal of conversations, or where recording would not be possible, full recording combined with written notes is the best approach.

However, the process of transcription itself involves a degree of analysis that is often underestimated or even ignored. This is particularly true when transcription is parcelled out to audiotypists to save time. Listening to recordings involves a degree of interpretation and selection and so involves an element of analysis. The transcripts of the same interview made by different transcribers can contain significant differences for this reason.

In addition to this aspect of transcription analysis, the sequential nature of interviews means that thoughts generated during prior interviews may come to influence the conduct of subsequent interviews. This may be more or less explicit. Just as in the case of field note-taking, so in interviewing the qualitative researcher needs to keep a record of their provisional interpretations of interviewee responses. Given the more open-ended nature of qualitative interview questions and schedules, it is rarely the case that such interviews will follow the same sequence from one interview to the next. It is important for the researcher, therefore, to keep a record of what they take from each interview as a means of identifying what it is they are bringing to the next.

In the case of conversation analytic research, the process of transcription takes on an added significance, as it is the attention to the fine-grain detail of talk (sequences of interaction, pauses and overlaps) that provides conversation analysis with the material it seeks to analyse. Specific attention will be paid to this in the section 'Doing conversation analysis' in Chapter 20.

Texts and secondary sources

Texts used as sources may be of two types:

- Primary texts: texts not produced for the purposes of research, that is, newspapers, diaries, letters.
- Secondary sources: texts generated by previous researchers.

In both cases selection for the purposes of the current research represents a set of prior analytical choices, and the texts once selected require further analysis.

The use of text as a qualitative data source highlights a number of general issues about QDA as well as having matters of its own to contend with. The transformation of a variety of experiences (talk, observations, memories and so on) into text is a near universal step in the process of qualitative research. It is not usually the first step, as encountering these sources precedes recording them, and recording such experiences may or may not be in text form in the first instance. Nevertheless, transformation into text, the transcription of experience into units of communicative meaning (that is, words and sequences of words), is itself both an act of analysis and often the prerequisite for subsequent forms of qualitative analysis.

Images as texts

Can images be reduced to textual accounts of them or, more importantly, can this be done without losing much of the image's content? The same question can be asked of music and much else in human behaviour that is non-verbal. The relationship between words and images has generated a significant debate within qualitative research. This debate over the content of images has shifted away from art history towards a more sociological approach to the meanings given to images by those who use them in various ways. As such, we might reasonably say that attributing meaning to images is the same as attributing meaning to text (Box 18.3). Both are problematic, but they may not be fundamentally different. A number of the most recent computer software packages designed to assist in the process of QDA make explicit attempts to facilitate the analysis of images.

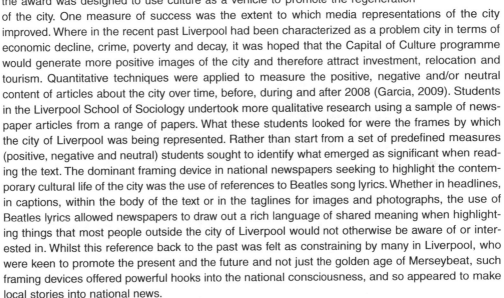

BOX 18.3 CONSIDER THIS

Beatles references as framing devices in the representation of Liverpool: Capital of Culture

In 2008, the city of Liverpool was designated European Capital of Culture. In part the award was in recognition of the city's significant cultural heritage, and in part the award was designed to use culture as a vehicle to promote the regeneration of the city. One measure of success was the extent to which media representations of the city improved. Where in the recent past Liverpool had been characterized as a problem city in terms of economic decline, crime, poverty and decay, it was hoped that the Capital of Culture programme would generate more positive images of the city and therefore attract investment, relocation and tourism. Quantitative techniques were applied to measure the positive, negative and/or neutral content of articles about the city over time, before, during and after 2008 (Garcia, 2009). Students in the Liverpool School of Sociology undertook more qualitative research using a sample of newspaper articles from a range of papers. What these students looked for were the frames by which the city of Liverpool was being represented. Rather than start from a set of predefined measures (positive, negative and neutral) students sought to identify what emerged as significant when reading the text. The dominant framing device in national newspapers seeking to highlight the contemporary cultural life of the city was the use of references to Beatles song lyrics. Whether in headlines, in captions, within the body of the text or in the taglines for images and photographs, the use of Beatles lyrics allowed newspapers to draw out a rich language of shared meaning when highlighting things that most people outside the city of Liverpool would not otherwise be aware of or interested in. Whilst this reference back to the past was felt as constraining by many in Liverpool, who were keen to promote the present and the future and not just the golden age of Merseybeat, such framing devices offered powerful hooks into the national consciousness, and so appeared to make local stories into national news.

Texts and actions

While transcriptions of interview data directly relate to the production of words by those being researched, field notes seek to record other forms of action as well as just talking and writing. Descriptions of actions other than talk, whether these are the descriptions given in talk by interviewees or descriptions made by the researcher of the actions of others, the relationship between text and other actions is a complex one that cannot be reduced to simplistic forms of representation. In the process of QDA the researcher needs always to bear in mind the difference between an account and the action itself. The researcher's interest may be in seeking to gain a true account of non-verbal events, or they may be more interested in the meanings given to such events by respondents. Alternatively, the researcher may be more interested in the ways respondents seek to represent events, which may not be the same thing as what they themselves think or believe, let alone what they actually do (Box 18.4).

BOX 18.4 CONSIDER THIS

How much social significance can be read into a cultural artefact anyway?

David (2006) notes that in recent years social researchers have become increasingly concerned not to be seen to reduce cultural products to social structures, to explain art, literature and musical works as simply reflections of the social circumstances of their production. To say that the work of Charles Dickens, Mozart or Picasso work should best be understood as the result of the eras in which they were produced has generated the criticism that social scientists are too busy showing the connection between the work and its context to notice what is really interesting about the work itself. It has traditionally been the preserve of art historians and other cultural historians to seek to account for cultural artefacts (books, paintings, musical compositions etc.) in terms of each cultural form's own traditions and principles. This sense of explaining culture 'in its own terms' sought to emphasize how internal criteria of judgement and quality drive the creative process, not external criteria such as economic forces, moral values and political movements. Interestingly, in the last two decades art historians have taken a greater interest in accounting for art with reference to the economic, political and social context, even whilst social scientists have started paying more attention to the 'meanings' and small-scale interactions occurring within artistic communities. Like ships passing in the night, these two research traditions highlight a tension in relation to the interpretation of cultural artefacts. Whether or not a researcher seeks to restrict interpretation or open it to wider and deeper social explanations, it is essential to keep in mind that whilst it is very easy to generate interpretations; they must be critically interrogated and efforts must be made to justify them.

These differences between action, interpretation and representation may be resolved through the choice only to focus upon the representations themselves, as acts of storytelling or accounting (Box 18.5). The attempt to give a picture of the world may be interesting in itself. The fact that some people seek to tell their stories in certain ways may tell us a great deal about the resources they have at their disposal and the strategies they believe will be successful. The differences in strategy adopted by different groups and individuals may be a sufficient focus of attention for the researcher. Alternatively, the researcher may want to analyse the relationship between accounts and the reality of people's behaviour. In this case they may wish to adopt forms of triangulation, such as a combination of interviews and observations. In this way the choice of data collection methods will depend upon what it is that the researcher wishes to analyse.

BOX 18.5 RESEARCH FOCUS

Pierre Bourdieu and the danger of reducing action to text/meaning

The French sociologist Pierre Bourdieu (2004) draws attention to the vanity of intellectuals who seek to turn all human life into 'text'. Whilst the world of intellectual practice is one where actions, events, relationships and things are to be translated and interpreted into abstract formulations, this does not mean that real life is fully comprehensible by such means alone. Just as qualitative researchers criticize quantitative research for 'reducing' life to numerical relationships between variables, so Bourdieu suggests that researchers in general have a tendency to reduce social life into what they know best, and about which they are best qualified to judge. In the case of qualitative researchers, what they know best is not numbers, but the interpretation of language. Whilst much qualitative research, such as in grounded theory, ethnography, case study research and most inductive interviewing, seeks to understand language and meaning in context, such methods still rely on such context being collected in the form of text most of the time. Even when visual recordings are made of actions, and where material artefacts are collected alongside text (whether in the form of field notes, memos or interview transcripts), such non-textual data will then have to be translated into text for the purpose of qualitative (i.e. textual) analysis. Bourdieu draws attention to the fact that social life is made up of practices, and should best be understood as practice rather than as text, even whilst practices cannot be 'recorded' as such, and must be transcribed into text at some stage. The qualitative researcher must render practices into textual form, but this should not lead the researcher to the convenient misconception that reality is simply text. Even talk and written text have to be understood as performative, rather than simply as a grammatical construction. Whilst some scientists believe that the universe is in fact made of numbers, and some social researchers really believe that the social world is made of meanings, the pragmatic researcher is well advised to be more cautious in equating data with the reality that data seek to give us access to. Numbers and meanings help us to comprehend the world, but it would be a mistake to think that they were the world. If only things were that simple.

Analysis of data collected individually or by team research

Because QDA and data collection are very often interlinked in the cyclical process outlined above, it is important for the process to be made clear throughout. This is highlighted in the case of team research, but is no less true when the data are collected and analysed by a single researcher. The act of team research simply forces the reflexive process into one of open communication. What the individual researcher needs to keep track of, in the context of team research, requires that the members of the team regularly update each other on the ongoing process of interpretation as it emerges and feeds into each other's conduct. This allows for coordination as well as deepening the process of reflection by which new insights from current rounds of data collection are fed into subsequent rounds.

Some rules of thumb and advice on process and practice

David Silverman (1993: 197–208) suggests six rules for the conduct of QDA:

1   Don't mistake a critique for a reasoned alternative (highlighting tensions and even contradictions in the accounts and actions of those being researched does not in itself demonstrate irrationality or the need for those being researched to change).

2 Avoid treating the actor's point of view as an explanation (how someone describes their reality is not necessarily the same thing as the reality itself, as explanations have purposes).

3 Recognize that the phenomenon always escapes (no account of accounts is ever total).

4 Avoid choosing between all polar oppositions (either/or is rarely an adequate account of complex realities and is more likely to mislead than to clarify).

5 Never appeal to a single element as an explanation (while axial themes may emerge, focus upon a single core is more likely to distort analysis than to provide insight).

6 Understand the cultural forms through which 'truths' are accomplished (if respondents say the same thing, this may say as much about shared ways of presentation as it does about any underlying reality).

In the second and third editions of the same work Silverman (2006) had modified the list to eight reminders:

1 Take advantage of naturally occurring talk.

2 Avoid treating the actor's point of view as an explanation (the same as his earlier point 2).

3 Study interrelationships between elements (linked to point 5 above).

4 Attempt theoretically fertile research.

5 Address wider audiences (beyond academic circles).

6 Begin with 'how' questions – then ask 'why'.

7 Study hyphenated phenomena (look for interconnections).

8 Treat qualitative research as different from journalism.

Silverman (2005: 173) identifies four ways to develop the analysis of qualitative data within a developmental sequence where data analysis begins at the same time as data collection and where the two progress hand in hand. These four aspects are:

1 Focus on data which are of high quality and are easiest to collect.

2 Focus on one process [at a time] within those data.

3 Narrow down to one part [at a time] of the process.

4 Compare different subsamples of the population.

What Silverman is suggesting here is how to start the ball rolling. By focusing upon a rich stream of initial data the researcher can develop ideas in provisional analysis that can then be compared with other research sites and groups. Initial judgements may emerge from the first rich source, but any such initial analysis is to be critically challenged in subsequent rounds of data collection. The choice of a rich initial source allows for relatively robust initial findings, but this robustness is for the purpose of heavy later challenge, not a taken-for-granted basis for interpreting what will be encountered next.

Bruce Berg (2007: 308) points out that the act of 'deciphering' text is essential in all qualitative data. The term 'deciphering' refers to the fact that words do not always mean the same thing, while at the same time different words can be used to mean the same thing in other situations. As such it is never enough to say 'look, here is the same word or phrase and therefore here is a connection or a shared meaning'. The researcher has to justify their claims to have identified connections and their claims to have identified differences in talk, just as they have to justify claims to have identified the 'meaning' of single texts. Berg suggests, in the first instance, that any claim to have identified a meaningful pattern must be demonstrated with at least three examples. One of the prime criticisms of qualitative research is the use of choice quotes to promote particular conclusions. The use of a minimum of three examples for each alleged finding at least forces the researcher to demonstrate what they mean by a pattern, in terms of both its incidence and its content. Such evidencing also helps avoid the equating of the researcher's way of seeing with the ways in which respondents see events, as the researcher has to show what it is that they are basing their claims upon. Such evidencing acts to make analysis more accountable and also more reflexive. Conversation analysis disputes the necessity of such 'exampling', but for specific reasons that will be discussed in Chapter 20.

Miles and Huberman (1994) adopt the expression 'think display' as their motto in the conduct of QDA. This is a suggestion not only to think about how best qualitative data can be represented, but also to recognize that it is in the act of representation that analysis is actually achieved. By means of visual reduction the complexity of qualitative data can be rendered comprehensible, in rather the same way that quantitative data are rendered comprehensible by means of tables, graphs and statistical procedures. More will be said about Miles and Huberman's approach to QDA in Chapter 19, but here it is useful to identify the range of displays they suggest. These authors identify matrix displays (grids) and network diagrams (flows and links) as the two most useful representational devices. They go on to identify forms of display that operate to describe and explore single cases or the comparison between cases. They also identify methods of representation that facilitate analysis at the level of explanation and prediction, either within cases or between cases.

All the above authors devote a great part of their accounts of QDA to the question of coding, and this is not surprising. Coding is perhaps the single most significant act in the process of qualitative analysis. Coding involves the identification of common themes (words, phrases, meanings) within the data being analysed. Every time the same theme is mentioned it is tagged (electronically or otherwise). Then all instances where the tag (code) has been made can be compared. Alternatively, the cross-referencing of two such tags can be used to highlight the incidence (or lack of incidence) of cases where the two themes occur together. These codes allow links to be made and are a form of data reduction, the highlighting of key points within the vast mass of the overall data. More quantitative forms of content analysis seek to count the number of times a theme is coded or the number of times two codes occur in close proximity. More qualitative forms of content analysis use coding not just to count the number of occurrences, but also to allow exploration of what is going on when such occurrences happen. Various things can be selected for coding. Miles and Huberman suggest the following list of basic coding prompts:

- themes

- causes or explanations

- relations among people

- emerging constructs.

Some coding is predefined; a set of codes is developed and applied to the data. Another form of coding is called open coding. Glaser and Strauss's grounded theory is associated with the open coding approach, though Strauss (Strauss and Corbin, 1990) has been more willing than Glaser (1992) to suggest initial prompts to act as initial code selecting devices. Glaser, Strauss and Corbin agree on elementary sensitizing concepts like who, what, where, how, when and why. Every time a name appears in the text this can be coded as an example of a 'who' code, and so on. Some see this as pragmatic, while others see it as prescriptive and distorting. Fielding and Lee (1998: 33) offer four tips for open coding (generating the codes to be used in the act of reading through the data, rather than generating the codes in advance):

1 Constantly question the data.

2 Data selected for coding must be treated microscopically (that is, in detail).

3 Coding should immediately generate memos of theory building.

4 Analytic import of categories must always be shown, not assumed.

Advocates of discourse analysis often accuse other researchers of adopting too mechanistic an approach to coding. Discourse analysts suggest that more depth can be achieved by detailed analysis of singular cases or small samples than by systematic coding of larger amounts of textual data. However, even such an in-depth approach involves selection and analysis of elements within the materials selected. Both require forms of coding. This may be informal, but it is a form of coding nonetheless.

Fielding and Lee (1998) mention memos. Memos are notes that researchers leave for themselves as they go through the data assigning codes to segments. If they come across an interesting extract they may wish to make a note that this phrase or description seems to relate to other extracts in a new way or that it seems to link or challenge an established theory. Memos can be notes in the margins of a page, sticky labels attached to transcripts, or subfiles within a computer package. Memos will be discussed in more detail in Chapter 21.

Two key dimensions of qualitative analysis: direction and purpose

The most important decisions in qualitative analysis are how to integrate analysis with the data collection process, and what it is the research seeks to achieve. Qualitative data collection involves the accumulation of large quantities of mainly textual material, and a significant part of the data analysis process involves the attempt to reduce this volume by means of selection and organization. Data collection itself involves selection and organization of whom to observe, interact with or speak to, what to record and when. As such the process of narrowing down occurs prior to any collection, and the choices about how to focus research once data collection begins continue this process of reduction by selection.

Direction of research

To what extent should the research process be open to redirection in the light of ongoing analysis throughout the various rounds of data collection? If each interview or day in the field were to be followed by a period of reflection over the meaning of the new data collected, and if these new tentative conclusions were then used to restructure the next interview or day in the field, it is possible that if these early interviews were unrepresentative then these encounters would move research away from other valuable insights that would have occurred if a steady course had been maintained. Alternatively, the choice to pursue a course of continuity may lead to other opportunities to pursue 'hot' leads being missed when they present themselves. The danger of redirecting the research too early all too often lies in the willingness of the researcher to trust hunches that they feel the data are telling them, while the reverse danger lies in trusting your initial hunches even in the face of contrary evidence from early encounters. Keeping a reflexive record, via memos and a research diary, allows the researcher to confront these dangers and to seek a balanced response to these competing pressures.

There is no simple solution to this problem, but in the process of learning the ropes for the first time, two rules of thumb may be drawn upon. The first can be taken from Chapters 5 and 11 (on qualitative data collection), that of data saturation. When thinking about how many data are enough in the context of qualitative research, it is not possible to draw easily on the sampling theories used in quantitative research. The grounded approach therefore uses the predictive ability of emerging theories as a yardstick to measure their usefulness and the usefulness of continuing to collect new data on that question. If a tentative explanation suggests itself, and this explanation suggests a change of research focus, it may be useful to continue along the same track as before to see if the next few encounters lead to the same conclusion. If so, follow the new direction. If not, carry on along the existing line of data collection. Of course, the use of data saturation was initially suggested to show when research might reasonably come to an end. The level of saturation that might be reached after a considerable amount of time is going to be far greater than that which might be reached in the early stages. If a new question arises early on in the data collection process, it is unrealistic to believe that it could draw upon the amount of supporting evidence that may be available to a researcher much further down the track. How much evidence might be needed to support a provisional conclusion such that it would justify a change of course? Here we might draw upon Berg's earlier rule of thumb concerning the evidence needed to support a tentative theory. Recall that Berg (2007: 308) suggests it is best to be able to show at least three independent examples of what you feel is evidence in favour of a conclusion before you can realistically suggest that it justifies a change of research direction. Early on in the research process this rule of three may act to balance the tension between an overly rapid change of course and too rigid a continuation with a preconceived research focus.

Purpose of research

Before the cycle of data collection and analysis can begin, the researcher needs to be clear what their analysis is actually aimed at achieving. Some important distinctions are worth repeating. Is it the intention of the researcher to describe, compare, explain or predict? Similarly, with reference to these possibilities, what is it that the researcher seeks to describe, compare and so on? Is it to be the accounts given by respondents? Is the researcher more interested in the beliefs of those they seek to research, or is the research to be aimed at behaviour and action – what people actually do, as distinct from what they say or believe? When designing a research question, the researcher needs to have identified which of these options they are aiming for. It may very well be the case that in the course of conducting research the emphasis of the research will change. The choice to focus attention upon action, belief and/or expression is distinct from the issue of deduction and/or induction regarding the substance of the research, but the two are related.

The process of reduction and organization that makes up data analysis is not simply the attempt to boil down the data collected to a manageable size. That manageability can be done in a number of ways. Reduction by the use of certain codes, chosen to highlight certain features of the data, will act to reduce the visibility of other aspects of the data. Clear identification of what the researcher seeks to achieve may at least reduce the risk of reduction, hiding what may be of significance to their project, but which was not identified early enough.

As has been pointed out already, the act of analysis early on may act to redirect the research. Similarly, the act of coding redirects the attention of the researcher from certain themes within the data towards others. Clarity of purpose allows greater reflection upon the inherent dangers involved in data reduction.

Content analysis versus forms of discourse analysis

The classic example of the clash between content analysis and discourse analysis can be found in discussions of mass media (see Anderson et al., 2004). At one extreme there are those who seek to identify the quantity of space given to certain things in different newspapers or the quantity of time given over to certain themes within different broadcast programmes. It may be found, for example, that 20 per cent of news coverage is devoted to stories about crime. That would be an example of highly quantitative content analysis. At the other extreme, there are the attempts to identify the construction of an individual crime story. How are the players in the story represented? Who and what are included and/or excluded from the coverage? How are images and words brought together to create the impression of fear, sympathy, security or mystery? This would be an example of discourse analysis. The two approaches have come to represent the ends of a spectrum, with much passion being expressed about the validity or weakness of each extreme.

Within qualitative research there is a fierce debate over the value of forms of content analysis. Content analysis assumes that it is possible to identify content in terms of units: one unit of data being an example of one thing, while another unit of data is either an example of the same thing or it is not. Article one is a crime story, while article two is not a crime story, for example. Once you have been able to identify which units of data belong to which categories, it is then possible to count them to see how many or how much of each type there are/is. To some qualitative researchers this attempt to reduce social reality to a bunch of things that can be counted is a misguided attempt to turn qualitative research into quantitative research in the quest for respectability. To others the attempt to identify units within a large amount of data such that differences and similarities can be identified is essential to any thinking.

Those who oppose what they see as the imposition of quantification into qualitative research prefer to use forms of discourse analysis. Discourse analysis covers a wide range of things, from semiotics to narrative analysis. What these forms of analysis have in common is a resistance to mechanistic reduction of meaning to measurement (in numbers).

Berg (2007) identifies himself with those who seek to develop qualitative forms of content analysis. It is not necessary to fall into the traps that constrained researchers who adopted simplistic quantitative forms of content analysis in the past. The common accusation levelled against quantitative forms of content analysis was that they relied on classifications that were often deeply flawed. If you were analysing crime coverage in the media and simply assumed a consensus notion of what a crime story is, you would potentially ignore a great deal of diversity. The coverage of military killings might not be included on the grounds that such killings were not defined as crimes by the journalists. But does that mean that they were not crimes? Who is to define? Some news media might report certain terrorist actions as crimes, others as acts of war. The fact that there is a difference of definition may be significant. Does the researcher use the definitions adopted by the different media or should they adopt their own classification? On what basis should such an alternative model be devised? Berg's claim is that forms of content analysis in these instances are not flawed because they seek to count and measure the level of certain things. Rather, the fault lies in the construction of the units they seek to add up. There are better ways of constructing such units. Interestingly, what Berg is suggesting here is that what makes qualitative research qualitative is not the absence of counting, but the more inductive form of data collection and data classification. Classification achieved by more grounded methods allows the researcher to explore and develop more valid systems of coding.

Berg (2007) suggests that while he is a qualitative researcher who still believes in the value of content analysis (and therefore the whole coding enterprise), others do not see things the same way. He cites David Silverman as a qualitative researcher who rejects content analysis and counting in favour of more discursive and narrative-based forms. While it is true that Silverman advocates forms of data analysis that do not fit with mainstream content analysis (especially his advocacy of conversation analysis), this is not to the exclusion of content analysis. Silverman's (1993) discussion of the works of Miles and Huberman and his accounts of QDA software (all of which are built around forms of content analysis) show that, while more sceptical than Berg, he still accepts the use of counting and coding for certain analytical ends. The divide is not as great as is often made out.

In the next chapters, the logic of qualitative forms of content analysis will be looked at. Chapter 19 first hinges around the practice of coding, then addresses the attempt to use coded data to develop more sophisticated forms of analysis than simply coding and showing the incidence of coded themes. Chapter 20 deals with forms of narrative, semiotic, deconstructionist and conversation analysis. Chapter 21 outlines how to use the QDA software package NVivo 8. Chapter 22 examines approaches to the conduct of qualitative visual analysis.

Summary

The relationship between qualitative data collection and QDA may be deductive or inductive. However, quite often it can be a cyclical combination of both. While the purpose of research will have emerged at the literature review stage, early rounds of data analysis may shift the direction of research, that is, the way in which the purpose is interpreted and pursued.

A useful point can be made here. Those using qualitative content analysis believe it avoids both the reductionism of quantitative content analysis and the limited attention to generalizability of discourse analysis. They claim that a greater understanding of the data is acquired by 'coding up' from the data rather than imposing codes upon the data or 'coding down'. This is said to increase the validity of the codes chosen. This requires a more in-depth reading and rereading of the data prior to coding. This process is, in many respects, similar to what discourse analysts seek to achieve. While suggesting that a more holistic encounter with the data allows the best impressions to be formed, qualitative content analysis still suggests the need for such impressions to be examined through formal coding and comparison. This resembles the formality of quantitative analysis. However, the difference between deductive code generation that guides most quantitative content analysis and the more inductive (or in fact cyclical) forms of code generation that guide qualitative content analysis is an essential distinction. The separation between discourse analysis and qualitative content analysis is not as clear-cut as it might appear once such distinctions within content analysis are taken properly into account.

Questions

1 What distinguishes qualitative content analysis from quantitative forms of content analysis?
2 How might each of the rules of thumb suggested by David Silverman help the would-be qualitative researcher avoid misinterpretation of their data?
3 What characteristics unite the diverse variety of data that can be analysed by qualitative means?

Further reading

Berg, Bruce L. (2007) *Qualitative Research Methods for the Social Sciences*, 6th edn. Needham Heights, MA: Allyn and Bacon.

Glaser, Barney and Strauss, Anselm (1967) *The Discovery of Grounded Theory: Strategies for Qualitative Research*. Chicago: Aldine.

Silverman, David (2006*) Interpreting Qualitative Data*, 3rd edn. London: Sage.

Strauss, Anselm and Corbin, Juliet (1990) *Basics of Qualitative Research: Grounded Theory Procedures and Techniques*. London: Sage.

NINETEEN

CODING QUALITATIVE DATA: QUALITATIVE CONTENT ANALYSIS

Chapter Contents

Content analysis has a long tradition in quantitative research, and has been strongly criticized in this form by qualitative researchers (see Anderson, 1997). However, there is also a tradition of qualitative content analysis which has sought to bridge the divide between deductive forms of quantitative content analysis and the more inductive and small-scale research of discourse analysis. This tradition of qualitative content analysis seeks to draw upon the advantages of both of the other traditions and to overcome their weaknesses. This chapter provides an account of qualitative content analysis, centred around the core theme of coding in qualitative research, and goes on to outline an array of techniques for, and types of, coding in the analysis of qualitative data.

Coding

Coding is the process of applying codes to chunks of text so that those chunks can be interlinked to highlight similarities and differences within and between texts. Codes are keywords, themes or phrases that may or may not correspond to actual terms in the text being analysed. If a set of interviews that investigated people's ideas about democracy was analysed, some codes might be words such as 'democracy', 'voting' and 'participation'. These words may be the words the interviewees used themselves, or the terms the researcher chooses to use to sum up or represent a range of similar findings that the researcher feels 'go together'. Similarly, in the analysis of field notes or texts taken from other sources, the choice of codes may draw upon a number of sources, within and beyond the texts themselves.

Coding enables data reduction. By flagging up those chunks of text where key themes seem to recur, the researcher is able to narrow their focus of attention from the whole of a text to just those areas they feel are significant. By identifying whether there are patterns between the chunks coded for a particular theme, the researcher can test the strength of potential accounts, descriptions and/or explanations. Descriptions, explanations and so on are forms of reduction. They are attempts to give a brief summary or model of a much larger set of phenomena. Data collection is an attempt to streamline a complex set of events into a set of manageable things for the researcher to analyse. Coding is the most common subsequent step in the attempt to organize those data so as to allow further reduction in the process of analysis.

Coding is not just about the application of codes to chunks of text. Codes not only need to be selected. Codes also need defining so that the researcher is clear what it is that they are claiming whenever a code is applied. Common sociological categories such as 'family', 'class', 'ethnicity' cannot simply be applied. The researcher needs to produce clear definitions of what these categories are being used to mean, either prior to coding or in the process of coding itself. Of course, these definitions may change in the course of the research, but a record of these changes needs to be kept, so the initial usage needs to be recorded. Memos are the most common method of recording these ideas about coding (see Chapter 11).

A brief history of coding in qualitative research

Coding is an integral part of quantitative research. The capacity to identify any kind of numerical relationship, whether that be simply identifying the number of times something occurs or the strength of the link between one thing happening and another thing happening, depends upon the ability to identify those things and to record them as such. Coding is the foundation of quantitative research. If you can't code it, you can't count it. Coding is also a crucial element within qualitative forms of content analysis. While content analysis can be rigidly quantitative, forms of content analysis have been developed to allow the mapping of patterns within qualitative data in a way that avoids reducing meaning simply to the number of times a particular textual term occurs within the texts being analysed. Nevertheless, there is always the danger that coding – the application of codes to segments of text for the purpose of mapping patterns – may lead to meanings being fragmented and coded segments being abstracted from the context which gives that text its meaning. Those who pursue a strong discourse analytic approach argue that this is the greatest weakness of content analysis, however much the researcher tries to avoid the failings of quantification.

Fielding and Lee (1998: Chapter 2) provide an account of the development of 'formal' methods of qualitative data analysis (QDA). Analytical induction emerged as an attempt to develop systematic qualitative methods of case study analysis which sought to generate 'universal' claims without resort to large-scale samples and statistical inference (the attempt to claim generality on the basis of a 'sufficient' and randomly selected sample). Developed by Florian Znaniecki in the 1920s and 1930s (Fielding and Lee, 1998: 21–3), analytical induction involves the formulation of a research question and a tentative hypothesis. This is then tested in relation to a single case study. Does the hypothesis fit? If yes, then retest the same hypothesis. If no, then reformulate or reject the original hypothesis, and test the new one. Eventually, a robust defensible thesis will emerge by means of continual reformulation. Keen-eyed readers will note that this is the same technique that Glaser and Strauss repackaged many years later under the title of 'grounded theory'. Critics point out that such an approach is as deductive as it is inductive (testing reformulated predictions), and that it is not explained how each single case is 'analysed' so as to say whether the original hypothesis is either supported or challenged.

BOX 19.1 STOP AND THINK

Coding and counting

The expression 'If you can't code it, you can't count it' can be interpreted in a number of different ways. Quantitative researchers see the need to count instances of things as fundamental to the ability to make any significant claim about the world, but the prior necessity to be clear what it is that is to be counted reminds us that quantification does require a prior act of qualitative judgement as to what there is to be counted. Ironically the qualitative researcher, who seeks to adopt a more inductive approach to coding, will want to read through their transcripts and field notes looking for instances of text they consider to have shared meaning. This exercise in looking for such shared meaning is a primitive form of counting. That something appears to repeat, that it recurs, is elementary counting, and the decision that some meanings seem more recurrent than others takes this elementary counting a little further. As such, deductive forms of quantitative research require an initial qualitative moment of defining codes, whilst inductive forms of coding are built upon prior form of elementary counting. All research is a form of mixed method, even if some research is more explicit about this than others.

It was around this time that researchers from the Chicago School of urban social research began using a range of techniques that we today would recognize as 'coding'. Segments from interview transcripts containing similar themes or phrases would be grouped together for comparison, and researchers conducting field studies would draw up summary sheets identifying the key events and themes of a particular encounter or interaction (Fielding and Lee, 1998: 23–4). Others engaged in open-ended interviewing from a number of academic and commercial fields also had to develop methods for teasing out the key themes from large volumes of textual data. Under a range of different names, what would now be called coding developed apace.

Fielding and Lee (1998: 25) identify the work of Becker and Geer (1960) and Becker et al. (1961) in relation to research into the training of medical students as the first sustained discussion of the value of coding. In the context of research into medical and scientific training, the perception that qualitative research was only capable of generating anecdotal accounts of events needed to be overcome. The desire to demonstrate a degree of rigour in the movement from data to conclusions led to a more systematic account of coding. Fielding and Lee conclude that while it was Becker and Geer who 'mainstreamed' coding, it was Glaser and Strauss (1967) who made it popular in their account of grounded theory.

BOX 19.2 HINTS AND TIPS

Using coding to signpost rather than to reduce

In qualitative analysis, codes are often used not to denote facts but to 'break up' the data (Strauss and Corbin, 1990). Such codes represent 'perspectives' of the researcher rather than clear-cut empirical contentful categories (Becker and Geer,

(Continued)

1960). According to Becker and Geer, these perspectives and the 'areas to which they apply' are only 'tentatively identified' when the coding begins. Coding is then done by going 'through the summarized incidents, marking each incident with a number or numbers that stand for the various areas to which it appears to be relevant'. Consequently, the coding of text does not serve to condense relevant information and to decide whether a certain person or event falls under a certain class of events or persons, but simply serves to make sure 'that all relevant data can be brought to bear on a point'. Here, the function of coding is restricted to signposting: codes are stored together with the 'address' of a certain text passage and, drawing on this information, the researcher can locate all the possible information provided by the textual data on the relevant topic. (Kelle, 1997: Section 3.9)

Generating a coding frame

A coding frame is a catalogue that identifies all the codes to be applied to the data in order to identify patterns within the data. Just as in quantitative research, the development of a coding frame may come before the analysis of the data or through the process of analysis itself. The development of a coding frame involves a number of choices and approaches. These are discussed below.

Types of coding

If coding is the act of identifying a series of 'tags' which are attached to or emerge from chunks of text in order to allow links between those chunks to be highlighted and explored, how are codes to be classified? A number of methods and types of coding can be identified.

Latent and manifest codes

Manifest codes refer to specific terms that recur within the text data collected. Manifest codes are terms that are in the data themselves. Latent codes are terms or themes that the researcher identifies beneath the surface of the text. Terms like 'lonely', 'isolated' and 'unfriendly' may recur in the text. The researcher may feel that, having read the full transcripts or because of their prior review of the literature, these three terms are all referring to the same thing. Rather than having three codes, the researcher may feel that beneath the surface there is sufficient commonality that a single code should be applied to all instances where any one of these three terms is used, even where there is no common terminology in the text itself.

Sociological and *in vivo* codes

In vivo codes refer to terms that are in the language of those either interviewed or observed, or who wrote the texts being collected by the researcher. This is in many ways the same thing as what was referred to above as manifest codes. However, the distinction being drawn here is slightly different. Sociological codes are themes drawn not from the language of those being researched, but instead from the language of the researcher's theoretical background. Just as in the above case, where three terms used by interviewees might be identified by the researcher as meaning the same thing, so the researcher might conclude that what a series of interviewees are touching on in their surface talk (or in whatever other form of text source the researcher is using) can be linked together through the use of a more theoretical term. This is similar to the notion of symptoms and diagnosis. What a number of different patients describe in different ways may appear to the doctor as symptoms of a common condition. The doctor classifies these things in terms of their theoretical account of the surface symptoms rather than in terms of the range of surface appearances or descriptions given. While *in vivo* codes remain true to the diversity of self-description or experience, sociological codes seek to identify underlying commonalities. The danger of *in vivo* codes lies in them becoming lost in multiple terms for the same thing. The danger of sociological codes is to rush too quickly into reducing diversity to already existing theoretical pigeonholes. The researcher must seek to balance this tension as best they can in the particular conditions of the research they seek to carry out.

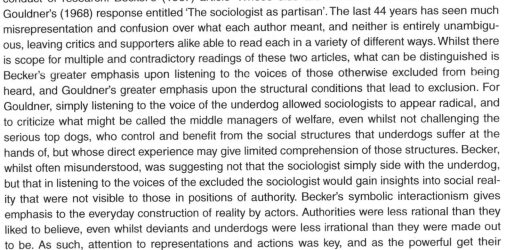

BOX 19.3 RESEARCH FOCUS

The Becker–Gouldner debate and its implications for qualitative data analysis

One of the most significant debates in sociology in the last 50 years was between Howard Becker and Alvin Gouldner concerning the nature of 'partisanship' in the conduct of research. Becker's (1967) article 'Whose side are we on?' stimulated Gouldner's (1968) response entitled 'The sociologist as partisan'. The last 44 years has seen much misrepresentation and confusion over what each author meant, and neither is entirely unambiguous, leaving critics and supporters alike able to read each in a variety of different ways. Whilst there is scope for multiple and contradictory readings of these two articles, what can be distinguished is Becker's greater emphasis upon listening to the voices of those otherwise excluded from being heard, and Gouldner's greater emphasis upon the structural conditions that lead to exclusion. For Gouldner, simply listening to the voice of the underdog allowed sociologists to appear radical, and to criticize what might be called the middle managers of welfare, even whilst not challenging the serious top dogs, who control and benefit from the social structures that underdogs suffer at the hands of, but whose direct experience may give limited comprehension of those structures. Becker, whilst often misunderstood, was suggesting not that the sociologist simply side with the underdog, but that in listening to the voices of the excluded the sociologist would gain insights into social reality that were not visible to those in positions of authority. Becker's symbolic interactionism gives emphasis to the everyday construction of reality by actors. Authorities were less rational than they liked to believe, even whilst deviants and underdogs were less irrational than they were made out to be. As such, attention to representations and actions was key, and as the powerful get their voices heard well enough already, so the sociological attention to the underdog's voice adds what

(Continued)

would otherwise not be heard. Progressive social change could be best advanced if we better understood what makes people act the way they do. Gouldner's sociology takes a more structural approach to inequalities, and so he is less interested in the meanings people hold than he is in the realities they are subject to. For him, simply recording the voices of the underdog is liberal niceness, but with limited value. Gouldner suggests what he calls 'objective partisanship', by which he means a sociology that is committed to the universal objectives of human fulfilment. If you believe the social world is fundamentally built from interactions and beliefs then you should use *in vivo* coding when undertaking qualitative content analysis. You should be looking for the ways people represent and construct their lives themselves. If you believe action and belief are best understood as located within social structures and institutions, then you will more likely want to engage in forms of socio-logical coding, locating what people say within 'deeper' overarching categories. The significance of the Becker–Gouldner debate runs throughout the following coding distinctions as well.

Deductive and inductive (and open) coding

Deductive coding involves the production of a list of categories by which data are to be coded prior to the collection of the data themselves. In so far as there is always an element of selection in any form of social research, and in so far as the researcher is always influenced by their culture in how they see the world they research, there is always an element of deductiveness about coding. Inductive forms of coding involve the generation of codes after the collection and initial reading of the data themselves. This may be at a number of stages in the data collection process. Either the first round of data collected is read to allow the researcher to generate a list of initial codes from which to give provisional conclusions, or the coding process is left until the data have all been collected. Early use of inductive coding becomes the basis for subsequent deductive forms of enquiry. This cyclical process is the basis for both analytical induction and grounded theory, though it is the latter that is more commonly practised (in broad terms). In the context of grounded theory the initial process of inductive coding is referred to as 'open coding' (see Chapter 11). Most texts on qualitative research suggest it is important to engage in forms of analysis from the very beginning of the data collection stage. However, it is also commonly announced that it is not good to be too pre-emptive in the kinds of coding that are done in early rounds of the cycle. This raises another set of questions about the types of code that can be generated.

Summary codes and pattern codes

Summary codes are often also called first-level codes. These codes focus on general characteristics of a population, situation or encounter. The most elementary of these might be the what, where, when, how and who type questions that allow the researcher to get a basic hold on what they have generated. This grasping applies in individual interviews, in notes on specific fieldwork encounters or from a single text (such as a newspaper article or letter). However, once such basic information has been coded, these summaries can be used to enable quick and easy comparisons between single cases. Summary codes are generally considered relatively non-distorting. In other words, such summaries do not seek to impose a particular agenda on the text. Fear that early coding may lead the researcher to become too focused too soon on one set of issues rather than another is offset by the belief that summary coding is not seeking to identify specifics. On the whole, summary codes are prescriptive and do not derive from the text itself. Wanting a record of who, what, when and so on is seen as a general interest. However, the specifics of a particular research project may lead to the formulation of some general summary questions which relate specifically to the project at hand. A study of undergraduate students may wish to record the stage at which the student is in their degree, for example. This will allow for some provisional organization of the data being collected. As has been pointed out earlier, it is not uncontroversial to use summary coding. Barney Glaser (1992) argues that even elementary codes used for initial organization of early rounds of data collection can become too prescriptive and that all codes not developed from the data themselves should be kept under suspicion at the very least. This view is not widely shared and many would argue that it is not possible. Nevertheless, the dangers of prescriptive coding should not be ignored, and the use of summary codes rather than pattern codes may not be enough to avoid the dangers of substantive or pattern coding being developed too early.

Pattern coding is also called specific coding or depth coding, and moves beyond what is called summary coding. Pattern coding seeks to highlight the existence of underlying patterns within the data. It is designed to get to the heart of what is going on in the data, or at least what is going on in terms of what the researcher is interested in, or what the researcher becomes interested in through the course of data collection and initial forms of analysis. This creates a tension. One cannot identify patterns without looking; and where and how does one look to see what is supposed to be beneath the surface? The initial application of summary codes will have involved the researcher in a preliminary scanning of the text. This should breed a degree of familiarity with the text's content without focusing the researcher's attention in one direction or another. The development of provisional pattern codes emerges from this familiarity, but a more detailed reading of the text may be required at this stage (whether this occurs after the first round of data collection, after the second round or at the end of the data collection process).

While summary codes seek to map the content of the text in terms of general characteristics, pattern codes are designed to enable the investigation of relationships within the specific content. This usually involves the identification of specific recurrent themes within the text – themes that can then be investigated both for their relationship with particular summary code characteristics (that is, male/female, age, location and so on) and between themselves.

Axial codes and systematic codes

Axial codes are codes that the researcher selects to represent and to highlight what they perceive to be the core issues or themes within the text they are analysing.

Whether the researcher is generating such axial (or 'meta', that is, higher-order) codes in a preliminary form applied to early rounds of data collection, or whether these axial codes are being developed in a more final sense after all the data have been collected, it is the case that axial codes imply a hierarchical ordering of codes. What this means is that axial codes highlight large units of meaning within which there will be lower-level codes. In a study of student activity a series of axial codes may be developed such as classroom time, private study time, paid work time and leisure time. This first-level coding could be said to apply a single first-level code called 'time', which then leads to a series of subcodes. Within each of these sub-codes there may need to be a set of further subcodes. This creates a series of pyramids or cascades. The principle behind axial coding is that through the selection of a core set of themes, coding can allow the most significant underlying issues to be made more manifest. The idea is that the most important (or axial) issues are shed light on while other issues are placed in the background.

Systematic coding involves the attempt to go through the text to be analysed and to identify all the emerging themes that the researcher can find. Rather than making a choice as to which is the key theme or set of themes, systematic coding attempts to be less pre-emptive, and to allow selection and reduction to occur more slowly and after initial coding has taken place rather than during initial coding. Only after the data have been coded in this way is it possible to test the significance of potential links between codes in a systematic way. There is a danger with axial coding that the researcher simply feels that there is a significant factor at work in their data, and they then code for it. This process highlights the instances in the text where that factor arises, while other factors not coded for are overshadowed. The researcher is then in danger of making their prediction appear to come true. Systematic coding seeks to avoid this situation by starting with the more modest aim of marking as many themes as the researcher thinks they can find, only to select and reduce at a later stage. Axial coding may be developed in subsequent rounds, if this is seen as appropriate.

The counter-argument to the above point is that it is never possible to code for every theme within a text as there are likely to be a near infinite number of potential themes that could be selected, especially when there is a significant amount of text to analyse. As such, it can be pointed out that a selection process is inevitable between themes the researcher thinks are important and those they do not. In the end, therefore, there will always need to be a pragmatic balance between the 'principles' of axial and systematic coding. This does not mean that a researcher cannot choose to move closer to one ideal or the other. It only means that they can never achieve either ideal.

Individual or group coding

It is a good idea, whenever possible, to seek some form of collaboration when engaged in the selection of codes. If the researcher is working with others as part of a research team, it makes sense for all members of the team to engage in an initial reading of a selection of the data collected. Each member of the team then needs to identify what they think the core codes are that need to be applied, or which 'emerge'. The team can then meet to discuss the schemes each member has identified and, with luck, this process should lead to a more developed coding scheme. Alternatively, the researcher can ask people whom they were researching to collaborate in identifying the core themes. When it is possible, the research may benefit from follow-up interviews that pursue this aim. Colleagues, fellow students and academic staff are alternatives, or might simply offer valuable additional insights.

The sum of these different approaches to coding is schematically presented in Table 19.1.

TABLE 19.1   Researcher-driven or data-driven coding: six dimensions of overlapping tension

Latent versus manifest	Does the researcher feel they can identify something underlying surface appearances?
Sociological versus *in vivo*	Does the researcher feel that sociological language better accounts for what is being said than the language actually being used by participants?
Deductive versus inductive	Does the researcher start with a coding frame drawn from prior literature and research?
Pattern versus summary	Does the researcher seek to select what they identify as important, or simply seek to map the whole?
Axial versus systematic	Is coding structured into a hierarchy or is it flat?
Group versus individual	How many researchers get to decide?
Researcher-driven versus data-driven coding	The sum of these distinctions maps onto questions of causation versus interpretation, structure versus action, theory testing versus theory building in the conduct of social research

Culling and refining: expansion and reduction

The common advice that there should not be too many codes and not too few, in addition to the advice that one should not start too late in analysis, while at the same time one should avoid being too pre-emptive in rushing to analytical conclusions, may seem to offer very little concrete advice about when and how to proceed. This is truly a grey area, one that the researcher needs to reflect upon and seek to clarify in their practice.

Perhaps the best advice to the beginner is to start with a very rough sketch of as many potential themes as seem to emerge from a reading of the texts in front of you. Code for these. From these it should be possible to make links and connections between the wealth of themes. In so doing some themes will stand out, while others will come to appear less significant. Some themes will drop out; others will be merged together. This refinement process will allow a degree of reduction without eliminating potentially valuable themes. Make a note of the themes that have been tied together in this process. In your revised coding scheme you will need to give definitions of the codes you have selected and these definitions will need to include mention of the other themes that have been incorporated. It may be the case later that some of these incorporated themes may prove more significant and will need to be extracted and made into separate codes, so keep your records precise. Depending upon how you choose to mix the data collection and the data analysis, the process of refinement and expansion will vary.

Higher forms of code-based analysis: matrices and network diagrams

Matthew Miles and A. Michael Huberman (1994) provide a wealth of illustration on the art of presenting qualitative data in ways that facilitate analysis. Their motto is 'think display'. They suggest two main forms of representational device: matrix and network displays. A matrix display is a table with rows and columns. By placing one or more variables in the columns and one or more variables in the rows, it is possible to create a grid into which cross-tabulations can be placed (that is, the results of each crossover between rows and columns). Data entries might be numerical figures, quotations, categorical responses, keywords or coded values depending on the nature of the variables being cross-tabulated (see Table 19.2 and Table 19.3). Once the data have been reduced by means of coding, it is possible to extract specific aspects of the data to fill the spaces created within a matrix. Once information is presented in this way, patterns may become easier to identify and certain links between themes may present themselves for further analysis. Content in the intersections can be either textual or numerical.

TABLE 19.2   Table of individual characteristics

Sample characteristics	Age	In paid work Y/N	Attitude to study
Student A	(Numerical figure)	(Categorical response)	(Point on ordinal scale,
Student B			quotation, keyword or
Student C			coded value)

TABLE 19.3   Table of group characteristics by gender

Attitude to change	Nurses	Doctors	Managers
Male	(Summary of findings)		
Female			

Network displays seek to represent flows and processes of connection. While matrices show the content of a situation, network diagrams focus upon sequences and relationships more explicitly.

A network display may seek to depict the flow of events in a singular instance, or the variety of options taken by different individuals or groups (see Figure 19.1).

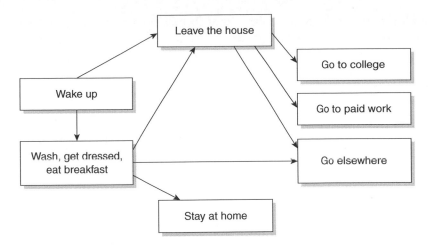

FIGURE 19.1 Starting the day: network diagram

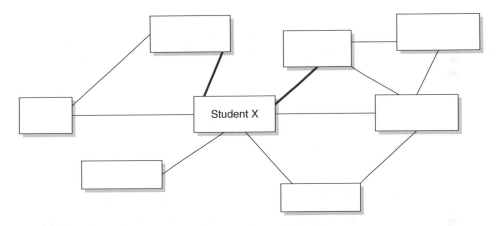

FIGURE 19.2 Network diagram showing associations with friends (thick lines) and acquaintances (thin lines); line thickness can be used to represent level of friendship by any arbitrary measure

This may be an individual or a group. A network diagram may seek to only describe a set of events or it may seek to map critical incidents or even causal processes. Network diagrams can depict a wide variety of phenomena, not just time. Flows of ideas, money, information and relationships between people can all be mapped using network diagrams (see Figure 19.2).

Miles and Huberman suggest four distinct ways in which such representational devices can be used in the process of QDA. The first level is what they call within-case displays. Here data from one case is presented. A case may be an individual or an organization or one location within fieldwork. There are two types of within-case displays. The first seeks to explore and describe the characteristics of a case. The second seeks to highlight processes and causes at work within the case. The second level of display is what Miles and Huberman call cross-case displays. Cross-case displays seek to highlight similarities and differences between cases. Cross-case displays can also be focused upon exploration and description or causation and prediction.

Example of the use of matrix displays

The Guardian and the Daily Mail are very different newspapers, with different editorials and readerships. Ten articles from each newspaper were coded in a matrix display (Table 19.4) and this qualitative content analysis was then further reduced (Table 19.5).

There are four dominant themes in my evaluation of the texts:

1 student finance (much more in The Guardian than the Mail)

2 the value of a degree (covered in both papers equally)

3 disruptive student behaviour (much more in the Mail – which addresses alcohol and religion – than The Guardian – which only focuses on alcohol)

4 standards falling (heavier coverage in the Mail).

In identifying these themes it was possible to select a subset of the articles in order to compare each theme as it was covered in the two newspapers (Table 19.6). This much smaller subset allowed for in-depth discourse analysis (see Chapter 20), but at the same time allowed that the selection of this small sample for in-depth analysis was representative of the range of material in the wider sample of newspapers.

A much more detailed matrix display (as is possible when the number of articles being coded is reduced), whilst still focused on the representation of qualitative coding, can present a range of themes, quotes, binaries, constructions, representations, representatives and claims making in relation to the four key themes. Table 19.7 shows the greater level of detail that can be presented in such a matrix display. This example of Miles and Huberman's mantra 'think display' created the basis for a detailed form of discourse analysis that will be discussed in the next chapter.

Some rules of thumb in the construction of matrix displays

Miles and Huberman (1994: 239–42) provide a series of rules of thumb and questions for the researcher to ask themselves. The first set concerns the content and purpose of the display device (1994: 240–1):

1 Descriptive versus explanatory.

2 Are the categories in your rows and columns in a sequence or not?

3 Are you seeking to present the sequence of events or what is going on at a particular time?

4 What are your categories/variables: people, groups, things or actions?

5 How many levels of connection are you seeking to make?

6 What are your units to be made up of (numbers, quotes, ratings and so on)?

7 Single-case versus multiple-case data.

TABLE 19.4 Two sets of ten newspaper articles about students

	Art. 1	2	3	4	5	6	7	8	9	10
Guardian	Sex industry Feminist students University groups Anti-pornography Beauty contests on campus Objectification in uni shops Photograph of four women in street at night	How do student loans work? Cost calculations Savings versus repayments Written to help 'your daughter'	Students lower tone in some areas Badger Hill in York Scruffy No quotas or planning Area schools in decline	Degree study still leads to higher pay But different for different subject areas Differences higher than elsewhere in Europe	Does Wikipedia dumb down higher education? Pros and cons Hostility and support Need for a new set of protocols to regulate and promote good practice Picture of Wiki logo	University to ban gay marriages on campus Christian-based university college Law may prohibit the prohibition on grounds that if ceremonies are to take place in a location then the sex of the partners cannot be grounds for discrimination	How to use the system of fees and loans to your best advantage Expansion of admission and decline of financial support, but scope to get in and get on Elite universities seek to recruit from wider base	US high fees fund scholarships 'The Pursuit of Happiness' Will Smith Elite school scholarships Harvard uses these cases to ask for rich alumni to contribute donations The case of Palvik 'the system rewards merit and hard work'	Students in the UK who will face debts of up to £25,000 Splits between old and new universities over scale of additional top-up fees and over fears for low-income access Explainer: facts and figures about debts	Top-up fees 'will hit poor middle class' Research those below the rich but above eligibility for grants will be squeezed Minister defends

(Continued)

TABLE 19.4 (Continued)

	Art. 1	2	3	4	5	6	7	8	9	10
Daily Mail	Campus crack-down on free beer for uni students Photo of students drinking Unis warn local clubs and pubs to rein in promotional events that encourage excessive drinking	Student paper pulped over Mohamed cartoon Cardiff university student mag. Seen as offensive Photo of angry bearded men with placard 'Slay those who insult Islam'	University professor pleads with clubs not to encourage binge drinking Reading University VC seeks responsible behaviour from all concerned Smiling bearded man	Radical Muslims 'Using universities to spread extremism' Ruth Kelly, communities secretary admits Muslim community leaders taking some action and joining the govt call for action Ruth Kelly smiling	Third of graduates don't need degree for work Higher Education Statistics Agency figures show figures are for one year after graduation Are there more graduates than graduate jobs?	Elite universities under pressure to accept vocations students Unis could be 'bullied' into accepting vocational qualifications Focus is on Oxford and Cambridge universities under pressure and their defence of the A level system New unis defend vocational bridge between theory and application	Tuition fees price middle-class students out of university Introduction of tuition fees saw student applications in England drop by five percent in the first year Student numbers amongst groups eligible for grant rose while middle-income homes saw applications decline Poor students see grades offered for access fail to get them in Gender gap as women become 54% of intake	University students who skip lectures could be thrown out Possibility of legally binding contracts upon students to attend classes Oxford, Nottingham Trent and Chester introduce these schemes this year NUS leaders are critical of a scheme that ties students to behave when they get increasingly little from university staff and resources, yet have to pay ever greater fees for their	'Force universities to take more minority students' calls Trevor Phillips, head of the Commission for Racial Equality Half the Russell Group universities had fewer than 30 Black Caribbean students each and 123/165 UK unis had less than 1% Defence made that if they had enough A levels they'd be treated equally Govt threat to force unis to let more minorities in Photo of	Top universities may lose funding unless they admit more deprived students Claims that this will force universities to adopt 'social engineering' to reduce the dominance of the middle classes Russell Group expresses fear that equality funding will be cross-subsidized from money that 'ought' to go into research budgets Photos of

TABLE 19.5 Qualitative coding in a reduced matrix display

	Art. 1	2	3	4	5	6	7	8	9	10
Guardian	Feminism on campus today	How do student loans work?	Students lower tone in some areas	Degree study still leads to higher pay	Does Wikipedia dumb down higher education?	University to ban gay marriages on campus Christian-based university college	How to use the system of fees and loans to your best advantage	US high fees fund massive provision of scholarships	Students in the UK who will face debts of up to £25,000	Top-up fees 'will hit poor middle class'
Daily Mail	Campus crack down on free beer	Student paper pulped over Mohammed cartoon Cardiff	University professor pleads with clubs not to encourage binge drinking	Radical Muslims 'using universities to spread extremism'	Third of graduates don't need degree for work	Elite universities under pressure to accept vocational students	Tuition fees price middle-class students out of university	University students who skip lectures could be thrown out	Force universities to take more minority students	Top universities may lose funding unless they admit more deprived students

TABLE 19.6 A matrix display of selected articles for subsequent discourse analysis

	Student finance	Value of degree	Student disruption	Standards falling
Guardian	Articles 2 and 7	Article 4	Article 3	Article 5
Mail	Article 7	Article 5	Article 1 (beer) and 2 (religion)	Article 6

The next set concerns designing a matrix (1994: 241):

1 What data do your research give you to play with?

2 Get colleagues to read through and suggest themes.

3 Produce a sheet with all matrix possibilities.

4 Don't put too many variables in any one table.

5 Keep revising and expect so to do.

6 Reorder (put some rows in columns and vice versa to see what emerges).

7 Stay open to the option of adding new variables.

8 Balance between fine grain and losing yourself in the detail.

9 Any one question may need many matrices.

Rules of thumb for matrix data entry are (1994: 241–2):

1 Be clear about level of data (individuals, families, organizations and so on).

2 Remember that all data display is a reduction.

3 Use codes to locate key material.

4 Keep a clear record of reduction process for future checking.

5 Explain process in legend.

6 Show missing data clearly in matrices.

7 Don't lock up data matrix too early.

8 Use text and numbers.

9 Be careful with scaling.

10 Get colleagues to review from start and throughout.

Content in any box within a matrix display may be numbers of incidents, it may be a description, or it may be a key quote as illustration.

Finally, the rules of thumb for drawing conclusions from matrix data are (1994: 242):

1 Squint analysis at the outset.

TABLE 19.7 A more detailed matrix display of qualitative coding from a subset of articles selected

	Student finance	Value of a degree	Student disruption	Standards falling
Guardian	**Article 1** Daughter is student. Parents want to know how to help with loans Article explains options Parents are high earners Advice to keep loan going Assumes graduate will get good job and promotion Seems neutral but builds upon the above assumptions and graduate work and affluent parents Uncritical of system **Article 7** Author is VC at UCL 'facing facts' 'we need sophisticated approach' HE is valuable investment 'Top-up fees are a realization' of issues 'Taxpayer shows no collective desire' 'Competition for treasury funds ... fiercer' 'global competition' 'talent not a genetic trait' Rationing by income is wrong Unis have helped social mobility over the last 50 years and new fees and bursaries will further this Grads will pay only when income exceeds x Fees not reduced demand Need to overcome fears of increasing fees further. This is the challenge (1) need blind admissions (2) impact on students and families needs to be phased in (3) move away from treasury dependence	**Article 4** 'Degrees continue to pay off' UUK evidence £160k av. over A level holders 340 for medics 250 engineers 52 for humanities 35 for arts 25% premium according to PricewaterhouseCoopers Large HE expansion not dented this Highest value added for men from poorer backgrounds, but women across the board (relative to non-graduate women who are the very lowest paid) Seen as evidence that 'controversial' loans scheme is legitimate Lowers up-front costs and provides for poorest Diana Warwick (UUK) and Bill Rammell claim as success.	**Article 3** 'Hostilities on the homefront' Non-student Hobman fears 'Balkanization' 11/80 homes 'We feel' 'we' 'our' house prices fall claim York Uni claims improvements 11 councils claim problems Nottingham Action Group (NAG) Cllr Trimble – uni is waking up 8 unis now have community offcrs Multi-occupancy problems Hobman fears local shops will become takeaways and video shops Local school numbers down 'I'm not anti-student' Fear of 3000 more York students Uni rejects problem claim NUS rep says students go to poor housing, don't create it £27m	Small elite US college history department bans Wikipedia entries from student report assessments. Wiki reaching 'epidemic proportions' iPod overtakes library 'Predictable culture clash' between 'whiskery "old" authoritarian wielding the censor's scissors' and 'cyber-libertarians' Think Catholic Church versus Galileo Has kicked up a storm, but should be recalled that ban is only for use as reference in assessment, not from use Defence of Wiki in knowledge economy 'keep it fluid' Pros and cons Distinguished prof from college says for all its faults Wiki still useful, when understood for what it is Author agrees Parallel drawn with US war of independence against the censor

(Continued)

TABLE 19.7 (Continued)

	Non-naïve Russell Group moving forward via evidence and analysis			
Mail	**Article 7** 'Tuition fees price middle class students out of university' 'Pupils from better off families hit hardest' crippling £20,000 debts' 'As many as 10,000 middle-class youngsters are deferring' 'Experts said many had decided a university degree is not worth the financial sacrifice. They said middle income families have been worst affected' 'Unprecedented downturn' in entrance 4.5% Marked class differences Social engineering 'where deserving applicants are sidelined in favour of pupils with inferior qualifications' Lower income groups up from 31.4 to 31.7% Bill Rammell was positive	**Article 5** 'Third of graduates don't need degrees for work' Many stack shelves, wash dishes or work in bars Higher Ed Stats Agency 34.4% of 04–05 grads went into 'non-graduate' work A level students may now think twice Wes Streeting (NUS) surprised as govt always says there are not enough graduates Intro of HE top-up fees problematic. 65.6% included software designers, teachers, solicitors, and retail managers 34.4% inc bars, kitchens, secretaries, farm and factory labour, postal staff Overall graduate unemployment rose but is still half that of non-graduates. 93.1–93% in last year of gad emp. Bill Rammell positive. Boris Johnson suggests not to be put off	**Article 1** 'Campus crackdown on free beer for uni students' Photo of two male white students drinking pints of beer Subtitle 'Another day another liquid lecture at uni' 'cheap booze' 'hangover' in lectures 'rite of passage' Reading VC Prof Downes warns bar owners that uni does not condone promotion of commercial organizations on its property Uni claims to promote enjoyment, safety and good community relations Uni spokeperson claims bus distributed free lager outside one hall of residence **Article 2** 'Student paper pulped over Mohamed cartoon' 'recalled', 'trainee journalists' Cardiff *Gair Rhydd* = *Free Word*, editor + 3 suspended from SU SU spokeswoman on freedom + responsibility 'SU very much regrets any upset caused or disrespect shown' SU has launched an investigation, 200 of 10,000 copies unaccounted for. Photo of shouting bearded men with poster 'Slay those who insult Islam'	**Article 6** 'Elite universities under pressure to accept vocational students' 'Universities could be "bullied" into admitting applicants with job-related diplomas instead of A levels' They are worried Ministers insist new vocational diplomas will be rigorous. Tearing down the wall between academic and vocational Encourage more to stay on post-16 Schools minister Jim Knight 'our very best and brightest young people may feel a diploma suits them better' 'Cool reception' Dr John Hood Oxford VC 'We typically do not accept vocational qualifications' A level as gold standard Alan Smithers Buckingham Uni – 'Govt has increasingly threatened university autonomy' i.e. quotas from ind. schools Picture of Cambridge college quad

2   Read through to notice and make note of apparent patterns.

3   Write text (memos) on emerging conclusions as you spot them.

4   Use content analysis summary tables to avoid over-reduction.

5   First conclusions always need revision.

6   Seek to verify, triangulate, contrast and gain feedback.

7   Always check cases before moving to cross-case comparisons.

8   Illustrate conclusions, but be representative, don't pick just juicy quotes.

9   Beyond empirical verification, seek to confirm theoretical models.

10   Document conclusion-drawing procedures and ask colleagues to comment.

11   Ask what data the reader will need to confirm your account.

Within-case displays: exploring and describing

Miles and Huberman (1994: 90–142) identify a wide range of representative devices by which to facilitate description of complex qualitative data. These can be organized into six broad types, as detailed below. Data to be presented in such a visual form may have different levels of ordering. Miles and Huberman distinguish between ordered and partially ordered forms of display. For example, data organized along a timeline, or which are presented in relation to age, would be called 'ordered'. Partially ordered displays present coded themes that emerged within a case study, but not in any sequential order (for example, types of work: building, teaching, administration, sales). A checklist table allows the content of a situation to be examined.

Context charts and checklist matrices

A context chart is a network diagram that seeks to show the range of groups or individuals or topics that made up the 'situation' being studied. It is a map of what was going on and who the players were, with lines to show relations between them. A checklist matrix is a grid into which a similar array of information is presented without the attempt to give it an order. A checklist matrix seeks to list all the key codes/categories that emerged from the case.

Time ordered displays

Time ordered displays include event listing, critical incident charts, activity record, decision modelling, growth gradients and time ordered matrices. The use of time as an ordering scale of matrices, or network diagrams, allows for the production of representations that show how events or ideas unfolded. An event listing and an activity record are similar to a checklist with the added dimension that events are listed in time order. Decision modelling is a network diagram that moves across a timeline. This form of network diagram is often referred to as a flow chart.

Role ordered displays

Here in the case of matrix displays, one axis of the grid is made up of a listing of the key roles of participants in the case being studied, while the other axis lists other significant categories that relate to the different roles (level of commitment, level of training, level of funding, for example). The intersection would contain quotes, the researcher's summary of the responses or keyword/coding values that related to the intersection of that role, and category of data. In this way it is hoped that the differences between roles, or those that perform those roles, can be more easily identified.

Role-by-time matrices

The ordering of both axes allows one dimension of potential difference to be matched to a second. For example, did teachers change their overall view about a particular class over the course of a year, while their view of other classes stayed the same? Role by time is only one potential pair.

Conceptually ordered displays

This includes thematic conceptual matrices, folk taxonomies and cognitive maps. A thematic conceptual matrix seeks to highlight links between theoretically interesting themes coded for in the data analysis. Folk taxonomies seek to map how participants view their worlds. How do those researched categorize their environment? What do they see going together and what things are seen as separate? Folk taxonomies can be represented either within matrices or in network diagrams. Cognitive maps are representations of how people view their space, or how they understand change. What things go where? What routes do which people follow? What and where are the boundaries? How do boundaries change? Who belongs and who is an outsider? What and who led to a particular outcome? If these themes are coded for within each interview or observation, the results can be drawn out in matrix or network diagrams.

Effects matrices

Where a cognitive map seeks to show via network diagrams how a person or a group understands a situation, and some of these situations will be 'outcomes' emerging over time, an effects matrix seeks to highlight how different groups or individuals see the same event or set of events. One axis is used to represent different players, while the second axis sets out dimensions of the change process or perception of the outcome. The grid then allows comparison of different groups' perceptions of an outcome and their accounts of how it came about.

Within-case displays: explaining and predicting

While not making generalized explanations, within-case displays may seek to highlight the process of causation in specific cases. Identifying a cause involves three levels:

- identification of a sequence of events that leads to an outcome
- identification of 'constant conjunction', the recurrent nature of a 'sequence' leading to an outcome
- identification of the 'mechanism', the way in which the sequence actually leads to the outcome.

Causally oriented matrices or network diagrams have a time-based dimension. A case dynamics matrix 'displays a set of forces for change and traces the consequential processes and outcomes. The basic principle is one of preliminary explanation' (Miles and Huberman, 1994: 148). One axis sets out preceding factors and the other axis sets out a series of outcomes. How often do the preceding factors lead to instances of the outcomes listed? The grid can be filled with numbers or descriptions. 'A causal network is a display of the most important independent and dependent variables in a field of study … and of the relationships among them … The plot of these relationships is directional, rather than solely correlational. It is assumed that some factors exact an influence on others. X brings Y into being or makes Y larger or smaller' (1994: 152–3). Exploratory matrices and network diagrams may lead the researcher to design case dynamics matrices.

Cross-case displays: exploring and describing

Cross-case displays are similar to within-case displays. Partially ordered displays (which use the same categories for each case) can be used to draw out potential similarities and differences, whether made in the form of numerical charts or content analytic summary tables.

Case ordered displays are matrices in which along one axis are arranged the cases being examined and along the other axis are arranged one or more key variables emerging from the data. By so doing it may be possible to identify particular characteristics about cases that allow all cases to be arranged in some kind of rank order. Such rankings may be in terms of outcomes (degrees of success or failure, for example) time taken to achieve an outcome, size of organization, number of a particular type of incident, and so on. By developing such rankings the researcher may identify common and divergent features between cases. Two-variable case ordering matrices, contrast tables, scatterplot diagrams and time ordered displays develop this logic of comparison. Comparative decision tree modelling again uses the methods of single-case analysis to produce a number of network diagrams that can then be compared (see Miles and Huberman, 1994: Chapter 7).

Cross-case displays: ordering and explaining

The methods for cross-case displays that aim to enable explanation build upon the earlier forms discussed. This is both in the development of plausible variables to test against one another and in terms of the displays best suited to bringing out causal processes, constant conjunction and explanatory mechanisms (Miles and Huberman, 1994: Chaper 8).

Summary

Qualitative forms of content analysis involve the selection of codes and their application to sections of the textual materials under analysis. Patterns can then be identified between the coded segments, and the location and incidence of certain codes can be mapped in relation to other codes (and by association, with the producers of those texts or with those the texts were produced about). Coding may serve to identify patterns within or between cases, and can be used to map descriptive and/or causal relationships. Coding forms the basis for the production of tables and network diagrams. Content analysis can be conducted 'by hand' or by using qualitative data analysis software (such as NUD*IST).

 ■ **Questions**

1   What distinguishes a matrix display from a network diagram?
2   What is qualitative about coding in qualitative data analysis?
3   How do some dispute the claim that content analysis can never be truly qualitative?

■ ■ **Further reading** ■

Berg, Bruce L. (1998) *Qualitative Research Methods for the Social Sciences*. Needham Heights, MA: Allyn and Bacon.

Kelle, Udo (1997) 'Theory building in qualitative research and computer programs for the management of textual data', in *Sociological Research Online* 2(2), http://www.socresonline. org.uk/socresonline/2/2/1.html.

Miles, Matthew and Huberman, A. Michael (1994) *Qualitative Data Analysis*. London: Sage.

Strauss, Anselm and Corbin, Juliet (1990) *Basics of Qualitative Research: Grounded Theory Procedures and Techniques*. Thousand Oaks, CA: Sage.

TWENTY

SEMIOTIC AND NARRATIVE FORMS OF DISCOURSE ANALYSIS, AND DOING CONVERSATION ANALYSIS

By the end of this chapter you will be able to:

- Distinguish between a range of non-content analytic forms of qualitative data analysis.
- Conduct forms of semiotic analysis.
- Conduct forms of deconstructive analysis.
- Conduct forms of narrative analysis.
- Conduct forms of conversation analysis.

This chapter outlines the principles and practical techniques involved in those forms of qualitative data analysis which do not stop at the formal techniques of coding that are associated with qualitative content analysis. The traditions of semiotics, deconstruction and narrative analysis, collectively referred to as discourse analysis, share with conversation analysis a rejection of what they see as the imitation of quantitative methods within qualitative content analysis. It is important, however, to note that, despite the rhetoric, qualitative data analysis in practice is more typically a mix of content and discourse analysis.

Semiotic and narrative forms of discourse analysis

Jonathan Potter and Margaret Wetherell (1994) suggest that what distinguishes discourse analysis (DA) from forms of content analysis is that while coding represents a fundamental part of analysis in content analysis, coding only represents a provisional part of data preparation in DA. They argue that 'unlike the sort of coding that takes place in traditional content analysis, the coding [in DA] is not the analysis itself but a preliminary to make the task of analysis manageable' (1994: 52). It should be noted that Potter and Wetherell are here discussing DA of a large quantity of interview, text and field recording data. In this case, they argue that it is useful to carry out forms of content analysis to identify key themes. In other contexts, where the researcher is seeking to analyse only a relatively small quantity of text, formal coding for the purposes of reduction may not be seen as useful. Even where coding is applied, DA gives a priority to overall themes and meanings within the data, and not to the incidence of particular words or phrases as such (Box 20.1).

BOX 20.1 CONSIDER THIS

The analytical paradigm with a thousand faces

'Discourse analysis' contains much in common, yet is separated by a cloud of different names, terminologies and supposed principles. Much of what holds such diversity together is opposition to quantitative methods. Below I highlight just the most popular variants within the discourse analytic 'stable' (yes, the metaphorical character of such terminology is not accidental, and for many discourse analysts is unavoidable).

Critical discourse analysis

This school (Wodek, 2007) uses fieldwork methods of collecting real-world language, and uses a variety of analytic techniques to identify and critically challenge the ideological representations of dominant groups. United in their critique of ideological misrepresentation, this network of researchers use the full range of analytical techniques outlined below and throughout this chapter.

Deconstruction

The identification of conceptual excess within language, i.e. where one supposedly coherent term is used to mean more than one thing, or where metaphors are passed off as concepts (see below).

Discourse analysis

In its narrow sense, this term is often used to refer to the work of Michel Foucault and those that followed him (such as Said, 1984). Foucault sought to show how 'serious texts' such as medical, psychiatric, penal, pedagogical and other 'disciplinary manuals' came to guide the practices of institutions and professions in shaping both how different groups were seen and treated, and how such treatment groups would then come to see and act themselves. Framing the figure in the discourse, constructing the person to be 'treated', uses knowledge as a form of power. Edward Said applied Foucault's discourse analytical approach to the colonial construction of the oriental 'other'.

Dramaturgical analysis

An approach to meaning focusing on the interactional situation in which utterances and practices take place. The most prominent exponent of the dramaturgical approach was Erving Goffman (1959). His approach to meaning in the context of performance, stage and audience emerges out of the symbolic interactionist tradition, can be linked therefore with hermeneutics, and is at odds with more formalist and structuralist approaches where meaning is to be found in semantics and/or grammar.

Formalism

In the years just before and after the Russian Revolution of 1917, Russian formalism challenged biographical and contextual readings of texts, searching instead for the basic units of meaning, both of narrative development (see below) and of characters (see the application of Vladimir Propp's seven archetypal characters to George Lucas's *Star Wars* in Box 20.12).

Frame analysis

Initially proposed by Erving Goffman in 1974, frame analysis was a rather vague symbolic interactionist approach to the interpretation of such things as advertising texts. The relatively unclear 'methodology' in Goffman has been increasingly replaced by versions of 'frame analysis' that are more systematic. For some this has led to something close to qualitative content analysis (see Chapter 19), whilst for others frame analysis is more akin to Foucauldian discourse analysis (see above). Contemporary frame analysis is commonly used in the study of social movements and in tandem with forms of network analysis. Where network analysis seeks to map the interactions between individuals and groups in the success and/or failure of social movement mobilization,

(Continued)

(Continued)

frame analysis seeks to map how different groups with differing constructions of 'the issue' manage or fail to manage their differences in the creation of a common frame, through which they seek to mobilize support and orient media representations of the topic. Contemporary frame analysis uses the kinds of qualitative content analysis (coding), semiotics and narrative analysis that are discussed in this chapter and in the previous chapter.

Genealogical analysis

Michel Foucault (1977), drawing upon Nietzsche, used the concept of genealogy to highlight the way historical accounts always plot a path backwards from the present. This path is always a selective one, focused on the issues and events most relevant to present concerns and in accordance with current beliefs about the direction of history (usually a narrative of why 'we' are the logical outcome of developmental tendencies). Such histories render the present a quasi-natural outcome of past events by ignoring the paths that started in the direction of alternatives. For Foucault, genealogy was a method for highlighting the contradictory histories of those elements of human life that are often seen to have no history at all (natural justice, sexuality, madness and family, for example).

Genre analysis

The attempt to identify conventions and rules by which certain types of form and content are either acceptable or required in certain fictional constructions. Genre represents an implicit or explicit contract between audience and producer over what is expected in certain forms of fiction. The requirement to provide something original within established parameters of expectation represents the challenge of mainstream entertainment, and also within various avant-gardes. The application of genre analysis to the study of non-fiction media such as news production (on paper or in broadcast media), and in wider social science analysis of life histories, for example, has allowed for the identification of conventions by which representation is managed, whether that is to a wide audience, a small circle of intimates or to oneself. Do you tell your life as a romantic comedy, a tragedy, a psychological thriller or a gritty piece of social realism?

Grounded theory

A mixing of qualitative content analysis with more developed forms of discourse analysis, with the particular characteristic that analysis and data collection are conducted in an iterative spiral rather than being left to carry out after data have been collected.

Hermeneutics

Originally referring to the interpretation of classical and biblical texts, hermeneutics in the social sciences is associated with interpretivism and phenomenology. This tradition is divided on the question of whether *verstehen* (understanding) should be sought at the level of the individual, within the text, within social contexts of interaction, or within the institutions of a culture or language. Those adopting an interpretivist approach within the social sciences today (such as Clifford Geertz, 1973) carry out analysis that they call 'thick description' of detailed ethnographic field notes and field interviews. More literary and philosophical forms of hermeneutics tend to focus upon the creation of self-referential systems of meaning within 'culture', and by culture they tend to mean the canonical texts of a given society. Hans-Georg Gadamer (1989), for example, suggests that the practice of hermeneutic analysis is to identify the horizon that limits what it is possible for a person within a particular time and place to imagine. Critical hermeneutics was developed in response to this suggestion that it was not possible to think critically outside one's own culture. Jürgen Habermas's 'universal pragmatics' (1984; 1989) is a version of critical theory that fuses hermeneutics with a Marxian critique of ideology. Habermas's work is one of the foundations of contemporary critical discourse analysis (see above).

Narrative analysis

This form of discourse analysis (which will be discussed in more detail below) focuses upon either the use of sequence within text to construct meaning, or the way language is used to represent temporal sequence. The latter will almost always involve the former. Narrative forms may be used to make a persuasive argument, to construct the representation of two sides of an argument, only to use the narrative sequence to actually allow one side of the argument to come out on top. Narrative devices are routinely used in telling the stories of individual lives and social change, whilst media accounts and politicians routinely use narrative sequence to construct a preferred reading of events and to make certain outcomes, decisions and suggestions appear virtuous or at least necessary.

Semiotics and structuralism

Semiotics and structuralism study internal relationships within semantic units of language based upon the study of signs that link concepts with words and symbols, and whose meaning is given through oppositions between signs within language. Semiotics and structuralism study how we come to know things only through the sense of what something is not, rather than through any unmediated relationship with a reality 'out there'.

Thematic analysis

A form of qualitative content analysis that is somewhat similar to what grounded theorists call either axial coding or theoretical coding, and which also gives strong emphasis, as does grounded theory, to the need to spend considerable time with the data, working out what themes actually emerge from the data rather than can be imposed upon it from the researcher's own beliefs. In so far as thematic analysis seeks to develop deeper-level themes than simply surface codes, it is not dissimilar to discourse analysis in general, except in its tendency to be more systematic in documenting how themes emerge. This will usually involve the systematic production of matrix displays of increased depth and detail (see previous chapter and later on in this chapter for how increasingly complex matrix displays are developed). Thematic analysis is the closest of all discourse analytic techniques to qualitative content analysis.

Jonathan Potter (1997: 155) argues that the aim of DA is to identify the meaning of talk and text in general terms and that this often involves the identification of surface themes recurrent in the text (Box 20.2). However, it is not the purpose of DA to remain at the level of surface characteristics. Its aim is depth exploration rather than the counting of examples. This gives greater emphasis to the singular, and analysis of one phrase or one advertisement may require less attention being given to its generality within all talk or all advertisements.

Diachronic and synchronic analysis of language

Semiotic discourse analysts tend to focus on the way words have meaning in relation to other words within a language at a particular moment in time. This is very often through the identification of distinctions, and in particular through the construction of binary oppositions. The study of language as a structured system of meaning is called synchronic analysis. The study of how language changes over time is referred to as diachronic analysis. Whilst semiotic forms of discourse analysis tend to focus on the synchronic aspect, narrative forms of discourse analysis do not always focus on how language changes over time, as they are often more interested in how language is used to tell stories about other changes over time. However, it is useful to recall that when researching the past, the accounts given today and the recorded accounts made in the past itself may tell you as much about how our language has changed as they do about the wider social changes that language may be a part of, but which we also hope language can give us insight into.

Outlined below are two forms of DA, semiotics and narrative analysis. Potter (1997) highlights the fact that there are many research traditions that call themselves discourse analysis. Here we will focus upon the analytical methods employed by the two dominant forms in the social sciences. Semiotics addresses the analysis of meaningful objects at a fixed moment in time. Narrative analysis addresses the analysis of change and movement across time. As has been pointed out in Box 20.1, despite the variety of names the practical conduct of discourse analysis does amount to permutations of a relatively simple set of approaches and foci.

Semiotic analysis

Semiotics or semiology is the study of signs. Signs are physical things (lines of ink, objects on the sides of the road or vibrations in the air) that carry meaning. How are such objects to be analysed? Semiotic analysis starts from the premise that anything that contains meaning, or which can be given meaning by an interpreter, can be called a 'text'. A text is anything that can be 'read', and 'read' means the act of taking a meaning from the thing being read. As such, the principles of textual DA can be applied not only to the written and/or spoken word, but also to all forms of readable objects such as music or film or television, architecture or fashion. What are these principles?

How to read a sign!

Within semiology, or semiotics, a sign is read as a combination of elements. A sign must have three elements:

- a signifier
- a signified
- the sign itself.

A signifier is a physical thing that has been given a meaningful content. A word is a physical sound or the physical combination of lines on a page or screen. A word is the signifier or carrier. Note that the same meaning will be carried by a different word in different languages, so the signifier has no necessary link to the meaning it carries. The signifier may be an image or object of any kind, as long as it has been given the role of conveying a certain meaning through its use. A signified is the meaning (concept) that is carried by the signifier. The sign is the combination of the signifier and the signified.

The final element in this equation is the referent (the thing to which a meaning might be said to correspond in the real world). The word 'cat' may be a signifier for the idea of a certain type of animal. It might be assumed that the idea is equally bound to real things out there in the world. However, the link between sign and referent is much more complex than one of correspondence. Semiotics is concerned with how signs, signifiers and signifieds link together in texts (of all kinds) to create meaningful systems. It is less concerned with the link between words and things beyond language (see Box 20.3).

BOX 20.3 STOP AND THINK

Signs and symbols

Semiotics or the study of signs is not just reserved for words and languages. It can also be applied to other forms of symbolic object. A word has a physical form, whether in sound or written form, but it is also part of a language system with semantic content and a relationship to a grammatical structure (syntax). A language is the combination of such a system of semantics and syntax. However, not everything that carries meaning can be located within such a system of syntax (grammar). Road signs carry meaning but do not have a grammatical structure; they have only a series of visual marks (signifiers) that stand for particular meanings (signifieds). In this sense a road sign is a sign like a word, but it has no grammar. Road signs exist within a system of such signs, but this system does not have the complexity of a proper language. Road signs can even carry metaphorical or mythical meaning. The road sign for 'No Entry' (in many countries a red circle with a white horizontal line through it) is often used to signify the power of a dominant group to restrict the freedom of subordinates in general. Whilst road signs are organized within systems of signs, even if these do not have the grammatical structure of a language, such signs are more systematic than many symbols. Many objects carry symbolic meaning within a particular culture, whether that culture be a whole society, a small community or family group, or just a couple of friends.

What do the gold chains worn by rap and hip-hop artists symbolize? This question may be approached in terms of what the wearer intends or what the observer understands, or in terms of the history and culture that has shaped both, even if neither is fully aware of such influences.

A common theme in semiotic analysis is to highlight how texts operate through the creation of oppositions within the text itself. Oppositions can be created by combining certain concepts under one unifying theme and then distinguishing this unity by setting up an opposite, which again unifies a certain set of themes (Box 20.4).

BOX 20.4 CONSIDER THIS

Binary thinking

Words are handy symbolic devices that allow human beings to refer to things and actions when they want to communicate with other human beings, but that is not the whole story. Words refer to concepts, and often in an unclear and complex fashion, and concepts are defined in relation to other concepts, not directly in relation to things external to language. Discourse analysis gives primary attention to the use of binary oppositions between concepts in the conduct of meaning making in social activity. The boundaries of the term 'love' can only be constructed in relation to other terms such as 'hate', 'indifference', 'friendship' and 'desire'. Being relational and not fixed, such a term, as with all terms, remains fluid for all our attempts to pin it down.

In a war 'our side' is brave, fearless and committed, and the enemy is warlike, crazed and fanatical. We cause collateral damage, whilst they engage in mindless killing. We make an alliance whilst they form an axis. Good and evil, them and us, progress and backwardness, male and female, old and young, black and white, imperialist and communist (in the binary opposition of the Cold War), even Pepsi Cola and Coca Cola, Nike and Adidas; such pairings highlight the power of binary thinking.

Semiotic analysis involves the examination of texts to identify the relationships within and between signs. Within signs there is the creation of unity. Between signs there is the creation of opposites. Creating the impression that something is black or white, in other words that it is either one thing or the other, or that a situation involves the clash of one unity against another unity, is a common characteristic of texts. This may be seen as creating impressions of the world that serve to reinforce certain ideas about what is true, good and beautiful. The task of the semiotician is to identify the mechanisms by which such impressions are manufactured.

At one level it is enough to identify the use of certain signs within texts and to identify how certain signs are built up and set against each other to create a 'representation' of reality. However, the most significant aspect of semiotic analysis lies in the study of myth (Lévi-Strauss, 1979; Barthes, 1967; 1973) and difference (Derrida, 1972; and for very useful introductions to Derrida and deconstruction, see Norris, 1982; 1987).

Myth

The concept of myth in DA refers to the situation where a sign becomes a signifier. This sounds odd and not in line with our common understanding of what a myth

Signifier	Signified	
(e.g. word: 'Snake')	(e.g. concept: 'Snake')	
Sign (denoted at surface level But can become a *Signifier* of a deeper connotation	*Signified* (at the deeper level) The Snake sign stands for the concept of Evil	
Sign (for Evil) When surface denotation comes to signify deeper connotation the sign becomes a *Myth*		

FIGURE 20.1 Denotation and connotation: signs and myths

is. For example, the word SNAKE acts as signifier for the signified concept of SNAKE (reptile with no legs). So the SNAKE sign is the combination of the signifier SNAKE (word) and the signified SNAKE (concept). But the SNAKE sign can be used for more than just recalling the concept of a legless reptile. In many cultures the snake stands for evil: in this case the SNAKE sign has come to stand for the concept/idea of EVIL. Here, then, the SNAKE sign is no longer just the combination of a SNAKE signifier word and a SNAKE signified idea/concept. The SNAKE sign acts as a signifier for a new signified concept, EVIL (see Figure 20.1).

It is not just in the study of classical mythic terms like 'snake' that we should look for mythic language. The study of advertising images highlights the way men and women, children and adults, suntans and shoes, dogs, hats and cars all come to take on the power of mythic signs, being filled with deeper meanings than just what is on the surface. Newspapers create mythic representations of criminals, which are constructed through images and language that build upon one sign to carry the meaning of another. Reading text and images for myths is one core dimension of semiotic forms of DA. News coverage, advertising, talk and text of all kinds can be 'read' for their mythic constructions – not that advertisers have the power to make audiences 'get' their message (see Boxes 20.5 and 20.6).

BOX 20.5 RESEARCH FOCUS

Why advertisers can't make us behave like Pavlov's dogs

Ivan Pavlov showed how dogs could be 'conditioned' to associate the sound of a bell with the arrival of food through regular association. As such, after sufficient conditioning the dogs salivated at the sound of the bell because they had come to link the bell with being fed. Primary conditioning refers to the making of associations between primary (already existing) desires and beliefs and new ones through systematic association.

(Continued)

(Continued)

Secondary and other levels of conditioning involve the attempt to make subsequent associations with previously conditioned desires and beliefs. For all their sophistication, advertisements are in large part trying to conduct forms of conditioning at various levels. But human beings are not so easily conditioned as dogs, in part because they cannot be confined in laboratories as were Pavlov's dogs, but also crucially because the process by which humans interpret messages such as advertisements involves far greater reflexivity and cross-referencing within their language, memory and culture. Because simple semiotic units of meaning exist only in complex webs of language it is never possible to programme human beings simply by presenting them with a regular pattern of association. Human beings always bring a wealth of other meanings to bear on each encounter and as such advertisers routinely find that only a fraction of their target audience get the message they are trying to put across, and even their getting the message does not mean all those individuals will then go out and buy the product.

BOX 20.6 CONSIDER THIS

The figure in the discourse: archaeology or ideology?

The conduct of discourse analysis can be seen as an attempt to unearth 'the figure in the discourse'. How does the figure of 'the student' emerge from the welter of material written about students today? How is the figure of the criminal, the pregnant woman, the child built up within text? The study of discourse for the purpose of identifying such emergent figures – the ideal-typical, stereotypical or archetypal patient, inmate or employee – has been taken in two very different directions by (1) those who wish to study such social construction work in rather the same way that an archaeologist would unearth the remains of an ancient civilization; and (2) those that seek to study representations in the attempt to criticize misrepresentations and to expose 'the truth' that hides behind such distortions. Michel Foucault's 'archaeological' approach refused to seek 'truth' as something external to 'representations'. For Foucault, powerful representations were integral to the construction of those who were being represented, rather than being misrepresentations that hid or repressed true identities that lay beneath. For critical discourse analysts the truth/misrepresentation distinction remains important, and their goal is to debunk misrepresentation and expose the truth.

Deconstruction

The concept of difference focuses attention also on the construction of myth-like combinations of meanings, but in a slightly different way. Derrida's method of deconstruction involves the identification of tensions within texts over the meaning of key terms. Rather than identifying the incidence of certain terms and concepts to highlight their associations and significance, the deconstructive method seeks to show that where the same term is used on a number of occasions in a text, that term often carries very different meanings. Derrida calls this the identification of *différance*. While, again, certain parallels with content analysis exist, such as the search for recurring terms, the purpose of deconstruction is to show how such terms are rarely able to contain themselves (being loaded with different meanings in different places – or sometimes with divergent meanings at the same time). While content analysis highlights recurring language to suggest connections, deconstruction highlights disconnections within recurrent use of the same language. For Derrida, all concepts are words overlapping with other words (see Box 20.7).

BOX 20.7 CONSIDER THIS

Words standing in for other words

Derrida makes the strong claim that all apparently clear and coherent terms are in fact metaphors masquerading as concepts, and that the appearance of philosophical and scientific clarity is always based at least in part on literary devices. Here are the most important such literary 'tricks':

- *Metaphor*: where one thing stands for another. The moon may be used to stand for the feminine. To say that rising unemployment is a 'tidal wave', or that immigrants are 'flooding' into the country, or that young people are 'wild animals', allows meaning to be migrated (another metaphor) from one set of terms to another. Talk of a 'demographic time-bomb' when we are discussing changes in the relative balance of births and deaths is pure metaphor; sometimes the term is linked to the idea that there are too many babies, and at other times the same metaphor is used to refer to there being not enough children to care for tomorrow's ageing population.
- *Metonym*: where an attribute of the thing being referred to is actually stated instead. Marks of gender, class and ethnicity are routinely used as markers of identity and taken to signify underlying characteristics.
- *Synonym*: where two terms are seen in most respects to mean the same thing. By a process of semantic differentials, associations can be created by slippage rather than reasonable argument. In the past the terms 'wife' and 'housewife' would be routinely equated such that the role of a married woman would be assumed to be one of domestic labour. Democracy, the West and the United States of America are often conflated as synonymous, when there are many reasons why this set of equations should be challenged.
- *Simile*: where a parallel is drawn between one term and another. Whereas it would be a metaphor to say that someone was a lion, it is a simile to say they are as brave as a lion, or that their love is like a red, red rose. Simile is routinely used to persuade by means of similarities and has the same power to create associations without logical support as does the use of synonym.
- *Synecdoche*: where a part is taken to stand for the whole, or vice versa. A crown may be used to stand for the monarchy, or the king for the nation, the apple for the tree etc. The logical fallacy of composition is routinely breached by means of synecdoche. If one black man can become the president of the United States, this is taken to show that all black men (and women) are free from discrimination and oppression in the United States. Stuart Hall et al. (1978) noted that British newspapers in the 1970s routinely printed photographs of violent criminals if they were black, but not if they were white, thereby creating the impression that a common characteristic of young black men was violent criminality, and vice versa.

(Continued)

- *Analogy:* where a parallel is drawn between two things that are said to have similar outcomes, even if the process is not the same. For example a famine in a part of Africa might be described as genocide if indifference and non-intervention are said to be driven by ethnic discrimination. The deadly outcome is the same, even if the deaths are not the result of direct acts of mass murder aimed at eliminating a particular group. Some Orthodox Jews claim that intermarriage between Jews and non-Jews, which leads to children that Orthodox Jews do not consider to be fully Jewish, represents a hidden Holocaust. Catholics use the same analogy with the Holocaust to describe the legalization of abortion. Feminists suggest that selective abortion in India, which has led to there being many millions fewer female babies than would have otherwise been the case, represents a female Holocaust. Analogy works by likening outcomes or functions. For example a bat's wing and a passenger jet's wing have the same function, but very different structures. Analogy is often falsely equated with homology, where the parallel is structural. A bat's wing and a human arm are homologous in structure, but different in function. We could make an analogy between a peacock's tail and human beings getting dressed up for a night out, but the two things are not homologous, any more than are numerous other parallels that are routinely drawn between nature and society.

The deconstructive method is to read text in fine detail and to focus analysis upon a very small number of details where it can be shown that the meaning of the text contradicts itself or overflows. Derrida uses the term 'aporia' to refer to such occasions. Such terms are placed 'under erasure', that is they have a line drawn though them to flag their contradictory meanings, and the consequence for the text of such multiple meanings is then explored in the wider text. As there is no clear and true language to set against that which must be placed under erasure, Derrida's method is to 'write under erasure', highlighting the contradictions, but never being free to write or think outside the limits of language itself. It is Derrida's contention that the words we use are not ones whose meaning we choose ourselves. As such, words do not correspond to a set of pre-existing mental feelings in our heads. For example, the term 'love' is one we use to express what we think is our inner feeling. We might have an inner feeling and believe that love is the word that best expresses the feeling we already have. But when we use the term 'love', we soon find that it is a word with so many meanings. For Derrida, words never express things or capture them. Words are always linked to other words and not directly to things. Words do not correspond to the world and are at best metaphors. A metaphor is one sign, which stands for another sign. Looking at a text we can highlight the use of metaphor. Often a metaphor is presented as though it were a concept that simply mapped onto reality in a direct way. But for Derrida language can never be a mirror on the world beyond language. Just as 'rose' is a word that can signify love, so 'love' is a word whose meaning is made up of links with other words. Trying to say what words really mean usually involves spirals or metaphor, simile and connection/comparison. All words carry the baggage of their links to other words and their metaphorical character always imports surpluses of meaning that add to, change and open the terms up to mean more than they might at first appear to. If the words we use do not contain coherence, and carry within them all kinds of circulating meanings, the idea that human beings simply say what they think and feel becomes problematic. Derrida sought to shock people out of their common-sense 'logocentrism' (the belief that words simply reflect prior thoughts outside language and in our heads) by asserting that writing always comes before speaking. This was of course only a metaphorical expression.

Myth and metaphor are in many respects similar and highlight the core of the discourse analytic method. It is to seek out the methods by which meanings are constructed within the text itself, how a sense of reality and order is maintained and presented through textual material (images, objects as well as words).

Manning and Cullum-Swan (1998) and Potter and Wetherell (1994) provide useful hints for the use of DA semiotics (see Boxes 20.8 and 20.9). These are hints that can be applied generally. Other specific themes will emerge from particular texts and combinations of texts once these initial steps are undertaken. Once again, it is useful to stress that in order to achieve these, a degree of coding of data may be useful if there is a large amount of text. This coding will be very similar to the open forms of inductive coding carried out in grounded forms of content analysis. The gulf between qualitative content analysis and DA should not prevent pragmatic use of useful tools as long as such tools do not become an end in themselves.

BOX 20.8 CONSIDER THIS

Applications of semiotics

Peter Manning and Betsy Cullum-Swan (1998) highlight the possibility of applying semiotic approaches to the study of McDonald's fast food restaurants. This could be through the study of the restaurants' menus (the organization of items into groups that reflect certain cultural values). It could be through a study of the experiences of those who go there (which could be based upon interviews of ethnographic participation and observation). Alternatively, it could be through an account of the company's attempts to manage its representation through advertising (by means of textual data collection and analysis).

BOX 20.9 CONSIDER THIS

Combining discourse analysis with other qualitative methods

Potter and Wetherell (1994) combine ethnographic, interview and textual materials in their discourse analysis of a television programme about cancer care. They provide a five-point list of themes for the discourse analyst. The list develops elements of the above discussion of signs and metaphors:

1 using variation as a lever
2 reading the detail
3 looking for rhetorical organization
4 looking for accountability
5 cross-referencing discourse studies.

Narrative analysis

Semiotics focuses attention upon what is called the 'synchronic' aspect of language. This means the structure of language at a given moment in time, the way signs are organized around each other to create a symbolic world of meaning. Thus it has paid less attention to what is called the 'diachronic' aspect of language, that is, how language changes over time. The meaning of signs can be studied in terms of their relation to other signs either at a given moment or as they change over time. The focus upon time and change is addressed more fully in forms of narrative analysis, although it should be pointed out that much of narrative analysis focuses upon stories recounted in the present of events and lives that occurred in the past. As such they are focused not solely upon changes in the use of language, but upon the way language is used to describe change. Narrative analysis is also interested in the constructions of meaning given at the point of telling. The relationship between the version of events as told now and the process of a life that such a story might seek to tell is a controversial one (see Box 20.10).

BOX 20.10 RESEARCH FOCUS

Careers, cycles, generations and personal narratives

Erving Goffman (1961) famously charted the career path of psychiatric patients through denial, resistance, acceptance and conformity to the role of being mentally ill. Accepting the role was said by the professional carers to be the precondition for getting better. The narrative is in the institutional expectation, in the patient's experience and in the researcher's account of both. Others have used the notion of career in the analysis of narrative accounts of illness and recovery (see Chapter 9 on autobiography). Life history and auto/biographic research will often focus upon the life cycle, with interview schedules geared to following the life course or path that the individual has followed. Research into the experience of generations or individual life histories will often adopt such a narrative structure. However, narrative analysis may also focus upon the way time is recounted or explained by the person being researched. Here narrative is about the way the story is told, and this is not the same as narrative as the history being recounted. Notions of career, life cycles and generations suggest social life has a narrative character beyond simply the way any one person will tell their story, yet the way individuals tell the stories of their lives using various narrative devices is not entirely separate from this. However, it is also not the same. Narrative analysis may attend to one or the other or both combined.

Catherine Kohler Riessman (1993) outlines a set of core analytical approaches to narrative in social research. Narrative analysis requires that the researcher collects data that are open ended in terms of the storyteller's account of events. This may be in the form of either open-ended interviews or textual data such as diaries, letters or autobiographical material. As Kohler Riessman was once told by an interviewee whom she had asked to explain a particular aspect of their life: 'Well, you know, that's a really long story' (1993: vi). To allow the analysis to focus upon this long story the data must be open ended.

Analysis involves more than just a focus upon the content, a chronology of events. The focus of narrative analysis is less on the events as on the way the events are described and located together in a meaningful account. While content may not always be disregarded, attention should also be paid to the telling. Kohler Riessman suggests three analytical foci: life stories, critical events and the poetics of telling. Although each is given a different priority in the work of different researchers, all three in fact combine in the analysis of all storytelling.

Themes for the researcher to attend to are the elements within a story, the sequence in which the elements are combined, the relationships drawn between the elements, and the plot devices and genre styles in which the stories are put together. All these elements can be analysed by means of the semiotic approaches discussed above, but the overall aim of narrative analysis is to give a sense of the storytelling itself (see Box 20.11).

BOX 20.11

NARRATIVE, PLOT, CHRONOLOGY, STORY

Jane Elliott (2005) points out the distinctions to be made between the following elements:

- *Chronology*: a set of events listed in sequence (temporality).
- *Narrative*: a set of events with an implied set of relationships between them (causality, even if only inferred).
- *Story*: the unilinear sequence of events in time.
- *Plot*: the sequence by which information is revealed, which may not be unilinear as storytellers may often start from the conclusion and then go back to the beginning, leave certain things out until the end, or just jump around between outcomes, causes, actions and contexts.

Elliott (2005: 9) goes on to discuss Labov and Waletzky's identification of the six essential characteristics of a 'fully formed narrative'. There six elements are:

- *Abstract*: a summary of the narrative – its meaning in a nutshell.
- *Orientation*: a contextual summary of what, when, where and who.
- *Complicating action*: the things that actually unfolded.
- *Evaluation*: an interpretation of what the action that unfolded meant.
- *Resolution*: how things actually turned out in the end.
- *Coda*: which places the meaning of the story in the context of the present (what this means for us today).

Analysis may also focus upon the coherence of an account, and tensions can be examined within particular accounts or between different accounts of the same event. Criteria by which stories are evaluated may be both those of internal validity, the coherence of the account, and external validity, the degree to which one account matches or differs from others.

Whilst much attention has been paid to the structures and devices used to tell stories within the traditions of literary scholarship and film studies (see Box 20.12), the value of these insights can be usefully applied to the study of how individuals recall their lives, how governments seek to construct their justifications for actions, and how professional bodies and media outlets seek to represent social change and the options that are available for the future.

BOX 20.12 CONSIDER THIS

Narrative, formal positions and structural oppositions in the first 20 minutes of *Star Wars*

George Lucas's (1977) original theatre release version of *Star Wars* (later to become *Episode IV: A New Hope*) opens with the line: 'A long time ago in a galaxy far, far away …'. Then follows the stylized title words 'Star Wars'. We can be sure that this film is within the science fiction genre. A rolling prologue then recedes into a star-speckled backdrop, the first line of which informs us: 'It is a period of civil war'. More background information locates the coming plot within a longer (but still, as yet, rather restricted) back story. Much is not revealed here as to the story into which we are being tossed. Numerous allusions are made over the coming minutes by various characters to what has clearly been a long-standing conflict, but at present the audience is only partially aware of the full context in which the action is set. As the prologue fades, the shot descends. A small spaceship moves rapidly into shot far above an unknown planet. It is flying away from us, rapidly followed by a second far larger craft which soon comes to dominate the screen. The first ship is under attack and is helpless against its far larger pursuer. We are thrown into the midst of a state of disequilibrium. It is only after 16 minutes that we see the hero's 'ordinary world' (a very dull world, he claims). This state of equilibrium has yet to experience the disruption that events we see above the planet are soon to bring.

The little rebel ship is captured, imperial stormtroopers crush resistance, and two droids escape to the planet below, one carrying a message from the ship's passenger, the imperial senator Princess Leia. Leia is captured by the evil Darth Vader who is searching for stolen plans for the Empire's new weapon, the death star. Leia denies knowledge. On hearing of an escape pod's launch Vader sends troopers to the planet, believing, correctly, that the Princess has sent the plans there. Vader tells the officer in charge: 'There will be no-one to stop us this time', implying a back story not yet revealed in the plot.

A shot of the imperial cruiser cuts via a diagonal curtain sweeping splice to the planet's desert surface, the escape pod, a path leading away from it, and the two droids now some distance from the landing point. The droid's argue. R2D2 squeaks, while C3PO repeats what he is saying, supposedly in rebuke, but of course in reality for the audience to understand. He is a translator after all. R2D2 claims he is on a mission. The two go in separate directions, as C3PO will not follow his companion. 'No more adventures,' he says, again implying past events that precede the plot itself.

A montage of wandering shots implies a long journey before C3PO, in front of a dinosaur-like skeleton, sees a transporter and imagines himself (gender implied but not specified) saved. A splice edit (like curtains closing) takes us from this to R2D2's journey into a rocky valley. He is watched, then followed, then stunned and captured by small cloaked and hooded creatures. R2D2 is carried to these Jawas' transporter, which of course is where C3PO, and many other droids, are also being held. Stormtroopers examine the pod landing site and identify droid parts and the path leading away from it. The next scene sees the droids unloaded at the farm of Luke Skywalker and his uncle Owen and aunt Varoo. Will the droids' path lead the Empire here?

Luke helps his guardians, but would clearly rather be playing pilots with his friends. He agrees however to do his chores first. The farmers buy C3PO and R2D2. In cleaning R2D2 Luke triggers Princess Leia's holographic message: 'Help me Obi-Wan-Kenobi; you're my only hope.' Luke is transfixed. This is Luke's call to adventure, the coming together of his mundane life on the planet's surface and the monumental events that are going on above his head.

Spaceships, droids, laser beams, starscapes and alternative worlds, alien creatures and strange costumes confirm that this film is within the science fiction genre, yet the classical orchestration – in its general themes and with its heroic string arrangement to introduce Luke Skywalker, trembling strings to introduce the threatened princess, clashing brass for the imperial stormtroopers and Darth Vader's appearance, a weaker string version of the same melody for the doomed rebel troopers defending the princess – tells us that this is also an epic. *Star Wars* is a 'high-concept' film and creates its own epic/sci-fi genre/tradition, yet even as it does create its own language, characters, settings, myths and history, this film conforms to classic models of narrative, character and plot development.

Tzvetan Todorov's basic grammar of narrative, as discussed in *The Poetics of Prose* (cited in Williams, 1998), extends Aristotle's theory of plot (an account of events with a beginning, middle and end). Todorov suggests narrative needs equilibrium, its disruption and subsequent return or reformation. Interestingly Todorov suggests that narrative structure requires these steps, but that their telling does not need to be linear (Williams, 1998: 53–4). So, in *Star Wars*, it takes 16 minutes for us to first see the hero's initial point of equilibrium, whilst the preceding time depicts the events that are going to destroy it. For the audience, via the plot, disruption (the Empire's violation of its own senate) comes before we are shown Luke's farming life.

Luke's family conflicts, over chores, the harvest and wasteful playtime, has him caught inside family obligation. He lives in a regulated space, with conflict at an emotional level, and where resolution takes place through compromise and reconciliation with his loved ones. This 'narrative of integration' can and is set against the counter 'narrative of order' unfolding above Luke's head and soon to descend upon him. Alien forces have undone the old order and seek, by violent means, the destruction of its defenders. Will Luke join this narrative of order, leave his home, and use violence to destroy the Empire, or will he stay and help his family? The early minutes of *Star Wars* play both of Thomas Schatz's (1981, cited in Denzin, 1991) narrative archetypes against each other. This heightens the tension in Luke's choice, not just to take up the narrative, but to choose between possible narratives. Only later do we learn that Luke's familial and galactic narratives are in fact one and the same.

The inversion of equilibrium and disruption that sees Luke's ordinary world only after 16 minutes means that the hero's journey only really begins at the 20 minute mark where he witnesses Leia's call for help. We, the audience, know much more than Luke at this point. At this point Luke is only really drawn to rescuing the princess because she is beautiful and because he is bored of farming. He does not even think to go looking for Obi-Wan, content until provoked only to dream of adventures. As such the first 20 minutes of Star Wars give us only the hero's ordinary world, his call to adventure and his initial refusal to heed the call. Other steps on Christopher Vogler's (1998) adaptation of Joseph Campbell's (1993) archetypal mythic narrative journey are yet to come. Vogler notes that George Lucas explicitly acknowledged Campbell's *The Hero with a Thousand Faces* in developing the narrative structure in *Star Wars*.

Within the opening period we are introduced to key characters – the plucky R2D2 and the complaining C3PO, the evil Darth Vader, a vulnerable princess, an adventurous Luke Skywalker – and

(Continued)

we hear of the mysterious Obi-Wan-Kenobi. We have then a hero (Luke), a nemesis (Vader), a friend (C3PO), a dispatcher (the messenger R2D2), a princess (Leia) and a donor (Obi-Wan, though at this point he has yet to give Luke his father's light sabre or teach him the gift of using the force). The princess's father and the rather dubious potential friend/rival to Luke (Han Solo) are yet to enter the plot and thereby complete Vladimir Propp's *Morphology of the Folktale* (1979). While critical of Propp's formalism, Lévi-Strauss's (2001) attention to the semantic content rather than the generic form of structural oppositions at work in mythology can be applied in complementary fashion. Good and evil, the light and dark sides of the force, are represented through the rebel alliance and the Empire, in the small ship caught by the big ship, in Leia's small but defiant resistance to Vader's towering power, and in Leia and Luke's white garb as distinct from Vader's black. Imperial stormtroopers (who oddly wear white armour) remain masked and faceless, as do Vader and the devious Jawas, while rebel troopers, Leia and Luke show their humanity in their faces.

Star Wars redefined and rekindled the science fiction genre in the late 1970s, yet it did so through a return, quite openly acknowledged by its director, to narrative, characterization and structural semiotic features of classic myth. This hero's journey does then conform to stories from a long time ago, but not just from a galaxy so very far, far away.

Summary comments on discourse analysis

David Silverman (2000: 824–5) suggests five questions that any researcher should ask themselves about their DA. He is discussing DA of interview data, but the list could be easily applied to the analysis of other forms of qualitative data, such as textual data, images and field notes.

1 'What status do you attach to your data?' Do you think of them as a window to the world beyond the talk or as a performance to be analysed as a social event in itself?

2 'Is your analytic position appropriate to your practical concerns?' Are you obscuring more than you are revealing with the conceptual models you bring to the data?

3 'Do interview data really help in addressing your research topic?' Would other data collection tools give you better access?

4 'Are you making too-large claims about your research?' What can you really justify?

5 'Does your analysis go beyond a mere list?' Have you moved beyond content to a sense of the underlying meaning in the discourse?

Doing conversation analysis

Conversation analysis requires recordings of naturally occurring talk (conversation between at least two persons). Conversation analysis transcription involves a much more elaborate set of indicators to identify the length of pauses, tones of voice, interruptions and simultaneous talking and so on than would be required in other forms of analysis (see Chapter 10). Because conversation analysis is based upon the examination of very small 'units' of conversation rather than the contents of large amounts of materials, the first question is: how do sections of talk get selected for such detailed treatment? The second question is: what does the analysis in conversation analysis amount to? These two questions are in reality interlinked as the selection of fragments is in large part dependent upon the analytic concerns of conversation analysts. Identified below are the themes which conversation analysts seek to highlight within talk and which they then seek to identify and explore through detailed transcription and further examination.

John Heritage (1997: 161–82) outlines six themes that constitute the focus of attention for conversation analysis:

1   *Turn-taking organization.* Conversation displays an orderliness that demonstrates the orientation of participants to each other and their shared expectations about how turn-taking is to be managed.

2   *Overall structural organization of the interaction – in specific cases.* The management of conversation involves the application of general expectations and orientations to unique encounters. The study of particular conversations highlights that people are not merely reciting scripts, but are creatively managing unique situations through the deployment of general principles.

3   *Sequence organization.* Conversations have beginnings and they conclude. Rather than focusing upon the intentions brought by participants to their conversations, something that is not directly manifest in the talk itself, conversation analysts are interested in the movement within a conversation from introductions, through the interaction, towards a completion and cessation of the talk. How do the parties to the conversation establish themselves, identify themselves, negotiate the presentation of information or requests for it? How do the parties to the conversation negotiate their exits? How are outcomes arrived at? Such processes highlight conventions and expectations which participants deploy and respond to.

4   *Turn design.* When someone responds to the previous speaker, they are following certain expectations and are demonstrating an orientation to the speaker. When a question is asked, or when someone speaks in a certain way, a reply is expected. In replying, the person replying is responding to the expectation. However, the way in which they respond is not determined by the question being asked, even if certain expectations are present. A reply may take a number of forms and move the conversation in a number of different directions.

5   *Lexical choice.* What words are chosen and how are they used? How might such choices influence the course of the conversation and what effects might they have?

6   *Epistemological and other forms of asymmetry.* Parties to a conversation do not bring the same resources or interests to the interaction. While such things as power, resources and motives are not the focus of conversation analysis as such, they become

of interest in conversation analysis when they are manifested in talk itself. A number of asymmetries draw attention to such differences:

(a) Asymmetries of participation occur when the shared expectations within a particular interaction mean that one party is given priority to speak either without being spoken back to or with little response from the other parties.

(b) Asymmetries of interactional and institutional know-how or routine occur when one party to a conversation demonstrates that they are practised in the discussion of the topic, while the other party demonstrates a lack of experience about the topic. Alternatively, parties may manifest different levels of interest in the conversation, or different levels of awareness or even consciousness.

(c) Epistemological caution and asymmetries of knowledge occur when those granted a certain status within the conversation seek to avoid commitment to a particular course of action or account of events. This may involve the use of distancing devices, technical language or claims to particular forms of privacy.

(d) Rights of access to knowledge are contested within talk, both in the form of requests for or denials to access and in the deployment of illicit forms of access, such as reference to secrets, invitations to secrets and the sharing of gossip.

Through attention to these themes by means of applying forms of content and discourse analysis to small segments of naturally occurring talk which have been transcribed in ultra-fine detail, the conversation analyst seeks to discover the complex order-creating activities that occur within talk. George Psathas (1995) sets out seven principles for the conversation analyst. While Heritage's list above sets out the kinds of surface phenomena that are looked for within talk, Psathas (1995: 2–3) provides an outline of the deeper processes which conversation analysts claim can be identified through theorizing the surface phenomena:

1 Order is produced order.

2 Order is produced by the parties *in situ*.

3 The parties orient to that order themselves; that is, the order is not an analyst's conception.

4 Order is repeatable and recurrent.

5 The discovery, description and analysis of that produced order is the task of the analyst.

6 Issues of how frequently, how widely, or how often particular phenomena occur are to be set aside in the interest of discovering, describing and analysing the structures, the machinery, the organized practices, the formal procedures, the ways in which order is produced.

7 Structures of social action, once so discerned, can be described and analysed in formal, that is, structural, organizational, logical, atopically contentless, consistent and abstract terms.

The goal of conversation analysis, then, is to demonstrate that talk displays a set of mechanisms and expectations whose application in various situations is specific, but whose nature is universal to talk. Conversation analysis is not interested in large-scale comparative samples as it seeks to generate a catalogue of specific analyses or how specific pieces of talk operate. Each such study should be published alongside the transcribed outline of the piece of talk being studied. Accumulation occurs over time and not in particular studies. While each study seeks to show the principles and expectations operating in that piece of talk, general principles emerge from the accumulation of specific case studies.

Given these orientations, the selection of pieces of text for detailed transcription and analysis may occur in one of two ways. Either extracts of talk are selected at random or the researcher carries out provisional forms of either content analysis or discourse analysis to identify the issues they are interested to examine in more detail. In principle, any selection should be as good a choice as any other as there is no attempt to have a representative sampling method. Given that all extracts of talk are talk, and all talk (as conversation) is assumed to display principles and expectations on the part of the participants, any piece of conversation should do. However, studies of particular organizations or issues by conversation analytic means (such as studies of doctor–patient interactions or parent–child interactions) may require attention to those types of conversation. In reality, conversation analysts engage in forms of selection that usually amount to informal content and discourse analysis and are sometimes formally so.

The question of what constitutes a piece of talk is an interesting one. How long is a bounded unit of conversation? Of course, we might reasonably suggest that at the minimum level a unit of conversation would be a matched pair of talk–response. Much attention has been paid to adjacency pairs (call–response pairs in which the call successfully – in most cases – generates an 'appropriate' response). Examples of adjacency pairs are many. Greetings tend to elicit a return greeting. Questions tend to elicit answers. Closing a conversation tends to elicit a counter-closure. Invitations tend to elicit replies. Complaints tend to elicit apologies or justifications. Beyond pairs, the amount of conversation that constitutes a sequence is determined by the closure effected by the participants. This does not require that a sequence is always the length of the conversation it is a part of. Shorter sequences of talk that have their own boundaries can be identified within longer conversations. Conversation analysts seek to identify segments that display their own boundaries.

David Silverman (2000: 831) provides guidance on how to do analysis in conversation analysis:

1 Always try to identify sequences of related talk.

2 Try to examine how speakers take on certain roles or identities through their talk (for example, questioner–answerer or patient–professional).

3 Look for particular outcomes in the talk (for example, a request for clarification, a repair, laughter) and work backwards to trace the trajectory through which a particular outcome was produced.

Silverman also identifies common errors in conversation analysis:

1 Explaining a turn at talk by reference to the speaker's intentions (except in so far as such intentions are topicalized in the conversation).

2 Explaining a turn at talk by reference to a speaker's role or status (for example, as a doctor or a man or a woman).

3 Trying to make sense of a single line of transcript or utterance in isolation from the surrounding talk.

Doing discourse analysis: newspaper articles about students

In the newspaper articles on students discussed in Chapter 19 and which were coded for in the matrix displays in Tables 19.4–19.7, the four themes of student finance, the value of a degree, student disruption and standards falling were identified. Elementary discourse analysis on each of these four themes is presented here.

Semiotic elements

Student finance   The two *Guardian* articles construct loans as a positive development, and they deal with the positive conditions of a supposedly typical student/graduate whose parents are relatively affluent, and who will get a good job based on their qualification. The second article asserts that loans are a positive development or inevitable 'realization' of global competition, treasury limits, taxpayer reluctance and general benefit to all. The 'problem' to be overcome is misguided fear. Loans and extending top-up fees benefit everyone. Demand has not been cut. Elite universities are not 'naïve' and will be guided by 'evidence and analysis'. The author is 'facing facts'. All these constructions present loans and the further extension of fees as a general benefit. Even the social mobility supposedly achieved by 50 years of grants will be extended by their abolition. Curiously, the new scheme is said to place financial responsibility with the student, but only once they earn enough to pay it back, yet one of the things that needs to be done to allow increased fees is to phase in the financial impact on 'families and students'.

In contrast the *Mail*'s focus is upon this 'impact' on 'families and students' of the middle class. The *Mail* points to a drop in student admissions of 4.5 per cent as evidence of student reluctance to take up debts, and the decline is greater for students from 'middle-class families'. Debts of £20k are 'crippling', recruitment falls are 'unprecedented', and a rise from 31.4 to 31.7 per cent in admissions from less-well-off backgrounds is said to be significant evidence that 'hard working families' in the middle are being squeezed. The use of the term 'middle class' is ambiguous, with reference being made to 'the better-off' and then to 'middle-income' groups as being the ones to suffer most. The *Mail* seems to blur the upper and middle into a general 'middle' and sets these against the poor, who it also claims are being given unfair access via 'social engineering', 'where deserving applicants [again from the undefined middle class] are sidelined in favour of [poorer] pupils with inferior qualifications'.

In general terms *The Guardian* aligns the poor and the rich, while the *Daily Mail* presents the poor as an undeserving threat to the 'middle class' (unclearly specified). Where *The Guardian* articles use rhetorical claims to reason, evidence and analysis set against irrational opposition, the *Mail* adopts a rhetorical language of angry common sense.

Value of a degree   This pair of articles is most interesting for the sheer divergence of their constructions of the very same question. *The Guardian* cites evidence over the life course of yesterday's graduates, while the *Mail* cites research looking at the first year of today's graduates' employment.

While life course earnings must be based on previous cohorts (who graduated in the significant past) and such cohorts graduated at a time when they were a tiny minority, it is claimed that PricewaterhouseCoopers' research shows that the 'premium' on having a degree has not changed even as graduate numbers have risen. How this has been calculated is not explained. That men from poor backgrounds and women in general gain most from a degree relative to members of those groups without degrees is explained as being largely the result of how little non-graduates in such groups earn rather than how much graduates from such groups do, and it is pointed out that the 'premium' is primarily gained by those with certain high-status degrees rather than across the board. Nevertheless, the article is concluded by two very positive statements from a senior academic and the education minister who both claim the research as supporting their policy of increasing loans and fees.

The *Mail* cites different research to show that over a third of graduates in 2004–5 went into 'non-graduate' jobs. It cites a student representative who declares surprise given government claims that there are plenty of graduate jobs. The *Mail* cites a number of manual and routine service sector jobs as examples of such 'non-graduate' employment, but does not question the nature of the 'graduate' jobs it cites, i.e. managers and teachers. Most managers do not have degrees and most teachers did not have them until recently. The meaning of 'graduate job' is curiously taken for granted, when the article is supposedly critical of claims that degrees are necessary for many of the jobs graduates actually do. The article cites research showing that graduate unemployment is half that of non-graduates.

These two articles, using different methods, come to diametrically different conclusions, highlighting that evidence does not determine opinion, and that the choice of evidence can easily be made to support one view or its exact opposite. The use of 'experts' and the quotation of statistics is common practice in the construction of claims. It allows the author to claim that what is said is more than just opinion; it is the view of an authority who has the right to assert their view as factual. The figure of the expert is an important one in discourse analysis but, as we can see, different perspectives find different experts to support their constructions, so the authority provided by one expert can be undermined by carefully setting it off against the view of another expert. This is rather what happens in 'courtroom dramas'.

Student disruption   *The Guardian* article on students lowering the tone of neighbourhoods starts with the claims to such disruption, with suggestions of 'Balkanization' (the break up of once apparently stable communities into hostile fragments – as occurred in the recent break up of the former Yugoslavia), house price decline, the threat to local shops and schools, and the poor state of multiple occupancy housing. It then goes on to cite a number of areas where this is said to be an issue. It then sets such claims off against counter-claims that university and student presence actually improves areas, and that students move to cheap housing rather than make houses cheap by moving to them. The one article that highlights problems with students is fairly doubtful over the claims being made that students are a problem.

The two articles on student disruption in the *Mail* are ironic in their diametric opposition to one another: one relating to heavy drinking, the other to religious sensitivities. The article about cheap beer presents a series of caricatures of student drinking along with a stereotypical image and caption about 'another liquid lecture'. A university vice-chancellor is said to be championing good behaviour, enjoyment and community relations in warning local bars not to promote cheap drinks to students. The example of free lager being given out is set against the claim that universities do not promote commercial organizations on campus. Students are presented as gullible, universities as moral and protective, local bars as predatory. Given the introduction of high tuition fees, and the increased commercial and consumer-driven forces in higher education, this image of the university playing *loco parentis* is a very particular and selective construction.

The second *Daily Mail* article concerns a student magazine and uses the term 'pulped' in its headline, but 'recalled' in the body of the article. The headline suggests a more extreme event. Interestingly the article cites the student union spokeswoman who explains why the student editor and three others were suspended from the student union for printing the cartoon, apologizes for any upset and offence, and defends the policy of freedom and responsibility (i.e. restraint) which curtailed free speech in the interests of avoiding offence. In this sense the article does not pass any judgement as to the merits of the course of action taken. However, the article ends with a picture of bearded Muslim men protesting and holding a placard which reads 'Slay those who insult Islam.' There is no indication that these men are protesting specifically against the student newspaper in Cardiff, but the inclusion of this image sets up a strong binary opposition between liberal self-censorship and radical religious 'extremists' who do not appear to respect the rights of others to have views divergent from their own. As such the article suggests one group balances freedom and responsibility, while the other is dogmatic and irresponsible.

Standards falling   In brief *The Guardian* gives coverage to the possibility that standards are falling, but in fact concludes that this is not the case. The *Daily Mail* has no such reservations, and using terms like 'bullied' and 'threatened' suggests that the government is pushing the acceptance of vocational qualifications upon universities, who are themselves keen to rely on the 'A level as gold standard'.

In general it is interesting to note that both newspapers quote students themselves, and both cite the education minister. Despite this, the two newspapers present very different accounts: *The Guardian* is more positive about both students and the minister's policies and claims, while the *Mail* tends to be more critical of student behaviour, standards and qualifications, and of the education minister Bill Rammell's claims that his policies are working. Again, what this highlights is that simply noting the content (i.e. reference and quotation from students and the minister) would not tell us much about the construction of the articles in which they are included. This is why discourse analysis is so valuable in getting past simple content.

Narrative elements

The value of narrative analysis is that it draws attention to more than just the elements within a discourse (the semantic meanings of different phrases or representations); narrative analysis attends to the flow by which those elements are combined (into syntactic structure). Some of this has already become clear in some of the above analysis of discourse. These narrative elements will be highlighted here.

In a number of articles, narrative sequence is used either to establish a proposition and then to support it, or to establish a proposition and then to knock it down. The *Daily Mail* uses the former strategy in all its articles, establishing with its headline not just the theme to be addressed, but also the frame through which the story is to going to be told. This is less true in *The Guardian*, which tends to use rather cryptic headlines that don't give a direction to the story and often don't even give a clear idea of what the story is about. The *Mail* tells you what it thinks in advance. *The Guardian* hopes its headlines will force you to read the article to find out. In two of *The Guardian* articles the initial proposition (that students lower the tone of neighbourhoods and that Wikipedia is undermining standards) is established as a claim, only to be systematically taken apart, with other evidence and expert views being used to pull apart the original suggestion. The three other articles start as they mean to continue, with support being added to further the initial proposition. These two strategies work in different ways, but each has the effect of asserting one view as correct and its opposite as being incorrect. It is interesting that in none of *The Guardian* articles is the notion of neutrality and balance in evidence. These are characteristics that liberal newspapers like *The Guardian* claim to promote, but while in some articles different views are expressed, when this happens the narrative structure is always set in place such that one group of opinions is set up to be knocked down by the other, rather than leaving each side equal ground to make their case and respond to the other. The *Daily Mail* articles always follow a strong line of argument, though in one case there is a twist in the tail. Where four articles establish their view from the start, the article on the withdrawing of the student newspaper in Cardiff is given a very neutral coverage, with voice given to the student union who decided to 'censor' the magazine. It is only the addition of the photograph at the end of the article that creates a binary opposition that throws into stark relief all that has gone before. This final framing acts to redefine what we have just read, from being a question of whether or not the cartoon should have been allowed or not, to a counter-position between those who would have such a discussion at all, and those that appear not to want dialogue but only to kill those who would offend their view. The neutrality displayed over the rights and wrongs of 'pulping' the magazine seems only to reinforce the framing of the protesters at the end as 'unreasonable'.

In short *The Guardian* and the *Mail* most often use a simple narrative structure in which an initial framing of the issue defines the article and is reinforced throughout. *The Guardian* deviates in two of its five articles, setting up a narrative of proposition to act as foil for a counter-proposition. The *Mail* deviates only once from the simple narrative form when it uses the 'twist in the tail' narrative structure in which one story is told, only to be turned upside down at the very last minute.

One last dimension of narrative can be mentioned here, and that is the use of stories about change. Routinely, authors talk about the past and the present and the relationship between them. Are things presented as getting better or getting worse? The article on Wikipedia in *The Guardian* starts by recounting the 'old chestnut' that student standards are falling (note my use of a narrative device to set this theme up as an old cliché), only to invert the narrative and go on to claim that today knowledge is becoming more free and more dynamic (all positive narrative forms). Then the metaphor of the American War of Independence sets Wikipedia in a tradition, a historical narrative of radical challenge for liberation. The articles on graduate employment play on narratives of expectation. Didn't we all expect there to be more graduate jobs and better pay for graduates? *The Guardian* supports an ongoing progressive narrative, while the *Mail* suggests things are getting worse. Expressions such as 'increasingly threatened' and 'unprecedented downturn' all set up narrative structures that suggest the change is not just happening now, but is part of a bigger trend. As such a small fall in student recruitment can be constructed as part of a longer-term decline, which makes it appear more significant. Defenders of the status quo will suggest things are specific 'blips' when a drop occurs, but will be the first to defend evidence of upturns as showing a positive trend. The minister, the vice-chancellor and the head of Universities UK all use this device. The claims that areas where students live tend to be run down is spun in two ways. One side claims that students lower the tone and value of areas they move into, while students and universities assert that because students are poor they move to areas that are already cheap and run down. The association between students and cheap housing does not prove which is causing what. Each side seeks to assemble the elements into a narrative such that the chicken and egg is set out so as to support their view.

Summary

Whilst discourse analysts are critical of the content analytic reduction of qualitative data to tables and charts via coding, discourse analysts often use coding techniques to contextualize the more detailed analysis they seek to carry out on either single texts or small subsamples of material. Discourse analysis can be pursued in a number of different ways, each with a distinct focus of attention. Semiotic analysis focuses on the construction of associations and differences within signs. The analysis of 'mythic' signs seeks to identify the way in which particular texts (words and/or images) carry deeper connotations than are manifestly denoted within surface content. Deconstruction focuses attention on the multiple meanings at work within seemingly coherent and singular textual productions (words or longer segments). Rather than looking for the deeper meaning, deconstruction seeks to show the absence of a deeper meaning below a surface level filled with multiple, often contradictory, meanings. Narrative analysis aims to identify the devices by which a text constructs time, genre, sequence, cause and effect, content and context. If we take someone's life story literally (as a true picture), we might overlook the literary devices at work within their storytelling.

Conversation analysis has its own rules for the presentation and analysis of naturally occurring talk. Most importantly, what is sought is an account of the machinery at work within the talk that relies neither on assumptions about the context beyond the talk nor on the assumed motivations of the talkers. Conversation analysis seeks to analyse the talk itself.

 ■ **Questions**

1 What is a 'myth' in semiotic analysis?
2 What aspects of language are of principal interest in deconstruction or narrative analysis, and how are these analysed?
3 To what extent can such divergent approaches as semiotics, conversation analysis, narrative analysis and deconstruction be used together, or with forms of content analysis?

■ ■ **Further reading** ■

Barthes, Roland (1967) *Elements of Semiology*. London: Cape.

Elliott, Jane (2005) *Using Narrative in Social Research: Qualitative and Quantitative Approaches*. London: Sage.

Kohler Riessman, Catherine (1993) *Narrative Analysis*. London: Sage.

Wodek, Ruth (2007) 'Critical discourse analysis', in Clive Seale, Giampietro Gobo, Jaber Gubrium and David Silverman (eds), *Qualitative Research Practice*. London: Sage. pp. 185–201.

TWENTY ONE

USING COMPUTER SOFTWARE: WORKING WITH NVIVO 8

Chapter Contents

By the end of this chapter you will be able to:

- **Create and manage data files within NVivo 8 project folders.**
- **Code files by creating and organizing nodes.**
- **Display results of coding.**
- **Create and use memos, attributes and models.**
- **Conduct a variety of simple and complex data searches within projects.**

Using the software

Nigel Fielding and Raymond Lee (1998: 13) discuss what they called the 'epistemological suspicion' which many qualitative researchers have in relation to computer assisted qualitative data analysis (QDA) software (CAQDAS). This fear is expressed in terms of the dangers of transforming QDA into quantitative data analysis. This rejection is, in many respects, similar to the rejection of content analysis by some qualitative researchers. However, as has already been pointed out, this rejection of content analysis is often over-played. Qualitative content analysis seeks to allow categories to emerge from the data, rather than being imposed in advance of data collection.

The use of computer software to assist QDA is advocated on the grounds that it speeds up the process of searching data, highlighting relationships, coding, modelling and building theory from the data. CAQDAS can be challenged for precisely these reasons, as many advocates of qualitative research believe that qualitative analysis should take time and is a craft. Such critics would question the view that doing things faster is always an advantage.

The use of computer software in quantitative data analysis is now more or less taken for granted, but the same criticism can be raised against statistical packages as are raised against qualitative data organizing software. Making it increasingly easy to store and analyse large amounts of data has led many researchers (beginners and more advanced) to ask meaningless questions. Lack of contact with the data themselves and a lack of understanding of the actual process of analysis leads to the production of meaningless outputs: garbage in, garbage out. Of course, this can be achieved with or without computer software, but the less time spent with the data themselves, the easier it is to ask meaningless questions. As such, software packages for anything have their dangers, but the advantages should not be ignored. It is not the intention of this chapter to tell the reader that they should or should not adopt CAQDAS. However, it is the case that without having tried it, it is not possible to judge. It is better, therefore, to understand the options and then decide.

A wide range of CAQDAS is available. These tools have emerged in recent years from simple text managers to more advanced and integrated packages that allow for coding, memoing, modelling and exploration of relationships. By far the most popular software currently available is QSR NVivo, formerly QSR NUD*IST (which stood for Non-numerical Unstructured Data * Indexing Searching and Theorizing). This software package will form the basis for the following discussion, though some attention will be given to a number of other specialist software packages that social researchers may want to be aware of. It is important to note that NUD*IST has undergone a number of updates. The following introduction seeks to enable the user to get started and be confident enough to learn more complex functions for themselves. If you have an older version of the package, the instructions below are still applicable. At the basic level, the upgrades have not involved significant change. However, what the programs do at the higher levels and how they present it will appear different from earlier versions. If you are using an older version of the software, you will have to remember this. If the exact name or location does not appear, then have a look around the window and in the menus. In the case of button name changes, the correct option should be fairly clear, though you may need to root around a little. If you have no package to work with, it is possible to download a free demonstration version by going to the QSR website at www.qsrinternational. com. This will enable you to follow the instructions below and to test each package if you are still undecided as to which to use or whether to use them at all.

The most confusing initial aspect of NVivo 8 is the range of options and the specific terminology and commands needed to operate within the system. The three most important ways of operating within NVivo are its *menu bars* along the top of each window, the *toolbars* below the menu bar in most cases, but sometimes at the bottom of the window, and the *context menus*. Context menus are opened by holding down the right mouse button. Context menus offer options relevant to the window you are in at any given time. Specific commands can also be executed using the function keys, but this option will not be discussed here as all these commands can be achieved by the first three methods outlined above. With more experience and with reference to the online **Help** you may wish to explore this option further.

NVivo provides extensive onscreen **Help** and tutorial advice online. This outline seeks to get you to the point where you can explore and use the package yourself with a reasonable degree of confidence. For more comprehensive and advanced information other sources are available. If you acquire a personal copy of the NVivo 8 software, the user guide and reference guide provide detailed explanations of every aspect of the package. Note that, if you are using NVivo under an academic or other site licence, you may not have direct access to these guides. If this is the case, then the user guide is available separately (Richards, 2002a; 2002b). Another useful text is Pat Bazeley and Lyn Richards's *The NVivo Qualitative Project Book* (2000), which comes with a CD-ROM that allows the reader to practise with examples on a no-save version of the software even if they do not possess the full package themselves. Other useful texts have been written by Pat Bazeley (2007), Lyn Richards (2005) and Ann Lewins and Christina Silver (2007).

This introduction takes you through the key aspects of QDA using NVivo:

1   creating a project

2   documents and document management

3   coding: nodes and links, stripes and reports

4   cases and attributes

5   memos

6   models

7   searching.

Note that all of what will be discussed relates to what has already been said about the nature of QDA. The software is designed to facilitate processes discussed in previous chapters. Of course, it is important to recall that no qualitative software will do 'analysis' quite in the sense that the term 'analysis' is usually used in quantitative research. What NVivo 8 is able to do is allow the researcher to organize and clarify a large amount of information so as better to see the connections that exist and discount those that may appear superficially to be present. Software allows the researcher to explore options and connections more easily. It does not do the thinking for you! The researcher is still the one who has to do the interpretation and the analysis. This should not be forgotten.

Creating a project

Before creating an NVivo 8 project you will need to clarify a few things about the textual data you are going to be working with. The data might be interview transcripts, newspaper transcripts, field notes or notes taken about archival materials. If you want to follow this guide to using NVivo 8 but do not have any data to work with, it will be a good idea to generate some. For the purpose of practice this material might be some newspaper articles downloaded from the internet, or some notes you have typed up from a book or article. Any textual material will do. If it is not currently in a computer text format you can type the material directly into NVivo 8 files (as will be explained shortly). Alternatively, NVivo 8 will allow you to copy Microsoft Word files and a number of other text document formats directly into NVivo files. Once you have some textual material, in electronic form or not, you can proceed to opening the **Launch Pad**.

On opening NVivo 8 you will be presented with the **Launch Pad** window (see Figure 21.1). This window contains a set of menu bars and toolbars but in fact these are all inactive apart from four functions, three of which are available as large buttons on the lower left side of the screen. From the **Launch Pad** you can choose to open an existing project (recent projects are also listed half way down the left hand side), create a new project folder (in which to store files and all the work you will undertake upon such data), look through the available **Help** options or exit

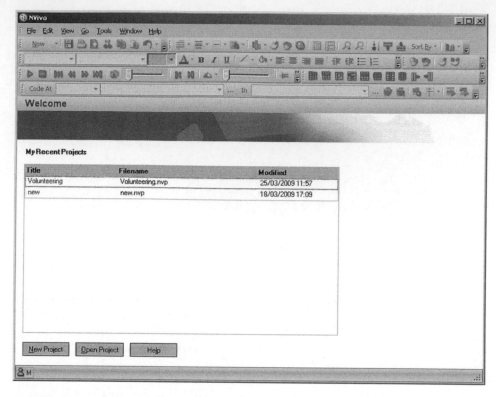

FIGURE 21.1 NVivo 8 Launch Pad window

NVivo. A project is one set of files and the analysis you carry out on them. You will need to create a project in order to then import or create textual files within it, which you can then analyse.

Click once with the left mouse button the option you require. If you want to create a new project, click the **New Project** button. You will be presented with the **New Project** dialogue box. You are then asked to give your project a title and a description. Do this and click **OK**. The new project will appear in the recent project title list within the **Launch Pad** window. If you have already created a project and are going back to it, then click the **Open Project** button when you first open the **Launch Pad**. You will then be asked to choose the project and go to where it is currently stored using the down arrow in the text box presented in the **Open Project** window.

Documents are the files containing textual materials you have collected. This might be interview transcripts, fieldwork notes, observations, media texts, letters and so on. It is best to keep specific texts as separate documents. If you have a series of field notes written at various times, keep each one as a separate document. If you have a series of interviews, keep each interview as a separate document. You can organize these documents into groups and hierarchies inside NVivo 8, as we will see.

Documents can be imported into NVivo 8, or they can be created in NVivo 8. If your textual material is in non-computer form, then you can create a new document and type in the content yourself (see below). If you have your textual materials in word-processing software files, you can create copies of the materials as NVivo 8 documents. In the past you had to save copies of your existing files in rich text format (.rtf) before importing them into NVivo 2.0 (and plain text format for N6). This allowed the software to read and convert content into old NVivo/N6 files (Box 21.1). NVivo 8 allows direct copying of Word (and many other text file formats) into NVivo files (.nvp).

BOX 21.1 HINTS AND TIPS

Saving a file to rich text format (for older versions of NVivo and N*)

To save a document as rich text format, open the document and select **Save As** from the **File** menu. Then, in the **Save As** window, select rich text format using the down arrow and scroll bar in the **Save as type** text box at the bottom of the window. Give the new copy a new name and select where it will be saved before clicking the **Save** button. The new .rtf document will be created and the original will also remain. With your textual materials ready to type up or with a copy of each file converted to .rtf, you are now ready to create NVivo/N6 documents.

Figure 21.2 shows what the **Project Pad** looks like. The project we will be working with here has been named 'New'. You will want to give your project a name suitable to what you are working on. As you can see, the **Project Pad** is set out like a virtual filing cabinet. A range of the options within the menu bars and toolbars are now active. The screen below the menu bars and toolbars is divided into three main parts:

- The bottom left section is set out like the drawers in a filing cabinet. Highlighting any one of these is like pulling out that drawer, and what is contained in that drawer then becomes visible in the section above.

- The second part of the screen is also on the left, but in the middle, between the first-level filing cabinet drawers and the toolbars. This part of the screen will highlight the sections within each virtual drawer below it. Highlighting a section in this middle level of the filing system calls up the content of those folders in the third section of the screen.

- The right hand side of the screen shows the lowest level of storage, the actual content.

Figure 21.2 shows the 'New' **Project Pad** open with the **Sources** 'drawer' highlighted, and within this the **Internals** documents are highlighted. As a result, on the right hand side the 10 newspaper article files about students (recall Chapters 19 and 20) are displayed. Click on any one of the document files contained and the file itself opens up below the list of documents.

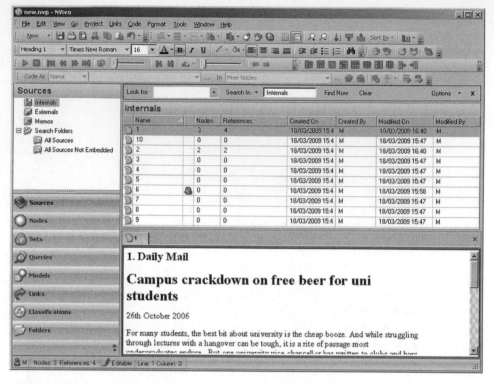

FIGURE 21.2 NVivo 8 Project Pad window – with internal sources highlighted

Figure 21.3 shows the 'New' **Project Pad** open with the **Nodes** drawer open and within that the **Tree Nodes** folder is open. Nodes are the coding themes, concepts and categories that the researcher identifies and tags through the texts they study (see below).

Documents and document management

To import an existing file from outside NVivo (such as a Word document or a rich text format document) into the project you are working within, or which you have just created, select **Import Internals** from the **Project** menu at the top of the window. This will bring up the **Import Internals** dialogue box (see Figure 21.4). Use the **Browse** option to locate the file you want to import into your NVivo project and select it. Then click on **OK**. Note within the dialogue box the option to make the newly imported document into a 'Case'. Defining a document as a case means that you can subsequently assign 'Attributes' to it. If all or some of your documents represent individuals or organizations or other cases, making an imported document into a case allows you to subsequently create a set of attributes about those cases (such as gender, age, ethnicity, income, employment type etc.).

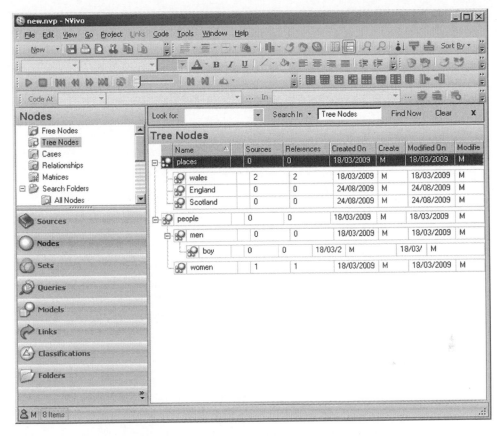

FIGURE 21.3   NVivo 8 Project Pad window – with internal sources highlighted

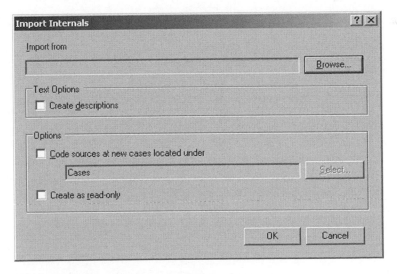

FIGURE 21.4   NVivo 8 Import Internals dialogue box

Attributes are like categorical variables (see Chapter 13) and, where documents pertain to cases, it may be useful to analyse attributes in a way similar to cross-tabulations in statistical analysis. This will be discussed in more detail below. You may not feel that cases and attributes are useful, but it is useful to recall that if you do want to assign attributes you need to designate your documents as cases at the point at which you create them or import them into NVivo.

If you want to create a blank NVivo document, which you will then type the data directly into, click on the **New** button at the far left side of the first toolbar, or use the **New Internal > Document** option within the **Project** menu. Note that in addition to documents, NVivo allows for the importation of audio and video files (which you may wish to explore yourself at a later point). A new blank document can also be created using the right hand mouse button when **Internals** is active.

Inside **Sources** and below **Internals** is the **Externals** folder. External documents are NVivo document files that summarize existing files which are either too large or of the wrong format to allow importing into NVivo or which summarize materials not available in any electronic format. A picture file might be an example of the former. External documents create files that the researcher can then fill with relevant ideas about what it is they cannot directly import into the software. As will be seen, links can be made between NVivo files and the original unimported files such that the researcher can jump in and out of their project materials to check their ideas.

Below **Externals** within **Sources** is the **Memos** folder. A memo is a note the researcher makes to themselves, either in the data collection process or in the analysis process. Memos are then linked to documents or passages within documents, or to codes that the researcher develops. Linking memos to other documents will be discussed later in this chapter. The researcher may create memos whilst coding a document with a specific link to that internal or external document. Memos are useful in tracking the process of analysis, especially when conducting a grounded approach to theory building.

New documents (either created or imported) are initially arranged alphanumerically in the right hand side of the **Project Pad** whilst **Sources** is the open section. Documents can be either kept in this alphanumerical sequence or reorganized as you choose within the **Source** window or copied into **Sets**. If you have a large number of documents already, or if meaningful sets already suggest themselves to you, create sets now. You can always rearrange them later. Otherwise, you may wish to leave documents in the all documents folder for now. Sets allow the researcher to organize documents into groups that are meaningful in terms of the research process or its emerging key concepts. To create a set, select **Sets** in the cabinet structure on the bottom left hand side and use either the **New** button, the right mouse button or the **New Set** option within the **Project** menu. This will open up a **New Set** dialogue box, where you need to provide a name for the new set. Once you have clicked **OK** the new set will appear within the **sets** selection. You can now copy and paste existing documents to the newly created set, adding sets to structure the organization of your data as you see fit. A quick way to add documents to your newly created set is to use the **Add Set Members** option within the

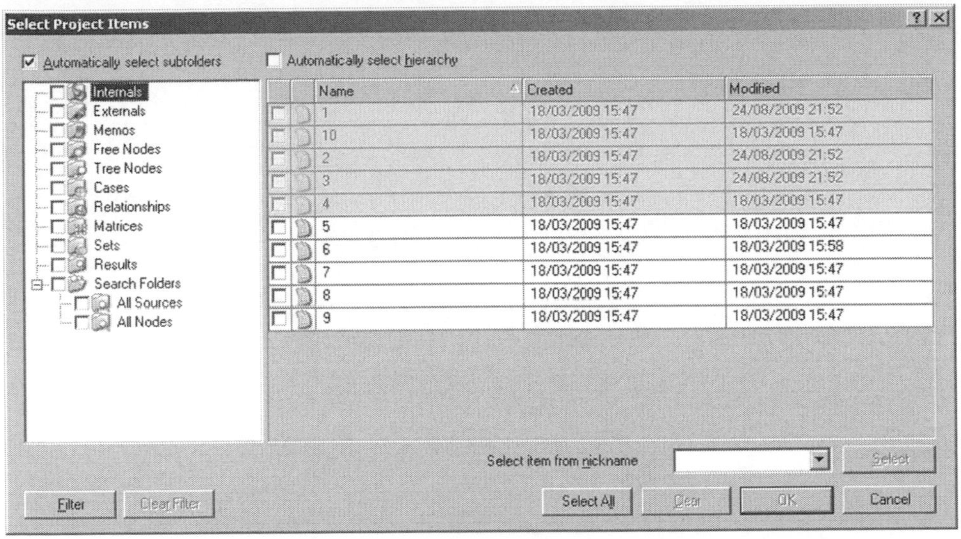

FIGURE 21.5   Select Project Items dialogue box

Project menu or from the right mouse menu that becomes available when any particular set is highlighted. Selecting **Add Set Members** offers you a dialogue box with a menu of all available documents to select from (see Figure 21.5).

Note that in Figure 21.6 the space between the listed items within the *Daily Mail* set and the currently open content of item 3 is filled with three little tags, highlighting that all three of these documents are currently active, with item three currently at the front. You can have a series of such items (documents in this case) open at any one time and you can easily flick between them.

In addition to saving documents and projects, it is useful to back up projects, that is, create dated copies that can be returned to if subsequent problems arise. This is achieved by selecting **Copy Project** from the **File** menu, and then selecting where to save the copy through the subsequent dialogue box.

Coding: nodes and links, stripes and reports

Within NVivo, documents can be coded through the creation of nodes and the linking of words, passages and whole documents to those nodes. Other kinds of links can also be made between documents. As has been discussed before, coding is the basis of content analysis and can be either deductive (the application of prior codes drawn from theory to textual data), inductive (codes being drawn from the texts themselves) or through the grounded folding of data collection and theorizing. NVivo 8 allows either top-down or bottom-up coding, and any combination of the two. The researcher creates nodes to hold categories for thinking about their data, and if they wish, coding of documents. These may be terms that emerge from

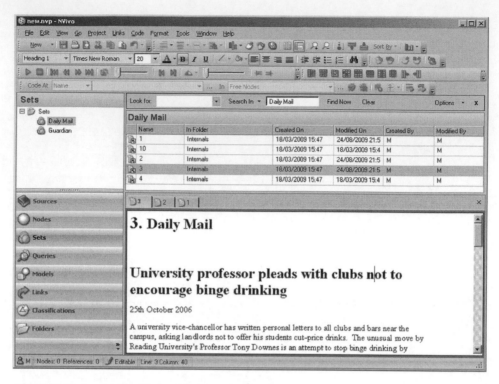

FIGURE 21.6 Project Pad window showing Sets

the texts being analysed, or terms that the researcher generated from prior literature. Coding is done (see below) by the researcher reading through all documents within their project, placing references (as will be explained below) at the node to all relevant items of text. This is the electronic equivalent of going through paper documents and marking text with a highlighter pen, using a different colour for each code. Then it is possible to 'ask' NVivo (using various techniques to be explained below) to show references and patterns that may exist between the themes coded for.

Bottom-up coding is where the researcher generates their codes during or after reading their texts. Top-down coding is where the researcher sets up their codes by creating nodes in advance of reading their texts. Once nodes have been created, references to other segments of text can be added. Nodes can be reorganized, internally and externally. Coding stripes make patterns more visible. All these options are discussed below.

Coding up from the text

With one or more documents in place it is possible to browse them, that is, open the file to read the contents. With a document open, from within either **Sources** or **Sets** the researcher can read the document. Coding up from the text means looking for things within the text to use as elements within a coding frame, or

FIGURE 21.7 Highlighting text in a document activates the Coding bar

what NVivo calls 'nodes'. In Figure 21.7 the phrase 'binge drinking' has been highlighted. The researcher may start to think that drinking alcohol is a theme routinely associated with students in the media, and that such drinking is often labelled as 'binge drinking', making the association between students and drinking even more negative.

By using the left hand mouse button the researcher can highlight a single word, or a whole paragraph, or in the case of Figure 21.7 a phrase. When any text is highlighted within a document, immediately the **Coding** bar becomes active. To create a new node from the text up, however, we do not want to choose an existing node, but rather create a new one, so we use the right mouse menu when the desired segment of text is highlighted (see Figure 21.8). Selecting **Code Selection > At New Node** requires that you then give the new node a name. The new node will then be stored in the **Nodes** section of the virtual filing cabinet (between **Sources** and **Sets**). Initially this node will be a free node and will be coded only to the one piece of text you linked it to. Subsequently, you can link this node to other

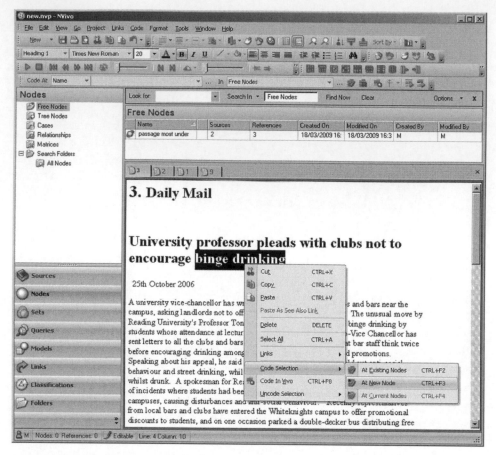

FIGURE 21.8 Creating a new node from the text up

segments of text throughout the project and reorganize the node within a tree structure if you wish (see below). If you had chosen the **Code In Vivo** option immediately below the **Code Selection** option (see Figure 21.8) NVivo would have created the node for you with the string of text selected as the node's name. This node would have then been created just like any other.

Coding may develop up from the text in a number of different ways (recall Chapter 19). The researcher may seek to code for interesting themes that emerge as they browse texts or they may wish to read through a number of documents before deciding what codes to choose and what segments of text to code. In either case, once a node has been created it is easy to highlight new segments of text and to instruct NVivo to link that segment to an existing node.

Within NVivo, nodes are organized either as free nodes or into 'trees' and 'sub-trees' (directory metaphor) which are also called 'parents' and 'children/siblings' (family metaphor). At first we will look at free nodes, which are not organized in any hierarchical or meaning-based way. Later we will look at the creation of nodes in the areas of trees and cases. Text can be coded up from the data in two main ways: by using the word(s) in the text (*in vivo*) or by typing in the researcher's chosen name for the node.

Coding from the top down

It is perfectly possible to create free nodes, tree structures and sets prior to coding the data themselves within NVivo. Whether this is because the researcher has a prescribed list of codes they want to use, or because they have begun to analyse their data 'by hand' prior to using the software, is not important here. If the researcher chooses, they can create nodes, trees, cases and sets which have no initial content. Creating a new free node (a free node is a node not located in a tree structure) is achieved with the **Nodes** section open in the bottom left corner of the **Project Pad** and with the **Free Nodes** folder open above this. A new node can be created using either the **New** button, the right mouse menu or the **New Free Node** option within the **Project** menu. You will then be asked to give the new free node a name within a **New Free Node** dialogue box. You can then provide a description for the node if you wish. Click **OK** and the new free node will be added (in alphanumeric sequence) to the existing list of free nodes, which are displayed on the right hand side of the **Project Pad** when the **Free Nodes** folder is open (see Figure 21.9).

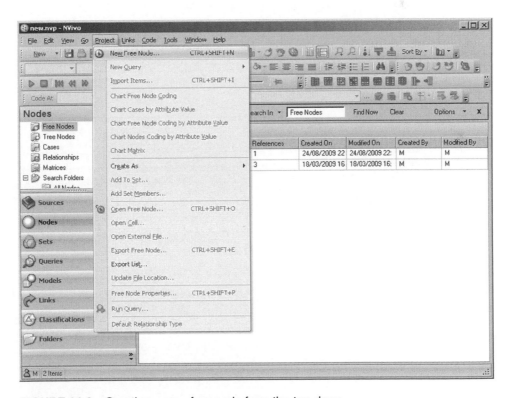

FIGURE 21.9 Creating a new free node from the top down

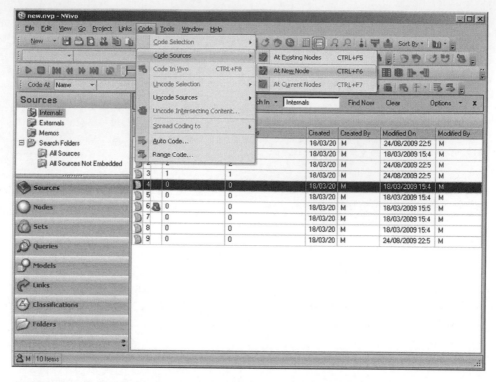

FIGURE 21.10 Linking a whole source document to a new node

NVivo has another way of linking a whole document to a node. From inside the **Sources** folder, highlight a document. Using either the right mouse menu when the document is still highlighted or using the **At New Node** option within the **Code** menu a node can be created and automatically linked to the whole source document (see Figure 21.10). You can then link (code) other sources or segments of sources to that node (see next section). Select the node you want to link to. This window can also be accessed to link any place in the text to a node, using the **NodeLink** button on the toolbar at the top of the individual document window.

Coding text at existing node/codes

Making a link (coding) between a segment of text within a source and an existing node within NVivo requires the researcher to have the document open in the **Sources** section (browser) on the right hand side of the **Project Pad**. They then need to highlight the word, phrase or segment of text they wish to code at the existing node. Once the text is highlighted, the options on the **Speed Coding** bar become operational. First it is necessary to select the node you want to have the new item of text coded at. If the node you want to code at is one of the last 10 nodes used or created, you can select it using the down arrow next to the text box

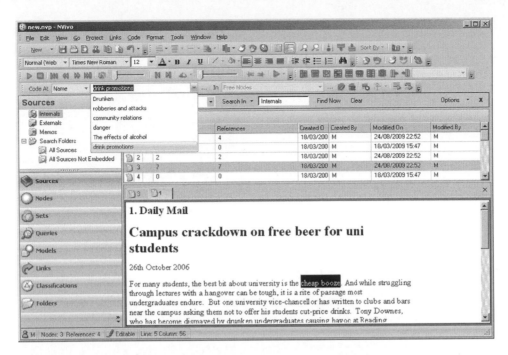

FIGURE 21.11 Coding at an existing (recently used or created) free node

on the **Speed Coding** bar (see Figure 21.11). If the node you want to code to was not used or created within your current session (since you last opened the project) the node can be selected using the **Code Selection > At Existing Node** option within the right mouse menu and in the **Code** menus. These menus give you the option to uncode if you want to deselect a link between a node and a segment of text.

Once nodes have been created and segments of text have been coded at those nodes, it becomes possible for the researcher to examine this coding. You may for example wish to see all the text that has been coded at a particular node. To do this, select the node you wish to display the coding for (see Figure 21.12). One thing that you might find when displaying the selections of text that have been coded to a particular node is that the segments on their own are rather too narrow to allow the researcher to compare their meanings. For example, in Figure 21.12 four elements of text have been coded to the node 'community relations' but some segments are very narrow and others wider, and the meaning of 'community relations' is not clear in each case. By highlighting all the coded text in the display window and selecting the **Coding Context** option within the right mouse menu, you can choose to widen the text around the coding as you think fit (see Figure 21.13). Be aware that if you use the **Spread Coding to** option within the **Code** menu, and then choose to widen the text around the initially coded segment, these changes will be permanent and you will not be able to go back to the narrow coding you had initially selected. As such, it is better to code narrowly and use the right mouse **Coding Context** option when seeking to contextualize your

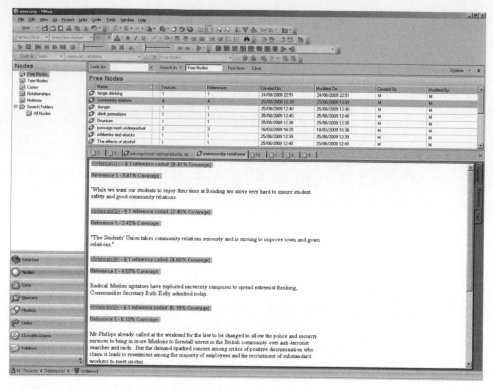

FIGURE 21.12 Showing the source text coded at a particular node

text selections. Coding to large chunks of text will make things harder when comparing large numbers of coded segments, and as you can expand your context if necessary (as just explained) then coding narrowly with the option to contextualize is the more flexible choice.

If you are coding up from the text you may generate a large number of nodes that are not organized in any particular fashion. These are free nodes. This accumulation of nodes may lead to two things. The first is the realization that the content of your nodes needs reorganizing (that your coding needs to be reallocated). The second is the realization that the nodes need to be placed in a more structured order (that you need to move from free nodes to tree nodes).

Reorganizing the contents of nodes

We have already seen how to uncode a passage or word in a document. Simply highlight the coded text and uncode it using the **Uncode** option in either the right mouse menu or the **Code** menu. To delete a node altogether, it is necessary to highlight the node in the right pane of the **Project Pad** and, using either the right mouse menu or the **Edit** menu, select **Delete**.

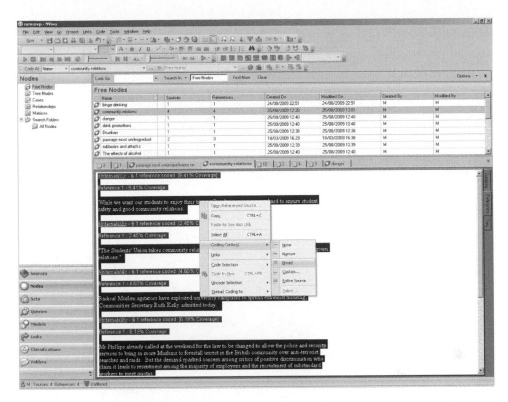

FIGURE 21.13 Selecting the broad context for sections of text coded to a node

In order to merge two nodes together, in the right pane of the **Project Pad** highlight the node to be merged (called the 'source') and then select **Cut** (or **Copy**) from either the right mouse (context) menu or the **Edit** menu. Using the left mouse button, highlight the node that you wish the first node to be merged with (called the 'target'). Then, from the right mouse context menu or the **Edit** menu on the menu bar, select **Merge Into Selected Variable** or **Merge Into > Selected Variables**. In the **Merge Variables** dialogue box you have various options to tick as to what will be merged, and on clicking **OK** the two existing codings from the source variable will be merged into the target variable. The option to merge attributes and memos is also available at this point. The question of what attributes are will be dealt with in the next main section. In addition to the coding, any hyperlinks from the source node will be added to those of the target node under the target node's name.

If it is felt that some of the current coding at a particular node is better removed, or coded to another node, it is necessary to go through the text coded within the node. In each instance, select the coded text in the node window; code it to the more suitable node and then uncode it via the **Uncode** button as described above.

Reorganizing the management of nodes (trees and sets)

Free nodes are the usual first step in coding up from the text. However, once a number of nodes/codes have been set up, it may become clear that some nodes/codes are subsets of others, or would be better ordered in that way. For example, missing friends back home might be one subset of homesickness in general, while missing family might be another. Missing family could, of course, be broken down into further subsets. Community relations might in fact best be divided into a number of subnodes rather than being kept as a single unified category. The organization of nodes/codes into trees allows for such a hierarchical organization of nodes/codes.

With the **Nodes** section of the virtual filing system open it is possible to select the **Tree Nodes** folder in the mid left hand section of the **Project Pad**. This will open up the **Tree Nodes** explorer window on the right hand side of the **Project Pad**. You can either create a tree structure out of new nodes, or copy existing free nodes (and their existing content) over from the **Free Nodes** folder by means of cut and paste. Figure 21.14 shows how a node already copied from the **Free Nodes** folder can then be pasted into a tree node structure. In this case it was felt that various nodes relating to student drinking could be organized into a tree structure. With the **Tree Nodes** folder open it is possible to create a new node using the **New** button, the **Project** menu or the right mouse context menu. In the case of Figure 21.13 the new tree node to be at the top of the new structure was called 'Drinking'. By using the **Copy** option in the **Free Nodes** folder it was then possible to select the 'drink promotions' node and paste it into the tree structure below the top level node 'Drinking'. By making a copy of the node to be pasted, highlighting the node that the copied node is to be placed below, and then selecting the **Paste** option, the copied file will be located below the highlighted node (Figure 21.14). It is worth noting that once a tree structure has nodes located above and below each other within a hierarchy, small plus (+) or minus (−) icons appear to the left of those nodes that have other nodes below them. When the tree structure is opened up fully to reveal what is nested below each level within the hierarchy, minus signs appear; clicking these collapses that level of the hierarchy so that those elements below are hidden, and a plus sign appears that will allow you to expand the hierarchy again if you so wish. Nodes above and below each other are referred to as parents and children, or branches and sub-branches. Nodes located at the same level are referred to as siblings.

To create a new node within an existing tree structure, simply highlight the node that you wish the new node to be situated below and select the **New > Tree Node** option from the toolbar, or the **New Tree Node** option from either the **Project** menu or the right mouse context menu. You are then presented with a **New Tree Node** dialogue box in which you are required to give the new node a name and have the option to also give a description.

If you wish to move an existing free node to become the top of a new tree structure, then the process is the same as was described above for copying a free node as a child/branch within a tree structure already in place.

Once a new node has been created, text can be coded to it in the normal way using the various techniques already discussed. If an old free node has been moved

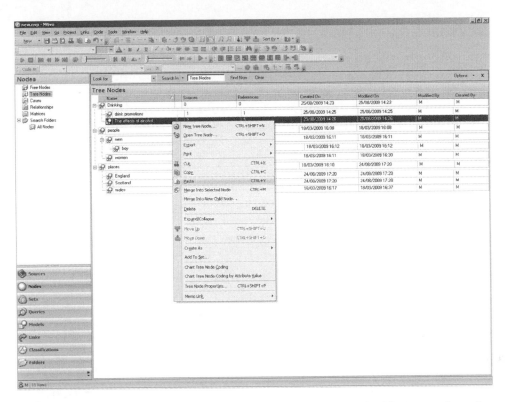

FIGURE 21.14 Pasting a copy of the free node Robberies and Accidents as a branch of The Effects of Alcohol node, itself a branch (alongside Dring Promotions) of the tree structure Drinking

to become a child within a tree, then its existing coding to documents and text will be carried over into the tree structure. Sometimes the content of the newly located node can be left as it is. However, it will often be the case that in creating a tree structure the text coded at a node moved into the new tree structure will need to be split up between the siblings. For example, in creating the subcategories of 'Friends' and 'Family' within a general category of 'Homesick', the links to the 'Homesick' node will need to be split between the subcategories. Browsing a node's coding (using the node browser window) allows the researcher to recode relevant passages to each of the child nodes. Because the free node will retain all the original coding, it is always possible to go back and see what you started from, even after you have chopped the contents of your pasted tree node around.

Node sets allow for the organization of nodes in groups that are not sufficiently hierarchical to be located in a tree node structure. It is important to recall that the structure of the node folder is such that the icons for a particular node can be placed in a number of different places. After copying and pasting the icon of a free node into a tree node structure, or into a set or a case node folder, that icon will then appear in both places. Cutting a free node and then pasting it somewhere else will remove that node from its original location. It is advisable to use copy and paste rather than cut and paste as your **Free Nodes** folder remains as a general location for all your nodes, even when you have undertaken all sorts of other activities and organizations of your data. Sets can allow for provisional explorations of connections without excluding future possible reordering work.

Coding stripes and highlighting

When you have coded your text, one initial method of looking over the content of your codes, the context in which your coded material is situated, and the relationships between the materials coded within a text, is to use coding stripes. Coding stripes are a graphic device to show what areas of text have been coded at which nodes. Stripes are coloured lines running the length of coded passages (see Figure 21.15). The use of coding stripes provides a useful visual summary of what is overlapping with what. To view coding stripes, select the **Coding Stripes > Selected Items** option within the **View** menu. If you have already carried out a coding stripes selection you may need to clear this by selecting the **Coding Stripes > None** option and then going back and selecting **Coding Stripes > Selected Items** again with a blank slate as it were. The **Select Project Items** dialogue box is then displayed and from here you can select which nodes you want to show. If you have copied nodes from the **Free Nodes** folder into a **Tree Nodes** structure, remember not to select both as this will produce two stripes for the same coding. Once you have selected the nodes you wish to display stripes for, click **OK**. The selected nodes will then have their coding stripes displayed down the right hand side of the document browser. Note also that in Figure 21.15 in addition to coding stripes a number of nodes have had their coding highlighted in the text itself. Just above the **Coding Stripes** option within the **View** menu is the **Highlight** option. By this means it is possible to select one or more nodes and to have the text coded at those nodes displayed in the document browser. The **Highlight** option is useful in some situations but, as the highlighting all comes out in the same shade, such highlighting can blur the boundaries between segments of text coded at different nodes, where coding stripes highlight the different nodes in different colours whilst marking proximity and overlap through the relative position of each vertical line. The researcher can choose for themselves how and when to use these different options.

Cases and attributes

Attributes are characteristics that apply to 'cases' (people, places, events and so on). Recall that a document (source) can be designated as a 'case' only at the point at which it is imported into NVivo, so if you wish to use the attributes functions within this software, it is necessary that you tick the **Cases** box in the **Import Internals** dialogue box (see Figure 21.4). People have attributes such as age, residence, income, attitude towards politics and so forth. Attributes in NVivo are characteristics that the researcher chooses to pay particular attention to and are assigned a range of values (for example, age values, values for the number of rooms

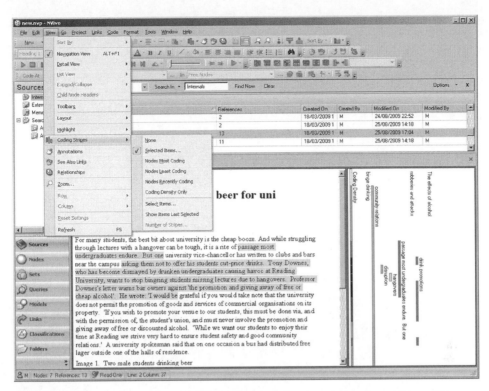

FIGURE 21.15 Coding stripes highlight what has been coded under which nodes

in that person's home, or values for the number of times each week they exercise). Each source document designated as a case is assigned one of the values attached to each particular attribute. For example, in the case of a student experience project, each student document (each student's response being recorded in one document and designated as a case) could be assigned values for the attributes age, gender, experience and living (in other words, type of accommodation). For age the values would be bands of age (an ordinal variable). For gender the value would be nominal (either male or female). For experience the value options might be positive, negative or both. For accommodation the value options could be student housing or family home. Giving each document attribute values enables the production of attribute matrices (see discussion of Miles and Huberman in Chapter 19). Attribute matrices highlight the variation within the group according to the attributes selected. The basics of attribute creation and matrices production are outlined below. The NVivo **Help** menus give extensive explanation of the more advanced use of attributes, and these processes will not be discussed here.

Creating attributes and values

When you import a source document and make it a case, NVivo creates a special type of node for that file. Just as you might go through ordinary documents

FIGURE 21.16 Within the Case Node folder opening the Casebook

coding to nodes within your **Free Nodes** and **Tree Nodes** folders, so documents that have been made cases have this special node as well. The coding that will be assigned within this case node represents the values of the attributes that each case has. Case documents can be coded to free and tree nodes just like any other document. Only source documents designated as 'cases' can have attribute values coded for. Figure 21.16 shows six case nodes created for six source documents. Selecting the **Cases** section from the lower left side of the **Project Pad** allows case nodes to be viewed in the browser window. Each source document contains the profile of an academic sociologist, and contains information they put down on their web page. As such, each document is a textual representation of how that academic presents themselves to the world within the limits that their university places on how they can do so. Looking through these profiles it was decided that

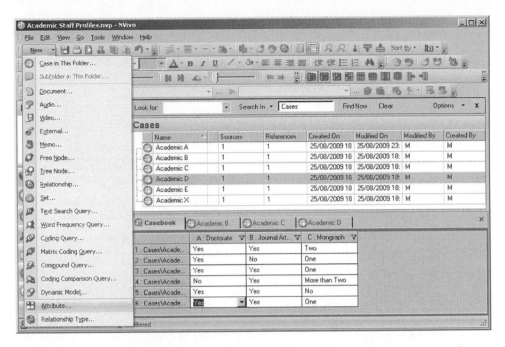

FIGURE 21.17 Creating a new attribute in the Attribute Casebook

key academic attributes were a doctorate (PhD), monograph books, and articles published in international peer-reviewed academic journals. These attributes can be given values (such as yes/no, a number, a band). Detailed qualitative analysis might allow the researcher to judge the status of the university from which an academic received their doctorate, the status of their book publisher, or the relative impact of the journals they write in, but here it will be kept simple. Figure 21.17 shows the case folder open with three attributes created. Each row represents a case, and creating new attributes will create columns. An attribute is created by selecting **New > Attribute**. The **New Attribute** dialogue box has two parts. The first part (**General**) asks you for a name and description. The second part (**Values**) asks you to specify the values. Figure 21.18 shows the second part of the dialogue box. Default values of **Unassigned** and **Not Applicable** can be added to (with valid values) using the **Add** button, which creates rows that you can write values into. In Figure 21.18 the values **Yes** and **No** have been added in relation to the attribute of whether an academic has a doctorate or not. The default is that a value has not been assigned, and when the attribute is created (by clicking **OK**) you can then assign the correct values for each case in the casebook by selecting the correct values in the cell where that case (row) crosses that attribute (column).

Attribute tables constitute one form of the matrix diagrams discussed earlier in relation to the presentation of qualitative research data (see Chapter 19). Various options exist for the editing of tables created in this way. This will involve some

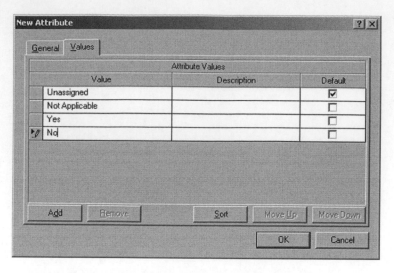

FIGURE 21.18 Adding values to an attribute

degree of either editing down when selecting from the **Explore Document Attributes** route or editing up when starting from the **Attributes** icon of a particular document. Rows and columns can be selected or deselected, values edited, and formatting changed to create made-to-measure tables, which can then be exported into other software formats (for example, word-processing or statistical packages). More detail can be found using the NVivo **Help** pages.

Memos

Memos are notes to oneself, or an audit trail of ideas emerging in the course of research. Memos can be linked to either nodes or documents. Node memos are documents where the researcher can record the process by which a node emerged and changed over the course of the analysis. Document memos record additional information the researcher may feel they want to record about the text. Memos are not the 'data' texts, and when it comes to searching the data using the **Search** tool, texts that are marked as memos can be excluded from the scope of the search, or specified as included. This allows the researcher to input their comments without those comments becoming a part of the data.

To create a new memo, highlight the source document or node that you want the memo to link to and follow **Links > Memo Link > Link to New Memo**. You can give the new memo a name and the memo text box allows you to record your thoughts (see Figure 21.19). You can add to these whenever you wish, and can view any memo by double clicking on the memo icon which will be displayed alongside the name of any document or node that has such a memo in the relevant browser. You can create a link to an existing memo in just the same fashion as above, only choosing the **Link to Existing Memo** and then selecting the desired

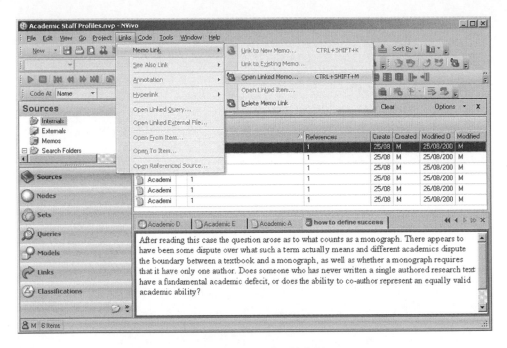

FIGURE 21.19 Highlighting a Memo Link via the Link Menu

memo accordingly. You can create and link to existing memos also using the right mouse (context) menu when a document or node is highlighted.

It is also possible to make memos and link them to segments of a source document in the same way as has just been explained in relation to whole documents.

Hyperlinks and other links: external links and external documents

In older versions of NVivo and N* the creation of links to external documents was relatively complex, but now it is possible to simply insert a hyperlink into a source document or into a memo as you might into a word-processing document or a web page. Select any segment of text, then select the **Links > Hyperlink > New Hyperlink** option. The subsequent dialogue box will ask you for the web address, which you can then either type in or browse for. If, alternatively, you wish to link to an electronic document held outside NVivo but within your computer, such as a file that cannot be imported into NVivo for size or formatting reasons, then follow the **Links > See Also Link > New See Also Link** option, and select the document from your computer drives.

Models

NVivo offers the facility to create visual representations of relationships and patterns that begin to become apparent as the researcher explores the links

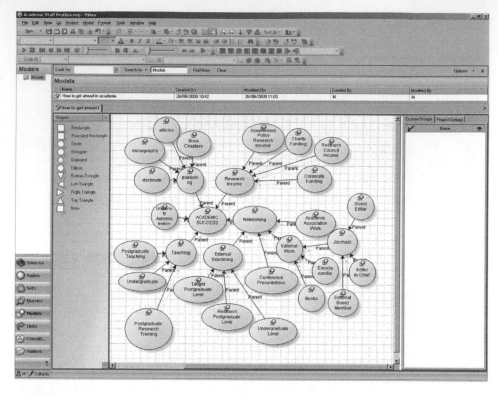

FIGURE 21.20 A model displaying the tree node structure for Academic Success

between various texts, nodes and cases. From the **Project Pad** click on the **Models** button. This opens up the **Models** explorer window (see Figure 21.20). The left pane of the **Models** explorer allows you to select existing models (if any have already been created within the project), to create new models and/or to name files. To create a new model, select **New > Dynamic Model in this Folder**. The **New Model** dialogue box will ask you for a name and description, and once given and **OK** is clicked, a blank model grid becomes available to work within. The model can be constructed within the right pane of the window. Here it will be explained how a simple model can be put together. With more experience you should be able to develop more sophisticated models, but a grasp of the basic ideas is sufficient here.

In the model presented in Figure 21.20, the tree structure of the 'Academic Success' project is displayed in its hierarchical format. Within the **Models** explorer window you can either add shapes and lines to create your own model or else select nodes and documents from the project you are working in and place these in relation to one another in the model. Using either the **Models** menu or the right mouse context menu, select either **New Shape** or **New Project Item** depending on which you want to add. If you select **New Project Item** a dialogue box will then ask you to choose which documents and/or nodes you want

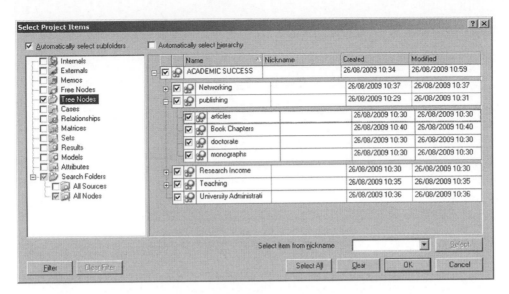

FIGURE 21.21 Selecting project items (in the case tree nodes) to build a model

to add (see Figure 21.21). Once the items you want to use have been selected, you will be asked whether you want to show relations and other features of these items (such as the items that might be nested within or below them). Click **OK** and the items and their links will be inserted into your model. You can then add other elements and shapes, as well as move the items around to create a visually clearer representation of the relationship you are seeking to model.

The models you create are saved as you go along, and you can make multiple models and mix elements from different models once you have created shapes and patterns that do what you want them to. You should practise with making models by playing with both the shapes and the project item options. Models are useful tools for setting out your initial hunches about your data, and can be useful as you go along in working out in your own mind what is going on, and how your analysis is developing. Models are one way of visualizing the relationship between ideas and are therefore a very useful way of making abstract ideas visible, both to aid the researcher's thinking and also to allow them to share their emerging ideas and to generate discussion about them. Models have the same value in communicating 'finished' theorizing.

Searching

NVivo allows you to search in three main ways. Cases and attributes are a search form that is structured in advance and has been discussed already. The other two main forms of searching are find searches and query searches. Find searches allow the researcher to locate project items such as source documents, cases and nodes.

FIGURE 21.22 Using the Find bar within the List Pane to locate documents or nodes

Query searches on the other hand allow the researcher to locate content from within such items (such as text or coding within source documents).

Find searches

NVivo 8 has a **Find** bar at the top of the list pane (see Figure 21.22). Typing in the name of a source document or node that you are interested in and clicking on the **Find Now** option will search for that project item (sometimes referred to as an 'operator'). If you want to restrict the fields in which the search is carried out, use the **Search In** dropdown menu. If you want to save the results of such a find search, then select the items within the results that you want to save (holding down the **Control** key and selecting each item in turn with the left mouse button) and select **Create As > Create As Set** from within either the **Project** menu or the right mouse context menu (see Figure 21.23). You will then be asked to give the new set a name and a description. It will be saved with all other sets in the **Sets** section of the **Project Pad**. Find searches can also be initiated through the **Tools** menu options.

Also within the **Find** bar is the **Options** button from which you can choose to carry out an **Advanced Find** search. This allows you to select the characteristics and the range of project items to be searched. For example it would be possible to search only through the case documents where the value for the 'doctorate' variable was **Yes**. Within the **Advanced Find** menu is also the **Group Find** option. NVivo defines **Group Find** as follows: 'Grouped Find enables you to list selected items and find the items related to them. For example, you can list: sources and the nodes that code them; Select the sources to include in the scope; Select the required range of nodes; The resulting list only includes nodes that are in the selected range and that code the source; Select the required range of nodes; The resulting list only includes nodes that are in the selected range and that code the source; Nodes and the sources they code; Attribute values and the matching cases; Nodes or sources and the items they have a relationship with; Nodes or sources and the items they link to; Project items and the models they appear in' (NVivo 8 **Help** menu).

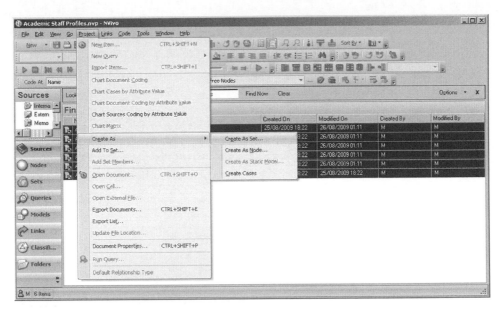

FIGURE 21.23 Saving selected items as a set using the Project > Create As > Create As Set option

Query searches: simple, compound and matrix

Text searchers are more likely to show you the interesting qualitative relationships that you are interested in, as you are able to examine the patterns within the data themselves. Whilst a find search can show you all the text coded to a particular node or within a particular document, the query search options give you scope to undertake more in-depth searching, and may be used either as a way to code or as a way to move beyond coding to more discursive analysis of the relationships within the text language.

Within the **Queries** section of the **Project Pad** select **New Query > Text Search** if you want to undertake a simple search for a particular item of text (see Figure 21.24). This text search option allows you to look for individual words or phrases, variations of words (using the **Wildcard** feature in the **Special** menu: see Figure 21.25), where different related words occur, or where certain words appear close together. The **Special** menu offers a range of useful means to achieving interesting search outputs and is worth exploring. Use the **Help** menu also to learn how best to take advantage of these various options, which are based on Boolean searching and Venn diagrams. The very basic forms of such searching are AND and OR. An AND search will only return items where both selected terms are present, whilst an Or search will return items when either one or the other term is present. Within the **Text Search Query** dialogue box, within the **Query Options** folder, you can choose whether to save the results of your search in a number of different node formats, or to simply preview the results without saving them.

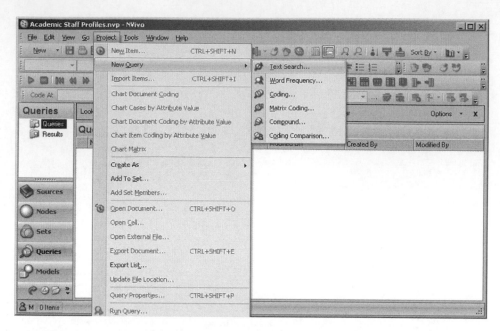

FIGURE 21.24 Selecting a New Query > Text Search within the Queries window

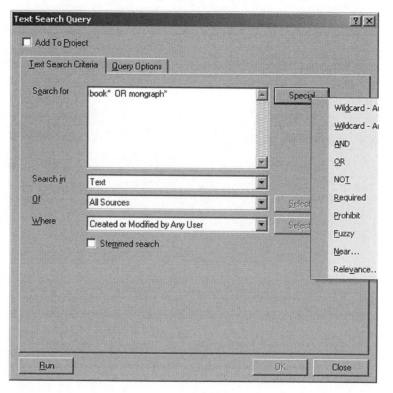

FIGURE 21.25 Using special features in a text search query

As you can see in Figure 21.24, there are a range of other **Project > New Query** search options. **Word Frequency** queries show the number of times an expression is used, whilst **Coding** queries bring up the number of times a node has been coded for. These are both very useful search options for exploring your data. **Matrix Coding** allows for cross-tabulations of a sort similar to attributes and values within cases.

One of the most useful query search options in NVivo is the **Compound** search option. This allows all sorts of choices about how to search for relationships between text in your data. For example, if you wanted to see how often two elements of text were located close together within source documents, then a **Compound** search allows you to identify two text elements and ask to see all the instances where those two elements are located close to each other. The degree of proximity can be specified narrowly or widely and the exact space can be defined. You can also choose which sets of source documents to search when conducting such a search. As such, if you had many newspaper articles about students, you might want to see how certain key terms related to each other. Is it the case that references to foreign or overseas students are linked to negative or positive associations, words and expressions? Selecting **Compound Query** from the **Project** menu brings up a dialogue box in which you can specify a number of criteria. First you need to specify whether the search will be a text search or a code search using the first dropdown menu box. From there, you can specify the search terms to be used via the **Criteria** option. Figure 21.26 has the **NEAR Content** option selected within the second dropdown menu. If this option is selected you will then have to select the kind of 'near' you are interested in. The **Options** button allows you to choose. The option selected here is **Custom Context**, and this then requires further specification in terms of number of words, surrounding paragraph, or within a whole source document.

Analysis?

What NVivo 8 is able to do is allow the researcher to explore the relationships that exist within their data. What it is best able to do is to allow clearer presentation of patterns within what is often complex and tangled textual material. This is the meaning of analysis in this context. What the term 'analysis' does not mean in this context is the intellectual process of identifying what such patterns might mean and whether or not they are significant. This is still the task of the researcher.

Alternative QDA software

NVivo 8 is certainly the most popular dedicated qualitative data analysis software. However, this does not, by definition, make it the best package for every person or for every job. Different tasks may require different tools, and different users may find different software packages more to their taste. One thing to remember is that much of the elementary work of qualitative data analysis can be done just as easily

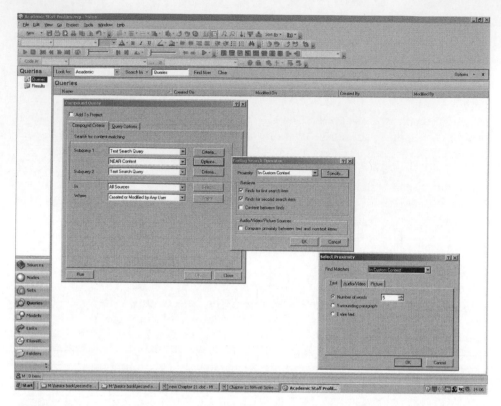

FIGURE 21.26 Specifying the custom context to define 'Near' in a compound text search

using a word-processing file as it can using a dedicated software package. If you do not want more than basic word and phrase searching, then there is little value in investing in QDA software. Similarly, if you have only a very small amount of data, analysis by means of reading and rereading the data, making memos by hand, and squint analysis, followed up by written reflections upon the findings, may give as much insight as any software. Still, dedicated software has its uses and here two other QDA software packages will be briefly mentioned.

ATLAS.ti

This software package is in many respects similar to the NVivo 8 software. What makes ATLAS a little different is the emphasis given in its design to the analysis of graphical, image and audio file data. The constructions of files, coding, memos and searching are all supported within ATLAS, as they are in NVivo 8. What ATLAS focuses upon is the capacity to index a number of graphical, image, textual and/or audio files within a project for the purpose of coding, searching and analysing. NVivo 8 is most useful for text files in the more limited sense of the term 'text' (that is, just written words – without scope to import even formatting conventions). Most of what NVivo 8 is designed to allow analysis of is just plain text. NVivo, however, does allow for any document to contain hyperlinks to files which are themselves not able to be imported into NVivo itself. These documents can then be given content that describes and records the key features of the original file. And the links can be coded and assessed to bring up the picture, video and so on. This is much the same as what ATLAS enables. Through ATLAS it is possible to apply codes to specific non-text files, and then to search these codes for patterns. While this attention to the searching of non-text files is smoother in ATLAS than in NVivo 8, it is not something that cannot be paralleled in either. The reverse is also true. ATLAS allows the researcher to carry out processes similar to the coding, memoing and searching procedures available in NVivo. For further details go to www.atlasti.de.

The Ethnograph

The Ethnograph in its original format was one of the earliest QDA software packages. It retains some of the earlier simplicity of formatting that sets it apart from the more complex formats of software packages that try to offer everything all in one. The Ethnograph allows the creation of projects, the importing, creation, storage and indexing of files, the coding of those files, the creation of a code book of free and tree-based codes, and the searching of the project's files for patterns in the distribution of codes. It is not as complex and offers fewer additional functions, but is quick to learn and use. For more information go to http://www.qualisresearch.com/.

Summary

Qualitative computer software enables the researcher to manage large amounts of textual data and to conduct forms of content analysis. The forms of content analysis that such software can facilitate cover the spectrum from highly deductive forms of quantitative content analysis to highly inductive forms of qualitative research. In each instance data analysis involves making a link between codes and particular instances of text within the data. Links and patterns between items coded in such a way can then be highlighted, mapped and modelled using various functions within the software. While qualitative data analysis software offers speed and efficiency in the mapping of large quantities of textual data, it is still the case that the process of coding requires that the researcher works through their data files, making the links that will then form the basis for analysis. Computer assisted qualitative data analysis is still a labour-intensive activity. In addition, while computer assisted qualitative data analysis offers speed and efficiency in the coding and exploration of large quantities of textual data, such software cannot 'analyse' data either in the philosophical sense of drawing logical and meaningful conclusions from data, or in the mathematical/statistical sense of providing clear, simple formulas or numerical patterns that 'sum up' the data. In so far as many qualitative researchers are suspicious of any attempt to reduce the social world down in such a way, this may not be seen as a problem. To the extent that such software may encourage the researcher to search for simplistic patterns in large quantities of data, some fear the creeping encroachment of a quantitative mentality into qualitative research. Others welcome such a move. The essential first step in such debates is to be informed enough to decide for yourself.

 **Questions**

1 What are the basic steps in the conduct of qualitative data analysis using NVivo?
2 What other qualitative data analysis software is available besides NVivo? You may wish to consult the World Wide Web to extend your answer to this question.
3 What are the strengths, limitations and dangers of using computer software packages designed to assist in the conduct of qualitative data analysis?

Further reading

Bazeley, Pat (2007) *Qualitative Data Analysis with NVivo*. London: Sage.

Lewins, Ann and Silver, Christina (2007) *Using Software in Qualitative Research: A Step-by-Step Guide*. London: Sage.

Richards, Lyn (2002) *Using NVivo in Qualitative Research*. London: Sage.

Richards, Lyn (2005) *Handling Qualitative Data: A Practical Guide*. London: Sage.

TWENTY TWO

VISUAL ANALYSIS

Aims

By the end of this chapter you will be able to:

- **Distinguish a visual experience and visual analysis.**
- **Identify the three main areas of attention in visual analysis.**
- **Recognize the main traditions of visual analysis.**

- **Be able to relate different forms of visual analysis to forms of data collection.**
- **Link visual analysis with the analysis of other forms of data.**
- **Critically evaluate the claim that visual material is not reducible to other forms of cultural meaning and effect.**
- **Address the question of whether or not modern Western society is a uniquely 'visual culture'.**

Introduction

The suggestion that we should never judge a book by its cover rather neatly sums up the attitude of many social scientists when it comes to the value of visual data. There is and has always been a strong suspicion that the visual is superficial and that what the researcher needs to do is get past such impressions and get to the 'real' causes or meanings that underlie phenomenal impressions. Yet, many expressions equate seeing with believing. The empirical tradition in science is replete with the equating of data with observations, which is another word for seeing. Experimental research is a form of observation where the researcher records observations numerically. Ethnographic forms of observation are 'written up' so that the data become the words recorded. Expressions such as 'seeing is believing' and 'do you see what I mean?' are badged as forms of common sense which the scientist should seek to 'look beyond', to use another visual metaphor (see Chapter 20). The suggestion that a picture tells a thousand words is greeted with the response that any picture we see in the media is going to have been posed, selected and possibly even manipulated in order to present events in line with a prior agenda that can best be understood by analysis of the textual discourses surrounding the image, rather than in the composition of the image itself. Whilst for some the most interesting discourses are those that surround the production of images, for others it is the discourses that surround the way an image is received and interpreted by audiences that should command attention. For a long time the content of the image itself was relegated to a rather marginal position in social science. Whilst art critics and design historians might discuss composition, and whilst archivists of the media and fashion might take an interest in the way photographs were composed and how the content of style changed, social scientists got on with the 'real' business of the statistically measurable causes and the linguistically explorable meanings that they considered to be the real basis of social life.

In many ways this has not changed. This chapter will suggest that indeed visual analysis is not visual analysis in the same way that statistical analysis analyses numbers or that textual analysis analyses words. Visual analysis relies on the use of numerical and/or textual translation, even when it actively seeks to avoid the reduction of images to other levels of social explanation and description. It will however be noted that, for some, visual analysis blurs into the conveyance of visual experience as a proxy for direct experience, a form of *verstehen* or 'being there' that the researcher believes visual images will allow their audience to share in.

Here the visual is used in a fashion almost akin to its common-sense usage as direct 'see what I mean' indexing of reality. This chapter will suggest that visual analysis is the analysis of the significance of the visual itself (its composition and content). Such analysis of the visual may rely upon textual and numerical modes of analysis, but this is not the same as saying that the visual is reducible to the causes or meanings that produced it, or into which it is received by audiences, or even the words and numbers by which an image can be described.

Images need to be understood in terms of the technologies that allowed their production (if they are humanly produced images), the social conditions of their production, their composition and their reception. As this chapter will suggest, different approaches to visual analysis are more significant for each of these four focuses of attention, but any attempt to understand images that ignores the element of compositional content ignores the specific significance of the visual, and as such is not really visual analysis at all. That is not to say that studies of media production or audience reception of images is not valid research. To put this simply, whilst many are suspicious of visual analysis, we should also note that even the most detailed account of an image (whether this be a photograph, a film, a painting, or even the view out of your window or from the top of your favourite hill) does not have the same effect on us as the image itself. A particular editing technique or perspective shot in a film, or the position we are given to assume as viewer in a painting, affects how we see things. These are all devices that can be described in language and/or numbers, but this does not mean that it is the description in language or numbers that is having that effect. It is only that such analytical devices are the only ones we have to comprehend the compositional features and content of images. That such devices do not always work should be set against the fact that they often do. We are influenced by the capacity of images to evoke feelings and to convey meanings that would be less well attained in words alone, or at least that is the possibility that makes visual analysis worthwhile, even whilst this should be complemented with attention to image production and reception.

Ethnography: visual analysis or experience

Visual data may take the form of already existing images, whether from research participants' private archives of photographs, or from mass and new media. Alternatively, the researcher may take their own photographs and films, or draw up their own maps and diagrams of their research field. In this section I will discuss visual analysis in ethnography because it addresses both forms of visual data analysis. Sarah Pink (2001) notes that observation-based ethnographic research has, strangely perhaps, typically regarded field notes as its primary form of data collection. The researcher observes, but then translates these sensations into text, and this text then becomes the data which the researcher seeks to analyse, whether this be in a grounded or a post-fieldwork fashion. She quotes C. Wright Mills: 'The modern project of ethnography has largely been "to translate the visual into words"' (2001: 96). Pink rejects the suggestion that this must be so, and suggests that the visual represents a separate 'mode' of data that do not 'merely' illustrate text. 'Images and words contextualized each other' (2001: 96). This raises interesting questions.

Pink is suspicious of attempts to reduce images to text, and this reflects her wider suspicion of positivism and reductionism in general. She writes: 'The idea that subjective experience can be translated into objective knowledge is itself problematic for reflexive ethnography. Therefore an "analysis" through which visual data becomes written academic knowledge has little relevance. Instead, ethnographers need to articulate the experiences and contexts from which their field notes, video recordings, photographs and other materials were produced' (2001: 97). It is being suggested here that visual data can be useful in conveying the 'subjective experience' of both those observed and the observer, even whilst textual 'articulation' is needed to describe what was going on, and even whilst text should not be used to 'explain' it. Pink is very aware that 'images' don't travel easily. She suggests: 'When they move from one context to another they are, in a sense, "transformed"; although their content remains unaltered' (2001: 95). Here lies the reflexive dilemma that all ethnography encounters. If the purpose of ethnography is to understand how a group, culture or community lives, and to do so in a holistic fashion, how then can such a whole 'way of life' be expressed to someone who was not there? They will only ever receive something less than the whole experience, and so will be unable to 'make sense' of the account given by the ethnographer, or if they do make sense it will be based on their own way of life. Visual data hold out the possibility of giving the ethnographer's audience something of the context, of the world in which particular actions and accounts make sense. The reflexive ethnographer knows that visual images do not translate fully, and that they require textual analysis, but there is the belief still that something is carried in the image that is not lost in the migration from field to home world.

Pink's questioning of the value of objectivist accounts in the social sciences frees her to place attention upon conveying the experience of the field for both researcher and researched. As such, for her, visual analysis often gives way to the exploration of experience by means of reflection upon visual records. This may involve asking the researched to reflect upon their personal visual archives, or the researcher reflecting upon their own visual data. These are both valuable research activities, even if the latter requires the researcher to be reflexive about their own reflexivity and increases the danger of becoming self-absorbed. If you have ever had to sit through a showing of someone else's holiday photographs and been bemused by the level of significance and meaning your 'friend' seems to be able to find in them, you will be aware that for all their belief that the meaning is in the image, it is very often only so for them. At least with the holiday photos, you can skim through them relatively quickly and have gained no real idea of what it was like; whereas to have to listen to endless holiday stories and remain equally ignorant of any really significant meaning might take hours. Cynics suggest that statistical tables perform the same function.

The problem for ethnography, that of how to convey a holistic sense of what went on to those who have no knowledge of the context in which such actions took place, and the place of visual analysis in overcoming this difficulty, cannot be resolved by assuming either that images carry meanings in an unproblematic fashion, or that images are simply screens upon which people project their own existing beliefs. Attendance to the significance of the visual allows the researcher to explore the middle ground between the extremes of objective experimental conceptions of visual data as an empirically transparent snapshot of reality, and subjectivist approaches that suggest that images have no carrying capacity and are simply filled with whatever context they happen to be read within. The remainder of this chapter will focus upon those analytical techniques that have sought to engage with the content of visual images and the relationship between composition and the contexts of image production and reception.

Modalities and methods

Gillian Rose (2001: 30) provides a useful typology of sites and modes of visual analysis. She suggests three modes of analysis and three sites of analysis. The three modes are focuses of attention: the technical possibilities (from oil paint to photography, and from the motion picture to television, with additional gradations such as the advent of the fast shutter camera or colour film and computer-based graphic manipulation); the actual composition of a work (its content and structure); and the social relations in which the work is located. All three modes can be studied in the three sites: production, content and audience reception. Very little social research has been carried out in relation to the technical modality of visual images. Instead most visual analysis in the social sciences focuses upon the relationship between composition and social modalities and the sites of production, content and reception. Different forms of visual analysis attend to different dimensions of this complex set of relationships.

Production, producers and technology

In Rose's presentation of the field of visual analysis (see Figure 22.1) there are no analytical traditions mentioned in the whole 'technical modality' column. This is in large part because social scientists have tended to focus upon the social modality. They have only recently begun to take a firm interest in the compositional modality, which was for a long time left to the humanities (whether this is art, film, architecture, criticism or history). Social scientists tended to focus upon the social contexts in which cultural products were manufactured, maintained and consumed, but did not have much to say about content. Art historians were critical of those attempts to explain cultural content in terms of social context, as a form of reductionism; and as social scientists were keen to avoid the reduction of their social domain to technological explanations, they gave technological issues a wide birth. Recently (David, 2006), art critics and historians began looking to social explanations to understand the content of cultural products,

	Technical modality	Compositional modality	Social modality
Site of production	How was it made?	Genre	Who, when, for whom, and why?
		Discourse analysis II	
Site of image itself	Visual effects	Composition *Compositional interpretation*	Visual meanings
		Content analysis	
		Discourse analysis I	
		Psychoanalysis □ Semiology	
Site of audiencing	Transmission, circulation and display	Viewing position offered, and relation to other texts	How interpreted, by whom and why? *Audience studies*

FIGURE 22.1 Re-visualizing the graphic visualization of visual research methods

and social scientists began to move the other way and explore the relative autonomy of the work of art.

Nevertheless, it should be borne in mind that technology plays a significant part in what is possible at the level of composition and social context. As has been suggested earlier, the idea that today's society is a more visual culture than previous eras is premised upon electricity and the chemistry that enabled photography and film. The combination of artificial light and images means that we can see more today than ever before. We sleep less than ever before. Whilst the advent of the photograph and the light bulb did not compel the subsequent development of society into its present configuration, the term 'affordance' allows us to point out that so much of how we live our lives today would not be possible but for these technical transformations in the scope of our visual experience.

This is not only at the level of technical production possibilities (the special effects possible using oil paint, camera lenses, digital recording equipment etc.), but also at the level of audience reception. Technical possibilities matter, but social scientists are suspicious of claims that such affordances determine outcomes. Hollywood narrative cinema parallels the development of new technologies, from spooling cogs, to outdoor cameras, to increasingly powerful special effects techniques. It is often said that 'mainstream' films are driven by special effects not meaning. That Hollywood films focus on image over meaning is to have global appeal beyond just English-language speakers. This is one reason that some social researchers think the content of visual culture is not worthy of attention (as it is generic and reducible to other social forces). Those that suggest there is value in the study of visual culture suggest that significant differences do exist in composition and that such differences have significant implications and even effects. Whilst technical possibilities should therefore be kept in mind, most attention has been placed on composition and reception.

Compositional analysis and content analysis

Gillian Rose (2001: 32) distinguishes between the 'good eye' of the art critic as connoisseur, and the rather more squinting eye of the content analyst. Whilst the connoisseur seeks to embody the feeling and knowledge of what is just right, to discern the sublime or beautiful within the totality of the image, the content analyst seeks to break the work down into its component elements.

Nevertheless, the two traditions of approaching the visual artefact in terms of its composition or its content are not entirely distinct and the social researcher may easily work with elements of both. Attention to materials used (whether these be types of paint, canvas, film or computer technologies) can highlight aspects of how an image creates the impression that it does. Colour has many facets that can be either noticed or coded for. Hue, saturation, lightness or darkness of colour or shading, harmony or contrast in colours used, the effect of using a restricted palette or even just monochrome or black and white, all add to the character of the composition. In addition to colour, artists use a range of devices to create optical illusions, most particularly the impression of depth, which can be achieved by means of either atmospheric perspective (the use of shades of blue to imply receding depth) or geometric perspective (the impression that objects are shrinking as they move towards a vanishing point on an artificial horizon line). Placing the horizon line high, low or in the middle of the vertical plane will create the impression of looking down upon, up towards or straight at the objects in the foreground, whilst angles and the relative locations of the objects in the image position the viewer in particular ways that they are not free to displace, even if they can resist the position that such a perspective is offering them to take up. Focal objects (in particular sources of light) draw the viewer's eye, whilst the dynamic tension of the golden mean (an off-centre position of a ratio of 1 to 1.6) is routinely used to focus the viewer's attention upon the action or element that the artist wishes to be the core of the image's meaning and significance. Using symbols, icons and metaphorical devices is another way that the composer may seek to embed meaning in their work, even if this meaning is not consciously read by the viewer. It may be one of the most powerful features of visual images that such colour, structure and use of symbolism are not consciously understood by the viewer (and thus are open to unconscious influence); but then again, what might have persuaded by the back door, as it were, might just as well get missed or go right over the viewer's head.

Whilst the traditional art critic or art historian shied away from mechanical forms of content analysis in favour of the impression of a natural awareness of what was significant and what was not, and whilst the act of breaking down an image into a series of elements may feel like an act of philistine reductionism, there is no good reason why such a breakdown cannot then be used to allow for a more detailed account of how the elements are combined within the overall composition. Just as qualitative content analysis can provide a firm foundation for more detailed and subtle forms of discourse analysis, so qualitative forms of image content analysis can provide the detail that precedes the depth that can be achieved by forms of semiotic and discursive analysis, as will be touched on in later sections of this chapter.

BOX 22.1 STOP AND THINK

Peace murals

Use the internet to look up 'The People's Gallery' and 'The Bogside Artists'. Take some time to examine these images and to read about the context in which they were produced, how they were made, and the reception they have received. In the context of this discussion of composition and content analysis, try to identify how the images work internally to create meaning and to organize the perceptions of the viewer. Examine the Peace mural (Figure 22.2). Here an oak leaf is merged with a dove, and is placed on a background of coloured squares that move from dark in the bottom left to light in the upper right. The eye is naturally moved towards the light. The dove is a near universal symbol of peace. The city in which the image is located is named (in one interpretation at least) after a glade of oak trees. Whilst the meaning of this image cannot be fully given outside the history, politics, geography and culture in which it was created, in which it is located and through which it is viewed, neither should the power of such a composition in itself be ignored.

Figure 22.2   Peace mural

Cinematic devices

Rather as the art critic will seek to identify the composition of a painting, photograph or other art object by means of those elements described above, so the film critic develops a heightened sensitivity towards the devices at work within the composition of a moving image. Key to such devices are *mise-en-scène* (scene dressing), location, casting and acting, make-up, editing, camera perspective and movement, framing, shot distance and scene/shot duration. Scene dressing and location create the environment in which events take place, and play a significant part in creating the atmosphere into which action will be located and framed. A domestic setting, a Wild West location, or the 1970s can be conveyed very differently depending upon how the scene is set. Casting particular actors for their iconic status, for their signature style or for their ability to convey certain human emotions and/or characteristics will again impact upon the composition of the finished product. That real people would look like freaks through a camera lens and under a spotlight means that even movie stars require make-up and, increasingly, surgical forms of cosmetic enhancement to make them look like the people we would want to identify with on the screen. Filming as though looking from the point of view of one of the protagonists creates a powerful sense of being inside the action, whilst panoramic perspective shots allow the viewer to feel they have an overview of the situation. Shooting from above, below or straight at the actors, close up, mid range or long distance again acts to move the audience into various positions in relation to the action. Editing between point of view shots creates tension, whilst the speed of editing creates a sense of pace. The opening nine minutes of *Pink Floyd's The Wall* contains around 100 edits, with the first shots lasting minutes and the final shots less than one second. The viewer is carried from sedate dreaming into nightmarish chaos, in part through the use of such accelerating editing. The crash zoom was first used in martial arts films, and supplemented a particular form of splicing between characters that had been popular. Panning and tracking shots capture and enhance action and movement, whilst cranes and zoom lenses allow for focus and emphasis. The art of film criticism cannot be reduced to a simple content analysis of techniques used, but such content analysis may represent the best first step in capturing the way in which a film director uses an array of visual devices to construct a sequence of images in order to tell a story with more than just words. The case of *The Wizard of Oz* is a powerful illustration of how film making technique can be used to tell a story, and in its opening four scenes to presage what is to come even without letting the audience know that they are being let into the secret (see Box 22.2).

BOX 22.2 CONSIDER THIS

The Wizard of Oz (or at least the first four scenes)

The first four 'scenes' of Victor Fleming's *The Wizard of Oz* (1939) are dominated by rolling clouds, gradually darkening. They first appear behind the opening credits, then behind the 'dedicated to the young at heart' prologue, and then above Dorothy, and her

(Continued)

dog Toto, as she runs fearfully home, only to be ignored, humoured and then lectured variously on using her brain, her courage and then just to stay out of trouble. Only at the end of scene four, as Dorothy comes to the end of her first song, does a break in the clouds appear, only to be snuffed out by thick black clouds as the wicked Arbela Gulch, from whom Dorothy and Toto were running in the first place, arrives to have Toto destroyed. The light and dark, closure yet distance evoked by these clouds offers both an oppressive proximity and the dream of escape beyond the glowing horizon. They also indicate that a storm is coming.

After the credits and prologue, scene three opens with an establishing shot of Dorothy and Toto running into shot and away from the camera along a dusty undulating road towards a farm bathed in light on the horizon. Fenceposts and telegraph poles along with the road lead the eye to this vanishing point of hope in a classical example of linear perspective. Dorothy is small in this open and rolling landscape and cloudscape. She turns to face the camera and her supposed pursuer. She crouches and we cut to a medium close-up at her now crouching level, as she checks Toto for injuries and explains to him (but really to the audience) that 'she' (as yet unspecified) has not yet caught up with them, and that 'she' has tried to hurt Toto.

A panning shot then follows Dorothy across the skyline and fenceline through the gate and into her aunt and uncle's farm. A slight jolt takes us a little closer to the three figures, one relaying Toto's plight, the other two more concerned with their chicks. Displaying concern for the chicks at first, Dorothy, gaining no attention to her tale, walks away. The camera follows her movement and, as she looks over her shoulder, a cutaway shot shows us what she is walking towards: three farm hands fixing a wagon. A cut in shot shows one farm hand tending his smarting finger, while a second shows his two colleagues showing little sympathy. The next slightly wider frame sees Dorothy given advice about using her brain by the very ragged and gangly looking man thoughtless enough to let his finger get caught. Distracted by the advice he is giving, and as Dorothy walks out of shot, 'Hulk' hits his own finger with a hammer and spins around in pain like a scarecrow in a high wind.

Dorothy is next seen climbing onto the fence of the pigsty and walking, tightrope style, along it while 'Zeek' advises her to confront her pursuer with courage. A crane shot elevates our perspective, while exaggerating the distance between Dorothy and the advice she is meant to be hearing. A medium close-up of Zeek focuses our attention upon the incongruity of his fine talk and his actions in pouring pig feed out of a bucket. Her back towards Zeek and the camera, a medium-distance shot shows Dorothy teetering along the fence top, proclaiming that she is not afraid, and then falling in amongst the pigs. We follow Zeek as he goes in and carries Dorothy out, and then as he sits sweating out of fear, while the others gather into a group shot and mock him.

Auntie Em enters the group shot and breaks it up. As she chastises the third hand, the camera pans up and across to focus upon these two figures. As the third hand and Hulk leave, the camera follows Em back and down to the seated Zeek with Dorothy between them. Zeek is sent off to the pigs and the camera now zooms in to follow Em and Dorothy as they walk away from it. Auntie Em advises Dorothy to find a place without any trouble. Em continues her movement away from the camera, while Dorothy turns back to it. We are then given a close-up of Dorothy's face and upper body as she muses over the possibility of such a happy place. A full-length shot allows us to see Dorothy give Toto a scrap of food. Chickens mill at her feet. She has her feet on the ground even as her head is now visibly clipping the horizon between the mundane world and the sky. The camera zooms up slowly as Dorothy raises her eyes skyward and contemplates somewhere above the rain. Leaning on a haystack, with her head now above the horizon and truly in the clouds, we can still see Dorothy's body alongside the farm animals nearby. This camera shot carefully places Dorothy between the physical and the mental worlds, a dull farmyard and a fluffy dream.

Dorothy starts to sing 'Somewhere Over The Rainbow'. We retain the same angle and proximity as the camera follows her from haystack to thrasher wheel, eyes still skyward, but as we reach this new location the camera lowers and the angle tilts upward. In so doing the camera takes in more sky behind Dorothy's head and the horizon drops away. Dorothy seems to be floating up into the sky. But then we see that the new angle is in fact a perspective shot as we are then given the reverse shot looking down upon Toto, who looks and strains his body upward towards Dorothy. Does Toto share Dorothy's escape into the clouds or will he be left behind on the ground (or worse, under it)? He wags his tail. We return to a shot of Dorothy, head equal to the horizon now, as if she cannot leave without Toto. She continues to sing and Toto jumps up onto the seat of the thrasher while Dorothy sits at a lower level. The camera moves down and its angle elevates once more. Now Toto's and Dorothy's heads are both in the clouds. They both look to the sky. Dorothy turns to Toto, proclaiming her wish to escape 'somewhere over the rainbow' and, as she reaches out a hand, so he reaches out a paw. They touch and then look to the sky. The perspective shot shows that they see sunbeams bursting through the clouds. A bluebird sings. Hope ascends. Dorothy ends her song: 'If happy little bluebirds fly; beyond the rainbow, why can't I?' The camera elevates its angle further, and Toto is now totally in the sky as Dorothy turns and embraces him. Will they escape together after all? In the last line of the song 'fly' and 'I' rhyme, but should it not have been 'we'? Will Toto be left behind? We now cut away to Arbela Gulch, Toto's nemesis, riding her bicycle to the farm under increasingly black clouds. She has come for Toto.

The use of camera angles, proximity, cutins and cutaways as well as reverse shots and perspective shots powerfully convey dynamics of place and escape, togetherness and potential separation, in relations between characters and between characters and situations. The set is most powerfully dressed with landscape and cloudscape, the farm scene and the coming storm, Dorothy's gingham dress, with its echoes of rural innocence, and Arbela Gulch's black hat, with its echoes of witchcraft.

As a musical, non-diagetic music, in particular Dorothy's playful and mischievous motif and Mrs Gulch's stabbing and predatory motif, is accompanied with diagetic singing. That Dorothy's singing is from within the scene itself, even while the orchestra playing with her is not visibly on the farm, blurs the distinction between diagetic and non-diagetic sound. This blurring is the very definition of the musical as a genre.

Performances are caricatures. Dorothy is headstrong and foolhardy; the farm hands are clearly a scarecrow, a cowardly lion and a tin man in waiting; Dorothy's aunt and uncle are caring and defiant, yet tired and powerless; while Mrs Gulch is clearly a poker-backed and wicked witch whose bicycle is obviously a proxy for her broomstick. Toto is a cute little dog.

A storm is brewing, the wicked witch is on her way. Dorothy and Toto want to escape, but we don't know where, how or whether they will manage to escape together. The grownups care, but are too concerned with mundane things. Can dreams really come true for the young at heart? Are we to be trapped in shades of grey, or will there be Technicolor over the rainbow? The use of cinematography, editing, light, sound, performance and *mise-en-scène* set up the enigma of Dorothy's and Toto's fate and an anticipation which draws the audience into it. The question is posed, 'Will they escape?', but more importantly the audience is left not only asking the question, but also emotionally needing to know the answer. The choice of black and white in these early scenes intensifies both the drab aspect of the everyday world, and the extremes of light and dark, of hope and fear that invade it.

(Continued)

Relatively slow editing, fast talking and a tendency to use fixed camera positions, at least relative to today's film makers, give the film a dated quality, as does the use of black and white in its early scenes. The way the film impacted upon its audience in 1939 would have been different than for us today, not least in the film's depiction of the dustbowl years of the Great Depression, the hunger of the farm hands, the threadbare old couple keeping a roof over their heads, and the demonic power of the local élites. Dorothy's dream of finding a better life would have resonated differently at a time when many were being forced onto the road to find new livelihoods, or were struggling to keep hold of what little they could protect. As such, while today we might see these opening scenes as wistfully contrived devices to foster a trivial sentimentality towards a girl and her pet dog, the techniques and their effects in 1930s America were powerful and political within the struggle to rebuild America through the New Deal.

Keith MacDonald on 'building respectability'

Keith MacDonald (1989) undertook a content analysis of buildings belonging to self-regulating professional associations. Part of the business of self-regulation is the creation of the impression of long standing, stability, respectability and authority. MacDonald wanted to see whether the buildings in which such associations had their head offices carried such messages, and if so, how. He identified 11 variables by which a building could be measured for its message of 'conspicuous consumption', one means of asserting wealth and power. Two related to the site where the building was located, whilst eight related to the building itself and one to the status of the architect commissioned to design the building. Each variable was ranked between −1 and +3, with a rank of 0 for 'present but not striking'. The eight variables for the building's 'visual' message were (1) size; (2) expensive/imposing exterior; interiors that (3) were expensive/imposing; (4) displayed large amounts of wasted space; (5) afforded leisure/lounging, relaxing, entertaining; (6) offered the impression of scholarship (such as a library of old volumes and space to study); (7) were filled with art/antiquities; and finally (8) that the building had a high profile (a celebrity ranking: prizes, fame, considered a classic). MacDonald was able to count the points scored for each building for each criterion to identify which building had the most powerful visual message of respectability. However, in reality what this use of content analysis allowed him to do was reflect on the more interesting qualitative significance of the combination of elements, and to show that within the discourses of professional bodies there is a recurrent attention to the power of visual image in the creation of an impression of respectability.

Semiology and Saussure: colour is relational

As has been noted in Chapter 20, semiotics is the study of signs, and these can be textual or purely visual. Because Saussure and Barthes were more concerned with semantics (the meaning contained within signs) than with syntax (the grammatical structuring of language), their work can be readily applied to non-linguistic symbols and images. Whilst semiology is partially concerned with the 'syntagmatic' (grammatical) creation of meaning through syntax, it is far more concerned with the 'paradigmatic' meaning of signs, the contrast that is created between the use of one sign relative to another. As such, the discussion about semiology and in particular the relationship between sign, signifier, signified and myth discussed in Chapter 20 should be recapped if you want to conduct a semiotic analysis of visual data. One thing that can be added here is that colours, like words, are relational for both Barthes and Saussure (Silverman, 2006: 252). This is triply so for semiotic analysts. First, just as words have no direct relationship with referents, so the way we classify colours is not simply the naming of discrete bands of light wavelengths. For Saussure and Barthes, the boundary around the word/concept 'cat' is not naturally given. Whether we include tigers, fluffy toys, long-dead fossilized ancestors of today's domestic pets etc. will be a matter of dispute. That we bundle a certain cluster of related things together under the title 'cats' is something that goes on within culture, and is not prescribed for us simply by reproductive exclusivity (and if we were to choose that criterion to define a 'cat' this choice would still have been one amongst many other possible and not necessary choices). We might think colour was different, that it represents a purer physical thing, but how we choose to slice the colour spectrum into segments with names is culturally specific. As such then, colours (the names we give to slices of the visible light spectrum) are more like slices of an apple (we have to cut them) than slices of an orange (which is naturally segmented inside). This leads to the second parallel between words and colours, and this is that not only do we slice the spectrum in culturally specific ways, but also we use names that both enforce such selective segmentation and give additional meaning to such segments of colour. Names like indigo, scarlet, peach, navy blue, sky blue and battleship grey invest meaning into colours. The use of the terms 'black' and 'white' to refer to human skin colour is arbitrary and yet acts as an attempt to naturalize and polarize differences between people. Third, colour is relational in its application. The choice to use one colour within a composition rather than another is both possible and significant, and the relative use of colours together can effect contrast, harmony or tension.

In addition to colour, symbols also exist in relation to other symbols and do not carry meaning directly from their referential characteristics (their physical features). Semiotic analysis of images works through the contrast of binary oppositions between symbols rather than looking at the relationship between signs and their referents. The content of a sign is defined by what is defined not to be covered rather than through any internally exhaustive list of what is to be included. Masculinity is defined as what is not feminine and vice versa, even when the internal content of such a binary pair remains open to dispute. A powerful illustration of this power of binary opposition was given by Judith Williamson (1978; cited in Rose, 2001) in her attempts to 'decode advertising' in the 1970s (see Box 22.3).

BOX 22.3 CONSIDER THIS

Judith Williamson: No. 5 and Babe

In one example from Williamson (1978) two advertising images are contrasted. Both are for perfume. One, for Chanel No. 5, contains a full-head shot of the then 'middle-aged' actress Catherine Deneuve. The other, for Babe, contains a full-body action shot of the actress Margaux Hemingway dressed in a martial arts outfit undertaking a karate kick. Each advertisement seeks to associate their product with their chosen female celebrity, but what Williamson points out is that it is the contrast between the two women that marks the contrast that the advertisers are seeking to create between their two fundamentally similar products (a mixing of flowery and spicy smells). Deneuve represents mature sophistication whilst Hemingway represents youthful energy, and the viewer is as much invited to identify against what they don't choose as they are to identify with what they do (Figure 22.3). Rose concludes: 'Thus two bottles of perfume are sold not only in terms of what they apparently are (sophisticated or youthful) but also in terms of what they apparently are not (youthful or sophisticated)' (2001: 87). If you look in the mirror and see old, you are invited to repackage this lack of youth by means of a product that associates sophistication with a mature overcoming of youth. If you look in the mirror and feel unsophisticated and out of control, you are invited to see yourself as energetic and youthful. You are invited to see yourself in such a way, subject to the correct purchase. You are invited or hailed to see. You may not succumb, but we should be aware of the semiotic power of images to position the viewer within a system of signs, and not just in relation to one image. The rejection of one identification may actively align the viewer with its binary opposite.

CD		MH
Catherine Deneuve	≠	Margaux Hemingway
=		=
Chanel No. 5	≠	Babe

FIGURE 22.3 Binary opposition in advertising (Williamson, 1978: 29; cited in Rose, 2001: 87)

Discourse analysis and visual images

The distinction made by Gillian Rose (in Figure 22.1) between discourse analysis I and discourse analysis II is between an attention to the construction and representation of social relationships within images, and the integration of such image-based representations and constructions within institutional practices of power and control. Here Rose draws upon two meanings of the term 'discourse'. One uses the term to refer to representations in abstraction, whilst the other uses the term to include both the representations and the practices which act upon such representations and which are themselves legitimated by discursive constructions of the way things are. These two domains are connected in the work of Michel Foucault, but the two elements can be separated out. Foucault's attention was always directed to what he called 'serious text', by which he meant texts which were taken up and used as the basis for disciplinary regimes, such as prisons, schools, hospitals or asylums. Such institutions gained the right to regiment people's lives because they claimed that they were acting upon expertise, itself expressed and formulated in such 'serious texts' as medical handbooks, psychiatric manuals, penal policy documents and pedagogical research. He was not interested in texts and images in isolation, or in popular cultural forms such as newspapers, television or advertising. Those that study popular cultural 'texts' (and often the term 'text' is used to include images) will typically do so using a semiological approach, and this can be seen as a part of discourse analysis, but such techniques as frame analysis, thematic analysis and critical discourse analysis can be applied to images in a fashion similar to that set out in Chapter 20.

Figures in the discourse

It might be better here to say 'discourses in the figure'. If discourse analysis of text seeks to identify the construction of particular figures in the language (the stereotypical criminal, the ideal-typical psychiatric patient, the delinquent child, the hysterical woman etc.), using discourse analysis to research visual images might be said to be looking for the meanings that are being presented by the selection of particular images. Gillian Rose (2001: 151) uses the example of Victorian newspaper depictions of prostitutes. Whether as victim or villian, these women are presented as abnormal, with a particular tendency to graphically depict grisly deaths. Without having to express open support for such outcomes, the message is delivered that 'the wages of sin are death'. However, Rose, in relation to the Victorian artist William Powell Frith, notes that images cannot be read simply, as we do not know from the image itself whether it was designed to depict, condone or condemn, to idealize, demonize or naturalize the world it represents or constructs.

Many Victorian viewers would have been familiar with theories of facial features and personality types that we today would miss if they were present within a nineteenth-century painting. Similarly, patrons and artists in the middle ages and early modern period would have shared a knowledge of symbols and mannerisms by which social relations of power and order could be naturalized in art. Today, audiences and film makers share a significant if tacit understanding about what they will be exposed to in different genres of film.

Maps and the cartographic gaze

Cultural geographers have drawn attention to the power of maps in shaping representations of the world. Edward Soja (1989) in his account of postmodern geographies questions the possibility of ever creating neutral and objective maps, and of course maps have been central to the presentation and maintenance of power within states and empires, as well as in exploration, war and colonization. The relationship between space and place, the former supposedly physical with the latter being such physical space imbued with meaning and social organization, is itself shaped by the maps we have to locate ourselves. Medieval maps depict the most important elements at the centre and make them physically bigger than other things. Modern cartography was meant to replace this with 'accurate maps', but this did not make them either neutral or non-ideological. The most striking example of this is the Mercator Projection, named after the Dutch cartographer Gerardus Mercator. This mid-sixteenth-century map of the world stretched out the land masses of the three-dimensional globe onto a two-dimensional map such that the equator runs across the middle while the poles are stretched out across the whole top and bottom of the map. This map became the 'standard' for global navigation, but had the effect of stretching northern and southern land masses, making them far larger than their actual size warranted relative to equatorial territories. That this representation of the world coincided with the distribution of power in the world was no accident. That a Chinese cartographer might have placed the Chinese Pacific coastline towards the top, and so enlarged China, making Europe and Africa relatively small, with the Americas enlarged at the bottom, or that someone from the Americas might have done things the other way up, points to the fact that the projection chosen was no accident. That Europe is both central (Asia to the east and the Americas to the west) and enlarged is in many ways similar to medieval maps and iconic paintings where kings are depicted as giants and where territories are scaled in terms of their relative importance rather than in any direct relationship to their actual size.

Orientalism, panopticism and archives

Edward Said's book *Orientalism* (1984) applied Foucault's approach to serious text to the academic study of 'the orient'. In the nineteenth century, Western colonial powers sought to secure and extend their control over non-Western (oriental as opposed to Western occidental) societies through knowledge of the 'other'. Knowing the 'other' was as much the construction of subjected peoples and cultures in such a way as to justify their subjugation, as it was to present the West as their natural and superior opposite. Whilst such academic study supposed itself to be rational and scientific, it was also deeply ideological and partial. The use of visual images was a crucial part of creating the impression of the orient as fundamentally irrational, dangerous, primitive, lazy and decadent. Those societies that were known to have had complex civilizations long prior to the rise of Western power were presented as languid, decaying and antiquated. Those that were said not to have had large-scale agriculture, state structures, towns or industry were presented as childlike or even subhuman. Visual representations were crucial to the naturalization of such representations. That the British flooded China with opium could be conveniently set to one side, when images depicted the opium pipe smoking Chinaman as either lazy and so in need of compulsion, or 'inscrutable' and so in need of being watched. Such images chimed with calls for further colonial intervention and later for tighter immigration controls. Representations of Africans as wild, ferocious and savage acted to legitimate violent conquest and slaughter. Anyone familiar with the films *Zulu* and *Zulu Dawn* will be familiar with the depiction of white soldiers gunning down endless ranks of Africans armed only with spears in such a fashion as to make those with the guns look like the heroes. While Said was interested in the serious texts produced by colonial administrators, state officials and academic researchers, the constructions of non-Europeans, in text and in catalogues of images, were not very dissimilar to the hideously racist media representations of non-Europeans that were considered acceptable and even true until very recently, and continue to be reinvented to this day. Said's personal and academic interest in Western representations of Palestinians, Arabs and Muslims in general remains very topical.

Another dimension of visual analysis stems from Foucault's interest in 'serious text', i.e. representations that serve to organize regimes of control (such as prisons or asylums). This is the way visual surveillance is central to the maintenance of such regimes. Foucault's most famous illustrations of knowledge/power and the use of the visual are the medical gaze and the panoptic prison. If premodern visual power was gained through making the powerful more visible, whether through thrones, towers, cathedrals or simply drawing them bigger on any illustration, the modern world reverses the gaze. Where once the hospital and the leper colony were where people went to be left alone to die, and the dungeon was a dark hole where the prisoner remained hidden, the modern hospital, asylum and prison turned the spotlight of knowledge upon the inmate. The medical gaze and the panoptic prison were designed to cure through knowledge, which was itself to be gained by means of surveillance, and in the case of the prisoner the internalizing of the sense that they were always visible (being watched). When we hear that modern society is a visual culture, we might automatically think of all the things that are produced for us to watch, but for Foucault modern society is a visual culture because it is one in which we are always being watched. The way that images are used to warrant control is central to Foucault's questioning of Western ideas of ever expanding freedom. Whether it is CCTV monitoring, photo ID cards, or even the self-monitoring that we undertake when we look in the mirror and think we really ought to eat less cake, we are part of a visual culture of surveillance. The part played by constant visibility in the organizing of our daily lives opens up a whole new realm of connections for visual analysis. Just how many mirrors do you have? Who is allowed to watch you, and when are you allowed to have privacy? Does your image belong to you? Is Big Brother really watching you?

Finally, Rose (2001) and Pink (2001) highlight in different ways the significance of archives, whether personal, institutional or research generated, as records and organizing systems not only for image storage, but also in providing rationales for the way people are understood, controlled, treated and/or managed. The study of the visual organization of museums, archives and galleries, personal photo collections and other image collections, as well as of researchers' visual data storage and presentation strategies provides an important set of sites for the further conduct of visual discourse analysis.

Audience reception

How people interpret visual material moves away from a direct engagement with visual analysis towards analysis of text and talk, but such research remains significantly linked to visual research. Approaches to audience response can be broken down into four main strands: mass society and psychoanalysis approaches; two-step flow models; uses and gratifications accounts; and structural (political economy) 'cultural capital' accounts of the viewer. These four approaches to visual analysis will only be touched on briefly in this work, but they open up interesting and divergent possibilities for engaging with visual material and cultural works more generally.

Mass society theory and psychoanalysis

Mass society theories in the social sciences start from the premise that urban, industrial and commercial conditions broke people away from traditional communities and left them fragmented and individualized, and therefore vulnerable to manipulation by newly emerging mass media and mass political parties. Whether it was Hollywood fantasy or Nazi and communist propaganda, the assumption that viewers were vulnerable to such manipulation meant that attention was primarily paid to the power of the medium, and its message. The most significant form of such attention was the application of Freud's theory of psychoanalysis to film. Gillian Rose (2001) provides a very useful introduction to this approach to visual analysis, though her account pays most attention to the representation of gender and the scope for gender identification in film, where earlier mass society writers had paid more attention to the political manipulation of unconscious desires for subjection. What Rose highlights is a tension within psychoanalytic approaches between those who see in film a reflection of patriarchal relations between men and women, where men are encouraged to be active whilst women are pacified and rendered the objects of voyeuristic and often sadistic fetishism; and those who see in film the reflections of the anxieties and insecurities underlying and undermining male dominance in society. Interestingly, whilst psychoanalysis was initially a form of therapeutic engagement with individuals, psychoanalytic approaches to visual analysis seek to apply Freud and his followers' work to the screen itself. They do not research the viewer. Rather, they attribute to the viewer feelings, identifications, fantasies and desires based on the analysts' reading of psychoanalytic theory, even though, using different interpretations of such theory, such analysts draw very different conclusions about the impact of visual material and what Freud called 'scopophelia' (the pleasure of looking). Whilst the suggestions made by psychoanalysis regarding fixations, complexes and infantile regression etc. are useful, the way that visual material such as film impacts upon its audience is not easily reduced to any single account. That early film goers, encased in the darkness of a cinema auditorium, staring up at the iconic figures of the silver screen, could be likened to infants emerging from the womb into the presence of idealized parental figures is an interesting possibility; but how should we understand the many alternative ways in which audiences engage with film and other visual material today, the familial television in the living room, the small screen in the bedroom, or the mini-screen as we travel?

Two-step flows and focus groups

It was exactly in order to locate the individual's reaction to cultural influence within the particular circumstances of their lives, and not simply in relation to a general account of social conditions or psychological universals, that Eluha Katz and Paul Lazarsfeld (2006) developed their account of personal influences, which is more generally referred to as the two-step flow model. Whilst Katz and Lazarsfeld were more interested in political influence, their approach can be applied to the impact of any other kind of cultural materials, such as film, television or radio. The two-step flow seeks to identify the dynamics of influence by which individuals engage with such things as film through dialogue with their friends, family and colleagues. Within such networks there are more or less dominant players, whose interpretation of such things carries a significant weight in shaping the views of those around them, but they themselves are also open to influences. From this perspective it is never enough to interpret the text or image alone, if you want to understand how people experience such things. Central to the conduct of such research has been the use of the focus group (see Chapter 7) as such a method is ideal for the study of group dynamics.

Uses and gratifications – and ethnography

The claim that people are manipulated by visual and other media products is more forcefully rejected by those who suggest that people actively choose the things they engage with and, far from being influenced, it is audiences who demand the things they want and reject what they either disagree with or do not enjoy. Discussion of this issue is most heated around the issues of pornography and violent images, and whether such images cause or increase the incidence of sexist attitudes and behaviour and physical violence in real life. Does increased 'exposure' to such material induce desires or reduce inhibitions? Much research has been undertaken on these questions and no simple answer has been forthcoming, because whilst there is a clear association between viewing sexist and violent images and sexist and violent behaviour, it is not clear whether the former increases the incidence of the latter, or whether the disposition towards the latter also increases the preference to consume the former. Men who enjoy violent behaviour are more likely to choose to watch violent films, and those with sexist attitudes towards women are more likely to access pornography. This is well known. Whether this exposure will increase the chances of them acting on their preferences and beliefs, or have the opposite effect, substituting fantasy for real behaviour, is highly controversial. Those who advocate the uses and gratifications approach take the latter view. They start from the view that people are robust individuals with the ability to make up their own minds, and that they make choices that aim to fulfil their existing desires. Deeply critical of mass society theories of people as cultural dupes, puppets at the mercy of hidden social forces, uses and gratifications theory tends to use ethnographic fieldwork and interviews in order to explore how people create their own reality and fulfil their own ambitions and desires (see David Gauntlett and Annette Hill, 1999).

Pierre Bourdieu and cultural capital

The work of Pierre Bourdieu (1986) has sought to locate taste as a marker of social status, and as such the way that different people choose to engage with cultural arte-facts such as painting, photography, theatre or film in different ways is understood not as the result of personal preference or personal influence, but rather in relation to other systems of social hierarchy, most particularly class. Bourdieu's approach engages with the claim that people select and interpret in accordance with strategies of use and gratification, but that such strategies can only be understood when we locate individuals within the social system that offers different opportunities depending upon where in that system you are located. One simple key to understanding taste is to identify how much it would cost to acquire it. Those able to devote large amounts of time, energy, knowledge and other resources (personal, financial, status and social networks of connection, for example) to the development of their tastes will tend to prefer those cultural forms that require the most, whilst those with fewer resources will tend towards a taste for those things that they can afford. As such, wealthier people will tend towards opera and classical music, classical fine art, architecture and furniture, as well as wine, foreign films and complex literary and poetic forms; middle-class people will feel at home with photography, jazz, modern art, middle-brow theatre and fiction; and those with few resources to spare will tend to enjoy cultural forms that require least investment to be able to engage with them, such as soap operas, blockbuster films, gossip magazines and popular music. If it takes years of background learning, travel and interacting with knowledgeable people to acquire the necessary confidence to buy original works of art, then becoming a connoisseur becomes a marker of all these things, and as such is something a person with such resources may choose to become, and feel good about so doing. Those who cannot afford to do so may simply reject such snobbery and embrace their more democratic values. Bourdieu was not unaware that the same snobbery could be said of the aca-demic who has spent years acquiring the skills to see the world more clearly than everyone else, and typically seeks qualifications to prove they are better. All these acquisitions are what Bourdieu calls 'cultural capital'. Explorations of the relationship between various forms of cultural capital and their connections with taste represent another useful approach to the study of how people engage with visual material.

Photo elicitation and grounded analysis

Showing people visual material as a way to elicit data in the form of their reactions and reflections is another valuable technique, even if it is not visual analysis as such.

It can become a part of visual analysis when the researcher uses this technique either to generate analysis from respondents or to cross-reference their own provisional interpretations. These are therefore valuable forms of grounded data analysis, building analysis from repeated interaction with research participants. An interesting tension exists between realists and constructivists as to the results that can emerge from such analytical engagement between visual data and research participants. Victoria Alexander (2008) cites the 1986 work of Collier and Collier, who used photographs of weaving techniques to engage weavers in a South American cultural context about the symbolic and practical aspects of such work. For these ethnographers the use of photo elicitation allowed them to get to the truth more fully. Sarah Pink (2001) takes issue with this realist expectation and suggests that such techniques generate as much diversity of interpretation as they do convergence. For Pink, the value of such photo elicitation is precisely to bring out such diversity of meaning constructions, not to generate closure around any one true meaning.

Summary

Just as tables and charts are used in the presentation of numerical and textual data, so visual material can provide a valuable additional form of representation in either a talk or a written publication. As has been detailed above, the relationships between visual analysis and visual experience, between visual data and their analysis through words and numbers, and between the analysis of visual material and that of other forms of data, have been the sites of many debates, most of which have not been fully resolved. Whether visual material carries a meaning from its production to its recipient, or whether it is all in the eye of the beholder, is as significant in analysing visual data as it is in deciding how useful the presentation of such visual material will be in allowing the audience for your research to understand what was going on. As this chapter has shown, the way images require textual support when relocated from their original context limits the claim that images carry a meaning independently of any accompanying description; yet at the same time discussion of photography, painting and film has showed how the image cannot be reduced to its textual description either. Yet this second observation, that the visual constructs meaning through content and composition, challenges the idea that any image could ever act as a neutral window through which reality can pass neutrally to the viewer. Visual analysis is important as image cannot be reduced into text; yet visual analysis cannot stand alone, as an understanding of its production and its reception require an awareness of more than simply what is in the image.

 ■ **Questions**

1 **Can images be analysed visually in the way that words can be analysed textually or numbers can be analysed statistically? What does it mean to analyse an image, and how can this be done?**

2   Is content analysis really at odds with composition, semiotic analysis and/or discourse analysis, or can it be usefully combined with other approaches?

3   Can an image be studied in its own terms, or in relation to the people who made or experience it?

■ ■ Further reading ■

Barthes, Roland (2000) *Mythologies*. London: Vintage.

Pink, Sarah (2001) *Visual Ethnography: Images, Media and Representation in Research*. London: Sage.

Rose, Gillian (2001) *Visual Methodologies*. London: Sage.

Williamson, Judith (1978) *Decoding Advertising: Ideology and Meaning in Advertising*. London: Marion Boyars.

TWENTY THREE

INTRODUCTION TO QUANTITATIVE DATA ENTRY

Chapter Contents

Introduction to quantitative data entry

This is the first of five chapters that will guide you through key stages associated with undertaking quantitative data analysis. In this chapter we detail how to enter your survey data into a software analysis package. In Chapter 16 we outlined how quantitative data need to be prepared for statistical analysis. This process involves developing a code book that details the conversion of survey data into a numerical format that can be used for statistical calculations. There are three data types or levels of measurement – nominal, ordinal and interval/ratio – with each data type having mathematical properties (Box 23.1). If you are reading this chapter before having read Chapter 16, you are strongly advised to visit the earlier chapter in order to ensure that you are familiar with the basic principles of coding.

BOX 23.1 STOP AND THINK

Summary of the mathematical properties of different data types

Data type	Characteristics
Nominal	Categories that have no particular order to them, just a list of different types, e.g. different newspapers
Ordinal	Categories that can be placed in a rank order, lowest to highest or highest to lowest, e.g. five-point attitude scale
Interval/ratio or scale	Data on a continuous scale. Values can be placed in rank order and the distance between the values is equal and known. Interval variables have no true zero point, e.g. temperature, whereas ratio variables have a true zero point, e.g. number of children in a household

Following on from the present chapter, the next four chapters introduce you to a range of analysis techniques most commonly used in social science research. These chapters will cover the following data analysis topics:

- The essentials of quantitative data analysis, describing single variables (Chapter 24).

- Bivariate analysis, describing and exploring relationships between two variables, and expanding the analysis to consider multiple variables (Chapter 25).

- Inferential statistics and hypothesis testing to enable judgements as to the generalizability of sample findings to the population (Chapter 26).

- Data management techniques commonly used to develop and expand analysis (Chapter 27).

Each chapter includes reference to the Northern Ireland Life and Times Survey (NILT) and the availability of a teaching data file from the 2006 survey. This file is downloadable from the NILT website (see Box 15.2). It provides an accessible dataset that you can use to practise data analysis techniques and interpret the findings before you start analysing your own research data.

In each of these chapters a distinction will be drawn between the 'technical' or 'doing' aspects of the analysis process and the higher-level understanding and reflection on why and when the analysis is appropriate, and how to interpret your findings. Particularly, attention will be given to the exploration of causality when exploring relationships. The strength of relationships can be assessed by measures of associations. Inferential statistics allow the researcher to assess the likelihood of survey findings being found in the population through hypothesis and significance testing. Within each section there are a number of tips and analysis tasks for you to undertake using the Northern Ireland Life and Times Survey teaching dataset. These provide you with an opportunity to try out what you have learnt before embarking on analysing your own research data.

Before we proceed with taking you through the steps of actual data entry, we are going to consider the range of data analysis packages available.

Quantitative data analysis software

A number of specialist software applications are available to support quantitative data analysis. These include Minitab for Windows, IBM SPSS Statistics 19, SAS and STATA. Details of each of these packages can be found at the company websites of www.minitab.com, www.spss.com, www.sas.com and www.stata.com, respectively. In an academic setting the choice of software package is often between IBM SPSS Statistics 19 and Minitab. In terms of basic analysis there is little difference in the operational characteristics of these two. The main difference comes in the ability of IBM SPSS Statistics 19 to manage variables collected from multiple answer questions and arrange these into sets for analysis purposes. The data management techniques are sufficient in IBM SPSS Statistics 19 to undertake a wide range of more advanced statistical analysis. IBM SPSS Statistics 19 does offer a student version of the software that has a restriction on the size of the data files. Alternatively many academic institutions are able to offer these packages for student use as part of their course of study. If you are a university student, contact the computing service at your host institution for further information on availability.

IBM SPSS Statistics 19 is widely used by business, market and social researchers. This provides the basis for each of the following sections making reference to the IBM SPSS Statistics 19 commands. An overview of the structure of IBM SPSS Statistics 19 will first be given. At the time of writing there are a number of different versions of IBM SPSS Statistics 19 and earlier versions of the software called SPSS for Windows in circulation. Earlier versions have some variations in the appearance of windows and dialogue boxes. It is also likely that subsequent versions will be developed. Notwithstanding a complete overhaul of the IBM SPSS Statistics 19 program, it is probable that the commands in this book will still be largely relevant to future versions and the reader should be able intuitively to find the relevant command without difficulty.

If specialist software such as IBM SPSS Statistics 19 and Minitab is not available to you, it is possible to undertake much of the basic analysis outlined in this chapter using the spreadsheet package Microsoft Excel using the pivot table functions, charts and Analysis Toolpak (see MS Excel for more information).

There are also other non-commercial software packages available to social science researchers. Open source software can be downloaded free of charge from the host website. Unlike the commercial packages, such software generally does not use a graphic user interface (GUI). Instead the user performs analysis functions using the command language, and this software is generally supported through free online tutorials and downloadable materials. In addition there are newsgroups of users where you can contribute to current applications or seek advice from other users. One readily available package is called R. This is available for download from the Comprehensive R Archive Network (CRAN) website (http://cran.r-project.org/index.html) or from many mirror websites around the world. For example in the United Kingdom R can be downloaded from http://www.stats.bris.ac.uk/R/. Other specialist software includes MLwiN (see the Centre for Multilevel Modelling at http://www.cmm.bristol.ac.uk/) for more sophisticated modelling techniques.

Data entry

The first stage in analysing data is to enter the research data, e.g. survey response, as coded data into a IBM SPSS Statistics 19 data file. This process requires an understanding of variables, levels of measurement and coding (see section 'Variables and levels of measurement' in Chapter 13, and section 'Developing a code book' in Chapter 16).

In primary data collection, the data entry process consists of creating a data file. The format of the data file is that responses are entered into variables. The universal standard format for data files is that variables are placed in columns and the responses for each individual case are placed in rows. Variables run 'across' the data file in columns and cases run 'down' the data file in rows.

TABLE 23.1   Example data file format

Columns ──────────────────────────────▶			
IdCase	**Sex**	**Age**	**Health**
1	Female	25	Good
2	Male	20	Good
3	Male	28	Poor
4	Male	40	Fairly good
5	Female	65	Poor

Rows points downward at the left of the data rows.

Survey number (IdCase)   ☐

Are you?   ☐ Male

☐ Female

How old are you?   ☐ Enter age in years

How would you rate your current health?   ☐ Good

☐ Fairly good

☐ Poor

In Table 23.1 an example of the structure of a data file is shown with the category response data included. For illustrative purposes we are showing the structure of the data file with the original uncoded data. Below the table are the three original survey questions for the data. The data file displays the responses of five individuals (the cases) to three questions relating to their sex, age and current self-assessed health status (the variables). Note also that an additional variable has been included, IdCase, that codes an identifying number for each case. It is good practice to always include such a variable in a data file as it enables entered data to be cross-checked with the original questionnaire or interview responses at a later date. Without the inclusion of the identification variable it becomes difficult to track back cases to an original response.

It is technically possible to enter individual responses to each question as text: for example, for the variable Sex the responses would be 'Female' or 'Male'. However, the normal practice is to numerically code the responses for each variable. Instead of entering the text 'Female' a code of 1 would be entered; likewise for 'Male' a code of 2 would be entered. This not only reduces the amount of time required for data entry, it also reduces the size of the data file. In addition – and the most important reason – converting the responses to a numeric value extends the range of statistical analysis procedures open to the researcher. This process of coding is just one of a number of aspects of quantitative research that can be uncomfortable to the social researcher, as concerns can be expressed over the reduction of an individual response to a numeric value. Coding data should never replace the understanding of the original question and why it was asked.

TABLE 23.2 Example code book and the coded data file

Variable	Codes
IdCase	Enter actual questionnaire number
Sex	1 = Female, 2 = Male
Age	Enter actual age value
Health	1 = Good; 2 = Fairly good; 3 = Poor

IdCase	Sex	Age	Health
1	1	25	1
2	2	20	1
3	2	28	3
4	2	40	2
5	1	65	1

BOX 23.2 STOP AND THINK

Remember that the process of coding data involves the creation of a code book (see section 'Developing a code book' in Chapter 16). For categorical variables, nominal or ordinal, each category response is coded and entered in the data file. For interval and ratio variables, the numeric value is simply entered into the data file.

From the extract of a data file shown in Table 23.1, the resulting data file is shown in Table 23.2. An extract from a code book for these variables is also shown in the table so that you can again see the link between the two stages. See also Box 23.2.

Variables for a multiple response question

So far we have shown you how to set up variables in a data file for questions that elicit a single response from the participant. For example, if you asked an individual person 'How old are you?', the response would be recorded in years, such as '23 years'. However, as we have already discussed, some question formats may allow or require the respondent to give more than one response. An example would be a question that asks the respondent to 'tick all relevant' from the list below, or an open question that the researcher then codes after collecting the data, known as post-coding.

In these instances the responses need to be clearly broken down into the appropriate number of different variables. The number of different variables required will be determined by how the responses were coded (see section 'Coding for multiple response questions' in Chapter 16). At a later stage in the process, these variables can be placed together in a multiple response set for analysis purposes.

Which of the following daily newspapers have you read in the last 7 days?
Please tick all applicable.

Financial Times ☐
New York Times ☐
Washington Post ☐
Melbourne Age ☐
Times of India ☐
South China Morning Post ☐
Other (please state) ☐

FIGURE 23.1 Example of a Multiple Response Survey Question

Figure 23.1 shows an example of a multiple response question about daily newspapers that were read in the last week. For coding purposes each newspaper is given its own variable, and the responses are coded as 1 for 'Yes' (ticked as read) and 2 for 'No' (not ticked and therefore assumed not read).

These variables and corresponding codes for each case are entered into a data file, as shown in Table 23.3. As can be seen, the standard format of variables placed in columns and case responses in rows has been applied.

Concerns are sometimes expressed about accidentally underestimating the number of variables required for a multiple response question, particularly if one is not using the 'Yes' or 'No' format. This, however, is not a problem as it is easy to insert an additional variable into a dataset at a later date.

Data entry errors

It is important to be aware that during the data entry process it is possible for the researcher to make a data entry error by entering an incorrect code. Due care and attention to detail are essential. An error at the data entry stage could remain undetected or hidden until the later stages of the data analysis process, or simply never discovered. Within the overall project management of the research there should be a sufficient amount of time allocated for checking the data. It is good

TABLE 23.3 Example data entry of a multiple response question

Financial Times	*New York Times*	*Washington Post*	*Melbourne Age*	*Times of India*	*South China Morning Post*	*Le Monde*	**Other**
2	2	1	2	2	2	1	2
2	2	2	2	2	2	2	2
1	2	2	2	2	2	2	2

practice to double check a proportion of the cases. In the commercial research world this is undertaken using specialist data entry software where cases are re-entered and any anomalies are flagged. For an individual student project, a manual double checking of the data entry will be sufficient. We suggest that you check the data entry of approximately 10 per cent or one in ten of cases. If there are few errors found then this would be sufficient checking. If however you find substantial data entry errors then a more detailed check of a subsequent 20 per cent of cases would be advisable. If there continue to be further errors then a full data entry check should seriously be considered.

Even after the double data entry check there are a number of additional checks that can be undertaken to further search the data for potential errors. The most common, and easiest, data entry error to detect is when a code is entered that falls outside the expected range for that variable. For a nominal or ordinal variable the coding frame will state that the codes should run from a minimum value, for example, 1 for 'Male', to a maximum value, for example, 2 for 'Female', with specific missing value codes, for example −99 for 'Did not respond'. An entered value which does not meet these conditions, also known as a wild code, for example a value of 3, should trigger an investigation by the researcher. In the case of primary data collection this will involve a referral back to the original questionnaire or interview response. Other data errors may come to light because of the researcher's knowledge of the entire research project and particular sample characteristics. For example, a study of young people's voting preferences focused on a sample of 18- to 25-year-olds. The age of the respondent was recorded and for one case an age of 52 was entered; this was clearly incorrect for the original target sample. Locating data entry errors that fall outside the expected range is most easily achieved by being vigilant when entering data.

Data entry errors that are the most difficult to detect are those that fall within the existing expected coded range but are incorrect. For example, when coding the sex of a case the entered code is 2 for 'Male', when in fact the respondent was 'Female' and a code of 1 should have been entered. The only way of minimizing these types of error is to double enter a proportion of the cases. The time constraints of the research project will inevitably determine the feasibility of undertaking this type of rechecking. Beyond this, though, one can remain vigilant to the possibility of these types of entry errors by scanning the data file for inconsistencies when both entering and analysing the data. For example, in a survey focusing on the ill-health of patients attending a general practice, the sex of the respondent was recorded together with the presenting health issue. Unknown to the researcher, for one respondent the sex had been incorrectly recorded as male when it should have been female. This respondent was presenting with a gynaecological problem. Analysis of the sex variable would not reveal this error, and neither would analysis of the presenting ill-health variable. However, analysis of the relationship between the sex variable and the ill-health variable in a contingency table (see Chapter 25 for further discussion) would reveal that there was one male respondent suffering from gynaecological problems. Other logical inconsistencies can occur with routing questions: for example, has someone ticked 'No' to a routing question that would then involve them not completing a number of questions, but has then completed those questions? Maybe the original routing question should have been ticked as 'Yes'.

If the researcher suspects that there may be inconsistencies in the data, then analysis of the relationships between two categorical variables using a contingency table can be carried out. Correcting the error will involve referral back to the original data collection source, for example, a survey questionnaire. As long as each case has been given a unique identification number which has been entered as a variable (for example, IdCase) in the data file it is easy to relate the error back to the correct case. If the identification number of the original case has not been recorded or if access to the original data collection tool is not possible, for example, in the case of secondary data sources (see below), then the only course of action is to recode the entry as missing data.

Often these inconsistencies will only present after the researcher has undertaken a fair amount of analysis. Remember that once the error is detected and then corrected or removed, the change to the variable will require any existing analysis to be undertaken again.

Familiarization with IBM SPSS Statistics 19

These sections contain a brief introduction to the key elements of IBM SPSS Statistics 19. First we familiarize you with the layout and overall structure before moving on to the process of creating a new data file in SPSS and entering coded data. If you are operating an earlier version, for example SPSS v.17 or 18, the majority of commands and instructions in this chapter will still be of relevance.

Starting IBM SPSS Statistics 19

If the IBM SPSS Statistics 19 application is stored on your own PC, you will be able to open it from the **Start** button. Alternatively, if you are using IBM SPSS Statistics 19 from a network service, for example, a university network, then you will need to refer to local instructions for accessing the application.

IBM SPSS Statistics 19 creates a number of different windows that the user will switch between depending on the data management or analysis task undertaken.

When the IBM SPSS Statistics 19 application is first opened, the default setting is to display a new **Data Editor** window. The **Data Editor** is where coded survey data are inputted and stored. The data window is saved to files that are automatically given a .sav file extension. The data file must be retrieved at the beginning of each IBM SPSS Statistics 19 session in order for data management and analysis to begin. The data window itself is divided into two views: the **Data View** contains the coded data and the **Variable View** contains information on each of the variables in the data file. These two views can be accessed via the tabs in the bottom left corner of the IBM SPSS Statistics 19 **Data Editor** window (see Figure 23.2).

BOX 23.3 HINTS AND TIPS

IBM SPSS Statistics 19 **Viewer** earlier file formats

If you have used earlier versions of SPSS and are reading this section to familiarize yourself with the latest software, then you will need to be aware that newer versions have a different format for output files. The new file format is .spv replacing the old .spo format. This means that if you have any old versions of output files that you wish to view in SPSS v.16 or later, you will be unable to automatically open them in these later versions. In order to open .spo output files you will need to install SPSS SmartViewer software. See the IBM SPSS Statistics website for further details.

The results of statistical and data analysis procedures are displayed in the **Viewer** window. The viewer is divided into two frames: the left frame is the index to the **Viewer** contents, and the actual contents are displayed in the right frame. Each frame can be navigated using the respective scroll bars. Results in this window are saved to files that have a .spv file extension. See Box 23.3 for information on the file format for earlier versions of IBM SPSS Statistics 19 **Viewer** window.

In addition to the **Data Editor** and **Viewer** windows one can also create SPSS Statistics 19 syntax files. These windows are where files containing SPSS Statistics 19 commands can be compiled and are generally used when undertaking complex statistical calculations or analyses that are repeated over time. A syntax window is saved to files with a .sps file extension. The use of IBM SPSS Statistics 19 syntax files is not specifically covered in this text, although reference is made to their use in the section 'Weighting data' in Chapter 27.

One can move between the different windows by selecting the required window from the taskbar or alternatively from the **Window** menu.

The majority of IBM SPSS Statistics 19 commands are contained within the menus at the top of the screen. The menus alter depending on the active or current window. A brief description of each of the menus and the window(s) they are associated with is shown in Table 23.4.

Data entry using SPSS Statistics 19

This section contains details on creating a new data file in IBM SPSS Statistics 19. It will cover the following topics: defining a new variable, saving the data file, importing existing data files and other data file formats. If you have not already done so, open the IBM SPSS Statistics 19 application from the **Start** menu button. Your local setup will determine the exact location of IBM SPSS Statistics 19 in the menus. IBM SPSS Statistics 19 will automatically open a new blank data file. If a dialogue box opens asking 'What you would like to do?', click on **Cancel**.

TABLE 23.4   Description of IBM SPSS Statistics 19 menus

Menu	Description
File menu (all windows)	Commands relating to opening, saving and closing all types of files. Information retrieval on data files. Printing files. Exiting the IBM SPSS Statistics 19 program
Edit menu (all windows)	Standard copy, cut and paste commands. Search facilities. Page and output breaks. Preferences for controlling the IBM SPSS Statistics 19 session
View menu (**Data Editor** window)	Enables the user to customize their IBM SPSS Statistics 19 environment in relation to the icons on the toolbars, commands in the menus, font type and size, grid lines and data labels (**Data View** only) displayed. Customize the columns displayed in the **Variable View** and switch between **Variable View** and **Data View**
View menu (**Viewer** window)	Commands relating to viewing the different elements in the index (left frame)
Data menu (all windows)	Commands relating to the definition of variables, file management, and case selection and weighting
Transform menu (all windows)	Data transformation commands: computing new variables, recoding values
Insert menu (**Viewer** window only)	Enables the user to insert different elements into the viewer, for example, page breaks, additional text
Format menu (**Viewer** window only)	Controls the alignment of text objects, for example, left, right, centre
Analyze menu (all windows)	Statistical commands are contained in this menu. For example, frequencies, cross-tabulations, descriptive statistics and so on
Direct Marketing	A IBM SPSS Statistics 19 tool used to identify customer segment using cluster analysis. This will not be used in this book
Graphs menu (all windows)	A variety of graph commands including bar, line, pie, histogram
Utilities menu (all windows)	Other IBM SPSS Statistics 19 facilities including variable information
Add-ons menu (all windows)	Provides information on other IBM SPSS Statistics 19 products and links to a variety of information sources, included web based
Window menu (all windows)	Use this menu to move between different IBM SPSS Statistics 19 windows
Help menu (all windows)	The IBM SPSS Statistics 19 online **Help** facility

Creating a new data file

The first step in creating a new data file is to define each of the variables. IBM SPSS Statistics 19 requires a variable name to be assigned to each variable. The name can be up to eight characters in length. It must not contain any mathematical operators (*/+—=), blank spaces or punctuation marks (/;:,.).

A variable name can directly reflect the variable itself, for example, Age, Gender. If there are many variables it may be advantageous to give a variable name relating to the question number, for example, Q1, Q2, Q3a, Q3b.

A variable label can be assigned to each variable. Unlike the variable name which is restricted to eight characters, the variable label can be longer, allowing for a more detailed description. The maximum variable label permitted is 255 characters.

The type of data can be defined, and for coded data this would be numeric. However, other data types including text, dates and currency are available.

The format of the data type can be defined. For numeric data you can control the format of the data in terms of the number of decimal places and the actual size or width of the number. The default setting is to have a width of eight and two decimal places. If the codes for nominal and ordinal variables are whole numbers, then it is good practice to set the number of decimal places to zero for these variables. If codes range from 0 to 9, then the width can be set to 1. Remember that the width will need to be greater if missing values are to be included. For example, using –99 to represent missing values requires a column width of three. Other data types are also available, including dates, scientific and string formats.

For nominal and ordinal variables, value labels can be assigned to define each of the categories. While it is not essential to allocate value labels, they will appear in the results, aiding interpretation and presentation. If value labels are not assigned, the code will be displayed. Value labels should also be included for missing codes.

The format of the column refers to how wide the column appears in the **Data View**. While not essential, it can be a useful feature to maximize the number of variable columns displayed at any one time in the window.

The appropriate level of measurement can be assigned to each variable, scale (interval or ratio), ordinal or nominal.

Defining a new variable

The first stage is to define each of the variables in the data file. Switch to the **Variable View** window (Figure 23.2). Each variable will be defined in the row. For each row there are 11 columns that define the variable: **Name**, **Type**, **Width**, **Decimals**, **Label**, **Values**, **Missing**, **Columns**, **Align**, **Measure** and **Role**. The list order of variables in the **Variable View** will be the order that they appear in each column in the **Data View**.

To define a new variable in **Variable View**, click in the first empty cell under the **Name** column. Enter a variable name, for example, 'Sex'.

Click, or use the tab key, to move to the **Type** column. The default setting is numeric. To alter to a different type, click on the small square with three dots that appears in the cell when you have selected the **Type** column. A **Variable Type** dialogue box will be displayed; select the required type and click on **OK** to close the box. Most survey data are converted into numeric codes. It is possible in IBM

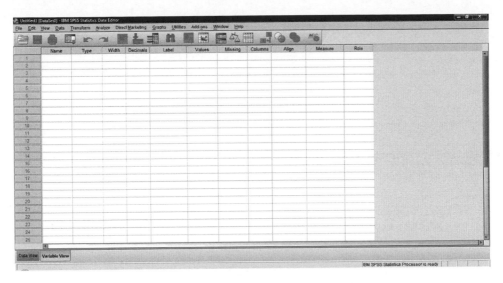

FIGURE 23.2   IBM SPSS Statistics 19 Data Editor Variable View

SPSS Statistics 19 to create alphanumeric or string, currency, scientific notation, dates and times variables.

Again click, or use the tab key, to move to the **Width** column. The width controls the maximum number of digits that can be entered for a value. For example, if the numeric codes ran from 1 to 12 with –99 as the missing value, then the minimum required width would be three: [–] [9] [9]. If the variable was storing values to two decimal places, for example, a weekly salary recorded in dollars and cents or pounds and pence sterling was 322.45, the width required would be six: [3] [2] [2] [.] [4] [5].

In the **Decimals** column the number of decimal places of the code can be set. In the case of coding using only whole numbers, the decimal places can be set to zero by typing 0 into the cell. It is acceptable to leave the default setting of two decimal places as this will not affect future analysis; however, it does allow for the possibility of an accidental data entry error, for example, typing in 1.1 when 1 was required.

The column **Label** is where the variable label is entered. For example, 'Sex of respondent'. There is an option to check the spelling of variable labels. To spell-check the variable label, make sure that your label entry is still selected. From the **Utilities** menu select **Spelling** (see Figure 23.3) and then as appropriate select the required spelling from the suggestions list.

The column **Values** is where the value labels for categories in nominal or ordinal variables can be assigned. Value labels can be set for both valid and missing codes. To enter value labels, click on the small square that appears when you move the **Values** column. A **Value Labels** box will appear (Figure 23.4).

To enter value labels, first click in the box next to **Value** and enter the code of the first category, for example, 1. Next click in the box next to **Label** and enter the value label for that code, for example, 'Female'. Now click on **Add**. Repeat this

FIGURE 23.3   Variable label spellcheck

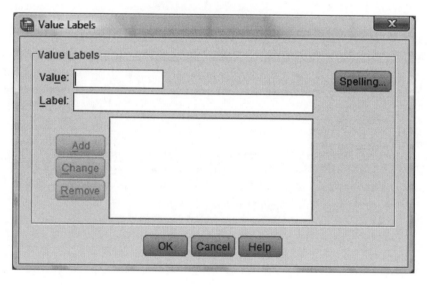

FIGURE 23.4   Value Labels dialogue box

process to enter value labels for all categories in the current variable. Labels can be edited by highlighting them in the list. Edit the code or label accordingly and then click on **Change**. Labels can be deleted by highlighting the required variable and clicking once on **Remove**. There is an option to undertake a spellcheck of each value label. Click on **Spelling** and as appropriate select the required spelling from the suggestions list. The spellcheck box will close when a change has been selected.

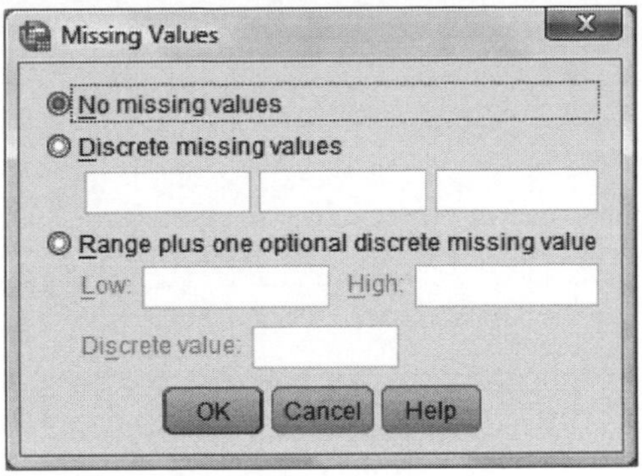

FIGURE 23.5 Missing Values dialogue box

Alternatively if no change is required, click on **Cancel** to return to the **Value Labels** dialogue box. Once completed, click **OK** to return to the **Variable View**. Value labels cannot be set for interval/ratio variables as the data are continuous.

The **Missing** column is used to define missing values. Missing values are codes that have been used to define non-response. The coding frame will contain details of the non-response codes. For the current variable, click once in the **Missing** column and then click on the small square that appears in the cell. The **Missing Values** box will be displayed (Figure 23.5).

There are a number of options for defining missing values. The default setting is 'No missing values'. There are two different ways of defining missing values. The first is to define up to three discrete missing values. The second is to define a range of missing values that could include one discrete value outside the defined range. Select the combination that best suits the type of missing codes you wish to define. Where there are one to three missing values, the first option should suffice. Where there are more than three missing values, ensure that the codes are sequential (for example, –6, –7, –8, –9) and use the second option to define the range. When the missing values have been defined, click on **OK** to return to the **Variable View**. In order to distinguish between different types of missing values in the final results, remember to assign a value label to each of the codes; see earlier on value labels.

The **Columns** and **Align** columns allow the width of the column and the alignment of the codes to be defined. It is normally sufficient to leave these on their default setting, but they can be altered to aid data entry. In the **Measure** column the level of measurement for each variable can be defined by selecting the appropriate option. The options are **Scale** (interval/ratio), **Ordinal** and **Nominal**. Finally, the **Role** column allows you to define the role of the variable in your analysis. For example, an input variable would be an independent or predictor variable in a regression model. At this stage it is not necessary to define the role. You can leave the setting at the default, **Input**, or change it to **None**.

Once the variable has been set up, click on the next row down in the **Name** column to continue the variable definition process for each of the subsequent variables in the code book.

Saving the data file

To save the data file, select the **File** menu and **Save**. Alternatively, click on the floppy disk icon. In the dialogue box, select the directory or drive in which you wish to save the data file. Enter a new file name in the **File Name** box. Click on **Save**.

Importing existing data files

Analysis of an existing data file can be undertaken in IBM SPSS Statistics 19. How the data file is imported into IBM SPSS Statistics 19 will be determined by the format of the data file. The increasing use of IBM SPSS Statistics 19 as a data management and analysis tool has resulted in many data files being available in a IBM SPSS Statistics 19 data file format. Indeed many data archives now routinely provide data in such a format. It is, however, possible to import data that have initially been stored in other applications. IBM SPSS Statistics 19 has filters that will enable it to read in data from file formats that include MS Excel, symbolic link files and MS Access. Where no direct filter exists, it is often possible to write out the data from the original application into one of these file formats.

To open a file in a different format, from the **File** menu select **Open** and **Data**. In the dialogue box from the **Files of Type** box, alter the type to the required format for the file you wish to import (for example, .xls). Locate the directory or floppy disk for the file. Highlight the file and click on **Open**.

Other data file formats

In a IBM SPSS Statistics 19 data file the data are held in a matrix format consisting of rows containing cases and columns containing the coded data in a variable. This matrix format is common to most data files and is accepted by most of the data analysis applications available. Generic file formats accepted by IBM SPSS Statistics 19 include tab delimited, comma separated and space separated. A variety of file formats specific to other spreadsheet and database package formats are also accepted and include Lotus, dBase, SLK, SAS, Systat and MS Excel. IBM SPSS Statistics 19 reads all MS Excel file formats. However, if there is more than one worksheet in the Excel workbook, only one worksheet can be read into a single IBM SPSS Statistics 19 data file. Multiple IBM SPSS Statistics 19 data files can be created, one for each of the worksheets. If you have more than one IBM SPSS Statistics 19 data file for a research project, it is possible to merge the files together. The techniques for merging data files are outlined in the following section.

Merging data files in IBM SPSS Statistics 19

Data from IBM SPSS Statistics 19 data files can be merged in two ways: by adding cases and by adding variables.

Adding cases

An existing data file can have additional cases added from a second IBM SPSS Statistics 19 data file. This can be a useful technique if you are working as a research team and have multiple people undertaking the data entry. Two people can be entering complete records of data into two separate IBM SPSS Statistics 19 data files. For example, survey questionnaires of 100 respondents might have been distributed between two people who will each enter 50 cases into two separate data files. These two data files are then merged together prior to the analysis phase. Files merged by cases ideally require the same variable names in the two separate data files and for each case to have its own case identifier in order that the researcher can check that the merge has been performed correctly. The IBM SPSS Statistics 19 command for merging files by adding cases is via the **Data** menu: select **Merge Files** and **Add Cases**. The command requires that you have the first data file opened in IBM SPSS Statistics 19. Table 23.5 shows the before-and-after files of merging data using **Add Cases**.

Adding variables

The second approach involves merging additional variables to cases in a data file. This is a useful technique if you are involved in an experimental or a longitudinal research design where you are undertaking measures on the same set of respondents at different points in time. In an experimental design, data will be collected pre- and post-experiment. In a longitudinal design, respondent data are collected at time point one and then again at a later time point two. The initial data collected (for example, pre-experiment or time point one) will be entered into one IBM SPSS Statistics 19 data file. The data file will record the research data and there will be a variable recording the unique case identifier of each respondent, e.g. IdCase. A second IBM SPSS Statistics 19 data file (for example, post-experiment or time point two) will also have the same unique case identifier variable plus the post or time point two research data stored in different variables. Files merged by adding variables require each case in the two data files to have the same unique identifying number. This enables each case to be correctly matched to the same case with the same number. This process is achieved as IBM SPSS Statistics 19 will sort both data files into ascending order by the unique identifier number.

Table 23.6, data file one contains the variables relating to individuals' sex, age and health status. Data file two contains follow-up data on the same respondents collected one year later: the data collected at time point two are age and health. The age and health variable names have been adjusted in each dataset to clearly distinguish between them. Each age and health variable has a corresponding 1 and 2, where 1 is the initial survey and 2 the follow-up survey one year later. The final data file contains the original cases, 1 to 5, with the five variables of Sex, Age1, Health1, Age2 and Health2.

TABLE 23.5   Merging data files by adding cases

Before: data file one

IdCase	Sex	Age	Health
1	1	25	1
2	2	20	1
3	2	28	3
4	2	40	2
5	1	65	1

Before: data file two

IdCase	Sex	Age	Health
6	2	33	3
7	2	41	3
8	2	52	1
9	1	31	2
10	1	24	2

After: merged by adding variables data file

IdCase	Sex	Age	Health
1	1	25	1
2	2	20	1
3	2	28	3
4	2	40	2
5	1	65	1
6	2	33	3
7	2	41	3
8	2	52	1
9	1	31	2
10	1	24	2

The IBM SPSS Statistics 19 command for merging files by adding variables is from the **Data** menu: select **Merge Files** and **Add Variables**. The command requires that you have the first data file opened in IBM SPSS Statistics 19.

Using secondary data sources

We have already discussed in Chapter 16 how you can locate and access secondary data sources (see section 'Locating and accessing secondary quantitative data' in Chapter 16). Gaining access to the data may involve a formal registration

TABLE 23.6   Merging data files by adding variables

Before: data file one

IdCase	Sex	Age1	Health1
1	1	25	1
2	2	20	1
3	2	28	3
4	2	40	2
5	1	65	1

Before: data file two

IdCase	Age2	Health2
1	26	3
2	21	2
3	29	2
4	41	2
5	66	1

After: merged by adding variables data file

IdCase	Sex	Age1	Health1	Age2	Health2
1	1	25	1	26	3
2	2	20	1	21	2
3	2	28	3	29	2
4	2	40	2	41	2
5	1	65	1	66	1

process in order to obtain the data file, which is generally in a IBM SPSS Statistics 19 file format, together with the relevant code book and survey information. The supporting information is often referred to as meta-data. Reading this information is as important as accessing the actual data file itself. The data file can be opened in IBM SPSS Statistics 19 for analysis. Data deposited at the archive will have already undergone a level of data cleaning from the primary research for which it was used. However, one should not assume that the file is 'clean' and one must be alert to possible inconsistencies and errors. Although the researcher has not actually entered the data, the same process of checking the data should be undertaken. The additional benefit of doing this is that it will also familiarize the researcher with the data file before undertaking any analysis.

Where the researcher does not have access to the original survey paperwork, data entry errors can be removed from subsequent analysis by recoding those particular cases as missing. Good practice would be to recode such values as new missing values in order to distinguish them from other types of missing value.

Using the Northern Ireland Life and Times Survey data

The quantitative data analysis chapters include optional exercises that use data from the Northern Ireland Life and Times Survey (NILT) 2006. See Box 15.2 for details on how to access the teaching data file and other related information.

Boxes 23.4 and 23.5 contain information on getting started with IBM SPSS Statistics 19 using the NILT data file. They provide an opportunity to familiarize yourself with the IBM SPSS Statistics 19 environment prior to creating your own data files. See also Box 23.6.

BOX 23.4

ANALYSING NILT: OPENING THE NORTHERN IRELAND LIFE AND TIMES SURVEY TO FAMILIARIZE YOURSELF WITH IBM SPSS STATISTICS 19

With the IBM SPSS Statistics 19 software installed and the NILT 2006 data file downloaded, you can open the data file by double clicking on it.

If this does not work then open IBM SPSS Statistics 19 on the PC. IBM SPSS Statistics 19 will be found either as an icon on your desktop or from the Windows **Start** button. From the **Start** button select **All Programs** and IBM SPSS Statistics 19 from the program list. Depending on how IBM SPSS Statistics 19 is installed on your computer, you may find it contained within a folder.

With the IBM SPSS Statistics 19 program open, from the **File** menu select **Open** and from the revealed menu select **Data**. In the dialogue box now locate the NILT06teach.sav file, click once on the file to highlight and click on **Open** (see Figure 23.6).

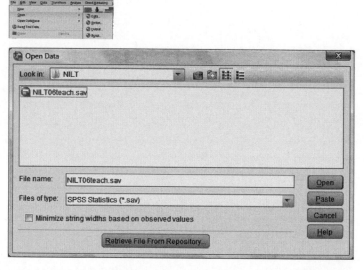

FIGURE 23.6   Opening the NILT06teach.sav IBM SPSS Statistics 19 data file

---

The data file should now be open. The data will populate the **Data Editor** window: see Figure 23.7 for an example.

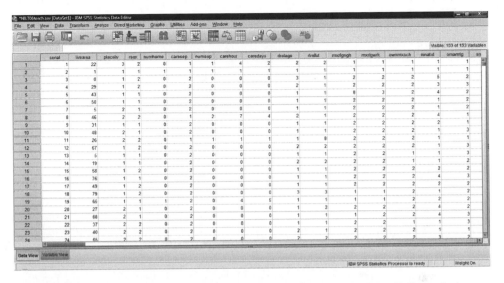

FIGURE 23.7 NILT dataset open in the IBM SPSS Statistics 19 **Data Editor** window

---

BOX 23.5

ANALYSING NILT AND FAMILIARIZATION WITH NILT

Open the NILT data file as in Box 23.4.

Use this IBM SPSS Statistics 19 data file to understand the IBM SPSS Statistics 19 environment. You can use this data file to explore how each of the variables has been set up.

To gain the maximal benefit from this process it is advisable to return to the NILT website (www.ark.ac.uk/nilt) and download the main questionnaire for NILT 2006. This file is in pdf format and can be easily opened for viewing. Make a note of how each of the survey questions relates to each variable in the NILT data file. You can gain an insight into the coding used and how the variables have been organized, particularly for multiple response and matrix questions. As part of this process, experiment with some of the IBM SPSS Statistics 19 commands that we have highlighted already. This dataset provides you with an opportunity to explore the data file and to see what some of the IBM SPSS Statistics 19 command options do. If you accidentally edit or delete the content of the data file it does not matter, as you can download a fresh copy of the data file from the website. Far better to make mistakes with this data file then risk damaging your own research data!

BOX 23.6 HINTS AND TIPS

File management

Since IBM SPSS Statistics 19 creates different types of files it is worth considering how you are going to organize the storage of these files. It is also advisable to make a backup copy of your original data file before you start the data analysis. This is considered good practice and is particularly advised when using IBM SPSS Statistics 19, as some procedures can alter the data file itself. In addition, always having the original copy provides a safety net should anything go wrong as you become familiar with using the software for the first time.

You will also be producing more than one output file during the course of your analyses, so it is advisable to plan how to manage these multiple files in a sensible manner. We would recommend that you create a project folder for your data analysis and within this folder create a subfolder, for example 'research data', that contains your data file, and a second subfolder labelled 'analysis'.

In the 'research data' folder, create one original data file. Make a copy of this data file (right click on the file and select copy and then paste; a file named 'copy of ...' will appear in the folder) and use this copy of the data file for your analyses. You can always rename the file to something more meaningful, for example, 'working data file'.

Use the 'analysis' folder to store the IBM SPSS Statistics 19 output files. Each time you open IBM SPSS Statistics 19 you create a new output window into which the results of your analyses are stored. When you save each output file into this folder, give it a clear and unique label. Avoid using the default file names as these always start with 'Output One', otherwise you will overwrite any previous files saved with this file name, losing vital data analysis and results!

Summary

In this chapter we have explained the process of entering data for analysis purposes. Data entry is the initial stage in the process of analysing survey data and it requires an understanding of variables, levels of measurement and coding. There are many statistical software packages available and the practice of data entry is similar for most of them. We have shown you how to undertake data entry using IBM SPSS Statistics 19. The first phase of data entry in IBM SPSS Statistics 19 requires variables to be defined. Many survey questions require a single variable in the data file. Survey questions that produce multiple responses require more than one variable and the social researcher must allocate enough variables for these questions. The development of a thorough code book prior to using IBM SPSS Statistics 19 should address these issues. Code books can take a number of formats, typically involving a coded version of the original questionnaire or a separate document that gives a detailed breakdown of the coding for each variable in the data file. The second phase is the actual entering of data, normally numeric codes, into the data file. Care needs to be taken to ensure that the data entry is as accurate as possible to limit difficulties in the subsequent analysis stages.

 ■ **Questions**

1 What are the key stages in preparing your research data for data entry?
2 What are the advantages of including variable labels and value labels in your IBM SPSS Statistics 19 data file?

■ ■ **Further reading** ■

Field, Andy (2009) *Discovering Statistics using SPSS for Windows*, 3rd edn. London: Sage.

Fielding, Jane and Gilbert, Nigel (2006) *Understanding Social Statistics*, 2nd edn. London: Sage.

Fowler, Floyd, J. (2008) *Social Research Methods*, 4th edn. London: Sage.

Pallant, Julie (2006) *SPSS Survival Manual: A Step by Step Guide to Data Analysis using SPSS for Windows*. Crows Nest, NSW: Allen and Unwin.

TWENTY FOUR

QUANTITATIVE DATA ANALYSIS: DESCRIBING SINGLE VARIABLES

Chapter Contents

Aims

By the end of this chapter you will be able to:

- **Understand how social statistics can be used to make sense of your quantitative research data.**
- **Understand a range of univariate analysis techniques available for different levels of measurement.**
- **Analyse categorical variables using frequency tables.**
- **Use appropriate measures of central tendency and dispersion to summarize the distribution of values.**
- **Understand standardized scores.**
- **Produce graphical presentations of data using appropriate charts and graphs.**

In this chapter we are going to explore the foundations of quantitative data analysis or social statistics. This chapter will introduce you to social statistics in general and how you can consider approaching the analysis phase of your research. Analysing data can be thought of as a series of blocks that build in complexity as you explore in more depth your research data and in so doing answer your original research question(s). Data analysis should be theory driven using your existing knowledge base, derived from the earlier stages in the research process, to guide the analysis that you undertake and specifically the variables you explore. The opposite to this is a data-driven analysis process in which all data collected are 'available' for your analysis. The number of variables collected often renders this an unmanageable process and one that can easily cause confusion as you try to make sense of the data.

At the first stage of analysing and understanding the quantitative data we will focus on the most frequently used data analysis techniques to describe individual variables. This process will involve getting to know your research data in terms of the range of values collected and how they are distributed. It will enable you to describe the data and to also consider the appropriateness of more advanced data analysis techniques that we explore in the subsequent chapters.

Social statistics

The analysis of quantitative data is also known as social statistics and is accompanied by a range of statistical and analytical terminology. The analysis process involves the researcher gaining an understanding of the data collected and exploring different elements of those data. The field of social statistics is thus concerned with managing, manipulating and analysing numerical data collected from a wider research process. From the preceding chapters we have seen how this process involves making decisions about research design, sampling, developing suitable measurement tools, ethical issues and effective data collection management. All of these aspects need to be considered when interrogating and making sense of the data.

It was C. Wright Mills who coined the phrase 'sociological imagination' as awareness of the relationship of the individual to wider society and to history. Academic specialist research focuses on a wide range of societal issues from across the social, political and economic domains. For example, sociologists focus on issues of conformity to social norms; economists are interested in how individuals make economic choices and their decision-making processes; and political commentators explore issues of polling outcomes in relation to voters' reactions to a downturn in the economy or overseas military campaigns. By collecting data on the individual and specific aspects of their behaviour, knowledge, attitudes and choices, the researcher can then consider them within a wider picture. For example, what may voter choice tell us about perspectives on the economy and social inequality?

Movement from the smaller picture to a wider understanding involves bringing together a solid research foundation, sociological imagination, and statistical imagination. As with sociological imagination, statistical imagination involves seeing the part (the individual case) as one element of a wider picture (society). Ritchey defines statistical imagination as an 'Appreciation of how usual or unusual an event, circumstance or behaviour is in relation to a larger set of similar events and an appreciation of an event's causes and consequences' (2008: 3). Unlike the laboratory experiment, the complexities of the social data collected in a real world require a sociological imagination to interpret and make sense of statistical findings.

The narrative of understanding the data is of equal importance to the correct application of different statistical techniques.

Social statistics both collects and summarizes data, known as descriptive statistics, and also considers the data findings in relation to a wider context using probability theory, known as inferential statistics. All data analysis requires you to think critically and systematically, to weigh up the data evidence before you, and to interpret the findings correctly. It will require you to make a judgement as to how frequent or infrequent or how usual or unusual an occurrence of an event is.

Key stages in the data analysis process

Quantitative data analysis can be broken down into five broad stages.

1 *Knowing your data.* This initial stage, and the focus of this chapter, is concerned with exploring individual variables in the dataset, and identifying trends in the data using descriptive statistical techniques and graphical representations of the data.

2 *Exploring relationships and differences in the data.* This stage, covered in Chapter 25, concentrates on describing differences and similarities between different groups of cases. For survey data this can involve making comparisons based on the biographical characteristics of individuals. Have men or women expressed a different range of attitudes? For experimental research this can involve comparisons between pre- and post-experimental measures, and for longitudinal research comparisons between two or more time points or cohorts.

3 *Making inferences via inferential statistics and hypothesis testing.* This stage, covered in Chapter 26, involves using inferential statistical techniques to estimate likely population parameters and to undertake hypothesis testing. For instance, from a known sample mean of average household income you can estimate the range within which the average household income for the population will fall.

4 *Modelling data and predicting outcomes from your research.* This stage, also covered in Chapter 26, involves using research data to model relationships in the data. These models can be used to understand the influence of different variables on outcomes and also to make predictions. For instance, from your sample data you can build a model to understand how age is related to individual income. Using the model from an individual's age you can predict the income of an individual based on their age.

5 *Data manipulation.* This stage, covered in Chapter 27, involves you making changes to your research data in order for you to be able to best analyse those data. While it appears as the final stage, it is more likely that you will actually have to undertake different types of data manipulation throughout the process of data analysis. For instance, you may wish to recategorize an income variable into income groups.

Knowing your data: describing single variables using univariate analysis

The first stage in the data analysis process is to describe and summarize the single variables in the dataset. This analysis uses descriptive statistics and is also known as univariate statistics. This is an exciting phase in the research as this is the first opportunity for 'getting to know the data'. It allows you as the researcher to start to look for trends in the data and to think critically how the findings can be interpreted and interrogated further at a later stage. Just as in qualitative analysis you should keep a research diary, noting down the analysis you have undertaken, why you focused on those data and your interpretations of the data. This can help inform the narrative that you will use to answer the research question(s). Regardless of research topic, this initial analysis allows you to note down anything that is noticeable about the data. Perhaps you will see values or category responses that are grouped or follow a particular trend which either confirms what you expected or contradicts your initial research hunches.

For instance, the distribution of responses to fear of crime in relation to two different types of crime – petty theft and physical assault – reveal very different responses, with fear of physical assault often higher than theft. In your research diary you should note these observed differences together with hunches or theories on why these differences may exist, perhaps related to age or gender. Also note how you progress the analysis to the next stage to provide evidence that supports or refutes your ideas. Here you can include how your findings compare to existing research and how you can explain your findings. For example, consider the analysis of a question which asked people about how they travelled to the university campus on a daily basis. This analysis revealed that over 70 per cent of the respondents travelled by car. This trend was surprising as other evidence provided by the university as part of a green travel policy suggested that only 20 per cent used the car. How can you make sense of this difference? What was the evidence base for the original green travel policy, and is it robust and reliable? What was the sampling technique and how were respondents recruited? Could it be accounted for by sampling error? Is it a reflection of the survey question: for example, was the question wording robust and reliable? Are there any other factors that could offer an explanation of your trend findings? How might you wish to explore this finding further?

Univariate analysis also allows the researcher first to detect data entry errors, second to describe and report the data, and third to determine the suitability of the data for possible future statistical testing. Where the data form a new indicator or measurement tool, the findings can be compared to the results of existing research to provide some preliminary analysis as to the reliability and validity of the measure.

The level of measurement of each individual variable will guide the univariate analysis to be undertaken. This analysis involves selecting from a range of measures including counts, percentages, measurements of distribution and spread, and graphical presentations in chart form. For categorical variables, nominal and ordinal, univariate analysis will initially involve producing a count and percentage of the number of cases that fall within each category. This summary information is presented in a frequency table format with the corresponding count and percentage displayed next to each of the categories in the variable. Graphical presentation of categorical data will involve bar charts and pie charts.

For interval and ratio variables, univariate analysis will begin with establishing the range of values, minimum and maximum, and the calculation of the average or mean value. Appropriate graphical presentation of interval variables will be stem and leaf diagrams, box plots, histograms and line graphs.

Once the basic analysis has been undertaken, the researcher can develop the analysis to look at how the values are spread in each of the variables. For example, are values clustered around one particular value? Are there more men than women in the sample? Are individual incomes clustered within a specific range? Finally, how confident can we be that the findings in our survey, taken from a sample, are representative of the population?

Frequencies and percentages

Frequencies

The starting point in the process of analysing categorical variables, nominal or ordinal, is to produce a frequency count of the number of cases that responded to each of the variable categories. One would normally start by selecting variables that will enable the researcher to describe the sample: for example, gender, marital status, employment status, occupation. From this the variables relating to the key questions can be described, and then finally the other variables in the data file. Examples of frequency tables for three different types of variable are shown in Table 24.1. Table 24.1a shows a nominal variable, gender, with two categories, male and female. Table 24.1b shows a nominal variable with five categories: four marital status categories and one missing category. Table 24.1c shows an ordinal variable with four categories and two different types of missing category.

From Tables 24.1a and 24.1b the frequency count of the variables 'gender' and 'marital status' reveal that of a sample of 1500 students, 600 were female and 900 were male; 1200 students were single, 150 were cohabiting, 50 were married, 40 were divorced or separated, and 60 students failed to answer the question, that is, data are missing as they did not respond.

Table 24.1c displays the responses to a question on personal safety around the university campus. The specific question was: 'How safe do you feel walking alone around the campus during daylight hours?' The question had four categories from which respondents could select very safe, fairly safe, a bit unsafe and very unsafe: 700 students felt very safe, 400 students felt fairly safe, 250 students felt a bit unsafe and 100 students felt very unsafe. In addition there were two missing categories. The first of these categories was 'not applicable', where respondents did not use the campus in daylight hours and the question was therefore irrelevant to

TABLE 24.1 Examples of frequency tables: gender, marital status safety

(a) Gender of students

Gender	Count
Male	900
Female	600
Total	1500

(b) Marital status of students

Marital status	Count
Single	1200
Cohabiting	150
Married	50
Divorced	40
Missing: did not respond	60
Total	1500

(c) 'How safe do you feel walking alone around the campus during daylight hours?'

Safe	Count
Very safe	700
Fairly safe	400
A bit unsafe	250
Very unsafe	100
Missing: not applicable	30
Missing: did not respond	20
Total	1500

Source: university student survey, 2009

the way in which they engaged with the campus. Thirty students were in this category. The second missing category was 'did not respond' where students had declined or failed to give a response. Twenty students were in this category.

Note that Table 24.1c is based on a survey shown in Figure 16.4. In that survey, Q2 asked if the respondent visited the university campus during daylight hours; Q3 then asked how safe they felt walking alone around the campus during daylight hours. The 'missing not applicable' category in Table 24.1c refers to the individuals who answered 'no' to Q2, i.e. they did not visit the campus during daylight hours.

Percentages

While a frequency count can tell us how many of the respondents fall into each of the categories, it is limiting in that it will not allow you to easily make comparisons between different samples. For instance, in the student survey example the researcher might wish to assess if changes to university security arrangements over the past year had had a positive impact on students' feelings of personal safety while on the campus. This could be assessed by comparing the responses from the current survey to a student survey conducted the year before. However, the previous year's survey had been conducted on a smaller sample of 900 students compared to 1500 for the current year. Comparing the category counts is clearly problematic as N (sample size) is different for each year. In order to make meaningful comparisons the relative proportion of students that responded in each of the four safe/unsafe categories needs to be compared. Calculating a percentage for each of the categories will enable such comparisons to be made.

The formula for calculating a percentage is

$$\% = \frac{\text{category count}}{N} \times 100$$

where N is the total number in the sample, and the category count is the observed value for a particular category.

Three types of percentage can be calculated. The first is based on the total sample size; the second is based on the total number of valid cases for that variable (total sample size minus the number of missing cases for the variable); and the third is a cumulative percentage, which is the sum of the valid percentages as one moves down the categories. The default category order is the ascending order of the category codes. Taking the earlier example (Table 24.1c), of how safe students felt walking around the university campus during daylight hours, Table 24.2 shows the calculated total percentage, valid percentage and cumulative percentage. Formulas for each are shown in square brackets.

Using IBM SPSS Statistics 19 to produce frequency tables

IBM SPSS Statistics 19 will calculate the count, percentage valid percentage and cumulative percentage using the **Frequencies** command. This section contains instructions on how to produce a frequency table for a nominal or ordinal variable in IBM SPSS Statistics 19.

The first step when undertaking data analysis is to open the data file. To open a data file from the **File** menu, select **Open** and **Data**. In the dialogue box, select the directory or drive where the file is located. Highlight the data file and click on **Open**.

To calculate a frequency table, from the **Analyze** menu, select **Descriptive Statistics** and **Frequencies**. A frequencies box will be displayed (Figure 24.1). On the left hand side of the box, all the variables contained in the opened data file will be displayed. The format shown is the variable label followed by the variable name in square brackets [ ]. The variable from which a frequency table will be produced needs to be moved from the left hand side to the right hand side of the box under **Variable(s)**.

To move the variable, highlight the required variable and click once on the arrow button ⬜ to move the variable name to the section under **Variable(s)**. Click

TABLE 24.2 'How safe do you feel walking alone around the campus during daylight hours?': count, total percentage, valid percentage and cumulative percentage

How safe	Count	Total %	Valid %	Cumulative %
Very safe	700	46.7% [700/1500 * 100]	48.3% [700/1450 * 100]	48.3%
Fairly safe	400	26.7% [400/1500 * 100]	27.6% [400/1450 * 100]	75.9% [48.3% + 27.6%]
A bit unsafe	250	16.7% [250/1500 * 100]	17.2% [250/1450 * 100]	93.1% [48.3% + .6% + 17.2%]
Very unsafe	100	6.7% [100/1500 * 100]	6.9% [100/1450 * 100]	100% [48.3% + 27.6% + 17.2% + 6.9%]
Missing: not applicable	30	2.0% [30/1500 * 100]		
Missing: did not respond	20	1.3% [20/1500 * 100]		
Total	1500	100%		

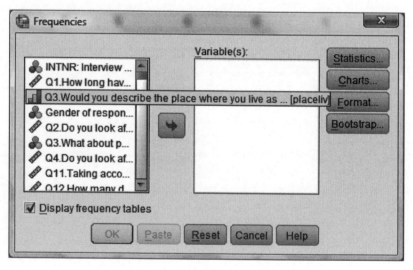

FIGURE 24.1 IBM SPSS Statistics 19 Frequencies dialogue box

on **OK**. More than one variable can be selected at a time. To select consecutive variables, click once on the first variable and then hold down the **Shift** key and click on the last variable required. To select non-consecutive variables, click on the first variable and then hold down the **Ctrl** key before selecting the other required variables. The frequency table will be calculated and displayed in the **Output Viewer**. See also Boxes 24.1 and 24.2.

Table 24.3 contains an example of the frequency table output in IBM SPSS Statistics 19. Two tables are produced. The first table 'Statistics' displays the number of valid and missing cases for the variable; additional statistical tests, if selected, would also appear in this table.

The second table displays the count and percentages of the variable Sex. The title of the table contains the variable label; in the table this is 'Sex of respondent'. The value labels are in the first column; in the example these are 'Male' and 'Female'. The term 'Valid' is also displayed next to the value labels to show that these are actual observations for these categories. The 'Frequency' column shows the

TABLE 24.3   Example of a IBM SPSS Statistics 19 frequency table output: sex of the respondent

Statistics

N	Valid	130
	Missing	0

Sex of respondent

		Frequency	Percent	Valid percent	Cumulative percent
Valid	Male	70	53.8	53.8	53.8
	Female	60	46.2	46.2	100.0
	Total	130	100.0	100.0	

frequency or count, that is, the number of respondents selecting each category. The 'Percent' column shows the percentage calculated on the total sample count of 130. The 'Valid percent' column shows the percentage based on the total valid count excluding the number of missing cases. There are no missing cases for this variable, so the 'Valid percent' is identical to the 'percent'. The 'Cumulative percent' column shows the cumulative percentage, which simply adds the valid percentages in ascending order. At the bottom of the table the number of missing cases is displayed (here none). This information is important when using the percentage and valid percentage columns. One would normally report the valid percentage in a written report.

Measures of central tendency

Measures of central tendency are concerned with identifying a typical value that best summarizes the distribution of values in a variable. There are three such measures. The mode is the most frequently occurring value in a variable. The median is the middle value when all the valid values for a variable are placed in ascending order. The mean, commonly referred to as the average, is the value derived from adding all the values in the distribution together and dividing by the total number of values. Examples of each measure are shown below.

The mode

In this example, 11 students have been asked their age in years. The results are:

18   26   24   19   34   33   28   37   28   28   37

From looking at the distribution of values we can ascertain that the most frequently occurring age value is 28 years, recorded three times. Where there are two most frequently occurring values in a distribution, the distribution is referred to as being bimodal. More than two modes in a distribution are called multimodal. The use of the mode is fairly limited, due to its focus on the most frequently occurring values and not all the values in the distribution.

The median

Taking the same age distribution as in the previous example, the median can be calculated by rearranging the ages into ascending rank order:

18   19   24   26   28 | 28 | 28   33   34   37   37
                          | 6th |

The middle position or median of the distribution is the sixth observation, as there are five observations either side.

Where there is an even number of observations in a distribution, the middle position will fall between two values. To calculate the median, add the two middle values together and divide by 2. In the following example the distribution has been reduced by one to 10 by removing the final case with an age of 37 years:

$$18 \quad 19 \quad 24 \quad 26 \quad \boxed{\begin{array}{cc} 28 & 28 \\ \text{5th} & \text{6th} \end{array}} \quad 28 \quad 33 \quad 34 \quad 37$$

$$(28 + 28)/2 = 28$$

Like the mode, the calculation of the median is not based on the entire distribution.

The mean

The mean or arithmetic mean is the most frequently used statistical measure of central tendency. In the literature it is often written as $\bar{x}$. It is based on the summation of all the values in the distribution divided by the number of occurrences. Thus the formula for the mean is

$$\bar{x} = \frac{\sum\limits_{i}^{n} x_i}{n}$$

where $\bar{x}$ is the mean or average; capital Greek sigma Σ means sum; x_i are the individual observed values; Σ_{x_i} between i and n means sum all values of x, for example $x_1 + x_2 + x_3$; and n is the sample size.

The mean for the age values in the example would be:

$$\bar{x} = \frac{18+19+24+26+28+28+28+33+34+37+37}{11} = 28.36$$

Using the mode, median and mean

Care should be taken when calculating the measures of central tendency. The level of measurement of the variable should guide the choice of measure. For interval and ratio variables the mode, median and mean can all be calculated, though it is normal just to use the mean. However, one must be aware that as the calculation of the mean is based on all values in the distribution, the extreme values, also referred to as outliers, at either end of the distribution will severely impact on the mean value. If outliers are identified it may be that the median is a better representation. A common example of where outliers can affect the mean is income.

For ordinal variables the median is a useful measure of central tendency as it is itself based on placing the rank order categories. Depending on the nature of the ordinal variable, it can be appropriate to apply the measurement techniques of interval/ratio variables. These are often applied when dealing with attitudinal scales, especially if they are combined into a single index score (see section 'Likert scales' in Chapter 15).

For nominal variables the mode is the appropriate measure of central tendency. Since this is the most frequently occurring category, the mode can be easily identified from the frequency table. It will be the category that has the highest number of counts.

Measures of dispersion

Measures of central tendency, while providing summary statistics for a sample, do not allow the researcher to comment on the distribution of the original values. It is not possible to conclude that two samples which have the same mean actually have values distributed in the same way.

Measures of dispersion provide information on how values are spread in a distribution. The following measures of dispersion can be applied to interval or ratio levels of measurement.

The range

When reporting interval/ratio variables one would be interested in the minimum or lowest and the maximum or highest valid values recorded. From these valid values the range can be established. The range is simply the maximum minus the minimum value. For example, if in a survey of 100 students the minimum age was 19 years and the maximum age was 55 years, the range would be 36 years (55 – 19).

For nominal variables the value codes, while having a numerical ascending order, are merely representing categories. Since the categories cannot be placed in any order, it does not make sense to calculate a range. For ordinal variables, the range is already known from the value codes assigned to each category. The range is limited in describing a variable, as it does not convey the most typical value or how the values are distributed within the range. An alternative approach is to calculate the interquartile range.

The interquartile range

The interquartile range (IQR) provides the researcher with more information on how the values within the range are distributed. This is particularly useful for analysing interval variables. It involves placing the values in rank order from lowest to highest, as for the range. The range is then divided into four equal percentiles or 25 per cent blocks (see Figure 24.2).

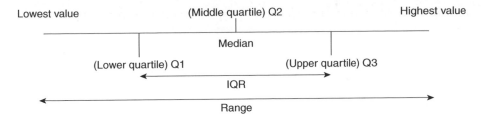

FIGURE 24.2 Interquartile range

The 25th quartile (25 per cent) is Q1, the 50th quartile (50 per cent) is Q2, which is also the median, and the 75th quartile (75 per cent) is Q3. The IQRs are the values that are placed between Q1 and Q3. Unlike the range, which is calculated on the lowest and highest values, thus susceptible to extreme values, the IQR is affected less by possible extreme values. For example, in a survey of 100 students the minimum age was 19 and the maximum age was 55. All 100 ages were placed in rank order from lowest to highest. The 25th percentile was located. The value of age at this 25th percentile was 24. At the 75th percentile the value of age was 45. The IQR is calculated as the difference between 45 years and 24 years. The IQR was therefore 21 years.

Variance

Variance is a commonly used measure of dispersion. Its calculation is based on the mean and involves finding the distance between each of the values and the mean. Since the mean is derived from these values anyway, it is hardly surprisingly that if you were to sum, or add together, all the distances of values that fall above the mean (+) with all the distances of values that fall below the mean (−), the result would be zero. The statistical fix for this is to square the distances, as mathematical convention states that when two negative numbers are multiplied together they become a positive number. The effect of this is to turn all the negative distances that fall below the mean into positive numbers. The full equation for calculating the variance s^2 is:

$$s^2 = \frac{\sum\left(x_i - \bar{x}\right)^2}{n-1}$$

where x_i are the observed values, $\bar{x}$ is the mean, n is the sample size and $\sum$ is summation (adding all values together).

The larger the variance, the further the observed values are dispersed from the mean. A variance of zero would mean that all observed values had the same value as the mean. One of the difficulties with calculating the variance is that because the calculation involves squaring the differences in distance from the mean and the observed value, the resulting values are not in the same units as the original values. This makes interpretation difficult. However, if the variance is then square rooted, this returns the values to the same units. The square root of the variance is known as the 'standard deviation' and is represented in statistical notation as s.

Standard deviation

The calculation for standard deviation is:

$$s = \sqrt{\frac{\sum (x_i - \bar{x})^2}{n - 1}}$$

where x_i are the observed values, x is the mean, n is the sample size, $\sum$ is summation (adding all values together) and $\sqrt{}$ is the square root.

Standard deviation units are the same as the original data. For example, if the variable is age recorded in years, the calculated standard deviation can be interpreted as years. Like variance, a large standard deviation means that the data are spread out from the mean, whereas a small standard deviation means that the data are concentrated around the mean. Since variance and standard deviation are based on the mean, and consequently all the observed values for a variable, both are susceptible to extreme values that appear at either end of the distribution, known as 'outliers'. Outliers can be identified and, if appropriate, removed from the analysis.

In addition, the shape of the distribution is also a factor to be considered. If the data are skewed in a particular direction, for example, more values at the top end of the distribution than the lower, then the median may be a better measure of central tendency. Standard deviation is an important calculation in relation to the normal distribution curve (see section 'The normal distribution curve and the central limit theorem' in Chapter 26).

Measures of the shape of a distribution

Two measures can be calculated that will indicate the shape of the distribution of an interval or ratio variable: skewness and kurtosis. The shape of a distribution refers to the resulting trend line when the data are plotted on to a line graph, or the shape of the distribution when the data are presented in a histogram. Details on producing line graphs and histograms are given late in this chapter.

Calculating skewness will indicate the position of the lower and higher values in the distribution, which have the effect of pulling the shape of a distribution to the lower or higher ends or tails. A negatively skewed distribution will have a greater number of observations at the higher values, pulling the distribution to the right or higher end. A positively skewed distribution will be the opposite, with a greater number of observations at the lower values, pulling the distribution to the left (see Figure 24.3). Values that are equally distributed will be symmetrical. An example of a symmetrical distribution is the normal distribution curve as in Figure 26.1.

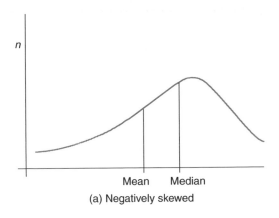

(a) Negatively skewed

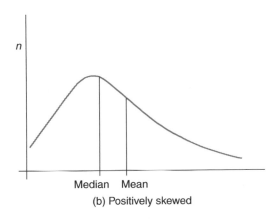

(b) Positively skewed

FIGURE 24.3   Skewness

Negatively skewed distributions will have a mean value that is less than the median value. Positively skewed distributions will have a mean value that is greater than the median value. It is therefore possible to assess the shape of the distribution by examining the values for the median and mean in addition to assessing the value for skewness. From the earlier section you know that the mean is susceptible to extreme values at either end of the distribution. For negatively skewed distributions the lower extreme values have the effect of pulling down or lowering the mean. For positively skewed distributions the higher extreme values pull up or raise the mean. Where distributions are greatly skewed, the median may be a more accurate measure of central tendency. As well as the measure of skewness, graphical presentations of the data allow for the distribution shape to be assessed. The most popular chart to use is the histogram. In addition, box plots allow the visualization of extreme values at both the lower and the higher end (see later in this chapter).

Calculating kurtosis will indicate how the values are distributed around the mode. The more tightly clustered are the values around the mode, the more 'pointed' the distribution. This is known as positive kurtosis, sometimes referred

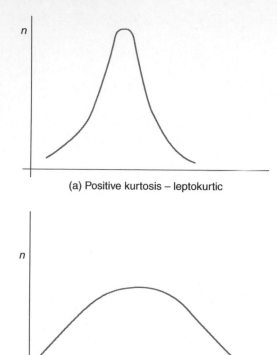

(a) Positive kurtosis – leptokurtic

(b) Negative kurtosis – platykurtic

FIGURE 24.4 Kurtosis

to as leptokurtic. The more loosely distributed are the values around the mode, the flatter and wider is the distribution (Figure 24.4). This is known as negative kurtosis or platykurtic. An even distribution is known as mesokurtic.

Using IBM SPSS Statistics 19 to calculate measures of central tendency and dispersion

There are a number of methods for calculating measures of central tendency and dispersion in IBM SPSS Statistics 19.

The Frequencies command   A frequency table can be produced with additional summary statistics calculated. From the **Analyze** menu, select **Descriptive Statistics** and **Frequencies**. Highlight the required variable from the left variables list and click once on the arrow button ▣ to move the variable to the section under **Variable(s)** (see Figure 24.1). To calculate measures of central tendency and dispersion, click on the **Statistics** button. A **Frequencies: Statistics** dialogue box will be displayed (Figure 24.5).

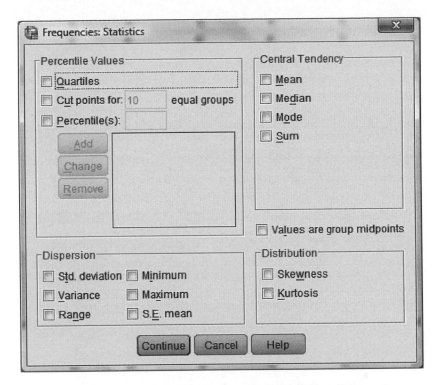

FIGURE 24.5 IBM SPSS Statistics 19 **Frequencies: Statistics** dialogue box

This box is divided into subsections; within each there are a number of statistical options that can be selected by clicking in the corresponding box. A tick in the box states that the option has been selected. Under **Percentile Values**, the IQR values can be calculated by selecting **Quartiles**. Under **Dispersion**, the measures of standard deviation (**Std. deviation**), variance (**Variance**), range (**Range**) and minimum and maximum (**Minimum, Maximum**) calculations can be selected. Under **Central Tendency**, the mean (**Mean**), median (**Median**) and mode (**Mode**) can be selected. There is also a sum option (**Sum**) that will simply provide a total of all values for each of the selected variables. Under **Distribution**, the values of skewness (**Skewness**) and kurtosis (**Kurtosis**) can be selected. Once the required statistics have been selected, click on **Continue** to return to the previous **Frequencies** dialogue box (Figure 24.1). If a frequency table is not required, remove the tick next to **Display frequency tables**. Finally, click on **OK** to execute the command. The corresponding results will be displayed in the **Viewer** window. The first summary statistics table will now contain the additional statistics requested.

An example of a summary statistics table is shown in Table 24.4. In this example the analysis is of an interval variable, Age, measured in years. Measures of central tendency and dispersion appropriate for this data type were selected. The results show that there were 130 valid cases with no missing cases. The lowest age was 16 years and the maximum age 93 years. The mean age was 47.27 years and the data

TABLE 24.4 Summary statistics using IBM SPSS Statistics 19

Age	Statistics	
N	Valid	130
	Missing	0
Mean		47.27
Median		46.00
Mode		26[a]
Std deviation		18.326
Variance		335.842
Skewness		.176
Std error of skewness		.212
Kurtosis		−.850
Std error of kurtosis		.422
Range		77
Minimum		16
Maximum		93
Percentiles	25	31.00
	50	46.00
	75	62.25

[a]Multiple modes exist; the smallest value is shown.

were slightly positively skewed with a skewness value of 0.176. Note that we can also conclude that the data are positively skewed from the calculation of the median being less than the mean. To calculate the IQR, subtract the value for percentile 25 (quartile 1) from the value for percentile 75 (quartile 3): here this is 62.25 – 31.00 = 31.25 years.

The Descriptives command An alternative method of producing summary statistics is to use the **Descriptive Statistics** command in IBM SPSS Statistics 19. This method does not produce the frequency table and the quartiles for calculating the interquartile range. From the **Analyze** menu, select **Descriptive Statistics** and **Descriptives**. The **Descriptives** dialogue box will be displayed (Figure 24.6). As with the previous IBM SPSS Statistics 19 command, first highlight the required variable(s) on the left hand side and click once on the arrow button ⏩ to move the variable across to under **Variable(s)**. To select the summary statistics, click once on the **Options** button. A **Descriptive: Options** dialogue box will be displayed (Figure 24.7). This box is divided into subsections, each containing a number of different options. At the top there are the two options of **Mean** and **Sum**. As with previous dialogue boxes, the option can be selected by clicking in the corresponding box. A tick in the box states that the option has been selected. Under **Dispersion** the standard deviation (**Std. deviation**), variance (**Variance**), range (**Range**), minimum (**Minimum**) and maximum (**Maximum**) values can be selected. Under **Distribution**, kurtosis (**Kurtosis**) and skewness (**Skewness**) can be selected. Finally, under **Display Order** the format of the results can be altered. The

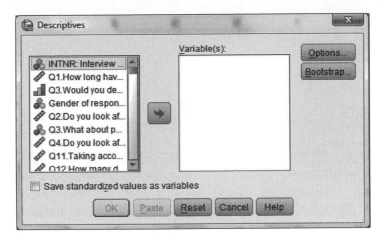

FIGURE 24.6   IBM SPSS Statistics 19 Descriptives dialogue box

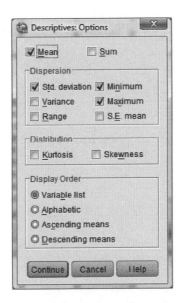

FIGURE 24.7   IBM SPSS Statistics 19 **Descriptives: Options** dialogue box

default setting is to display the results for each selected variable in the same order as the variable list (**Variable list**). Other options are to display, in alphabetical order (**Alphabetic**), or in order of the smallest calculated mean (**Ascending means**) or largest mean (**Descending means**) of each variable. Unless there is a specific reason for rearranging the variable display, do not alter the default setting of **Variable list**. Other measures of central tendency, the median and the mode are not available, and if required the **Frequencies** command should be used. Click on **Continue** to return to the previous **Descriptives** box and click on **OK** to execute the command. An example of the IBM SPSS Statistics 19 output using **Descriptives** is shown in Table 24.5. For a caution see Box 24.3.

TABLE 24.5 Example of Descriptive Statistics IBM SPSS Statistics 19 output

Descriptive Statistics

	N	Range	Minimum	Maximum	Mean	Std. Deviation	Variance	Skewness		Kurtosis	
	Statistic	Statistic	Statistic	Statistic	Statistic	Statistic	Statistic	Statistic	Std. Error	Statistic	Std. Error
Respondent's age	130	77	16	93	47.27	18.326	335.842	.176	.212	–.850	.422
Valid N (listwise)	130										

EXERCISE CAUTION WHEN USING IBM SPSS STATISTICS 19 TO CALCULATE MEASURES OF CENTRAL TENDENCY

IBM SPSS Statistics 19 will allow you to calculate a mean for any variable including a nominal variable such as 'Gender', even though it is not appropriate for this level of measurement. The calculation of the mean is based on the value codes for each category, in this case 1 = Male and 2 = Female. The mean will fall somewhere between these two values, for example, 1.45. Calculating a mean for a nominal variable is clearly meaningless as you cannot interpret this value. For nominal variables, the coding used for data entry is a convenience and the qualitative nature of the variable should determine the interpretation of the responses.

Further frequency table and descriptive exercises using the NILT data set can be found at chapter 24 tasks.

Standardized scores

Standardized scores are particularly useful as they allow for comparisons between two interval variables with different distributions or measures. They are routinely used in health, social care and educational settings to assess the position of one case, for example, one individual's weight score, or the deprivation score of a ward in a local authority in relation to the overall distribution of values. Standardized scores are also used in more advanced statistical analyses that involve modelling data for the purposes of predicting different outcomes. Using standardized scores resolves the difficulty of having different variables with different measurement characteristics. For example, consider household income and the number of children in a household. These have different characteristics and magnitudes; the number of children in a household is likely to be five or fewer, while household income is measured in thousands of pounds.

Standardized scores involve calculating the distance that an observed value is from the mean and converting it into standard deviation units. Standardized scores are also called Z-scores.

For a worked example of how to calculate standardized scores and how to calculated z scores in IBM SPSS Statistics 19 see Chapter 24.

Graphical presentation of single variables

The graphical presentation of data using charts enables the researcher to get an overall feel for the data. Differences and trends can be easier to interpret when the data are presented in a chart format. The researcher can also include particular charts in the final report both to evidence the research findings and to convey a particular aspect of the data to the reader. Different graphical techniques are available according to the level of measurement or data type. The following sections will detail the appropriate charts for interval, ordinal and nominal variables.

Charts for interval variables

A number of graphic methods are available that will provide a visual interpretation of the range of a variable. This section details the flow charts most commonly used. All are easy to produce in IBM SPSS Statistics 19.

Histograms

The histogram is one of the most frequently used graphical presentations of interval or ratio data. It is particularly useful where you have data with a wide range of values. Histograms are drawn based on grouped frequency distributions. A frequency distribution counts the number of observed cases for each value in the distribution. A grouped frequency distribution places observed values into groups and counts the number of observed cases in each of the groups. In a histogram these groups of values are known as intervals and are represented by a bar on the histogram.

Intervals are consecutive and the values of each interval should not overlap with the next interval. In a histogram each interval is displayed as one bar on the x-axis (horizontal) and each bar touches the next bar as the data are continuous. The y-axis (vertical) displays the count or frequency of cases that fall into the data range represented by the bar. An example of a histogram for a variable of property prices is shown in Figure 24.8.

Imagine we were involved in a research project that was looking at issues of homelessness in a city area. One area of exploration in this project would be around issues of private residential property ownership, availability and affordability. As part of the research project we could examine the sale value of properties sold within the previous six-month period and calculate the ratio of average property price to average income to establish availability and affordability. However, property prices have wide variation as they are dependent on the type, size and location of the property. So a more detailed analysis of the property price data could address the affordability of different property types. The price data of all completed sales for residential property were gathered over the six-month period. The minimum sale was £70,000 and the maximum sale was £320,000. The mean sale price was £204,000. A total of 530 sales took place.

To calculate a grouped frequency distribution and a histogram you would undertake the following steps. Calculating a grouped frequency distribution involves:

TABLE 24.6   Property prices grouped data, June–December 2009

Intervals (£s)	Frequency
> 100k	6
100–124,999	15
125–149,999	42
150–174,999	70
175–199,999	80
200–224,999	125
225–249,999	135
250–274,999	52
275–299,999	3
300k +	2
N	530

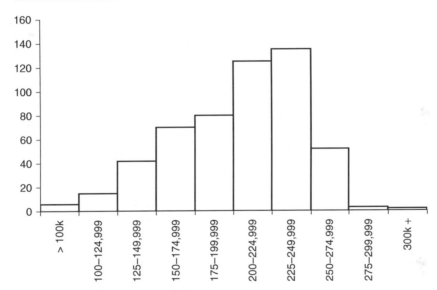

FIGURE 24.8   Histogram of property sales, June–December 2009.

1   Sorting the data into rank order, i.e. lowest to highest, to find the minimum and maximum values.

2   Determining the number of groups or intervals. You would normally start by determining the lowest and highest groups and then dividing the remaining distribution of values into groups of equal widths.

3   Counting the number of observed cases with values that fall within each of the groups/ intervals.

Table 24.6 shows the grouped property prices and the observed cases within each. There are 10 groups or intervals for these data. The lowest interval is less than

£100k, and the highest interval is £300k or higher. Each group needs to be discrete with no overlap. Values here are shown to the nearest whole pound. The intervals and frequency for each group are displayed in the histogram in Figure 24.8.

The grouped frequency table and the histogram enable us to assess the distribution of sold property prices. The histogram shows that a small number of property sales are less than £125,000, with the majority of sales falling between £150,000 and £225,000. Clearly some properties will be more affordable than others, with the number of properties sold also providing interesting insights. The next stage in the analysis would be to identify income data to provide evidence that can contribute to affordability issues, together with an analysis of properties made available for sale as an indicator of market supply.

Histograms should not be confused with bar charts (see 'Bar charts' later in this chapter). Histograms should be used to provide a visual presentation of the distribution of values for an interval/ratio variable. The bars in a histogram touch as the data are continuous. Bar charts are for categorical variables where each category in the variable is represented by a bar; however, since each category is discrete, the bars need not touch.

Stem and leaf diagrams

Stem and leaf diagrams can be used to display interval variables that have at least two significant places: for example, currency or percentages in tens and units. The first significant unit is the stem and the second the leaf. Stem and leaf diagrams are particularly useful in identifying variables where there is more than one mode.

Table 24.7 displays a stem and leaf diagram for the variable Age. The stem represent units of 10 years and the leaf represents single units of 1 year. In the first line there are 6 observations; these are 16, 16, 17, 17, 18 and 19 years. In the second line there are 22 observations; the first eight of these are 20, 20, 20, 21, 21, 22, 23 and 24 years.

Box and whisker plots

Box and whisker plots graphically present the summary measures of median, quartiles and interquartile range for an interval-level variable. Box and whisker plots are often referred to as box plots. The box plot represents the data values placed in rank order from lowest to highest values. The values are represented on the y or vertical axis. The median is displayed as a horizontal line within a box. The lower and upper edges of the box represent the lower quartile (Q1 or 25 per cent) and upper quartile (Q3 or 75 per cent) respectively. Therefore the box represents the interquartile range or middle 50% of cases. Within the box is a line that represents the median value. The single lines that extend beyond the box are known as the 'whiskers'. The whiskers will represent the minimum and maximum values of the variable. These two lines also represent the lower 25 per cent and upper 25 per cent

TABLE 24.7   Example of a stem and leaf diagram for Age of respondent

Frequency	Stem and leaf
6.00	1. 667789
22.00	2. 0001123456666667778889
21.00	3. 000113344555568888889
23.00	4. 00011123333455666777999
19.00	5. 1113444555666677899
24.00	6. 000222233334444556667999
10.00	7. 0112336678
4.00	8. 3345
1.00	9. 3

Stem width: 10
Each leaf: 1 case(s)

of cases in the distribution. A box plot is shown in Figure 24.9 and represents the same variable Age as shown in the stem and leaf diagram in Table 24.7. The y or vertical axis displays values that are age measured in years.

The box and whisker plot can be used to assess the distribution of values in the variable. To interpret the plot, first look at the box itself. The box represents the interquartile range. This will tell you where the middle 50 per cent of cases are located within the overall distribution of values in the variable. A box that is not positioned in the middle of chart and is either at the lower or upper end is an indication of a skewed distribution. Differences in the length of the lower and upper whiskers provide a further indication of skewness.

The position of the median line within the box and in relation to the upper and lower whiskers indicates how the values are clustered within the interquartile range. If the median line is in the middle of the box with an equal distance to the lower and upper horizontal lines, then this indicates a distribution that is equally distributed with symmetry, as is the case with a normal distribution. If the median line is towards the upper half of the box with a shorter distance to the upper horizontal line of the whisker, then this would suggest that more cases are clustered towards the upper end of the distribution values. Conversely if the median line is closer to the lower horizontal line, then this suggests that more cases are clustered towards the lower end of the distribution values.

Figure 24.10 displays a box plot of house prices for two neighbourhood areas in a city. The house prices in each area have a different distribution. The properties sold in Neighbourhood One, represented by the plot on the left, consist of one- or two-bedroom flats and terraced houses with two or three bedrooms. Compare this to the box plot for Neighbourhood Two that shows the distribution of houses sold in a desirable suburb of the city, where there is a greater mix of housing stock that includes flats, and houses that are terraced, semi-detached and detached, with on average a greater number of bedrooms.

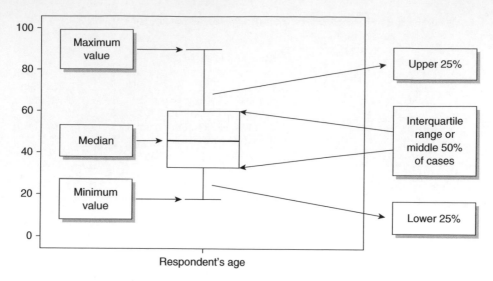

FIGURE 24.9 Example of a box and whisker plot for Age of respondent

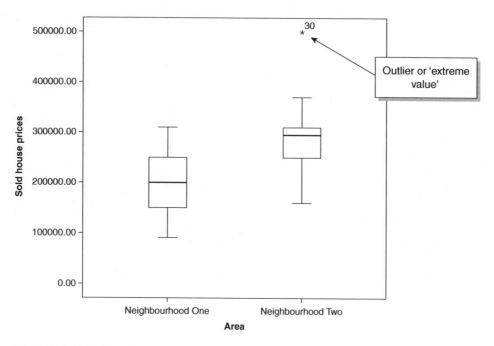

FIGURE 24.10 Two box plots showing different distributions for sold house prices (£)

In Neighbourhood One the lowest house value is £91,000 and the highest is £310,000. The mean house price is £204, 345 and the median, represented by the solid line in the box plot, is £200,000. Here the mean and the median are similar. Looking at the box plot for Neighbourhood One we can see that the box,

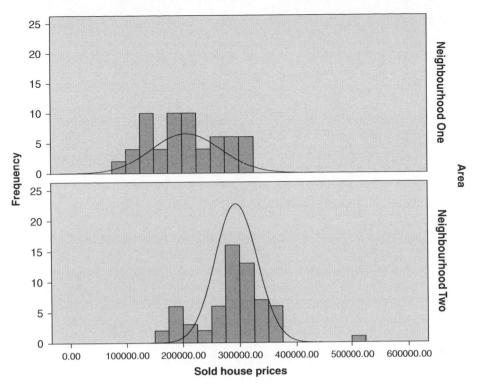

FIGURE 24.11 Two histograms showing different distributions. Sold house prices £s.

representing the interquartile range, is in the middle of the distribution, with the distance between the upper and lower whiskers almost identical. The median line is in the middle of the box, indicating the data are normally distributed; this is reinforced with a skewness of only 0.214. Data that approximate to a normal distribution will have median and mean values that are very close. The corresponding histogram for Neighbourhood One house prices is shown in Figure 24.11, top chart. By comparing the two different charts you can see how the two different representations of the data are visualizing the data. We can see from the histogram that the distribution is quite flat.

The box plot and histogram for Neighbourhood Two show an entirely different distribution of values that, as we would expect from our prior knowledge of the neighbourhood property profile, reflect a much higher house price. In Neighbourhood Two the lowest house price is £160,000 and the highest house price is £500,000. The highest value is an outlier or extreme value which has been flagged on the box plot as falling outside the boundary of the upper whisker and is clearly identifiable on the corresponding histogram in Figure 24.11. There is a slight difference between the mean house price of £286,193 and the median house price of £295,000; however, the mean value will have been affected by the outlier.

In relation to Figure 24.10, the box plots for an interval variable by the categories in a nominal variable can be produced in SPSS 19. From the **Graphs** menu, select **Legacy Dialog** and **Boxplot**. Click on **Simple** and select **Summaries for groups of cases**, and then click on **Define**. Place the interval variable, e.g. sold house prices, under **Variable**, and the grouping Variable, e.g. neighbourhood area, under **Category Axis**. Click on **OK** to execute the command.

One point to note about box plots in IBM SPSS Statistics 19 is that the application will identify the whiskers based on the minimum and maximum values that IBM SPSS Statistics 19 has calculated as falling within 1.5 box lengths from the upper and lower edges of the box. Values that fall outside the calculation are assessed as being 'outliers' or extreme values in the distribution and are plotted on to the box plot itself. While this is a useful function in IBM SPSS Statistics 19, it does mean that the user needs to take care to correctly interpret the whiskers on box plots where outliers are marked.

In relation to Figure 24.11, the histograms for an interval variable by the categories in a nominal variable are produced in IBM SPSS Statistics 19 by the following commands. From the **Graphs** menu, select **Legacy Dialog** and **Histogram**. Place the interval variable, e.g. sold house prices, under **Variable** and the grouping variable, e.g. neighbourhood area, under **Rows**. Click on **OK** to execute the command.

Line graphs

Line graphs are an alternative to histograms for the presentation of interval variables. Unlike histograms, line graphs will not group the data into ranges. On the *x*-axis (horizontal) are the values entered in the interval variable, organized into ascending order. For every value recorded for the interval variable, the count of the number of cases with that variable is plotted against the *y*-axis (vertical). When all values and their frequencies have been plotted, a line is drawn between the plots to create a line graph. An example of a line graph for the Age of respondent is shown in Figure 24.12. Line graphs are not always a suitable graphical presentation for interval data, as sometimes the data produce a very 'spiky' graph that is difficult to make sense of.

Using IBM SPSS Statistics 19 to create charts for interval variables

The following three sections detail the techniques available in IBM SPSS Statistics 19 for producing stem and leaf diagrams, box plots, histograms and line graphs.

Creating stem and leaf diagrams and box plots
The technique for producing these two charts in IBM SPSS Statistics 19 will also, by default, calculate the descriptive statistics that we produced by a different technique earlier. From the **Analyze** menu, select **Descriptive Statistics** and **Explore**. The **Explore** dialogue box will be displayed (see Figure 24.13).

First highlight the required variable(s) on the left hand side and click once on the first arrow button 🔜 to move the variable across to the section under **Dependent List**. In the bottom left of the dialogue box under the section **Display**,

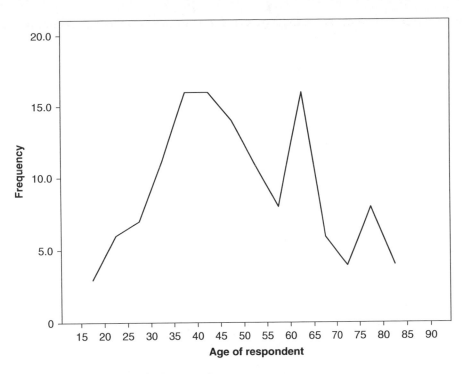

FIGURE 24.12 Example of a line graph

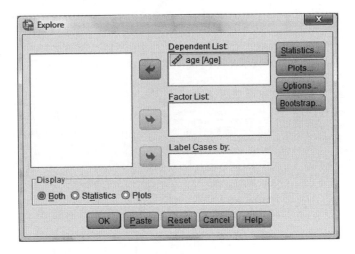

FIGURE 24.13 IBM SPSS Statistics 19 **Explore** dialogue box

check that **Both** is selected. This will produce both a stem and leaf diagram and a box plot. Click on **OK** to execute the command. The **Viewer** window will display an **Explore Descriptives** table, a stem and leaf diagram and a box plot. An example of the descriptive statistics produced from the **Explore** command is shown in

TABLE 24.8   Example descriptive statistics from the Explore command Descriptives

Descriptives

			Std error	Statistic
Age	Mean		47.27	1.607
	95% confidence interval for mean	Lower bound	44.09	
		Upper bound	50.45	
	5% trimmed mean		46.90	
	Median		46.00	
	Variance		335.842	
	Std deviation		18.326	
	Minimum		16	
	Maximum		93	
	Range		77	
	Interquartile range		31.25	
	Skewness		.176	.212
	Kurtosis		−.850	.422

Table 24.8. A box plot and a stem and leaf diagram for the same variable are shown in Figure 24.9 and Table 24.7 respectively.

Creating histograms   The easiest method to produce bar charts in IBM SPSS Statistics 19 is to use the **Frequencies** function. Select the **Analyze** menu and **Descriptive Statistics** ➡ **Frequencies**. The **Frequencies** dialogue box will be displayed (Figure 24.1). From the left hand side, highlight the interval/ratio variable(s) for which histogram(s) are required, and click once on the arrow button ➡ to move the variable across to under **Variable(s)**. Click on the **Charts** button. A **Frequencies: Charts** dialogue box will be displayed (see Figure 24.14).

This box is divided into two sections, each containing a number of options. Under **Chart Type** a number of different chart options are listed. A chart can be selected by clicking in the corresponding circle. Click on the circle next to **Histograms**. The second section **Chart Values** will remain grey and unavailable, as these options are not available for the histogram function. Click on **Continue** to return to the previous dialogue box and then click on **OK** to execute the command. IBM SPSS Statistics 19 will automatically calculate the interval widths and will also display the mean, standard deviation and valid count. For more general details on editing, see section 'Editing IBM SPSS Statistics 19 charts' later in this chapter.

Creating line graphs   From the **Graphs** menu select **Legacy Dialog** and **Line.** The **Line Charts** dialogue box will be displayed. Select **Simple** and click on the **Define** button. From the left hand side, highlight the interval/ratio variable for which a line graph is required and click once on the arrow button ➡ to move the variable across to under **Category Axis**. Under the section **Line Represents** select either **N of Cases**, to display counts, or **% of cases**, to display percentages. If you wish to include a title, click once on the **Titles** button and enter an appropriate title next to **Line 1**, then click

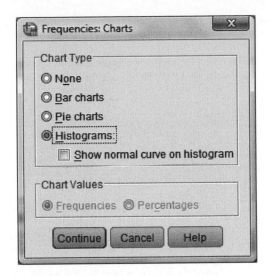

FIGURE 24.14   IBM SPSS Statistics 19 **Frequencies: Charts** dialog box

on **Continue** to return to the previous dialogue box. Finally, to ensure that any values defined as missing are excluded from the line graph, click once on the **Options** button. Under **Missing Values,** remove the tick next to **Display groups defined by missing values.** Click on **Continue** to return to the previous dialogue box. Click on **OK** to execute the command. A line graph will be displayed in the **Viewer** window. An example is shown in Figure 24.12. The line graph can be edited using the **Chart Editor** (see section 'Editing IBM SPSS Statistics 19 charts' later for more details).

Charts for categorical variables

Charts that are used to graphically present categorical variables, nominal or ordinal, are bar charts or pie charts.

Bar charts

A bar chart consists of two axes, x (horizontal) and y (vertical). Along the x-axis, bars will be placed to represent each of the categories in the variables. Along the y-axis, a measure is placed that will represent the observations for each category. The measurement can be a count N or a percentage of the total sample (see Figure 24.15).

Pie charts

Pie charts can be used graphically to display the proportion of cases that are in each category of a single categorical variable. A pie chart is a circle that is divided into segments. Each segment represents one category in the variable. The size of

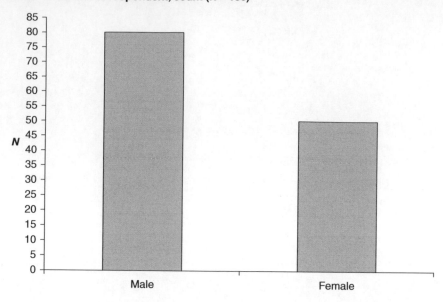

Chart 1: Gender of respondent, count (*N* = 130)

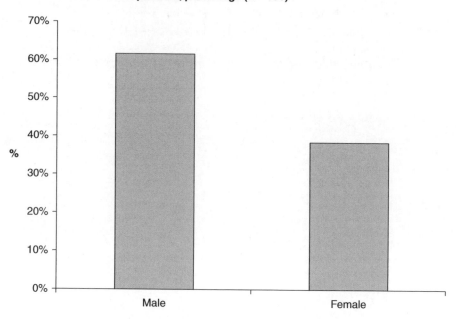

Chart 2: Gender of respondent, percentage (*N* = 130)

FIGURE 24.15   Two examples of bar charts

Both charts are displaying the same data, the gender of the respondents in the sample. Chart 1 is displaying the counts (*N*) and Chart 2 the percentages (%).

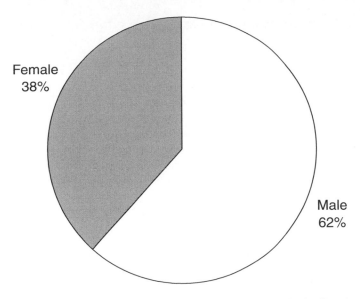

Female
38%

Male
62%

FIGURE 24.16 Example of a Pie Chart with percentage data labels. Gender of Respondent (*N* = 130)

the segment is calculated according to the number of cases that fall in the category. The larger the segment, the more cases in the category. Pie charts should not be used for variables that have over five or six categories or where there are a relatively small number of counts in many of the categories. In such occurrences the segment will be too narrow and it will be impossible for the reader to assess the number of cases that fall within it (Box 24.4). When this occurs either use a different chart, present the findings as a frequency table or, if appropriate, collapse the categories with a small number of counts into an 'other' category; see Chapter 27 for more details on recoding. A pie chart provides a quick visualization of the proportions of each category. An example of a pie chart is shown in Figure 24.16.

BOX 24.4 HINTS AND TIPS

Using pie charts

The use of pie charts to present research data should be given careful consideration. While pie charts provide a very useful means of representing categorical data, they are restrictive when there are many categories in the variable. Over six categories can often prove problematic, and/or where there are small category counts, resulting in very small pie segments. The decision to use pie charts should be determined by the distribution of observations for that variable and the researcher making a sensible decision as to whether a pie chart is preferable to a bar chart.

Using IBM SPSS Statistics 19 to create bar charts and pie charts

The following two sections detail the techniques available in IBM SPSS Statistics 19 for producing bar charts and pie charts.

Creating a bar chart   The easiest method to produce bar charts in IBM SPSS Statistics 19 is to use the **Frequencies** function.

From the **Analyze** menu, select **Descriptive Statistics** and **Frequencies**. The **Frequencies** dialogue box will be displayed (Figure 24.1). From the left hand side, highlight the nominal or ordinal variable(s) for which bar charts(s) are required and click once on the arrow button ![arrow] to move the variable across to under **Variable(s)**. Click on the **Charts** button. A **Frequencies: Charts** dialogue box will be displayed (see Figure 24.14). Under **Chart Type** click on the button next to **Bar charts**. The second section, **Chart Values**, is available for bar charts. Select either **Frequencies** or **Percentages**, depending on the values you wish to be displayed on the y-axis of the bar chart. Click on **Continue** to return to the **Frequencies** dialogue box. One final decision to be made is whether a frequency table is required in addition to the bar chart. It is likely that in your preliminary analysis you will have already produced a frequency table, and if this is the case, to stop a second table being produced click in the box next to **Display frequency tables** (Figure 24.1). The tick should now be removed. You will need to select this option if you wish to produce frequency tables at a later stage in the current IBM SPSS Statistics 19 session. Click on **OK** to execute the command. The chart will be displayed in the **Output Viewer** window.

Creating a pie chart   The procedure for producing pie charts in IBM SPSS Statistics 19 is almost identical to that for bar charts. From the **Analyze** menu, select **Descriptive Statistics** and **Frequencies**. The **Frequencies** dialogue box will be displayed (Figure 24.1). From the left hand side, highlight the nominal or ordinal variable(s) for which pie charts(s) are required and click once on the arrow button ![arrow] to move the variable across to under **Variable(s)**. Click on the **Charts** button. A **Frequencies: Charts** dialogue box will be displayed (see Figure 24.14). Under **Chart Type,** click on the button next to **Pie charts**. Under **Chart Values,** select either **Frequencies** or **Percentages**, depending on the values you would like displayed as labels on the pie chart. Click on **Continue** to return to the **Frequencies** dialogue box. If no frequency table is required, remove the tick next to **Display frequency tables** (Figure 24.1). Click on **OK** to execute the command. The pie chart will be displayed in the **Viewer** window and can be edited using the **Chart Editor** (see next section).

Editing IBM SPSS Statistics 19 charts

Various aspects of IBM SPSS Statistics 19 charts can be edited using the **Chart Editor**. Common elements of IBM SPSS Statistics 19 charts that may require editing include the default colour schemes for bars, font types and sizes, line patterns, axis labels and

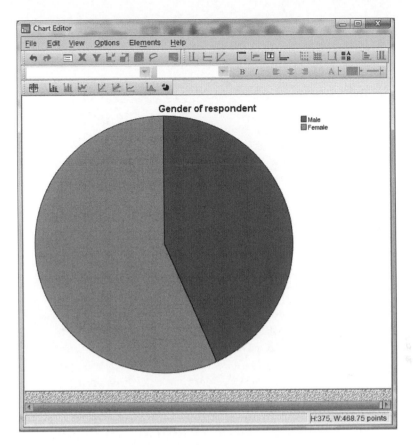

FIGURE 24.17　IBM SPSS Statistics 19 **Chart Editor** window

categories. The type of chart and the final requirements for report and presentation purposes will determine the exact editing. This section describes some of the key features of the **Chart Editor**. The **Chart Editor** is easy and intuitive to use. To open the **Chart Editor**, switch to the **Viewer** window by selecting the **Window** menu and **2 Output window name**. Locate the chart to be edited and double click anywhere on the chart. This will open the **Chart Editor**. Note also that some of the menus available have changed. An example of the **Chart Editor** is shown in Figure 24.17.

The chart can be edited using the various functions available on the toolbar, using the commands from the menus, and simply by double clicking in the area on the chart that you want to change. Once you have clicked on that element the process is really quite intuitive, and hence we have decided that no further instruction is required here – except to remind you that the best charts are those that are clear and simple. The most useful command in **Chart Editor** is the **Properties** box which will appear when you double click on an element, or by selecting **Properties** from the **Edit** menu. The **Properties** box allows you to change the colour of bars, segments and lines.

Once the edits are complete, return to the **Viewer** window by closing the **Chart Editor** window. Select the **File** menu and **Close**.

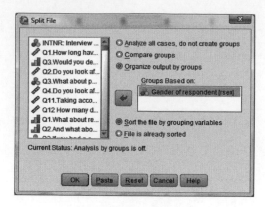

FIGURE 24.18   IBM SPSS Statistics 19 **Split File** dialogue box

Univariate analysis for different groups

Often for comparison purposes you may wish to report on the responses of different groups. There are a number of ways of undertaking this in IBM SPSS Statistics 19. One of the easiest methods is to make use of the **Split File** command. This technique involves temporarily dividing the data file into different groups. The division is defined by the categories contained in a nominal or ordinal variable in the data file. For example, if you wished to calculate the mean and standard deviation age for men and for women, the technique would involve splitting the data file into two groups, men and women. The statistics would then be calculated for each group. The groups would be defined by an existing variable; in this example, the variable 'Sex'.

This technique is particularly useful when the variable to be compared between the different groups is interval, for example, age or salary. It can be utilized for other levels of measurement, though consider using the techniques discussed in Chapter 25 on bivariate analysis.

Using **Split File** in IBM SPSS Statistics 19

Select the **Data** menu and **Split File**. A **Split File** dialogue box will appear (see Figure 24.18). Select the option **Organize output by groups**. From the left hand side, highlight the variable whose categories will define each of the sub groups, for example 'Sex', and click once on the arrow button to move the variable across to under **Groups Based on**.

Check that the option **Sort the file by grouping variables** is selected. Click on **OK** to execute the command. In the bottom right corner of the IBM SPSS Statistics 19 **Data Editor** window, **Split File On** should now be displayed. Any analysis undertaken now will be divided according to the categories in the variable selected. An example of descriptive analysis of age undertaken when the **Split File** is set to 'Sex', thus dividing the results into 'Male' and 'Female', is shown in Table 24.9.

TABLE 24.9 Example output of descriptive statistics using Split File

Sex = Male

	N Statistic	Range Statistic	Minimum Statistic	Maximum Statistic	Mean Statistic	Std. Statistic	Variance Statistic	Skewness Statistic	Std Error	Kurtosis Statistic	Std Error
Age	70	68	16	84	46.54	19.334	373.788	.051	.287	-1.258	.566
Valid N	70										

Sex = Female

	N Statistic	Range Statistic	Minimum Statistic	Maximum Statistic	Mean Statistic	Std. Statistic	Variance Statistic	Skewness Statistic	Std Error	Kurtosis Statistic	Std Error
Age	60	74	19	93	48.12	17.199	295.800	.431	.309	-.212	.608
Valid N	60										

To return to analysing all cases as one group, the **Split File** command needs to be switched off. Select the **Data** menu and **Split File**. From the **Split File** dialogue box (Figure 24.18), select the option **Analyze all cases, do not create groups**. Click on **OK** to execute the command. In the bottom right corner of the IBM SPSS Statistics 19 **Data Editor** window the **Split File On** should no longer be displayed.

Summary

The first stage in the analysis process is to describe and summarize single variables, enabling you to become familiar with the data and to detect any data entry errors. It is important that the analysis undertaken is appropriate for the level of measurement of the variable being analysed. Nominal variables can be summarized using a frequency table, calculating the mode and presenting the data as bar charts and pie charts. Ordinal variables can be summarized using frequency tables, the median, and again by presenting data as bar charts or pie charts. Interval and ratio variables have a full range of statistical measures available. These include the measures of central tendency and dispersion. Interval and ratio data can be presented graphically in a histogram, stem and leaf diagram, box plot and line graph.

 **Questions**

1　What are the appropriate measures of central tendency for each level of measurement, and why is it important that the correct statistical measures are applied?
2　What are the appropriate means of dispersion for each level of measurement?
3　What are the appropriate charts for presenting nominal data, ordinal data and interval data?

Further reading

Fielding, Jane and Gilbert, Nigel (2006) *Understanding Social Statistics*, 2nd edn. London: Sage.

Field, Andy (2009) *Discovering Statistics using SPSS for Windows*, 3rd edn. London: Sage.

Pallant, Julie (2006) SPSS *Survival Manual: A Step by Step Guide to Data Analysis Using SPSS for Windows*. London: Allen and Unwin.

TWENTY FIVE

DESCRIBING AND EXPLORING RELATIONSHIPS BETWEEN TWO VARIABLES

Chapter Contents

| Aims |

By the end of this chapter you will be able to:

- **Analyse relationships between two variables using appropriate techniques.**
- **Create and interpret contingency tables in IBM SPSS Statistics 19.**
- **Present data in a contingency table as a multiple bar chart.**
- **Create and interpret scatterplots.**
- **Calculate and interpret appropriate measures of association in IBM SPSS Statistics 19.**

Bivariate analysis: causality and association

This chapter will focus on techniques that enable the researcher to describe and explore relationships between two variables, also known as bivariate analysis. Chapter 13 discussed the relationships between variables and how the researcher can explore and test those relationships. Bivariate analysis is concerned with the actual process of exploring the relationships between variables. A common problem for the first-time researcher is the sense of being overwhelmed by the data and the possibilities of relationships to explore. Your analysis should be theory driven rather than data driven. In a purely data-driven approach it would be possible to explore relationships between all variables in the dataset; however, a better theory-driven approach uses a process guided by the original research question. If you are unclear as to what analysis to undertake, then return to the original research question and your identified hypotheses.

The chapter will first focus on describing relationships between categorical variables (nominal and ordinal) and between two interval variables. In addition to describing a relationship, measures of association can be calculated to measure the strength of the relationship. Different measures of association are available and their use is determined by the level of measurement of the two variables in the relationship. The final section of this chapter examines how the analysis of two variables can be expanded to introduce a third variable – a technique known as elaboration.

In Chapters 12 and 13 we outlined different research designs. In an experimental design the independent or control variable(s) are manipulated and the changes in the dependent variable are measured. Changes in the dependent variable are the outcome of the manipulation of independent variables. In a cross-sectional design the researcher collects data at one point in time and is unable to manually manipulate independent or control variables. Instead, the survey will include the collection of independent and control variables, or the facesheet data on the questionnaire, which are then used to statistically control the dependent variable. This analysis enables associations to be explored. When we explore associations or relationships between variables we are statistically controlling, or holding constant, the independent variable in order to observe differences in the dependent variable.

In order for the statistical controls to be appropriate, we need to check that the time order or temporal order of the variables is such that the independent variable occurs in time before the dependent variable (Box 25.1). Within this we also need to consider the length of time involved. Variables that occur close together in time may have more or less association than those which occur further apart in time. The researcher will need to judge such time order issues. For instance, a research project evaluated the impact of a public information event being run by a local fire brigade. People attending the event were given information on how to make their homes 'fireproof safe'. A short survey was conducted, designed both to measure the knowledge retained by the attendees and to gauge their views on the usefulness of the event. A further study was conducted on the same individuals six months later. Perhaps unsurprisingly, the results showed that people had retained less knowledge six months later compared to the initial survey; however, both survey results reported that the usefulness of the event remained high amongst attendees.

BOX 25.1 HINTS AND TIPS

Unsure about the independent variable?

There is a convenient time order between independent and dependent variables. Since the independent variable influences the dependent variable, an independent variable will occur in time before the dependent variable. Furthermore, in the social sciences many of the independent variables are drawn from the personal attribute questions, or facesheet data, on the questionnaire.

In statistical analysis we refer to association as an observed change in the independent variable corresponding to an observed change in the dependent variable. We use a narrative explanation to discuss this association and to present a case that there is a causal relationship between these two observed variables, i.e. that the independent variable is the cause and the dependent variable is the effect. It is the responsibility of the researcher to draw conclusions as to whether there is sufficient evidence from the measured association to conclude that causality exists. Data and statistical techniques can support the researcher so far; however, there are unfortunately no easy solutions to the underlying issues of association and the assumptions of causality. The complexity of the social world, and indeed the natural world, means that many research projects are required in order to gather enough evidence for robust conclusions to be drawn. Table 25.1 lists the different statistical terminology used to describe independent and dependent variables.

TABLE 25.1 Independent and dependent variables: terminology

Variable	Also known as (a.k.a.)
Independent	X variable
	Cause
	Predictor
	Explanatory
Dependent	Y variable
	Effect
	Outcome
	Response
	Criterion

Contingency tables: analysing relationships between categorical variables

The most common technique used to describe and explore relationships between variables is the contingency table or cross-tabulation, reflecting that many of the variables collected by social scientists are categorical, either nominal or ordinal. Rather than describing characteristics of single variables, for example the number of individuals in paid employment, or the number of full-time and part-time workers in a sample, cross-tabulations allow for more detailed exploration of responses by different subgroups and exploration of hypotheses on the relationships between variables. For example, do more men than women work full-time? Can we identify variables that may affect this relationship? Here we are examining the work status responses controlling for the sex of the respondent.

The cross-tabulation or contingency table consists of placing one variable in the column and one in the row. The standard convention is to place the independent variable in the column and the dependent variable in the row. Following this convention is a matter of individual preference, and there is no strong reason to adhere to it; however, it is a simple technique for ensuring that the researcher is clear as to the possible relationship between variables.

The independent variable is the variable that is identified in the hypothesis to be acting upon and influencing the dependent variable. Likewise, the dependent variable is the variable that is hypothesized as being influenced by the independent variable. We use the independent variable as the control for the dependent variable. Taking the earlier example of differences in employment between men and women, the hypothesis is that sex determines whether a respondent works full-time or part-time. Hence gender is the independent variable, and working full-time or part-time is the dependent variable. Table 25.2 shows an example of this relationship.

Table 25.2 shows the four cells (a)–(d) that correspond to the variables: working full-time or part-time, and sex. The counts of the number of cases that fall within each category are displayed in the cells of the table. For example, in cell (a) the count of the number of men who work full-time is 40; in cell (b) the

TABLE 25.2 Example of a cross-tabulation: working full-time or part-time by sex, count ($n = 120$)

Working	Sex		
	Male	Female	Row total (marginal)
Full-time	40 (a)	30 (b)	70
Part-time	20 (c)	30 (d)	50
Column total (marginal)	60	60	120

count of the number of women who work full-time is 30. If you follow the rule of placing the dependent variable in the row and the independent variable in the column, then it will follow that the row total, often referred to as 'row marginal', will contain the total count for each of the categories in the dependent variable, for example, full-time and part-time. The column total, or column marginal, will contain the total count of the categories in the independent variable, for example, gender of respondent. As with frequency tables, a category count and total count enable a percentage to be calculated. Within cross-tabulations there are three different totals from which percentages can be calculated: column, row and total.

The column percentage The column percentage is calculated based on the column marginal for each column in the table. The column percentage for each cell in the table is shown in Table 25.3 with corresponding calculations shown in brackets. Interpretation of Table 25.3 displaying column percentages would be as follows: 66 per cent of men work full-time and 33 per cent of men work part-time. An equal proportion of women work full-time, 50 per cent, and part-time, 50 per cent.

TABLE 25.3 Example of a cross-tabulation: working full-time or part-time by gender, column percentage ($n = 120$)

Working	Gender		
	Male	Female	Row total (marginal)
Full-time	66% (40/60*100) (a)	50% (30/60*100) (b)	58% (70/120*100) (R1)
Part-time	33% (20/60*100) (c)	50% (30/60*100) (d)	42% (50/120*100) (R2)
Column total (marginal)	100% (C1)	100% (C1)	$n = 120$ 100% (Total)

TABLE 25.4   Example of a cross-tabulation: working full-time or part-time by gender, row percentage ($n = 120$)

Working	Gender		
	Male	Female	Row total (marginal)
Full-time	57% (40/70*100) (a)	43% (30/70*100) (b)	100% (R1)
Part-time	40% (20/50*100) (c)	60% (30/50*100) (d)	100% (R2)
Column total (marginal)	50% (60/120*100) (C1)	50% (60/120*100) (C2)	$n = 120$ 100% (Total)

The row percentage   The row percentage is calculated based on the row marginal for each row in the table. Table 25.4 shows the row percentages with the corresponding calculations shown in brackets. Interpretation of the row percentages would be that of those working full-time, 57 per cent were male and 43 per cent were female, whereas 60 per cent of part-time workers were female and 40 per cent were male.

The total percentage   The total percentage is calculated based on the total count of valid cases in the table. This is displayed in the bottom right corner ($n = 120$). The total percentage for each cell in the table is shown in Table 25.5 with corresponding calculations shown in brackets. Interpretation of the table would be that of the total count of 120 individuals, 33 per cent were full-time working males, 25 per cent were full-time working females, 17 per cent were part-time working males and 25 per cent were part-time working females.

Creating contingency tables in IBM SPSS Statistics 19

To produce a contingency table or cross-tabulation, first identify the two variables that are going to be examined. Open the data file containing these variables. From the **Analyze** menu, select **Descriptive Statistics** and **Crosstabs**. A **Crosstabs** dialogue box will be displayed (see Figure 25.1).

A contingency or cross-tabulation table consists of a number of rows and columns. To produce the table a variable needs to be allocated to both a row and a column. On the right hand side of the box there are two sections, one for row and one for column. Variables from the list need to be placed in both these sections. The independent variable should be placed in the column and the dependent variable placed in the row.

TABLE 25.5 Example of a cross-tabulation: working full-time or part-time by gender, total percentage (n = 120)

Working	Gender		
	Male	**Female**	**Row total (marginal)**
Full-time	33% (40/120*100) (a)	25% (30/120*100) (b)	58% (70/120*100) (R1)
Part-time	17% (20/120*100) (c)	25% (30/120*100) (d)	42% (50/120*100) (R2)
Column total (marginal)	50% (60/120*100) (C1)	50% (60/120*100) (C2)	100% (Total)

To move the first variable, dependent, into the row section, from the left hand side highlight the nominal or ordinal variable required and click on the top arrow button ⊡ to move the variable across to under **Row(s)**. To move the second variable, independent, into the column section, from the left hand side highlight the nominal or ordinal variable required and click on the second down arrow button ⊡ to move the variable across to under **Columns(s)**.

There are three buttons on the right side of the **Crosstabs** box: **Statistics**, **Cells** and **Format**. The **Statistics** button contains commands on statistical analysis techniques, including chi-square (see section 'Using IBM SPSS Statistics 19 to calculate chi-square' in Chapter 26). The **Format** button contains a command on controlling the category order of the row variable and it is rarely used. The **Cells** button contains commands that control the calculated data displayed in the table and enables the user to select row, column or total percentages. Click on the **Cells** button. A **Crosstabs: Cell Display** dialogue box will be displayed. Under **Percentages** select one or more of the available percentages: **Row**, row percentage, **Column**, column percentage and **Total**, total percentage.

Under **Counts** the default setting is **Observed** to display a count of the observed frequencies in each cell of the table. When calculating a chi-square the **Expected** count would also be selected (see Chapter 26 for more on this statistical technique). Leave the **Observed** option selected. Click on **Continue** to return to the **Crosstabs** dialogue box. Click on **OK** to execute the command. The **Crosstab** table will be displayed in the IBM SPSS Statistics 19 **Viewer** window. An example of a **Crosstab** displaying cell counts and column percentages is shown in Table 25.6.

Interpreting the table Interpreting a cross-tabulation will involve you analysing the percentages in the table. The table allows you to assess the evidence for the original hypothesis or your idea about the relationship between the independent and dependent variables. If the convention of placing the independent variable in

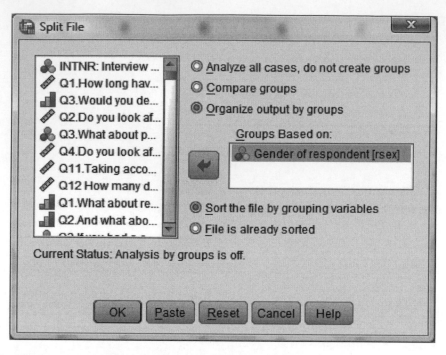

FIGURE 25.1 IBM SPSS Statistics 19 **Crosstabs** dialog box

the column and the dependent variable in the row is followed, then you will need to compare the column percentage between each of the categories in the independent variable. Any differences in the column percentages for each row will indicate that there is a relationship between the two variables. The larger the numerical difference between the two percentages, the more strongly related the variables.

Further example of cross-tabulation In Chapter 24 we looked at the results of a university student survey that examined how safe students felt walking around a university campus during daylight hours. Frequency tables allowed us to examine the number of male and female respondents and the distribution of responses on a four-point scale from very safe to very unsafe (Table 24.1). The next stage in the analysis would be to explore if there is a difference in how safe male and female students feel walking around the campus. Given that both the corresponding variables, gender and how safe students feel, are categorical, a cross-tabulation would be the appropriate analysis tool to use. Our question, or hypothesis, is that sex influences how safe a student feels walking around the campus. Based on existing research from the literature we could also be more specific here and write the following hypotheses. If a student is male then they will feel more safe walking around the campus. If a student is female then they will feel less safe walking around the campus. Here we are specifying a direction to the hypothesis, whereas in the initial hypothesis we were stating that there is just a difference in

TABLE 25.6 Example of a IBM SPSS Statistics 19 cross-tabulation: gender by how safe students feel walking alone around the university campus in daylight hours

Case Processing Summary

	Cases					
	Valid		Missing		Total	
	N	Percent	N	Percent	N	Percent
Safe * Gender	1450	96.7%	50	3.3%	1500	100.0%

Safe * Gender Cross-tabulation

			Gender		Total
			Male	Female	
Safe	Very safe	Count	570	220	790
		% within Gender	65.5%	37.9%	54.5%
	Fairly safe	Count	230	150	380
		% within Gender	26.4%	25.9%	26.2%
	A bit unsafe	Count	50	130	180
		% within Gender	5.7%	22.4%	12.4%
	Very unsafe	Count	20	80	100
		% within Gender	2.3%	13.8%	6.9%
Total		Count	870	580	1450
		% within Gender	100.0%	100.0%	100.0%

how safe male and female students feel walking around the campus, known as non-directional hypothesis. For these hypotheses, sex is the independent variable and how safe walking around the campus is the dependent variable.

The cross-tabulation for this analysis is shown in Table 25.6. The first thing to note is that there are 50 missing cases which are in the categories listed in Table 24.1c. This leaves an overall total number of cases of 1450 in the analysis. Sex, as the independent variable, has been placed in the table column; and the 'how safe', as the dependent variable, placed in the row. Column percentages have been selected to allow comparisons between male and female students to be made. Examination of the percentages shows that there are differences in how safe male and female students feel. We can see that the majority of male and female students felt either very or fairly safe. We can calculate the combined figures for both categories by adding together the column percentage for male and the column percentage for female for these two categories. For male students this is 65.5% + 26.4% = 91.9% and for female students this is 37.9% + 25.9% = 63.8%. More male students felt very safe, 65.5%, than female students, 37.9%. Only a small proportion of male students felt fairly unsafe or very unsafe, 8% (5.7% + 2.3%). This compares to over one-third, 36.2% (22.4% + 13.8%), of female students who felt fairly or very unsafe.

Our conclusions, based on the survey findings, are that there are differences in how safe male and female students feel walking around the university campus and that overall male students feel more safe than female students. Of course we would need to interrogate the data further to explore possible factors that may explain these findings. For example, how does feeling safe relate to frequency of student visits to the campus? Frequent users may feel safer as they are more familiar with their surroundings. How does feeling safe relate to personal experiences of being a victim of crime? How many students have actually been the victim of a crime on or off the campus?

Graphical presentations of data in a contingency table   Data from a cross-tabulation can be presented as a multiple bar chart. Each category in the independent variable will have a bar for each category in the dependent variable. A legend will normally be displayed with the multiple bar chart to inform the reader as to which of the bars represents each of the dependent categories. An example of a multiple bar chart of the data in Table 25.6 is shown in Figure 25.2.

Producing multiple bar charts   There are a number of methods for creating a multiple bar chart. The easiest method is to use the **Crosstab** command. From the

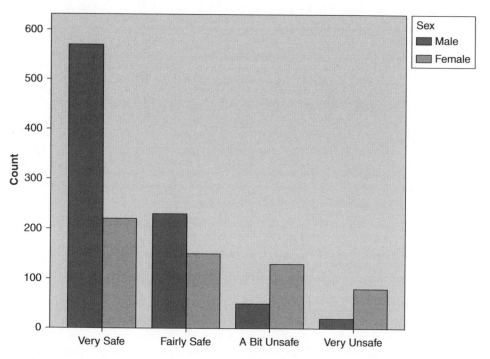

FIGURE 25.2   Multiple bar chart of Table 25.6, counts

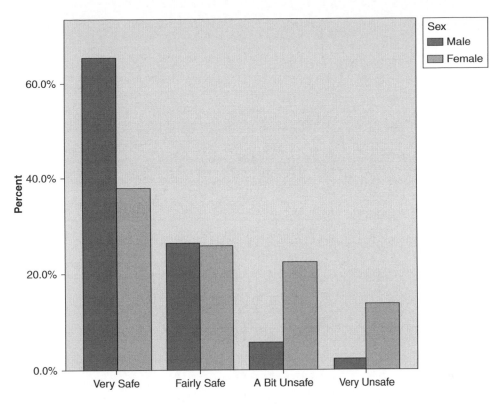

FIGURE 25.3 Multiple Bar Chart of Table 25.6, column percentages.

Analyze menu, select **Descriptive Statistics** and **Crosstab**. In the **Crosstab** dialogue box, follow the procedure for producing cross-tabulations by placing the independent variable under column and the dependent variable under row. Place a tick next to the option **Display clustered bar charts**. If tables have already been produced or are not required, also place a tick next to **Suppress tables**. Click on **OK** to execute the command.

The bar chart in Figure 25.2 has a *y* (vertical) axis that is plotting the frequency counts in each of the categories of male very safe, female very safe, male fairly safe, female fairly safe etc. The difficulty with bar charts displaying counts is that the height of each bar does not take into account the different total counts of the independent variable categories. In this example, the total number of males in the table is 870 and females is 580. It is therefore better to produce a bar chart displaying the percentages of male and female where the bars are the column percentages from Table 25.6. This chart is shown in Figure 25.3.

Producing multiple bar charts displaying percentages   There are two methods available to produce multiple bar charts with percentages in IBM SPSS Statistics 19. One method involves using the **Chart Builder** function. The second method uses the **Legacy** charts function and is, in the authors' opinion at least, the quickest and easy method to use.

From the **Graphs** menu, select **Legacy Dialogs** and **Bar**. Highlight the **Clustered** option. Check that under the section **Data in chart are** the first option **Summaries for groups of cases** is highlighted. This should be the default setting. Now click on **Define**. In the **Define clustered bar** dialogue box, move the independent variable (for example, gender) to the box under **Define clusters by**. Move the dependent variable (for example, how safe walking around campus) to the box under **Category axis**. In the section **Bars represent** select the **% of cases** option. If you wish to enter a chart title click on **Title**, enter a title and click on **Continue** to return to the previous box. Now click on **OK** to execute the command.

Measuring associations: phi and Cramer's *V*

There are statistical techniques that will provide a summary statistic of the relationship between two variables. These statistics are known as measures of association and indicate the strength of the relationship between the two variables. Different types of measures of association are available are according to the data type of the two variables in the relationship. There are a large number of different correlation coefficients designed to take account of matters such as level of measurement and the number of categories in the variables (de Vaus, 2002a: 267). A full discussion of the different types of correlation coefficient can be found in Fielding and Gilbert (2006), de Vaus (2002a) and Bryman and Cramer (2000).

The measure of association appropriate for cross-tabulations where both the independent and dependent variables are nominal are phi and Cramer's *V*. Phi should be applied to cross-tabulations where both nominal variables are dichotomies. A dichotomy is a variable that has only two categories. Cramer's *V* can be used in cross-tabulations where one or both variables has more than two categories.

The calculation of phi and Cramer's *V* is based upon the chi-square statistic. The chi-square statistic is calculated for the purposes of hypothesis testing, and a discussion of chi-square can be found in Chapter 26. The basis of the chi-square statistic, and thereby also phi and Cramer's *V*, is the comparison of the observed or actual count for each cell in the cross-tabulation with the expected count for each cell if there was no association between the two variables. The mathematical calculations to obtain phi and Cramer's *V* are beyond this book. Since IBM SPSS Statistics 19 will calculate both measures of association, the important aspect is the interpretation of the statistic itself.

The value of phi and Cramer's *V* will fall between 0 and 1. A value of 0 would indicate that there is no association between the two variables. A value of 1 would indicate that there is a perfect association. Rarely will values for phi or Cramer's *V* of 0 or 1 be found. Instead the value will be somewhere between the two. Values closer to 0 indicate a weak or low association and values closer to 1 indicate a stronger or high association. Bryman and Cramer (1997) suggest the following for interpreting the measures of association: 0.19 or less is very low association; 0.20

to 0.39 is low association; 0.40 to 0.69 is modest association; 0.70 to 0.89 is high association; and 0.90 to 1 is very high association.

Calculating phi and Cramer's *V* in IBM SPSS Statistics 19

The easiest method is to use the **Crosstab** command. From the **Analyze** menu, select **Descriptive Statistics** and **Crosstab**. In the **Crosstab** dialogue box, follow the procedure for producing cross-tabulations by placing the independent variable under column and the dependent variable under row. To calculate chi-square, click on the **Statistics** button. In the section under **Nominal**, select the **Phi and Cramer's V** option in the top left corner. Click on **Continue**. Click on **OK** to execute the command. An example of the phi and Cramer's *V* calculated in IBM SPSS Statistics 19 is shown in Table 25.7. These are the measures of association calculated for the how safe walking around the campus by gender table (Table 25.6). Since this table is greater than 2 × 2, Cramer's *V* should be applied. The value of Cramer's *V* is 0.365. Interpretation of this value suggests that the association is low.

TABLE 25.7   Example of phi and Cramer's *V* calculated in IBM SPSS Statistics 19

Symmetric Measures

		Value	Approx. Sig.
Nominal by Nominal	Phi	.365	.000
	Cramer's *V*	.365	.000
N of Valid Cases		1450	

Analysing relationships between interval/ratio variables

The techniques discussed so far have been appropriate for analysing relationships between two nominal variables. Analysis of interval/ratio variables has been restricted to single variables or statistical measurements of interval variables between different subgroups. The analysis of the relationship between two interval/ratio variables requires a different statistical technique called correlation. Correlation is a measure of the association. Correlation analysis involves measuring the degree to which one interval/ratio variable is related to another interval/ratio variable. Where a change in one variable is related to a change in the second variable, it is referred to as covariance. When one is undertaking correlation analysis in IBM SPSS Statistics 19, the dependent and independent variables need to be specified. Correlation analysis of interval/ratio variables involves the calculation of the Pearson product-moment correlation coefficient or Pearson's *r*. The value of the correlation coefficient will vary between −1.00 and +1.00, reflecting the strength and direction of the association between the two interval variables. A correlation of +1 indicates a perfect positive association between the two interval variables. A correlation of –1 indicates a negative association between the two interval variables.

Calculation of the correlation coefficient should be undertaken in conjunction with a scatterplot of the two variables. A scatterplot allows the researcher to visualize the covariance between the two variables. This is important, as correlation coefficients should only be calculated on linear relationships. A linear relationship is one that plots a straight line or approximates to a straight line. Increases in the independent variable correspond with an increase or decrease in the dependent variable. A non-linear relationship could be where the values of the dependent variable increase and then decrease for different values of the independent variable. An example of a non-linear relationship is an individual's average yearly income over the life course. In general we would expect income to rise with age as the person gains more working experience and promotion in the workplace. Income will then decrease upon retirement.

The issues of association and causality are still applicable with interval-level data. While a correlation coefficient allows us to assess the relationship between two variables, it does not allow us to state with certainty that the relationship between the two variables is causally linked, and neither does it allow us to make any judgement on the direction of causality between the two variables. So while there may be a positive association it may be due to a third unknown variable (or more) that is influencing the relationship between the two variables; and, even where there is a positive or negative association between the two variables statistically, we do not know which variable is influencing the other. Of course we may write a narrative or hypothesize about the order of the relationship between the two variables.

The following two sections cover, first, calculating scatterplots using IBM SPSS Statistics 19; and, second, the calculation of Pearson's *r* correlation using IBM SPSS Statistics 19.

Scatterplots

Scatterplots give a visual representation of the relationship between two interval variables. A scatterplot consists of two axes, *x* (horizontal) and *y* (vertical), one axis for each variable. Typically, the independent variable *x* is placed on the horizontal axis and the dependent variable *y* is placed on the vertical axis. The values of the *x* and *y* variables are plotted for each case on the respective axes of the scatterplot. The distribution of the plots will indicate the relationship between the two variables.

For a positive relationship, high values for one variable will correspond with high values for the second variable. A negative relationship would be indicated by a high value on one of the variables corresponding to a low value on the second variable (see Figure 25.4). The relationship may be linear (in a straight line) or curvilinear (in an arc). It is important to determine that the relationship is linear as only these relationships should be analysed using the correlation technique Pearson's *r*. Scatterplots will also provide a visual representation of outliers, i.e. extreme values.

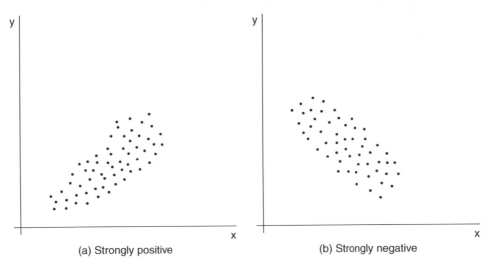

(a) Strongly positive   (b) Strongly negative

FIGURE 25.4   Scatterplots, positive and negative relationships

Creating scatterplots in IBM SPSS Statistics 19

To produce a scatterplot, from the **Graph** menu select **Legacy Dialogs** and **Scatter/ Dot**. In the **Scatterplot** dialogue box, select **Simple Scatter** and click on the **Define** button. The **Simple Scatterplot** dialogue box will be displayed. From the left hand side, highlight the dependent variable and click once on the top arrow button 🔲 to move the variable across to under **Y Axis**. Now highlight the independent variable and click once on the second arrow button 🔲 to move the variable across to under **X Axis**. An additional option is to include a title for the scatterplot. If you wish to include a title, click on the **Titles** button and type in a title in the top box. Click on **Continue** to return to the **Simple Scatterplot** dialogue box. Click on **OK** to execute the command. The scatterplot will be displayed in the IBM SPSS Statistics 19 **Viewer** window. An example of a IBM SPSS Statistics 19 simple scatterplot is shown in Figure 25.5.

Interpreting scatterplots   Interpretation of the scatterplot will involve a careful analysis of the distribution of the plots. The resulting plot can be compared to those in Figure 25.4 showing a negative and a positive relationship. The scatterplot should allow you to check for outliers and the shape of the scatterplot. Outliers appear as isolated plots that are some distance from the majority of plots, and they are important as they may affect any subsequent statistical analysis. Scatterplots may also reveal clusters of plots in a particular area on the plot, showing that many cases fall in a particular value range. The use of markers (see next section) may reveal intervening variables that could explain this pattern. By examining the scatterplot you may be able to visualize a line of best fit or summary line. Could a straight line be drawn or would a curved line be better suited? One of the

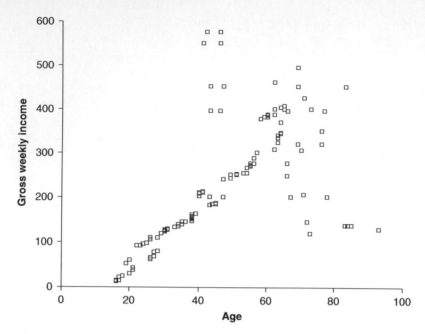

FIGURE 25.5   IBM SPSS Statistics 19 simple scatterplot

problems with scatterplots is that it becomes difficult to assess the relationship when there are a large number of cases.

Setting markers in scatterplots   One very useful technique available in IBM SPSS Statistics 19 is to request that the plot marks on the scatterplot are colour coded for each case according to the characteristics of a third categorical variable. For example, a scatterplot was used to examine the relationship between an individual's income and their age. The plot markers could be set to distinguish between men and women. In order to achieve this a variable containing the categories of men and women would need to be included in the data file. In the **Simple Scatterplot** dialogue box there is a section called **Set Markers by**. From the variable list place the distinguishing variable, for example Sex, in the box underneath.

Measuring associations: correlation coefficient or Pearson's *r*

Correlation coefficients allow the researcher to summarize the relationship between two variables. These sections will focus on Pearson product-moment correlation, often referred to simply as Pearson's correlation or Pearson's *r*. Another way of thinking of this is: how much do values of one variable associate with values in a second variable? For example, does income vary according to the age of the respondent? Look back to Figure 25.4 on the different relationships using scatterplots to get a visual representation of this.

Pearson's r can be used where both the independent and dependent variables are interval/ratio. There is an important assumption behind Pearson's r that you must be aware of and check for at the initial analysis phase, particularly if you want to undertake significance testing: see Chapter 26 for more details on this. The assumption is that the sample data for both variables is normally distributed. A large sample will normally be sufficient for this to be assumed (Field, 2009: 177). Where you have a small sample, visualizing the data for both variables using histograms and box plots will help you assess the distribution of values. If the variable data are not normally distributed then Spearman's rank, the non-parametric alternative, can be used instead (see later in this chapter).

Calculating Pearson's r in IBM SPSS Statistics 19

Using IBM SPSS Statistics 19 to calculate Pearson's r for two interval variables, from the **Analyze** menu select **Correlate** and **Bivariate**. The **Bivariate Correlations** dialogue box will be displayed. From the left hand side, highlight the first interval variable in the relationship and click once on the arrow button ⊡ to move the variable across to under **Variables**. Highlight the second interval variable and again click once on the arrow button ⊡. Under **Correlation Coefficients** check that the **Pearson** box is ticked. This is the default setting; if it is not selected, click once in the corresponding box. Under **Test of Significance** leave the default setting as **Two-tailed**. (For an explanation of the meaning of two-tailed, see section 'One-tailed and two-tailed tests' in Chapter 26.) Make sure that there is a tick next to the box **Flag significant correlations**. Click on **OK** to execute the command. A correlation coefficient matrix will be displayed in the IBM SPSS Statistics 19 **Viewer** window and an example is shown in Table 25.8.

Interpreting Pearson's r   The Pearson's r correlation for the relationship between age and income in Table 25.8 is 0.632. This is a modest association. With a two-tailed significance of less than 0.01, this association is significant at the 1 per

TABLE 25.8   Example of a correlation coefficient matrix in IBM SPSS Statistics 19

Correlations

		Age	Gross weekly income
Age	Pearson correlation	1	.632**
	Sig. (2-tailed)	. .	000
	N	130	130
Gross weekly income	Pearson correlation	.632**	1
	Sig. (2-tailed)	.000	.
	N	130	130

** Correlation is significant at the 0.01 level (two-tailed).

cent level. (Hypothesis testing is discussed in the section 'Hypothesis testing: single variables and relationships between variables' in Chapter 26.)

Analysing ordinal and interval/ratio relationships

Pearson's *r* can also be used in relationships of interval/ratio and ordinal variables if there are a large number of categories in the ordinal variable. Field (2009), Argyous (2000), Kanji (1999) and Blalock (1960) provide details of other correlation coefficients available for different data types or levels of measurement. Correlation coefficients for interval and ordinal variables, and for two ordinal variables, include Spearman's rank order correlation and Kendall's tau-b.

Spearman's rank order correlation, also known as Spearman's rho, is the non-parametric version of Pearson's *r*. It can be used when the variable data are ordinal or when interval/ratio data are not normally distributed and statistical testing is required. The difference between Pearson's *r* and Spearman's rho is that rather than the association being calculated on the actual variable data, it is instead based on the rank position of each piece of data. Ordinal variables, as you may recall from Chapter 23, are variables where the categories are placed in a rank order; hence there is a logical connection between the level of measurement and how Spearman's rho is calculated.

Calculating Spearman's rho in IBM SPSS Statistics 19 uses the exact same procedure as for Pearson's *r*. The only difference is that when you reach the **Bivariate Correlations** dialogue box, under **Correlations Coefficients** select **Spearman** and deselect Pearson. Interpretation of the correlation matrix is similar to that for Pearson's *r*.

Kendall's tau can be used for ordinal data when samples are small and there are a large number of tied ranks (Field, 2009: 181). The term 'tied ranks' means that many of the scores when ranked have the same rank position. In IBM SPSS Statistics 19 **Kendall's tau** is the third option under **Correlation Coefficients**.

Expanding the analysis of categorical data

The techniques discussed so far have focused on the description of single variables and the exploration of relationships between two variables. In order to explore and understand further the relationship between two variables, the researcher needs to think of why the relationship exists, how the are variables associated, and whether there are any other variables that impact on the relationship. Can the relationship be applied to all cases in the dataset, or is it stronger or weaker in different subgroups? Elaboration analysis is suitable for exploring such relationships in categorical, nominal or ordinal data.

Elaboration and spurious relationships

Elaboration analysis involves using a series of techniques to explore the extent to which a relationship is affected through the introduction of other variables. Does the relationship still exist, and to the same degree, when a third control variable is introduced? For example, if a relationship is found between full-time and part-time work and hourly pay (grouped), is the association the same when applied to men only compared to women only? Alternatively, is the same relationship maintained when 'type of work' is applied as a third variable? Or does the relationship disappear, suggesting that type of work is the variable impacting on hourly pay?

In our earlier example from the survey of university students (see Table 25.6) we concluded that there was sufficient evidence to suggest a difference in how male and female students feel walking around the campus. However, is this conclusion, or 'our model' for understanding the data, too simplistic? What other factors may be of influence? One factor that may be of importance is how familiar students are with the university campus. Measuring the concept of 'familiarity' would be quite difficult and in this survey no specific questions were asked. However, a suitable proxy measure could be how long the student has studied at the university. This data could be gathered by asking a question such as, 'Is this your first year at university?', with category responses of 'Yes' and 'No'. The corresponding variable can be introduced into the cross-tabulation as a third control variable which we can use to explore for differences in how safe students feel by sex, controlling for length of time enrolled as a student. Students in their first year of study will be less familiar with the university campus than students who have been at the university for longer. We will look at the results of introducing the third variable in Table 25.9. Before we do this, we need to consider the problem of spuriousness.

When undertaking data analysis we need to be alert to the possibility of the presence of spurious relationships. Spurious simply means false. Our data analysis allows us to identify and explore relationships; an identified relationship is said to be spurious when our association between two variables is not due to a direct cause-and-effect relationship but is actually due to a third variable, known or unknown. Elaboration techniques such as introducing a third variable into a cross-tabulation allow us to build a more complex understanding of our data and to consider the possibility of spuriousness.

The following technique for elaboration analysis involves examining the relationship between two categorical variables controlling for a third categorical variable. It is an extension of the contingency table analysis in Table 25.6.

Elaboration techniques using IBM SPSS Statistics 19: cross-tabulations

Introducing a third variable into a cross-tabulation will enable the researcher to assess the extent to which the two initial variables in the cross-tabulation are causally related. To introduce a third control variable into the contingency table, the **Crosstabs** command is used. From the **Analyze** menu, select **Descriptive Statistics** and **Crosstabs**. A **Crosstabs** dialogue box will be displayed (see Figure 25.1).

Follow the same procedure as in the section 'Creating contingency tables in IBM SPSS Statistics 19' in this chapter. Place the dependent variable under **Row(s)** and the independent variable under **Column(s)**. In addition, place the third control variable in the third box under **Layer 1 of 1**. Click on the **Cells** button and in the **Crosstabs: Cell Display** dialogue box under **Percentages** select **Column**. Column percentages are selected because the independent variable has been placed in the column. Click on **Continue** to return to the **Crosstabs** dialogue box. Click on **OK** to execute the command.

An example of a cross-tabulation controlled for a third variable is shown in Table 25.9. This is the table of 'how safe do you feel walking around the university campus during daylight hours' by 'sex' by 'first year of study'. The IBM SPSS Statistics 19 cross-tabulation table contains two partial tables. The first partial table shows the responses of Sex by Safe for students enrolled in their First Year. The second partial table shows the responses of Sex by Safe for Other students (students who are not in their first year). (Note the caution in Box 25.2.)

We can see that the sex differences in how safe the students feel are similar to

BOX 25.2 HINTS AND TIPS

You will notice from the example of using elaboration techniques that the counts for each cell in the table become smaller as the data are divided further between the categories of the control variable (Table 25.9). As the number of cells in a table increase the number of observed counts in each cell diminishes, and this is one of many reasons why a sufficient sample size is important from the outset. Where small cell counts become problematic, it is possible to combine existing categories together to create a large *n* for that new category (see section 'Recoding categorical variables' in Chapter 27).

those in the original top-level table in Table 25.6. Overall male students feel safer than female students for both first-year enrolled and those enrolled at the university for more than one year. For first-year students, 50.0% of male students and 23.3% of female students felt very safe. This compares to 70.1% of male students and 53.6% of female students who felt very safe and had been at the university for over a year.

The introduction of the 'first-year student' variable has revealed some other interesting differences that allow us to explore the data in greater depth. We can see that a larger proportion of students who have been enrolled at the university for over a year, both male and female, feel very safe or fairly safe, compared to those enrolled in their first year of study at the university. This table suggests that both gender and whether the student is in their first year are important influences on how safe students feel walking around the university campus.

TABLE 25.9 Example of a cross-tabulation controlling for a third variable: gender, by how safe students feel walking alone around the university campus in daylight hours, by first-year student

Safe * Gender * Year Cross-tabulation

Year				Male	Female	Total
				Gender		
First Year	Safe	Very safe	Count	100	70	170
			% within Gender	50.0%	23.3%	34.0%
		Fairly safe	Count	50	80	130
			% within Gender	25.0%	26.7%	26.0%
		A bit unsafe	Count	40	100	140
			% within Gender	20.0%	33.3%	28.0%
		Very unsafe	Count	10	50	60
			% within Gender	5.0%	16.7%	12.0%
	Total		Count]	200	300	500
			% within Gender	100.0%	100.0%	100.0%
Other	Safe	Very safe	Count	470	150	620
			% within Gender	70.1%	53.6%	65.3%
		Fairly safe	Count	180	70	250
			% within Gender	26.9%	25.0%	26.3%
		A bit unsafe	Count	10	30	40
			% within Gender	1.5%	10.7%	4.2%
		Very unsafe	Count	10	30	40
			% within Gender	1.5%	10.7%	4.2%
	Total		Count	670	280	950
				100.0%	100.0%	100.0%

Summary

Bivariate analysis involves describing and exploring relationships between two variables. The analysis techniques used will depend on the level of measurement of the variables. Relationships between two categorical variables (nominal or ordinal) can be explored using contingency tables and presented graphically by using a multiple bar chart. Analysis of two interval variables requires the technique of scatterplots to produce a visual representation of the relationship which can then be described. Measures of association enable the researcher to summarize the strength of the relationship between two variables. Different measures of association are appropriate for the level of measurement of the two variables. Depending on the original research question, the social researcher may be interested in expanding the analysis to consider more complex relationships involving a third variable. Elaboration analysis involves introducing a control variable that allows the influence of this third variable to be assessed. Where the original relationship between two variables disappears on the introducing of the control variable, the relationship is said to be spurious.

 ■ **Questions**

1 Contingency tables or cross-tabulations can be used for what level of measurement?
2 Describe the following elements of a contingency table: column marginal, row marginal and total count.
3 Identify each of the measures of association discussed in this chapter and summarize under what circumstances they can be calculated.

■ ■ **Further reading** ■

Argyous, George (2000) *Statistics for Social and Health Research: With a Guide to SPSS.* London: Sage.

Field, Andy (2009) *Discovering Statistics using SPSS for Windows*, 3rd edn. London: Sage.

Vogt, W. Paul (2005) *Dictionary of Statistics and Methodology: A Non Technical Guide for the Social Sciences*, 3rd edn. London: Sage.

TWENTY SIX

INFERENTIAL STATISTICS AND HYPOTHESIS TESTING

Chapter Contents

| Aims |

By the end of this chapter you will be able to:

- **Understand the importance of inferential statistics in the analysis of quantitative data.**
- **Calculate and analyse confidence intervals using IBM SPSS Statistics 19.**
- **Understand what is meant by hypothesis testing.**
- **Analyse the mean difference between two groups using a *t*-test.**
- **Analyse the relationship between two categorical variables using the chi-square test.**
- **Understand the principles of modelling using simple linear regression.**

In Chapter 25 we focused on describing relationships and differences using a range of different techniques. In this chapter we concentrate on how we can use inferential statistics to help us make further sense of data. Inferential statistics focus on techniques that involve making inferences when generalizing data from a sample to the whole population. Inferential statistics can be used to estimate population characteristics, or parameters, from sample data and to establish if the observed relationships and differences in sample data are likely, statistically, to be found in the population.

Inferential statistics

Inferential statistics are based on the assumption that a probability-based simple random sampling technique is used to draw a sample, that is, everyone in the population has an equal chance of being selected. A discussion of different types of probability sample can be found in Chapter 14. A sample must be selected carefully to minimize sampling variability and sampling error. Sampling variability refers to the selecting of repeat samples from the same population which will produce different means and standard deviations.

Sampling error refers to the notion that an estimate from a sample will not be the same as the population value. Sampling error will be dependent on the size of the sample and the variability of the variable in the population. A random sample will 'on average' have characteristics that resemble the population. Any differences between the observed sample characteristic and the known population value are the result of randomness. The terminology used in inferential statistics makes the distinction between *statistic* when referring to the sample, and *parameter* when referring to the population. For example, the mean income of a sample is known as the sample statistic, and the mean income of the population is known as the population parameter. Different statistical symbols are used for sample and population statistics:

- Sample statistics (Roman script): mean x, standard deviation s, proportion p.

- Population parameters (Greek script): mean μ, standard deviation σ, proportion π.

Where the sample has been selected by a random sampling technique, then the above can be assumed to be true. However, given the difficulties for some studies in obtaining a sampling frame, the researcher will need to make a professional judgement as to whether their sample is sufficiently representative of the population to enable the techniques in inferential statistics to be used. Details of how the sample was selected should be included in the research findings to enable the reader to assess if this is the case.

Parametric and non-parametric

Inferential statistics can be divided into two types of statistical test. Parametric tests are based on the assumptions of a normal distribution curve, as discussed below, and in using them in your analysis you are assuming that the data meet these underlying assumptions. Parametric tests are normally applied to interval data. Sometimes they are also used with ordinal data when the researcher is satisfied, or can successfully argue, that the ordinal data can be treated as if they were interval (Bryman and Cramer, 1997: 117). Data that are nominal or ordinal, or where the population characteristics do not meet a normal distribution or the sample is too small, require the use of non-parametric tests. Non-parametric tests are based on other types of distributions and have different shaped curves.

The normal distribution curve and the central limit theorem

One of the key elements in the use of inferential statistics is the normal distribution curve and the principles of the central limit theorem. The main principle of the central limit theorem is that taking repeated measures from different random samples will result in many sample means being close to the true population mean, and fewer sample means being further away from the population mean. For example, suppose from a known sampling frame we take a 10 per cent random sample of a population of working individuals and record their

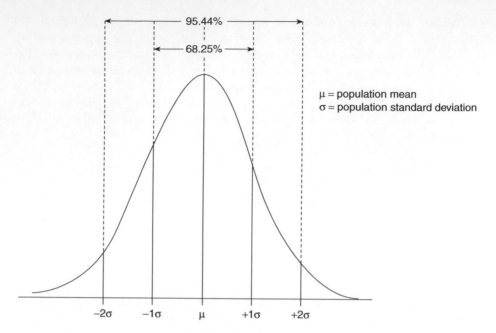

FIGURE 26.1 The normal distribution curve

income. We could then calculate the mean income of that sample. We then repeat the sampling and recording of income data for a further 100 samples taken from the same population. According to the central limit theorem, we should find that more of the calculated mean incomes will fall around the population mean income, with fewer samples falling a long way from this mean. This distribution of sample means will approximate to the normal distribution curve, a theoretical curve that is bell-shaped (see Figure 26.1). The shape of the normal distribution curve is the same; variations occur only in the mean and standard deviation (or spread).

Standard error

A further feature of the central limit theorem is that if the mean is calculated from all the sample means, its value will approximately equal the population mean. If we can calculate the mean of the sample means, then we can also calculate a standard deviation. The standard deviation of the sample means is known as the standard error and is expressed as SE. The central limit theorem states that the formula for the standard error of the population is

$$SE = \frac{SD_{\text{population}}}{\sqrt{n}}$$

The smaller the value of the standard error of the mean, the better the sample mean is as an estimate of the population mean. In practice we will not know what the SD of the population is; however, if the sample is large enough (Fielding and Gilbert, 2006, cited about 100), it can be approximated using the sample standard deviation:

$$SE = \frac{SD_{sample}}{\sqrt{n}}$$

This is an important feature as it enables the researcher to assess the accuracy of a calculated sample mean. The larger $SE(\bar{x})$, the less likely the mean from one sample is to be a good representation of the population mean. Since the distribution of sample means approximates to the normal distribution, we can make use of some of the properties of the normal distribution curve to calculate the likely range that the population mean will fall in, estimated on the sample mean. These involve the calculation of confidence intervals.

Confidence intervals

Since the distribution of sample means approximates to the normal distribution curve, we can use the properties of the normal distribution curve to estimate how accurate are the statistics drawn from our sample. To put it another way, we can decide how confident we can be that the findings in our sample can be generalized to the population. The normal curve states that 95 per cent of the area under the curve, or cases, will fall between −1.96 and +1.96 standard deviations.

In the normal distribution of sample means we know that the sample means will fall around the true population mean μ. We know that 95 per cent of the sample means will lie within plus or minus 1.96 standard deviations from the population mean. Therefore from the population mean we could calculate the range that we would expect our sample mean to fall 95 per cent of the time. However, in research we actually want to calculate the reverse. We know the sample mean and we want to calculate the range within which we would expect the population mean to fall from our sample mean with a level of confidence of 95 per cent. We can calculate a confidence interval and estimate how likely it is that we have identified the correct confidence interval for a specific level of confidence or level of significance. A 95 per cent level of confidence means that we would expect our confidence interval results to be correct 19 out of 20 times. We can express it the other way around: that we would expect to be wrong or be in error only 1 in 20 times. This measurement of expected error is known as the level of significance (Box 26.1). Level of significance is 100 per cent minus the level of confidence, for example, 5 per cent. This can also be expressed as a decimal with the statistical notation of p: for example, $p < 0.05$ (less than 5 per cent) or $p > 0.05$ (more than 5 per cent).

BOX 26.1 HINTS AND TIPS

Statistical terminology can sound similar and yet mean different things.

- *Level of confidence or confidence level* is a measure of how statistically confident you are that the calculated measurement is correct. It is normally expressed as a percentage, e.g. 95 per cent.
- *Level of significance or significance level* is a measure of the expected error. This can be expressed as a percentage, e.g. 5 per cent, or as a decimal, e.g. 0.05. Levels of significance are also referred to as the *p*-value.
- *Confidence intervals* are a measure of possible values (lower and upper values) within which a population parameter is expected to fall with a stated level of confidence or significance.

Confidence intervals are estimations of the lower and upper values in which we would expect a known population parameter to occur with a stated level of statistical significance. Below we show how to calculate a confidence interval for a mean value.

Manual calculation of confidence intervals for a mean

The equation for calculating the 95 per cent confidence interval for a mean is

$$\bar{x} \pm 1.96 \times \frac{s}{\sqrt{n}}$$

where s is the standard deviation, n is the count and $\bar{x}$ is the sample mean. This can be further summarized as

$$\bar{x} \pm 1.96 \times \text{SE}\,(\bar{x})$$

As we take the sample mean to be the best representation of the population mean, we can use the standard error of the mean. From this we can calculate the confidence interval at the 95 per cent level by multiplying $\text{SE}(\bar{x})$ by $+1.96$ and -1.96.

The following is a worked example. Calculating the standard error of the sample mean $\text{SE}(\bar{x})$ of age from a sample of 150 individuals with a mean age of 32.5 years and a standard deviation of 5.5 years, we find $\text{SE}(\bar{x})$ to be 0.449 years. Taking the sample mean to be the best estimate of the population mean, we can calculate the confidence interval at the 95 per cent level as follows:

$$32.5 \pm 1.96 \times 0.449 = 32.5 \pm 0.88 \text{ at the 95\% level (31.62, 33.38)}$$

To conclude, we can be 95 per cent confident that the population mean age will lie between 31.62 years and 33.38 years.

Using IBM SPSS Statistics 19 to calculate standard error and confidence intervals

From the **Analyze** menu, select **Descriptive Statistics** and **Explore**. Highlight the variable to be analysed and click on the arrow button ⮞ to move it to under **Dependent List**. Click on the **Statistics** button. The **Explore: Statistics** dialogue box will open. The default **Confidence interval for the mean** is set at 95 per cent. This should normally be sufficient, but if you are working to 99 per cent confidence, alter the figure. Click on **Continue**. Under **Display** select **Statistics**, unless plots are required as well, in which case leave **Both** selected. Click on **OK** to execute the command. A **Descriptives** box will be displayed containing the standard error (**Std. Error**), mean, and calculated 95 per cent confidence interval (**Lower bound, Upper bound**).

Hypothesis testing: single variables and relationships between variables

Hypothesis testing, also referred to as significance testing, enables researchers to make judgements as to whether there is enough evidence from the survey data to generalize the findings to a population. Many different hypothesis tests are available. Some involve comparing the observed values of a single variable from the survey data with a theoretical model about the distribution of the values in the population. For interval variables the theoretical model would be the normal distribution curve. Other hypothesis tests are available to compare the observed values in a relationship between two variables with a theoretical model of that relationship.

In order to decide which hypothesis test to use, the researcher needs three pieces of information. The first is the level of measurement, or data type, of the variable(s). The second is the number of samples. These can be one sample, two samples or many samples, often referred to in the literature as k samples. The third piece of information is, where there are two or more samples, whether the samples are independent or dependent, also referred to as related, paired or matched. The easiest way of understanding dependent and independent samples is through illustrating the two most common occurrences in social research.

An example of two samples that are dependent is a study involving the pre-testing and post-testing of a group of individuals or cases. Here two samples of data are collected: pre-test data values and post-test data values. The data are related since they are collected from the same cases.

An example of two samples that are independent is a cross-sectional research design that seeks to examine the relationship between two variables. When examining the relationship between two variables, the researcher considers one variable to be independent, the cause, and the second variable to be dependent, the effect. The survey data are divided into two samples by the categories in the independent variable: for example, the variable 'sex' with two categories, male and female. The samples for male and female are unrelated, since the individuals in the survey can only belong to one of the samples.

Hypothesis testing requires the establishment of two opposing hypotheses: the null hypothesis H_0 and the alternative or research hypothesis H_1. The null hypothesis is that there is no difference between observed or survey values and those in the theoretical model. The alternative or research hypothesis is that there is a real difference between the observed or survey values and those in the theoretical model.

For example, a cross-section research design collected data on two variables, the sex of the respondent, male or female, and the working status of the respondent, full-time or part-time. The null hypothesis is that there is no difference in the working status of men and women. The alternative or research hypothesis is that there is a difference in the working status of men and women.

The logic of null hypothesis testing requires that we begin by 'assuming' a particular pattern in the population. This pattern will be the opposite to that which we 'expect' (on the basis of theory and so on) to find (de Vaus, 2002a: 167). The basis of hypothesis testing is then to test if there is enough 'evidence' from the sample data collected to reject the null hypothesis. By rejecting the null hypothesis the researcher can 'accept' the alternative or research hypothesis. The 'evidence' used to make the judgement is the level of significance of the test statistic. In Chapter 14 probability samples were discussed, and in the present chapter the use of confidence intervals has been outlined. Levels of significance, or statistical significance, allow the researcher to make a judgment as to how confident they can be about the findings in the sample data being found in the population. In the social sciences, if the level of significance for the test statistic is less than 5 per cent ($p < 0.05$), then the null hypothesis can be rejected. Sometimes a level of significance of less than 1 per cent ($p < 0.01$) is used.

Making errors in hypothesis testing

There are two possible errors to be made in hypothesis testing.

A type I error is an incorrect rejection of the null hypothesis, where the conclusion was that there was a real difference when one does not exist. The chance of this happening is the result of the significance level selected. If a 5 per cent level (0.05) is selected, then we have a 1 in 20 chance of falsely rejecting the null hypothesis. At the 1 per cent level (0.01) we would have a 1 in 100 chance of falsely rejecting the null hypothesis.

A type II error is an incorrect acceptance of the null hypothesis, where the conclusion was that there was no real difference when a difference did exist. The chance of a type II error is unknown. The chances of making a type I error can be reduced by selecting a higher level of significance, say 1 per cent instead of 5 per cent. However, the higher the significance level, the greater the chance of making a type II error.

One-tailed and two-tailed tests

Hypothesis testing is divided into one-tailed and two-tailed tests. The difference between these is that one-tailed tests impose a specific direction on the alternative

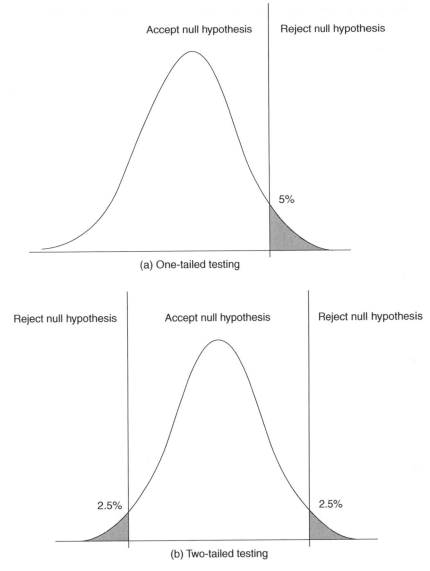

FIGURE 26.2   One-tailed and two-tailed hypothesis testing

hypothesis, and two-tailed tests are non-directional in the alternative hypothesis (see Figure 26.2). For example, in a one-tailed test, H_1 is that men have a higher monthly gross income than women. In a two-tailed test, H_1 is that there is a difference in the monthly gross incomes of men and women. In both instances, H_0 would be that there was no difference in the monthly gross incomes of men and women. The researcher must have good evidence or theory to be confident of the direction that the test should be applied. If the direction is incorrect, this will result in the false acceptance of the null hypothesis. In the majority of instances the direction cannot be assumed and a two-tailed test should be employed.

The independent samples *t*-test

A common parametric hypothesis test used by social researchers when they want to compare the mean scores of two different groups of cases is the independent samples *t*-test (Box 26.2). It is a test that you use to assess an interval/ratio variable (e.g. age, income) by a categorical variable that contains two groups for comparison (e.g. gender). For example, if you had calculated descriptive statistics which included the mean age for men and women, the next stage would be to calculate an independent samples *t*-test to assess if the observed difference was statistically significant (Box 26.3). The independent samples *t*-test is a calculation based on the mean, standard deviation and sample sizes for both groups (see Field, 2009: 334–6 for a detailed explanation).

There are some assumptions that you need to consider when considering using this *t*-test:

BOX 26.2 HINTS AND TIPS

If you need to make comparisons between the mean score of an interval/ratio variable for more than two groups then you use analysis of variance (ANOVA) techniques. See Field (2009: Chapter 10) for more information.

BOX 26.3 HINTS AND TIPS

Be careful to not confuse the independent samples *t*-test with either the dependent samples *t*-test or the one-sample *t*-test. The dependent samples *t*-test is used where the test data are collected from the same participants at two points in time, hence they are dependent samples. An explanation of the dependent samples *t*-test is provided later in this chapter. The one-sample *t*-test is used to assess the distribution of a single variable in relation to a known population parameter using the *t*-distribution. See Field (2009) for a more detailed explanation of both.

1 The level of measurement of the dependent variable should be interval or ratio.

2 A random sampling technique has been used to collect data from the population.

3 Independence of observations: it is assumed that the response made by the participants (cases) are not influenced by the other participants. Typically this assumption can be

challenged if the research data have been collected on participants who have been in a group setting and interacted with each other.

4 Normal distribution: it is assumed that the populations from which the sample is drawn are normally distributed. The distribution of your sample scores can be assessed by examining the data using a histogram.

5 Homogeneity of variance: this means that the population from which the sample has been taken have equal variances. So, for example, in the population we would expect that the distribution of income values for men and women will have equal variance and the shape of the distribution will be similar. There is a statistical test that allows you to test for violation of this assumption, called the Levene test of equality of variances. This test statistic is calculated automatically in IBM SPSS Statistics 19 and the software subsequently calculates two *t*-test statistics where one is adjusted for unequal variances.

Calculating an independent samples *t*-test in IBM SPSS Statistics 19

For the independent sample *t*-test, the null hypothesis H_0 is that there will be no difference in the mean between the two groups. The alternative hypothesis H_1 is that there is a difference in the mean between the two groups. For example, the null hypothesis is that there is no difference in the mean age of men and women. Here the dependent variable is age and the independent variable is sex.

As mentioned earlier, IBM SPSS Statistics 19 also allows you to test for the homogeneity of variance. For the Levene test for equality of variances the null hypothesis H_0 is that there is no difference in the variance of the two groups. For example, there is no difference in the variance of age for men and women.

To perform both tests in IBM SPSS Statistics 19, from the **Analyze** menu select **Compare means** and **Independent-Samples T Test**. An **Independent-Samples T Test** dialogue box will be displayed (Figure 26.3). Highlight the dependent variable, for example, Age, and click on ➡ to move across to under **Test Variables**. Highlight the independent variable, for example Sex, and click on ➡ to move across to under **Grouping Variable**.

The next stage is to define the codes of the two groups in the independent variable. Click on **Define Groups** and a dialogue box will be displayed (Figure 26.4). The boxes next to **Group 1** and **Group 2** may automatically display the two valid codes for the grouping variable. For example, **Group 1** is 1 (code for Male) and **Group 2** is 2 (code for Female). If the correct codes have not been entered, you will need to type each code in the corresponding boxes as required.

Click on **Continue** to return to the main dialogue box. Now click on **OK** to execute the command.

Interpreting the output   IBM SPSS Statistics 19 will produce two boxes of statistical information as in the example shown in Table 26.1. In the group statistics box the mean and standard deviation for the dependent variable, Age, for each of the two groups, Male and Female, are given. We can see that there are 130 cases, 49

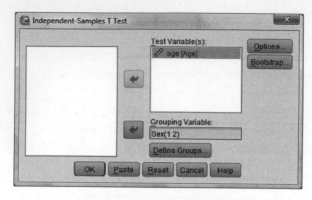

FIGURE 26.3 Independent-Samples T Test dialog box

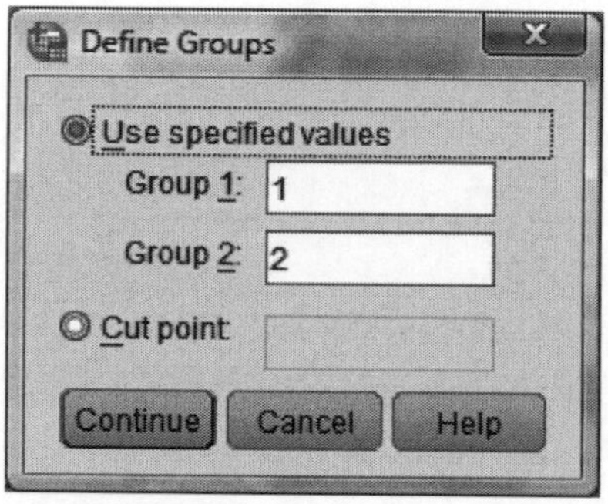

FIGURE 26.4 Define Groups dialog box

male and 81 female. The mean age of the males was 47.02 years and for the females 48.99 years. The variance for men and women is similar: standard deviation 16.57 years and standard deviation 16.48 years. The average age of the women was slightly higher than for men.

The next stage is to determine the null hypothesis for the Levene test to establish if the assumption of homogeneity of variance has been violated. The null hypothesis for Levene's is that there is no difference in the variance of age distribution for men and women. For the Levene statistic, examine the second independent samples test box and look at the F-value and the significance (Sig.) level. We can see that $F = 0.003$ and the significance level p is 0.958. With the significance level greater than 0.05 we can accept the null hypothesis for the Levene test and assume that the variances are equal.

The next stage is to determine the null hypothesis for the independent samples t-test. The null hypothesis for the t-test is that the men and women have the same mean age. Since we know from Levene that equal variances can be assumed, read across the first row from 'Equal variances assumed' to look at the value of t, the degrees of freedom and the significance level (two tailed). Here $t = -0.658$, d.f. = 128, and the significance level $p = 0.512$. With the significance level greater than 0.05 we therefore accept the null hypothesis and conclude that there are no significant differences in the mean age of men and women.

TABLE 26.1 IBM SPSS Statistics 19 example of independent sample *t*-test output

Group Statistics

	Sex of …	N	Mean	Std. Deviation	Std. Error Mean
Age of respondent	Male	49	47.02	16.576	2.368
	Female	81	48.99	16.484	1.832

Independent Samples Test

		Levene's Test for Equality of Variances		*t*-test for Equality of Means						
									95% Confidence Interval of the Difference	
		F	Sig.	t	df	Sig. (2-tailed)	Mean Difference	Std. Error Difference	Lower	Upper
Age of respondent	Equal variances assumed	.003	.958	-.658	128	.512	-1.967	2.990	-7.883	3.948
	Equal variances not assumed			-.657	100.937	.513	-1.967	2.994	-7.906	3.972

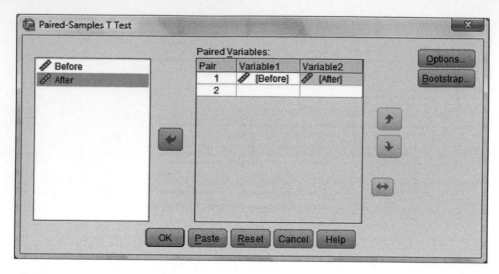

FIGURE 26.5 Paired Samples dialogue box

The dependent samples *t*-test

The dependent samples *t*-test, also known as the paired samples *t*-test, is a parametric test and is to be used if you have collected data on the same cases at two different time points. This is also known as repeated measures and is appropriate to be used for research data from experimental designs. For example, you have measured a sample of individuals' political opinion of the elected government before the chancellor's budget statement, and you then take a second measurement on the same individuals one month later after the budget statement has been made. The assumptions of the dependent samples *t*-test are that the data are interval/ratio and the difference between the two scores, the before-and-after measurements, should be normally distributed (Field, 2009: 329). So, in this example there may be a set of ordinal responses to a series of attitudinal statements. These responses can be combined into a single 'opinion' index that is an interval data type, see section 'Calculating new variables' in Chapter 27. Producing a histogram and box plot of the new 'difference' variable would allow you to assess the distribution. For the dependent *t*-test the null hypothesis H_0 would be that there is no difference in, for example, political opinions pre- and post-budget. The alternative hypothesis H_1 is that there is a difference in political opinion.

Calculating a dependent samples *t*-test in IBM SPSS Statistics 19

To perform a dependent samples *t*-test in IBM SPSS Statistics 19, from the **Analyze** menu select **Compare means** and **Paired-Samples T Test**. The **Paired-Samples T Test** dialogue box will be displayed (Figure 26.5). Highlight the two

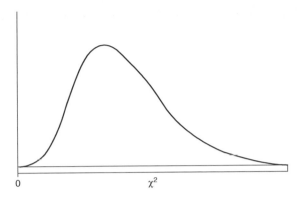

FIGURE 26.6 Chi-Square distribution curve

Source: Stanford University School of Medicine.

variables, shown as Before and After in Figure 26.5. Click on the first variable, Before, and click on ⬇ to move it across to under **Variable1**. Now click in the box under **Variable2**. Click on the second variable, After, and click on ⬇ to move it across to under **Variable2**. An alternative method for doing this is to highlight both variables (click on the first variable, hold down the **Shift** key, and click on the second variable) and then click on ⬇. Click on **Options** if you need to change the confidence level from 95 per cent (the default setting). Click on **OK** to execute the command. The resulting IBM SPSS Statistics 19 output can be interpreted in the same way as for the independent samples *t*-test, except that there is no Levene's to discuss first.

The chi-square test for categorical data

The most common hypothesis test used by social researchers is the chi-square test for independence. This is a test that is applied to a relationship between two nominal variables. It ascertains whether there is enough evidence from the survey data to state with statistical confidence that there is a relationship between two variables. The chi-square test statistic has a different curve to that of a normal distribution curve (see Figure 26.6). The curve is positively skewed to the right, reflecting that this is a distribution of categorical data. The exact shape of the curve will depend on the number of degrees of freedom. Degrees of freedom reflect the amount of variability there is in the table: large values result in a more spread distribution, and very large values result in a curve that is similar in shape to a normal distribution (Agresti, 2009: 226–7).

To describe the relationship between two nominal variables, contingency tables can be produced in IBM SPSS Statistics 19. In order for the researcher to assess whether the observed differences in the table are significant, and hence

TABLE 26.2 Contingency table example: Car Ownership by Sex

Actual count

Own a car?	Male	Female	Total
Yes	848	162	1010
No	218	247	465
Total	1066	409	1475

Expected count

Own a car?	Male	Female	Total
Yes	$\dfrac{1066 \times 1010}{1475} = 729.9$	$\dfrac{409 \times 1010}{1475} = 280.1$	1010
No	$\dfrac{1066 \times 465}{1475} = 336.1$	$\dfrac{409 \times 465}{1475} = 128.9$	465
Total	1066	409	1475

generalizable, a chi-square test can be performed, represented by χ^2. This is a non-parametric test and involves comparing the observed values with the values expected if there was no association between the two nominal variables. It enables the researcher to make a judgement as to whether the observed differences are real differences and not due to the fluctuations that occur by chance, known as 'probability', as a result of the sample selected. The formula for calculating the expected frequency count for each cell is:

$$\text{expected frequency} = \frac{\text{column total} \times \text{row total}}{\text{grand total}}$$

Table 26.2 shows a contingency table for the relationship of car ownership by sex. The first stage in exploring this relationship is to describe the differences. A chi-square test can then be performed. The null hypothesis H_0 is that there is no difference in car ownership between men and women. The alternative hypothesis H_1 is that there is a difference in car ownership between men and women. The first part of Table 26.2 shows the actual count. The second part shows the expected counts if there was no association between the two variables, Car Ownership and Gender.

Calculating chi-square

The chi-square statistic is calculated using the following formula:

$$\chi^2 = \frac{\Sigma (O_i - E_i)^2}{E_i}$$

where O_i is the observed count, E_i is the expected count and Σ is summation.

TABLE 26.3 Manual calculation of chi-square

O	E	(O–E)	(O–E)²	(O–E)²/E	χ²
848	729.9	118.1	13,947.61	19.11	
162	280.1	–118.1	13,947.61	49.80	
218	336.1	–118.1	13,947.61	41.50	
247	128.9	118.1	13,947.61	108.20	218.61

For each cell in Table 26.2 the expected count is subtracted from the observed count. This value is squared and divided by the expected count. This is repeated for each cell in the table, and the resultant values are summed together. This calculation is shown in Table 26.3.

The value of χ^2 is 218.61. If χ^2 is 'big', then there is a large difference between the observed and expected counts. However, it is difficult to assess how big is 'big', as the value of chi-square is a product of the number of cells and cell counts in the table. In order to determine this, the degrees of freedom for the table need to be calculated. For a contingency table the degrees of freedom (d.f.) are calculated as

d.f. = (no. of rows – 1) × (no. of columns – 1)

In a 2 × 2 table the degrees of freedom would be (2–1) × (2–1) = 1.

If you do not have access to computing software to calculate chi-square, the next stage would be to look up on a chi-square table the critical value for 1 d.f. These tables are available in most data analysis texts or from specialist statistical tables texts (for example, Lindley and Scott, 1995). If χ^2 is greater than or equal to the critical value, then the null hypothesis can be rejected. If χ^2 is less than the critical value, the null hypothesis cannot be rejected. Looking up the chi-square distribution at 5 per cent (0.05) significance for 1 d.f., the critical chi-square value is 3.8415. Since the calculated chi-square, or test statistic, value is higher than this, we can reject the null hypothesis and accept the alternative or research hypothesis that there is an association between car ownership and sex.

Some guidelines should be applied when using chi-square (Box 26.4). The first is that there needs to be a minimum number of expected counts in each cell of the table. The minimum expected count is five, and if more than 20 per cent of cells in the table contain an expected count of less than five, then either more data will need to be collected or recoding techniques will need to be used to combine categories. The difficulty with the latter is that this technique reduces the sensitivity of the data.

BOX 26.4 HINTS AND TIPS

When calculating a chi-square test for independence always:

1 Identify the independent and dependent variables.
2 Write down the null hypothesis and the alternative or research hypothesis.

(Continued)

3 Always produce a contingency table with observed counts, expected counts, and percentages based on the independent variable. These will be column percentages if you have placed the independent variable in the column.

4 Always interpret the data in the contingency table as well as the chi-square result.

5 When reporting the chi-square result, remember to cite the degrees of freedom and the significance level.

6 Remember that if the significance level is greater than 5 per cent (or 0.05) then you must accept the null hypothesis of no difference. If the significance level is less than 5 per cent (or 0.05) then you can reject the null hypothesis and conclude that any observed differences in your table are statistically significant.

7 Remember that chi-square has some limitations if more than 20 per cent of the cells in your table have an expected cell count of less than five. All is not lost if this happens, as you can look to recode the categories, see section Recording Categorical Variables in Chapter 27.

Using IBM SPSS Statistics 19 to calculate chi-square

IBM SPSS Statistics 19 makes the calculating of chi-square very easy. Instead of one having to look up the critical value for chi-square for the degrees of freedom in a table, IBM SPSS Statistics 19 will calculate the level of significance for that value of chi-square based on the degrees of freedom.

To calculate chi-square in IBM SPSS Statistics 19, the first stage is to select the **Crosstabs** command and place the independent variable in the column and the dependent variable in the row. In the **Crosstabs** dialogue box, calculate the expected frequencies by clicking on the **Cells** button. The **Cells** dialogue box will appear. Under **Counts**, select **Expected**. Click on **Continue**. To calculate chi-square, click on the **Statistics** button. Select the **Chi-Square** option in the top left corner. Click on **Continue**. Click on **OK** to execute the command.

Table 26.4 shows an example IBM SPSS Statistics 19 output of a cross-tabulation and chi-square. It is based on the earlier example of car ownership by sex. In the output, the chi-square statistic is shown as 'Pearson chi-square'. The value given is 218.441. The slight variation between this and the earlier manual calculation is simply due to rounding numbers calculated to two decimal places.

The IBM SPSS Statistics 19 output in Table 26.4 includes a range of other calculated statistics. In instances of a 2 × 2 table IBM SPSS Statistics 19 will, in addition to Pearson's chi-square, also calculate a continuity correction. Tables that have independent and dependent variables with only two categories respectively are treated statistically as special cases, particularly when sample sizes are large or small. Yates's contingency correction can be used for these 2 × 2 tables where the table total is more than 40, or between 20 and 40 with expected frequencies of five for each cell (Cramer, 1994: 83). The use of this correction is not widely accepted; Field (2009: 691) summarizes the discussion that it may overcorrect the problem and recommends that it is worth avoiding.

TABLE 26.4   IBM SPSS Statistics 19 example of cross-tabulation and chi-square

		HOHSEX	Male	Female	Total
Car owned	Yes	Count	848	162	1,010
		Expected count	729.9	280.1	1,010.0
		% within HOHSEX	79.5%	39.6%	68.5%
	No	Count	218	247	465
		Expected count	336.1	128.9	465.0
		% within HOHSEX	20.5%	60.4%	31.5%
Total		Count	1,066	409	1,475
		Expected count	1,066.0	409.0	1,475.0
		% within HOHSEX	100.5%	100.0%	100.0%

Chi-square tests

Value	d.f.	Asymp. sig. (2-sided)	Exact sig. (2-sided)	Exact sig. (1-sided)
Pearson chi-square	218.441[b]	1	.000	
Continuity correction[a]	216.595	1	.000	
Likelihood ratio	209.327	1	.000	
Fisher's exact test			.000	.000
Linear-by-linear association	218.293	1	.000	
N of valid cases	1475			

[a]Computed only for a 2 × 2 table.
[b]0 cells (0%) have expected count less than 5. The minimum expected count is 128.94.

For tables with small samples, the condition of use of chi-square where the expected count is less than five and where 20 per cent of the table cells have expected counts of less than five is often violated. The Fisher's exact test corrects for these sampling distribution difficulties. Where certain conditions are met, both Yates's and Fisher's are automatically calculated by IBM SPSS Statistics 19. This does not automatically mean that you should include them as part of your analyses, and their use should be considered accordingly (see Field, 2009: 690–1 for a more detailed explanation). If you are unsure as to whether it is appropriate for your data to make use of Fisher's exact test or Yates's continuity correction, continue to report the chi-square statistic only.

The two-tailed significance level for Pearson's chi-square, Fisher's and Yates's is displayed as 0.000. This means that the significance level is less than 0.01. The null hypothesis can be rejected at the 1 per cent level and the alternative hypothesis accepted.

Reporting chi-square findings

Reporting χ^2 should be in addition to an interpretation of the contingency, which would normally involve reporting the column percentages. You should clearly state the purpose of the test, the null hypothesis and the research hypothesis. Report the chi-square test result, the degrees of freedom and the significance level of the result. State whether these results allow you to accept or reject the null hypothesis.

From the worked example we could report that in the sample 79.5 per cent of men owned a car compared to 39.6 per cent of women (Table 26.4). A chi-square test was performed to assess whether these observed differences are significant. Two hypotheses were established. The research hypothesis is that there is a difference in car ownership between men and women. The null hypothesis is that there is no difference in car ownership between men and women. The chi-square statistic is 218.44, the degrees of freedom are 1 and the reported significance level is 0.000. At the 1 per cent level the null hypothesis can be rejected. It is therefore unlikely that men and women have the same proportion of car ownership in the population, in which case we can conclude that there is an association between car ownership and gender. Note that chi-square does not tell you anything about the direction or strength of the relationship, only that it is statistically significant. The direction of the relationship can be ascertained from interpreting the column percentages in the table, and for strength the measures of association phi and Cramer's V.

Chi-square example: walking on campus

In Table 25.6 we looked at differences in the levels of how safe male and female students felt walking alone around the university campus in daylight hours. We found that there were differences, with male students overall feeling more safe than female students. The next step in the data analysis would be to calculate a chi-square test of independence for this table. The null hypothesis H_0 is that there is no difference in how safe male and female students feel walking around the campus. The alternative hypothesis H_1 is that there is a difference in how safe male and female students feel walking around the campus. The same table has been reproduced in IBM SPSS Statistics 19, this time showing observed and expected counts together with the chi-square test results (Table 26.5). The chi-square statistic is 193.188, the degrees of freedom are 3 and the reported significance level is 0.000. At the 1 per cent level the null hypothesis can be rejected. We can conclude that there is a significant difference in how safe male and female students feel walking around the campus in daylight hours.

Other hypothesis tests available

The chi-square test for independence is used for relationships between two nominal variables. It can also be used for a relationship between a nominal and an ordinal variable, and is acceptable to use for two ordinal variables, although there are more appropriate hypothesis tests available for this and other levels of measurement. For two ordinal variables a Mann–Whitney, Wilcoxon or Kruskal–Wallis

TABLE 26.5 Sex by how safe students feel walking alone around the university campus in daylight hours: chi-square test for independence

Safe * Sex Cross-tabulation

| | | | Sex | | |
			Male	Female	Total
Safe	Very safe	Count	570	220	790
		Expected Count	474.0	316.0	790.0
	Fairly safe	Count	230	150	380
		Expected Count	228.0	152.0	380.0
	A bit unsafe	Count	50	130	180
		Expected Count	108.0	72.0	180.0
	Very unsafe	Count	20	80	100
		Expected Count	60.0	40.0	100.0
Total		Count	870	580	1450
		Expected Count	870.0	580.0	1450.0

Chi-Square Tests

	Value	d.f.	Asymp. Sig. (2-sided)
Pearson Chi-Square	193.188[a]	3	.000
Likelihood Ratio	194.537	3	.000
Linear-by-Linear Association	181.802	1	.000
N of Valid Cases	1450		

[a] 0 cells (0%) have expected count less than 5. The minimum expected count is 40.00.

test may be undertaken. There are a number of other tests available for a nominal variable with more than two categories and an interval variable. These include analysis of variance (ANOVA). For further details on these and other hypothesis tests see Argyous (2000), Field (2009) or Bryman and Cramer (2000).

Data modelling techniques

Data models in empirical social science research enable researchers to consider the complex relationships between different social data that have been collected. Models use statistical techniques to provide a framework to make sense of this complexity. Models are used in many other academic and professional disciplines. For example, architects and town planners routinely build scale models of buildings and landscaped areas to help understand build requirements and consider how individuals interact with their surroundings. While the architect's model will be a physical scale model, the general principle of using a model to understand, test and predict is the same for statistical data models. In the natural sciences, scientists are using climate and environmental data to understand and predict future climate change using models that contribute to the global warming debates.

The aim of this section is to introduce the principal ideas of modelling data using a simple linear regression model. At the end of this section a summary of other modelling techniques is given and further reading is suggested. Modelling techniques, like other statistics, are dependent on the level of measurement or data type of your research data. There are different techniques for analysing interval-level data compared to ordinal data. In the social sciences a combination of data types is quite common and there are data transformation techniques available to deal with this issue.

From the quantitative analysis techniques we have explored so far in Chapters 24, 25 and 26, one of the challenges for the social researcher is managing the different types of data analysis undertaken. We have examined individual single variables, understood their distribution and spread of values, explored differences and relationships between two variables, and considered the influence of a third variable in that relationship. These produce many different sets of results that all need to be sifted, sorted and interpreted. For instance, every single variable will have descriptive statistics, tables and charts; each bivariate relationship will have a contingency table or correlation matrix and scatterplot. Multivariate analysis introducing a third variable will produce additional tables and outputs. For example, an analysis of data from the university student survey on crime and safety would focus on understanding differences in experiences and concerns about different crimes. The analysis would seek to explore the differences between male and female students, where they lived and how much time they spent on campus. The research analysis may explore if there is a causal link between past experiences of crime and current fear of crime levels.

Even though a high volume of results is produced, these stages are crucial in your understanding of the research data and should always form the foundations of your analysis. From this analysis you will identify the key variables and gain valuable insights that will enable you to address your research question, accepting or rejecting hypotheses and considering those findings in relation to the underpinning theory. However, one of the limitations of these techniques is that they do not allow you to easily explore the relationships and complex interactions that exist between variables. Depending on the research question and the depth of analysis required, the next stage is to consider modelling your data. 'Statistical modelling is an important analytical tool as it enables social researchers to consider in a coherent and unified procedure complex inter-relationships between social phenomena and to isolate and make judgements about separate effects of each' (Tarling, 2009: 1).

Tarling (2009: 1) summarizes four main reasons why social researchers use modelling techniques to understand their research data:

1   To improve understanding of causality and the development of theory through the testing of competing theories.

2   To make predictions – particularly useful in risk assessment relating to policy decisions.

3   To assess the effect of different characteristics – particularly useful where there are multiple independent variables, e.g. age, gender, that influence particular outcomes such as fear of crime.

4 To reduce the dimensionality of data. Where many variables exist, techniques are available to manage these variables to identify latent variables that measure the underlying concept.

The variables that are included in statistical models are based on theory. Variable selection should always be theory driven rather than data driven. A model will consist of a dependent or outcome variable, for example, a fear of crime measure, and one or more independent variables or predictors that influence the outcome, for example, age, gender, area of residence. The researcher decides the variables to be included in the model and their status as independent or dependent variables. The empirical data collected are then subjected to statistical techniques to assess how much explanation the model provides.

The aim of a statistical model is to produce a model of the least complexity that provides the maximum amount of explanation. An example of a common modelling technique, simple linear regression, is discussed in the next section.

Simple linear regression analysis

Simple Linear Regression (SLR) analysis attempts to establish the relationship between two scale variables in order to calculate a predictive equation enabling the value of the dependent variable to be determined from a given value of the independent variable.

Regression analysis requires the two variables to be clearly defined as independent and dependent, according to the theoretical model defined by the researcher. The following presents a basic introduction to the principles of linear regression. You are advised to consult a specialist quantitative data analysis and statistical analysis text, for example, Field (2009) or Tarling (2009), if you wish to undertake this analysis. In this section we provide an overview of the technique. There are some underlying assumptions associated with applying SLR techniques to data. Briefly, these assumptions are:

1 Your dependent and independent variables should be interval.

2 The variables should ideally not be influenced by outliers.

3 The individual variables should be normally distributed.

4 The correlation of the two variables should be linear. This can be ascertained by looking at the scatterplot of x against y: the plot should be positively or negatively correlated in a linear (straight line) direction.

Regression is closely associated with the scatterplot and correlation coefficient. It is concerned with finding the line of best fit between two variables in a scatterplot. The line of best fit is defined as a straight line that is placed on the scatterplot in a position that minimizes the distance between the line and each plot. Since it

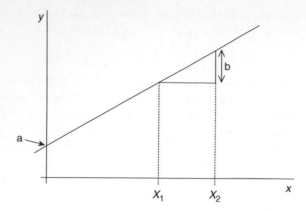

FIGURE 26.7 The regression line

would be impossible to manually place this straight line in a position that would account for all plots and distances from the line, a regression equation is used to determine the line of best fit. The regression equation is

$$y = a + bx$$

where y is the dependent variable, x is the independent variable, a is the intercept (the point at which the line of best fit crosses the vertical or y-axis) and b is the slope of the line, determined as the rate of change in y for a change in x. This is represented in Figure 26.7.

The regression model plots a line of best fit. As you can see, some of the cases will fit better than others, i.e. be closer to the model (the regression line). The model will explain some of the relationship between the two variables but not all of it. For this reason an error term e needs to be included in the equation of the regression model: e is the part of the relationship that the model cannot explain. A model of good fit will explain a high proportion of the relationship, so minimizing the e. The equation now is

$$y = a + bx + e$$

A multiple regression technique is available for use when there are more than two interval or ratio variables, with more dependent variables and multiple independent variables. Additionally, it will enable you to determine which of the variables is a better predictor of the dependent variable. For details on using this technique, see Field (2009), Tarling (2009), Bryman and Cramer (1997), de Vaus (2002a) and Rose and Sullivan (1996).

Calculating linear regression in IBM SPSS Statistics 19

IBM SPSS Statistics 19 will calculate the regression coefficients and also provide an indicator of how well the independent variable is a predictor of the dependent

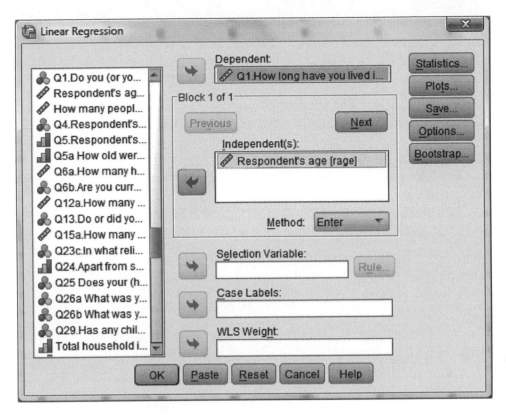

FIGURE 26.8 IBM SPSS Statistics 19 **Linear Regression** dialogue box

variable, reported as R^2. In addition, confidence intervals will be calculated to assess if the linear regression model is statistically significant and can be generalized to the population.

The instructions on how to calculate regression using IBM SPSS Statistics 19 are as follows. From the **Analyze** menu, select **Regression** and **Linear**. The **Linear Regression** dialogue box will be displayed (Figure 26.8). From the left hand side, highlight the dependent variable in the relationship and click once on the arrow button to move the variable to under **Dependent**. Highlight the independent variable and click once on the second arrow button to copy the variable across to under **Independent(s)**. Next to **Method** select **Enter** from the available list. Click on the **Statistics** button. In the **Linear Regression: Statistics** dialogue box, check that under **Regression coefficients** the **Estimates** is selected and that **Model Fit** is selected. Click on **Continue**. Click on **OK** to execute the command. A regression model will be displayed in the IBM SPSS Statistics 19 **Viewer** window, and an example is shown in Table 26.6.

Interpreting the output The example output in Table 26.6 is a regression model of age and income per week. The output is quite complex and is divided into three

TABLE 26.6   IBM SPSS Statistics 19 Linear Regression output

Model summary

Model	R	R square	Adjusted R square	Std error of the estimate	Sig.
1	.632	.400	.395	105.98893	.000[a]

[a] Predictors: (constant), Age.

ANOVA[b]

Model		Sum of Squares	d.f.	Mean square	F	Sig.
1	Regression	958558.8	1	958558.805	85.329	.000 [a]
	Residual	1437908	128	11233.653		
	Total	2396466	129			

[a] Predictors: (constant), Age.

[b] Dependent variable: gross weekly income.

Coefficients[a]

Model		Unstandardized coefficients B	Std Error	Standardized coefficients Beta	t	Sig.
1	(Constant)	8.538	25.803		.331	.741
	Age	4.704	.509	.632	9.237	.000

[a] Dependent variable: gross weekly income.

different boxes. The key areas that you need to interpret from the IBM SPSS Statistics 19 output are as follows. In the 'Model summary' box under the 'R Square' column (R_2), the value is 0.4. This means that the regression model of age as the one variable predicting income explains 40 per cent of the variation between age and income. This suggests that it is a reasonable model for explaining income differences. In the 'ANOVA' box the statistical significance can be assessed by looking in the far right column under 'Sig.'. The value is 0.000, which means that this model explains 40 per cent of the variation in income and is significant at the 0.001 per cent level. There is less than one in a thousand chance of these findings occurring by chance. However sixty per cent of variation is not explained by the model. In the 'Coefficients' box a lot of data is presented. In the first row '(Constant)' read the data in the cell under B for a, and in the second row 'Age' read the data under B for b. In this example a is £8.54 and b = £4.70. The regression equation would therefore be:

income = £8.54 + £4.70 × age

This equation can also be used for prediction. For an individual age 20 inserting the value of 20 into the equation would give a predicted income of £8.54 + (£4.70*20) = £102.54. We know from the value of R^2 that this model is a reasonable predictor of income and that factors other than age contribute to income. This model could

BOX 26.5 HINTS AND TIPS

Plotting the linear regression line on a scatterplot

In IBM SPSS Statistics 19 it is possible to fit the linear regression line on to a scatterplot:

- First produce the scatterplot and then open the plot in **Chart Editor**.
- From the **Elements** menu, select **Fit Line** at **Total**.
- The **Properties** dialogue box will open.
- Select the **Fit Line** tab.
- Under **Fit Method** select **Linear**.

be expanded upon to build a more complex multiple linear regression (MLR) model. (See also Box 26.5.)

Developing models with more than one dependent variable allows you to build greater complexity into the model that will, hopefully, result in the model explaining a higher proportion of the variation in your data. Determining the variables to be included in the model will need to be theory driven as the aim of developing the model is to provide as much explanation as possible with the simplest model. The variables that you select need to be based on your knowledge of the social context. The simplest model will be the one which has the least number of variables and which retains the maximum amount of explanation. You will need to remember that, in the social sciences, achieving a high level of explanation is difficult given the complexity of the social world. In the following section we briefly outline some of the other modelling techniques available. It is beyond the scope of this textbook to provide detailed explanations of these other techniques, and suggested references have been provided.

Other modelling techniques

There are different modelling techniques available to help you make sense of your data. The selection of the model will depend on the type of data you have collected and what you are trying to achieve through the development of a model.

Multiple linear regression

Multiple linear regression (MLR) models are an expansion of the simple linear regression technique to include more than one independent variable x. For each x variable in the model there is a separate b coefficient. The equation is

$$y = a + b_1 x_1 + b_2 x_2 + b_3 x_3 \ldots + b_i x_i + e$$

MLR models follow the same principles as SLR models. In MLR models the dependent variable needs to be interval. The independent variables can be interval or they can be categorical if the variables are dummy variables (see the next paragraph for an explanation of dummy variables). Since there can be two or more independent variables, MLR techniques can also include inter-action effects in the model. For example, in a model predicting individuals' income we could have a series of variables; these could include their gender, whether they have degree-level education and whether they are in current employment. The model could include the individual contribution of gender, degree education and employment to income levels, and also the interaction of gender with employment, gender with degree, and degree with employ-ment. Running the model will allow the researcher to assess which, if any, of the interactions make a significant contribution to understanding factors influencing income.

Dummy variables are categorical variables that are transformed into binary variables and are also known as indicator variables. Dummy variables are coded as 1 (an event occurs or a criterion is met) and 0 (an event does not occur or the criterion is not met). Dummy variables provide a useful means of using linear regression models with non-interval data. For categorical variables that already have only two categories, for example, gender with male or female, the variable can easily be transformed into the appropriate format. The code 1 is normally applied to the category of interest which you wish to use as the refer-ence or baseline measure. So for example if I was interested in how women compare to men I could make men my baseline and I would code this category as 0. Where categorical variables have more than two categories, more than one dummy variable needs to be included. The number of dummy variables to be included is the number of categories in the original variable minus 1, repre-sented as $k-1$ in the literature.

Logistic regression

Logistic regression is also a linear regression technique and is used when the dependent variable y is binary, where 0 corresponds to when an event does not occur and 1 to when an event does occur. For example, 0 is not currently in employment and 1 is in employment; or 0 does not own a car and 1 does own a car. Logistic regression models are based on probabilities, odds and logs. In order to use these techniques you will need to have an understanding of these statistical terms. The model allows the researcher to calculate the probability or odds of a specific event occurring based on the independent variables in the model. Multinomial logistical regression techniques are available for dependent variables with more than two categories.

Multi-level modelling

Multi-level modelling techniques should be considered if you have collected data that have hierarchical or multi-level structure. The easiest way to explain what is meant by this term is to give an example. A research project has collected exam performance data from pupils across different schools that are run by two different local authorities. Data have been collected on individual pupils; however, the data themselves can be organized into different levels. Data can be organized by local authority. They can be organized at school level, and within schools they can be organized into classrooms. These modelling techniques allow you to produce models that consider the different levels of the data.

Further reading for modelling techniques

We would suggest reading a combination of two different types of text to develop your knowledge of modelling techniques. For an excellent introduction to their use with detailed examples using social science, see Tarling (2009). Both Field (2009) and Agresti and Finlay (2008) provide detailed statistical guidance on the modelling techniques.

Summary

Inferential statistics enable the social researcher to make generalizable claims about their research findings. Parametric tests are based on the assumptions of the normal distribution curve and are normally applied to interval data and in some cases ordinal data. Non-parametric tests are based on other types of distribution and are to be used for nominal and ordinal data or where samples are small. Both parametric and non-parametric testing require the defining of a null hypothesis and an alternative or research hypothesis. The hypothesis test will involve establishing if there is enough evidence from the sample data to reject the null hypothesis. There are different hypothesis tests, depending on the level of measurement of the data and the nature of the sample data collected. An important aspect of using inferential statistics and hypothesis testing is that it is possible for the researcher to make an error by either falsely accepting or rejecting the null hypothesis.

 ■ **Questions**

1 Why are inferential statistics useful to social researchers?
2 Describe the terms 'null hypothesis' and 'alternative or research hypothesis'.
3 Under what circumstances would you consider applying an independent samples *t*-test?

■ ■ **Further reading** ■

Agresti, Alan and Finlay, B. (2008) *Statistical Measures for the Social Sciences*, 4th edn. London: Pearson.

Argyous, George (2000) *Statistics for Social and Health Research: With a Guide to SPSS.* London: Sage.

Field, Andy (2009) *Discovering Statistics using SPSS for Windows*, 3rd edn. London: Sage.

Howell, David C. (2007) *Fundamental Statistics for the Behavioral Sciences.* London: Wadsworth.

Lindley, Dennis V. and Scott, William F. (1995) *New Cambridge Elementary Statistical Tables*, 2nd edn. Cambridge: Cambridge University Press.

TWENTY SEVEN

DATA MANAGEMENT TECHNIQUES

Aims	

By the end of this chapter you will be able to:

- **Describe the different types of data manipulation used to analyse quantitative data.**
- **Demonstrate recoding interval variables into categorical variables using IBM SPSS Statistics 19.**

- **Demonstrate recoding categorical variables using IBM SPSS Statistics 19.**
- **Demonstrate how to create subsets using IBM SPSS Statistics 19.**
- **Demonstrate how to create and analyse multiple response sets using IBM SPSS Statistics 19.**
- **Weight datasets in IBM SPSS Statistics 19.**

The data analysis covered so far has involved analysing variables as they have been defined and entered into the data file. This chapter concentrates on introducing some data management techniques that will allow the researcher to develop and expand the analysis. These techniques can allow for a more detailed exploration of quantitative data. We will examine the following techniques:

- recoding variables in IBM SPSS Statistics 19

- calculating new variables in IBM SPSS Statistics 19

- case selection and subsets

- multiple response sets

- matching data files

- weighting data.

Recoding data

Recoding variables in IBM SPSS Statistics 19 is a technique that is particularly useful when the original variable is not in a format that the researcher considers appropriate for the analysis. Different types of recoding can be undertaken. For example, a variable 'age' coded in actual years could be recoded into a variable 'age groups', where cases are placed into specific age groups. Again, a variable on the most feared crimes against individuals might list 30 different crimes, and the researcher may wish to reduce the number of categories to make the data more manageable for analysis by grouping 'like' crimes together. This technique can also be used when it has not been possible to successfully run a chi-square test due to more than 20 per cent of cells containing an expected cell count of less than 5. The recoding of the test variable will involve the collapsing of categories together, enabling the chi-square test to be successfully applied, albeit with a reduction of variability in the variable.

There are two ways to recode interval data into discrete groups, for example, ages into age groups. The first is to directly recode the original variable. The second is to recode the data from the original variable into a new variable. The first technique will result in the original data being lost from the open data file. The second procedure ensures that the original variable is left untouched and can be used for future analysis. Consequently, always recode a variable into a new variable.

Using IBM SPSS Statistics 19 to recode variables

The process of recoding a variable is first to note the original level of measurement of the variable to be recoded. See section 'Hierarchical order with levels of measurement' in Chapter 13 for a full discussion. This order means that interval or ratio levels of measurement can be recoded into an ordinal level of measurement, which in turn can be recoded into a nominal level of measurement. Recoding of lower-order levels of measurement to higher orders is not possible. For example, it is not possible to recode a nominal variable into an interval variable. The following is an example of recoding an interval variable into two categorical variables: exam scores in percentages (ratio) can be recoded into grades A–F (ordinal), which in turn can be recoded into a pass/fail (nominal).

Second, for nominal or ordinal variables, refer to the original code book and frequency of counts for each category. In all cases of recoding, reference to the original coding frame is essential. One must be aware of the level of measurement, the coding, the range of codes and the coding used for missing values. It is also strongly advisable to produce a frequency table and/or descriptive statistics of the original variable before proceeding with recoding.

Third, the researcher must have a clear understanding of exactly how the variable data are going to be recoded. The following sections will detail the procedures for recoding interval data into categorical data and recoding categorical data.

Recoding interval data into categorical data

Recoding an interval variable into a categorical variable, ordinal or nominal, is one of the most common data manipulation techniques. It is particularly useful where the researcher wishes to explore relationships between two variables when the dependent variable is ordinal or nominal and the independent variable in its original data type is interval. For example, the researcher wishes to explore attitudinal responses to using public transport by the age of respondents. The attitudinal variable is ordinal, coded on a scale of 1 = low usage to 5 = high usage of public transport. The age variable is coded in years, and the researcher wishes to recode the ages into age bands or ranges in order to explore possible differences in attitudes to using public transport by different age groups.

The exact categories used in the recoded variable will be determined principally by two factors. First, the categories identified will be those that are of interest to the researcher in exploring the research question. These are likely to be determined by any categories used and findings that have emerged from previous research. The second factor is how the values in the original variable are distributed. Categories will need to take into account minimum and maximum values, and how the values are distributed, i.e. the shape of the distribution. Where the distribution is positive, with a greater number of values falling at the lower end of the distribution than at the upper end, categories may be selected that reflect the distribution. Determining the exact number of categories to include will depend on the distribution. Recommendations on the maximum number of categories vary; some researchers cite no more than nine categories. What is important is that you check that each category has a sufficient number of observations, or counts of cases, to enable you to draw meaningful conclusions. Remember also that some statistical tests have a minimum number of expected counts: see the chi-square test for independence in Chapter 26. The norm is that with the exception of the lowest and highest categories, the remaining categories will be divided into equal widths. For example, in a survey of sold house prices in the last 12 months the minimum house price is £91,000; the maximum house price is £310,000; and the remaining house prices are distributed fairly evenly between these two values. We could create the following categories where, with the exception of the lowest and highest categories, the widths are £50,000: less than £100,000; £100,000–£149,999; £150,000–£199,999; £200,000–£249,999; £300,000 plus. You will notice that each of these categories is discrete, with no overlap. The figures for house prices are normally rounded to the nearest whole pound (£). If one is recoding prices that involve pounds (£) and pence (p) then the category definitions would need to reflect this. For example, the second category would need to be defined as £100,000.00–£149,999.99.

When you undertake any recoding exercise it is vital that you double check that the recoding is correct and has not inadvertently missed out some values. One of the easiest techniques to check the recode is to run a cross-tabulation or contingency table of the original variable by the recoded variable. An example of the cross-tabulation of the house prices variable by the recoded categories is shown in Table 27.1. If the recode has been undertaken correctly then the counts for each of the original values should fall into the appropriate new category, as shown.

Using IBM SPSS Statistics 19 to recode interval variables

The following worked example will involve recoding the interval variable Age (coded in actual years) into a new variable Age2 (ages grouped in age ranges). From earlier analysis of the Age variable, the researcher knows that the minimum age is 16 years and the maximum age is 94 years. There are no missing values. They have decided that the Age2 variable will contain the respondents' ages grouped into the following six categories: 16–19, 20–29, 30–39, 40–49, 50–59, 60 plus. Each of the new categories will need to be given a code from 1 to 6, where 1 = 16–19 years and 6 = 60 plus years.

From the **Transform** menu, select **Recode into Different Variables**. The **Recode into Different Variables** dialogue box will appear (see Figure 27.1).

From the left hand side, highlight the variable that is to be recoded: in this example it is the variable Age – and click once on the arrow button ⮞ to move the variable across to under **Input Variable > Output Variable**. The next stage is to define the new variable or 'output' variable. In the section **Output Variable,** click in the box under **Name** and type in the variable name Age2. To assign a variable label to this new variable, click in the box under **Label** and

TABLE 27.1 Checking interval data recoded into categories using cross-tabulations

		House prices in categories					
		Less than £100,000	£100,000–£149,999	£150,000–£199,999	£200,000–£249,999	£250,000–£299,999	£300,000 or more
Actual house price (£)	91,000	2	0	0	0	0	0
	120,000	0	2	0	0	0	0
	122,000	0	2	0	0	0	0
	125,000	0	2	0	0	0	0
	137,000	0	2	0	0	0	0
	140,000	0	2	0	0	0	0
	145,000	0	2	0	0	0	0
	149,999	0	2	0	0	0	0
	160,000	0	0	2	0	0	0
	165,000	0	0	2	0	0	0
	175,000	0	0	4	0	0	0
	180,000	0	0	4	0	0	0
	190,000	0	0	2	0	0	0
	200,000	0	0	0	2	0	0
	205,000	0	0	0	2	0	0
	210,000	0	0	0	2	0	0
	220,000	0	0	0	2	0	0
	235,000	0	0	0	2	0	0
	240,000	0	0	0	2	0	0
	250,000	0	0	0	0	2	0
	270,000	0	0	0	0	2	0
	285,000	0	0	0	0	2	0
	290,000	0	0	0	0	2	0
	295,000	0	0	0	0	2	0
	305,000	0	0	0	0	0	2
	310,000	0	0	0	0	0	4
Total counts		2	14	14	12	10	6

enter the variable label 'Age of respondent recoded'. Now click once on the **Change** button to paste this information into the **Input Variable > Output Variable** section.

The next stage is to define the categories for the Age2 variable. Click once on the **Old and New Values** button. A **Recode into Different Variables: Old and New Values** dialogue box will be displayed (see Figure 27.2). The box is divided into

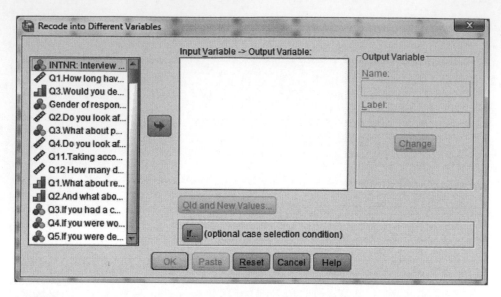

FIGURE 27.1 IBM SPSS Statistics 19 **Recode into Different Variables** dialogue box

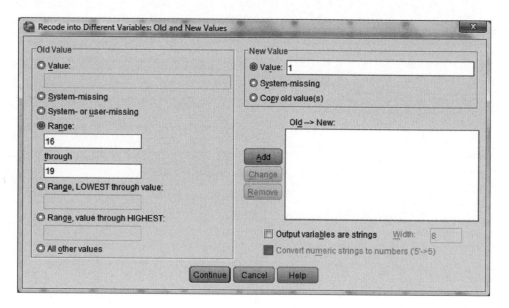

FIGURE 27.2 IBM SPSS Statistics 19 **Recode into Different Variables: Old and New Values**

two halves. The left hand side is where the **Old Value**(s) are specified and the right hand side is where the **New Value**(s) are entered.

To recode the data for the first age category, 16–19 years, first under **Old Value** click on the first **Range** option. Enter the value 16 in the box underneath, and the value 19 in the box under **through**. Under **New Value**, in the box next to **Value** enter the new code 1. Click once on the **Add** button. In the box under **Old > New**, '16 thru 19 > 1' should appear. This process has defined the first age category of 16–19 years. The process now needs to be repeated for the next four age categories of 20–29 (code as 2), 30–39 (code as 3), 40–49 (code as 4), 50–59 (code as 5). For the final age category 60 plus, under **Old Value** select **Range, value through HIGHEST**. Enter 60 in the left box. There is no need to specify the highest value, 94, as this option will automatically select the highest value. Under **New Value**, in the box next to **Value** enter the new code 6. Click once on the **Add** button.

Recoding missing values   This variable has no missing values; see the next section for details on how to manage missing values when recoding variables.

When all the observed and missing values have been recoded, click once on the **Continue** button to return to the **Recode into Different Variables** dialogue box. Click on **OK** to execute the recode command.

The new variable Age2 will be calculated and displayed in the **Data Editor** window. It can be located in the far right column of the **Data View** window and at the bottom of the variable list in the **Variable View** window. In the **Variable View** window, value labels should be assigned to each of the new age categories.

The final stage of the recoding process is to produce a frequency table for the new variable Age2. This will enable the researcher to check that the recoding is correct by checking that the count and percentage for each of the age categories is as expected. The percentages for each age category should correspond to the cumulative percentage of the upper value in each age range taken from a frequency table of the original variable Age.

Finally, remember to save the data file, as a new variable has been created. In the **Data Editor** window, select the **File** menu and **Save**.

Recoding categorical variables

The same recoding technique can be used to recode a categorical variable. There may be occasions when an existing categorical variable needs to be recoded for the purposes of the analysis you wish to undertake. You may wish to combine certain categories in a categorical variable, for example, combining categories with very small counts into one 'other' category. Alternatively, you may wish to recode a category to 'missing' to remove it from the analysis. These techniques may also be appropriate when undertaking measures of statistical association, such as chi-square, when cells with small expected counts are problematic. The technique is essentially the same as in the earlier example of recoding interval variables. Before undertaking the recoding you must be absolutely sure of the code that is used for each category and which codes you wish to combine or remove. As before, you are strongly advised always to recode to a new variable in order to preserve the original data.

Using IBM SPSS Statistics 19 to recode categorical variables

In the following example the categorical variable Victim contains a four-point ordinal scale of responses to the 'How worried are you about being a victim of crime?' question. A copy of the frequency table for this variable is shown in Table 27.2.

From the frequency table and code book we know that the coding is 1 = very worried, 2 = worried, 3 = not very worried, 4 = not at all worried, and –99 = missing, refused to answer. In this exercise the categories 'very worried' and 'worried' are going to be combined (1 and 2), the categories 'not very worried' and 'not at all worried' are going to be combined (3 and 4), and finally the 'refused to answer' (–99) category will continue to be coded as missing. The new categories will then be 1 = worried, 2 = not worried and –99 = missing.

From the **Transform** menu, select **Recode into Different Variables**. The **Recode into Different Variables** dialogue box will appear (see Figure 27.1). If previous recoding has been undertaken in the current IBM SPSS Statistics 19 session, click once on the **Reset** button to clear the settings.

From the left hand side, highlight the variable that is to be recoded, for example, the variable Victim, and click once on the arrow button 🔘 to move the variable across to under **Input Variable > Output Variable**. The next stage is to define the new variable or output variable. In the section **Output Variable** click in the box under **Name** and type in the variable name Victim2. To assign a variable label to this new variable, click in the box under **Label** and enter the variable label 'Victim recoded'. Now click once on the **Change** button to paste this information into the **Input Variable > Output Variable** section.

The next stage is to define the categories for the Victim2 variable. Click once on the **Old and New Values** button. A **Recode into Different Variables: Old and New Values** dialogue box will be displayed (see Figure 27.2). The box is divided into two halves. The left side is where the **Old Value**(s) are specified and the right side is where the **New Value**(s) are entered.

To recode 1 (very worried) and 2 (worried) into the first new category 1 (worried), first under **Old Value** click on the first **Range** option. Enter the value 1 in the box underneath, and the value 2 in the box under **through**. Under **New**

TABLE 27.2   Frequency table of the variable Victim: 'How worried are you about being a victim of crime?'

Frequency			%	Valid %	Cumulative %
Valid	Very worried	100	32.8	34.5	34.5
	Worried	120	39.3	41.4	75.9
	Not very worried	60	19.7	20.7	96.6
	Not at all worried	10	3.3	3.4	100.0
	Total	290	95.1	100.0	
Missing	Refused to answer	15	4.9		
Total		305	100.0		

TABLE 27.3   Frequency table of the recoded variable Victim2

Frequency			%	Valid %	Cumulative %
Valid	Worried	220	72.1	75.9	75.9
	Not worried	70	23.0	24.1	100.0
	Total	290	95.1	100.0	
Missing	System	15	4.9		
Total		305	100.0		

Value, in the box next to **Value** enter the new code 1. Click once on the **Add** button. In the box under **Old > New**, '1 thru 2 > 1' should appear.

Repeat this process for the second category, recoding 3 and 4 into a new category of 2 (not worried), entering the range 3 through 4 and the new value 2.

Recoding missing values   The final category from the original variable to recode is the 'missing, refused to answer' category, coded as –99. There are two ways of dealing with this value. The first is to simply copy the existing value, –99, and in the new variable Victim 2 set the missing value to –99. The second is to define –99 as a missing value in the **Old and New Values** dialogue box (Figure 27.2).

To copy the existing value under **Old Value**, in the box next to **Value**, enter –99. Under **New Value**, select **Copy old Value(s)**. Click once on the **Add** button. When the new variable is created, remember to set a missing value of –99 and a value label of –99 = refused to answer.

To define –99 as 'missing', under **Old Value**, in the box next to **Value** enter –99. Under **New Value** select **System-missing**. Click once on the **Add** button. The –99 is recoded as a system 'missing' value and will appear as a blank entry in the data file. No value label is required.

The new variable Victim2 will be calculated and displayed in the **Data Editor** window. It can be located in the far right column of the **Data View** window and at the bottom of the variable list in the **Variable View** window. In the **Variable View** window, value labels should be assigned to each of the new age categories.

The final stage of the recoding process is to produce a frequency table for the new variable Victim2. This will enable the researcher to check that the recoding is correct by checking that the count and percentage for each of the age categories is as expected. The frequency table for Victim2 is shown in Table 27.3.

Finally, remember to save the data file, as a new variable has been created. In the **Data Editor** window select the **File** menu and **Save**.

Calculating new variables

There are occasions when it may be advantageous for the researcher to calculate a new variable based on one or more existing variables. First, the data the researcher would like to analyse may not exist and they may need to calculate a new variable based on variables that do exist. Second, two or more variables may be added together to form an index, for example, taking multiple indicators and combining them into one measurement. Third, an existing variable may be manipulated to give it a greater weight in the analysis: for example, when creating an index based on multiple indicators, the researcher considers one of the variables to have double the weighting of other variables and it should therefore be multiplied by a factor of two. The rationale for computing a new variable must be clearly stated in the research report and, where appropriate, references to existing theories and literature should be given to justify the data manipulation. These techniques are particularly useful when undertaking secondary analysis where the researcher is unlikely to find the variable data in the exact format required.

Using IBM SPSS Statistics 19 to compute a new variable

In this example the researcher is interested in creating an index of environmental awareness. The data collected do not contain a variable on environmental awareness. However, there are four variables based on questions that asked the respondent to rate on a scale of 5 (very important) to 1 (not very important) the importance of the following: use of renewable energy sources; reduction in fossil fuel emissions; reduction in car journeys; and the availability of domestic recycling schemes. The responses were coded into four variables, env1, env2, env3 and env4 respectively. The researcher has decided to add the four variables together to create an overall index of the importance of environment issues. The first stage was for the researcher to check that the numerical coding was in the same direction for each of the variables. With 'very important' coded as 5 and 'not very important' coded as 1, for all variables this means that higher values in the final index will correspond with a higher overall importance value. If the coding did not run in the same direction, a recoding procedure on the individual variable(s) would have to be undertaken before the index was computed.

To calculate the environmental importance index a new variable called 'index' is going to be created using the **Compute** command.

The compute command can only be accessed when viewing the **Data** window. Select the **Window** menu and **1-'filename' IBM SPSS Statistics 19 Data Editor**. Select the **Transform** menu and **Compute**. The **Compute Variable** dialogue box will be displayed (see Figure 27.3).

Under **Target Variable**, enter the new variable name, 'Index'. Click on **Type & Label**. Next to **Label** enter the variable label 'Environmental Index'. Leave the **Type** set as **Numeric**. Click on **Continue** to return to the **Compute Variable** dialogue box.

The variables to be combined into the 'index' variable are to be placed in the section under **Numeric Expression**. For 'index' the numeric expression will be

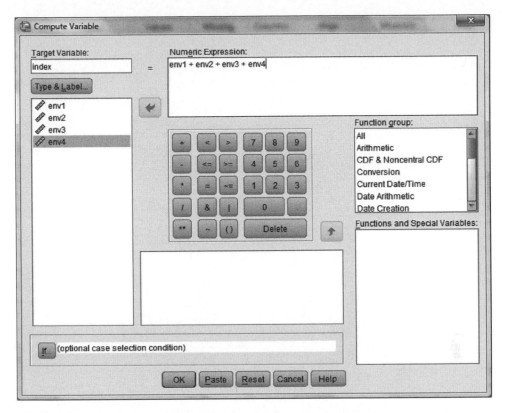

FIGURE 27.3 IBM SPSS Statistics 19 **Compute Variable** dialogue box

env1 + env2 + env3 + env4. To build this expression, first highlight the variable env1 and then click on the arrow button ⊞ to move the variable across to the section under **Numeric Expression**. Enter a + by either clicking on the + button from the middle section or typing in +. Now highlight the second variable env2, again click on the arrow button ⊞ to move the variable across, and again enter a +. Repeat this process until all the variables are entered. Click on **OK** to execute the command. A new variable 'index' will appear in the **Data Editor** window. Save the data file by selecting the **File** menu and **Save**.

Selecting cases and creating subsets of data

There may be occasions when undertaking data analysis that only a particular sample group of the data needs to be examined, for example, men only. More complex filtering parameters can be entered based on two or more variables. Cases that do not meet the filter conditions can be either temporarily removed or permanently removed. If the permanent option is selected, care must be taken not to overwrite the original data through saving the data file.

Using IBM SPSS Statistics 19 to create subsets

From the **Data** menu, choose **Select Cases**. Under the **Select** section, highlight the option **If condition is satisfied**. Click on the **If** button. The **Select Cases: If** dialogue box will be displayed (see Figure 27.4). Highlight the variable to build the selection criteria and click the arrow button 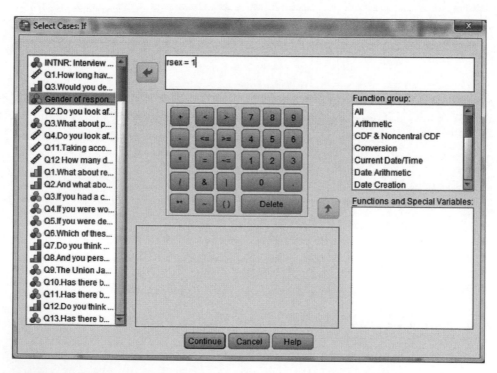 to move the variable into the right box. Next build the expression. The example in Figure 27.4 shows the expression 'rsex = 1'. This will select all cases where rsex = 1 and the code 1 represents females. This expression would create a subset of females only.

The Boolean operators AND and OR can be used to combine two or more variables. The following is an example of the expression that would select a subset of men aged 31–40 using the two variables 'sex', coded 1 = male, 2 = female, and 'age', coded 1 = 16–20 years, 2 = 21–30 years, 3 = 31–40 years, 4 = 41 years plus:

sex = 1 AND age = 3

An expression to select a subset of 16–20 year olds or 31–40 year olds only would be:

Age = 1 OR age = 3.

As well as equals to =, the mathematical operators = > equal to or greater than, = < less than or equal to, > greater than, < less than, and ~ = not equal to, are available.

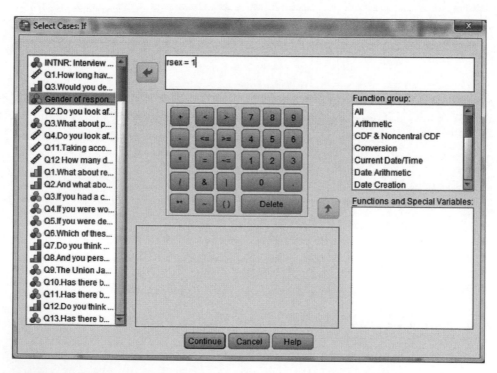

FIGURE 27.4   IBM SPSS Statistics 19 **Select Cases: If** dialogue box

Once the expression is complete, click on **Continue** to return to the previous **Select Cases** dialogue box. In this dialogue box, under the section **Unselected Cases Are**, select **Filtered** to temporarily remove unselected cases, or **Deleted** to permanently remove the unselected cases. Click on **OK** to execute the command. Where cases are filtered, the cases filtered out can be viewed in the **Data Editor** window as the corresponding row number has a diagonal line through it. To return to analysing all cases, remove the filter by selecting the **Data** menu and **Select Cases**. Under **Select**, highlight **All cases**. Click on **OK** to execute the command to return to analysing all cases.

Creating multiple response sets in IBM SPSS Statistics 19

Survey questions that result in multiple responses require multiple variables to be created in IBM SPSS Statistics 19. See sections 'Coding for multiple response questions' in Chapter 16, for more detail on these variables. Variables can then be placed together in a multiple response set for analysis purposes. The sets can then be analysed using multiple response frequency tables and cross-tabulations. This section will detail how to create multiple response sets and produce frequency tables and cross-tabulations of these sets.

The first stage of the multiple response procedure is to define the variables in a set. First, identify the variables to be merged into the set, using the coding frame for reference. From the **Analyze** menu, select **Multiple Response** and **Define Variable Sets**. A **Define Multiple Response Sets** dialogue box will appear. Under **Set Definition** there is a list of all variables in the current dataset. One at a time, highlight the variables to be included in the set and click on the arrow button 🔽 to move them to the section under **Variables in Set**. Repeat this process until all the required variables are moved to this section. Under **Variables are Coded As** the coding used for these variables needs to be defined. If a coding scheme of Yes/No has been used for each variable in the set, select **Dichotomies** and in the box next to **Counted Value** enter the code used for Yes, for example, 1. Alternatively, if a coding scheme of 1 to a maximum code of n has been used for each variable in the set, select **Categories**. In the box next to **Range** enter the lowest coded, for example, 1, and in the box next to **through** enter the maximum coded, for example, 6. The next stage is to create a set name. Next to **Name** enter a multiple response set name. It can be up to seven characters in length as it will be automatically prefixed with a $ symbol. Next to **Label** enter a multiple response set label. Click on **Add** to create the set – it will appear in the right box – and finally to remove the dialogue box click on **Close**.

Producing frequency tables and cross-tabulations of multiple response sets

Frequency tables and cross-tabulations of multiple response sets cannot be created using the commands outlined in Chapters 24 and 25. Instead, the following procedure should be used.

To create a frequency table, from the **Analyze** menu select **Multiple Response** and **Frequencies**. In the **Multiple Response Frequencies** box under **Multiple Response Sets**, highlight the required set and click on the arrow button ➔ to move it to the section under **Table(s) for**. To exclude missing values from the table, under **Missing Values** select either **Exclude cases listwise within dichotomies** or **Exclude cases listwise within categories**. The selection will depend on the coding used. Click on **OK** to execute the command. A frequency table for the multiple response set will appear in the **Output Viewer**.

To create a cross-tabulation, from the **Analyze** menu select **Multiple Response** and **Crosstabs**. In the **Multiple Response Crosstabs** box, both variables and multiple response sets are displayed on the left hand side. When exploring a relationship using multiple response sets, the set will be the dependent and the variable the independent. The conventions for placing the independent in the column and the dependent in the row can still be applied to these cross-tabulations. Highlight the required multiple response set and click on the first arrow button ➔ to move to the section under **Row(s)**. Highlight the required independent variable and click on the second arrow button ➔ to move to the section under **Column(s)**. The coding range for the variable will need to be defined. Highlight the variable under **Column(s)** and click on **Define Ranges**. In the dialogue box, enter the minimum and maximum code values. Click on **Continue**. To define the content of the cells in the table, click on **Options**. Under **Cell Percentages** select the row, column or total required. Under **Percentages Based On** select whether the percentages are to be based on the number of **Cases** or **Responses**. It is likely that you will require **Cases**. Click on **Continue** and click on **OK** to execute the command. A cross-tabulation will appear in the **Viewer** window.

Weighting data

A small-scale research project undertaken by an undergraduate social researcher would not normally be expected to consider issues of weighting of the collected data to account for under- or over-representation. However it is worthy of a mention here because the NILT dataset that is used in the IBM SPSS Statistics 19 task boxes is a weighted dataset. The purpose of this section is not to provide a detailed breakdown for the weighting technique used for NILT. Instead this is a brief introduction to the technique.

Weighting is a technique that is applied to data in order to adjust the dataset to take into account biases due to sampling error. While sampling technique can help minimize sampling bias, issues of non-response can impact on the final characteristic of the sample in the data file. For example, social researchers may find that they have a data file that has either over- or under-representation by age, gender, ethnicity or socioeconomic status. Sample bias can have an impact on data findings, particularly when analysis is looking to estimate the population characteristics through the calculation of confidence intervals. A thorough analysis of the data will enable the researcher to assess if there is bias in the sample and if it is a particular problem for the analysis to be undertaken.

If sampling bias is considered problematic and if there is sufficient reliable data available on the population characteristics (for example from Census data or other population-based surveys), then it is possible to perform a calculated correction to the data based on one or more of the key variables. This is the technique known as weighting.

An overview of the weighting process is now explained using a hypothetical example. This example is based on correcting for sample bias using one key variable, gender. The weighting calculation is based on a simple calculation. More complex weighting calculations can be used, and anyone wishing to explore this area in more detail is referred to the recommended reading at the end of this chapter.

A researcher has conducted a postal survey of 1000 residents in the City of Plymouth. Despite using a stratified sampling technique and offering incentives for those returning the survey, preliminary analysis of the survey results has revealed that there is a discrepancy in the distribution of men and women in the survey sample compared to the known city population at the last Census. As shown in Table 27.4, there is an over-representation of men and an under-representation of women.

TABLE 27.4 Sample and population characteristics: City of Plymouth, resident survey

Gender	Plymouth sample %	Plymouth population % (Census 2001)
Male	54.75	48.84
Female	45.25	51.16

Weighting data using IBM SPSS Statistics 19

Weighting involves calculating a constant value for each category, in this case men and women, which is applied to the data file to correct for the discrepancy between the sample proportion and the known population proportion. As part of this process a new weight variable is created in the IBM SPSS Statistics 19 data file and then applied using the IBM SPSS Statistics 19 **Weight Cases** command.

The weight value for each category is the population percentage divided by the sample percentage. From Table 27.4, the weight value for men is 48.84/54.75 = 0.892; and the weight value for women is 51.16 / 45.25 = 1.131.

The next stage of the process is to create a new weight variable in IBM SPSS Statistics 19 and allocate the value 0.892 to cases that are male and the value 1.131 to cases that are female. While it is possible to manually go through the data file, a much easier method is to use the IBM SPSS Statistics 19 syntax (command) language. To open a **Syntax** window, from the **File** menu select **Open** and **Syntax**. Type in the following syntax command, with full stops at the end of each line. In this example WT refers to the new variable. For the variable Sex, 1 is the code for Male and 2 is the code for Female.

Compute WT = 0.
If (Sex = 1) WT = 0.892.
If (Sex = 2) WT = 1.131.

To execute these comments, highlight the text. From the **Run** menu, select **Selection**. The command will be executed and a new variable called WT will be calculated and displayed in the data file.

The final process is to apply the new WT variable to the IBM SPSS Statistics 19 weighting command. From the **Data** menu, select **Weight Cases**. In the dialogue box, select **Weight Cases by** and place the WT variable in the box next to **Frequency Variable**. Click on **OK**.

Summary

Manipulating quantitative data enables the researcher to explore the data to greater depths. The recoding of variables allows for improved data handling and can enable the researcher to apply hypothesis testing to variables that in their original format were not appropriate. Recoding is particularly valuable when a nominal variable has a number of categories which contain a small number of counts, allowing for these categories to be combined into one larger category. In large datasets the technique that allows the researcher to select certain cases to create a subset is particularly useful when wanting to make comparisons between different groups based on more than one variable. IBM SPSS Statistics 19 allows the researcher to combine variables from a survey question that has multiple responses into one set. The resulting multiple response set can then be analysed as a frequency table or contingency table. Finally, the chapter examined weighting as a technique for correcting for sample bias in the dataset.

 ■ **Questions** ▬▬▬▬▬▬▬▬▬▬▬▬

1 How can recoding a categorical variable to a new variable with a smaller number of categories aid hypothesis testing?
2 When is it appropriate to create multiple response sets in IBM SPSS Statistics 19?
3 Under what circumstances would you consider using the Weight Cases function in IBM SPSS Statistics 19?

Babbie, Earl and Halley, Fred (2007) *Adventures in Social Research: Data Analysis Using SPSS for Windows*. Thousand Oaks, CA: Pine Forge.

Fielding, Jane and Gilbert, Nigel (2006) *Understanding Social Statistics*, 2nd edn. London: Sage.

For a more detailed account of assessing sample bias and different techniques used to weight data in SPSS see:

De Vaus, D. (2002a) *Analyzing Social Science Data*. London: Sage. Read Chapter 21 'How to Judge the Extent and Effect of Sample Bias' and Chapter 22 'How to Weight Samples to Adjust for Bias'.

PART FOUR

PRESENTING RESEARCH

TWENTY EIGHT

PRESENTING RESEARCH FINDINGS

Chapter Contents

| Aims |

By the end of this chapter you will be able to:

- **Produce an appropriately structured research report.**
- **Demonstrate how to present qualitative research findings.**
- **Demonstrate how to present quantitative data in appropriate tables and figures.**
- **Provide a written interpretation of your research findings**
- **Prepare and undertake a verbal presentation of your research findings.**
- **Understand how to structure your presentation.**
- **Understand the different visual techniques which you can use to enhance a presentation.**

The written report

This chapter will consider the various issues related to presenting your research in a written report and as a verbal presentation to an audience. There are many points to consider and it is important that you allocate enough time to both preparing and writing a report. You must also give careful consideration to the overall structure, content, presentation and written interpretation of your research findings.

Different types of written report

The structure of the written report can take a number of different forms depending upon the audience that you are writing for. The report should include details of all elements in the research process with a greater emphasis placed on some elements depending on the intended audience. A report written as part of an academic course of study is likely to have predefined sections and subsections. A report resulting from a piece of commissioned research, for example, for a local government agency or a private company, is unlikely to have a predefined structure; the researcher will have to make decisions about the inclusion of different elements based upon the organization's requirements.

An additional consideration is the terminology and tone of the writing required for different audiences. An academic report should include a detailed discussion of the methodological approach taken and include a reflective evaluation of the research undertaken. A report for a local government agency is unlikely to require such a detailed inclusion of the methodological approach; the focus will be more on the research method, the data collection tools, and the research findings and their interpretation with, where applicable, policy recommendations. A report for such an agency may also benefit from the inclusion of an executive summary at the front of the report summarizing the key findings and policy recommendations.

General structure of report

- *Title page*. The title should accurately reflect the research project. Include a subtitle if it helps to clarify the project. The name of the author(s), the organization and a date should also be included.

- *Acknowledgements*. The acknowledgements should contain thanks to those individuals and organizations that have enabled the research to take place. They should also contain a generic thank you to all the participants in the data collection phase of the research.

- *Contents page*. The contents page should contain a list of the main sections and subsections included in the report. The relevant page number for the start of each section and subsection should also be included.

- *List of tables and figures*. A list of all tables and figures should be included in a separate index. The tables and figures should each be numbered sequentially. The relevant page number for each table and figure should be included.

- *Executive summary*. This is an optional section in a report and is often used where the report is going to be read by an audience that will be appreciative of a summary of the main points of the research findings without having to digest the entire report. Executive summaries can vary in length from say two pages to six pages. The executive summary should contain a brief summary of the research approach and the main research findings. If the remit of the report includes making some recommendations for future research, these can also be summarized in this section.

- *Abstract*. The abstract is a short summary that provides a brief introduction to the research problem, the methodological approach and methods adopted, and the main conclusions. It should be no longer than 150–250 words.

- *Introduction*. The purpose of this section is to briefly introduce the research problem, the aims and objectives of the study, the hypotheses to be explored and so on.

- *Literature review*. This section should contain a review of the literature researched in relation to the research problem, together with a summary of previous research in the area.

- *Methodology and methods*. This should cover all the technical aspects of the research process, including methodological approach, research design, concepts and how they were operationalized, measurement tools developed or used, sampling, methods, data collection, and data and statistical analysis undertaken. Issues arising during the research process should also be detailed in this section: for example, where organizational constraints or gatekeepers restrict the research process. Any political or ethical considerations can also be highlighted in this section.

- *Research findings*. The research findings section will detail the data collected. The structure of this section will be dependent on the research aims, objectives and hypotheses, and on the quantitative or qualitative nature of the data. See sections 'Presenting qualitative data findings' and 'Presenting quantitative data results' later in this chapter.

- *Discussion*. The discussion section should bring together the main research findings and the key elements of the literature review. The discussion should focus on answering the original research problem, comparing the research findings with previous research in the area, and offering new insights or explanations. Reflections on the limitations of the research can also be discussed at this stage, together with recommendations for future research in the area. New literature or data should *not* be introduced in the discussion section.

- *Conclusions*. The conclusion should summarize the main findings of the research, the debates undertaken in the discussion section, and the recommendations for future research. Where the research is focused on policy issues, policy recommendations can be included here.

- *References*. A references section should contain details of the materials that you have specifically referred to in the form of quotes in the report.

- *Bibliography*. A bibliography should contain details of all materials that you have used during the course of the research project.

- *Appendices*. Appendices can contain a variety of information related to the research project, but not central to the main report: for example, a copy of the survey questions, interview schedule, covering letters, interviewer prompt cards and so on. Results (charts, tables, quotes) that are omitted from the main results section may also be included.

Report layout and format

The following provides some general points for consideration when typing up a report. When presenting a report, the most important element is *consistency* in the layout and format. You should refer to local guidelines for specific criteria when preparing your report.

- *Report sections and subsections*. These should be numbered and the text enhanced to bold and/or italic. The most widely used format is 1, 1.1, 1.2, 1.3, 2, 2.1, 2.2, 2.3 and so on. The numbering sequence can go to a third level, for example, 1.1.1, 1.1.2, 1.1.3; however, this increases the complexity.

- *Tables.* Tables contain data presented in rows and columns. Throughout the report the tables must be labelled and numbered sequentially, starting at 1: for example, Table 1, Table 2, Table 3. After the table and number, the table title should be included, for example, 'Table 1: Sex of respondent', 'Table 2: Daily newspaper read by sex of respondent'.

- *Charts.* Charts are used to present data graphically. As for tables, charts should be labelled and numbered sequentially, starting at 1. The numbering of tables and charts is separate. The normal convention is to use a Figure 1, Figure 2, Figure 3 format. After the Figure and number, the chart title should be included, for example, 'Figure 1: Marital status of respondent'.

- *Font, font size and line spacing.* Fonts are divided into two types, serif and san serif. An example of each is Times New Roman and Arial respectively. A feature of san serif fonts is that they are easier for some individuals to read and they provide a clear image when included in a slide presentation. The normal font size for text in a report is 12 point, and the line spacing should be one and a half or double.

- *Report length.* The length of a report will obviously vary according to the size of the research project and any local guidelines on word length, particularly for coursework-related dissertations.

Referencing sources in the bibliography

All sources – books, chapters in books, journal articles, newspaper articles and internet sources – must be referenced. A number of systems are used for referencing; the two most common are the Harvard system and the numeric system, also known as the footnote/endnote system. The footnote system involves placing references immediately at the bottom of each page. The endnote system involves references being placed at the end of the section or book. Both the footnote and the endnote system involve placing a superscript number next to the referenced text. This number then appears at the foot of the page, or at the section end or book end with the corresponding reference next to it. The number system normally starts at 1.

You are advised to check with the institution, organization or publisher to whom your research report is going to be submitted for the exact format they require. If no guidance is provided, you may use the following formatting suggestions based upon the Harvard system.

- *Book sources.* These must contain the following information: the author(s)' surname(s), initials, year of publication, title, place of publication and publisher. For example:

  May, T. (2001) *Social Research: Issues, Methods and Process*, 3rd edn. Buckingham: Open University Press.

- *Chapters in books.* For a chapter in an edited collection, the format is slightly different: chapter authors, year, chapter title, book author, book title, place of publication, publisher, page range. For example:

Stroh, Matt (2000) 'Qualitative interviewing', in D. Burton (ed.), *Research Training for Social Scientists*. London: Sage. pp. 196–214.

- *Journal articles.* Information to be presented in this order: author(s)' surname(s), initial(s), year of publication, article title, journal title, volume number, part number and page range. For example:

Bendelow, G. (1993) 'Pain perceptions, emotions and gender', *Sociology of Health and Illness*, 15 (3): 273–94.

- *Newspaper articles.* These follow a similar format to journal articles. Where the author's name is not included in the original article, the newspaper title should be given instead. So the information is: author's surname and initials (or newspaper title), year, article headline, newspaper title (if not used in place of author), day and month of publication, page number(s). For example:

Guardian, The (2002) 'Pickets "will not stop" army', 15 November: 2.

- *Internet sources.* These are slightly more complex to report, given the different levels of information available about the site and author. One possible format for referencing internet sources is to cite the author's surname, initial, (if available) year, date of page being written (if available), title of article or web page, website name, website address and date accessed. Website addresses are usually presented with no underline. Where the web address is particularly long, consider citing the website home page as this future proofs against lost pages due to website reorganization. For example:

Travis, A. (2002) '10-year-old offenders to be sent to foster homes', Guardian Unlimited, website at http://www.guardian.co.uk/uk_news/story/0,3604, 840592,00. html, accessed 15 November 2002.

Drafting and revisions

Writing a report can seem a daunting prospect, and often the new researcher feels overwhelmed by the scale of the task. It is advisable to start writing as soon as possible during the research process. Ideas and lines of argument may alter and can be subsequently amended. We recommend that you start by producing a rough draft of how you envisage the structure of the report. The guidance on standard sections provided in the earlier part of this chapter will help you in getting started. One way to begin is to sketch out the anticipated sections and subsections. Within each, write a few short paragraphs together with bullet points, if appropriate, that summarize the main content of those sections. It may be that you are only able to provide the most general of content guidance as you have yet to complete that section of the research process. For example, perhaps you are waiting for a particular journal article that you think may make an important contribution to the discussion in your literature review; or perhaps you are unable to provide a detailed structure for your data analysis sections as the data are still being analysed. Sketching out the various sections in this manner will enable you to see the whole structure of the report and will serve to remind you that the final report needs to be presented to the reader as a coherent whole and not as several disjointed sections.

From these initial thoughts on structure you can now move on to write a first draft of the report. The order that the report is written depends on the nature of the report and on what stage you are at in the research process. It is very rare that a researcher has the luxury of completing the research entirely before writing the report. In order to give yourself as much time as possible to review and revise the contents, start writing as early as possible. A logical approach to writing a report is to start by detailing the research aims and objectives, followed by a review of the relevant literature. The next sections would detail the methodology and methods employed in the research. Next to follow would be the presentation of the data, together with appropriate analysis and discussion of the findings. The discussion of the findings will seek to relate the research findings with the current literature, offering new thoughts and contributions to existing theories or development of new theories as appropriate. The abstract and conclusion, together with an executive summary if appropriate, will be the last of the main sections to be written.

Once you have produced a full draft report you should read through the complete report from beginning to end. Ideally you should find someone to comment on this draft. A third party should be more able to identify sections that are confusing to the reader, that require more explanation, or indeed that deviate from the main research aims. Sections can be revised and edited, or perhaps even deleted completely. Even if you have a third party to read through the report, you should check it carefully yourself. The most common areas that you should check for include spelling and grammar. Do not rely solely on the use of checkers supplied within word-processing packages. Make sure that the text is clear and easy for the intended audience to read through. If you are not sure of the point that you are trying to convey, then it can be virtually guaranteed that your intended audience will also be mystified. While you may think what you have written makes sense, someone unfamiliar with your research area may not understand it. On this point a balance does need to be struck between making the report accessible, but at the same time not removing the theoretical and higher-level discussion. Knowing your audience will guide you in this matter. If you find that sections are confusing or just simply do not make sense, try reordering the work or adding a suitable example. Pulling the section content apart to change the structure can often clarify matters, helping to determine the purpose of the section and the particular lines of thought or argument within it. You should not be afraid to edit your work drastically if required.

Finally, a word of warning should be offered. It is possible to spend too much time editing your report and undertaking changes that do not make a positive contribution to the final finished product. In such circumstances it is best to set a final deadline (assuming an external organization or a course work leader has not already set one) at which point all edits have to be completed and the final report presented.

Presenting qualitative data findings

Introduction: text and reduction

The most typical criticism of the presentation of qualitative data is that the audience is given a range of examples which do not allow them to comprehend whether those choice snippets represent the typical or the most extreme examples from the researcher's data collection. Whilst quantitative researchers may boil down their research findings into a one-line statistical conclusion, and so be accused of excessive data reduction, the other extreme is the qualitative researcher who presents a vast array of examples and drowns their audience in seemingly undigested data. Chapters 18 to 21 sought to show the range of techniques by which a degree of qualitative data reduction can take place, even if this process will never, and does not seek to, achieve the level of reduction possible with more numerical data. This section seeks to highlight how such techniques can be usefully deployed in the presentation of findings to an audience.

The discussion of presenting quantitative data results largely hinges on the formatting of various statistical, graphical and tabular forms for inclusion in textual documents. Analysis in quantitative research is largely bound up with the production of statistical 'results' that can then be presented. These 'results' are mainly generated today using computer software. The question of presentation is that of how best to show the 'results'. In the field of qualitative data analysis, computer software does not perform this kind of analytical function. Software can enable the researcher to organize their data in various ways to enable certain relationships to be presented more clearly, both to the researcher and to any other potential audience. Recall Miles and Huberman's (1994) motto 'think display'. This applies as much in the communication of one's findings as it does to their production.

While qualitative researchers are not able to generate statistical results to test the strength of an initial hypothesis, as has already been seen in Chapters 18 to 21, some qualitative researchers do use representational devices that mirror elements in the quantitative tradition of data presentation. The use of tables and network diagrams can identify the contents of a particular case in the same way that a frequency table and a graph might be used to map numerical data either at a particular moment or over a period of time. The production of matrix displays that map the crossover between codes or attributes within qualitative data parallels the production of cross-tabulations in quantitative data analysis.

It is important, however, to recall that there are different ways of 'doing' qualitative data analysis. The forms of qualitative content analysis advocated by Miles and Huberman (1994) and by Berg (1998) draw heavily upon forms of data presentation that involve qualitative data being 'reduced' to units of meaning that can be counted or at least located within tables and network diagrams (see Chapters 18 to 21). Those who carry out forms of discourse analysis will very often reject the primary value of such representational devices. Such researchers prefer in-depth textual forms of analysis that rarely rely upon visual forms of data reduction (that is, tables, graphs and diagrams). Those who conduct conversation analysis once again reject the attempt to use representational devices to 'reduce' data for the purpose of either comprehension or comparison. Rather, those in the tradition of conversation analysis seek to give the most elaborate presentation of the data possible within any written or spoken presentation of analysis. It is the aim of conversation analysis never to analyse more than is presented in the article or discussion. The full transcript of the conversation being analysed must always be presented along with the analysis. There is absolutely no attempt to use presentational devices to 'reduce' data. Quite the reverse.

As such, different aims are pursued by different researchers. Not all qualitative researchers seek to parallel the data reduction techniques typical of more quantitative traditions, and only some of these researchers use computer software to achieve this. Therefore, this section will look at a range of presentational devices. At the end of certain sections, the specific issue of transferring tables and diagrams from NVivo to word-processor documents will be discussed. The labelling of these tables and diagrams should follow a similar format to those required for quantitative tables and figures. This is discussed later.

Appropriate forms of presentation

Presenting the results of qualitative data analysis involves working with forms of textual material. Whether the data be the transcribed text of a series of recorded interviews, that of naturally occurring conversation, the notes taken by an interviewer at the time of interview, the field notes taken by an ethnographer, or the contents of primary texts (such as newspapers, letters or diaries), those data are fundamentally full of meaning. The type of text does not determine the way it should be analysed. That choice will be driven by the questions asked by the researcher. Content analysis is best able to help identify patterns of meaning across a relatively large quantity of text. Discourse analysis is best able to identify meaning in specific or small amounts of text. Conversation analysis is focused upon identifying the machinery at work in individual segments of conversation. The choice of focus determines the method of analysis to be used, though of course there is most often a combination of motives that leads to a mixing of methods. It is the choice of data analysis methods that determines the best form of data presentation to communicate findings to a wider audience.

Conversation analysis

The golden rule when presenting analysis of conversation from a conversation analytic perspective is always to include a full transcription of the naturally occurring talk that you are going to discuss. As was shown in Chapter 20, there are elaborate conventions for the presentation of talk such that the intricate machinery of pauses, intonation, interruption and turn-taking can be made manifest to those seeking to analyse the talk. Conversation analysts argue that the researcher should not draw upon inferences beyond the talk when seeking to explain it to an audience. As such, all the evidence necessary to draw the conclusions that the researcher draws should be available to the audience, whether this be the readers of a book, a chapter or an article, or the listeners to a spoken presentation. The audience is supposed to be able to share in the analytic process. The segment of text to be analysed is presented first, and the various dimensions of analysis (outlined in the section 'Doing conversation analysis' in Chapter 20) are given after that, with each conclusion linked explicitly to the appropriate lines of text in the talk. Each line of text is numbered to facilitate this process of analytic transparency. At present there is no generally available computer software designed to facilitate the transcription of naturally occurring talk into the form used by conversation analysts.

Content analysis and NVivo

The presentation of results generated by means of content analysis of qualitative data may draw upon a number of techniques designed to effect forms of data reduction that enable patterns to become apparent within large amounts of complex textual data. The three dominant forms of such reduction have been discussed in Chapters 18 to 21, both in general terms and with reference to their production within NVivo. The following discussion will outline each in turn, touching on their use and how they can be best produced for presentation purposes within NVivo. All three can be produced 'by hand' (that is, not using designated qualitative software), using paper and pencil or via other kinds of textual or graphics-based software. It is important to recall that content analysis may be used in the organization of data, elements of which can then be analysed in a more discourse analytic fashion. It is important, therefore, to think whether the use of the three techniques for presenting the findings of content analysis outlined below are to be the end of a particular presentation or merely the introduction (the contextualization) for a more detailed examination of particular sections of 'text' (see Introduction and the section 'Qualitative Data Analysis' in Chapter 18).

Numerical tables within qualitative data presentation   Tables in the presentation of qualitative content analysis serve much the same function as frequency tables and cross-tabulations in the presentation of quantitative data analysis. In the development of a written or spoken presentation of qualitative research, it is valuable to show the kinds of tables (that is, matrix displays) discussed in Chapter 21. Within-case displays and cross-case displays can be used to great effect in familiarizing an audience with the field of research. Context charts and checklist charts allow the audience to comprehend the characteristics of those who were researched. Time ordered displays can be used to familiarize the audience with both the research process and the events that were the subject of the research. Recall that tables should serve the purpose of communicating to the audience the findings of the research and the tables should be chosen accordingly. Do not seek to show every aspect of the data, the sample or the research process. The researcher needs to identify what is significant and select their tables in the light of this.

Tables can be created within NVivo from three main sources (see Chapter 21). The first is the creation of attribute tables. The second is using various forms of matrix intersection searches within the **Search** tool. Finally, there is the **Assay** function that allows numerical tables to be created that map the incidence of particular codes. Such tables need to be exported from NVivo into whatever software package is being used to write the presentation. For this to be achieved, it is necessary to transfer the NVivo file into a plain text file. With either the attribute table, matrix intersection table or assay table open, select **Export** from the **File** menu at the top of the window. This opens up the **Export Profile** window. Here it is necessary to locate where you want the new file to be stored. The default option is for the file to be reformatted as a plain text file via **Text file (*.txt)**. The contents of this file can then be exported into a word-processing file or a computer-based presentational software file. If, on the other hand, you wish to export the document into the statistical package SPSS (now IBM SPSS Statistics 19), it is necessary to deselect the default export option and select instead the **SPSS** option. This allows the data to undergo more elaborate statistical investigation if that is desired.

Non-numerical code search results   It may be useful to present tables that show the incidence of particular codes and values within the data collected. This allows the audience to see whether the particular phenomenon coded for was common or rare, evenly distributed or more prevalent in some groups than in others. However, there may be more to add than just a display of numerical distribution. You may wish the audience to understand the different meanings the same phenomenon had for different groups, or the different ways in which the same outcome was achieved, and so on. This will often require the presentation of textual data themselves. This may be in the form of tables that contain quotes or descriptions from or of the same individuals or groups concerning a range of different topics or over a range of different times (see Chapter 18). Alternatively, the researcher may choose to select specific quotes (from interview transcripts, field notes or primary textual sources) to illustrate their conclusions. Regarding the use of quotation as a device to illustrate a researcher's conclusion to an audience not fully familiar with the data, it is useful to recall Berg's (2007) rule of three (see Chapter 18). One supportive quotation does not prove anything and may not be convincing to an audience. The use of tables allows the range of findings to be presented. If this is done, then the use of a single quotation may add to the persuasiveness of the overall presentation. If tables are not used, then it is necessary to demonstrate to the audience why the selected quotation is considered representative of a more general pattern in the data. Alternatively, it is possible to say that selected quotations are illustrative of the uniqueness of particular individuals or groups. However, this claim still needs to be supported in the presentation in order to be persuasive. This can be achieved by discussion of the coding process and its outcomes. See below for discussion of this in the context of NVivo. The same principles apply when coding by hand.

It is not possible to construct tables containing textual data at the points of intersection between variables within NVivo itself, but specific quotations can be cut and pasted into other document formats relatively easily. What NVivo also allows is the conduct of searches that produce textual outputs. Within NVivo the conduct of node searches, Boolean searches, text searches and proximity searches all generate textual data that can be incorporated, by cutting and pasting, into presentation formats. The conduct of such searches also makes the task of selecting those quotes that best illustrate general patterns or specific differences easier for the researcher.

Network diagrams   Diagrams that illustrate timelines (whether of the research itself or of the lives or events being researched) or which illustrate relationships within the data are the equivalent of graphs in more numerical forms of data presentation.

Models created in NVivo can be exported from NVivo in the following way. The simplest method is to select the **Export Diagram to Clipboard** option from the **Model** menu of the **Model Explorer** window. This saves a copy of the model to the clipboard and this can then be pasted directly into compatible word-processing software.

Discourse analysis

Discourse analysis, as discussed in Chapter 20, takes a critical stance towards forms of data reduction that bring qualitative content analysis closer to quantitative forms of data analysis and presentation. Nevertheless, as was pointed out in Chapters 18 and 20, forms of qualitative content analysis can be usefully applied to large quantities of textual data to enable key themes to emerge that can subsequently be analysed in more depth, using selected examples, by discourse analytic means. As such, the presentation of general characteristics about a dataset in the form of tables and network diagrams may well usefully precede more discourse analytic work in a written presentation of findings. These tables and diagrams can be generated 'by hand' or using qualitative data analysis computer software packages.

For the presentation of discourse analysis itself, it is most common to use predominantly textual, that is, written, accounting techniques. More holistic descriptions of time spent in the field, of the practices, rituals and routines of a group observed, or of the life of a person interviewed, are not always usefully reduced to non-textual form. Much of the significance of a 'way of life' or 'way of seeing' would be lost in non-textual forms of data reduction. Also, the value of more open-ended forms of data collection would be lost if all the data were then packaged in more closed representational forms. The value of the more content analytic approaches to data presentation discussed above lies in enabling the researcher to identify general patterns in large amounts of data. Once done, forms of textual discourse analysis, discussed in Chapter 20, may be applied to the selected events, lives and situations. This application moves in two directions. First, specific examples can be explored in greater depth, and second, more general or holistic conclusions about the pattern of events can be presented.

Specific representational devices   Much discourse analytic work is carried out on visual images and material artefacts. In presentation of research on such items it is useful to present a selection of such images or visual representations of those artefacts. A study of gender representation in advertising may deploy content analytic techniques to identify the incidence of certain characteristics. The selection of such characteristics and the attempt to understand their significance by discourse analytic means can be presented most successfully to a wide audience by means of a discussion accompanied by one or more selected examples.

Ethnographic research may use a number of representational devices to convey the meaning that those studied attach to their lives and actions. These may be drawings made by the researcher themselves, or images drawn by those studied. While time in the field allows the researcher to get to know the way those around them see the world, someone reading a discussion of that fieldwork may benefit from visual pointers such as maps, drawings and photographs from the field.

Finally, within deconstruction there is a particular notation device used to draw the attention of the reader to the analytical questioning being applied to a particular concept (or metaphor masquerading as a concept). This is to place a line through a concept or term within a text being analysed. Such a term is then said to be placed 'under erasure'. It is this term that is being 'deconstructed', or taken apart.

Presenting quantitative data results

Writing descriptive accounts of quantitative results

The purpose of the results section is to convey the main findings of your research to the reader. It will form a large proportion of the overall size of the report. When you are writing up the results from quantitative data analysis, a number of issues should be considered. The first is, what are the main results that you want the reader to learn about? These should be clearly related to the original research objectives and presented in the same or broadly similar order as in the literature review and methodology sections. It is likely that through the process of exploring the data you will have collated much more data analysis than can be included in the final report. You will need to sift and sort your results accordingly. Likewise, you will need to make careful decisions about the tables and charts to be presented in the final report. A general rule is to only include those tables and charts that actually show a trend or relationship between two or more variables that relates to the original objectives. Limits on the number of tables and charts to be included in a report are sometimes suggested. The important point is that a balance must be maintained between the written interpretation and the tables/charts.

The researcher should avoid including tables and charts in reports that are not referred to in the written text. If you feel that you want to include some tables/ charts that are interesting but are not a key focus of the project, consider placing them in the appendices and make a short reference to their inclusion in the write-up. The style of descriptive account could be a simple written interpretation of the summary statistics and percentages in a frequency table or contingency table. A more analytical and contextualized explanation, offering a greater depth and possibly linking to the findings of previous research and theories from the literature review, can also be made. The key findings for the research data will inform much of the content of the subsequent discussion sections. The nature of quantitative data analysis generally requires that the written interpretations are normally undertaken in the passive voice, avoiding the use of 'I' or 'we'. There may be occasions, particularly when using multi-method or mixed method approaches, where the use of the active voice is appropriate.

Tables and IBM SPSS Statistics 19

In Chapters 24 and 25 frequency tables were used to provide descriptive summaries of single variables, and contingency tables or cross-tabulations were produced to explore the relationship between two variables. For both frequency and contingency tables, the format of the table produced by IBM SPSS Statistics 19 (here termed SPSS for convenience) is inappropriate for a formal report. The cells in the table contain a lot of data, all of which is not necessary for inclusion in the final report. SPSS row, column and total headings often fail to convey the exact meaning of the data. Tables of a suitable format can be produced within SPSS using the **Tables** command, or alternatively the table can be reproduced using the table function in a word-processing package, for example, MS Word. For both types of table the meta-data, containing the accompanying titles, labels and information on missing data, must be included to allow the reader to accurately interpret the presented data. The meta-data must be included for tables from both primary and secondary data sources.

A suggested format for both frequency and contingency tables is detailed below. This is only one of a number of appropriate formats and you should refer to local guidelines for your particular report. An important aspect of presenting tables is that the structure and format must be consistent throughout the report. Fink (1995c) provides some excellent guidance on how to present survey data in a report.

Frequency tables Frequency tables summarize the data for a single variable. The basic SPSS frequency table calculates the count, percentage, valid percentage and cumulative percentage for each variable category. The most common data to present are the valid percentage for each category in that variable, as this allows for comparisons between category responses to be made. Where sample numbers are exceptionally small it may be appropriate to present the count. If there is a large number of missing data, then presenting the percentage based on the total sample size may be more appropriate. The meta-data to be included with a frequency table are:

- *Table title.* The table title should start with the word 'Table' followed by the number of the table in the report, for example, Table 1. All tables in the report should be numbered sequentially, starting from 1. This should be followed by a title that accurately reflects the frequency table data presented. It should not include the original SPSS variable name. The table title should include, either on a separate line or in brackets, the total number of valid observations for the variable, expressed as $n = 100$. For example: 'Table 1: Sex of respondents ($n = 100$)'.

- *Category labels.* The labels for each category should be entered in full. Avoid replicating abbreviations that may have been used in the data entry phase, for example, '*dna*' for did not answer. The category labels should relate to the table title. Labels for the unit of analysis (valid percentage or count) should be entered in the appropriate column headings.

- *Footnotes.* Additional information can be placed in a footnote immediately underneath the table. Footnotes can include the number of missing cases for a variable; it is also appropriate to include this where the valid percentage has been calculated and presented in the main body of the table. If presenting tables from a secondary data source, for example, aggregated data from a university student survey, the footnote could contain the data source and year. Similarly, any technical aspects that you wish to draw to the reader's attention can also be included in the table footnote.

An example of a report-quality frequency table is shown in Table 28.1.

Contingency tables or cross-tabulations Contingency tables allow you to explore relationships between two variables. The standard format is that the

TABLE 28.1 Example of presenting a report-quality frequency table

(Table 1. Sex of respondents (n = 200)

Sex	Percentage
Male	32
Female	68
Total	100

Missing = 10
Source: University student survey, May 2009

independent variable is placed in the column and the dependent variable in the row (see Chapter 25 for an in-depth discussion). Cells in the contingency table can contain count, row percentage, column percentage or total percentage. Cells in a report-quality table will normally contain the column percentage only, since the independent variable is placed in the column. Column percentages enable the researcher to make comparisons between the different categories in the independent variable. Where the convention of placing the independent variable in the column is not followed, the cell percentage should be adjusted accordingly to row percentages.

With the independent variable in the column 'Column totals', 100 per cent should be included in the last row of the table to aid the reader in the interpretation of the table. Each column total will also need to include a count to allow the reader to see the number of observations in each of the categories in the independent variable. This will also enable the reader to calculate the individual cell counts from the column percentage. Where individual cell counts are exceptionally small, it may be more appropriate to present the count.

The meta-data to be included with a contingency table are:

- *Table title.* The table should start with the word 'Table' followed by the number of the table in the report, for example, Table 2. All tables should be numbered sequentially. The format for a contingency table title is dependent variable by independent variable. The title should not include original SPSS variable names. The total number of valid observations for the variable, expressed as $n = 120$, should be included in brackets or on a second separate line. For example, 'Table 2: Working Full-Time or Part-Time by Sex ($n = 120$)'.

- *Category labels for independent and dependent variables.* Labels should be entered in full, avoiding the use of abbreviations. If abbreviations are used because of limited space, a definition should be included in the table footnote. Labels for the unit of analysis (percentage or count) should be entered in the column headings, assuming the independent variable is placed in the column.

- *Footnotes.* Additional information can be placed in the footnote immediately underneath the contingency table. This information can include missing values, definitions of category labels, data source and year if using secondary data. As with frequency tables, any technical information can also be included as a footnote.

An example of a report-quality contingency table is shown in Table 28.2. See also Box 28.1.

TABLE 28.2   Example of presenting a report-quality contingency table

Table 2. Employment Status by Sex of Respondent (n = 120)

	Sex	
Employment status	Male %	Female %
Full-time	66.7%	50.0%
Part-time	33.3%	50.0%
Total	100.0%	100.0%
	($n = 60$)	($n = 60$)

Source: Survey of local residents, 2008

BOX 28.1 HINTS AND TIPS

Using SPSS to produce report-quality tables

The basic frequency and cross-tabulation tables produced in SPSS are of a limited quality for presentation in a formal report. These tables produced in later versions of SPSS (versions 15 onwards) can be copied and pasted into MS Word and then edited using the MS Word table function.

Alternatively, SPSS does have a report-quality table function within the package. This can be accessed from the **Analyze** menu, select **Tables** and **Custom Tables**. Variables can be dragged and dropped into the row and column elements of the table. Custom tables do require that each variable is correctly set up in SPSS. All variables need to have the correct measure assigned. All variables must have variable labels, and categorical (nominal and ordinal) variables need to have value labels for each code.

Charts and graphs The presentation of charts and graphs in a report is fairly straightforward. The main charts produced in SPSS for analysis are quite basic. An alternative approach is to take the data from frequency tables and contingency tables and enter them into a package that has a chart function within it, for example, MS Excel or MS Word.

The key aspects when presenting charts in a report are:

- *Chart title.* The chart title should follow the same format as for frequency and contingency tables for a single bar chart and multiple bar chart respectively. Charts are normally labelled as Figure 1, Figure 2 and so on.

- *Axis labels.* Edit axis labels where existing labels contain SPSS variable labels.

- *Bars.* Consider altering the bar colours and fill patterns to give a consistent appearance throughout the report. Give consideration to the colour of bars, particularly in multiple bar charts, if the report is going to be printed in black only, or if it is going to be reproduced in grey scale. The grey scale equivalents for some colours are extremely close together, making it difficult for the reader to distinguish between bars.

- *Footnotes.* Make use of footnotes to include the number of missing cases, definitions of category labels, data source and year if using secondary data. Footnotes can also be used to draw the reader's attention to any other issues related to the data: for example, if you want to remind the reader of a particular technical aspect related to the data.

Writing up the results from statistical tests In the report, statistical tests will normally be placed after the descriptive account of the variable(s). For example, a descriptive account of the relationship between two categorical variables would be stated before proceeding to undertake a statistical test, such as chi-squared. When including the results of statistical tests in academic reports you should clearly state the purposes of the test, the null hypothesis and the research hypothesis. Report the statistical test results in full; these include the test statistic, the degrees of freedom where applicable, and the significance level. Finally, accept or reject the null hypothesis based on these findings and the conclusions you can draw from them. An example of reporting a chi-square test can be found in the section 'Reporting chi-square findings' in Chapter 26.

Reporting both qualitative and quantitative research

So far in this chapter we have given you the basic information relating to how to present qualitative and quantitative data. This has been presented as two distinctive subsections. If you have undertaken research involving either qualitative or quantitative approaches then one of these subsections is likely to be sufficient for your needs. However, increasingly research is using both qualitative and quantitative approaches, and the mixing of research methods can present some challenges at the reporting and presentation stage.

There are two approaches you can take. Both are legitimate, and which you adopt will ultimately depend on your research findings, the nature of your research and what you are aiming to achieve in your report (or presentation).

The first approach, and the most obvious, would be to simply present the qualitative and quantitative data findings as two distinct sections. So, for example, you might present findings from the survey and findings from the interviews. Linkages between the data findings, that is cross-referencing, can be included. Adopting this approach will require a drawing together of the research findings at the end of the data and results section. For example, you would highlight areas of commonality or aspects of the research topic or subtopic that reveal different levels of understanding. The difficulty with this approach is twofold. First, it is too easy to forget this last stage and simply present the data as two distinct episodes of the research, almost as two separate research projects. The reader may quickly lose interest. Second, if you have a limited word count for your report then you may find that you very quickly start to struggle with keeping the words within the maximum limit.

The second approach is to adopt a thematic or topic-led approach. Here you introduce the reader in a systematic manner to each of the main topics or themes and subtopic areas or themes. Within each topic or theme you draw upon the evidence, both qualitative and quantitative. The structuring of the topics will be closely linked to your original research objects. The advantage of this approach is that it allows you to combine both broad (quantitative) and depth (qualitative) data to provide an interesting and engaging account.

Drafting, redrafting and final versions of the report

The overall assessment of a report will be judged not only by the quality of the research but also on the quality of the writing. Writing research reports, like writing essays, is a skill that can be developed and honed over time. The importance of planning the timeline of the report to enable you to make amendments cannot be understated. The more time you have to reflect on the content, to express the arguments and conclusions, and to tie together the different elements of the report so that it reads as a coherent whole, the more likely you are to produce a quality report. Writing under the pressure of an impending deadline is less than ideal and is unlikely to yield your best quality work, and neither will it give you the time to review, refine and reflect on your research argument.

A well-planned research write-up will mirror each stage of the research process. A draft literature review can be written during the early stages of the research. As the research develops and the research questions become more formalized the research approach can be written, including the section on methodology and methods. Once data are collected and analysed, the research findings can be written. You will need to consider the findings that are pertinent to your argument; not all the data you have collected and analysed will necessarily make it to the final versions. Throughout the research you need to ensure that there is a coherent thread that hangs each section together. Lots of metaphors are used to describe this. At its simplest it can be thought of as a washing line or power line cable. The line or cable needs to be visible and strong enough to carry out the function that has been assigned to it. In the instance of reports, the function is to carry the line of argument. Each section of the report needs to be linked with the argument. For example, in the discussion of the research methods a justification must be provided that is clearly related to the research question. Overall, you need to be considered, fair, persuasive, and convincing in guiding the reader through your research and towards accepting the conclusions that you have drawn.

It may be valuable to engage friends, perhaps to develop a reading circle where you read each other's reports and provide critical feedback. Do make full use of academic tutors to guide you through the writing.

Finally, you must include enough time to adequately proofread your work. It may be best to put the report to one side for a couple of days before returning to it with fresh eyes. This will help you identify areas that are less clear or where lines of argument could be made tighter or more convincing.

Box 28.2 provides a summary of common areas to consider when writing your research report.

BOX 28.2

AREAS TO CONSIDER WHEN WRITING AND REVIEWING YOUR REPORT

Title
Find a title that accurately reflects the research project and is engaging for the reader.

Signposting
Each chapter of the report needs to clearly state what is going to be discussed. Use subsections with appropriate headings to break chapters down into manageable chunks that are easy for the

(Continued)

(Continued)

reader to navigate. Where subsections are used, make sure that at the beginning of each chapter there is a brief sentence relating to each subsection to guide the reader. It is appropriate to cross-reference the reader to different chapters and sections where appropriate linkages exist. This will avoid unnecessary replication.

The research question
Have you given a rationale for why your research question is important and worthy of research?

The literature review
How does the literature relate to the research question? Have you been explicitly clear on the parameters of the literature review? Ensure that you have critically considered the available literature and not simply provided a summary of the existing literature. Are there any gaps in your literature review? Avoid overly long quotes from the literature, and ensure that you summarize the content in your own words.

Research design and methods
How do these relate to the research question? Why was a particular approach taken? Give an account for the research design and methods used. You will need to state how you identified research participants; include details of sampling techniques. Processes for developing the research design and methods need to be summarized, including ethical considerations, piloting, administrative processes, data entry and approaches to the analysis. Within this section consider any difficulties encountered, for example, gatekeepers or exceptionally low response rates, and how you overcame them. What were the limitations of your research?

Data analysis
Present data that address the original research questions. This is likely to mean that you will not present all the data you have collected or analysed. You will need to be selective, identifying those findings that illuminate your research questions.

Tables and figures need to have appropriate labels. This should include a table or figure number and a title. Check that the table/figure number you refer to in the written text actually refers to the correct table/figure. If you have tables/figures that you do not explicitly refer to in the written text, should they still be included? If the answer is yes then you need to write a commentary.

Discussion and conclusions
The discussion and conclusions should not simply be a summary of the data findings! Use the data findings to support your line of argument. If your findings contradict other research identified in the literature review, consider the reasons for this in the context of your research questions.

Bibliography
Check that the correct reference format has been used. Your institution will provide guidance on the format requirements. Cross-check that items in your bibliography are cited in the report. Any that have not been used should be removed. Conversely, if you have cited a source in the main text that does not appear in your bibliography, you will need to locate the exact details of that reference and include it in the bibliography.

Appendices
Include all relevant items. They will need to be clearly labelled and you will need to check that you have referenced them appropriately in the main report.

> **Format of the report**
>
> Have you met the requirements for the report format?
>
> Check that you have included the correct sections, requirements for page margins, page numbers, printing (single or double sided). There will be a minimum and maximum word limit. Remember to spellcheck the report.

Presenting verbally to an audience

The key to a successful presentation is to set out clearly the objectives that you wish your presentation to achieve. It is highly likely that the time allocated for a presentation will not allow you to go into every detail about the research you have undertaken and your findings. You will therefore need to make decisions as to what to include in your presentation. The audience you are addressing will in part determine the key points, or objectives, that you wish to convey. Remember that the audience expects to learn something about your research and this will be influenced by the amount of prior knowledge that they have of the process of social research and the substantive topic area investigated. Deciding on the level of knowledge the audience brings with them can be tricky. The more experience you gain from presenting research, the more confident you will become in making a decision as to the level of knowledge to assume. General advice when undertaking your first presentation is to assume that the audience has very little or no prior knowledge. This is particularly the case if your presentation is to a non-academic audience. Where you are presenting to an academic audience, some basic knowledge of the social research process and common concepts may be known. You can always skip over the more basic aspects of the research if it becomes clear that the audience is familiar with some aspects.

Having set the level of prior knowledge of the audience that you are going to assume, the next step is to decide on the intended objectives of the presentation itself. The audience is likely to want to know why you carried out the research, the research design, the research methods used, the main findings from the data collected, and how your conclusions inform or relate to current understanding and theory.

At this stage it is also advisable to consider any visual, audio or other sensory requirements of your intended audience. Where there are specific needs consult with appropriate local advisors. More general advice can be sought through a general web search for up-to-date advice and support materials.

Organizing the material

Organizing your material is a fairly straightforward process, as the presentation will follow a similar structure to a written report. The structure is likely to be:

- State background to the research project.

- Research aims/questions.

- Research design and methods employed.

- Key findings.

- Discussion of key findings in relation to existing literature and theory.

- Conclusions.

You will need to tailor the structure and content to the allocated time that you have for the presentation. If you do not have time to present the entire research project, select a number of key findings and focus on those. You will be able to assess the constraints of the time allocation by practising your talk.

Delivery of a presentation

There are a number of elements to successfully delivering a presentation:

- Use of visual aids.

- Content of visual aids.

- Body language and eye contact.

- Clarity and tone of voice.

Use of visual aids   There are a variety of visual aids available including flip charts, whiteboards, overhead projectors, computer LCD projectors, video and audio recorders.

Flip charts and whiteboards tend to be used more in situations where discussion and small-group work is taking place. They can be used for presentations where no other visual aids are available. The use of flip charts and whiteboards requires the presenter to have a supply of suitable marker pens and board erasers.

Overhead projectors and computer LCD projectors allow the presenter to prepare in advance OHP transparencies or a computer-based slide show. Where a slide show is prepared it is always advisable to have a backup of the slides printed on ordinary OHP transparency sheets.

Content of visual aids   Keep the content of slides, OHP or computer-based presentation simple:

- Use bullet point lists to highlight key points.

- Do not clutter the slide with too much text.

- The text should be at least 18 point. Remember that it needs to be seen by those sitting at the back of the room.

- Include graphs and tables as appropriate.

- Avoid the use of large tables. In these instances it is better to report the content of 'key' cells.

BOX 28.3 HINTS AND TIPS

Using PowerPoint

PowerPoint is frequently used slide show software from the MS Office suite. It has a tremendous array of different functions and slide formats. Functions can include animations of text, background formats and styles; Smart Art to produce a graphical visualization of a list; and video, audio and image fields. When constructing a slide show in PowerPoint it is advisable to use the different functions wisely and economically. Remember that the sole purpose of a presentation is to tell your story to the audience.

General advice when using PowerPoint is to select a background style that is quite plain, so that it does not detract from your main text. Think about the contrast between the colour of your background and the colour of the text. A pale coloured background (for example, pale yellow or pale blue) is a good contrast against which black text can be seen. Use different text colours and fonts sparingly. Having one or two colours for fonts and the same for font style is advisable. General advice is to have no more than five or six bullet points and/or a maximum of 40–50 words per slide.

Technical guides on how to use the different features of PowerPoint can be found at the Microsoft website under 'How to articles for educators'. See http://www.microsoft.com/education/howto.mspx.

When using a computer slide show, do not overuse the 'additional features' available through the templates. Flashing graphics, additional noise and multiple colour schemes can detract from the content of your research (Box 28.3).

Video and audio materials can provide a useful addition to a presentation. A short piece of video footage can be included to illustrate a particular point. Alternatively, some audio from an interview or group discussion can add context and life to the presentation. The use of video and audio materials also breaks up the presentation and gives the presenter a few welcome minutes of rest from speaking.

When designing the use of video or audio materials, make sure that:

- the selected materials are appropriate
- the video or audio clip is not too long.

Body language and eye contact   It is important that you build a rapport with the audience to increase your own confidence and to reinforce to the audience that you have something important to say and they should listen to you. The easiest way to achieve this is to engage with the audience through eye contact. Look around the audience and remember to smile, even if you are feeling very nervous.

In addition, eye contact with the audience will provide you with feedback on how your presentation is going: does the audience understand what you are saying? Finally, avoid annoying habits such as fumbling with a pen or jewellery.

Clarity and tone of voice   Speak clearly and confidently. If you are concerned that your nervousness will show through in your voice tone, try taking some deep breaths to calm your nerves. Try to avoid repeating phrases, for example, 'OK', 'right', 'cool'. You will probably not notice them, but your audience will! You will need to speak at a slightly slower pace than your normal speaking rate. The more nervous you are, the more likely you are to speak quickly, resulting in the audience becoming confused and the talk becoming shorter than originally anticipated. You can control the speed of your delivery by remembering to include pauses in your speech. Where you pauses, think a long pause. This will give your audience time to digest the points you have made before you continue.

Presenting the research

One of the most pressing issues for the presenter is whether they should read a pre-prepared script or try to remember everything they want to say. Neither of these two extremes is advantageous. A person who reads from a script runs the risk of disengaging from the audience as they read with their head buried in the paper they are holding. Likewise, unless the presenter is extremely confident and calm and has an excellent memory, the latter is also likely to fail. The reality will be somewhere in between. When first presenting it is likely that you will want to have detailed notes in front of you, and as experience grows the notes are likely to become briefer.

When preparing your speaking notes, consider the following:

- Make use of headers and subheaders to divide your talk into manageable sections. These may correspond with the keywords on your visual aids.

- Consider the use of index cards as they are smaller and easier to manage than large sheets of paper.

And finally, it is advisable to practise your talk to a group of supportive friends or colleagues. Practising the talk will enable you to judge whether the information you wish to present is possible within the allocated presentation time.

Summary

This chapter has outlined the main elements of presenting your research findings in a written report. When producing a report it is vital that you consider the intended audience you are writing for. A report for an academic course is likely to have predefined sections with equal emphasis on methodology, methods and research findings. Reports for non-academic audiences will vary from this structure. For example, they may be less interested in the methodology and more interested in the research findings and potential policy implications. It is important that you are clear from the outset, before writing your report, that you understand these requirements and the subsequent balance between the different elements.

A successful presentation is achieved by setting clear objectives as to the purpose of the presentation. The researcher needs to decide upon the elements of the research that they wish to share with the audience, as inevitably there will be time restrictions limiting discussion of all areas relating to the research. This will involve organizing the material appropriately and developing a structure that has a number of sections and subsections. The use of visual aids can enhance a presentation, give a professional look and give the presenter an additional confidence boost. It will be the confidence of the presenter that will ultimately determine the success of the presentation. Body language, clarity and tone of voice will convey how important your research is and that it makes a positive contribution to the subject area.

■ Questions

1 **Identify the key sections of a report and the type of information that should be included in them.**
2 **What are the key elements to a successful presentation?**
3 **What information should be included when presenting research findings in a table?**

■ ■ Further reading ■

Bradbury, Andrew (2006) *Successful Presentations*, 3rd edn. London: Kogan Page.

Byram, Lynda (1999) *Being Successful in Presentations*. London: Blackhall.

Becker, Lucinda and Van Emden, Joan (2004) *Presentation Skills for Students*. London: Palgrave.

Chivers, Barbara (2007) *A Student's Guide to Presentations*. London: Sage.

Fink, Arlene (1995c) *How to Report on Surveys*. London: Sage.

Hague, Paul N. and Roberts, Kate (1994) *Presentations and Report Writing*. London: Kogan Page.

Northey, Margot and McKibbin, Joan (2007) *Making Sense in the Social Sciences: A Student's Guide to Research and Writing*. Canada: Oxford University Press.

GLOSSARY

ABSTRACTS AND INDEXES.   Abstracts are summaries that sum up the content of a journal article (or other text). Abstracts used to be collected into large bound volumes that could be searched for using parallel volumes of indexes (alphabetical lists by author, title and subject matter). Now, much of this searching can be done on electronic abstracting and indexing services.

ACTION RESEARCH.   Research designed not simply to know the world, but to enable change. Action research is more than just policy-driven research; it seeks to implement policy through the research itself. See also *evaluation research, participant action research*.

ACTORS.   While an actor is said to engage in action, machines, plants, objects and so on only display behaviour (the position of animals is controversial in this spectrum). Action requires a consciousness capable of reflecting upon a course of action. While behaviour can be studied simply in terms of causal mechanisms, understanding action requires a knowledge of what the actor intended to achieve by their action, even if this is not the whole story. The capacity for self-reflection is seen by some as grounds for saying an actor is 'morally' responsible for their actions in the way that, for example, a thunderbolt is not responsible for its behaviour. This view is premised upon the belief that if an action was 'chosen', in the course of 'reflection', the actor could have chosen not to take that course of action. In other words, some believe that actors are at least in part able to determine (cause) their own actions and therefore should be held accountable for those actions. Others prefer to use the term 'subject' to refer to the human individual (consciousness as well as physical being) so as to avoid this attribution of something close to 'free will'. The term 'actor' is closely associated with the term 'agency', which again is often used to attribute self-determination to human beings, rather than seeing them as outcomes of the social arrangements they are a part of. Once again, critics highlight the fact that such a term assumes some kind of freedom of the will, something that cannot be proven, and is almost impossible to conceptualize, except in the base sense of feeling the urge to blame and punish (itself a form of social causation that justifies itself in the language of responsible actors).

ADJACENCY PAIRS.   Conversation analytic term referring to forms of talk where the first speaker's talk elicits a predictable response. The expectation built into such pairs is what is significant. Speakers can choose to deviate, but the expectation is still present. See also *conversation analysis, turn-taking*.

ADVOCACY. In a research context, advocacy describes the situation when the researcher role becomes merged with that of supporting the group being studied in a political or other sense. While *action research* refers to research that seeks to change those being researched, research as advocacy is more focused on changing the way others see or treat those being researched. This distinction is not rigid.

AGGREGATED DATA. Data that have been previously manipulated and summarized into *tables*.

AIDE-MÉMOIRE. List of themes, questions and keywords that an open-ended interviewer keeps with them during an *interview*. The purpose is to remind the interviewer of things to bring into the interview, or ways of developing a line of questioning, not as a strict script (which would be an *interview schedule*).

ALTERNATIVE HYPOTHESIS. Also called *research hypothesis*. Used in hypothesis testing. It asserts that there is a real difference between observed values and those expected in the theoretical model as stated in the *null hypothesis*.

ANONYMITY. Anonymity is where the identity of a research participant is not recorded for the purposes of research, or where records are destroyed once data collected have been recorded. Anonymity is not the same as *confidentiality*.

ARCHIVE, ARCHIVAL RESEARCH. Research based on existing data and other textual materials. This may mean working from a formal library or from the archives of organizations or individuals. Government records and personal letters and diaries may form the subject of archival research. Archival research now includes working with material held electronically, or which can be located electronically, but which has then to be located in physical archives.

ARTEFACT. Any product of human cultural production. In social research the word is used in two senses. First, it can refer to any cultural product recorded or collected for analysis by the researcher. Examples might include diaries, photographs, items of clothing or jewellery, cooking implements and/or newspapers. Second, it can refer to any research outcome that might be said to have been biased by the research process itself. If the researcher's questions, appearance, behaviour or simply their presence lead to distortions in results, these distorted results are referred to as research artefacts, rather than valid representations of reality.

ASSAY. Originally 'to assay' was to analyse the mineral content of a substance, such as in assessing the gold content. In social research an assay table sets out the number of times selected codes occur within selected cases.

ATTRIBUTES. Attributes are general properties possessed by one or more persons or objects. Recording and comparing attributes enables patterns to be identified if underlying similarities exist within or between groups.

AUDIENCE RECEPTION, AUDIENCE STUDIES. Research into how audiences interpret media images and messages. Most popular are *cultural capital* theories, the *two-step flow model* and the *uses and gratifications* approach.

AUTOBIOGRAPHICAL METHOD. Use of the researcher's own life story as a subject of research.

AVAILABILITY SAMPLING. See *opportunity sampling*.

AXIAL CODES. Codes that the researcher selects to represent and to highlight what they perceive to be the core issues or themes within the text they are analysing. Distinguished from *systematic codes*.

BALANCING. When the researcher is developing rank order categories for *closed-ended questions*, balancing ensures that there are equal numbers of positive and negative categories.

BAR CHART. A graphical presentation of data appropriate for nominal or ordinal variables. Consists of a series of bars on the *x*-axis (horizontal axis) with a count or percentage displayed on the *y*-axis (vertical axis). Each bar represents the count or percentage of observations in a category.

BASELINE. An established point from which to measure changes over time or between locations. The term can be used to refer to highly *quantitative* measures. For example, changes in unemployment in all OECD countries can be compared by translating each country's unemployment figure in a given year into the figure 100 and then calculating changes in each country year by year in relation to that standardized baseline *statistic*. More *qualitative* use of the term 'baseline' refers to the collection of data on attitudes and beliefs at one point in time to be compared with results gathered later (often after a particular policy initiative or programme).

BEFORE-AND-AFTER DESIGN. A research design in which all subjects are measured, pre-test, before being subjected to the manipulation of an *independent variable*. The subjects are then measured again, post-test. Pre-test and post-test findings are then compared. There is no control group.

BIASED. Bias occurs when *sample* characteristics are different to those found in a *population*.

BINARY OPPOSITIONS. Device for the creation of meaning through an either/or distinction within language rather than reference to an object external to language (in nature). In creating such oppositions culturally, particular meanings and identities are made to appear natural, and often hierarchies of good/bad are managed in the same way. Whilst some social researchers consider such binary thinking as a natural and inevitable feature of human culture, others seek to research the ideological manipulation such oppositions may be said to create.

BIOGRAPHICAL METHOD. The use of written accounts of lives as a source of data. Biographical method can be distinguished from *life history* interviewing, where the researcher interviews rather than reads accounts of lives. However, this distinction is not always maintained and the terms have become in part interchangeable.

BIVARIATE ANALYSIS. Analysis of quantitative data which describes and explores the relationship between two variables.

BOX PLOT. A graphical presentation for *interval* variables. Graphically represents the *median* and first and third *quartiles* as a box.

BREACHING. A term used in *ethnomethodology* to refer to deliberate attempts by the researcher to break social conventions in order to see how people cope and react to someone who does not conform to expected patterns. Such research is typically *covert*.

CARTOGRAPHY. The field of geography devoted to the making of maps and the study of map-making.

CASE. An individual unit being studied. A case could be a person, an institution, a household, an organization and so on.

CASE STUDY, CASE STUDY METHOD. Research that is non-*comparative*. A case study may focus on one individual, one area, one group or one organization. It is not designed to compare one individual or group to another. Though it is possible to conduct a series of case studies, each study would not be designed specifically to enable comparison with others.

CATEGORICAL VARIABLES. A term used for *nominal* and *ordinal* variables. The attributes of the data can be categorized.

CATEGORIES. The grouping of data in a unit, each member of which shares one or more characteristics. Categories require the ability to specify their boundaries. This involves criteria of *internal homogeneity* and *external discretion*.

CAUSALITY. See *causation*.

CAUSATION. In simple terms, causation is the process that makes an outcome happen. Causation is something more than just the fact that certain things happen regularly in a sequence. However, outcomes rarely have only one potential cause, and particular causal factors do not always lead to the same outcome. *Mediations* as well as *necessary* and *sufficient conditions* are important aspects of causal accounting. When testing a hypothesis the researcher tries to test the extent to which variation in one or more *independent variables* causes variation in one or more *dependent variables*.

CENSUS.   A survey of all cases in a population.

CENTRAL LIMIT THEOREM.   A mathematical theorem that states that repeated sample means, taken using a random sampling technique, will approximate to a *normal distribution curve*. It is used as the basis for *inferential statistics* and *hypothesis testing*.

CHARTS.   A form of visual display in which time/sequence, size, quantity, relationships or causal processes are represented. Bar or pie charts, histograms and scatterplots are examples of quantitative charts, while Gantt charts and cognitive maps are examples of more qualitative charts.

CHI-SQUARE TEST FOR INDEPENDENCE.   A *non-parametric test* of a *hypothesis* used to assess the statistical significance of findings. Enables the researcher to assess if sample findings are *generalizable* to a population. This is a suitable test for a relationship between two categorical variables. Involves comparing the expected values of no relationship between the two variables (*null hypothesis*) with the observed values (*alternative hypothesis*).

CLASSIC EXPERIMENTAL DESIGN.   In a classic experimental design, subjects are randomly allocated to two groups, the experimental group and the control group. Pre-test observations are made on both groups. Only the experimental group is then subjected to stimuli. Observations are then taken again on both groups, known as post-test.

CLASSIFICATION.   A classification system is a set of categories, often arranged in a scale, into which every member of the population can be located. See also *attributes*.

CLOSED-ENDED QUESTIONS.   Also called *standardized questions*.

CLUSTER SAMPLE.   A sampling method where a number of locations are selected from which individual units are then selected by *random sampling* or *non-probability-based sampling* techniques.

CODE BOOK.   Also called *coding frame*. Contains a list of the variables and coding for each variable in the survey dataset.

CODES. See *coding*.

CODING. The identification and application of codes to data. In quantitative data, coding refers to the application of numerical *values* to the different possible responses to questions in a *questionnaire*, for example. In qualitative research, coding refers to the selection and application of codes to segments of textual material so that all segments associated with a code can then be analysed together and patterns identified.

CODING FRAME. This is a list of all codes being used in a coding-based qualitative data analysis exercise.

COGNITIVE MAPS. These can be either mental maps held by those the researcher is investigating, or *charts* designed by the researcher to represent the mental maps of those being researched. Sometimes the researcher can use maps made by the researched.

COHORT STUDIES. A research design that involves data collection on the same subjects at two or more periods in time.

COLUMN MARGINAL. The column totals in a *contingency table*.

COLUMN PERCENTAGE. A percentage calculated in a *contingency table* where the percentage of a cell count is calculated according to the *column marginal* (also called column total).

COMMUNITY STUDIES. Research aiming to understand the 'way of life' of a particular community, often involving *field research* and *life history* interviewing.

COMPARATIVE ANALYSIS. This is where data from different locations or groups are analysed to identify similarities and differences at a given time.

COMPARATIVE DESIGN. A research design that focuses on identifying differences and similarities between two or more groups.

COMPOSITIONAL ANALYSIS. The study of the structure and content of cultural artefacts, such as paintings, novels or films. Compositional analysis developed initially in art history and literary studies, but its initial opposition to attempts to 'understand' creative works by reference to anything outside the artefact (whether this be the biography of the author or the social conditions of its creation and reception) has more recently given way to mixed methods.

CONCEPT. A theoretical unit that needs to be translated from an abstract idea into something that can be identified and measured if it is to be researched.

CONFIDENCE INTERVALS. Based on the *central limit theorem* and the properties of the *normal distribution curve*. They enable the researcher to estimate the accuracy of the sample statistics and whether the findings can be generalized to the population.

CONFIDENTIALITY. Where personal information is collected by a researcher, confidentiality refers to the non-disclosure of that information to parties other than the research team (or in some cases specified others). Confidentiality is not the same as *anonymity*.

CONSEQUENTIALIST ETHICS. Ethical view that it can be legitimate to infringe on the ethical rights of those researched (such as deception or partial disclosure of the researcher's intentions) in cases where a greater good is achieved. This view contrasts with the *deontological* (or transcendentalist) ethical view.

CONSTANT COMPARISON. The *grounded theory* technique of building theory by continually comparing the latest round of data collection with ideas generated in previous rounds of data collection for the purpose of testing emerging ideas that might lead the research to be taken in new and fruitful directions.

CONSTRUCTIONISM. Also called social constructionism. See *phenomenology*. Some writers distinguish constructionism from a more radical social constructivism, but often the terms are used interchangeably. Constructionism focuses upon how people create their social reality through interaction with each other.

CONSTRUCT VALIDITY. A validity that is used to assess how well the measurement conforms to the theoretical model.

CONTENT ANALYSIS. The technique of *coding* textual data so that all instances where the same code has been applied can be either counted (in quantitative content analysis) or compared and further analysed (in qualitative content analysis).

CONTENT VALIDITY. A validity that is used to assess how well the measurement tool measures the different dimensions of a *concept*.

CONTINGENCY TABLE. Also called cross-tabulation. A two-way table that displays the relationship between two *categorical variables*. Each cell in the table displays the observations. The independent variable is normally placed in the column and the dependent variable in the row. Row percentages, column percentages and total percentages can be calculated for each cell in the table.

CONTINUITY CORRECTION. Also called Yates's contingency correction. A hypothesis test used to test the significance of the findings between two *categorical variables*. Can be used in place of the *chi-square test for independence* in 2 × 2 tables with small cell counts.

CONTROL VARIABLE. A variable that influences the relationship between the *independent* and *dependent variables*. Referred to as the Z variable in mathematical notation.

CONTROLLED CONDITIONS. Research procedures designed to allow only those variables that the researcher is interested in to vary, allowing relations between those variables to be studied more rigorously. Controlled conditions may distort the actions of those researched, and critics suggest *naturalistic* research conditions are often more valid.

CONVENIENCE SAMPLING. See *opportunity sampling*.

CONVERSATION ANALYSIS. Research tradition focused upon the collecting, transcription and analysis of naturally occurring talk. Conversation analysis aims to provide an account of the machinery in operation within talk by means of fine-grain analysis of talk without reference to context or motive, unless those things are explicitly deployed in the talk itself. Conversation analysis has developed a highly sophisticated form of *transcription notation* to facilitate this goal.

CORRELATION. Pattern of association between variables or the statistical measure used to identify such patterns. Correlations may be positive (increases in one variable are associated with increases in the other) or negative (increases in one are associated with decreases in the other). Correlations may be strong, weak or non-existent. A correlation may indicate a *causal* relationship, but not all correlations are causal.

CORRELATION COEFFICIENT. A measure of association that summarizes how two variables covary. There are different measures of association for the levels of measurement of the two variables. Pearson's r is used for measuring the association between two *interval* variables. Phi and Cramer's V are used for the measurement of association between two *nominal* variables. Kendall's tau-a, -b or -c are used for measuring the association between two *ordinal* variables.

COUNT. The frequency of observations.

COUNTERFACTUAL. A term often used in relation to *evaluation research* and related to *quasi-experimental design*. The counterfactual refers to the outcome if no intervention had taken place. For example, in an evaluation of a reoffending reduction programme the evaluation would compare the outcomes for offenders who went through the programme with those for a group that did not. The counterfactual of no intervention would examine the outcomes for a group of offenders who did not receive the programme. Assessing the counterfactual would need to consider individual case characteristics.

COVERING LETTER. A letter that accompanies a *self-completion survey* detailing the nature of the research project, completion and return instructions.

COVERT RESEARCH. Research where those being researched are not aware, or not fully aware, of the researcher's role. This may be by means of hidden observation, the recording of *non-intrusive data*, or covert *participant observation*.

CRAMER'S V. A measure of association used for examining the relationship between two *categorical variables*. Cramer's V is used in tables that are larger than 2×2. Normally interpreted in conjunction with a *contingency table*.

CRITERION VALIDITY. Refers to the checking of the performance of a measurement tool or *indicator*. The researcher performs some initial analysis on a measurement tool or indicator to check that it returns results that would be expected.

CROSS-CASE DISPLAYS. Graphical devices (tables, charts and so on) designed to highlight the existence or non-existence of patterns between cases, as distinct from *within-case displays*. There are both quantitative and qualitative forms of such devices.

CROSS-SECTIONAL DESIGN. A research design that involves collecting data from a sample at one point in time. Variations in particular characteristics of the sample are used to describe and explore relationships.

CROSS-TABULATION. See *contingency table*.

CULTURAL CAPITAL. Non-material and/or monetary 'assets' which accord status and enable access to various forms of social reward. Such assets as education, expertise, authority and skill can be traded directly for more material assets, but cannot be fully reduced to them. They must be earned (or be seen to be earned) rather than simply bought. The time and other resources required to acquire such cultural capital as good taste in wine, art and literature for example, or the qualifications necessary to practise law or medicine, make such domains relatively exclusive. Cultural capital can bolster baser forms of power, but also resists such reduction.

CUMULATIVE PERCENTAGE. A percentage that is derived from adding together the frequency percentage of values or categories in a *frequency table*.

DATA. Numerical or textual material generated and recorded in the research process for the purpose of analysis. Data are not 'out there' waiting to be collected. Data are the product of the research itself and are determined by the research process.

DATA ANALYSIS. The analysis of research data.

DATA COLLECTION. The period in the research project that involves engaging with a target sample or population from whom data are collected.

DATA ENTRY. Occurring after a period of data collection, data entry involves inputting data into an appropriate data file. For quantitative data this could be an SPSS data file. For qualitative data this could be the transcribing of interviews and their importation into an analysis package such as NVivo.

DATA REDUCTION. Forms of representational and analytical device used to reduce large amounts of numerical or textual material to forms from which patterns or the lack of patterns can be identified.

DATA SATURATION. A technique proposed within *grounded theory* to enable the researcher to identify when enough data have been collected. Through *constant comparison* of data and emerging theories the researcher is able to make tentative predictions (or emergent hypotheses) about what new rounds of data collection will generate. When these predictions are continually confirmed the researcher can conclude that enough data have been collected.

DATASET. All data collected by one or more projects and integrated for the purpose of analysis.

DATA TYPE. See *level of measurement*.

DECONSTRUCTION. Form of *discourse analysis* focused upon the highlighting of multiple meanings within the seemingly coherent concepts deployed in literary, political, philosophical and other texts. Deconstruction challenges the view that authors deploy language. Rather, language is seen to flow through its 'users'.

DEDUCTION. The generation of logical conclusions from rational premises. Forms a key step in *hypothetico-deductive methods* (hypothesis testing) of research and is the opposite of *induction*.

DEDUCTIVE CODING. The generation of the codes to be used in coding data prior to any analysis of the data themselves.

DELPHI GROUP. *Focus group* in which the participants are selected for being experts in the field to be discussed.

DEONTOLOGICAL ETHICS OR TRANSCENDENTALIST ETHICS. Ethical stance opposed to the *consequentialist* view that the ethical rights of those being researched can be legitimately violated if the consequence is to bring about a greater good. The deontological view argues that ethical rights cannot be traded.

DEPENDENT SAMPLES *T*-TEST. A *parametric test* used to assess the statistical significance of findings between two sets of measures collected on the same cases at two points in time. For example, a research project measures the average reading scores of a class of pupils prior to the teacher using a new reading teaching technique. The pupils are then assessed after the technique has been used for a period of time. The reading scores pre and post are tested. Here the reading scores are the dependent variable and the differences between the two measurement periods are used to assess statistical significance.

DEPENDENT VARIABLE. Variable that a researcher predicts will be affected by the variation of another variable (this other variable being called the *independent variable*). Referred to as the Y variable in mathematical notation.

DEPTH VALIDITY. See *validity* (*internal*).

DESCRIPTION. Mode of data presentation that does not seek to 'explain' why things are as they are, only to show what is going on. See also *descriptive statistics*.

DESCRIPTIVE STATISTICS. Statistics that enable the researcher to identify and explore patterns in the data collected, as distinct from *inferential statistics*.

DICHOTOMY. Also called dichotomies. A categorical variable that has only two response categories: for example, yes/no, male/female, true/false.

DISCOURSE ANALYSIS. Form of qualitative data analysis focused upon the meaning of textual data. Discourse analysis is critical of more quantitative forms of *content analysis* that seek to count the incidence of particular units of meaning within a text. *Semiotics*, *deconstruction* and *narrative* analysis are forms of discourse analysis.

DUMMY VARIABLE. A variable that contains only two categories which are coded 0 (the event does not occur) and 1 (the event has occurred). Continuous and categorical variables can be recoded into dummy variables for use in modelling techniques. See *multiple linear regression* and *logistic regression*.

ELABORATION. Process of analysing relationships between the independent variable and the dependent variable which seeks to uncover the effects of a *control variable*. Seeks to uncover *spuriousness*.

EMERGENCE. Term drawn from *grounded theory*, and used widely in qualitative research, to refer to the technique of concept selection, formation and refinement that builds up from data collection. The researcher seeks to allow useful key terms to 'emerge' from relatively open-ended early rounds of data collection. This use of *induction* is then followed by more *deductive* forms of data collection that seek to evaluate the significance of the newly identified concepts.

EMPIRICAL. Reference to the collection of data (by various means), rather than drawing conclusions only from the manipulation of theoretical propositions.

EPISTEMOLOGY. The branch of philosophy dealing with the grounds by which knowledge about the world can be gained and assessed. See also *ontology*.

ETHICS. Branch of philosophy and field of everyday thinking dealing with questions of what is morally right and wrong.

ETHNOGRAPHIC, ETHNOGRAPHY. Research tradition based upon forms of *naturalistic* data collection. Commonly associated with anthropological fieldwork, that is, time spent 'living' with a community. Ethnography draws upon a wide range of data collection methods, but its rationale lies in the premise that the researcher should go to those they research, rather than the researched enter contrived research conditions set up by the researcher.

ETHNOMETHODOLOGY. Research tradition established by Harold Garfinkel and others, focused upon identifying the methods used by people to establish and maintain a sense of social order through forms of social interaction. Ethnomethodology rejects social structural accounts of social order and is keen to show how such 'fictions' are maintained and deployed in everyday life.

EVALUATION RESEARCH. Research oriented towards measuring organizational performance, whether against quantitative standards or in terms of more qualitative indicators of satisfaction.

EXCLUSIVENESS. When developing *categories* for closed-ended questions, the researcher needs to ensure that respondents can only select one of the categories. Particular care needs to be taken with categories that represent numerical ranges. For example, with age ranges ensure that there are no overlaps in the age categories.

EXHAUSTIVENESS. The available *categories* in closed-ended questions need to contain an appropriate range of responses. Where appropriate, exhaustiveness can be ensured by included a final 'other – please state' category.

EXPECTED COUNT. Also called expected frequency. The expected value if there were no association between two *categorical variables*. Should be calculated for the *chi-square test for independence*. The expected counts are the values expected if the *null hypothesis* were true.

EXPERIMENTAL RESEARCH. Research designed to test a hypothesis, usually through the establishment of *controlled conditions* and the manipulation of independent variables to measure changes in dependent variables.

EXPLANATION.   Account that suggests a causal process behind data collected.

EXPLORATION.   Research that is designed not to test a hypothesis by *deductive* means, but which instead aims to explore a field in a more *inductive* way.

EXTERNAL DISCRETION.   What makes the contents of one category distinct from the contents of another category. If a case could be placed in more than one category, then those categories do not display external discretion. See also *internal homogeneity*.

EXTERNAL VALIDITY.   The extent to which research findings can be generalized to the population and different social settings.

FACE-TO-FACE INTERVIEW.   See *interview*.

FACE VALIDITY.   Refers to the assessment of whether the measurement tool is a suitable measure of a concept.

FACILITATOR.   Person who leads a focus group. Sometimes called moderator. The facilitator's job is to frame the discussion, ask initial questions, and 'manage' the flow of conversation. Depending upon the goals of the research and the dynamics of the group, the facilitator may wish to encourage less vocal members of the group to participate, or allow more vocal participants to 'lead' or 'dominate' discussion.

FACTS.   Real things in the world or statements about reality that are 'true'. Facts are supposedly neutral with regard to whether such things are morally right or wrong. The idea that factual statements can be made that do not contain value judgements has been questioned by some.

FEMINIST METHOD.   Research methods building upon the principles of feminist theory and ethics, and therefore designed to avoid detachment, domination and exploitation in the conduct of research, and to promote women's consciousness and empowerment in society. Feminist method is primarily qualitative and often *participant action research* oriented. Some advocates and critics have, however, questioned the assumptions that qualitative methods are intrinsically more suited to women and that qualitative approaches are always the best methods for highlighting, and therefore challenging, the subordination of women in society.

FIELD RESEARCH, FIELDWORK.   Research carried out in naturally occurring settings rather than in controlled conditions. See also *ethnography*.

FISHER'S EXACT TEST.   A hypothesis or significance test appropriate for exploring the relationship between two *categorical variables* that are dichotomies (2×2 tables) where the expected counts are small (<5 per cell).

FOCUS GROUP INTERVIEW. Interview with a group of people at the same time, and usually in the same place (though forms of teleconferencing can also be used). Distinct from the one-to-one *interview* format, the focus group may be geared to assessing group dynamics, but is more often interested in generating a range of opinions. Many forms of focus group exist.

FREQUENCY. See *count*.

FREQUENCY TABLES. Tables presenting the distribution of values within a single quantitative variable.

GATEKEEPERS. Persons within a research process whose assistance enables the researcher to access those they want to research, or others they want to research if the gatekeeper is themselves part of the researcher's sample. Gatekeepers may hold formal positions of responsibility within the accessing process, or they may be well-connected and helpful 'locals' within the environment the researcher enters.

GAZE. A socially constructed way of seeing that also acts to socially construct what is seen. Disciplines such as the medical, prison and school systems create organized forms of seeing, examining, monitoring and testing that not only affect the way patients, prisoners and pupils are seen, but also feed into the way they are treated and shaped by such treatment. The tourist gaze refers to the creating of both a way of seeing 'other places' and the way such seeing has transformed the places designated as tourist destinations.

GENERALIZABILITY. Also known as external validity. The extent to which findings from the researcher's *sample* can be claimed to accurately reflect the characteristics of a wider *population* of those groups the researcher sampled from. Factors affecting generalizability are the quality and quantity of the sample and the variance within the sample collected. Statistical measures of *significance* are designed to test these characteristics.

GENRE. Literary styles, often deployed in everyday text and talk, that frame specific content within a more general form of storytelling (for example tragedy, comedy, thriller, political drama, soap opera).

GRAPHS. Visual representations of data.

GROUNDED THEORY. Approach developed by Barney Glaser and Anselm Strauss (1967) by which theory emerges from exploration of a field rather than in advance. Theories emerging from the field are then tested by *constant comparison* in subsequent rounds of data collection until a point of saturation is reached.

HERMENEUTICS.   The study of meaningful objects or actions. Originally the term was used in biblical study, but in the modern age it has come to be applied to the more general study of literature and culture. Hermeneutics is associated with qualitative social research in general, and with *phenomenology* in particular.

HISTOGRAM.   A graphical presentation for use with interval variables. Variable values are divided into ranges and these ranges are displayed as adjoining bars on a chart. Histograms should not be confused with *bar charts* which are for *categorical variables*.

HYPOTHESIS.   Tentative theory that makes a prediction which can then be tested. See also *deduction* and *hypothetico-deductive method*. Hypothesis testing is the opposite of *induction*.

HYPOTHESIS TESTING.   Also called significance testing. A statistical technique that allows for generalizations to be made from a sample to the wider population. It involves developing an alternative hypothesis and a null hypothesis. The collected sample data are then tested to see if there is sufficient evidence to enable the null hypothesis to be rejected, and thereby the alternative hypothesis to be accepted. There are different hypothesis tests for different levels of measurement.

HYPOTHETICO-DEDUCTIVE METHOD.   Research method in which theory (that is, prior literature on the subject) is used to generate a *hypothesis*, which is then tested by *empirical* means.

ICON.   An image that stands for or represents something external to it either directly or by analogy. See also *symbol*.

INDEPENDENT SAMPLES *T*-TEST.   A *parametric test* used to compare the mean scores of two different groups of cases. It is a suitable test where the *dependent variable*, or test variable, is interval/ratio and the *independent variable* is categorical (e.g. gender).

INDEPENDENT VARIABLE.   Often referred to as the cause (see *causation*), assumed to be the variable influencing changes in the *dependent variable*. Referred to as the X variable in mathematical notation.

IN-DEPTH INTERVIEWS.   Interviews that use open-ended and often relatively unstructured questioning to explore a topic in significant detail from the interviewee's perspective.

INDEX.   See *indicators*.

INDICATORS.   Empirically measurable variables that are used to gauge the extent of an underlying phenomenon. Often a range of variables is combined to create a more sophisticated indicator: for example, income, housing tenure, access to transport and so on could all be part of a 'rural poverty' indicator.

INDUCTION. Philosophical field of generating conclusions where pure logical relationships between premises are insufficient. In social research, inductive methods are those that generate theory from evidence, rather than generating testable theory from rational extensions from existing theory. Opposite of *deduction*.

INDUCTIVE CODES. Codes that the researcher chooses on the basis of reading the data, such as in content analysis. See *induction*.

INFERENTIAL STATISTICS. Statistics that allow the researcher to make inferences on the likelihood of the sample findings being replicated in the population. Involves *hypothesis testing*.

INFORMED CONSENT. Consent refers to the expressed willingness of those being researched to participate. Informed consent is consent that is based upon a full disclosure by the researcher, in terms those being researched can understand, of the aims, methods and intended uses of the research.

INTERNAL HOMOGENEITY. The extent to which all those assigned to a particular category are the same, or sufficiently similar, at least in the terms specified by the *operationalization* of that category.

INTERNAL VALIDITY. Concerned with establishing whether no other factors, on which data may or may not have been recorded, could explain the research findings. Sampling technique and measurement tools can compromise internal validity.

INTERNET SELF-COMPLETION SURVEY. A self-completion survey that is distributed via the internet. Can be sent by e-mail to respondents or placed on a web page.

INTERQUARTILE RANGE. The middle 50 per cent of values in a *range*. Values should be placed in ascending order from lowest to highest. Calculated by taking the upper (75th) *quartile* value from the lower (25th) quartile value.

INTERVAL. A *level of measurement* where data are measured on a continuous scale. The term may also be used to refer to both interval and *ratio* data. Data can be placed in rank order and can be subjected to mathematical calculations. Interval data do not have a *true zero point*.

INTERVIEW. Traditionally a face-to-face talk based on the data collection method, though telephone and computer interviewing are also popular. Interviews may be one-to-one or group based, and may be more or less formal or *structured* (that is, with a rigid set of questions in a specified sequence, set out in an *interview schedule*) or informal/unstructured (less rigid and based upon a looser *aide-mémoire*). *Standardized questions* require an answer that is one of a selected series of options. Unstandardized questions require more open-ended answers. See also *interviewer effect, interviewer bias*.

INTERVIEWER EFFECT, INTERVIEWER BIAS. Potential for the social characteristics and behaviour of the interviewer to distort the responses of the interviewee.

INTERVIEW SCHEDULE. Written outline of the questions to be asked in an *interview*. A highly *structured* and *standardized* interview schedule would be more or less the same as a *questionnaire*, except that the interviewer would be the one to ask the questions and record the answers.

***IN VIVO* CODES.** When one is *coding* textual data by reading the text before generating the codes, *in vivo* codes are actual words or phrases used in the data themselves.

KENDALL'S TAU. A measure of association used to summarize the relationship between two *ordinal* variables. There are three versions of this measure: tau-a, tau-b, and tau-c.

KEYWORDS. Search terms used when conducting a *literature search*. These are rather like codes used in analysis of textual data. Keywords may emerge prior to the literature search, or in the process of the *literature review* of previously found materials.

KURTOSIS. A statistical measure that indicates how values are distributed around the *mode*. Positive kurtosis indicates that values are more tightly clustered around the mode. Negative kurtosis indicates that values are more loosely distributed.

LATENT CODES. Codes used in the analysis of textual data that refer not to particular surface characteristics in the text, but to underlying phenomena the researcher believes exist beneath the range of surface terms being used in the text. The researcher may believe a range of different terms being used all relate to an underlying theme.

LEPTOKURTIC. A term used to describe positive *kurtosis* where a distribution is tall and peaked.

LEVEL OF MEASUREMENT. Variables can be distinguished in terms of the level of mathematical scaling that can be carried out on those data. *Nominal* data have no mathematical sequence. *Ordinal* data can be arranged in an order, but levels of difference between units cannot be specified. *Interval* data are ordered and the difference between the units can be numerically specified. *Ratio* data are similar to interval data, with the added feature that the numerical scale on which units are located has a true point. This means that the difference between unit values can be calculated in proportion (5 metres is half of 10 metres). Level of measurement determines the statistical tests that can be carried out on the data.

LIFE HISTORY. Interview form in which the focus is the life story of the person being interviewed. Such *interviews* tend to be structured around the life course, but are otherwise relatively open-ended.

LIKERT SCALES. An attitudinal scale used in survey questions. Involves the construction of a number of statements with the same scale responses, for example, a five-point scale from strongly agree to strongly disagree. The scale responses are then scored and can be combined into one total score.

LINEAR REGRESSION. A technique used to describe the relationship between two variables based on calculating the line of best fit. Both the independent and dependent variables need to be interval or ratio.

LINE GRAPH. A graphical presentation for *interval* data. The frequency of observations for each interval value is plotted on to a graph. Particularly useful for representing trends, especially economic trends.

LINE OF BEST FIT. A predicted line that best summarizes the covariance between two interval variables. Used in *correlation* and *regression* analyses.

LITERATURE REVIEW. The process of evaluating the output from a *literature search*. Of course, identifying a text as being relevant to the researcher requires that searching involves a degree of reviewing. The two are never fully separate.

LITERATURE SEARCH. The process of identifying and locating existing published research and theory on the subject the researcher is interested in researching. See also *literature review*.

LOGISTIC REGRESSION. A data modelling technique used when the dependent variable is categorical or nominal.

LONGITUDINAL DESIGN. A research design that involves collecting data on cases over an extended period.

MAIL OR POSTAL SURVEY. A *self-completion survey* that is distributed via the postal service.

MANIFEST CODES. Codes generated for the analysis of textual data which are themselves directly linked to the expressed content of the data. Opposite of *latent codes*, and often the same as *in vivo codes* (but not always).

MATRIX DISPLAY (GRID). Table used for representing the incidence of crossover between codes and attributes (that is, general codes), between codes, or between codes and particular units (individuals, groups or organizations). Matrix tables can be structured around time.

MATRIX QUESTIONS. Individual questions that have the same response categories can be organized into a *table*. Particularly useful in the design of *self-completion surveys*.

MEAN. A *measure of central tendency*. All the values in a distribution are added together and divided by the number of observations. The mean is affected by extreme values.

MEASUREMENT TOOLS. See *indicators*.

MEASURE OF CENTRAL TENDENCY. A single statistical measure that summarizes the distribution of values in a variable. There are different measures of central tendency according to the *level of measurement* of the data. See *mean, median, mode*.

MEASURE OF DISPERSION. A statistical measure that summarizes the amount of spread or variation in the distribution of values in a variable. See *standard deviation* and *variance*.

MEASURES OF ASSOCIATION. Statistical measures that summarize the relationship between two variables. There are different measures of association according to the *levels of measurement* of the two variables. See *correlation, Pearson's r, Kendall's tau-a, -b or -c, Spearman's rank order correlation* (rho), *phi, Cramer's V*.

MEASURES OF SIGNIFICANCE. See *hypothesis testing*.

MEDIAN. A *measure of central tendency*. Scores are placed in rank order, from lowest to highest. The value in the middle position is the median. Where two values occupy the middle position, they should be added together and divided by 2. Used for ordinal variables and sometimes interval variables. Unlike the mean, the median is not sensitive to extreme values.

MEDIATIONS. Intervening variables that impact upon the influence of *independent variables* and *dependent variables*. Mediations may inhibit, enhance, change or cancel out causal mechanisms at work between other variables.

MEMOS. Notes made by the researcher in the process of data collection and/or data analysis. Memos may be separate, linked to particular data, or collected to form a research diary (an account of the research process itself).

MESOKURTIC. A term used to describe *kurtosis* where the distribution is symmetrical.

METHOD. The actual process used to collect data. See also *ontology, epistemology, methodology*.

METHODOLOGY. General principles and traditions of data collection. See also *ontology, epistemology, method*.

MISSING VALUES. Data that have not been recorded.

MIXED METHODS. Also called multi-method. Research design using more than one data collection technique. This may or may not involve the mixing of qualitative and quantitative data.

MODE. A *measure of central tendency*. It is the most frequently occurring value in a distribution of scores.

MODELS. Mapping devices designed to represent the relationship between key elements in a field of study. Models may be predictive, causal or descriptive, and may be discursive, mathematical or graphical.

MODERATOR. See *facilitator*.

MONOGRAPHS. Term used to refer to a book devoted to outlining a single research project. In its narrower usage the term refers to a single book devoted to outlining the conduct and findings of a particular ethnographic or case study project.

MULTI-METHOD. See *mixed methods*.

MULTIPLE LINEAR REGRESSION. A data modelling technique used where the independent and dependent variables are on a continuous interval or ratio scale and a linear relationship between the independent and dependent variable(s) is assumed. Models with only one independent variable are known as *simple linear regression* models.

MULTIPLE RESPONSE QUESTIONS. Survey questions that ask respondents to select more than one item from a category list.

MULTIPLE RESPONSE SETS. SPSS allows for variables derived from *multiple response questions* to be combined for analysis purposes into a multiple response set.

MULTI-STAGE SAMPLING. A sampling technique that involves case selection at different stages. For example, a *random sample* of universities is selected. Within this university sample, a further random sample of students is selected.

MUTUALLY EXCLUSIVE.   Phrase used to refer to *categories* whose content does not overlap.

MYTH.   Semiotic term for when a *sign* becomes the *signifier* for a deeper meaning (such as SNAKE standing for Evil). See also *semiology*.

NARRATIVE.   The construction of process/sequence within a text. *Narrative analysis* seeks to study the textual devices at work in such constructions.

NARRATIVE ANALYSIS.   Form of *discourse analysis* dealing with the construction of *narrative* sequence within *text*.

NATION-STATE.   A state that is characterized by defined geographical borders and a government that has sovereign power.

NATURALISM, NATURALISTIC.   Research that takes place outside *controlled conditions*.

NECESSARY CONDITION.   A factor that is essential to an outcome. See also *sufficient condition*.

NETWORK DIAGRAM (FLOWS AND LINKS).   Graphic representational model designed to show links between variables or codes within a dataset.

NODES.   Term referring to *coding* terms in NVivo (qualitative data analysis software). Nodes can be organized into trees, sets or cases, or they can remain as free nodes.

NOMINAL.   A *level of measurement* where response categories cannot be placed into any specific order and no judgement can be made about the relative size or distance of one category to another.

NON-EQUIVALENT CONTROL GROUP.   A quasi-experimental research design in which subjects are divided into experimental and control groups according to naturally occurring features.

NON-EXPERIMENTAL RESEARCH DESIGN.   Research designs that do not adhere to the experimental designs that originated from the natural sciences.

NON-INTRUSIVE DATA COLLECTION.   Collection of data that does not involve interaction with those to whom the data refer. Examples might be forms of hidden *observation*, collection of *official statistics*, or analysing the contents of people's rubbish bins.

NON-PARAMETRIC TESTS.   Non-parametric tests are statistical tests that are based on distributions other than the *normal distribution curve*. They are used where the population characteristics do not meet the normal curve and/or the *sample size* is small.

NON-PROBABILITY-BASED SAMPLING. Sampling methods that do not select cases randomly from a *sampling frame* of all members of the target population. See also *snowball sampling, opportunity sampling, purposive sampling*.

NON-RESPONSE. Failure of a case to provide a response to a question. Non-response can occur for a number of reasons: poor question construction can mean that the respondent is unable to answer; the question is not applicable; or refusal to answer. Non-response is recorded as missing data.

NORMAL DISTRIBUTION CURVE. The normal distribution curve is a theoretical curve whose properties are that it is bell-shaped with the population *mean* in the middle.

NORMATIVE. A statement containing or based upon an ethical judgement. Opposite of *positive*.

NUD*IST. See *NVivo/N6*.

NULL HYPOTHESIS. Used in *hypothesis testing*. States that there is no difference between the observed values and those found in the stated theoretical model.

NVIVO/N6. Qualitative data analysis software packages descended from NUD*IST (Non-Numerical Unstructured Data * Indexing Searching and Theorizing).

OBJECTIVE, OBJECTIVITY. A proposition that is not biased or distorted by particular motives. Science seeks to present the 'truth'. Objectivity is the lack of a *standpoint*. Not every social researcher accepts that this detachment is either possible or desirable.

OBSERVATION. Form of data collection based upon recording observable events, whether in *controlled conditions* (such as in an experiment) or in *naturalistic* field conditions. Observation may be *overt* or *covert*, participant based or not.

OFFICIAL STATISTICS. Numerical data collected by government agencies and departments. A valuable source for *secondary research*.

ONE-TAILED TEST. A directional statistical test that states the direction of a test. For example, in a survey of males' and females' weekly income, a one-tailed test would state that one group, males, had a higher weekly income than the second group, females.

ONTOLOGY, ONTOLOGICAL. Branch of philosophy concerned with questions of what exists, or questions of being. See also *epistemology, methodology, method*.

OPEN CODING. Coding of textual data whereby the researcher reads through the text (of either open-ended questioning or primary texts), coding what they consider to be significant items as they go along. After this the researcher may choose to reorganize their *coding frame* by other forms of coding. Open coding is the opposite of *prescriptive coding*.

OPEN-ENDED OBSERVATION. Observation-based data collection method where the researcher seeks to allow important issues to emerge from time spent observing, rather than beginning with a fully prestructured set of things to look for, count or focus attention upon. As such, open-ended observation is a form of *induction*-based data collection.

OPEN-ENDED QUESTIONS. Questions that do not require the respondent to choose between a prescribed set of answers.

OPERATIONALIZATION. The 'translation' of theoretical concepts into measurable categories and variables.

OPPORTUNITY SAMPLING. Also called convenience or availability sampling. Selecting members of a sample as and when such members present themselves, such as stopping people in the street. Such sampling often involves *quota sampling*.

ORDINAL. An ordinal *level of measurement* is applied to categorical variables whose response categories can be placed into a rank order of importance: for example, *rating scales*. No mathematical calculations can be made in relation to the distance between the categories.

ORIENTALISM. The name given to the European study of Africa and Asia in the nineteenth and twentieth centuries. Heavily bound up with European colonialism, the creation of a *binary opposition* between a supposed occidental (Western) reason and oriental (Eastern) irrationality and backwardness was and some think continues to be used to justify domination.

OUTLIERS. Values in an *interval* variable that are at the extreme lower or upper end of a distribution. Outliers will influence the *mean* value.

OVERT RESEARCH. Research where those being researched are aware that the researcher is collecting data. Opposite of *covert research*.

PANEL STUDIES. A research study that surveys representative samples at two or more points in time.

PANOPTICISM. A particular form of *gaze* named after Jeremy Bentham's panoptic (all-seeing) prison design, in which guards at a central observation point were able to view each prisoner's cell whilst themselves being obscured. The principle of total observation was meant to instil discipline. It has been suggested that modern societies install forms of such all-seeing panopticism into everyday life with all manner of surveillance technologies.

PARAMETER.   A parameter is a *statistic* that is calculated from the *population*.

PARAMETRIC TESTS.   Statistical tests that are based on the assumptions of the *normal distribution curve*. They are normally applied to *interval* data.

PARTICIPANT ACTION RESEARCH.   Research where the researcher becomes involved in seeking to facilitate the goals of those being researched, and those being researched become involved in the design and conduct of the research.

PARTICIPANT OBSERVATION.   *Naturalistic* fieldwork-based research where the researcher takes up a role within the group they are researching. This may be *covert* or *overt*.

PATTERN CODES, SPECIFIC CODES.   Coding focused upon drawing out the specific characteristics of the texts being analysed, as distinct from summary codes that focus upon generic characteristics, such as who, what, when, where and so on.

PEARSON'S *r*.   A measure of association used to explore the association between two *interval* variables. The measure will vary from –1 to 0 to +1. A value of 0 means no association, a value of –1 means a negative association, and a value of +1 means a positive association.

PERCENTAGES.   A percentage is the proportion of observations for a certain value in a variable, divided by the total number of observations for that variable, multiplied by 100.

PERSPECTIVE.   Artistic devices used to create the illusion of three-dimensional depth in a two-dimensional image. The two main techniques are using diminishing size and shapes that shrink in the direction of a vanishing point (geometric perspective) and using shades and blues to create the impression of distance (atmospheric perspective).

PHENOMENOLOGY.   Tradition of social research and theory that attends to the experience of the world from the point of view of people, and which is critical of claims that external causal processes operate to generate social reality. The social world is seen as a social construction, and an achievement of people. Closely associated with *constructionism* and opposed to *realism* and *positivism*.

PHI.   A measure of association used when exploring the association between two categorical variables that are *dichotomies*. Calculated for 2 x 2 tables. Values will vary between 0 and 1. A value of 0 means no association and a value of 1 means a perfect association.

PHOTO-ELICITATION. The use of visual materials to prompt respondents to discuss a topic in the process of data collection.

PIE CHART. A graphical presentation suitable for *nominal* or *ordinal* variables. The circle, or pie, is divided into a number of slices. The size of each slice is determined by the number of observations in each category.

PILOT, PILOTING. Pre-testing of research instruments such as *questionnaires* or *interview schedules* with a small subsample of the target population to identify weaknesses within the data collection instrument.

PLATYKURTIC. A term used to describe negative *kurtosis* where a distribution is flat.

PLURALISM. See *mixed methods, triangulation*.

POETICS. Linguistic devices used to generate rhetorical effects within language. Often used as a means of persuasion in everyday language and in research writing. The poetics of language is therefore both a topic to be studied and a source of bias.

POLYSEMY. Polysemy is the notion that texts can be interpreted in a variety of ways (often referred to in the context of media or *discourse analysis*).

POPULATION. All members of the category under investigation. Sometimes, for practical purposes, the population is defined as all members of the *sampling frame* available, but this excludes the hidden population (those not identified within the sampling frame). Where there is no reasonably comprehensive sampling frame to draw a *random sample* of the population from, the researcher will need to use a non-probability sample to access members of the population they are interested in.

POSITIVE, POSITIVISM. Focus upon facts without reference to ethical judgements about them. A positive statement is non-*normative*. Positivism is the belief that knowledge of the world can be detached from *ethical* evaluation.

POST-CODING. The numerical coding of responses to *open-ended questions*.

POST-PRIMARY RESEARCH. Data collection conducted after a first round of data collection, either by similar methods or by alternative methods. Often conducted for the purpose of checking the *validity* of primary research findings.

PREDICTION. A statement about the future that can be tested if stated in a rigorous form (that is, as a *hypothesis*).

PREDICTIVE VALIDITY. Research findings that make predictions about future events are said to have predictive validity if the predicted events are measured at a subsequent point in time.

PRESCRIPTIVE CODING, PRE-EMPTIVE CODING. Codes developed from the review of prior research and theory in a field and not from the data collected. If research is designed to test a hypothesis, codes will often need to have been specified in advance.

PRESENTATION. To deliver verbally the details and findings from a piece of research.

PRIMARY RESEARCH. Data collection carried out by the researcher or research team that will analyse it. Distinct from *secondary research*.

PRIMARY SOURCES. Textual (and sometimes numerical) sources that were not produced originally for research purposes. Letters, newspaper articles and diaries are examples.

PROBABILITY SAMPLING. A sampling technique where the probability or likelihood that a sampling unit will be selected from a sampling frame is known. Usually associated with a *random sampling* technique.

PSYCHOANALYSIS. School of thought founded by the Austrian physician Sigmund Freud, initially aimed at overcoming unconscious neurotic conditions through the use of the 'talking cure'. Its key concepts of unconscious conflict, guilt, resistance, fantasy and transference have been used in the analysis of cultural artefacts such as films and advertising.

PURPOSIVE SAMPLING. Sampling based on the researcher's understanding of the field and emergent interests in it. Non-random or *non-probability-based sampling* method often associated with grounded theory and other qualitative methods.

QUALITATIVE. Refers to forms of data, data collection and data analysis that give priority to one or more of the following: meanings over numerical measurement, induction over deduction, constructionism, or phenomenology (attention to small-group interaction) over objectivism or realism (attention to social structures and constraints), and depth over generalizability.

QUANTITATIVE. Refers to forms of data, data collection and data analysis that give priority to one or more of the following: numerical measurement over meanings, deduction over induction, objectivism or realism (attention to social structures and constraints) over constructionism or phenomenology (attention to small-group interaction), and generalizability over depth.

QUARTILES. The values in a distribution can be placed into rank order and then divided into four equal parts or quartiles.

QUASI-EXPERIMENTAL DESIGN. A research design that is often used when a classic experimental design is not achievable. There are many variations of quasi-experimental design. The main feature is that test groups are allocated according to naturally occurring features.

QUESTIONNAIRE. Also called self-completion survey. A question-based data collection instrument designed to be distributed and filled in by the person responding without the presence of an interviewer. Questionnaires are structured but can have a degree of variation in the level to which expected answers are standardized.

QUESTIONNAIRE SURVEY. See *survey*.

QUOTA SAMPLING. Form of convenience, availability or *opportunity sampling* where the researcher seeks to fill certain quotas of different types of people from those they meet, such as on the street.

RANDOM SAMPLING. Sampling based on the random selection of units from a *sampling frame* of the whole target *population* (or as near to this as possible). This method is designed to give each member of the population an equal chance of being selected and so to minimize *sampling error* or *sampling bias*.

RANGE. The difference between the highest value and the lowest value in a distribution.

RANKING QUESTIONS. Questions that ask a respondent to assign a rank order to a series of categories: for example, placing a list of different foods into order of preference from 1 = lowest preference to 5 = highest preference.

RATING SCALES. Response categories that require the respondent to position their response on a scale: for example, the five-point rating scale of strongly agree, agree, neutral, disagree and strongly disagree.

RATIO. A *level of measurement* for continuous data that has a *true zero point*. Often combined with and referred to as *interval* data.

REALISM. Approach to the study of the natural and physical world which holds that beneath appearances there are causal mechanisms at work. Opposed to both *positivism* and *phenomenology* or *constructionism*.

RECEPTION THEORY. See *audience reception*.

RECODE, REGROUP. Values taken from one variable are reclassified into a new variable. For example, an interval variable recording age in years may be recoded into age groups.

RELATIONSHIP. Term used to refer to an association between variables, concepts or categories. Relationships may be causal in nature, but the identification of a relationship may not be sufficient grounds to demonstrate or identify a causal process.

RELIABILITY.   When a data collection instrument records the same phenomenon, it is said to be reliable. This does not mean consistency of results every time, only consistency in the way, for example, a question is understood by interviewees. If a question was interpreted differently each time it was asked, or an experimental set of conditions were experienced differently by different participants, the responses generated could not be said to be reliable. Reliability can be tested during *piloting*.

REPORT.   To deliver the details and findings from a piece of research in a written format.

REPRESENTATION.   When one thing stands for something else. The parallel can be drawn between political representation and media representation. Critical approaches to representation seek to identify the biases built into systems of representation that claim to be neutral.

RESEARCH DESIGN.   Provides the framework for the research process involving the collection and analysis of data.

RESEARCH HYPOTHESIS.   See *alternative hypothesis*.

RESEARCH METHODS.   Research techniques employed to collect data.

RESEARCH QUESTION.   Term used to refer to the focus of a research topic. A research question may form the broad agenda within which a researcher develops a *hypothesis* in order to test a prediction by *deduction*. Alternatively, where the researcher does not choose to test a hypothesis, the term is used to refer to the alternative strategy of *induction*, where research is designed to explore a theme rather than test a prediction.

RESPONSE RATE.   The proportion of cases who respond to participate in research. This can only be calculated where the total number of units in the *sampling frame* is known. The calculation is the number of respondents, divided by the total number of sampling units, multiplied by 100.

ROUTING OR FUNNELLING QUESTIONS.   Questions that direct a respondent to answer specific questions in a survey.

ROW MARGINAL.   The row totals in a *contingency table*.

ROW PERCENTAGE.   A percentage calculated in a *contingency table* where the percentage of a cell count is calculated according to the *row marginal* (also called row total).

SAMPLE. A subsection of the total target *population* selected to participate in research. Various sampling methods seek to gain an accurate cross-section of the population, but differences in the nature of populations require different techniques in particular circumstances.

SAMPLE SIZE. The total number of sampling units, or cases, selected from the *sampling frame*.

SAMPLE STATISTIC. A statistical measure that is calculated from the sample data: for example, the mean age of a sample of 100 men.

SAMPLING. See *sample*.

SAMPLING BIAS. A sample can be biased if it over-represents and/or under-represents cases or groups of cases from the *population*. Bias can occur for a number of different reasons including *sampling error* and *non-response*. Sampling bias is problematic when the researcher wishes to apply *inferential statistics* to their data as these are based on the underlying assumption that the collected data are representative of the population being researched. *Weighting* techniques can be used to correct some sampling bias.

SAMPLING ERROR. The difference between the population *parameter* and the *sample statistic*. The smaller the sampling error, the more representative is the sample of the population. Sampling error is determined by the sample size and the variability of the variable being collected in the population.

SAMPLING FRAME. Database of all members of a target *population*, or as near to that goal as is possible. A sampling frame may already exist for some populations, or it may have to be created by the researcher in other cases. In some situations, no sampling frame can be generated and the researcher needs to adopt *non-probability-based sampling* methods. A sampling frame allows the researcher to use *random sampling* such that each member of the population has an equal chance of being selected.

SAMPLING UNITS. Cases that are selected for inclusion in the sample to be surveyed.

SAMPLING VARIABILITY. Samples drawn from the same population will produce different sample statistics. For example, repeated random samples from the same population will produce different *means* and *standard deviations*.

SATURATION. See *data saturation*.

SCALE. An alternative term for interval or ratio *levels of measurement*.

SCATTERPLOT. A graphical presentation of the relationship between two interval variables. For each case a position plot is marked according to the values for the *independent variable x* and the *dependent variable y*. The independent variable is on the horizontal axis and the dependent variable is on the vertical axis.

SCHEDULE.   A timetable that details the order of planned events.

SCOPOPHELIA.   Psychoanalytic term referring to the pleasure derived from looking, and often associated with fetishism.

SCORE.   The number of observed occurrences of a particular event or response. Also known as a count.

SECONDARY DATA.   See *secondary sources*.

SECONDARY DATA ANALYSIS.   Research based upon the reanalysis of data collected during previous research projects. See also *secondary research*. As there is no primary research stage in secondary data analysis, the terms 'secondary research' and 'secondary data analysis' are often used to mean the same thing, though in the strict sense the former term covers the wider aspects of research design and the selection and accessing of data sources and archives.

SECONDARY RESEARCH.   Research where the researcher uses the *primary research* of others to carry out secondary data analysis of their own. Also called *secondary data analysis*.

SECONDARY SOURCES.   Existing data, whether numerical or textual, that were gathered by others at some prior time for the purpose of research. Diaries and letters would not count. Also called secondary data.

SELF-COMPLETION SURVEY.   A quantitative research method that consists of a series of predetermined questions that are answered by a respondent. Normally consists of a mixture of closed-ended questions and open-ended questions.

SEMANTIC DIFFERENTIAL SCALES.   A scale that requires a respondent to indicate their position on an issue on a numerical scale between two extremes. The end of each scale represents an extreme position. An example is dull to fun with a 10-point scale of 0 to 9.

SEMIOLOGY, SEMIOTICS.   The science of signs, semiology studies the organization of meaning within language. A *sign* is the combination of a *signifier* and a *signified*. When a sign becomes a signifier for another deeper meaning, this is referred to as myth or mythic language.

SIGN.   A meaningful linguistic unit.

SIGNIFICANCE TESTING.   See *hypothesis testing*.

SIGNIFIED. A concept.

SIGNIFIER. A word/image or other representational unit.

SIMPLE LINEAR REGRESSION. Simple linear regression allows the researcher to build a model of the relationship between an *independent* and a *dependent variable*. It is concerned with finding the line of best fit between two *interval variables* on a *scatterplot*. See also *multiple linear regression*.

SKEWNESS. A statistical measure that indicates the position of lower and higher values of a distribution. A positively skewed distribution will have a greater number of observations at the higher values. Negatively skewed distributions will have a greater number of observations at the lower values.

SNOWBALL SAMPLING. Identifying subsequent members of a sample by asking current members of the sample to identify other participants with the required characteristics. Often used where no *sampling frame* can be identified or constructed. See also *non-probability-based sampling*.

SOCIAL CONSTRUCTIONISM. See *constructionism*.

SOCIAL CONSTRUCTIVISM. See *constructionism*.

SOCIAL STRUCTURES. Architectural/biographical metaphor seeking to highlight the objective constraints imposed upon individuals by social institutions such as the family, school, state or market.

SOCIAL SURVEY. A generic term used to describe *self-completion surveys* and *structured interview* methods.

SOCIOLOGICAL CODES. Codes that are based on theoretical concepts, not the language of those who generated the texts being analysed. The researcher may want to highlight theoretical links beneath the diversity of descriptions of what they believe to be the same thing. Opposite of *open coding* and of *in vivo coding*.

SPEARMAN'S RANK ORDER CORRELATION. Can also be referred to as Spearman's rho. A measure of association used where the relationship is between two ordinal variables or an *interval* and an *ordinal* variable. A value of 0 means no association, a value of −1 means a negative association, and a value of +1 means a positive association.

SPLIT FILE. A technique in SPSS for dividing the data into groups according to the categories in a nominal or ordinal variable. For example, grouping cases according to whether they are male or female.

SPSS. Statistical Products and Service Solutions. A data and statistical analysis software program.

SPURIOUS. Also called spuriousness. Occurs where a relationship between an independent and a dependent variable is either altered or removed by the introduction of a third or *control variable*. Spuriousness is detected through the process of *elaboration*.

STANDARD DEVIATION. A *measure of dispersion* that summarizes the spread of scores in a distribution. See also *variance*.

STANDARD ERROR. The *standard deviation* of the sample *means*.

STANDARDIZED QUESTIONS. Questions, whether in an *interview* or a *questionnaire*, which require the respondent to select from a prescribed set of responses. Opposite of *open-ended questions* (otherwise called unstandardized questions) and open coding at the data analysis stage.

STANDARDIZED SCORES. Also called Z-scores. The conversion of an *interval value* into a standard score. The resulting score is expressed in units of *standard deviation*. It is useful when comparing an individual's score on two measures where each has a different mean and standard deviation.

STANDPOINT. A perspective from which to see the world and which influences the way you see things. Objectivists seek to detach science from such a position. Standpoint theorists have rejected this view, seeing *objectivity* as the ideology of the social engineer's standpoint.

STATISTIC. A numeric summary of a range of *values*.

STEM AND LEAF DIAGRAM. A technique for exploring the values in an *interval* variable. Unlike other techniques for interval variables (*histogram, box plot, line graph*), the stem and leaf diagram displays the actual data.

STRATIFIED SAMPLING. Selecting in advance to represent particular social groups or strata within the sample, and in particular proportions (often based on prior knowledge or estimations of the distribution of those strata within the target population). A useful technique when seeking to select small groups whose representation within a random sample may be statistically insignificant, but whose characteristics are of particular interest to the researcher.

STRUCTURED INTERVIEW. An interview where the interviewer asks a series of predetermined questions to the interviewee.

STRUCTURED QUESTIONS. A data collection instrument (*questionnaire* or *interview*) where the wording and sequence of the questions is prescribed. Opposite of the unstructured interview (which is rare). Semi-structured interviews involve a degree of flexibility in wording and sequence.

SUFFICIENT CONDITION. Factor whose presence is sufficient to bring about a particular outcome. There is no such thing as a singular sufficient condition. Often a factor may be a *necessary condition*, but other factors will also be necessary. Confusing necessary and sufficient conditions is a common logical error.

SUMMARY CODES. See *pattern codes, specific codes*.

SURVEY. A specific approach to collecting social data. It involves collecting the same data from all cases in a *sample* or from all cases in a *census*. The data collection techniques associated with the survey include the questionnaire, the telephone interview and the structured interview.

SYMBOL. An image or object which, by convention, stands for something else. See also *icon*. Symbols tend to be more abstract than icons, or it may be suggested that icons are the most concrete forms of symbolic representation.

SYSTEMATIC CODES. Systematic coding involves going through the text to be analysed and identifying all the emerging themes that the researcher can find. Distinct from *axial codes*.

SYSTEMATIC REVIEW. A form of *literature review* that uses a systematic approach to identify and synthesize the research evidence.

SYSTEMATIC SAMPLING. A probability sampling technique involving the selection of sampling units from a *sampling frame* according to the proportion of the sample size to the total units in the sampling frame. For example, if a sample of 10 per cent is required from a sampling frame of 1000, every tenth unit would be selected.

TABLES. Representational device used to present *frequencies* and *cross-tabulations* in the field of quantitative data and which are also used in the presentation of qualitative data, either for highlighting numerical aspects of textual data or in presenting selected textual materials. See also *matrix display*.

TELEPHONE INTERVIEW. A survey conducted using a telephone.

TENDENCIES. Where a significant, but not constant, relationship is observed between a preceding factor and a consequent 'outcome', a tendency is said to exist. While some poor people are healthy and some wealthy people are unhealthy, it is still true that there is a tendency for income to be positively associated with health.

TEXT, TEXTUAL. Any representational device that carries meaning. Text in the more restricted meaning refers to forms of writing, but has been extended in the form of textual analysis to refer to anything that can be 'read' (such as an advertisement, a piece of music or a film). This approach sees all social phenomena as 'text'. See also *discourse analysis, genre, narrative analysis, semiology*.

THEORETICAL SAMPLING. See *purposive sampling*.

TIME-ORDERED DISPLAY. When exploring a relationship between two variables, the researcher needs to ensure that the *independent variable* naturally occurs in time before the *dependent variable*.

TOTAL PERCENTAGE. A percentage calculated in a *contingency table* where the percentage of a cell count is calculated according to the total count of observations in the table.

TRANSCENDENTALIST. See *deontological ethics*.

TRANSCRIPTION. The transfer of spoken words into written text. Today this is usually from a recording device into a computer file.

TRANSCRIPTION NOTATION. Highly complex form of transcription developed by *conversation analysts* to capture the many subtle pauses, crossovers and changes of intonation characteristic of talk, but which are not easily conveyed within the normal conventions of transcription.

TRIANGULATION. Approaching the same topic from a number of different approaches. Triangulation may involve the use of more than one researcher or research team, more than one round of data collection, different types of data collection, or different theoretical frameworks.

TRUE ZERO POINT. The defining characteristic of a *ratio* variable. A true zero point allows for the following type of calculation to be made: if person A is aged 20 years and person B is aged 40 years, person B is twice the age of person A.

TURN-TAKING. The focus of attention in *conversation analysis* where the expectation is built into talk that one person speaks after another. From this seemingly trivial observation, conversation analysis develops interesting accounts of hidden expectations that are the machinery within talk.

TWO-STEP FLOW MODEL. Approach to audience reception which places individual belief within processes of group influence.

TWO-TAILED TEST. Non-directional statistical tests that do not impose a specific direction on the tests. For example, in a survey of males' and females' weekly incomes, a two-tailed test would test to see if there was a significant difference in the incomes of men and women. It would not state if males earned more than females, only that there was a difference.

TYPE I ERROR.   The incorrect rejection of the *null hypothesis*, where the conclusion was that there was a real difference when one did not exist. Used in *hypothesis testing*.

TYPE II ERROR.   The incorrect acceptance of the *null hypothesis*, concluding that there was no real difference when in fact a real difference did exist.

UNIVARIATE ANALYSIS.   Analysis of quantitative data that describes and summarizes a single variable.

UNSTANDARDIZED QUESTIONS.   See *open-ended questions*.

USES AND GRATIFICATIONS THEORY.   Approach to audience reception that highlights the way audiences choose what to view. Any link between media messages and audience beliefs is said to be the result of self-selection rather than media influence.

VALID COUNT.   The total number of valid responses made to a question and recorded in a single variable. The valid count is derived from the total count in a sample minus the count of missing data.

VALIDITY (EXTERNAL, INTERNAL).   External validity refers to the degree to which data from a *sample* are *generalizable* to the wider target *population*. Internal validity refers to the extent to which the data collected accurately reflect the reality of the beliefs or behaviours of those from whom those data were collected.

VALID PERCENTAGE.   A percentage that is calculated based on the total *valid count*.

VALUE FREEDOM.   Belief commonly held in the natural sciences that there are no meaningful *ethical* issues regarding the nature or use of its subject matter, the physical and natural world, and that research in those fields can be purely *objective*. This view is not common in the social sciences.

VALUE LABEL.   A descriptive label that is applied to the coded response categories of nominal or ordinal variables in SPSS.

VALUE NEUTRALITY.   The proposition that while any choice to research one topic rather than another contains a value-based element, once chosen it is possible and necessary to detach values from *objective* data collection and analysis.

VALUES (AS DISTINCT FROM FACTS).   Normative or *ethical* positions held either by a researcher or by those being researched. Values in this sense may be the subject of the research, the motivation behind research, or a potential source of bias in research. Some would argue that certain biases are 'correct', and are not therefore distortions.

VALUES (WITHIN A VARIABLE).   If a variable is any unit (characteristic, code or attribute) whose value can vary, values are a range of possible variations available to that variable.

VARIABLE.   Any unit of data collection whose value can vary. See *level of measurement*.

VARIABLE LABEL.   A descriptive label that is applied to all variables in SPSS.

VARIABLE NAME.   A name applied to a variable in SPSS.

VARIANCE.   The square of *standard deviation*.

VISUAL AIDS.   Equipment that the researcher can use to enhance a presentation: for example, using an overhead projector to present transparencies.

VISUAL ANALYSIS.   Methods designed to identify the meaning of images. These methods include semiotics, psychoanalysis, discourse and content analysis, compositional analysis and audience reception analysis.

VISUAL DATA.   Data that are non-numerical and non-textual in the sense of simply words (though often images are read as meaningful texts). Increasingly, film, photography, digital imagery and drawing are being used as data.

VISUAL EXPERIENCE.   Term used to distinguish the attempts to use visual analysis to identify meaning in images, and the claim that images convey emotional content, not reducible to language.

VISUAL REDUCTION.   The use of representational devices (tables, diagrams, maps and graphs) to allow patterns within complex textual or numerical data to stand out.

WEIGHTING.   This is a data manipulation technique that is applied to data to take into account biases in the data due to sampling error. While sampling technique can help minimize *sampling bias*, issues of *non-response* can impact on the final characteristic of the sample in the data file. If sampling bias is considered problematic and if sufficient reliable data are available on the population characteristics (for example from Census data or other population-based surveys) then it is possible to perform a calculated correction to the data based on one or more of the key variables.

WITHIN-CASE DISPLAY. Graphical devices (tables, charts and so on) designed to highlight the existence or non-existence of patterns within cases, as distinct from *cross-case displays*.

YATES'S CONTINGENCY CORRECTION. See *continuity correction*.

Z-SCORES. See *standardized scores*.

REFERENCES

Adorno, Theodor and Horkheimer, Max (1979) *The Dialectic of Enlightenment*. London: Verso.

Agresti, Alan and Finlay, B. (2008) *Statistical Measures for the Social Sciences* (4th edn). London: Pearson Education.

Alexander, Victoria (2008) 'Analysing Visual Materials', in Nigel Gilbert (ed.), *Researching Social Life* (3rd edn). London: Sage. pp. 462–81.

Aldridge, Alan and Levine, Ken (2001) *Surveying the Social World: Principles and Practice in Survey Research*. Buckingham: Open University Press.

Allan, S., Adam, B. and Carter, C. (eds) (1999) *Environmental Risks and the Media*. London: Routledge.

Ames, Genevieve M., Duke, Michael R., Moore, Roland S. and Cunradi, Carol B. (2009) 'The impact of occupational culture on drinking behaviour of young adults in the US Navy', *Journal of Mixed Methods Research*, 3 (2): 129–50.

Anderson, A. (1997) *Media, Culture and the Environment*. London: UCL.

Anderson, A., Petersen, A. and David, M. (2004) 'Communication or Spin? Source-Media Relations in Science Journalism', in Allen, S. (ed.), *Journalism: Critical Issues*, Milton Keynes, Open University Press. pp. 188–98.

Arber, S. (2001) 'Secondary analysis of survey data', in N. Gilbert (ed.), *Researching Social Life* (2nd edn). London: Sage. pp. 269–86.

Aries, Elizabeth and Seider, Maynard (2005) 'The Interactive Relationship Between Class Identity and the College Experience: The Case of Lower Income Identity', *Qualitative Sociology*, 28 (4): 419–33.

Argyous, G. (2000) *Statistics for Social and Health Research*. London: Sage.

Atkinson, J.M. (1978) *Discovering Suicide: Studies in the Social Organisation of Sudden Death*. Basingstoke: Macmillan.

Atkinson, J.M. and Heritage, John (1984) *Structures of Social Action: Studies in Conversation Analysis*. Cambridge: Cambridge University Press.

Atkinson, P. (1992) *Understanding Ethnographic Texts*. London: Sage.

Atkinson, R. (1998) *The Life Story Interview*. London: Sage.

Atkinson, R. and Flint, J. (2001) *Accessing Hidden and Hard-to-Reach Populations: Snowball Research Strategies*. Social Research Update Issue 33. University of Surrey.

Babbie, Earl and Halley, Fred (2007) *Adventures in Social Research: data analysis using SPSS for Windows* (2nd edn). Thousand Oaks, CA: Pine Forge.

Ball, S., Davies, J., David, M. and Reay, D. (2002) 'Classification and Judgement: social class and the "cognitive structures" of choice of Higher Education', *British Journal of Sociology of Education*, 23 (1): 51–72.

Balnaves, M. and Caputi, P. (2001) *Introduction to Quantitative Research Methods: An Investigative Approach*. London: Sage.

Banks, M. (2001) *Visual Methods in Social Research*. London: Sage.

Barnes, Barry (2000) *Understanding Agency: Social Theory and Responsible Action*. London: Sage.

Barr, H., Hammick, M., Koppel, I. and Reeves, S. (1999) 'Evaluating Interprofessional Education: two systematic reviews', *British Educational Research Journal*, 25 (4): 533–45.

Barthes, R. (1967) *Elements of Semiology*. London: Cape.

Barthes, R. (1973) *Mythologies*. London: Paladin.

Barthes, Roland (2000) *Mythologies*. London: Vintage Classics.

Bauman, Zygmunt (1991) *Modernity and Ambivalence*. Cambridge: Polity Press.

Bauman, Z. and May, T. (2001) *Thinking Sociologically*. Oxford: Blackwell.

Bazeley, Pat (2007) *Qualitative Data Analysis with NVivo*. London: Sage.

Bazeley, P. and Richards, L. (2000) *The NVivo Qualitative Project Book*. London: Sage.

Becker, H. (1967) 'Whose side are we on?', *Social Problems*, 14: 239–47.

Becker, H. and Geer, B. (1960) 'Participant observation: the analysis of qualitative field data', in R.N. Adams and J. J. Preiss (eds), *Human Organization Research*. Homewood, IL: Dorsey. pp. 267–89.

Becker, Howard (1986) *Writing for Social Scientists*. Chicago, IL: University of Chicago Press.

Becker, H. Geer, B., Hughes, E.C. and Strauss, A.L. (1961) *Boys in White: Student Culture in Medical School*. Chicago, IL: University of Chicago Press.

Becker, Lucinda and Van Emden, Joan. (2004) *Presentation Skills for Students*. London: Palgrave.

Bell, Colin and Newby, Howard (1971) *Community Studies: An Introduction to the Sociology of the Local Community*. London: Allen and Unwin.

Belson, William A. (1981) *The Design and Understanding of Survey Questions*. London: Gower.

Benson, Douglas and Hughes, John (1991) 'Evidence and Inference', in Graham Button (ed.), *Ethnomethodology and the Human Sciences*. Cambridge: Cambridge University Press. pp. 109–36.

Bentham, Jeremy (1879) *An Introduction to the Principles of Morals and Legislation*. Oxford: Clarendon Press.

Berelson, B. (1952) *Content Analysis in Communication Research*. New York: Hafner.

Berg, Bruce L. (1998) *Qualitative Research Methods for the Social Sciences*. Needham Heights, MA: Allyn and Bacon.

Berg, Bruce (2007) *Qualitative Research Methods for the Social Sciences* (7th edn). Needham Heights, MA: Allyn and Bacon.

Bergner, M., Bobbitt, A., Carter W.B. and Gilson, B.S. (1981) 'The Sickness Impact Profile: development and final version of a health status measure', *Medical Care*, 19: 787–805.

Beveridge, W. (1942) *Social Insurance and Allied Services*. London: HMSO.

Bhaskar, Roy (1979) *The Possibility of Naturalism*. Brighton: Harvester.

Black, D. (1992) *Inequalities in Health: The Black Report*. London: Penguin.

Black, T. (1999) *Doing Quantitative Research in the Social Sciences: An Integrated Approach to Research Design, Measurement and Statistics*. London: Sage.

Blalock, H. (1960) *Social Statistics* (2nd edn). Boston, MA: McGraw-Hill.

Blumer, Herbert (1956) 'Sociological Analysis and the "Variable"', *American Sociological Review*, 21 (6): 683–90.

Bouma, Gary D. and Atkinson, G.B.J. (1995) *A Handbook of Social Science Research*. Oxford: Oxford University Press.

Bourdieu, Pierre (1986) *Distinction: A Social Critique of the Judgement of Taste*. London: Routledge.

Bourdieu, Pierre (2004) *Science of Science and Reflexivity*. Cambridge: Polity.

Bowles, Samuel and Gintis, Herbert (1976) *Schooling in Capitalist America*. New York: Basic Books.

Bradbury, Andrew (2006) *Successful Presentations* (3rd edn). London: Kogan Page.

Brewer, John (2000) *Ethnography*. Buckingham: Open University Press.

British Sociological Association (2002) Statement of the ethical practice for the British Sociological Association. http://www.britsoc.co.uk/equality/Statement+Ethical+Practice.htm Accessed 02/02/2010.

Bryant, L., Evans, J., Sutton, C. and Beer, J. (2002) *The Experience of Rural Deprivation and Exclusion*. Plymouth: Social Research and Regeneration Unit, University of Plymouth.

Bryant, L., Sutton, C. and Bunyard, T. (2000) *The Integration of Sea Service: Evaluation Study*. Plymouth: Social Research and Regeneration Unit, University of Plymouth.

Bryman, Alan (1988) *Quantity and Quality in Social Research*. London: Routledge.

Bryman, Alan (2001) *Social Research Methods*. Oxford: Oxford University Press.

Bryman, Alan (2006) 'Integrating Quantitative and Qualitative Research: How is it done?', *Qualitative Research*, 6: 97–113.

Bryman, Alan (2004) *Social Research Methods* (2nd edn). Oxford: Oxford University Press.

Bryman, Alan (2008) *Social Research Methods* (3rd edn). Oxford: Oxford University Press.

Bryman, Alan and Cramer, Duncan (1997) *Quantitative Data Analysis with SPSS for Windows: A Guide for Social Scientists*. London: Routledge.

Bryman, Alan and Cramer, Duncan (2000) *Quantitative Data Analysis with SPSS for Windows Release 10: A Guide for Social Scientists*. London: Routledge.

Bulmer, Martin (1984) *The Chicago School of Sociology: Industrialization, diversity, and the rise of sociological research*. Chicago, IL: University of Chicago Press.

Bulmer, Martin (2008) 'The Ethics of Social Research', in Gilbert, Nigel (ed.), *Researching Social Life* (3rd edn). London: Sage. pp. 145–61.

Burgess, Robert G. (1984) *In the Field*. London: Allen and Unwin.

Burgess, Robert (ed.) (1993) *Education Research and Evaluation: For Policy and Practice?* London: Falmer.

Burton, Dawn (ed.) (2000) *Research Training for Social Scientists*. London: Sage.

Button, Graham (1990) 'Going up a blind alley conflating conversation analysis and computational modelling', in Pauline M. Luff (ed.), *Computers and Conversation*. London: Academic Press. pp.67–90.

Button, Graham, (ed.) (1991) *Ethnomethodology and the Human Sciences*. Cambridge: Cambridge University Press.

Calder, B.T. (1977) 'Focus groups and the nature of qualitative marketing research', *Journal of Marketing Research*, 42: 702–37.

Campbell, Joseph (1993) *The Hero with a Thousand Faces*. London: Fontana.

Chambers, Paul and Thompson, Andrew (2005) 'Public Religion and Political Change in Wales', in *Sociology*, Vol. 39, No. 1, 29–46.

Charmaz, Kathy (1990) 'Discovering Chronic Illness: Using grounded theory', *Social Science and Medicine*, 30: 1161–72.

Charmaz, Kathy (2006) *Constructing Grounded Theory: A Practical Guide Through Qualitative Analysis*. London: Sage.

Child, Sue (2003) *From Tellers to Sellers: An Ethnographic Study of Retail Banking*. PhD thesis. Plymouth: University of Plymouth.

Chivers, Barbara (2007) *A Student's Guide to Presentations*. London: Sage.

Cicourel, Aaron (1968) *Method and Measurement in Sociology*. New York: Free Press.

Clarke, Alan and Dawson, Ruth (1999) *Evaluation Research: An Introduction to Principles, Methods and Practice*. London: Sage.

Clifford, J. (1988) *The Predicament of Culture: Twentieth-Century Ethnography, Literature, and Art*. Cambridge, Mass: Harvard University Press.

Cohen, Stanley (1985) *Visions of Social Control*. Cambridge: Cambridge University Press.

Collier, John Jr. and Collier, Malcolm (1986) *Visual Anthropology: Photography as a Research Method*. Albuquerque, NM: University of New Mexico Press.

Collins, Harry and Pinch, Trevor (1998) *The Golem at Large: What You Should Know About Technology*. Cambridge: Cambridge University Press.

Collins, P. (1998) 'Negotiating Selves: Reflections on "Unstructured" Interviewing', *Sociological Research Online*, 3 (3) www.socresonline.org.uk/3/3/2.html

Coomber, Ross (1997) 'Using the Internet for social research', *Sociological Research Online*, 2 (2): http://www.socresonline.org.uk/socresonline/2/2 /2.htm

Corbin, Juliet and Strauss, Anselm (2008) *Basics of Qualitative Research* (3rd edn). London: Sage.

Cottle, S. (1993) *TV News, Urban Conflict and the Inner City*. Leicester: Leicester University Press.

Cottle, S. (1999) 'TV news, lay voices and the visualisation of environmental risks', in S. Allan, B. Adam and C. Carter (eds), *Environmental Risks and the Media*. London: Routledge. pp. 29–44.

Countryside Agency (2000) *Rural Services in 2000: Working for People and Places in Rural England*. Northampton: Countryside Agency.

Countryside Agency (1999) *Working for People and Places in Rural England*. Northampton: Countryside Agency.

Cramer, D. (1994) *Introducing Statistics for Social Research: Step-by-step Calculations and Computer Techniques Using SPSS*. London: Routledge.

Cresswell, John W. (2008) *Research Design: Qualitative, Quantitative and Mixed Methods Approaches* (3rd edn). London: Sage.

Crompton, R., Gallie, D. and Purcell, K. (eds) (1996) *Changing Forms of Employment: Organisations, Skills and Gender*. London: Routledge.

Dahl, Robert (1969 [1961]) *Who Governs? Democracy and Power in an American City*. New Haven: Yale University Press.

Dale, Angela, Arber, Sara and Procter, Michael (1988) *Doing Secondary Analysis*. London: Unwin Hyman.

David, Matthew (2002) 'Problems of participation: the limits of action research', *International Journal of Social Research Methodology: Theory and Practice*, 5 (1): 11–17.

David, Matthew (2003) 'The politics of communication: information technology, local knowledge and social exclusion', in *Telematics and Informatics*, 20 (3): 235–53.

David, Matthew (2005a) *Science in Society*. London: Palgrave.

David, Matthew (2005b) 'Distance Learning, Telematics and Rural Social Exclusion', in: Marshall, Stewart, Taylor, Wal and Yu Xinghuo ed(s). *Encyclopedia of Developing Regional Communities with Information and Communication Technology*. Hershey PA, Idea Group Reference, 205–9.

David, Matthew (2006) 'Romanticism, Creativity and Copyright: Visions and Nightmares', in *European Journal of Social Theory*, Volume 9, Number 3. pp. 425–33.

David, Matthew (ed.) (2007) *Case Study Research* (volumes 1–4). London: Sage.

David, Matthew (2008) 'You Think Bart Simpson is Real. I Know He's Only an Actor!', *Current Sociology*, 56 (4): 517–33.

David, Matthew (2009) *Peer to Peer and the Music Industry: The Criminalization of Sharing*. London: Sage.

David, Matthew and Kirkhope, Jamieson (2006) 'The Impossibility of Technical Security: Intellectual property and the paradox of informational capitalism', in Lacy, Mark and Witkin, Peter (eds), *Global Politics in an Information Age*. Manchester: Manchester University Press. pp. 88–95.

David, Matthew and Zeitlyn, David (1996) 'What are they doing? Dilemmas in analysing bibliographic searching: cultural and technical networks in academic life', *Sociological Research Online*, 1 (4): http://www.socresonline.org/socresonline/1/4 /2.html

Delamont, Sara (2007) 'Ethnography and Participant Observation', in Silverman, David (ed.) *Qualitative Research Practice*. London: Sage. pp. 205–17.

Dey, Ian (1999) *Grounding Grounded Theory*. San Diago: Academic Press.

Deacon, D., Pickering, M., Golding, P. and Murdock, G. (1999) *Researching Communications: A Practical Guide to Methods in Media and Cultural Analysis*. London: Arnold.

Delanty, Gerard (2002) 'Constructivism, Sociology and the New Genetics', *New Genetics and Society*, 21 (3): 279–89.

Delbridge, R. (1998*) Life on the Line in Contemporary Manufacturing*. Oxford: Oxford University Press.

Denscombe, Martyn (2007) *The Good Research Guide: For Small-Scale Social Research Projects*. Buckingham: Open University Press.

Denzin, Norman (1978) 'The logic of naturalistic inquiry', in Denzin, N (ed.), *Sociological Methods: A Source Book*. New York: McGraw-Hill.

Denzin, Norman (1991) *Symbolic Interaction and Cultural Studies: The Politics of Interpretation*. Oxford: Blackwell.

Derrida, Jacques (1972) 'Structure, sign and play in the discourse of the human sciences', in R. Machsey and Press E. Donato (eds), *The Structuralist Controversy*. London: Johns Hopkins University.

DETR – Department of the Environment, Transport and the Regions (2000) *Indices of Deprivation 2000*. Regeneration Research Summary, Number 31.

de Vaus, David (1996) *Surveys in Social Research*. London: UCL Press.

de Vaus, David (2001) *Research Design in Social Research*. London: Sage.

de Vaus, D.A. (2002a) *Analyzing Social Science Data: 50 Key Problems in Data Analysis*. London: Sage.

de Vaus, D.A. (2002b) *Surveys in Social Research* (5th edn). London: UCL Press.

Dolnicar, Sara, Laesser, Christian and Matus, Katrina (2009) 'Online versus paper: format effects in tourism surveys', *Journal of Travel Research*, 47 (3) : 295–316.

Durkheim, E. (1952) *Suicide: A Study in Sociology*. London: Routledge.

Ebeling, Mary and Gibbs, Julie (2008) 'Searching and Reviewing Literature', in Gilbert, Nigel (ed.), *Researching Social Life*. London: Sage. pp. 63–79.

The Electoral Commission (2008) *Scotland – Poll Position: Public Attitudes Towards Scottish Parliamentary and Local Government*. www.electoralcommission.org.uk/_data/assets/electoral_commission_pdf_file/0005/16169/ScotPollPosition_23369-17390_E_N_S_W_.pdf

Ellen, Roy F. (1984) *Ethnographic Research – A Guide to General Conduct*. New York: Harcourt Brace.

Elliott, Jane (2005) *Using Narrative in Social Research: Qualitative and Quantitative Approaches*. London: Sage.

Elias, Norbert (1978) *What is Sociology?* New York: Columbia University Press.

Ellis, Lee (1994) *Research Methods in the Social Sciences*. Madison, WI: WCB Brown and Benchmark.

Emmison, Michael and Smith, Philip (2000) *Researching the Visual: Images, Objects, Contexts and Interactions in Social and Cultural Inquiry*. London: Sage.

The Evidence for Policy and Practice Information and Co-ordinating Centre – EPPI (2009) http://eppi.ioe.ac.uk/cms/

Ericson, R.V., Baranek, P.M. and Chan, J.B.L. (1991) *Representing Order: Crime, Law and Justice in the News Media*. Buckingham: Open University Press.

Fairclough, R. (1995) *Media Discourse*. London: Edward Arnold.

Fern, E.F. (1982) 'The use of focus groups for idea generation: the effects of group size, acquaintanceship, and moderator on response quantity and quality', *Journal of Marketing Research*, 19: 1–13.

Ferrie, J., Martikainen, P., Shipley, M., Marmot, M., Stansfeld, S. and Davey-Smith, G. (2001) 'Employment status and health after privatisation in white collar civil servants: prospective cohort study', *British Medical Journal*, 322: 1–7.

Fetterman, David (1998) *Ethnography: Step by Step* (2nd edn). London: Sage.

Field, Andy (2009) *Discovering Statistics using SPSS for Windows*. (3rd edn). London: Sage.

Fielding, Jane and Gilbert, Nigel (2000) *Understanding Social Statistics*. London: Sage.

Fielding, Jane and Gilbert, Nigel (2006) *Understanding Social Statistics*. Second Edition. London: Sage.

Fielding, Nigel (1981) *The National Front*. London: Routledge.

Fielding, Nigel (1995) 'Ethnography', in N. Gilbert (ed.), *Researching Social Life*. London: Sage. pp. 154–71.

Fielding, Nigel and Lee, Raymond (1998) *Computer Analysis and Qualitative Research*. London: Sage.

Fink, Arlene (1995a) *The Survey Kit: How to Ask Survey Questions*. Thousand Oaks, CA: Sage.

Fink, Arlene (1995b) *The Survey Kit: How to Sample in Surveys*. Thousand Oaks, CA: Sage.

Fink, Arlene (1995c) *How to Report on Surveys*. London: Sage.

Flick, U. (1992) 'Triangulation revisited: strategy of or alternative to validation of qualitative data', *Journal for the Theory of Social Behaviour*, 22, 175–97.

Foster, J. L. H. (2007) *Journeys through Mental Illness: Clients Experiences and Understandings of Mental Distress*. New York: Palgrave Macmillan.

Foucault, Michel (1977) 'Nietzsche, Genealogy, History', in D. F. Bouchard (ed.), *Language, Counter-Memory and Practice: Selected Essays and Interviews*. Ithaca: Cornell University Press. pp. 139–64.

Foucault, Michel (2001) *The Order of Things*. London: Routledge.

Fowler, Floyd (1995) *Improving Survey Questions: Design and Evaluation*. London: Sage.

Frank, A. W. (1995) *The wounded storyteller: Body, illness and ethics*. Chicago: University of Chicago Press.

Fuller, Steve (2000) *The Governance of Science*. Buckingham: Open university Press.

Gadamer, Hans-Georg *(1989) Truth and Method*. New York: Crossroads.

Garcia, Beatriz (2009) 'Impact 08–the Liverpool model: a framework for impact research in Liverpool, 2008 European Capital of Culture', in A. Taormina (ed.), *Osservare La Culture*. Milan: Edizioni Franco Angeli.

Garfinkel, Harold (1984) *Studies in Ethnomethodology*. Cambridge: Polity.

Garrett, C. J. (1997) 'Recovery from anorexia nervosa: A sociological perspective', *International Journal of Eating Disorders*, 21: 261–272

Gauntlett, David and Hill, Annette (1999) *TV Living: Television, Culture and Everyday Life*. London: Routledge.

Geertz, Clifford (1975 [1973]) 'Thick description: toward an interpretative theory of culture,' in: ibid. (ed.) *The Interpretation of Cultures: Selected Essays*, New York, Basic Books. pp. 3–30.

Gellner, Ernest (1992) *Postmodernism, Reason and Religion*. London: Routledge.

Giarchi, G. (1999) *The Overshadowed Districts of East Cornwall*. Plymouth: University of Plymouth.

Giddens, Anthony (1971) *Capitalism and Modern Social Theory: an analysis of the writings of Marx, Durkheim and Max Weber*. Cambridge: Cambridge University Press.

Giddens, Anthony (1986) *Sociology: A brief but critical introduction*. London: Palgrave Macmillan.

Gilbert, Nigel (ed.) (2001) *Researching Social Life* (2nd edn). London: Sage.

Glaser, Barney (1978) *Theoretical Sensitivity*. Mill Valley CA: The Sociology Press.

Glaser, Barney (1992) *Emergence vs Forcing: Basics of Grounded Theory Analysis*. Mill Valley, CA: Sociology Press.

Glaser, Barney and Strauss, Anselm (1999 [1967]) *The Discovery of Grounded Theory*. Chicago: Aldine Transaction.

Goffman, Erving (1959) *The Presentation of Self in Everyday Life*. Harmondsworth: Penguin.

Goffman, Erving (1968 [1961]) *Asylums: Essays on the Social Situation of Mental Patients and Other Inmates*. London: Pelican Books.

Goffman, Erving (1974) *Frame Analysis*, New York, NY: Harper.

Gold, R.L. (1958) 'Roles in Sociological Fieldwork', *Social Forces*, 36: 217–23.

Government Statistical Service (1998) *Harmonised Concepts and Questions for Government Social Surveys: Update December 1997*. London: Office for National Statistics.

Gouldner, Alvin (1968) 'The sociologist as partisan: Sociology and the Welfare State', in *American Sociologist*, May, 103–16.

Gouldner, Alvin (1979) *The Future of Intellectuals and the Rise of the New Class*. New York. Macmillan.

Graham, Bill (2000) *Case Study Research Methods*. London: Continuum.

Gray, David. E. (2009) *Doing Research in the Real World* (2nd edn). London: Sage

Green, Nicola (2008) 'Formulating and Refining a Research Question' in Gilbert, Nigel (ed.), *Researching Social Life* (3rd edn). London: Sage. pp. 43–61.

Greene, Jennifer C., Caracelli, Valerie J. and Graham, Wendy F. (1989) 'Toward a conceptual framework for mixed-method evaluation design.' *Educational Evaluation and Policy Analysis*, 11(3), 255–74.

Greene, Jennifer C., Caracelli, Valerie J., and Graham, Wendy F. (2008) 'Toward a conceptual framework for mixed-method evaluation designs', in Plano Clark, Vicki L. and Creswell, John W., *The Mixed Method Reader*. London: Sage.

Greenlaw, Corey and Sharon Brown-Welty (2009) 'A Comparison of Web-Based and Paper-Based Survey Methods: Testing Assumptions of Survey Mode and Response Cost', *Evaluation Review*, 33 (5): 464–80

Griffiths, P., Gossop, M., Powis, B. and Strang, J. (1993) 'Reaching hidden populations of drug users by privileged access interviewers: methodological and practical issues', *Addiction*, 88: 1617–26.

Grim, Brian, Harmon, Alison and Gromis, Judy (2006) 'Focus Group Interviews as an Innovative Quanti-Qualitative Methodology (QQM): Integrating Quantitative Elements into a Qualitative Methodology', *The Qualitative Report*, 11 (3): 516–37.

Habermas, Jürgen (1984) *The Theory of Communicative Action* (volume one). Cambridge: Polity.

Habermas, Jürgen (1987) *The Philosophical Discourse of Modernity*. Cambridge: Polity Press.

Habermas, Jürgen (1989) *The Theory of Communicative Action* (volume two). Cambridge: Polity.

Habermas, Jürgen (1992 [1962]) *The Structural Transformation of the Public Sphere*. Cambridge: Polity.

Hague, Paul N. and Roberts, Kate (1994) *Presentations and Report Writing*. London: Kogan Page.

Hakim, Catherine (1982) *Secondary Analysis in Social Research: A Guide to Data Sources and Methods with Examples*. London: Harper Collins.

Hakim, Catherine (2000) *Research Design: Successful Designs for Social and Economic Research* (2nd edn). London: Routledge.

Hall, Stuart, Chitcher, Chas, Jefferson, Tony and Clark, John N. (1978) *Policing the Crisis: Mugging, the State and Law and Order*. Basingstoke: Palgrave Macmillan.

Halliday, J. (1998) *Developing Rural Indicators: Findings from a Project in the Blackdown Hills*. Exeter: Devon County Council.

Hammersley, Martyn (1995) *The Politics of Social Research*. London: Sage.

Hammersley, Martyn (1998) *Reading Ethnographic Research* (2nd edn). London: Longman.

Hammersley, Martyn (2000) *Taking Sides in Social Research: Essays on Partisanship and Bias*. London: Routledge.

Hammersley, Martyn and Atkinson, Paul (1995) *Ethnography: Principles in Practice* (2nd edn). London: Routledge.

Hansen, A., Cottle, S., Negrine, R. and Newbold, C. (1998) *Mass Communication Research Methods*. Basingstoke: Macmillan.

Harding, J. (2006) 'Questioning the Subject in Biographical Interviewing', *Sociological Research Online* 11(3) www.socresonline.org.uk/11/3/harding.html

Harries-Jones, Peter (1991) *Making Knowledge Count*. London: McGill Queens University Press.

Hart, Chris (1998) *Doing a Literature Review*. London: Sage.

Hart, Chris (2001) *Doing a Literature Search*. London: Sage.

Heaney, Michael and Rojas, Fabio (2006) 'The Place of Framing: Multiple Audiences and Antiwar Protests near Fort Bragg', *Qualitative Sociology*, 29: 485–505.

Heritage, John (1997) 'Conversation analysis and institutional talk: analysing data', in David Silverman (ed.), *Qualitative Research: Theory, Methods and Practice*. London: Sage. pp. 161–82.

Hewson, Claire, Yule, Peter, Laurent, D. and Vogel, Carol. (2003) *Internet Research Methods: A Practical Guide of the Social and Behavioural Sciences*. London: Sage.

Hine, Christine (2000) *Virtual Ethnography*. London: Sage.

Hodkinson, Paul (2008) 'Grounded Theory and Inductive Research', in Nigel Gilbert (ed.), *Researching Social Life* (3rd edn). London: Sage. pp. 81–96.

Homan, Roger (1991) *The Ethics of Social Research*. Harlow: Longman.

Horowitz (1967) *The Rise and Fall of Project Camelot – Revised Edn: Studies in the Relationship between Social Science and Practical Politics*. Cambridge MA: MIT Press.

Howell, David C. (2007) *Fundamental Statistics for the Behavioral Sciences*, International edition. London: Wadsworth Publishing

Hsu, L.K., Crisp, A. H. and Callender, J. S. (1992) 'Recovery in anorexia nervosa – the patient's perspective', *International Journal of Eating Disorders,* 11 (4): 341–50.

Humphreys, Laud (1970) *The Tea Room Trade*. London: Duckworth.

Husserl, E. (1962) *Ideas: General Introduction to Pure Phenomenology*. New York: Collier.

Internet World Stats (2009) Usage and Population Stats. http://www.internetworldstats.com/stats.htm

Israel, Mark and Hay, Iain (2006) *Research Ethics for Social Scientists: Between ethical conduct and regulatory compliance*. London: Sage.

Jacobsen, John Kurt (2000) *Technical Fouls: Democratic Dilemmas and Technological Change*. Boulder Colorado: Westview.

Jagger, Elizabeth (2001) 'Marketing Molly and Melville: Dating in a postmodern consumer society', *Sociology*, 35 (1): 39–57.

Jenkinson, Crispin (ed.) (1994) *Measuring Health and Medical Outcomes*. London: UCL.

Junker, B. (1960) *Fieldwork*. Chicago, IL: University of Chicago Press.

Kanji, G.K. (1999) *100 Statistical Tests* (2nd edn). London: Sage.

Kant, Immanuel (1997) *Critique of Practical Reason*. Cambridge: Cambridge University Press.

Kather, G. (2009) *'Good'/'Bad' Citizens on the Margins? An Ethnographic Study of Political Participation in Two Northern English Towns*, thesis submitted in accordance with the requirements of the University of Liverpool for the degree of doctor in philosophy, March 2009.

Katz, Eluha and Lazarsfeld, Paul (2006) *Personal Influence: The Part Played by People in the Flow of Mass Communications*. New Brunswick NJ: Transaction Publishers.

Kelle, Udo (1997) 'Theory Building in Qualitative Research and Computer Programs for the Management of Textual Data', in *Sociological Research Online,* vol. 2, no. 2, http://www.socresonline.org.uk/socresonline/2/2/1.html

Kvale, S. (2009) *Interviews: An Introduction to Qualitative Research Interviewing* (2nd edn). Sage: London.

Keefer, Jane (1993) 'The hungry rats syndrome: information literacy, and the academic reference process', *RQ*, 32 (3): 333–9.

Kmietowicz, Z.W. and Yannoulis, Y. (1998) *Statistical Tables for Economic, Business and Social Studies*. Harlow: Longman Scientific and Technical.

Kohler Riessman, Catherine (1993) *Narrative Analysis*. London: Sage.

Kuhn, Thomas (1970 [1962]) *The Structure of Scientific Revolution*. Chicago: University of Chicago Press.

Kuper, Adam (1973) *Anthropology and Anthropologists*. London: Allen Lane.

Lacan, Jacques (2001) *Ecrits: A Selection*. London: Routledge.

Lawson, Tony and Garrod, Joan (1994) *The Complete A–Z Sociology Handbook*. London: Hodder and Stoughton Educational.

Lee, Raymond (1993) *Doing Research on Sensitive Topics*. London: Sage.

Lee, Raymond (2000) *Unobtrusive Methods in Social Research*. Buckingham: Open University Press.

Lévi-Strauss, Claude (1979) *Myth and Meaning*. New York: Schocken.

Lévi-Strauss, Claude (2001) *Myth and Meaning*, London, Routledge.

Lewins, Ann and Silver, Christina (2007) *Using Software in Qualitative Research: A Step-by-Step Guide*. London: Sage.

Lindley, D.V. and Scott, W.F. (1995) *New Cambridge Elementary Statistical Tables* (2nd edn). Cambridge: Cambridge University Press.

Lipset, Seymour Martin, Trow, Martin A. and Coleman, James S. (1956) *Union Democracy*. New York: The Free Press.

Lofland, J. and Lofland, L.H. (1995) *Analyzing Social Settings* (3rd edn). Belmont, CA: Wadsworth.

Lofland, John (1996) 'Analytic ethnography: features, failings, and futures', *Journal of Contemporary Ethnography*, 24 (1): 30–67.

Lowith, Karl (1993) *Max Weber and Karl Marx*. London: Routledge.

Lynd, Robert L. and Lynd, Helen Merrell (1929) *Middletown: A Study in Modern American Culture*. Chicago: University of Chicago Press.

McDonald, H. and S. Adam (2003) 'A Comparison of Online and Postal Data Collection Methods in Marketing Research', *Marketing Intelligence and Planning*, 21 (2): 85–95.

McDowell, Ian and Newell, Claire (1996) *Measuring Health: A Guide to Rating Scales and Questionnaires*. New York: Oxford University Press.

Macdonald, Keith (1989) 'Building Respectability', in *Sociology*, Volume 23, Number 1–pp. 55–80.

Mann, Chris and Stewart, Fiona (2000) *Internet Communication and Qualitative Research: A Handbook for Researching Online*. London: Sage.

Manning, Peter and Cullum-Swan, Betsy (1998) 'Narrative, content and semiotic analysis', in Norman K. Denzin and Yvonna S. Lincoln (eds), *Collecting and Interpreting Qualitative Materials*. London: Sage. pp. 246–73.

Marcuse, Herbert (1991 [1964]) *One Dimensional Man*. London: Routledge.

Markham, Annette N. and Baym, Nancy. K. (2009) *Internet Inquiry: Conversations about Method*. London: Sage.

Marsh, Catherine (1988) *Exploring Data: An Introduction to Data Analysis for Social Scientists*. Cambridge: Polity.

Matsueda, Ross. (2007) 'Labeling Theory.' *Blackwell Encyclopedia of Sociology*. Ritzer, George (ed.). Blackwell Publishing. Blackwell Reference Online. 04 October 2009. http://www.blackwellreference.com/subscriber/tocnode?id=g9781405124331_chunk_g978140512433118_ss1-2

Matoff, M. L. and Matoff, S. A. (2001) 'Eating disorder recovery: Learning from the client's healing journey', *Women & Therapy*, 23 (4): 43–54.

May, Tim (1997) *Social Research: Issues, Methods and Processes* (2nd edn). Buckingham: Open University Press.

Mayhew, Henry (1961) *London Labour and the London Poor* (Four Volumes). London: Griffin.

Maynard, Mary (1998) 'Feminists' knowledge, and the knowledge of feminisms: epistemology, theory, methodology and method', in Tim May and Malcolm Williams (eds), *Knowing the Social World*. Buckingham: Open University Press. pp. 120–37.

Mazzocchi, Mario (2008) *Statistics for Marketing and Consumer Research*. London: Sage.

Menard, S. (1991) *Longitudinal Research*. Newbury Park, CA: Sage.

Miles, Matthew and Huberman, A. Michael (1994) *Qualitative Data Analysis*. London: Sage.

Milgram, Stanley (1974) *Obedience to Authority: An Experimental View*. London: Tavistock Press.

Millward, Peter (2008) 'Rivalries and racisms: "Closed" and "open" Islamophobic dispositions amongst football supporters'. *Sociological Research Online*, Volume 13, issue 6. http://www.socresonline.org.uk/13/6/5.html

Millward, Peter (2006) '"We've all got the bug for Euro-Aways": What fans say about European football club competition', *International Review for the Sociology of Sport*, 41 (3): 375–93.

Mills C. Wright (1940) 'Situated actions and vocabularies of motive', *American Sociological Review*, 5 (6): 904–13.

Mills, C. Wright (1959) *The Sociological Imagination*. Oxford: Oxford University Press.

Mills, C. Wright (2000 [1956]) *The Power Elite*. Oxford: Oxford University Press.

Moran-Ellis, J., Alexander, V.D., Cronin, A., Dickinson, M., Fielding, J., Sleney, J. and Thomas, H. (2006) 'Triangulation and integration: processes, claims and implications', *Qualitative Research*, 6 (1): 45–59.

Morgan, David L. (1997) *Focus Groups as Qualitative Research*. London: Sage.

Morgan, David L. (1998a) *The Focus Group Guidebook*. London: Sage.

Morgan, David. (1998b) 'Practical Strategies for Combining Qualitative and Quantitative Methods: Applications for Health Research', *Qualitative Health Research*, 8, pp. 362–76.

Morley, David (1980) *The 'Nationwide' Audience: Structure and Decoding*. London: British Film Institute.

Morse, Janice M. and Lyn Richards (2002) *Readme First for a User's Guide to Qualitative Methods*. London: Sage Publications.

Moser, C.A. and Kalton, G. (1971) *Survey Methods in Social Investigation* (2nd edn). London: Heinemann.

Mullins, A., McCluskie, J. and Taylor-Browne, J. (2001) 'Challenging the Rural Idyll: Children and Families speak Out about Life in Rural England in the 21st century'. NCH Report on behalf of the Countryside Agency.

Murphy, R. and Torrance, H. (eds) (1987) *Evaluating Education: Issues and Methods*. Buckingham: Open University Press.

Murthy, Dhiraj (2008) 'Digital Ethnography: An Examination of the Use of New Technologies for Social Research' *Sociology*, Vol 42, No. 5 pp. 837–55 http://soc.sagepub.com/cgi/content/abstract/42/5/837

Nettleton, S. and Burrows, R. (1998) 'Mortgage debt, insecure home ownership and health: an exploratory analysis', in M. Bartley, D. Blane and G. Davey-Smith (eds), *The Sociology of Health Inequalities*. Oxford: Blackwell.

Nettleton, S. and Burrows, R. (2000) 'When a capital investment becomes an emotional loss: the health consequences of the experience of mortgage possession in England', *Housing Studies*, 15 (3): 463–79.

Norris, Christopher (1982) *Deconstruction: Theory and Practice*. London: Methuen.

Norris, Christopher (1987) *Jacques Derrida*. London: Fontana.

Norris, N. (1990) *Understanding Educational Evaluation*. London: Kogan Page.

Northey, Margot and McKibbin, Joan (2007) *Making Sense in the Social Sciences: A Student's Guide to Research, Writing and Style*. Canada: Oxford University Press.

Oakley, Ann (2000) *Experiments in Knowing: Gender and Method in the Social Sciences*. Cambridge: Polity.

Office for National Statistics (2004) Rural and Urban Area Classification 2004, http://www.statistics.gov.uk/geography/nrudp.asp accessed 31/03/2009.

Office for National Statistics (2009) UK Census: Collecting the Information, http://www.ons.gov.uk/census/2011-census/collecting-info/index.html, accessed 23/11/09.

Oliver, S., Kavanagh, J., Caird, J., Lorenc, T., Oliver, K., Harden, A., Thomas, J., Greaves, A. and Oakley, A. (2008) *Health promotion, inequalities and young people's health: a systematic review of research*. London: EPPI-Centre, Social Science Research Unit, Institute of Education, University of London.

Oppenheim, A.N. (1992) *Questionnaire Design, Interviewing and Attitude Measurement* (2nd edn). London: Pinter.

Outhwaite, William and Bottomore, Tom (1993) *The Blackwell Dictionary of Twentieth Century Thought*. London: Blackwell.

Pallant, Julie (2006) *SPSS survival manual: a step by step guide to data analysis using SPSS for Windows*. London: Allen and Unwin.

Parsons, Talcott (1951) *The Social System*. London: Routledge.

Pawson, Ray and Tilley, Nick (1997) *Realistic Evaluation*. London: Sage.

Payne, J. in collaboration with Hyde, M., Giarchi, G. and Payne, G. (1995) *Regional Profile of the South West with Special Reference to Disadvantage and Poverty*. Community Research Centre, University of Plymouth and National Lotteries Charities Board South West.

Phippen, Andy (2007) 'How Virtual are Virtual Methods?', *Methodological Innovations Online*, Vol. 2. No. 1 http://erdt.plymouth.ac.uk/mionline/public_html/viewarticle.php?id=43&layout=html

Phippen, Andy, Davey, R. and Furnell, Steve. (2009) 'Should We Do It Just Because We Can?', Methodological and Ethical Implications for Information Revelation in Online Social Networks Methodological Innovations Online 4 (3) pp. 41–55 http://www.methodologicalinnovations.org/pdf/18-01-10/5.%20Phippen%20et%20al%2041-55%20.pdf

Phoenix, Cassandra and Sparkes, Andrew (2009) 'Being Fred: big stories, small stories and the accomplishment of a positive ageing process', *Qualitative Research*, 9 (2): 219–36.

Pilnick, Alison (2002) 'What "most people" do: Exploring the ethical implications of genetic counselling', *New Genetics and Society*, 21 (3): 339–50.

Pink, Sarah (2001) *Doing Visual Ethnography*. London: Sage.

Platt, Jennifer (1992) 'Cases of cases … of cases', in Ragin and Becker (eds) pp. 21–52.

Plano Clark, Vicki L. and Creswell, John W. (2008) *The Mixed Method Reader*. London: Sage.

Popper, Karl (2002 [1935]) *The Logic of Scientific Enquiry*. London: Routledge.

Porter, Sam (2002) 'Critical Realist Ethnography', in Tim May (ed.), *Qualitative Research in Action*. London: Sage. pp. 53–72.

Potter, Jonathan (1997) 'Discourse analysis as a way for analysing naturally occurring talk', in David Silverman (ed.), *Qualitative Research: Theory, Methods and Practice*. London: Sage. pp. 144–60.

Potter, Jonathan and Wetherell, Margaret (1994) 'Analysing discourse', in Alan Bryman and Robert Burgess (eds), *Analysing Qualitative Data*. London: Routledge. pp. 47–65.

Propp, Vladimir (1979) *Morphology of the Folktale*. Austin: University of Texas Press.

Psathas, George (1995) *Conversation Analysis: The Study of Talk-in-Interaction*. London: Sage.

Punch, K. (2005 [1998]) *Introduction to Social Research: Quantitative and Qualitative Approaches*. London: Sage.

Ragin, Charles (1992) 'Introduction: Cases of "What is a Case?"', in Ragin and Becker, Howard, S. (eds), pp. 1–17.

Ragin, Charles (1994) *Constructing Social Research*. Thousand Oaks, London, New Delhi: Pine Forge Press.

Ragin, Charles and Becker, Howard S. (eds) (1992) *What is a Case? Exploring the Foundations of Social Inquiry*. Cambridge: Cambridge University Press.

Ralph, R.O., Lambert, D. and Kidder, K.A. (2002) *The Recovery Perspective and Evidence-Based Practice for People with Serious Mental Illness: A Guideline Developed for the Behavioural Health Recovery Management Project*. http://bhrm.org/guidelines/Ralph%zerecovery.pdf

Redenbach, J. and J. Lawler (2003) 'Recovery from disordered eating: What life histories reveal', *Contemporary Nurse*, 15: 148–56.

Regan de Bere, S. (2003) 'Evaluating the implications of complex interprofessional education for improvements in collaborative practice: a multidimensional model', *British Educational Research Journal*, 29 (1): 105–24.

Regan de Bere, S., Annandale, S. and Natrass, H. (2000) 'Achieving health improvements through interprofessional learning in south west England', *International Journal of Interprofessional Care*, 14 (2): 161–74.

Renzetti, Claire M. and Lee, Raymond M. (1993) *Researching Sensitive Topics*. London: Sage.

Richards, Lyn (2002a) *Using NVivo in Qualitative Research*. London: Sage.

Richards, Lyn (2002b) *Using N6 in Qualitative Research*. London: Sage.

Richards, Lyn (2005) *Handling Qualitative Data: A Practical Guide*. London: Sage.

Ritchey, Ferris., J. (2008) *The Statistical Imagination: Elementary Statistics for the Social Sciences*. McGraw-Hill: New York

Roberts, B. (2002) *Biographical Research*. Buckingham: Open University Press.

Roberts, G. and Wolfson, P. (2004) 'The rediscovery of recovery: Open to all', *Advances in Psychiatric Treatment,* 10 (1): 37–49.

Robson, Colin (2002) *Real World Research: A Resource for Social Scientists and Practitioner-Researchers* (2nd edn). Oxford: Blackwell.

Rose, Gillian (2001) *Visual Methodologies*. London: Sage.

Rose, D. and Sullivan, O. (1996) *Introducing Data Analysis for Social Scientists* (2nd edn). Buckingham: Open University Press.

Rosenhan, David (1973) 'On being sane in insane places', *Science* 179 (70): 250–8.

Rossi, P.H., Freeman, H.E. and Lipsey, M.W. (1999) *Evaluation: A Systematic Approach* (6th edn). London: Sage.

Rossi, Peter H., Lipsey, Mark W. and Freeman, Howard E. (2004) *Evaluation: A Systematic Approach*. (7th edn) Thousand Oaks, CA: Sage

Rowntree, S. (1901/1980) *Poverty: A Study of Town Life*. New York: Garland.

Ruspini, E. (2000) *Longitudinal Research in the Social Sciences*. Social Research Update Issue 28. University of Surrey.

Sacks, Harvey (1992) *Lectures on Conversation*. Oxford: Blackwell.

Said, Edward (1984 [1978]) *Orientalism*. London: Penguin.

Sapsford, Roger (1999) *Survey Research*. London: Sage.

Sarantakos, Sotirios (1998) *Social Research* (2nd edn). Basingstoke: Macmillan.

Savage, Mike and Egerton, Muriel (1997) 'Social Mobility, Individual Ability and the Inheritance of Class Inequality', *Sociology*, 31 (4): 645–72.

Sayer, Andrew (1992) *Method in Social Science: A Realist Approach*. London: Routledge.

Sayre, R. (1994) *American lives: An anthology of autobiographical writing*. WI: University of Wisconsin Press.

Schlesinger, P. and Tumber, H. (1994) *Reporting Crime: The Media Politics of Criminal Justice*. London: Clarendon.

Scholz, Roland W. and Tietje, Olaf (2002) *Embedded Case Study Method: Integrated Quantitative and Qualitative Knowledge*. London: Sage.

Schutt, Russell (2001) *Investigating the Social World* (3rd edn). Thousand Oaks, CA: Pine Forge.

Schutz, Alfred (1972) *The Phenomenology of the Social World*. London: Heinemann.

Scott, A. (1994) *Willing Slaves? British Workers Under Human Resource Management*. Cambridge: Cambridge University Press.

Scott, John (1990) A *Matter of Record: Documentary Sources in Social Research*. Cambridge: Polity.

Seale, Clive, Gobo, Giampietro, Gubrium, Jaber F. and Silverman, David (eds) (2007) *Qualitative Research Practice*. London: Sage.

Schutz, Alfred (1967 [1932]) *The Phenomenology of the Social World*. Evanston Il: Northwestern University Press.

Shaw, Clifford (1966 [1930]) *The Jack Roller: A Delinquent Boy's Own Story*. Chicago: University of Chicago Press.

Shaw, Ian F., Greene, Jennifer C. and Mark, Melvin M. (2006) (eds) *The Sage Handbook of Evaluation*. London: Sage.

Sheehan, K (2001) 'Email Survey Response Rates: A review', *Journal of Computer-Mediated Communication*, vol 6, http://jcmc.indiana.edu/vol6/issue2/sheehan.html

Shucksmith, M., Roberts, D., Scott, D., Chapman, P. and Conway, E. (1996) Disadvantages in Rural Areas. Rural Research Report 29. London: Rural Development Commission.

Silverman, David (1993) *Interpreting Qualitative Data*. London: Sage.

Silverman, David (1998) *Harvey Sacks: Social Science and Conversation Analysis*. Cambridge: Polity.

Silverman, David (2000) 'Analysing talk and text', in Norman K. Denzin and Yvonna S. Lincoln (eds), *Handbook of Qualitative Research* (2nd edn). London: Sage. pp. 821–34.

Silverman, David (2005) *Doing Qualitative Research – A Practical Handbook* (2nd edn). London: Sage.

Silverman, David (2006) *Interpreting Qualitative Data* (3rd edn). London: Sage.

Simmons, R. (2001) 'Questionnaires', in N. Gilbert (ed.), *Researching Social Life* (2nd edn). London: Sage. pp. 85–104.

Singer, Peter (1990) *Animal Liberation*. London: Jonathan Cape.

Skocpol, Theda (1979) *States and Social Revolutions: A Comparative Analysis of France, Russia and China*. Cambridge: Cambridge University Press.

Skocpol, Theda (1982) 'Rentier State and Shi'a Islam in the Iranian Revolution', *Theory and Society*, volume 11, pp. 265–83.

Slater, Don and Miller, Daniel (2000) *The Internet: An Ethnographic Approach*. London: Berg.

Soja, Edward (1989) *Postmodern Geographies*. London. Verso.

Spitzer, W.O., Dobson, A.J. and Hall, J. (1981) 'Measuring the quality of life of cancer patients: a concise QL-Index for use by physicians', *Journal of Chronic Diseases*, 34: 585–97.

Stake, Robert (1995) *The Art of Case Study Research*. London: Sage.

Stake, R. (1998) 'Case Studies', in N. Denzin and Y. Lincoln (eds), *Strategies of Qualitative Inquiry*. London: Sage.

Strauss, Anselm and Corbin, Juliet (1990) *Basics of Qualitative Research: Grounded Theory Procedures and Techniques*. London: Sage.

Survey Resource Network http://surveynet.ac.uk/ accessed 10 June 2010.

Sutton, Carole (1994) 'Piloting a study of the medical condition Vulvar Vestibulitis', MSc. thesis, University of Plymouth.

Sveningsson Elm, Malin. (2009) 'How do various notions of privacy influence decisions on qualitative internet research?', in Markham, Annette N. and Baym, Nancy K. (2009) *Internet Inquiry: Conversations about Method*. London: Sage.

Swetnam, Derek (2004) *Writing Your Dissertation*. Oxford: Baseline Arts Limited.

Tarling, Roger (2009) *Statistical Modelling for Social Researchers: Principles and Practice*. London: Routledge.

Thomas, I.W. and Thomas, D.S. (1928) *The Child in America: Behaviour Problems and Programs*. New York: Knopf.

Thomas, R. and Purdon, S. (1994) *Telephone Methods for Social Surveys*. Social Research Update Issue 8. University of Surrey.

Thomas, William Isaa and Znaniecki, Florian (1996 [1919]) *The Polish Peasant in Europe and America*, ed. Eli Zaretsky. Chicago: University of Illinois Press.

Townsend, P. (1979) *Poverty in the United Kingdom*. London: Allen Lane.

Tashakkori, Abbas and Teddlie, Charles (2008) 'Introduction to Mixed Methods and Mixed Model Studies in the Social and Behavioural Sciences', in Plano Clark, Vicki L. and Creswell, John W. (2008) *The Mixed Method Reader*. Sage: London

Turkle, Sherry (1996) *Life on the Screen: Identity in the Age of the Internet*. New York: Simon and Schuster.

UK Data Archive, The (2002) www.data-archive.co.uk. Essex: University of Essex.

Vedder, Clyde (1951) 'Lonely Hearts Clubs Viewed Sociologically', *Social Forces*, 30 (2): 219–22.

Victor, Liz (2008) Systematic Reviewing. Social Research Update. Issue 54, Summer 2008. http://sru.soc.surrey.ac.uk/SRU54.pdf

Vogler, Christopher (1998) *The Writers Journey: Mythic Structure for Writers*, (2nd edn). Studio City California: Michael Wiese Productions.

Voas, David and Crockett (2005) 'Religion in Britain: Neither Believing nor Belonging', *Sociology*, Vol. 39, No. 1, 11–28.

Vogt, W. (1999) *Dictionary of Statistics and Methodology* (2nd edn). London: Sage.

Vogt, W. Paul (2005) *Dictionary of Statistics and Methodology: A Non Technical Guide for the Social Sciences* (3rd edn). London: Sage.

Ware, J.E. and Sherbourne, C.D. (1992) 'The MOS 36-item short-form health survey (SF-36) I: Conceptual framework and item selection', *Medical Care*, 30 (6): 473–83.

Weaver, K., Wuest, J. and Ciliska, D. (2005) 'Understanding Women's Journey of Recovering From Anorexia Nervosa'. *Qualitative Health Research*, 15 (2): 188–206.

Weber, Max (1930/original 1905) *The Protestant Ethic and the Spirit of Capitalism*. London: Unwin Hyman.

Weber, Max (1949) *The Methodology of the Social Sciences*. New York: Free Press.

Weber, W. (1975) *Roscher and Knies: The Logical Problems of Historical Economics*. New York: Free Press.

Whitehead, Margaret, Townsend, Peter and Davidson, Nick (1992) *Inequalities in Health: The Black Report and the Health Divide*. London: Penguin Books.

Whyte, William Foote (1943) *Street Corner Society: The Social Structures of an Italian Slum*. Chicago: University of Chicago Press.

Whyte, William Foote (ed.) (1991a) *Participatory Action Research*. London: Sage.

Whyte, William Foote (1991b) *Social Theory for Action: How Individuals and Organizations Learn to Change*. London: Sage.

Wilkinson, Sue (1998) 'Focus groups in feminist research: power, interaction and the co-production of meaning', *Studies International Forum*, 21 (1): 111–25.

Wight, D. (1994) 'Boys' thoughts and talk about sex in a working class locality of Glasgow', *Sociological Review*, 42: 702–37.

Williams, J. (1985) 'Redefining Institutional Racism' *Ethnic and Racial Studies*, 8(3): 323–48.

Williams, Jeffrey (1998) *Theory and the Novel: Narrative Reflexivity in the British Tradition*. Cambridge: Cambridge University Press.

Williams, Malcolm (2002) 'Generalization in interpretive research', in Tim May (ed.), *Qualitative Research in Action*. London: Sage. pp. 125–43.

Williams, Malcolm. (2003) *Making Sense of Social Research*. London: Sage

Williams, Malcolm and May, Tim (1996) *Introduction to the Philosophy of Social Research*. London: UCL.

Williamson, Judith (1978) *Decoding Advertising: Ideology and Meaning in Advertising*. London: Marion Boyars.

Willis, Paul (1977) *Learning to Labour: How Working Class Kids Get Working Class Jobs*. London: Saxon House.

Wodek, Ruth (2007) 'Critical Discourse Analysis', in Seale, Clive, Gobo, Giampietro, Gubrium, Jaber and Silverman, David (eds) *Qualitative Research Practice*. London, Sage, pp. 185–201.

Wolcott, H.F. (1973) *The Man in the Principal's Office: An Ethnography*. Prospect Heights, IL: Waveland.

Wright, Erik Olin (1997) *Class Counts: Comparative Studies in Class Analysis*. Cambridge: Cambridge University Press.

Yin, Robert K. (2004) *The Case Study Anthology*. London: Sage.

Yin, Robert K. (2009) *Case Study Research: Design and Methods* (4th edn). London: Sage.

Zeitlyn, David, David, Matthew and Bex, Jane (1999*) Knowledge Lost in Information*. London: British Humanities Press.

Zeller, R.A. (1993) 'Combining qualitative and quantitative techniques to develop culturally sensitive measures', in D.G. Ostrow and R.C. Kessler (eds), *Methodological Issues in AIDS Behavioral Research*. New York: Plenum. pp. 95–116.

Zimbardo, Phillip (2008) *The Lucifer Effect*. Warrenton Co: Rider and Co.

Znaniecki, Florian (1934) *The Method of Sociology*. New York: Farrar and Reinhart.

INDEX

Tables and figures are indicated by page numbers in **bold**.

Dale, A. et al., 15, 287, 292
data
  aggregated, 287, 289
  definitions, 18–19
  in grounded theory, 110
  qualitative and quantitative,
    82–3
  sample survey, 289
data analysis
  and data collection, 110
  mixed methods, 298–9
  qualitative *see* qualitative data
    analysis (QDA)
  quantitative: key stages, 471
data collection
  ethics, 211–12
  hypothetico-deductive method,
    216, 217
  primary or secondary?, 205
  and qualitative data analysis
    (QDA), 320
  in qualitative research *see* case
    study research; ethnography;
    focus groups; grounded
    theory; interviews; textual
    data
  in quantitative research *see*
    coding/codes; research
    design; sampling; surveys
  secondary quantitative, 287,
    289–90
  see also sampling
data entry, 448–53
  data file format, 448–50,
    449, 450
  errors, 451–3, **451**
  for multiple response questions,
    450–1, **451**
data management, 560–74
  calculating new variables, 567–9
  multiple response sets, 571
    frequency tables and cross-
      tabulations, 571–2
  recoding data, 560–7
  subsets, 569–71
  weighting data, 572–4
data modelling, 549–57
  dummy variables, 556
  linear regression, 551–5
  logistic regression, 556
  multi-level modelling, 556–7
  multiple linear regression
    (MLR), 555–6
  reasons for, 550–1
Data Protection Act (1998),
  212–13
data reduction, 339, 586, 588

data storage
  confidentiality, 47–8, 130,
    211–12
  from interviews, 129–30
  textual data, 188
  visual data, 188
databases for research, 62, 63, 64
David, M., 22, 34, 38, 39, 78, 114,
  157, 169, 328, 427
David, M. and Zeitlyn, D., 55
de Vaus, D., 210, 217, 228, 255,
  268, 518, 536, 575
deadlines, 24
deception in research, 35, 44, 45
decision-making evaluation, 302
deconstruction, 363, 370–3, 591
deduction and induction, 20,
  83–4, 87
deductive questioning, 19, 84
Delamont, S., 152
Delanty, G., 78
Delbridge, 153
Delphi groups, 10, 133, 139
Denscombe, M., 312
Denzin, N., 377
Department for Business,
  Innovation and Skills, 301
Department for Children, Schools
  and Families, 301
Department for Environment,
  Food and Rural Affairs,
  219, 301
Department of Health, 301
Department of Work and
  Pensions, 301
dependent samples t-test, 14,
  538, 542–3
  in IBM SPSS Statistics 19, 542–3
Derrida, J., 79, 368, 370, 372
description, 11
descriptive statistics, 471
Dewey, 191
Dey, Ian, 200, 202
dialectical materialism, 77
diaries, 181, 184
Dillman, D.A. et al., 315
direction of research, 333–4
discourse analysis
  vs. content analysis, 323, 334–6
  conversation analysis, 378–82
  deconstruction, 370–3
  example analysis: newspaper
    articles on students, 382–6
  forms of, 362–6
  meanings of 'discourse', 436
  myth, 368–70, 373
  narrative analysis, 374–8

discourse analysis *cont.*
  presentation, 590
  semiotic analysis, 105, 365,
    366–8, 373, 435
  and visual images, 436–9
discovery, 148, 192
discussion of findings in written
  reports, 582
displays, 331, 348–60
  cross-case, 349–50, 359–60
  matrix, 331, 348, **348**, 350–7,
    351–2, 353, 354, 355–6,
    358–9
  rules for construction, 350,
    354, 357
  within-case, 349, 357–9
Dolnicar, S. et al., 309
dramaturgical analysis, 363
dummy variables, 556
Durkheim, Emile, 15, 89, 289

e-mail surveys, 309, 310, 312
e-research *see* internet
Ebeling, M. and Gibbs, J., 67, 73
Economic and Social Research
  Council (ESRC), 16, 210
educational research, 93
effects matrices, 358–9
elaboration, 524–6
  in IBM SPSS Statistics 19, 525–6
Elias, N., 86
Ellen, R.F., 147
Elliot, J., 168, 375, 387
Ellis, L., 82
emergence, 110
Emmison, M. and Smith, P.,
  180, 189
emotional harm, 49
empiricism, 76
entry criteria, 24
ethical orientation of
  organizations, 7
ethics in research, 30–53
  anonymity, 47, 211–12
  basic philosophies, 41–3, 44
  conduct of researcher, 212–13
  confidentiality, 47–8, 115–16,
    211–12
  consent, 40–1, 42, 43–7, 212
  controversial cases, 31–3, 35
  critical theory, 37
  ethical oversight, 40–1
  ethics committees, 50, 115
  falsification and fabrication, 52–3
  human nature and values, 35–8
  internet, 213, 313–14
  morality, 30

Pearson's chi square, 546
Pearson's *r*, 519, 522–4
   in IBM SPSS Statistics 19, 523–4
percentages, 474–5
performance, 21
phi, 518
Phippen, A., 310
Phippen, A. et al., 314
Phoenix, C. and Sparkes, A., 109
photographs, 181–2, 184, 186
physical harm, 49
Piaget, Jean, 173
pie charts, 499, 501, **501**
   on IBM SPSS Statistics 19, 502
pilot surveys, 92, 97
Pink, S., 180, 425–6, 439, 443, 444
plagiarism, 52, 68–9
Platt, J., 167
plot, 375
political orientation of
   organizations, 7
politics of research, 38–9
Popper, Karl, 84–5, 173
populations, 226–7
   definition of, 20–1
   and sampling frame, 226
Porter, S., 152
positivism, 34–5, 76
Potter, J., 365, 366
Potter, J. and Wetherell, M.,
   362, 373
PowerPoint, 601
pragmatism, 191
predictions, 14–15
predictive validity, 268
presentation
   drafting and redrafting, 596–9
   from qualitative and quantitative
      research, 596
   qualitative research, 586–91
   quantitative data results, 591–6
   verbal, 599–602
   written reports, 580–5
primary data, 205
primary and secondary data, 103–4
privacy, 45, 46, 47–8
probabilities, 17
professional review - validation and
   accreditation, 302
Project Camelot, 33
protection from harm, 48–9
Psathas, G., 380
psychiatric patients research,
   32–3, 35
psychoanalysis, 440
Punch, K., 12, 268
punishment and reward, 34

purposive sampling, 232
Pyšňáková, Michaela 194-6

Qualidata Archive, 104–5
qualitative data analysis (QDA),
   320–37
   cyclical process, 324–5
   and data collection, 320, 324
   direction of research, 333–4
   discourse vs. content analysis,
      323, 334–6
   displays, 331, 348–60
      matrices, 348
      network, 348–9
   memos, 332
   notes and transcriptions, 325–6
   purpose of research, 334
   representation/display, 331,
      348–60
   rules for (Silverman), 329–30
   software, 389–422
   and team research, 329
   texts, 326–9, 331
      and Liverpool: Capital of
         Culture, 327
   see also coding/codes; discourse
      analysis
qualitative and quantitative
   research, 5, 13, 14, 81–98
   and beliefs about human nature,
      87–8
   classification, 90–4
   deduction and induction, 83–4
   distinction, 95–6
   falsification, 84–5
   generalizability, 86
   measurement, 94–5
   mixed methods, 96–8
   and numerical scientific
      methods, 88–9
   objectivism and constructionism,
      85–6
   phenomenology, 89–90
qualitative research
   case study research, 105, 165–77
   choice of research subject, 108–9
   ethics, 113–17
   ethnography, 147–64
   focus groups, 10, 107, 132–45
   grounded theory, 102, 109–13,
      191–202
   hypothesis testing, 106–9
   and induction, 102
   and institutions, 115
   interviews, 118–30
   presentation, 586–91
      content analysis, 588

presentation *cont.*
   conversation analysis, 587–8
   discourse analysis, 590
   forms of, 587
   non-numerical code results,
      589–90
   numerical tables, 588–9
   quotations as evidence, 589
   text and reduction, 586–7
   sampling, 111–13
   textual data, 179–85
   see also qualitative data analysis
      (QDA)
Quality of Life Index, 261
quantitative data: presentation,
   591–6
quasi-experimental design, 206–7
questionnaires, 19, 242–3
   e-mail, 244
   online, 244
   response rates, 243
   see also questions; surveys
questions
   bias, 124
   closed-ended, 253–63
      10-point and 100-point scales,
         259, **259**
      attitudinal/opinion
         responses, 258
      balancing categories, 256
      exclusiveness, 255–6
      exhaustiveness, 255, 257
      Likert scales, 259–61, **260**
      with a list of responses,
         257–8, **258**
      matrix question structure,
         261–3, **263**
      multiple response questions,
         261, **262**
      coding/codes, 283
      ranking questions, 261
      coding/codes, 283
      rating responses, 258, **259**
      response categories,
         253–5, **254**
      semantic differential
         scales, 259
      with two responses, 256–7
   demographic information, 264–5
   focus groups, 141–2
   language, 123
   open-ended, 121, 246, 253
      coding/codes, 283–4
   piloting, 123–5, 272–3
      warning signs, 272
   reliability, 266–8
      correlation techniques, 268

Printed in Great Britain
by Amazon.co.uk, Ltd.,
Marston Gate.